Praise for *Doctor Who: The Writer's Tale*:

★★★★★
'A funny, revealing insight into the
workings of the genius who puts the
show together'
Boyd Hilton, HEAT MAGAZINE

'The fans will adore it. Davies has engaged
with the book totally and there is full
disclosure from him about everything'
Esther Walker, THE INDEPENDENT

'Wonderful! Destined to be a Christmas bestseller…
We get an absolute snapshot into the mind of a
creative writer… It's a free flow of thought –
a stream of consciousness. It's a great book'
RICHARD & JUDY

★★★★★
'You can douse all the other books about
new *Who* in lighter fuel and spark up your
Zippo – this is all you need. It's the only
one that opens a door into the brain of the
series' showrunner'
Ian Berriman, SFX MAGAZINE

'It's the *Doctor Who Annual* for adults, and it's not nearly
enough, should have been 1,001 pages, because Davies
doesn't need to be writing fiction… to be a storyteller.
He's the Scheherazade of Cardiff Bay'
Veronica Horwell, THE GUARDIAN

'Remarkably open… Despite the self-deprecating
bonhomie, there's a ruthless confidence to Davies'
Robert Colvile, THE DAILY TELEGRAPH

★★★★★
'If you're an uber fan of the show… or an
aspiring (or even established) writer, this
book will very, very quickly fall into the
"can't put down" category'
Darren Scott, THE PINK PAPER

'A fascinating insight into the writing of
one of TV's biggest hits'
THE SCOTSMAN

★★★★

'Many writers dismiss the idea of
inspiration outright, simply stating their
formula for wild success as "apply seat of
pants to seat of chair". *The Writer's Tale* does
several impossible things, one of which is to
unravel the complexity of that very act'
Thom Hutchinson, DEATH RAY MAGAZINE

'Probably the best book ever written about scriptwriting.
It's certainly one of the clearest windows into
a writer's mind'
Douglas McPherson, WRITERS' FORUM MAGAZINE

'I can't recommend *The Writer's Tale* highly enough…
It's a genuine insight into the entire
television production process'
Scott Matthewman, THE STAGE

'This book is a treasury of wit, of truthfulness,
and of good sound storytelling sense'
PHILIP PULLMAN

'Far from just being a piece of national
treasure, it's one of the most precious
bundles of educational platinum that any
writer could set their lamps on. It reads like
an adventure, like real writing ought to'
PAUL ABBOTT

'I got my copy in Waterstone's yesterday. Five
pounds off! Not that I cared, cos I stole it'
STEVEN MOFFAT

DOCTOR · WHO

THE WRITER'S TALE
THE FINAL CHAPTER

DOCTOR·WHO

THE WRITER'S TALE
THE FINAL CHAPTER

The definitive story of the BBC series

RUSSELL T DAVIES
and BENJAMIN COOK

Hi Ben.

BOOKS

3 5 7 9 10 8 6 4

Published in 2010 by BBC Books, an imprint of Ebury Publishing. A Random House Group Company.

The Random House Group Limited Reg. No. 954009

Addresses for companies within the Random House Group can be found at www.randomhouse.co.uk

A CIP catalogue record for this book is available from the British Library.

ISBN 978 1 846 07861 3

The Random House Group Limited supports The Forest Stewardship Council (FSC), the leading international forest
certification organisation. All our titles that are printed on Greenpeace approved FSC certified paper carry the FSC logo.
Our paper procurement policy can be found at www.rbooks.co.uk/environment.

Mixed Sources
Product group from well-managed
forests and other controlled sources
www.fsc.org Cert no. TT-COC-2139
© 1996 Forest Stewardship Council
FSC

Commissioning Editor: Albert DePetrillo
Project Editor: Steve Tribe
Designer: Clayton Hickman
Cover design: Clayton Hickman
Production Controller: Phil Spencer

Printed and bound in the UK by CPI Mackays, Chatham ME5 8TD

BBC Books would like to thank the following for providing photographs and for permission to reproduce copyright material.
While every effort has been made to trace and acknowledge all copyright holders, we would like to apologise should there
have been any errors or omissions.

All images © BBC, except:
Plate section 1:
p1 (right) and p2 (left) courtesy courtesy of the *Doctor Who* Art Department
p3 (below left) © Darenote Ltd. Photographer William Baker
p4 (top, above left, above right) courtesy of William Baker
p5 (below) computer-generated imagery courtesy of The Mill
p6 (top) courtesy of Benjamin Cook
p6 (above left, above right) courtesy of Jennie Fava
p7 (below right) courtesy of Clayton Hickman
p8 courtesy of Adrian Rogers
Plate section 2:
p2 (left) courtesy of Indigo Television/ITV1
p4 (below) courtesy of Benjamin Cook

Front cover photography by Adrian Rogers
Illustrations by Russell T Davies

CONTENTS

BOOK ONE

PHILIP PULLMAN

I have never met Russell T Davies, but I like him, from the T on outwards. He steals from the best, which proves that he is both discriminating and unscrupulous; he is adventurous and humane, not a common combination; and most of all he's full of a boundless energy, which fizzes out of these pages like champagne. He's a genuine maker. Everybody knows *Doctor Who*, and *Queer as Folk*, and *Torchwood*. They made a difference: they have stamped his authority on the TV screen for a long time to come. My favourite among his stories is *Mine All Mine*, for the simple reason that it was charming, and it confirmed my long-held view that the Welsh are the sexiest people in the world.

But what's this book about? Specifically, it's about the writing – and the re-writing, and the talking about, and the thinking about, and the arguing about the scripts for a series of *Doctor Who*.

However, it's not the theme that's important. What matters are the insights and the vivid and illuminating comments that crop up on the way, as Davies examines the whole business of storytelling. Take the theme itself. Davies says – and he's dead right – 'Maybe that's when bad scripts are written, when you choose the theme first. I consider that I've something to say when I've thought about a person, a moment, a single beat of the heart, that I think is true and interesting, and *therefore* should be seen.'

That's true of novels, stage plays, films, short stories – any narrative that's made up in order to illuminate a theme has a quality of duty rather than joy. It's what Yeats called making the will do the work of the imagination.

He's also right – by which I mean, of course, that his opinion coincides with mine – on the subject of writer's block: 'I don't know why, but I sort of react with revulsion to that phrase. I imagine it to mean sitting there with No Ideas At All. For me, it feels more like the ideas just won't take the right shape or form.'

He's pugnacious, and rightly so, when faced with narrow-minded prejudice: the key is 'not to defend the work, because I think defence always sounds like an apology, but to go on the attack.' But he's also sensitive to the difficulties less experienced writers face when trying to deal, for example, with the relentless and merciless idiocy of internet 'criticism'. His attitude is, again, mine, and therefore resonantly true: 'Creating something is not a democracy. The people have no say. The artist does. It doesn't matter what the people witter on about: they and their response come after. They're not there for the creation.'

In fact, not only is Russell T Davies a great TV writer, a vigorous and creative producer, a wise and perceptive commentator on the profound business of storytelling, and I dare say (I have never met him) a figure of godlike and unearthly personal beauty, he is probably omnicompetent. Reading this excellent book I was more than once put in mind of the old song 'Abdul the Bulbul Amir'. The Bulbul's opponent in that epic conflict was Ivan Skivinsky Skivar, who 'could imitate Irving, play poker or pool, and perform on the Spanish guitar.'

Such a man is Russell T Davies. This book is a treasury of wit, of truthfulness, and of good sound storytelling sense, and well worth stealing from.

PHILIP PULLMAN
May 2008

RUSSELL T DAVIES

I can't drive, so I get a lot of taxis. Which means that five or six times a week I have this conversation:

'So what do you do then?'

'I work on *Doctor Who*.'

'As what? Are you one of the monsters?'

'No, ha ha, that's funny. No, I'm a writer.'

'Oh, right, nice.'

Pause, and then, every time, here it comes…

'So where d'you get your ideas from?'

At that point, I normally say that I buy them from The Ideas Shop in Abergavenny. But in fairness, it's a good question. With no good answer.

Writers never talk about this. You'll see us, in script meetings, talking about plot and character and motivation; you'll see us in the bar, talking about contracts and rivals and fonts; you'll see us in the gutter, complaining about money. (With all of us, all the time, wondering when the good luck will run out.) But the actual writing… oh no, no way, no one talks about that. Like it's sacrosanct. Or just too scary to look at.

But Benjamin Cook wanted to know! And wouldn't give up. So that's what we've tried to pin down here. The ideas. Those mad, stupid, vague, shape-shifting, hot, nagging, drive-you-barmy ideas. And as the idea for this book grew – you'll see it grow, on the page – then it gave me the chance to tackle another thing that was bugging me. Writing is such an industry now. In many ways, that's a good thing, in that it removes all the muse-like mystique and makes it a plain old job, accessible to everyone. But with industry comes jargon. I was aware that jargon was starting to fill those growing shelves of Writer's Self Help books, not to mention the blogosphere. Wherever I looked, the writing of a script was being reduced to A, B, C plots, Text and Subtext, Three Act Structure and blah, blah, blah. And I'd think, that's not what writing is! Writing's inside your head! It's thinking! It's every hour of the day, every day of your life, a constant storm of pictures and voices and sometimes, if you're very, very lucky, insight.

That's what I wanted to capture here, and that's why so much of this book is written at 2am, in the dark hours, when the storm's a-blowing and the rafters creak. It's not writing in theory; it's writing in action, in motion. In anguish! Ideas written down before anyone else could sit in judgement, or before I could reconsider them in the cold light of day.

I wonder. You might be surprised. It does get a bit wretched and angst-ridden at times. (Steven Moffat, *Doctor Who*'s next showrunner, read the manuscript and said, 'If you still want to be a writer after reading this, then you probably will be.') But for me, that's what writing is, coupled with the enormous joy of actually getting something made. Ben and I tried to capture the process live and unfiltered, in e-mails, and when it came to publishing this, we didn't go back and tidy up. We've tried to leave it as instinctive, impulsive and contradictory as… well, as the inside of your head. Okay, all right, we did go through the finished text to remove the scandal (3,000 words, including My Night With The Slitheen), the lies (2,000 words, including my belief that Arthur Miller nicked my idea for *The Crucible*) and the swearing (28,000 words, including some brand new ones), but, apart from that, we left it intact, to make it as honest as possible. Oh yes, and we removed one or two secrets about the future, because *Doctor Who* is an ongoing show, and hopefully always will be, for ever.

To see writing in motion, means writing as work – a real, proper job, with deadlines and constraints and setbacks, like any other profession. The writer doesn't sit in an ivory tower. Mine's kind of beige, if not nicotine, and the real world is always intruding. No, it doesn't intrude; that real world is part of the writing process too, so a lot of that is laid out for you here, during the most extraordinary time that we've ever had on *Doctor Who*, with the casting of Kylie Minogue and Catherine Tate and Davros and… oh god, I love this job! (Steven, I've changed my mind! Steven? What d'you mean, 'Russell who?')

The only problem with writing on-the-spot e-mails is that I don't stop and pause to give praise where it's due. The personal nature of this book means that I'm not being too objective, or kind. I take a lot of things for granted, so I don't stop to thank David, or Catherine, or the Heads of Department, or Lindsay, as she sews 500 buttons on 75 extras, or Mark the gaffer, as he hauls his lamps around in the rain, or the runners, as they juggle tea and scripts and abuse. They're the people who really get *Doctor Who* made, alongside the brilliant teams at *Doctor Who Confidential* and the Website, and Branding, and… oh, the thanks could fill a whole book. Albeit a rather dry book.

But right here and now, I just want to say thank you to Ebury, for having faith in us, and to Philip Pullman, for his wonderful words, with special thanks to Ben, for the idea, the support, the kindness and the friendship, and to Andrew Smith, the man who's hardly mentioned in here, because he's part of a different world, one which keeps me sane and makes the whole thing possible.

Oh, and then, by the way, the taxi driver always says, 'So do you think up the story and the actors make up the words?' I've gotta learn to drive.

RUSSELL T DAVIES
July 2008

INTRODUCTION

BENJAMIN COOK

'**I** love that image of this correspondence surviving a nuclear war,' Russell T Davies told me back in April 2007, two months into what would become a two-and-a-half-year-long exchange of e-mails and text messages. 'The last remnant of civilisation. "It's… glowing!"'

In the beginning, the Great Correspondence was supposed to be a magazine article. But we exceeded our word count by forty-fold, so it became a book instead. *Doctor Who: The Writer's Tale* was published in September 2008. The book's mission statement, if it had one (which would imply meticulous planning and a sense of direction, so it didn't), was to take a progressive look at not just the scriptwriting and storytelling processes, but also Russell's role as showrunner of the BBC's most imaginative, most exhilarating, most prized drama series – to find out what it's like to live, and write, under such a weight of expectation. In that first year, we tackled everything from the courting of JK Rowling to the snubbing of George Lucas, taking in chicken pox, press leaks, the companion that never was, Steven Moffat's thighs, and the loss of Russell's third-best pair of trousers in Soho.

Oh, and the writing. Obviously. It's all about the writing.

'I think Russell T Davies is the Shakespeare of today,' said David Tennant recently. But did Shakespeare write 31 episodes of *Doctor Who*? No. (Subs, please check.) Even the Bard would have baulked at the prospect of reviving a TV show in 2005 that was last popular in the '80s – decreasingly so at that – and transforming it into The Best Thing On Telly Bar None. And I bet Shakespeare wouldn't have agreed to e-mail me his scripts as he wrote them, page by page, night by night, and then answer a barrage of questions about how he did it, how he's feeling about it, and what he's going to write next. (Shakespeare probably couldn't even *work* a computer. What an idiot.)

Anyway, people seemed to quite like *The Writer's Tale*. I mean, other people. People who weren't Russell or me. (We'd been calling it the 'Great' Correspondence since February 2007 – ooh, the reckless optimism of youth!) The critics said nice things. Richard and Judy chose it for their Christmas Book Club. Revered newspaper columnist Charlie Brooker was inspired to devote an entire edition of his BBC show *Screenwipe* to interviews with TV writers. And the man who produces and writes for CBBC's talking cactus Oucho (see p.226) wrote us a letter to say that *The Writer's Tale* is one of his all-time favourite books. 'And if you ever want to interview the cactus,' he said, 'give me a call.' Okay. Thanks.

At which point, we began to wonder whether some sort of follow-up volume might *not* be an altogether terrible idea. We were, after all, still e-mailing, Russell and I. Like cockroaches that had survived the fallout. ('It's… glowing!') Or should we quit while we're ahead? A second time around, we'd be all too aware that our e-mails would *actually be published*, and *read*, by *real people*. Would we play up to our prospective readership? Look at me, would-be reader! Look at me! Or get woefully shy, and self-conscious, and tongue-tied? Would Book Two turn out to be an appalling piece of fluff?

Well, no. *The Writer's Tale: The Final Chapter* extends the Great Correspondence to September 2009, and the new material – 135,000 words' worth, across 350 pages, kicking off in March 2008 – is as candid, as honest, as impulsive and as revealing as Book One… which, by the way, is thrown in for good measure. Topics in Book Two include the killing of Ianto Jones, the preposterously secret Operation Cobra, an ABBA/*Torchwood* crossover, slagging off Prince Charles, the resurrection of Gallifrey, the arrival of Matt Smith as the Eleventh Doctor, and Russell's departure for foreign shores. The original *Writer's Tale* even feeds back into the TV series. Keep an eye on the abandoned 'Alien Watch' idea from Chapter 1.

The original book reproduced Russell's scripts for *Voyage of the Damned, Partners in Crime, The Stolen Earth* and *Journey's End*, in pre-first-draft form. But we wanted to give over as much of this paperback edition as possible to new material, so the scripts have largely been removed. Instead, the polished, shooting scripts for these episodes – along with *Midnight, Turn Left, The Next Doctor*, and the 2009 Specials – can be downloaded from our website (*www.thewriterstale.com*) for free!

Right. A few thank yous. Big thanks to Chris Costello, Max Letek, George Archer (he of the octopus tattoo – see Chapter 21), Nicky Lane and Adam Conway. More people are thanked in the Acknowledgements section opposite, but you'll only read that if there's a possibility you're one of them (you narcissist), so I'd like to single out Clayton Hickman, for his top-notch design work; Steve Tribe, for his extraordinary diligence; and Julie Gardner, without whom this book – and, frankly, the last five years' worth of *Doctor Who* – wouldn't have happened.

In my Introduction to the original *Writer's Tale*, I reserved my biggest thank you for Russell himself – 'for engaging with this project so passionately, so thoughtfully and so honestly, for not telling me to sod off at the start, and for capturing the madness, the fun and the struggle of writing. For telling it How It Is. Even the stuff that contradicts the other stuff.' Well, that all pretty much stands. Except I'd like to add that it takes a special kind of genius to make something – something like *Doctor Who* – that means so much to so many people. And you have, Russell. Never forget it. I mean that.

So then, here it is – *The Writer's Tale 2*. The final chapter. The end of an era. (Not, as Russell once suggested, 'the end of an *error*' – the misanthropist!) The last remnant of civilisation. Better than Shakespeare. Beloved by cactuses. ('God bless the cactuses!') It's absolutely, definitely, defiantly, the GREAT Correspondence.

BENJAMIN COOK
December 2009

ACKNOWLEDGEMENTS

The Writer's Tale: The Final Chapter would not have been possible without the invaluable help of some wonderful people. For giving us permission to include them in this book, heartfelt thanks to Paul Abbott, Pete Bennett, Pete Bowker, Chris Chibnall, Will Cohen, Phil Collinson, Bryan Elsley, Phil Ford, Mark Gatiss, Murray Gold, Bob Harris, Anne Jowett, Joe Lidster, Steven Moffat, Caitlin Moran, Andy Pryor, Helen Raynor, Gareth Roberts, Nicola Shindler, John Simm, Tracie Simpson, David Tennant and Piers Wenger. Special thanks to James Moran, for giving us permission to talk through the rewriting process. For photographic material, design drawings and other illustrations, thanks to Lindsey Alford, Jennie Fava, Samantha Hall, Arwel Jones, Brian Minchin, Jess Van Niekerk, Matt McKinney, James North, Adrian Rogers, Tom Spilsbury at *Doctor Who Magazine*, and Alex Thompson and Dave Turbitt at BBC Worldwide. Further thanks to Philip Pullman, Catherine Tate, Bernard Cribbins, Jill Atfield, Susie Liggat, Nikki Wilson, Bethan Evans at The Agency, Albert DePetrillo and the lovely Ed Griffiths at Ebury, the tireless Steve Tribe, the brilliant Clayton Hickman, and the incredible Julie Gardner.

ACKNOWLEDGEMENTS

... to say that *The Winter's Tale* is one of his all-time favourite books.

KEY TO REFERENCES

Episodes of *Doctor Who* aren't always given titles until close to transmission, so numerical production codes are used instead. Listed here in order of transmission (with each episode's writer in parentheses), the production codes to date are as follows:

1.1	**Rose** (Russell T Davies)	
1.2	**The End of the World** (Russell T Davies)	
1.3	**The Unquiet Dead** (Mark Gatiss)	
1.4	**Aliens of London** (Russell T Davies)	
1.5	**World War Three** (Russell T Davies)	
1.6	**Dalek** (Robert Shearman)	
1.7	**The Long Game** (Russell T Davies)	
1.8	**Father's Day** (Paul Cornell)	
1.9	**The Empty Child** (Steven Moffat)	
1.10	**The Doctor Dances** (Steven Moffat)	
1.11	**Boom Town** (Russell T Davies)	
1.12	**Bad Wolf** (Russell T Davies)	
1.13	**The Parting of the Ways** (Russell T Davies)	
2.X	**The Christmas Invasion** (Russell T Davies)	
2.1	**New Earth** (Russell T Davies)	
2.2	**Tooth and Claw** (Russell T Davies)	
2.3	**School Reunion** (Toby Whithouse)	
2.4	**The Girl in the Fireplace** (Steven Moffat)	
2.5	**Rise of the Cybermen** (Tom MacRae)	
2.6	**The Age of Steel** (Tom MacRae)	
2.7	**The Idiot's Lantern** (Mark Gatiss)	
2.8	**The Impossible Planet** (Matt Jones)	
2.9	**The Satan Pit** (Matt Jones)	
2.10	**Love & Monsters** (Russell T Davies)	
2.11	**Fear Her** (Matthew Graham)	
2.12	**Army of Ghosts** (Russell T Davies)	
2.13	**Doomsday** (Russell T Davies)	
3.X	**The Runaway Bride** (Russell T Davies)	
3.1	**Smith and Jones** (Russell T Davies)	
3.2	**The Shakespeare Code** (Gareth Roberts)	
3.3	**Gridlock** (Russell T Davies)	
3.4	**Daleks in Manhattan** (Helen Raynor)	
3.5	**Evolution of the Daleks** (Helen Raynor)	
3.6	**The Lazarus Experiment** (Stephen Greenhorn)	
3.7	**42** (Chris Chibnall)	
3.8	**Human Nature** (Paul Cornell)	
3.9	**The Family of Blood** (Paul Cornell)	
3.10	**Blink** (Steven Moffat)	
3.11	**Utopia** (Russell T Davies)	
3.12	**The Sound of Drums** (Russell T Davies)	
3.13	**Last of the Time Lords** (Russell T Davies)	
4.X	**Voyage of the Damned** (Russell T Davies)	
4.1	**Partners in Crime** (Russell T Davies)	
4.3	**The Fires of Pompeii** (James Moran)	
4.2	**Planet of the Ood** (Keith Temple)	
4.4	**The Sontaran Stratagem** (Helen Raynor)	

4.5	**The Poison Sky** (Helen Raynor)
4.6	**The Doctor's Daughter** (Stephen Greenhorn)
4.7	**The Unicorn and the Wasp** (Gareth Roberts)
4.9	**Silence in the Library** (Steven Moffat)
4.10	**Forest of the Dead** (Steven Moffat)
4.8	**Midnight** (Russell T Davies)
4.11	**Turn Left** (Russell T Davies)
4.12	**The Stolen Earth** (Russell T Davies)
4.13	**Journey's End** (Russell T Davies)
4.14	**The Next Doctor** (Russell T Davies)
4.15	**Planet of the Dead** (Russell T Davies & Gareth Roberts)
4.16	**The Waters of Mars** (Russell T Davies & Phil Ford)
4.17	**The End of Time: Part One** (Russell T Davies)
4.18	**The End of Time: Part Two** (Russell T Davies)

N.B. The transmission order of Series Four was revised after the initial scripting stage, but the production codes remained unchanged to avoid confusion.

On *Torchwood*, the production codes pertaining to specific episodes are as follows:

1.1	**Everything Changes** (Russell T Davies)
1.2	**Day One** (Chris Chibnall)
1.3	**Ghost Machine** (Helen Raynor)
1.4	**Cyberwoman** (Chris Chibnall)
1.5	**Small Worlds** (Peter J Hammond)
1.6	**Countrycide** (Chris Chibnall)
1.7	**Greeks Bearing Gifts** (Toby Whithouse)
1.8	**They Keep Killing Suzie** (Paul Tomalin & Dan McCulloch)
1.9	**Random Shoes** (Jacquetta May)
1.10	**Out of Time** (Catherine Tregenna)
1.11	**Combat** (Noel Clarke)
1.12	**Captain Jack Harkness** (Catherine Tregenna)
1.13	**End of Days** (Chris Chibnall)
2.1	**Kiss Kiss, Bang Bang** (Chris Chibnall)
2.2	**Sleeper** (James Moran)
2.3	**To the Last Man** (Helen Raynor)
2.4	**Meat** (Catherine Tregenna)
2.5	**Adam** (Catherine Tregenna)
2.6	**Reset** (JC Wilsher)
2.7	**Dead Man Walking** (Matt Jones)
2.8	**A Day in the Death** (Joseph Lidster)
2.9	**Something Borrowed** (Phil Ford)
2.10	**From Out of the Rain** (Peter J Hammond)
2.11	**Adrift** (Chris Chibnall)
2.12	**Fragments** (Chris Chibnall)
2.13	**Exit Wounds** (Chris Chibnall)
3.1	**Children of Earth: Day One** (Russell T Davies)
3.2	**Children of Earth: Day Two** (John Fay)
3.3	**Children of Earth: Day Three** (Russell T Davies & James Moran)
3.4	**Children of Earth: Day Four** (John Fay)
3.5	**Children of Earth: Day Five** (Russell T Davies)

On *The Sarah Jane Adventures*, the production codes pertaining to specific episodes are as follows:

1.X	**Invasion of the Bane** (Russell T Davies & Gareth Roberts)
1.1	**Revenge of the Slitheen: Part One** (Gareth Roberts)
1.2	**Revenge of the Slitheen: Part Two** (Gareth Roberts)
1.3	**Eye of the Gorgon: Part One** (Phil Ford)
1.4	**Eye of the Gorgon: Part Two** (Phil Ford)
1.5	**Warriors of Kudlak: Part One** (Phil Gladwin)
1.6	**Warriors of Kudlak: Part Two** (Phil Gladwin)
1.7	**Whatever Happened to Sarah Jane? Part One** (Gareth Roberts)
1.8	**Whatever Happened to Sarah Jane? Part Two** (Gareth Roberts)
1.9	**The Lost Boy: Part One** (Phil Ford)
1.10	**The Lost Boy: Part Two** (Phil Ford)
2.1	**The Last Sontaran: Part One** (Phil Ford)
2.2	**The Last Sontaran: Part Two** (Phil Ford)
2.3	**The Day of the Clown: Part One** (Phil Ford)
2.4	**The Day of the Clown: Part Two** (Phil Ford)
2.5	**Secrets of the Stars: Part One** (Gareth Roberts)
2.6	**Secrets of the Stars: Part Two** (Gareth Roberts)
2.7	**The Mark of the Beserker: Part One** (Joseph Lidster)
2.8	**The Mark of the Beserker: Part Two** (Joseph Lidster)
2.9	**The Temptation of Sarah Jane Smith: Part One** (Gareth Roberts)
2.10	**The Temptation of Sarah Jane Smith: Part Two** (Gareth Roberts)
2.11	**Enemy of the Bane: Part One** (Phil Ford)
2.12	**Enemy of the Bane: Part Two** (Phil Ford)
3.1	**Prisoner of the Judoon: Part One** (Phil Ford)
3.2	**Prisoner of the Judoon: Part Two** (Phil Ford)
3.3	**The Mad Woman in the Attic: Part One** (Joseph Lidster)
3.4	**The Mad Woman in the Attic: Part Two** (Joseph Lidster)
3.5	**The Wedding of Sarah Jane Smith: Part One** (Gareth Roberts)
3.6	**The Wedding of Sarah Jane Smith: Part Two** (Gareth Roberts)
3.7	**The Eternity Trap: Part One** (Phil Ford)
3.8	**The Eternity Trap: Part Two** (Phil Ford)
3.9	**Mona Lisa's Revenge: Part One** (Phil Ford)
3.10	**Mona Lisa's Revenge: Part Two** (Phil Ford)
3.11	**The Gift: Part One** (Rupert Laight)
3.12	**The Gift: Part Two** (Rupert Laight)

WHO'S WHO

WRITERS

Paul Abbott – creator of TV shows *Clocking Off, Linda Green, State of Play* and *Shameless*

Douglas Adams – 14 episodes of *Doctor Who* between 1978 and 1980, and script-edited the show at the end of the 1970s; best known as the creator of *The Hitchhiker's Guide to the Galaxy* series (initially for radio, later novels and a TV series); died 2001

Lindsey Alford – script editor on *Doctor Who* Series Three and Four, and *The Sarah Jane Adventures*

Sir Kingsley Amis – novelist, poet and critic; died 1995

Peter Bowker – TV includes *Blackpool, The Canterbury Tales* and *Casualty*

Charlie Brooker – comedian, presenter, *Guardian* columnist, and TV scriptwriter with credits including *Dead Set*

Chris Chibnall – *Doctor Who* 3.7, and head writer on *Torchwood* Series One and Two (1.2, 1.4, 1.6, 1.13, 2.1, 2.11, 2.12 and 2.13)

Paul Cornell – *Doctor Who* 1.8 and 3.8/3.9

Richard Dawkins – evolutionary biologist and popular science writer; cameoed as himself in *Doctor Who* 4.12

Bryan Elsley – co-creator of and showrunner on *Skins*

Jane Espenson – TV includes *Star Trek: Deep Space Nine, Buffy the Vampire Slayer* and *Battlestar Galactica*

John Fay – *Torchwood* 3.2 and 3.4

Phil Ford – *Doctor Who* 4.16 (with Russell T Davies), *Torchwood* 2.9, and head writer of *The Sarah Jane Adventures* (1.3/1.4, 1.9/1.10, 2.1/2.2, 2.3/2.4, 2.11/2.12, 3.1/3.2, 3.7/3.8 and 3.9/3.10)

Mark Gatiss – *Doctor Who* 1.3 and 2.7; also played Professor Lazarus in *Doctor Who* 3.6

Matthew Graham – *Doctor Who* 2.11

Stephen Greenhorn – *Doctor Who* 3.6 and 4.6

Bob Harris – TV includes *CSI: Crime Scene Investigation*; books include *Prisoner of Trebekistan: A Decade in Jeopardy!*

Robert Holmes – 64 episodes of *Doctor Who* between 1968 and 1986, and script-edited the show in the mid 1970s; died 1986

Matt Jones – *Doctor Who* 2.8/2.9 and *Torchwood* 2.7; script editor on *Queer as Folk* and *Queer as Folk 2*

Stephen King – contemporary horror fiction, science fiction and fantasy, and screenplays

Joseph Lidster – *Torchwood* 2.8 and *The Sarah Jane Adventures* 2.7/2.8 and 3.3/3.4

Tom MacRae – *Doctor Who* 2.5/2.6

Jimmy McGovern – creator of TV shows *Cracker, The Lakes* and *The Street*

Robert McKee – screenwriting guru

Brian Minchin – script editor on *Doctor Who* Series Four and *Torchwood*

Steven Moffat – *Doctor Who* 1.9/1.10, 2.4, 3.10, 4.9/4.10 and *Children in Need* mini-episode *Time Crash*, and Russell T Davies' replacement as showrunner on the 2010 series

Alan Moore – comic books include *Watchmen, V for Vendetta* and *From Hell*

James Moran – *Doctor Who* 4.3 and *Torchwood* 2.2 and (with Russell T Davies) 3.3

Peter Morgan – TV includes *The Deal* and *Longford*; movies include *The Queen, The Last King of Scotland* and the adaptation of his stage play *Frost/Nixon*

Terry Nation – 56 episodes of *Doctor Who* between 1963 and 1979; created the Daleks; died 1997

Philip Pullman – novels include the Sally Lockhart series and *His Dark Materials* trilogy

Helen Raynor – *Doctor Who* 3.4/3.5 and 4.4/4.5, *Torchwood* 1.3 and 2.3, and has script-edited both shows

Gareth Roberts – *Doctor Who* 3.2, 4.7, 4.15 (with Russell T Davies) and 2005's interactive mini-episode *Attack of the Graske, The Sarah Jane Adventures* 1.X (with Davies), 1.1/1.2, 1.7/1.8, 2.5/2.6, 2.9/2.10, 3.5/3.6 and (with Clayton Hickman) Comic Relief mini-episode *From Raxacoricofallapatorius with Love*

Gary Russell – script editor on *Doctor Who* Series Four, *Torchwood* and *The Sarah Jane Adventures;* author of behind-the-scenes books on *Doctor Who*

Robert Shearman – *Doctor Who* 1.6

Keith Temple – *Doctor Who* 4.2

ACTORS

Freema Agyeman – Martha Jones in *Doctor Who* Series Three and Four, and 4.18, and *Torchwood* 2.6, 2.7 and 2.8

Annabelle Apsion – TV includes *Soldier, Soldier, The Bill* and *Shameless*

Howard Attfield – Geoff Noble in *Doctor Who* 3.X; died 2007

Rakie Ayola – the Hostess in *Doctor Who* 4.8

Annette Badland – Blon Fel-Fotch Pasameer-Day Slitheen (Margaret Blaine) in *Doctor Who* 1.4/1.5 and 1.11

Tom Baker – the Fourth Doctor in *Doctor Who* from 1974 to 1981

John Barrowman – Captain Jack Harkness in *Doctor Who* Series One, Three and Four, and 4.18, and *Torchwood*

Mark Benton – Clive in *Doctor Who* 1.1

Brenda Blethyn – movies include *Secrets & Lies, Little Voice* and *Atonement*

Claire Bloom – the Woman (the Doctor's mother) in *Doctor Who* 4.17/4.18

Samantha Bond – Mrs Wormwood in *The Sarah Jane Adventures* 1.X and 2.11/2.12.

Nicholas Briggs – the voice of several monsters in *Doctor Who* and *The Sarah Jane Adventures*, most notably the Daleks, the Cybermen and the Judoon; also played Rick Yates MP in *Torchwood* Series Three

Kathy Burke – TV includes *Harry Enfield's Television Programme* and *Gimme Gimme Gimme*; movies include *Elizabeth* and *Kevin & Perry Go Large*

Simon Callow – Charles Dickens in *Doctor Who* 1.3

Peter Capaldi – Lobus Caecilius in *Doctor Who* 4.3 and John Frobisher in *Torchwood* Series Three

Debbie Chazen – Big Claire in *Mine All Mine* and Foon Van Hoff in *Doctor Who* 4.X

Chipo Chung – Chantho in *Doctor Who* 3.11 and the Fortune Teller in 4.11

Noel Clarke – Mickey Smith in *Doctor Who* Series One, Two and Four, and 4.18; also scripted *Torchwood* 1.11

Camille Coduri – Jackie Tyler in *Doctor Who* Series One, Two and Four, and 4.18

George Costigan – Max Capricorn in 4.X

Lindsey Coulson – Val Cane in *Doctor Who* 4.8

Nicholas Courtney – Brigadier (formerly Colonel) Alistair Gordon Lethbridge-Stewart in *Doctor Who* from 1968 to 1989, reprising the role (as Brigadier Sir Alistair Lethbridge-Stewart) in *The Sarah Jane Adventures* 2.11/2.12

Bernard Cribbins –Wilfred Mott in *Doctor Who* 4.X, Series Four and 4.17/4.18, and Tom Campbell in 1966 movie *Daleks' Invasion Earth: 2150 A.D.*

Mackenzie Crook – TV includes *The Office, Demons* and *Skins*; movies include the P*irates of the Caribbean* series

Timothy Dalton – the Time Lord President (Rassilon) in *Doctor Who* 4.17/4.18

Gareth David-Lloyd – Ianto Jones in *Torchwood* and *Doctor Who* 4.12/4.13

Alan Davies – Bob Gossage in *Bob & Rose*

Peter Davison – the Fifth Doctor in *Doctor Who* from 1981 to 1984 and 2007 mini-episode *Time Crash*

Dame Judi Dench – movies include *Mrs Brown, Shakespeare in Love* and the *James Bond* series

Ian Dury – lead singer of Ian Dury and the Blockheads; played Mr Scott in a 1998 episode of *The Grand*; died 2000

Christopher Eccleston – Steve Baxter in *The Second Coming* and the Ninth Doctor in *Doctor Who* Series One

Lee Evans – Malcolm in *Doctor Who* 4.15

Janet Fielding – Tegan Jovanka in *Doctor Who* from 1981 to 1984

Sir Michael Gambon – TV includes *The Singing Detective*; movies include the *Harry Potter* series

Sean Gilder – the Sycorax Leader in *Doctor Who* 2.X

Karen Gillan – A soothsayer in *Doctor Who* 4.3 and Amy Pond in the 2010 series of *Doctor Who*

Aidan Gillen – Stuart Jones in *Queer as Folk* and *Queer as Folk 2*

Burn Gorman – Owen Harper in *Torchwood* Series One and Two

Robson Green – TV includes *Soldier Soldier, Reckless* and *Touching Evil*

Susan Hampshire – Esme Harkness in *The Grand*

Mitch Hewer – Maxxie Oliver in *Skins*

Sir Anthony Hopkins – movies include *The Elephant Man* and *The Silence of the Lambs*

Dennis Hopper – movies include *Blue Velvet, Speed, Apocalypse Now* and *Easy Rider*

Nicholas Hoult – Tony Stonem in *Skins*

Glyn Houston – Professor Owen Watson in 1976 *Doctor Who* serial *The Hand of Fear* and Colonel Ben Wolsey in 1984 serial *The Awakening*

Charlie Hunnam – Nathan Maloney in *Queer as Folk* and *Queer as Folk 2*

Jessica Hynes (née Stevenson) – Holly Vance in *Bob & Rose,* Joan Redfern in *Doctor Who* 3.8/3.9 and Verity Newman in *Doctor Who* 4.18

David Jason – TV includes *Open All Hours, Only Fools and Horses* and *A Touch of Frost*

Peter Kay – the Abzorbaloff in *Doctor Who* 2.10

Sinead Keenan – Addams in *Doctor Who* 4.17/4.18

Craig Kelly – Vince Tyler in *Queer as Folk* and *Queer as Folk 2*

Sam Kelly – TV includes *'Allo 'Allo!* and *Porridge*

Jacqueline King – Sylvia Noble in *Doctor Who* 3.X, Series Four and 4.17/4.18

Alex Kingston – River Song in *Doctor Who* 4.9/4.10

Tommy Knight – Luke Smith in *Doctor Who* 4.12/4.13 and 4.18, and *The Sarah Jane Adventures*

Sarah Lancashire – Miss Foster in *Doctor Who* 4.1

Angela Lansbury – TV includes *Murder, She Wrote*; movies include *Beauty and the Beast*

Katy Manning – Jo Grant in *Doctor Who* from 1971 to 1973

James Marsters – Captain John Hart in *Torchwood* 2.1, 2.12 and 2.13

Sir Ian McKellen – movies include the *Lord of the Rings* and *X-Men* trilogies

Kylie Minogue – pop star and actress; Astrid Peth in *Doctor Who* 4.X

Dame Helen Mirren – movies include *Elizabeth I* and *The Queen*

Georgia Moffett – Jenny in *Doctor Who* 4.6

Colin Morgan – Jethro in *Doctor Who* 4.8

Sir Roger Moore – movies include seven outings as James Bond; TV includes *The Saint*

Naoko Mori – Toshiko Sato in *Doctor Who* 1.4 and *Torchwood* Series One and Two

David Morrissey – Jackson Lake ('the next Doctor') in *Doctor Who* 4.14

Eve Myles – Gwyneth in *Doctor Who* 1.3, and Gwen Cooper in *Torchwood* and *Doctor Who* 4.12/4.13

Gray O'Brien – Rickston Slade in *Doctor Who* 4.X

Peter O'Toole – Old Casanova in *Casanova*

Geoffrey Palmer – Edward Masters in 1970 *Doctor Who* serial *Doctor Who and the Silurians*, Earth Administrator in 1972 serial *The Mutants* and Captain Hardaker in *Doctor Who* 4.X

Francois Pandolfo – Quintus Caecilius in *Doctor Who* 4.3

Lynne Perrie – Ivy Tilsley (later Brennan) in *Coronation Street*; died 2006

Billie Piper – Rose Tyler in *Doctor Who* Series One, Two and Four, and 4.18

Amanda Redman – TV includes *At Home with the Braithwaites* and *New Tricks*

Clive Rowe – Morvin Van Hoff in *Doctor Who* 4.X

Christopher Ryan – Lord Kiv in 1986 *Doctor Who* serial *The Trial of a Time Lord* and Sontaran leader General Staal in *Doctor Who* 4.4/4.5

Daniel Ryan – Andy Lewis in *Bob & Rose* and Biff Cane in *Doctor Who* 4.8

Michelle Ryan – Lady Christina de Souza in *Doctor Who* 4.15

Colin Salmon – Dr Moon in *Doctor Who* 4.9/4.10

Lesley Sharp – Rose Cooper in *Bob & Rose*, Judith Roach in *The Second Coming* and Sky Silvestry in *Doctor Who* 4.8

John Simm – the Master in *Doctor Who* 3.11, 3.12/3.13 and 4.17/4.18

Elisabeth Sladen – Sarah Jane Smith in *Doctor Who* from 1973 to 1976, reprising the role in 1981 spin-off *K9 & Company*, 1983 anniversary Special *The Five Doctors* and in *Doctor Who* 2.3, 4.12/4.13 and 4.18, and *The Sarah Jane Adventures*

Matt Smith – the Eleventh Doctor in the 2010 series of *Doctor Who*

Brenda Strong – Mary Alice Young in *Desperate Housewives*

Kiefer Sutherland – TV includes *24*

Clive Swift – Jobel in 1985 *Doctor Who* serial *Revelation of the Daleks* and Mr Copper in *Doctor Who* 4.X

Catherine Tate – Donna Noble in *Doctor Who* 3.X, Series Four and 4.17/4.18

Gwen Taylor – TV includes *Duty Free, Barbara* and *Heartbeat*

David Tennant – Giacomo Casanova in Russell T Davies' *Casanova* and the Tenth Doctor in *Doctor Who* Series Two, Three and Four, and the 2009 Specials

Russell Tovey – Midshipman Frame in *Doctor Who* 4.X and 4.18

David Troughton – Private Moor in 1969 *Doctor Who* serial *The War Games*, King Peladon in 1972 serial *The Curse of Peladon* and Professor Hobbes in *Doctor Who* 4.8

Indira Varma – Suzie Costello in *Torchwood* 1.1 and 1.8

Jimmy Vee – *Doctor Who* credits include the Moxx of Balhoon (1.2), the Space Pig (1.4) and Bannakaffalatta (4.X); *The Sarah Jane Adventures* credits include Carl Slitheen (1.1/1.2), the Graske (1.7/1.8 and 2.9/2.10) and Nathan Slitheen (1.9/1.10)

Julie Walters – movies include *Educating Rita, Billy Elliot, Mamma Mia!* and the *Harry Potter* series

June Whitfield – Minnie Hooper in *Doctor Who* 4.17/4.18

Lee Williams – TV includes *Teachers* and *The Forsyte Saga: To Let*

Penelope Wilton – Monica Gossage in *Bob & Rose* and Harriet Jones in *Doctor Who* 1.4/1.5, 2X and 4.12

Barbara Windsor – TV includes *EastEnders*; movies include the *Carry On* series

Kate Winslet – Reet in *Dark Season*; movies include *Titanic, Eternal Sunshine of the Spotless Mind* and *Finding Neverland*

PRODUCTION

Jana Bennett – the BBC's Director of Vision since 2006

Peter Bennett – first assistant director on *Doctor Who* 1.12/1.13, 2.2, 2.4, 2.7, 2.11, 3.X and 4.17/4.18, and *Torchwood* 1.1 and 1.2; production manager on *Doctor Who* 4.6, 4.8 and 4.12/4.13; producer of *Torchwood* Series Three and (along with Tracie Simpson) the 2010 series of *Doctor Who*

Matthew Bouch – producer of *The Sarah Jane Adventures* Series One

Will Cohen – visual FX producer on *Doctor Who*

Phil Collinson – producer of *Doctor Who* Series One to Four

Mark Cossey – executive producer on *Doctor Who Confidential*

Nick Elliott – Controller of Drama at ITV from 1995 to 2007

Jennie Fava – second assistant director on *Doctor Who* 3.3, 3.6, Series Four and 4.14, assistant script editor on the 2009 Specials, and production manager on *Children in Need* mini-episode *Time Crash*

Peter Fincham – Controller of BBC One from 2005 to 2007

Jane Fletcher – BBC One's Head of Press from 2005 to 2007

Julie Gardner – BBC Wales' Head of Fiction and Drama, and executive producer of *Doctor Who*, *Torchwood* and *The Sarah Jane Adventures*

Murray Gold – composer of *Doctor Who*'s musical scores

Neill Gorton – special make-up and prosthetics designer on *Doctor Who, Torchwood* and *The Sarah Jane Adventures*

Michael Grade – Executive Chairman of ITV plc from 2007 to 2009; formerly Controller of BBC One (1984–1986), in which capacity he ordered an 18-month hiatus for *Doctor Who*

Sarah Harding – director of four episodes of *Queer as Folk*

Graeme Harper – director of six episodes of *Doctor Who* during the 1980s, as well as *Doctor Who* 2.5/2.6, 2.12/2.13, 3.7, 3.11, 4.2, 4.7, 4.11, 4.12/4.13, 4.15 and *Children in Need* mini-episode *Time Crash*

Ann Harrison-Baxter – producer of *Bob & Rose*, *The Second Coming* and *Mine All Mine*

Anna Home – the BBC's Head of Children's Television from 1986 to 1997

Julian Howarth – sound recordist on *Doctor Who* Series Three and Four, *The Sarah Jane Adventures* Series Two, and *Torchwood* Series Three

Jay Hunt – Controller of BBC One since 2008

Mike Jones – editor on *Doctor Who* since Series One

Verity Lambert – *Doctor Who*'s first producer, from 1963 to 1965; other TV producing credits include *Adam Adamant Lives!*, *The Naked Civil Servant*, *Minder*, *Jonathan Creek* and *Love Soup*; died 2007

Susie Liggat – producer of *Doctor Who* 3.8/3.9, 4.2, 4.4/4.5, 4.7, 4.11 and 4.14, and *The Sarah Jane Adventures* 1.X

Euros Lyn – director of *Doctor Who* 1.2, 1.3, 2.2, 2.4, 2.7, 2.11, 3.X, 4.9/4.10, 4.17/4.18 and 2005's *Children in Need* mini-episode *Born Again*, and *Torchwood* Series Three

Paul Marquess – TV producing credits include *The Bill* and *Family Affairs*; creator of *Footballers' Wives*

Charles Martin – director of *The Sarah Jane Adventures* 1.5/1.6 and 1.9/1.10, and two episodes of *Skins* Series Two

Charles McDougall – director of the first four episodes of *Queer as Folk*

Peter McKinstry – concept artist on *Doctor Who* since Series Two

Louise Page – costume designer on *Doctor Who* Series Two to Four, and the 2009 Specials

Andy Pryor – casting director on *Doctor Who* and *Torchwood*

Tessa Ross – Channel 4's Film and Drama Controller

Nicola Shindler – producer of *Queer as Folk*, *Bob & Rose* and *The Second Coming*, and founder of independent TV drama production company Red

Tracie Simpson – production manager on *Doctor Who* Series One to Four; producer (along with Peter Bennett) of 4.15, 4.17/4.18 and the 2010 series

Barbara Southcott – make-up designer on *Doctor Who* since Series Three

Richard Stokes – producer of *Torchwood* Series One and Two

James Strong – director of *Doctor Who* 2.8/2.9, 3.4/3.5, 4.X, 4.1 and 4.15

Colin Teague – director of *Doctor Who* 3.12/3.13 and 4.3, *Torchwood* 1.3, 1.7, 2.2 and 2.4, and *The Sarah Jane Adventures* 1.X

Edward Thomas – production designer on *Doctor Who, Torchwood* and *The Sarah Jane Adventures*

Mark Thompson – the BBC's Director-General

Jane Tranter – the BBC's Controller of Fiction from 2006 to 2008, who – as Head of Drama – oversaw the resurrection of *Doctor Who* in 2005

Jess Van Niekerk – production co-ordinator on *Doctor Who*

Piers Wenger – Julie Gardner's replacement as BBC Wales' Head of Drama and executive producer of *Doctor Who* from the 2010 series onwards

Nikki Wilson (née Smith) – producer of *The Sarah Jane Adventures* since Series Two, and *Doctor Who* 4.15; script editor on *Doctor Who* 4.4/4.5

Tony Wood – producer of *The House of Windsor* and *The Grand*

OTHERS

Benny Andersson – Swedish musician, composer and former member of 1970s/80s pop group ABBA

William Baker – Kylie Minogue's creative director

Russell Brand – comedian, TV and radio presenter and movie star

Simon Cowell – A&R executive and TV producer; talent judge on *American Idol*, *The X Factor* and *Britain's Got Talent*

Matt Dawson – former England rugby player and captain

Judy Finnigan – TV presenter and (with husband Richard Madeley) former host of regular TV chat shows

Jason Gardiner – choreographer and judge on *Dancing on Ice*

Ed Griffiths – Publicity Manager at Ebury Publishing

Rufus Hound – stand-up comedian and TV presenter

Gethin Jones – TV presenter best known for a stint on *Blue Peter*; cameoed as himself in *The Sarah Jane Adventures* 1.X, and played a Cyberman in 2.6 and a Dalek in 4.13

Anne Jowett – a Commissioning Editor at *Radio Times* magazine

Jimmy Krankie – one half of Scottish husband-and-wife comedy due the Krankies

Freddie Ljungberg – Swedish footballer and underwear model for Calvin Klein

Richard Madeley – TV presenter and (with wife Judy Finnigan) former host of regular TV chat shows

McFly – pop-rock band; cameoed as themselves in *Doctor Who* 3.12

Lee McQueen – winner of *The Apprentice* Series Four

Dannii Minogue – pop star and occasional actress; talent judge on *The X Factor*

Chris Moyles – radio DJ and TV broadcaster

Kirsten O'Brien – TV presenter and stand-up comic

Paul O'Grady – comedian and TV presenter; cameoed as himself in *Doctor Who* 4.12

Arlene Phillips – choreographer, former dancer and judge on *Strictly Come Dancing* from 2004 to 2008

Chris Rea – singer/songwriter

Craig Revel Horwood – choreographer, former dancer and judge on *Strictly Come Dancing*

Jonathan Ross – comedian, film critic, and TV and radio presenter

Britney Spears – pop star

Anthea Turner – TV presenter particularly known for *Blue Peter*, *Top of the Pops* and *GMTV*

Björn Ulvaeus – Swedish musician, composer and former member of 1970s/80s pop group ABBA

Richard Whiteley – TV presenter and journalist, famous for hosting Channel Four quiz show *Countdown*; died 2005

Wynnie la Freak – Manchester-based drag queen; appeared in *Bob & Rose*

BOOK ONE

CHAPTER ONE

DEFINITELY MAYBE

In which Mika is inspiring,
Skins is disappointing, and Russell
performs a triple loop on ice

FROM: BENJAMIN COOK TO: RUSSELL T DAVIES, SUNDAY 18 FEBRUARY 2007 07:19:48 GMT

AN IDEA

I've been thinking. I know, I know, but I was feeling dangerous. How about a magazine article on the writing of one or more of your *Doctor Who* scripts? The nuts and bolts of the process, from start to finish. Developing the story, the characters, the dialogue. An exploration of the painstaking creation process. What worked, what didn't, and why. I think it'd be fascinating. Or would it be too intrusive? And is there enough time? I'd want to chat to you about your ideas before you start writing (it could be this year's Christmas Special, or Episode 1 of Series Four, or another episode altogether), and exchange regular e-mails over the weeks and months that you spend scripting, honing, and developing the episode(s). I'd need to read, discuss, and compare various drafts. It'd be a unique and valuable look at the art of the television scriptwriter.

Thoughts?

P.S. Please say yes.

FROM: RUSSELL T DAVIES TO: BENJAMIN COOK, SUNDAY 18 FEBRUARY 2007 12:41:59 GMT

RE: AN IDEA

Well, that's a yes, then. You had me at hello.

Morning, Benjamino! Look at you, typing at first light on a Sunday. You're meant to be waking up hung over in the bed of two strangers called Hans and Milly. London isn't what it's cracked up to be. Anyway, yes to the writing thing. But I'd better warn you – I've never done anything like it before. If it feels too odd, I'd have to stop. My worry is, I never show my stuff to *anyone*. I just lock myself away and work. But the real problem is, I don't do my working out on paper. I don't often do treatments or breakdowns. It all exists in this great big stew in my head, because any story can go in any direction. It's not what you write, it's what you *choose* – and I'm good at choices. Paul Abbott always says that about me, bless him. He says that I make good choices – as opposed to someone who writes a first draft, and *then* focuses on what the story is about, what works and what doesn't. But I doubt that makes me a better writer. Paul tends to work it out on paper, and he's the Best Writer In The Land.

There's little physical evidence of the script process to show you. No notes. Nothing. I think, and think, and think… and by the time I come to write, a lot has been decided. Also, a lot hasn't been decided, but I trust myself, and scare myself, that it'll happen in the actual writing. It all exists in my head, but in this soup. It's like the ideas are fluctuating in this great big quantum state of Maybe. The choices look easy when recounted later, but that's hindsight. When nothing is real and nothing is fixed, it can go anywhere. The Maybe is a hell of a place to live. As well as being the best place in the world.

I filter through all those thoughts, but that's rarely sitting at my desk, if ever. It's all done walking about, going to town, having tea and watching telly. The rest of your life becomes just the surface, chattering away on top of the Maybe. It never turns off. (And bear in mind, the Maybe isn't just thinking about one episode. Right now, today, I've skipped ahead to Series Four, Episode 12's problem: what do the Lost People of Earth actually *do*? And that'll go on for, oh, the next year or so, until I start writing it in November.) I can't begin to tell you the thousand problems and their possible solutions, bubbling away at the same time. And the *doubts*. That's where this job is knackering and debilitating. Everything – and I mean every story ever written anywhere – is underscored by the constant murmur of: this is rubbish, I am rubbish, and this is due in on Tuesday! The hardest part of writing is the writing.

So, Ben, what I'm saying is: yes, let's do it (judging by how long I've gone on in this e-mail, we might even get a book out of it!), but so much of the process is invisible. When I start typing, those solutions lock in, and create the world of the story very fast – which is terrifying, because you're always waiting for the inevitable day when… they don't! Blimey, that'll happen. One day.

The thing is, you'll have to fight me feeling superstitious about the writing process. My trust in the Maybe feels almost superstitious. (Though I don't actually call it the Maybe; I just made that up now. And I'm not even superstitious. I was born atheist, me.) In considering a script, I might feel that saying those early options out loud to you automatically makes them more fixed, and might unbalance things. It's new territory, and that feels terrifying. Equally, so would the prospect of a night in with

Freddie Ljungberg, but I wouldn't say no to that either. (Actually, I don't even fancy him that much, but it's a good name to type, don't you think?)

RE: AN IDEA

'There will be no *Doctor Who* this year. Russell was too busy e-mailing Ben.'

I appreciate what you're saying about how you write – more in your head, less on paper – but I reckon it's better like that. It's the bits beyond the documents, beyond what's written down, that interest me the most. Literally, the thought processes. Not just what happened, but what's *happening*. Not just what goes into that great big stew in your head, but also what doesn't. I'm after a more progressive, imaginative, insightful exploration of the scriptwriting and storytelling process. Not much, then!

RE: AN IDEA

Right, you're on! I've been thinking about it all day, and it could be really exciting. Also, it's the article on writing that I've always wanted to read. Writers almost never talk about writing. Not ever. Even when I'm sitting there with Paul Abbott, getting drunk at three in the morning (long time since I did that – friendships perish under the *Doctor Who* schedule), we might complain about deadlines and commissioners and directors… but never the actual writing. We guard it. Perhaps it truly is superstition. Like saying Candyman out loud.

Would this year's Christmas Special script work? It's not a typical script: it has to be big and blousy and Christmas Day-y. It's half script, half event. But I'm not sure about the first episode of Series Four either, because that's introducing the Doctor's new companion – I like the name Penny (do you like Penny?) – and I might want to be left alone for that. Plus, you can give away too much information. Maybe discussions about a new companion, if put into print, would become part of fandom's rigid thinking. That actress would, in 20 years' time, still be asked in interviews, 'How do you feel about the fact that you were originally conceived to be a blind Sumo lesbian?'

Anyway, off to bed. Not because I'm tired, but because I'm reading a brilliant book, *Prisoner of Trebekistan*. The 'Trebek' is Alex Trebek, who's presented the US quiz show *Jeopardy!* for over 20 years. It's the story of a man who dedicated his life to getting on the show. It's so brilliant, and so funny, and even heartbreaking in small and beautiful ways. A man who's devoted to telly. No wonder I like it.

RE: AN IDEA

Yes, I like Penny.

SERIES FOUR BREAKDOWN

This is the Series Four Breakdown, compiled by Russell for the production team early in 2007. 'It's such a scary document, people might resign,' he joked at the time. Episodes 4.X, 4.1, 4.11 and 4.12/4.13 were to be scripted by Russell, 4.2 by Keith Temple, 4.3 by either Mark Gatiss (World War II) or James Moran (Pompeii), 4.4/4.5 by Helen Raynor, 4.6 by Stephen Greenhorn, 4.7 by Gareth Roberts, 4.8 by Tom MacRae, and 4.9/4.10 by Steven Moffat...

4.X – STARSHIP TITANIC

The *Titanic* In Space crossed with *The Poseidon Adventure*. The ship is on a Christmas Cruise, gets hit by meteorites, and the Doctor and survivors have to crawl through the wreckage and find out who caused the sabotage, while stopping the ship hitting the Earth below. It's not a proper recreation of the *Titanic*; it's more of a luxury hotel, with Olde Worlde trappings, plus Christmas decorations. The people on board, staff and passengers, aren't human; they're just visiting, like a cruise ship to the Bahamas. I'd like a new, one-off, spiky-faced little alien in black tie to be one of the survivors. Plus, the main monsters are the ship's robot staff – Golden Angels, beautiful, male, blank-faced masks. Also, the Judoon stomp in at the end to arrest the villains.[1] And there'll be a trip down to Earth, to a night-time shopping street with Christmas decorations – but it's deserted! No people. And maybe one scene on moorland at the end. With snow. Gotta have snow.

4.1 – NEW COMPANION

The Doctor meets his new companion, they solve an alien threat, and then sail off together. Modern-day Earth. Possibly a CGI monster.

4.2 – PLANET OF THE OOD[2]

A visit to their home planet, an ice-world, where the poor Ood are being sold into slavery by the human race. CGI-enhanced exteriors – wide-open vistas covered in snow. Factories where Ood are processed. Posh PR-type offices, where the whole enterprise looks legit, but underneath are dark, grimy rooms where the Ood are treated terribly. One huge warehouse space, full of Ood cages. Caves where the giant, pulsating, CGI Ood-brain is fermenting. Plus, a sequence of a man transforming into an Ood.

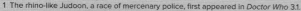

1 The rhino-like Judoon, a race of mercenary police, first appeared in *Doctor Who* 3.1.
2 The subservient Ood débuted in *Doctor Who* 2.8.

4.3 – NAZIS

World War II. Monsters on the loose in the Natural History Museum as a Nazi strike-force invades. FIRST DRAFT SCRIPT AVAILABLE, but with changes to come. The museum could be a London shoot for a few days, if we can use the interior of the Natural History Museum, but we'll need Cardiff corridors and rooms as well, if they can match. Plus, an *Indiana Jones*-type chamber hidden beneath, with sliding stone doors and stuff.

OR!!!

I am worried about recreating World War II again so soon.[3] This entire script could be replaced by...

4.3 – POMPEII

God help us! We could build a villa interior, some alien base inside the volcano, and a CGI Vesuvius, smoke and lava and all that, and Fire People might be possible... but the obvious worry is: we can stand in a bit of Welsh countryside and look at a CGI Pompeii from a distance, but I don't know how we can achieve any sort of exterior street/marketplace/whatever. We have to see people running from those ashes! But let's talk about it, because it's possible that we can write a script around our parameters. For once! And 'Pompeii' is such an irresistible headline.

4.4/4.5 – SONTARANS[4]

Martha calls the Doctor back home.[5] A huge British science project to repair the ozone layer is being infiltrated by the Sontarans. Big, sprawling science base. Maybe a military feel. These episodes might have quite a bit of military hardware, open battles between soldiers and Sontarans, guns, trucks, explosions. It's war! Also, secret Sontaran chambers where they're mass-cloning. The science project involves some device being attached to 'Every Home in Britain', like, say, a metal tube running from floor to gutter. Plus, back to suburbia with the companion's family.

4.6 – ALIEN PLANET

The Doctor, Martha, and the new companion. It's not a huge-vistas world; it's more contained. Maybe a broken-down world at war, huddled in bunkers, under fire. I'd love a new race of alien soldiers for this – all identical, like the Ood. Battle-scarred grunts in flight-suit-like costumes. Also, Martha goes back home at the end of this episode, requiring one suburbia-type scene.

3 *Doctor Who* 1.9/1.10 were set during the Blitz.
4 A warrior race of dome-headed aliens, the Sontarans featured in four *Doctor Who* serials between 1973 and 1985.
5 Martha Jones (played by Freema Agyeman) was the Doctor's travelling companion throughout Series Three.

4.7 – AGATHA CHRISTIE

The Doctor and Agatha hunt the murderer! Pure Agatha Christie. Country house, drawing rooms, wood-panelled corridors, below-stairs, etc. Nice and smart and gorgeous. It's probably set in 1966, but should feel old-fashioned, like a '20s/'30s thriller. But the gentry don't date much anyway. And a CGI monster on the loose.

4.8 – CENTURY HOUSE

A double-bank episode.[6] All Doctor. Companion-lite (she sits at home and watches the whole thing on TV with her mum; hopefully, one day's filming with her). The Doctor goes live on reality TV show *Most Haunted* to track down the ghost of the Red Widow. A big, old, abandoned, spooky house, like on a cliff top. OB vans and trucks with cables ringed around the house. Certain rooms will flashback to the 1950s or '60s. A big fire sequence towards the end – a couple of rooms burning.

4.9/4.10 – SPACE LIBRARY

An ancient, alien library on another world has been sealed off for centuries, until the Doctor joins an archaeological expedition on a mission to find out why. It's a Steven Moffat script (not available yet), so God help us! He says there are moving shadows (I'm worried that this means actual animation), and he describes the library as dark and dusty, abandoned, creepy, though it's alien and sci-fi at the same time. Events are connected to an ordinary modern-day boy in his bedroom.

4.11 – COMPANION ALONE

Double-bank. Doctor-lite. I'll try to keep this low-cost. Honestly.

4.12/4.13 – THE STOLEN EARTH

The season finale. Earth is transported halfway across the universe as part of a Dalek plot.[7] These episodes feature Martha, Captain Jack, Sarah Jane, Elton, and Rose.[8] Jackie and Mickey?[9] Also, can I have the rest of the Torchwood team, just for a couple of days? Plus, a futuristic space station complex where

6 Each series has contained at least one double-bank episode, featuring nominal appearances from one or more of the regular cast, so that another episode can be shot simultaneously, to save on filming days.
7 The Daleks – with their battle cry of 'Ex-ter-min-ate!' – first appeared in *Doctor Who* in 1963 and have featured in many subsequent episodes, becoming synonymous with the show.
8 Captain Jack Harkness (played by John Barrowman) travelled with the Doctor in Series One and Three, and is the central character in spin-off show *Torchwood*; Sarah Jane Smith (Elisabeth Sladen), companion to the Third and Fourth Doctors in the mid 1970s, returned in *Doctor Who* 2.3, and subsequently spin-off show *The Sarah Jane Adventures*; Elton Pope (Marc Warren) appeared in *Doctor Who* 2.10; Rose Tyler (Billie Piper) was the Doctor's companion throughout Series One and Two, before getting trapped on a parallel Earth with her mother and boyfriend in 2.13.
9 Rose's mother Jackie (played by Camille Coduri) and boyfriend Mickey (Noel Clarke) featured in Series One and Two.

lots of alien races are gathering for a conference. CGI: Bane, Krillitanes, Gelth, Isolus, everything we've got in the computer.[10] PROSTHETICS: Judoon, Slitheen, the Graske, the Moxx of Balhoon (well, his brother, the Jixx of Balhoon), Sisters of the Wicker Place Mat, plus a new female alien, a wise old counsellor, head of the space conference.[11] And Daleks, en masse. Lots of gunfire and exterminations. And the biggest Dalek spaceship interior ever – more like a Dalek Temple. Christ almighty! The skies over the Earth need to be changed to weird outer space vistas. Also, visible in the sky, a huge Dalek ship exterior. The size of a solar system! This will probably explode. Like they do.

And Davros.[12]

10 The Bane first appeared in *The Sarah Jane Adventures* 1.X; the bat-like Krillitanes in *Doctor Who* 2.3; the Gelth in *Doctor Who* 1.3; the Isolus in *Doctor Who* 2.11.
11 The Slitheen débuted in *Doctor Who* 1.4; the Graske at Christmas 2005, in interactive mini-episode *Attack of the Graske*; the doomed Moxx in *Doctor Who* 1.2, alongside a clan of background aliens nicknamed the Sisters of the Wicker Place Mat.
12 The (fictional) creator of the Daleks, mad-scientist Davros, first appeared in 1975 serial *Genesis of the Daleks*.

FROM: RUSSELL T DAVIES TO: BENJAMIN COOK, WEDNESDAY 21 FEBRUARY 2007 00:57:02 GMT

RE: AN IDEA

Penny it is! I like that too.

Right. The Great Correspondence. Let's start. I've been sitting here for about two hours thinking, go on, start writing to Ben. With the back of my head going, EEK! The scary thing is, it feels so exposed, balanced by the lovely thing that you're one of the few people I'd trust completely to do this with. The only other person I used to show script-in-progress was my Manchester script editor, Paul Abbott's wife, Saskia, because she lives with a writer.[1] She knows how barmy it is.

I'm just going to type and say *everything*. The moment I start censoring, it'll start to become 'written', and I think you need to know everything. I think that's the process you're after. I'm going to type what's in my head, and how it started developing today. No, not developing, but shifting. It's 4.1, the first episode of Series Four, and the creation of Penny. A good, iconic episode, but still a standard 45-minute length –

Of course, this big lump of Maybe coexists with thoughts on my two scripts for *The Sarah Jane Adventures* – which I'm dying to write, but I suspect time is running out. Plus, *Torchwood* Series Two, for which I'm supposed to be writing the Annual Return Of Suzie, coinciding with the 'death' of Ianto, but these plans are being stymied in the preparation stage, because Indira Varma is pregnant and Naoko Mori needs some time off.[2] The schedule is like a spinning wheel of alternative options, intruding into the thinking process. On top of all that there's the *Doctor Who* Christmas Special, the

1 Saskia Abbott script-edited both *Bob & Rose* and *Casanova*.
2 Torchwood operatives in Series One and Two include computer specialist Toshiko Sato (Naoko Mori), support man Ianto Jones (Gareth David-Lloyd) and, in 1.1, second-in-command Suzie Costello (Indira Varma).

Titanic In Space. (*Titanic II* – is that a good title?) For the past few days, I keep focusing on one of the central characters, an old historian-type figure – a nice, funny part, a man who's studied the Earth (these are aliens, sailing above the Earth, on a Christmas Cruise), and he gets all Earth history hopelessly wrong. 'They worship the Great God Santa!' He should wear round pebble glasses. A while back, I read that *Doctor Who* is one of the few programmes that David Jason lets his young daughter watch. Perfect guest star! Yesterday, we asked Andy Pryor, our casting director, to contact David's agent. The agent confirmed that, yes, David's daughter genuinely loves the show, so they'll talk to him, with the caveat that he's very busy, and with our fear that he'd cost a fortune. But that created today's shift onto *Doctor Who* 4.1, because *Sarah Jane* and *Torchwood* problems can park. And David Jason – well, we'd have to meet him and schmooze him, if it ever happens, so I leave that for a minute… and my mind skips onto 4.1, because that's sort of 'clean', untouched, and untroubled –

Well, no, the real truth is, I'm sitting here listening to Mika's album, *Life in Cartoon Motion*. I like Mika. Oh, a lot. Just listen to 'Any Other World', Track 6 of his album. I heard that today for the first time. *Click!* That's what shifted me onto 4.1. A piece of music. '*In any other world / You could tell the difference.*' That's a *Doctor Who* companion song! That's 'I'm going in the TARDIS'! And then those violins start. '*Say goodbye to the world you thought you lived in.*' That's Penny! I'm going to use that track on screen, as she decides to become the companion. The scene is written in my head. I can *see* it – where she is, how she walks, how I write the stage directions, the mood of it, the romance of it, the size of it. I can absolutely see it. Moments of clarity like that, when everything else is in flux, you cling to. You might remind me about that song one day and I'll just be like, 'Oh yeah, forgot.' Or more importantly – 'It didn't work.' But that's today's thought. Never mind schedules, and actors, and bollocks – I've found a companion's soundtrack! And I'm excited about Penny.

Thoughts I've had about Penny, prior to this: a bit older, maybe 30+ (are we losing all the little girls in the audience?), smarter, sassier. All of us loved Catherine Tate and that sort of repartee with the Doctor.[3] At the *Radio Times* Covers Party, Jane Tranter (the BBC's Controller of Fiction) said to me, 'Can't we bring back Donna for a few episodes?' Hmm, no. There are tentative Maybe plans for everyone to come back in cameos for 4.12/4.13, including Donna, so let's keep our powder dry for that. But we all liked Donna's equal-status sparkiness, independence, sharpness –

Hang on. Back to Penny. What's her job?! Journalist? It worked for Sarah Jane. In 4.4/4.5, there's going to be an Earth research base that needs investigating. Maybe.

Also, Penny is northern. It's my love of northern, and my ability to write that speech pattern. I actually miss it. But we've told Andy Pryor, 'Don't limit your thinking to northern.' That would be stupid. We've just got to get the best. Andy lives in his great

---

3 Catherine Tate played would-be-companion Donna Noble in 3.X.

big Casting Maybe all the time. He's already thinking. Sheridan Smith? Someone like a younger Sarah Parish? That ability to really banter with the Doctor, to match him. And to love him, actually. Under all this is my need to write The Doctor In Love again. I think we've handled it exactly right for Series Three: he'd never fall in love with Martha, because he can't just love the next woman to walk through the door, after Rose. That would cheapen the whole thing. Martha's unrequited love for the Doctor is beautiful. She deserves to grow out of that, so leaves, giving us a nice year-long bridge. Penny is walking into the Doctor's life at just the right time. (It fills me with horror, actor's lives and wages and destinies being decided on my whims, sitting here, looking for the right story. The Maybe isn't just ethereal; it actually employs people. Still, the show is the most important thing.) The first time that the Doctor sees Penny, it should be like – *wham!* Both hearts.

Northern also gives Penny a northern mother. Lovely! Maybe a bit posh. Maybe lottery-winner posh. I miss the funny mum. Little voice in the Maybe, a little doubt whispering away: 'You've *done* funny mum. Lots of funny mums, in fact. Rose's. Even Donna's. What about a funny dad?' But dads aren't funny. Yes, that's not fair, and probably not true. But tough. We're actually close to tackling that question that I always refuse to answer: where do you get your ideas from? *That's* why this correspondence fascinates me. Every writer says that they can't answer that question, but the ideas do come from *somewhere*. That conversation about funny mums happened in the foyer of Claridge's. That's when I thought, let's give Penny a funny mum. ('Where do you get your ideas from?' 'Claridge's!') Or what about a grandfather? Nice old bloke, gentle, sweet, telescope in his shed – he's always been the stargazer. He's the one who waves Penny off, tears in his eyes. It's all unashamed sentiment in the Maybe. I'd planned that grandad for Martha, vaguely, but he never appeared. He lingers on. They do that, the Characters In Search Of An Author.

Other thoughts: the story has to be set on Earth. I've always had this vague image of a housing estate – not a council estate, I mean suburbia – and a great big inverted bowl of a spaceship lands on top of it. Huge ship, covering and sealing off the estate. The space inside becomes night, whilst outside it's day. The ordinary turned into the extraordinary. That's very *Doctor Who*. Turning suburbia into terror. The police and army surround the bowl, but they can't get in, while on the inside – a hunt! An alien hunt. A creature is released – on purpose? Or is it a prison ship? Has the creature run amok and killed the crew, and it's crash-landed here? Nasty alien, vicious, give Penny something to really fight. Fast and deadly. Probably CGI. Make it able to climb on ceilings – that's always scary. Scuttling. Words like scuttling become good and important. I like that.

And in the middle of this estate, there's the Doctor. Taken as read.

That was the thinking… up until today. Thank you, Mika. Today it became: simplify. What if a spaceship crashed, and an alien is on the loose at night? No bowl.

A simple, sudden thought of, no, don't contain it; you can make this story wide and free. That made me start to write to you, because the process is starting. The process of going through options. The start of thinking about 4.1. And the stray thought, should Penny start this episode to camera, like a video diary? That's hard to sustain, but it's reaching for a different feel, using the stuff of every other drama. Not being limited to a straightforward telling of a sci-fi or fantasy story. The point is – I don't think that will happen, but I did have an exhilarating moment of thinking it *could* happen. That exhilaration carries over into the rest of the story, and creates these e-mails.

FROM: BENJAMIN COOK TO: RUSSELL T DAVIES, WEDNESDAY 21 FEBRUARY 2007 17:30:09 GMT

RE: AN IDEA

>> *Titanic II* – is that a good title?<<

Do you really want me to answer that, Russell? *Really?!*

I've just downloaded Mika's album. And I Googled him to see what he looks like. I found him in the end, on his official website, sat atop a piano, without shoes. He has oddly shaped toes. The impact of music on your writing, one art form inspiring another (there's a thought – do you see what you do as an art or a craft?), is interesting. Tell me if 'O Mio Babbino Caro' or the Prodigy's 'Smack My Bitch Up' influences today's work.

Also, I'd like to know more about how you name characters. How much importance do you attach to finding the right name? Would Rose have smelt as sweet by any other name? (Do you see what I did there? Eh? *Eh?*) Would we view her differently were she called Natalie? Or Rachael? Or Martha even? Are unusual names better? Can you start writing a character without a name in place?

One other thought, for now. You said, 'Words like scuttling become good and important,' but also you've had 'this vague image of a housing estate… and a great big inverted bowl of a spaceship lands on top of it.' So, do you prefer writing in words or pictures?

FROM: RUSSELL T DAVIES TO: BENJAMIN COOK, WEDNESDAY 21 FEBRUARY 2007 22:17:12 GMT

RE: AN IDEA

I won't be working tonight, because I've had a drink. Never work with drink. (That's me, not a rule. Paul Abbott does the opposite.) I've been for dinner with David and Phil.[4] We had such a good time, with some genuine *Doctor Who* discussion. But that's the first drink I've had in ages, so cor blimey! I'm not what I was.

Names. As I think of a character, I think of the name. I never spend time debating them, though I can pin all sorts to them in retrospect. Rose Tyler? I'd used Rose in *Bob & Rose*, so that name is like a good luck charm. There's the desire to make the series essentially British, and that's the most British name in the world. I was annoyed with

---

4 David Tennant (who plays the Doctor) and Phil Collinson (producer).

that ridiculous run of female *Doctor Who* companions with boys' or boyish names – Benny, Roz, Charley, even Ace. But that's all hindsight. I just thought, she's called Rose. Instantly, it felt right. On ITV drama *The Grand*, the executive producer made me change the lead woman's name, on a whim, from Judith to Sarah – and that character never felt right from that moment on. I never wrote her well enough. Honestly, I believe that.

Penny's mum is called Moira. There, I just thought of it now! Perfect name.

Look, I'm wary of anyone who's about to start writing ever reading something like this and thinking, that's the way to do it, that's what *I* must do. If you're going to write a script yourself, Ben, please don't think that you have to copy me. I don't think a creative process copies too much anyway. I think it finds its own way. Equally, I know the world is swamped with Robert McKee-type books on structure, and there might be, for all I know, a *How to Choose Your Characters' Names* self-help book. It probably exists. In America. You're just as free to sit down with a *Bumper Book of Baby Names* and choose one with a pin. Whatever works for you.

Now, music is very important to me. I always try to find an album that fits each thing that I write, and then I play it whenever I'm writing, repeating and repeating until I've stopped hearing it, really. It just sinks in, becomes part of the script. There's not always much variance with *Doctor Who*, because most episodes are some sort of action adventure, so often movie scores will do. They equal the size and energy that we try to show on screen. It's much harder with dramas that are more individual pieces of work. (Not that *Doctor Who* isn't personal to me, but there is an essential *Doctor Who*ness that isn't all my own creation.) *Queer as Folk* was Hi-NRG albums, to catch that sheer clubland drive and instil it into the drama. Those characters lived by that beat. *Bob & Rose* was written to *Play*, the classic Moby album. I must have played it tens of thousands of times. That album is urban, sexy, full of lonely hearts at night, just as *Bob & Rose* was full of taxicabs and chance meetings. And *The Second Coming* was Radiohead – experimental, anguish, dark, pain. That was fun!

>>Do you prefer writing in words or pictures?<<

Yes, very pictorial. A visual imagination isn't true of a lot of – very successful – writers, but I can draw, I was drawing before I was writing, so pictures are wired in. It's easy to say that applied to *Doctor Who*, because it's such a visual show, but it's true of everything I've written. *Bob & Rose*, Episode 1, the first ad break, beautifully shot, a crane lifting up as Bob and Rose's respective taxis go their separate ways. That was key. That image was in my head before anything was written. To get pretentious (why am I calling it pretentious, to describe something creative? Shame on me!), that moment sums up the whole show; not the sexuality shtick, but the randomness of it, that two-in-the-morning emptiness, out of which two people make a connection. Of course, sometimes the pictures don't come. It's easy, quoting that scene. There are plenty of ordinary scenes that aren't so memorable. Also, it's not just music + picture

+ character in separate beats. No, they're all interconnected. The pictures aren't just pictures; they're the tone, the wit, the style, the plot, the people, all in one.

Back to 4.1. As an update, not much has shifted. No real advances. Some days are like that. A lot of days. But I've been playing Mika constantly, always going back to Track 6. If I'm really not going to censor myself, then the sheer fancying of that man, right now, is powerful, ha ha! You see, I just said 'ha ha', because I find it embarrassing to relate. I've got to lose that as I go on, or it'll hold back the honesty. I reckon sex drives a lot of thinking and writing, for everyone. I do think being creative is *immensely* sexual. I think that's true of a lot of writers; they just don't talk about it. It's not just a passive, funny, 'I fancy Mika': it's a very vivid image of him. Oh, in every detail! Just very *real*. (A visual imagination is a great help here.) All those thoughts about sex are really, intrinsically, part of the process – an equal and steady beat underneath Penny's mum, alien hunts, and housing estates. The job is actually sexual. I really believe that.

Perhaps I've made the Maybe sound pure and holy, as though I go into a trance and think. People say that to me: Julie is always saying, 'You need thinking time.'[5] But it doesn't exist. The thinking is constant. Never mind Mika with his pants off; this Maybe has a thousand other voices saying, 'Must lose weight. Must stop smoking. Must phone my sisters more often.' Etc. Etc. Etc. Those voices aren't separate from whichever *Doctor Who* plot I'm considering; they're part of it. And look – that list is full of doubts. That's the thing about writing. It's all doubt. Doubts about plot, story, character, etc, let in every other doubt, the real doubts, about yourself, your very self.

I'm also sort of... hmm, pausing, wondering how to say this, but I'll say it anyway, it's ground work, and I think you have to know everything to get to the heart of the creative stuff... I'm sort of obsessive. About work, obviously. And smoking. And just look at this e-mail! Proof! A quick chat has turned into an essay. And I get like that about people. I'm not good at handling people. I'm very good at appearing to be Friend To All, but that's easy. But I rarely tell anyone, anywhere, what I'm really thinking, ever. I love my own company. I choose my own company. Because of that obsessive streak. Right now, I think I'm obsessing on these e-mails, and on you. Whether you like it or not. Still, it'll give us material.

Writing isn't just a job that stops at six-thirty. (Well, bad writers can do that.) It's a mad, sexy, sad, scary, obsessive, ruthless, joyful, and utterly, utterly personal thing. There's not the writer and then me; there's just me. All of my life connects to the writing. *All* of it.

That's scared you off, hasn't it? And all we got out of that was bloody Moira! Pages of cheap psychoanalysis, and we end up with a mother's name! That is, equally, why I love this whole bloody thing. Oh, don't think I'm mad and creepy. I'm wondering whether to send, or delete some stuff. Ah, send.

---

5 Julie Gardner, *Doctor Who*'s executive producer.

FROM: BENJAMIN COOK TO: RUSSELL T DAVIES, THURSDAY 22 FEBRUARY 2007 05:30:13 GMT

RE: AN IDEA

Dear Mad and Creepy,

Your candidness is definitely A Good Thing. Your frankness is refreshing, and much appreciated. Of course, I would say that. But *really*. It's more than I'd hoped for. Thank you. This is fast becoming the magazine article/book that *I've* always wanted to read.

FROM: RUSSELL T DAVIES TO: BENJAMIN COOK, THURSDAY 22 FEBRUARY 2007 16:46:33 GMT

HERE WE GO THEN...

Good, good, good. I was worried about your reply. Or whether you'd reply or not.

That was a mad e-mail, but also very true. I think I need to do that, to break down the walls a bit, because Glib Funny E-mail Voice is too easy to assume. Well, it's fun. But I need to get beyond that. Even the invention of the Maybe sounds mystical, and possibly glamorous. To make it feel more real, I have to open up that weirdness and compulsion, the darkness of the drive to write, as well as the fun stuff. It *is* painful. And that's good. It's funny, because when I read about other writers' seething fury or alcoholism or whatever, I actually think, blimey, I'm so vanilla. But I'm just barmy in different ways, I suppose.

I had a hell of a time from my mid 20s to mid 30s. Well, everyone does. But I was compulsive and obsessive, and that can get dangerous. I was out every night – really, every night, even Sundays – dancing, drinking, and off my head on God-knows-what. I'd be out till five in the morning, get into work at Granada at nine, throw up in the toilets, then go and be brilliant at my job. What a time! It was madness. (I'll draw a veil over a lot of it or this'll never be printed.) Then I had one calamitous night in 1997, three days after the death of Princess Diana. I actually, really, remember thinking, Jesus, if I die, I won't even make a minor headline, it's all Diana! But that cleaned me up completely. No therapy, no nothing. Just stopped. Well, no, not straight away, it took me three more years, but I got there in the end. I hardly even drink any more. God, I miss it. Really. Compulsive obsessive.

I wrote *Queer as Folk* as a hymn and testament to those days. Not a condemnation of them, but a salute. I'm proud of that. And only I really know that. Well, and you now. But that drive and compulsion, and even the self-destruction, is still there – all poured into the writing now, though still lurking.

Back to the plot! Last night, as I lay in bed, I found myself thinking, Penny should be jilted. In Scene 1. Leaving her raw and open, just ready for a dazzling Time Lord to enter her life. Imagine: a house, full of party guests; Penny is running around saying, 'Ssh, he's coming, hush everyone, lights off!' They all stand in the dark, her boyfriend – Gary, he's called Gary – walks in, lights on, *surprise!* He's standing there, blinking, shocked... as behind him, his *other* girlfriend – Roxanne – walks into the house, which they'd thought would be empty! Nice, cute, needs work.

Practical considerations (because this is where you have to be tough with a scene, and edit it before it's even written): for this scene to work, the lights have to be off, because Gary needs to think that Penny is *away*, assuming that they live together. Problem: you'd have to switch the lights off as he drove into the street, not as he approached the front door, or he'd know. So that means – what? – a minute, two minutes, in darkness, until he actually opens the door. That's a dead two minutes, right at the top of the episode. You can fill that dead time with Penny helping the set-up, whispering to her mate, 'He thinks I'm in Southport for the weekend,' but there's only so much of Penny saying 'Ssh' that you can take. Practical considerations are important when writing for the screen – even simple things, like the time it takes for a person to walk from A to B. Lots of scripts say: 'Gary gets into the car and drives off.' But think about how long that takes. You open the door, get in, adjust the gears and put the key in, do up your seatbelt, ignition, rev up, drive off – that's 30 seconds. The writer intended five seconds maximum, but it can't be done, not without a lot of camera set-ups. You can tighten the length of the process in the Edit by cutting to close-up (CU) keys, CU seatbelt going click, CU exhaust gunning fumes – but that's three extra shots already on what's meant to be a simple, one-line event. A lot of time is wasted on a thousand sets while directors and actors try to fix those sorts of problems.

But the most important worry is this: Penny lives in a house. With a boyfriend. Settled. I don't like that. It feels too old, too remote from those eight-year-old girls watching. Does the scene work in a flat? A flat is more like an eight-year-old's bedroom. Is the scene just too cute? But it's handy for pushing Penny to where I want her to be, emotionally. Alone. Brittle. Sad, but wistful. The result of that scene is a good image: night, city street, lamplight, taxis. Penny is walking along, heartbroken, being funny about it on her mobile to her friend, saying why-oh-why can't she meet the right man… as she walks past a police box.

FROM: RUSSELL T DAVIES TO: BENJAMIN COOK, SATURDAY 24 FEBRUARY 2007 11:47:11 GMT
RE: AN IDEA
I'm home. Manchester. But this is odd: I get welded to a place when I write, because it now feels weird not to be writing to you in my Cardiff flat. Manchester feels wrong, feels like starting from scratch somehow. I try to never carry a script from one city to another, because they feel very specific to either room. (But I left Mika in Cardiff. Damn! I'll have to download that later. I'm making do with Rufus Wainwright.)

I'd better update you on what's in my head. I feel daft calling it the Maybe right now, because it's all pretty empty. The other day, Julie put her foot down, brilliantly, and I am now writing *Torchwood* 2.1! But I've got *no ideas*. No bloody story. And it has to be in by the end of March. It's like looking into your head, into the store of ideas, and there's nothing there. I've a pre-titles sequence – a blowfish driving a sports car – but that's a one-off sequence to reintroduce the show. After the titles… nothing. *Nothing!*

And just when I want to be thinking about *Doctor Who* 4.1. It's hard to turn off one story while another is just starting. But it must be done.

There's a funny thing happening, too. This is what's really going on in my head. Yesterday, Julie, Phil and I get into the lift. We all turn to the mirror, fuss with our hair, we all sigh, and then hoot with laughter at ourselves. But then Phil says, 'I've got something terrible to tell you. Have you watched the very first *Doctor Who Confidential* recently? From 2005?' No. Oh God. 'You should see us,' he continues, 'all three of us – we look like *children*.' Ohhhh God! 'We look so young and happy.' And then he looks at me and says, 'Russell, you're sitting in that old flat, and your hair looks good, and you look beautiful.' Ohhhh. And we're falling apart with laughter, clutching each other in the corridor, but that loud crack you can hear is my vain old heart. I'm telling you this because *that* has been at the front of my head ever since. Right at the front. Blocking anything else. That's what I mean about work and life being indivisible. Never mind 2.1, 4.1, Christmas 2007… my head is full of that first *Confidential* documentary, wondering how knackered I am by all this work, all this sitting. Oh, I could cry. My sister says I lead an incredibly straightforward life. No car to worry about, mortgage paid off, certainly no money worries. But then a simple thing like 'You look beautiful' ruins days of thinking.

That's not entirely true. It works the other way sometimes. When my mum was dying, I was rewriting *The Second Coming*, and work was a good escape. It was nice to retreat into my head.

But I sat in the car back to Manchester yesterday, trying to *make* myself think about *Torchwood* 2.1. Except that doesn't work, it never works, you can't force it. I mustn't buy into that myth of delicate creativity, but that's what's happening. My mind just wriggles off somewhere else. It feels like flinching, to consider *Torchwood*. I *cringe*. And I know already that's a bad start. I'm not sure a truly good piece of writing ever comes from that sort of beginning. Poor *Torchwood*.

FROM: BENJAMIN COOK TO: RUSSELL T DAVIES, SATURDAY 24 FEBRUARY 2007 17:13:09 GMT

RE: AN IDEA

A question (a bit random, but bear with me): have you been watching *Skins*? It's E4's new 'teen drama'. I saw the trailers on TV last month – full of wild, feral, hormonal, house-ravaging revelry – and thought, blimey, this looks incredible! But it's not. Not yet. A few moments of genius aside, *Skins* is a bit of a misfire. It has so much potential, and there are glimpses of genius, but there's a real gulf between the show that everyone involved seems to think that they're making and the show that they're *actually* making. It's fascinating. It deserves to be better. And yet I watch it, week in, week out, hoping that it'll improve. I'm an optimist. Or an idiot.

FROM: RUSSELL T DAVIES TO: BENJAMIN COOK, SATURDAY 24 FEBRUARY 2007 18:08:19 GMT

RE: AN IDEA

I'm watching *Skins*. You do get glimmers of it working. Sid and Cassie are interesting characters (is that her name, the anorexic girl?), and sometimes Nicholas Hoult takes his clothes off, so *come on!* Be fair! What a mouth on that boy. But I do know what you mean.

FROM: BENJAMIN COOK TO: RUSSELL T DAVIES, SATURDAY 24 FEBRUARY 2007 20:54:21 GMT

RE: AN IDEA

Nicholas Hoult the actor is appealing in other stuff, but his *Skins* character, Tony, is so unlikeable. So *improbably* unlikeable. Can that be sustained? Or is Tony heading for redemption? To what extent do lead characters have to be likeable, do you think? Especially in serial drama, where you're asking an audience to stick with them week after week? The Doctor is a likeable character. A modern-day hero. And Rose Tyler – we like her a lot. Mickey and Donna weren't so likeable to begin with, but we warmed to them as they proved their worth. There can't have been many viewers, by the end of *The Runaway Bride*, who weren't rooting for Donna to accept the Doctor's invitation to travel on in the TARDIS. I'm with Jane Tranter on this one. Even the opening of 4.1, still waiting for a ticket out of Maybe, you've planned so that Penny's likeability is, deliberately, right there on screen from the off: she's on the phone to her mate, she's been jilted (we like her *because* she's been jilted – we've all been jilted), and you say she's 'being funny about it'. We like her for being funny about it. How important is it that we like Penny and Donna and the Doctor, and how significant is it that I don't like Tony from *Skins*?

FROM: RUSSELL T DAVIES TO: BENJAMIN COOK, SATURDAY 24 FEBRUARY 2007 21:42:09 GMT

RE: AN IDEA

Likeability. I've been thinking about your question during *Dancing on Ice* (did I ever tell you, I was *asked to be on that*? Actually skating! Julie is still laughing, to this day) – and I wonder, should a writer worry about likeability? It tends to be the concern of people outside the script, the producers and commissioners. Years ago, I invented a soap called *Revelations*. At the story conference, one of the commissioners from Carlton said, 'None of these characters seems very likeable,' and Peter Whalley, a wise old soap writer, just sat in the corner of the room, puffed on his pipe, and said, 'Likeability is very low on the list of useable adjectives.' Bless him.

However, *Doctor Who* is designed to incorporate likeable characters, because so much else is going on. You're creating monsters, plots, worlds, environments, so even fairly complicated characters like Rose are sketches, in a sense, to be filled in by good acting. A likeable character is shorthand, to get you into the story, fast. An unlikeable companion, for example, is going to rail against the conventions of the show, so holds you up. Even Donna had to mellow over the course of *The Runaway Bride*. For Penny, being jilted is instantly, automatically likeable, but we're talking about scenes of only a few minutes in duration, because really she's there to be chased by monsters. The jilting is shorthand. If she were awful, if she'd just jilted someone and was laughing about it (well, she's already a bit unbelievable, in this crude example), then she'd be much more complicated, and you'd spend a lot more time trying to get to know her and engage with her, but that isn't actually the point of 4.1. There are stronger voices saying, 'Get on with it! Where are the monsters?'

In other TV dramas... well, first off, most people *are* likeable, or go through the world with some construct of character that they hope is likeable. That's how you get through life. Even if you're an SS guard, you want to get on with other SS guards. The key with characters is to be *honest*. If a character's actions are believable, then that character will work. Notions of like or not-like become irrelevant. One of the finest ever examples of unlikeable characters is the movie *Dangerous Liaisons*. That's the story of two absolute monsters at war – vile, vicious people – and yet you love them, and weep for them both at the end. Brilliant writing. Those characters are so absolutely true to themselves, you end up admiring and understanding monsters.

Stuart Jones in *Queer as Folk* is like that. Without him, that show would have been The Everyday Lives Of Gays, and the whole thing would have died. But Stuart is selfish, cruel, cold, hedonistic... and fantastic! He's the star around which every other character satellites. Stuart is honest and straightforward, and knows himself very well, and knows what he wants. Oh, people *hated* him, vociferously at first, but he's attractive as a character, undeniably, because he's true. How many Stuarts are there on Canal Street? Dozens. *Hundreds!* More importantly, any one of us can, on a certain night of our lives, be like that, exactly like him. There are times when we would all do anything – drop our friends, stampede over people, defy convention – for the sake of getting a man. Or a woman. I don't simply mean that men like Stuart exist; I mean that we can all be like that sometimes. Every one of us. My job as writer is not to worry on behalf of an invisible consensus wondering about sheer bloody boring niceness. Allow the bastards to be lovely, allow the heroes to be weak, and then they'll come alive.

I know that you can't stand Tony from *Skins*, but I can see, or think I can see, what they're trying to do with him. He's got that Stuart Jones certainty, complacency, charm and good looks, and cuts through everyday events with an absolute ruthlessness – and I think we're meant to admire that, to love the monster. The problem, I think, is that I do not believe a 17-year-old boy like that exists anywhere in the world. *That's* my problem with Tony. I think that's yours, too. He's a collection of ideas, an ideal, a walking wish list, but trapped in the wrong age. If he were 20, 21, then maybe he'd seem more real – but even that's doubtful. In *Queer as Folk*, which was designed to be YOUNG! YOUNG! YOUNG! in its outlook, I had to make both Stuart and Vince 29 to make them believable. Tony doesn't stand a chance. He's simply too young to be that assured.

Maybe I'm wrong. Maybe I'm out of touch. Maybe boys like that do exist. Or maybe boys like that can be invented. It's got to be said, Ben, that *Skins* is popular with Da Kidz. Maybe we're just too old for it. Yes, even you! I just accused you of being old. I'm very happy now. I shall ice-skate away with a triple loop.

FROM: RUSSELL T DAVIES TO: BENJAMIN COOK, MONDAY 26 FEBRUARY 2007 01:51:01 GMT
RE: AN IDEA
I just saw a trailer for next week's *Skins*, in which it seems that Tony is kissing the blond gay boy, Maxxie. This is good drama, Ben! Stop fighting it! *Skins* wins.

I'm off to Brighton in the morning, Monday to Thursday, selling shows to Johnny Foreigner (it's the BBC Showcase, where Worldwide – the commercial arm of the BBC – flogs all its shows across the world), so that'll be interesting, to have a break, to see what I'm thinking by the time that's done, because my thoughts this weekend have been dominated by *Torchwood* 2.1. It's cancelling out everything else. The sheer white space of it. My mind is blank. It's more like fear and panic. It's so bad that I'm inclined to tell everyone this and pull out of the script. But I won't. I always think like this late at night. In the day, when Julie is looking at me, like I'm the one who can save them, then – I don't know – I'm too polite. That's ridiculous, isn't it? But I'm the man who fixes things. They don't need to hear my problems, just that I can fix theirs. That's more than a production problem. That's me. I don't tell people what I'm really thinking. Maybe things would be better if I did. People would help. But I just don't.

This is a rare problem. It's come along just as we happen to have started this process. It's not typical. But since I've already told you a lot of the things that I don't tell anyone, like the stuff that I got up to years ago (and I've skipped over some of it, and deleted stuff, cos, y'know, dignity and all that), you might as well know this…

In a crisis, another sly snake of a voice starts wheedling away. 'Go out and get off your head, *then* you'll think of a good idea,' it says. I used to do that, go out drinking in a crisis. I used to believe it worked. Actually, I can pinpoint certain evenings when it *did* work. I can point to exactly where I was standing in Manchester's Cruz 101 (downstairs, by the funny little stone well), off my head, when I thought of the frankly brilliant climax to Series One of *The Grand*. The thought was blinding. (It was simply this: both brothers are called Mr Bannerman! They've got the same name! You'd have to see the episode to make sense of that, but it was *so* clever.) It wasn't the alcohol or whatever I was on that night that made me think of that idea – I've created enough stuff since to know that I can do it on my own – but nonetheless the connection is there. Literally, a temptation. 'Just spend one night in Brighton, on your own, out in a club, not talking to anyone, just losing it, and see what you think up.' Bad voice. But it's always there. And I'm not 100 per cent clean. I don't want to sound like a saint here. Once a year or so, I still go out, on my own, I do get slaughtered, I end up God-knows-where… ha ha, pathetic… but then I can lock it away again.

I thought I'd tell you this because, well, that's the contract, and the things that are past are never really past; they're still going on in my head, all the time. But they're under control now. A lot of nights writing are spent not just thinking of plot, character, pace, etc, but also waiting till 2am or so, just waiting, sitting there with the script open but not actually working on it, finding anything else to do, sending trivial e-mails, eating, watching a bit of telly, whatever, by which time that snaky, tempting voice has given up – and then I can get back to work. It stops by 2am because that's when clubs used to shut, as simple and as literal as that. I know clubs are open all hours now, and I thank God it wasn't like that when I was younger or the pattern would be a thousand times worse.

Blimey, this is therapy. And so is writing.

FROM: RUSSELL T DAVIES TO: BENJAMIN COOK, MONDAY 26 FEBRUARY 2007 08:31:34 GMT

RE: AN IDEA

I just read last night's e-mail. How self-pitying! I suppose everyone sounds like that at 2am. I mean, it's all true, but putting that stuff into words sounds sort of fraudulent. Or embarrassing. I suppose I want you to think I'm marvellous, but I sound like an idiot. Hey ho. Still, glad I said it all. Just about.

Anyway, daylight, Brighton, ta-ra!

P.S. This morning, I thought: Penny *Carter*. Sounds nice.

FROM: BENJAMIN COOK TO: RUSSELL T DAVIES, MONDAY 26 FEBRUARY 2007 09:48:16 GMT

BRIGHTON

All writers are self-pitying. Discuss. (No, don't.) Thank you, again, for your openness. If tomorrow morning's headline is 'Family TV Writer Found in Brighton Gutter', I won't half feel guilty. I wonder, though, have you ever pursued 'suffering' in the hope of achieving some sort of, I don't know, creative epiphany? You say that *Queer as Folk* was inspired by your own experiences, but has it ever worked the other way round? Have you ever gone looking for trouble along with inspiration?

FROM: RUSSELL T DAVIES TO: BENJAMIN COOK, WEDNESDAY 28 FEBRUARY 2007 15:32:23 GMT

RE: BRIGHTON

I'm typing from Hull, from a cheap hotel where they've a computer in the bar. It costs a quid for 20 minutes. I was only in Brighton for one night, then my boyfriend's mother died. The poor soul. Oh, it's sad. I've been around to the house and all that, but they're all together now, brothers and sister, so I've retreated. Escaping back into work again.

>>have you ever pursued 'suffering' in the hope of achieving some sort of, I don't know, creative epiphany?<<

No. Honestly, that simple. Never. There's an underlying question of why – why did I end up so drunk and off my face on whatever all those years ago? – but honestly, during those dark times, not one part of my brain was thinking, I'm doing this for research. It's way too scary, too exciting, too mad, too needy for anything that ordered and logical. If only I could use that excuse! Nowadays, it's like I almost entirely disassociate that person from myself. Maybe it's best left sleeping. Just promise me, if it's midnight and I say, 'Sod it, I'm off to buy some Chinese red' or something, you'll say, 'STOP!!!' Mind you, it's been so long, they probably don't call it Chinese red any more. I'd come back with a takeaway sweet-and-sour.

Is that true, though? Did I just lie my way out of that? Okay, so I've never sought out an experience just so that I can use it in a script, but every experience, every single one, I'm thinking, this is interesting. And they do find their way into a script in the end. So which comes first? Blimey, that'll keep me awake.

Meanwhile, I had to take emergency measures. Given the time that I'll have to spend with my boyfriend, I took action on *Torchwood* 2.1 – and stole a plot! Lovely Joe Lidster (nice man, so enthusiastic) is being tried out as a writer on *Torchwood*, so about a month ago I gave him one of my standby plots: Spooky 24-Hour Supermarket. (Have you ever been in one at 3am? Weirdest places in the world – so bright and empty, and staffed by The Damned.) And Joe has been working on this script faithfully, though he has some way to go till it's TV-ready, but then I got on the train to Hull, and thought, clear as daylight – that's *my* plot, I need it, I'm having it. Made the calls. Done. Poor Joe ousted (we'll find him something else), but I've got a story. Smash and grab. Never done that before. Mind you, it's not a brilliant plot – it's more of a standard mid-series plot – and now I have to *make* it brilliant, with precious little time.

Also, on the train down to London on Monday, I was thinking about this year's Doctor-lite double-banker episode. I got an image: Penny and Moira driving into that estate in 4.1... what if, in *Sliding Doors* fashion, they'd turned left that day, but this time we have them turning right? What if she'd never met the Doctor, and 4.11 tells the story of that? Good idea!

There we go. My quid's almost up. Love from Hull.

FROM: BENJAMIN COOK TO: RUSSELL T DAVIES, WEDNESDAY 28 FEBRUARY 2007 23:47:13 GMT

RE: BRIGHTON

Greatest sympathies to your fella on the passing of his mum. That's horrible news.

Penny and Moira, *Sliding Doors* style? I think it was Robert Holmes who once said: 'We only ever use original ideas on *Doctor Who*, but not necessarily our own original ideas.' Clever man. With the sheer wealth of sci-fi material coming out of the US over the past 20 years, isn't it near impossible not to touch on story ideas that have been done already? Isn't this equally true for any writer, of any genre, in any medium? How much do you worry about that?

FROM: RUSSELL T DAVIES TO: BENJAMIN COOK, SATURDAY 3 MARCH 2007 16:24:50 GMT

RE: BRIGHTON

Do I worry about finding original ideas? Not at all. Within limits. For a start, there are no new stories, and long-running shows eat up a lot of plots. These plots haven't necessarily been seen on primetime BBC One. Material doesn't have to be new, just good. You might as well ditch all alternative-timeline stories because *A Christmas Carol* did it first. (Just how brilliant was Dickens in coming up with that? It's now replacing the Nativity as *the* Christmas story. What a man!) I'd feel revolted if the *start* of the process was, 'I like *Sliding Doors*, so let's do that.' But I went through a genuine sequence of thoughts that led me to a *Sliding Doors*-type of story – the need for a double-banker, Doctor-lite episode, etc – so I feel completely justified. I feel, and the story feels, fundamentally honest. (If I can learn from *Sliding Doors*' precedents, though, all well and good.)

Thursday night, driving back to Hull again, I had a sudden panic about 4.1. I'm thinking it's bollocks. But then last night – a million ideas! I'd been to the funeral, and the result, after a sad, stifling day, was that the Maybe went into overtime. (Later, thinking about that, I fell into that superstition of thinking you have to have a bad day in order to have a good day. Like there's a balance, a pattern, a God, which is bollocks, but you can't help thinking it. All writers are self-pitying, yes. And self-hating.) First off, the *Sliding Doors* episode – it's called *Turn Left* – is *brilliant*. Penny and Moira in that car. Fateful, casual decision: how's it quickest to get to Donna's grandad's? Turn left or turn right? In 4.1, she turns left. In 4.11, she turns right – so Penny never meets the Doctor. And she has a time-psych-thing-creature living on her back, feeding off this alt-life. Ooh, but certain people can see it – old women, psychics, Penny's nervous, quiet friend, glimpsing the beast in mirrors. Is Penny going mad?

Problem: life without the Doctor is dull. Nice idea, the alt-life, but what's *happening*? Apart from simply living that life? And the occasional glimpse-of-monster-in-mirror? Worrying about a monster on your back isn't enough. But what if the Doctor is dead? If Penny didn't meet the Doctor, then the Doctor died. (Which means that I must write a scene in 4.1 where Penny saves the Doctor. But I'd have done that anyway.) Penny in 4.11 becomes a bystander to the events of 4.1, trapped outside the bowl or whatever with the army and police. She sees the Doctor's body being carted away, some soldier saying, 'He gave his life, killing the creature' or something. The story becomes not just What If Penny Never Met The Doctor? but What If The Doctor Were Dead? A world without its protector. While Penny is continuing her 'normal' life, getting paranoid about a glimpsed beast on her back, the weather is getting warmer, strange reports on TV, aliens are moving in; we're getting invaded, and there's no Doctor to save us. With Earth falling, Penny needs to travel back in time to stop her original self from turning right.

But how does Penny travel in time? The thing on her back? No! The TARDIS! Of course! The Doctor is dead, but he left the TARDIS behind, so UNIT has gutted it.[6] A big empty warehouse, pool of lights at the centre, the police box, innards gutted, scientists all around. They can't really use the TARDIS, because it's beyond them, but they can make one person travel back in time – and they've worked out that Penny is at the heart of the nexus. Penny has to travel back to that road, on that day, to stop herself. But it needs a chase, so Penny is on foot. Running. I love running. Especially if the lead character is running. The cannibalised TARDIS equipment is faulty, she arrives back in time, but half a mile away, it's too late, the car is pulling out, so to stop the original car turning right… she runs in front of the traffic. She kills herself. Alt-Penny has to die. In dying, she fades away, with a blissful smile, because she never

6 UNIT (standing for Unified Intelligence Taskforce, formerly United Nations Intelligence Taskforce) is a fictional military organisation that has featured in *Doctor Who*, on and off, since 1968. Its purpose is to investigate and combat paranormal and extraterrestrial threats to the Earth.

existed. The traffic to the right screeches to a halt, original Penny and original Moira can't see what's happened, just some cars tailing back, so they have to turn left. And time goes back into its groove. [Major editorial worry – and this is rare, so it has square brackets – the story requires the lead audience-identification character, Penny, to throw herself under a car! Don't copy that, kids. Yikes, I can see trouble with that. I'll just have to write it carefully.]

Meanwhile, I was stuck on 4.6, pencilled in for Stephen Greenhorn to write. I really, really like that man. I was due a meeting with him next Friday to talk ideas, but cancelled it yesterday because my head was empty. I'd nothing to talk to him about. Part of me thinks, he's lovely, he loves us, just ask him for his own ideas. But maybe I'm too power-mad for that. Ha! This is interesting, though, because I've just read an interview with him in *Doctor Who Magazine*, which got me thinking.[7] I learnt more about Stephen from that interview than I ever have face-to-face. In *DWM*, Stephen says that it's unusual, writing *Doctor Who*, because the lead character never really changes, like he would in any other drama; he just changes the world around him. Very true. And yet… therefore… wouldn't it be brilliant to ask Stephen to write a story in which, well, the Doctor really changes? (The text of *DWM* feeds back into the series itself – I love this process!) We haven't got a Madame de Pompadour or *Human Nature*-type story in Series Four yet, so let's have something that really stretches David's limitless acting.[8] What can that be? Well, let's really go for broke…

A child. Give the Doctor a child! A daughter. Pre-titles sequence: the Doctor and Penny are trapped underground. Door explodes open. Smoke clears. Great big sexy Amazon of a woman standing there, loaded with guns, and says… 'Hello, dad!'

It's a war-torn world, an Earth colony in mid-invasion, she's leader of the rebels, she and the Doctor have to get to know each other, and lose each other, in the middle of gunfire and barricades and running. But how is she his daughter?! Even I don't want an ex-girlfriend/mother in the background. Ah, but it's sci-fi: she's a genetic scraping extrapolated into a fully grown woman. Somehow. Technically, his daughter. Ooh, technically a Time Lord. (She's got to die at the end, of course.) Or what if some remote probe scans the Doctor and Penny the moment they step out of the TARDIS, and then they meet this fully grown warrior woman who's *their* daughter? From a simple scan, the enemy, the aliens, create fully grown clone soldiers *who are your children*. A form of psychological warfare – you'd find it harder to gun down your own child. Hmm, bit odd. Bit short story. Bit mad. Bit cluttered, if it's Penny's child too. Do you see, in reaching to make something new, you can make it over-complex? At heart, *Doctor Who* is a Saturday night, primetime show. But, but, but… there might be something in there.

---

7 *Doctor Who Magazine* (*DWM*), first published as *Doctor Who Weekly* in 1979, is an official, four-weekly periodical about the show.
8 In 2.4, the Doctor falls in love with Madame de Pompadour; in 3.8/3.9, the Doctor becomes human.

Thinking of 4.6 and 4.11 simultaneously made me feel very happy. There's a lot of misery and worry in these e-mails, but last night felt excellent. I went to bed full of adrenalin, letting all these ideas buzz. But then, on the train back to Manchester this morning, I realised: 4.6 *isn't* a blank slate, you dope! It's actually tagged as the Martha Trapped In Space episode. She rejoins the Doctor on Earth in 4.4/4.5, but just as a mate, not as a companion, and then 4.5 ends with the TARDIS spinning off with her on board. The whole of 4.6 is supposed to be 'Take me home!' And I forgot. Damn. How could I forget? I've *promised* that to Freema Agyeman. Ah well. The Doctor's daughter is far, far better.

P.S. You were right, *Skins* is weird. In Thursday's episode, they went to Russia! *Why?!* It's the oddest hybrid of a drama and broad sitcom. Mind you, people say that about my stuff.

FROM: BENJAMIN COOK TO: RUSSELL T DAVIES, SUNDAY 4 MARCH 2007 11:17:56 GMT

'HELLO, DAD!'

The Doctor's Daughter! Well, that'll get some folk hot under the collar. But will they believe it? Go on, Russell, leak *The Doctor's Daughter*, and watch the internet explode! During the 1980s, the *Doctor Who* production team replaced an entry on the office planning board – or so the story goes – with a fake title, *The Doctor's Wife*, in an attempt to identify the culprit leaking information about the series to the press. Sure enough, before long, the redtops were reporting that *The Doctor's Wife* would feature in the next season. (But was the mole caught? That's what I want to know.)

When conceiving story ideas, are you ever aiming, specifically, to articulate social, political or religious points of view? You've conceived scripts with that in mind before… haven't you? You embarked on *The Second Coming*, for instance, to advocate atheism? And wrote *Queer as Folk* to represent gay men and gay issues on TV? Do you do that on *Doctor Who* ever? Can you? Or is it, above all, about the spectacle, the rush of adventure, the gunfire, the dark tunnels, the tough woman with guns, and all that running?

FROM: RUSSELL T DAVIES TO: BENJAMIN COOK, MONDAY 5 MARCH 2007 01:23:12 GMT

RE: 'HELLO, DAD!'

You do ask tough questions. That's good! It's tricky, that social/political/religious thing, because really that's *life*, that's *people*, that's *what you think about the world*, and that's why you want to write in the first place. It's not like there's a section of my mind that categorises things – like, this scene is about character, the next is all sociology. They're all in there, in one huge continuum.

If you're touching on big issues, you've got to keep turning these things, examining them, looking at the opposite of what you think. For example, as an atheist, I set out to include the 'Old Rugged Cross' sequence in *Gridlock* to show how good faith can be, regardless of the existence of God – how it can unite and form a community, and essentially offer hope.[9] That was my intention, or my starting point, and yet the real me came bleeding through, because it transpires that hope stifles the travellers. It stops them acting. By uniting, they are passive. The Doctor is the unbeliever. The direct consequence of the travellers in the traffic jam singing that hymn is that the Doctor realises that no one is going to help them. There is no higher authority. That's when he starts to break down the rules of that world by jumping from car to car. You could argue, therefore, that the travellers' faith is misguided.

It's great discussing this with David Tennant, actually. We fell into devil's advocate: he argued for the car-drivers being wrong and passive, and I argued for their goodness. But I think he's right. He got what the script is saying. But I didn't write *Gridlock* thinking,

---

9 *Doctor Who* 3.3 is set on New Earth, a planet in the far future, where the population is stuck in an infinitely huge, near-stationary underworld traffic jam, driving for an eternity in the hope of reaching the real city above.

this is my take on religion. My foremost thought, and my principal job, was to write an entertaining drama about cats and humans stuck on a motorway. Everything else just bleeds through. I do have opinions, I do have beliefs, and when I'm writing well – and that hymn sequence is one of my favourites, because the hymn *changes* the course of events – it's synthesised with my worldview. How can it be any other way? Yes, *Queer as Folk* is a massively political drama, and yet barely a political speech is made. Not directly. But every word is loaded. Every scene is about the place of gay men in the world. You could argue that it's entirely political. And it's *my* politics. It's all me, me, me.

Of course, I'm aware of the politics with the cheap, easy lines, like the 'massive weapons of destruction' reference in *World War Three*. But that barely counts: it's quick satire, hardly profound. (Although, it satirises a politician on TV lying to the country about needing a war; men have died for that, are dying now.) More often, I prefer a slyer approach. It boils down to that line in *Tooth and Claw*, my favourite line in the whole series, when Queen Victoria says of the Koh-I-Noor diamond, 'It is said that whoever owns it must surely die,' and the Doctor says, 'Well, that's true of anything, if you wait long enough.' Nice gag, fast, harmless – but actually, under that, it's lethal. That's what I really think about a ton of things: religion, superstition, mysticism, legends, all bollocks. That's a whole belief system, trashed. And I was conscious of that. I wanted to write that line. I was glad that I thought of a way of putting it so precisely, because it wasn't the time for a polemic.

I say the process is inevitable, but also I do think it's your job as a writer to say something about the world. Why else are you writing? I can't think of a script in which I haven't done that. I'm being disingenuous if I imply that it's accidental, because I look for those chances. I create them. Queen Victoria had been expressing her profound interest in the afterlife, ever since the dinner table. That's quite a belief system that the Doctor knocks for six with one fleeting line. The whole thing has a slight awareness of Rational Man versus Head of the Church. Of course, the *real* job of the episode is Man versus Monster (the werewolf, not Queenie), but I can't, I cannot, write just that.

FROM: BENJAMIN COOK TO: RUSSELL T DAVIES, MONDAY 5 MARCH 2007 22:19:55 GMT

RE: 'HELLO, DAD!'

You say that it's a writer's job to say something about the world ('Why else are you writing?'), but do you reckon that's true of all good writers? Or is it perfectly possible to write something brilliant, beautiful or intensely thought-provoking simply out of a desire to tell a ripping yarn, to entertain people? Isn't that why a lot of people start writing? Especially why a lot of people start writing *Doctor Who*? Then again, there are plenty of bad writers out there, so are they the ones that *don't* have something to say? (Even the phrase 'something to say' sounds overtly political.)

FROM: RUSSELL T DAVIES TO: BENJAMIN COOK, TUESDAY 6 MARCH 2007 02:34:07 GMT

RE: 'HELLO, DAD!'

I should start calling this BBQ – Ben's Big Questions. That last one is huge!

When I say something like 'It's your job as a writer', I'm grandstanding a bit or falling into lecture mode. I don't think of it as a job. In fact, I've never joined the Writers' Guild, out of some strange belief that this isn't a real job. Partly, I feel a fraud, as everyone does. But also it's because writing, I think, is nothing to do with unions or status or making money; writing is a compulsion. An obsession. You have to be arrogant to be a writer. You have to be able to walk into a commissioner's office and demand six million quid to make something. You have to believe that it's worth that, that it deserves to be made, that it deserves to be seen. I wouldn't be happy just writing this stuff in an exercise book and then leaving it for my own contemplation.

You're right, 'something to say' sounds political, but that doesn't mean I sit here thinking, oh, I must announce my thoughts about gay men, about Christianity, about life. Maybe that's when bad scripts are written, when you choose the theme first. I consider that I've something to say when I've thought of a person, a moment, a single beat of the heart, that I think is true and interesting, and *therefore* should be seen. It's because I can imagine *Queer as Folk*'s Nathan Maloney so full of repression, and desire, and lust, and martyrdom, that I have to write him. It's because I've seen, and sometimes been, Stuart Jones – it's because I understand him and want to convey that life – or because I don't understand him and want to explore him through writing.

Thinking about the show that I'm going to do once *Doctor Who* is over, known only, ridiculously, as *More Gay Men* (I don't even know what it's about, just gay men), I can imagine a man who is so enraged by something tiny – the fact that his boyfriend won't learn to swim – that he goes into a rage so great that, in one night, his entire life falls apart. It's not about the learning to swim at all, of course; it's about the way that your mind can fix on something small and use it as a gateway to a whole world of anger and pain. Huge things in life can extrapolate from small details. That's what I love. That's what I explore. If I write the Learn To Swim scene well – and it could be the spine of the whole drama – then I *will* be saying something about gay men, about couples, about communication, about anger. But that's the result, not the starting point. For me, anyway. You need to be a titanic genius of Jimmy McGovern-level to start with your theme. It might not even be true of him, actually, because look how quickly he boils down the Great Themes to ordinary people making ordinary mistakes in kitchens and pubs.

There's a great big streak of entertainer in me, but the truth is, if you're writing well, if the end result is brilliant or beautiful, then you *are* saying something about the world. You can't not be. *Fawlty Towers*? Comedy genius! But I could write a thousand-page thesis on what it has to say about frustrated middle-aged men, about England, about the 1970s, about dead marriages. It's brilliant because it's honest, and that means that it's resonating. Even something like *Only Fools and Horses*, a much plainer sitcom, is ineffably funny, but it *sings* when Del Boy says, 'This time next year, we'll be millionaires.' That's when people truly take it to their hearts. They recognise it. That's all of us. Even if you're blubbing at the Doctor and Rose on Bad Wolf Bay in *Doomsday*, you're empathising, you're feeling it, and there's an echo of every loss you've ever had in that.[10] If it's successful, it *is* saying something about you, about the world. I'm trying hard to think of something of which that's not true – and can't. Even the bloody *Teletubbies*! That's an extraordinary show, it's true brilliance, because somewhere in there they've captured the sheer strangeness, the joy, the bombardment, of being a toddler in a world of colour and shape and noise.

So why do it? Why write? Well, there's no choice. Thinking of these stories is just the way that my brain is shaped. It's hardwired. If I fell out of favour as a writer and ended up as a teacher or something, those stories would still be boiling away. I see them everywhere. I think of them all the time. Just today, I met a woman – who shall remain nameless – a nice, smiling, 80-year-old woman, really kind and quiet, and I sat with her waiting for a taxi. But the more we chatted, the more I thought, actually, you're not nice, there's something sour and hard at the heart of you, and you don't let it out; you just sit there smiling. It's not like I solved her conundrum, but she's in my head now, that fixed smile – and I am writing her. She'll pop up one day in something I write. I want to find out why she's like that. I want to push it further, to the day that she cracks. I want to see her let loose with other characters, to see what happens. That's what I do. That's why I do it.

I ended up thinking about 4.1 today. (Hooray! With a boo from the Christmas Special corner.) I thought about Penny's grandad. Way back in the '90s, before reviving *Doctor Who* was real, I had a sort of rough first new episode in my head, should the call ever come. A companion-to-be, all told from her point of view, and she's a young office cleaner, working at night in some sort of smart, high-rise city office, where she can't help noticing… well, maybe they have dinosaurs in the basement! But then I wondered whether dinosaurs are limiting, and I started to think of computer terminals that could move, casings that could ooze and creep after you, even swallow you. This led to thoughts about plastic, and then to Auton twins as the Big Bad Bosses, a man and a woman who would always hold hands, because their hands turned out to be fused.[11] Of course, the would-be-companion meets the Doctor (his first word to her is 'Run!'), and the story had an escape-by-window-cleaner's-cradle sequence – which I ended up using, actually, in *Smith and Jones*, but it was cut well before the final draft. But the point is, the companion had a grandad. He was funny. He played in a skiffle band in the local pub. At one point, the whole skiffle band would get involved in… well, I don't know, distracting a guard or something. Funny old codgers. All vague

---

10 Bad Wolf Bay in Norway, on a parallel Earth, is where the Doctor last saw Rose, at the end of *Doctor Who* 2.13. She told the Doctor that she loved him, but he was cut off before he could complete his reply.
11 The Autons – animated plastic, often in mannequin form – appeared in two *Doctor Who* serials in the early 1970s, and were resurrected by Russell for the first episode of the revived show (1.1).

images. Thing is, when they asked me to do *Doctor Who* for real, I junked all that, almost instantly. (Except for the Autons.) That putative companion – she had no name – felt too old, not everywoman enough. But I remembered her grandad today ('Where do your ideas come from?' 'Old ideas!')…

He's now *Penny's* grandad, the stargazer, the man with a telescope in his shed, someone who's been UFO-spotting all his life, now invigorated by this new world in which spaceships fly into Big Ben, Christmas Stars attack, etc. Instead of the skiffle band, maybe there's a gang of old codgers who all meet round his house. Instead of a Neighbourhood Watch, they're an Alien Watch. All a bit hopeless and funny – and then, when faced with real aliens in 4.1, they turn out to be magnificent and brave. Bit schematic. But it could work.

FROM: BENJAMIN COOK TO: RUSSELL T DAVIES, TUESDAY 6 MARCH 2007 02:50:39 GMT

RE: 'HELLO, DAD!'
I'm asking big questions, I know, but they'll get smaller, I promise. (Actually, I don't.) I tell you what…
    1) What's your favourite colour?
    2) If you were a pizza topping, which one would you be?
    3) What's it like in space?
    Better?

FROM: RUSSELL T DAVIES TO: BENJAMIN COOK, TUESDAY 6 MARCH 2007 02:59:45 GMT

RE: 'HELLO, DAD!'
    1) Blue.
    2) Pepperoni.
    3) Cold.
    Much better. Thank you.

CHAPTER TWO

CATHERINE, KYLIE, AND DENNIS

In which Kylie Minogue sings the Muppets,
Russell turns down a fifth series of *Doctor Who*,
and Charlie Kaufman is told to sod off

FROM: RUSSELL T DAVIES TO: BENJAMIN COOK, TUESDAY 6 MARCH 2007 23:58:01 GMT

RE: 'HELLO, DAD!'

Today was *mental*. I can't even begin to type it all right now. Sorry, Ben. I only got four hours' sleep last night, after watching all of last week's rushes, then getting up at 8am, so I'm exhausted. Mental days like this tend to come to nothing in the end, so we'll look back and think, that was so daft, none of it happened. But it's part of the job, so I'll update you tomorrow. I promise.

FROM: BENJAMIN COOK TO: RUSSELL T DAVIES, WEDNESDAY 7 MARCH 2007 00:11:02 GMT

RE: 'HELLO, DAD!'

Talk about leaving me on a cliffhanger! Never mind e-mailing me, Russell. For Christ's sake, get some sleep, and then you can fill me in on your mental Tuesday.

FROM: RUSSELL T DAVIES TO: BENJAMIN COOK, WEDNESDAY 7 MARCH 2007 12:06:51 GMT

MENTAL TUESDAY

Right. Mental Tuesday. First up, we got interest from Dennis Hopper. Yes, the Dennis Hopper. American movie star Dennis Hopper! James Strong met his agent on a plane or something, on his way back from the US, having done ADR with Ryan Carnes for the Dalek episodes.[1] What a showbiz tale! I could fit Dennis Hopper into 4.X, maybe, if I can work out who he can play. A nice little cameo? Or a proper big part, I don't know, like the ship's historian? Mind you, we should be so lucky. I'll believe it when I see it.

Secondly, back in the world of hard facts, Julie said that Billie Piper is up for doing four episodes next year. *Four!* I was hoping for one, two at best. Brilliant. Entirely out of leftfield. What a day! And as if that weren't enough…

As you know, we've been talking to Jane Tranter about how Donna-like Penny could be. Completely by chance, Jane had a meeting with Catherine Tate this week, just one of those general, bigwig, let's-work-together-more sorts of chats. But afterwards Jane phoned up Julie and said, 'All Catherine talked about was what a brilliant time she'd had on last year's *Doctor Who* Christmas Special. She went on and on about it. She could be up for a whole series. I think you're in with a chance.' Bollocks, of course. But it all went a bit mad. This all happened on Tuesday. I bloody love the idea – oh, I love Donna – so we asked Phil, who relished working with her on set, and then we asked David, and he just adores Catherine, and now Julie is booking in a lunch to see her! But it's madness. A woman that busy? With her own TV show? Making movies now? We'll never get Catherine for a whole series. Still, we can but try. At the very least, we might be able to get her back for 4.12/4.13. But this will probably just end up as a wistful paragraph in these e-mails. TV goes crazy sometimes.

P.S. Will you be at tomorrow's Dub of 3.4?[2] Murray Gold's Dalek Choir time! Though it might be rather strange to see you, because it feels like you live in my head now. In a good way, I think. See you in Cardiff.

FROM: BENJAMIN COOK TO: RUSSELL T DAVIES, FRIDAY 9 MARCH 2007 09:23:58 GMT

RE: MENTAL TUESDAY

Good to see you at yesterday's Dub. I love Dubs. How could I not? Watching *Doctor Who* on the big screen, stuffing my face full of BBC croissants, seeing you put your foot down ('You worked on that camera shake for hours, I know. But do you know what? You were wrong!'), and realising that Julie is the biggest *Doctor Who* geek in the room. She'd barely even watched the show three years ago!

Any further news on Catherine?

FROM: RUSSELL T DAVIES TO: BENJAMIN COOK, FRIDAY 9 MARCH 2007 13:49:19 GMT

RE: MENTAL TUESDAY

I'm feeling bleeargghhh. I must have picked up some bug. I've only just got up, after 16 hours' sleep! I feel pale. I want to go back to recording the Maybe, but I'm too busy

---

1 US-based actor Carnes, who played Laszlo in *Doctor Who* 3.4/3.5, directed by James Strong, was required to record additional dialogue (ADR) after principal photography had wrapped on the episodes. This is standard practice on TV dramas.
2 The Dub is the first time that the producers view an episode, on a big screen, with finished visuals, sound design, and Murray Gold's score.

feeling ill. Again, poor *Torchwood*. This is shameful, but I'm feeling too sick to even worry about it. However, I described the basics of 4.X to David yesterday evening; as I said it out loud, I *really* liked it, what little there is, so that's good. It's David's last day filming Series Three tomorrow. And it's John Barrowman's 40th birthday. I can't believe he's admitting to 40!

One other thing worth noting: in the lift at Broadcasting House yesterday, maybe you heard me turn to Julie and say, 'Wouldn't [name removed – let's call her Miss X] be a brilliant Penny?' She's a marvellous actress, with a rare flair for comedy. So that's snowballed. We've checked with Jane Tranter, and she loves her too. Hmm, we'll see. It might be another of those things that comes to nothing, but thinking about [Miss X] is good, because it sort of merges with Catherine Tate, and makes it clear to me that Penny should be funny. A bit of a klutz would be good. I can see Penny more clearly – not in the magical, pictures-of-the-mind way that radio enthusiasts bang on about, but a sort of vivid, moving blur. When you think of your friends, you don't *see* them, do you, but you register this strong sort of…? I don't know.

FROM: BENJAMIN COOK TO: RUSSELL T DAVIES, FRIDAY 9 MARCH 2007 15:32:09 GMT

RE: MENTAL TUESDAY

This strong sense of…? What is it that you register at this stage in a character's conception? In what way do you sense Penny? Can you hear her voice in your head already? Her speech patterns? Can you smell her? No, that's silly. (Then again, if I asked you what perfume Penny is wearing, would you know?) Do you know what she'd do in any given situation? And can you really think about her now without the faces of [Miss X] and Catherine Tate flickering away in your mind's eye?

FROM: RUSSELL T DAVIES TO: BENJAMIN COOK, SATURDAY 10 MARCH 2007 21:56:06 GMT

RE: MENTAL TUESDAY

The 'seeing' thing is hard to pin down. Characters really are blurs, but that doesn't mean they're vague; it means they're alive and unpredictable. And I don't carry actors' impressions and characteristics over, thankfully. There's a distinct Donna in my head, separate from Catherine. Even if [Miss X] were to become Penny, Penny has a life of her own. (I get annoyed when other writers say that characters have a life of their own, and now here I am saying it. I suppose what I mean is, Penny has a life beyond the actress that ends up playing her.)

When I wrote *Queer as Folk*, I had strong mental impressions of Stuart, Vince and Nathan, but then when I came to write *Queer as Folk 2*, long after they'd been cast and had acted in eight episodes, I still didn't write Aidan Gillen, Craig Kelly and Charlie Hunnam. The mental versions were far stronger and took over again. I wonder if that's weird. But it *is* like when you picture your friends, isn't it? You imagine their *essence*. I don't imagine their hair colour, or teeth, or clothes, or crow's feet; I sort of imagine their dynamic, the place that they occupy. Penny has that dynamic already. She came born with it. I'm talking, for example, about how to make her funny, but actually that's e-mail rationalisation after the event. Just look at her, from the moment she was conceived: she's jilted, walking past the TARDIS; with her posh mum, going to see her grandad, when she walks into an alien invasion. That's already essentially funny. Even her sadness isn't tragedy; it's light and sweet. She felt like that from the start, from the moment I thought of her.

But there's no smell. You've got me there! And I don't know where she went to school, what she had for breakfast, what knickers she's wearing, unless the scene needs me to know. If I do write Penny having breakfast, I'll write something that will fit her. (It's black coffee. She'd just have black coffee. If it weren't *Doctor Who*, she'd also have a cigarette. Yes, that's very Penny.) Some people draw up huge lists of that background stuff before they start writing. Well, I don't. That doesn't mean you shouldn't. It works for some people.

I suppose I do know already exactly what she'd do in given circumstances… with the proviso that anyone can do anything in any circumstance. You should never mark out a character so formally that their reactions are fully defined, because none of us is like that; we're slightly different every day, with different people, with each different mood. You have to keep turning characters in the light. One of my favourite Doctor moments ever is the opening of *Gridlock*, where he lies about Gallifrey having been destroyed. It's a tiny lie. He omits the fact that his home world is gone. But, for the Doctor, that's seismic. I had nothing interesting in that scene until I discovered that. I found a completely new way of understanding the Doctor, a new way of revealing his history, and better still a tiny piece of narrative that sustains the Doctor/Martha relationship throughout that episode. If characters keep turning, moving, thinking, shifting, if they aren't fixed, then they can do anything. Just like real people.

A prerequisite of a good story is that the audience watches the central character – or characters – change, even if the characters themselves aren't aware of that process happening. I'm trying to think of a film or drama in which that doesn't happen. I'm sure they exist, but… do you see? They've been forgotten. Even in something as simple as *High School Musical* – in fact, that's so simple and underwritten, the change is poking out of the carcass so even blind passers-by can give it a good feel. The school jock becomes an arts boy; the geeky girl breaks out of her math class; even the villainous valley girl, in the most appalling and sudden about-turn, becomes nice (that's a failed change, because it comes from nowhere, and demeans her). The template, *Grease*, does it even better, because you really *feel* them change in that. If a story is good, then someone changes. You can apply that principle from *Grease* to *Hamlet* to *Teletubbies*. There is no low-art and high-art divide here. My God, that scene in *Monsters, Inc.* where the monsters realise that their entire world is founded on hurting children – look at that for a change! Two galumphing cartoon characters making a shattering realisation about their world and their role in sustaining it. A truly epic moment. It's stunning.

FROM: BENJAMIN COOK TO: RUSSELL T DAVIES, SATURDAY 10 MARCH 2007 22:41:10 GMT

RE: MENTAL TUESDAY

>>I suppose I do know already exactly what she'd do in given circumstances… with the proviso that anyone can do anything in any circumstance.<<

If a character can do anything, what stops them becoming a sort of Everyman? What makes them distinct?

FROM: RUSSELL T DAVIES TO: BENJAMIN COOK, SATURDAY 10 MARCH 2007 23:15:54 GMT

RE: MENTAL TUESDAY

I suppose what I'm saying is that a character can act in any way *in character*. They can be good, bad, happy, sad, liars, lovers, but in a way that's still unique to themselves. To stretch the metaphor: keep turning them, but not so fast and so often that they become blurred.

FROM: BENJAMIN COOK TO: RUSSELL T DAVIES, SATURDAY 10 MARCH 2007 23:38:19 GMT

RE: MENTAL TUESDAY

Sometimes, surely, the fact that people are incapable of change is enough of a story in itself? Take Madame Ranyevskaya in *The Cherry Orchard*.

FROM: RUSSELL T DAVIES TO: BENJAMIN COOK, SUNDAY 11 MARCH 2007 00:03:44 GMT

RE: MENTAL TUESDAY

Yes, but the realisation of that is a change for the audience. I don't think Madame Ranyevskaya leaves *The Cherry Orchard* truly aware of herself or really having moved on from Act One, but the world has changed around her and other characters have grown in wisdom, so she acts as a still point – and that's equally powerful.

But I don't know that you can take this principle and apply it to drama too consciously. Can you sit down and say, 'I'm going to write about change! My theme is change'…? Rather, I think it's inherent in a story, any story. That's why they're stories. Things start on Page 1 and are different by the final page, or else why is the tale being told? The Goldilocks who runs away from the three bears is a very different girl from the one who started out into the forest. The change might not last, she might well go back to stealing other people's food and trashing their furniture, but that's why the story ends when it does.

FROM: RUSSELL T DAVIES TO: BENJAMIN COOK, TUESDAY 13 MARCH 2007 22:27:29 GMT

MENTAL TUESDAY II

Let the record state: Julie had lunch with Catherine today, assuming that she'd say she's too busy for a full series – but she *screamed*, and started planning how to move to Cardiff!!! *WHAT?!* I still don't believe this is going to happen. Surely Catherine's agent is going to rugby-tackle her? Imagine a whole season of Tennant and Tate! It's a casting director's dream. Can't be true. Can't be.

Also, I had to go into Peter Fincham's extremely posh office today, and explain why I will not be doing a Series Five. Ohh, he's not happy. It was very awkward. Mind you, it did strike me that he has no idea how much work *Doctor Who* actually is, how much work I actually do, and absolutely no awareness of the fact that so many of us have had to up sticks and go and live in Cardiff for years on bloody end. Instead, he just supports us with money and publicity and trust and… oh, I shouldn't complain, should I?

Since we started this project, it's been unusually busy and showbizzy on *Doctor Who*. It's normally 'Can we shift that scene to Penarth?' These are weird times. But it does help explain what I'm thinking. Which is not much, because now we're in a Penny/ Donna flux. Which woman is it going to be? But the Donna stuff is fun. I imagine that she failed to 'walk in the dust' after *The Runaway Bride*. That's what life is like, isn't it? You meet an amazing man, spend one night with him, think you're going to change your life… then you wake up the next morning and he's gone, there are bills to be paid, your flat needs cleaning, and you never quite get around to it. Poor Donna, she had her chance and blew it. If only she could have a second chance. (I could call 4.1 *Second Chance!*) Mind you, there's no way that Donna could come across the Doctor again by chance; she'd have to be *looking* for him. A very different entry for a companion. I'd have to dump the whole jilted-by-her-boyfriend strand that I'd planned for Penny. But the marvellous thing is, that strand is still true, because we've already done that with Donna in *The Runaway Bride*. Not just jilted, but betrayed by her man.

Anyway. I had a good meeting with Gareth Roberts today, about the Agatha Christie episode. Lovely ideas. But it's going to be tough, that one. I can tell. And a brilliant meeting with Matt Jones about *Torchwood*, leaving me thinking, damn, everyone's episode is better than mine. A rising bile of fear that I'm already *very* behind and will stay like this for months now, maybe for the whole year. I did no proper work at the weekend either. David was the only living soul I saw. But I had some nice thoughts about 4.X – obvious thoughts, but ones that I hadn't crystallised before, namely that a 'disaster movie' needs a supporting cast to climb through the wreckage, some of whom will live, some of whom will die, which means, of course, that some lovely people must die and some bastards will survive. I'm thinking we'll have a sweet, middle-aged or ageing couple – both will die. Heartbreaking. A feisty would-be companion – she'll survive. An arrogant young businessman – he might survive, because you'll want him to die. That sort of thing. Fab.

FROM: BENJAMIN COOK TO: RUSSELL T DAVIES, TUESDAY 13 MARCH 2007 22:54:09 GMT

RE: MENTAL TUESDAY II

Catherine Tate hasn't said no? That is so mad. But oh… Penny! (I almost used a sad smiley there. I feel dirty now.) This will sound pathetic, but I'll miss her. Donna would be AMAZING, and the repartee between Catherine and David to die for, but poor Penny Carter becomes just another Character In Search Of An Author. No second chances for Penny. No *first* chances, even. End of.

FROM: RUSSELL T DAVIES TO: BENJAMIN COOK, TUESDAY 13 MARCH 2007 23:18:44 GMT

RE: MENTAL TUESDAY II

That alone makes this whole e-mail chain worthwhile, because you must be the only other person in the whole world who will miss Penny. No one else had that stuff described to them. Not Phil, not Julie, not anyone. I don't like to flog it, because it sounds daft, but I really do miss her too. That lovely, lonely, wistful scene of her walking past the TARDIS late at night, in a city centre, in the rain – I know I hadn't done much with her, but that moment was crystallised perfectly. In a really strange corner of my mind, I honestly believe that she sort of exists somewhere. It really is that *Six Characters in Search of an Author* stuff. God, when I first saw that play – I'd barely ever written anything at that point – I was stunned by the central conceit, and really took it to heart, and now – and I'm never going to admit this again, and you can't print it anywhere, ever, because I sound like a nonce – I still believe that Penny Carter is walking past that TARDIS, but now she walks on and never meets the Doctor. That feels real.

FROM: BENJAMIN COOK TO: RUSSELL T DAVIES, TUESDAY 13 MARCH 2007 23:31:28 GMT

RE: MENTAL TUESDAY II
Shall we light a candle for Penny?

FROM: RUSSELL T DAVIES TO: BENJAMIN COOK, TUESDAY 13 MARCH 2007 23:37:51 GMT

RE: MENTAL TUESDAY II
You light a candle. I'll light a cigarette.

FROM: RUSSELL T DAVIES TO: BENJAMIN COOK, WEDNESDAY 14 MARCH 2007 22:45:53 GMT

RE: MENTAL TUESDAY II
Catherine's agent phoned today. We expected her to blast us with 'WHAT THE HELL D'YOU THINK YOU'RE DOING?! SOD OFF, CATHERINE IS BUSY!' But no, Catherine is definitely tempted. And then I spent an hour on the phone to Catherine herself. She *so* wants to do it! This is madness.

FROM: BENJAMIN COOK TO: RUSSELL T DAVIES, MONDAY 19 MARCH 2007 22:52:20 GMT

AN UPDATE
Russell! I'm dropping you a quick line to touch base. I hope all is well. (Has Catherine said yes yet?!) I imagine you're extra busy in the run-up to Wednesday's Series Three press launch, and then transmission next week...?

FROM: RUSSELL T DAVIES TO: BENJAMIN COOK, MONDAY 19 MARCH 2007 23:25:25 GMT

RE: AN UPDATE
Mark the date in your diary: today, Catherine Tate officially said yes! Bloody hell. This is so brilliant. What a cast!

But we've got to get it right. I'm worried about how other writers will handle Donna. Not Steven Moffat, obviously. But it needs a delicate touch not to go too funny or too broad... says the man who, in *The Runaway Bride*, had her swing across the Flood Chamber and smack into the wall! And when do we tell people? Everything leaks. Freema hasn't even débuted as Martha yet. This is going to get very complicated.

Announce this too soon and it'll mess up Freema/Martha. We've got to keep that début clean and successful, because Freema is so brilliant. She deserves a big launch. We can't clutter it by announcing the *next* companion. I think Penny will have to live on as a disguise: we'll ask people to write Penny as a placeholder name.

Catherine's casting has, at least, jumpstarted my thinking. I've been worried all weekend, back here in Manchester, because I've done very little thinking. Well, none. I worried that Manchester had become divorced from work, become a place where I switch off. But today I could click back a bit, because the news of Catherine's casting was so exciting. Of course, I also started thinking of problems: Donna would actively have to be looking for the Doctor, so she can't turn right in 4.11, as opposed to left in 4.1, and become The Woman Who Never Met The Doctor. It takes the charm off that 4.11 story slightly now that it's Donna instead of Penny. The magic of it has gone. Oh well. It's a strong story, and strong stories survive changes. (Have I told you that Rose will appear in 4.11, meeting Donna, because the parallel-world walls are breaking down? Bloody glorious.)

Meanwhile, major panic building on *Torchwood*. I'm running out of time. With all the press launch stuff happening this week, I'm just too busy. You wouldn't believe the amount of phone calls and planning that goes into a simple bloody launch. Oh, I don't even want to type about it. It just feels awful.

FROM: BENJAMIN COOK TO: RUSSELL T DAVIES, THURSDAY 22 MARCH 2007 15:13:46 GMT

THE PRESS LAUNCH
Well, last night was fun. I'm still buzzing. It was weird, all those celebs, wasn't it? Looking around and seeing Dawn French and Jonathan Ross and Jo Whiley, like one of those events that you see in the papers, only now it's for *Doctor Who*!

FROM: RUSSELL T DAVIES TO: BENJAMIN COOK, SATURDAY 24 MARCH 2007 16:44:56 GMT

RE: THE PRESS LAUNCH
The press launch was brilliant. Best thing was, I had a good few drinks with you, Phil and Andy, and *didn't* want to carry on and get leathered, which is really good for me. I'm saying this because, when I'm actually writing, I suspect there are going to be a few Dark Night Of The Soul e-mails – oh Lordy – so it's good to report the times when I feel happy. And *The Times*' Caitlin Moran was there, too. Did you see her? She said to me, 'You always write about unrequited love.' I've been thinking about that a lot since. Not sure what it says about me. Not sure that it's healthy.

In other news, Kylie Minogue wants to appear in *Doctor Who*.

Yes, Kylie Minogue! Ha ha ha ha.

I wish I could see your face as you read that sentence. Don't worry, it won't happen. Will Baker, Kylie's creative director, was at the press launch and said how marvellous it'd be to get Kylie in *Doctor Who*. He'd had a bit to drink, so I didn't believe it. But then he phoned Julie on Thursday and insisted he'd been serious. (I could waste time fancying Will, but he's way out of my league. He's just nice to look at.) 4.X was always going to have a one-off companion, or maybe a couple of one-off companions, but if it were Kylie… well, no, it won't be. Nothing will happen. But I might have to have lunch with Kylie, and that alone is worth it.

Plus, on Monday, I've got to phone Dennis Hopper, who *is* interested. This is so weird. Kylie Minogue and Dennis Hopper! We really did start this e-mail correspondence at the best time ever. It's never this mad!

FROM: BENJAMIN COOK TO: RUSSELL T DAVIES, SATURDAY 24 MARCH 2007 17:00:10 GMT

RE: THE PRESS LAUNCH
Kylie Minogue? Oh, c'mon! For the next spin-off series, please can I have Kylie and Dennis travelling the universe in a camper van, solving murder mysteries? Thanks.

FROM: RUSSELL T DAVIES TO: BENJAMIN COOK, SATURDAY 24 MARCH 2007 17:32:35 GMT

RE: THE PRESS LAUNCH
I forgot to tell you, I had the strangest clashing of the Maybe/real world the other day, in a way that doesn't happen often. I was walking down Oxford Street, and someone shouted hello, came running up for a kiss and a hug and all that – and it was [Miss X]! In the last days of Penny Carter's short half-life, [Miss X] had advanced *way* up the list of possible Pennys. We'd run [Miss X]'s name past Peter Fincham, and it turns out that he *loves* her, and her dates are free, so for a couple of days, while I never believed that the Catherine Tate thing would happen, the lovely [Miss X] really, really became Penny for me. Meeting her in Oxford Street completely out of the blue… oh, it was bizarre. I'm not kidding, and you're the only person who might properly understand this, I actually found it hard to talk to her. It was like looking at Penny. The fact that Penny would never exist. The fact that [Miss X] would never even *know* this. She was talking about what she was up to, but I was, literally, stumbling and stammering and failing to say all the nice polite things that I should have said. I just mumbled a bit, with this weird collision in my head, and then walked away, thinking how strange it all is…

FROM: RUSSELL T DAVIES TO: BENJAMIN COOK, MONDAY 26 MARCH 2007 23:41:45 GMT

RE: THE PRESS LAUNCH
Crumbs! This has been a mad day. So mad that it's made me say 'crumbs'. All the way to London… TO MEET KYLIE MINOGUE!!! To sell her the next Christmas Special. Then all the way back to Cardiff. This is INSANE!!!

Kylie was lovely. And tiny. I even sang a duet with her. No kidding. We were talking about the Muppets, and she said, 'What's that song that Kermit's nephew used to sing on the stairs?' I sang the first line, she sang the second, and then we both sang the entire verse! Bloody crazy. She liked the sound of Christmas, but visibly baulked at the thought of three/four weeks' filming, so we'll see. Her life seems so barmy and mad that she might forget about it all tomorrow. Although, she's sitting down to watch *The Runaway Bride* tonight. Imagine that! But still, Julie and I were on top form, so I know we couldn't have done more to convince her, and that makes me happy enough. We did good work.

Also, Julie saw Billie yesterday afternoon, and Billie is definitely saying four episodes. Julie ran past her the option of staying on board after 4.13, and then doing the Christmas Special 2008 – filmed as part of our Series Four run, God help us – which would allow her to come back as and when, and film further Specials alongside David. But that's all in a state of flux. If a lot of Series Four is building up to Rose's return, I'm thinking, do we film a scene for 4.1, right at the end, a glimpse of Rose? End of 4.1, story over, danger past, the Doctor standing by the TARDIS, about to give Donna one of those classic 'come aboard' speeches, but Donna interrupts, 'Hang on a minute,' and runs off, leaving the Doctor stranded. That's quite funny. She runs over to the crowd – police, army, ambulances – looking for her mum, just so that she can give her the car keys. In a rush, a panic, Donna shoves the keys at a woman in the crowd – 'Her name's Sylvia Noble. Give her these. It's that red Toyota over there' – and runs off to her new life. Reveal the woman that she gave the keys to: it's Rose! Just standing, watching, waiting. That could be nice. Or too inward-looking? But thrilling! There's an undoubted 'ooooh!' in that moment.

Yes, 4.1 might need tricks like that. I'm worried that the events in the Medusa Cascade in 4.12/4.13 are much harder to foreshadow than 'Vote Saxon' in Series Three.[3] Is Series Four's running thread quite un-runnable? What do you think?

FROM: BENJAMIN COOK TO: RUSSELL T DAVIES, MONDAY 26 MARCH 2007 23:56:02 GMT

RE: THE PRESS LAUNCH
You've met Kylie? (Yeah, well, I met McFly last month, so... er... there! Yeah, Russell – McFly!) Were you able to tell Kylie much about who she'd play?

I've just got back from watching Catherine interview David on stage at the Duchess Theatre, Covent Garden, for Radio 4 show *Chain Reaction*. They were brilliant together. Hilarious. They talked tons about *Doctor Who*, and said nice things about you, which will probably be cut out of the broadcast show, and didn't let slip that they'll be back on our screens, together, for the duration of Series Four. Mad, mad times indeed.

Two things:

1) What is the Medusa Cascade?

2) Rose Tyler at the end of 4.1? Of course I love it! But then, I'm a ming-mong.

---

3 Mr Saxon is a running reference throughout Series Three, foreshadowing the Master's return at the end of the series in his guise as UK Prime Minister Harold Saxon (played by John Simm).

FROM: RUSSELL T DAVIES TO: BENJAMIN COOK, TUESDAY 27 MARCH 2007 00:18:33 GMT

RE: THE PRESS LAUNCH

1) The Medusa Cascade is where 4.12/4.13 takes place. It's just an area of space. The Earth is stolen, along with five other planets, and taken to the Medusa Cascade to form a ring that makes up a great big, um, Dalek energy-converter thing to, er, do things. Kill everything, probably. They've always wanted to be the supreme life form, so why not invent a multi-planet-sized energy-converter-bomb thing that sterilises the entire universe, leaving only them alive? Audacious! The Master mentions the Medusa Cascade in 3.13. He says, 'You sealed the rift at the Medusa Cascade,' nicely placing a Big Rift there, because with universe-walls breaking down, and Rose returning, that's going to be needed somehow.

2) Good. Me too.

I just busked with Kylie. I was phoned up at 1am. 'Kylie wants to meet you *today*. She's flying to Stockholm tomorrow.' I got on the train, which turned out to be full of fans on their way to see *Chain Reaction*. (How funny you watched that, knowing what you know.) Then I met the great lady, and I said… well, that they're aboard a spaceship called the *Titanic*, it's hit by meteorites, it destroys Buckingham Palace at the end (she loved that), and her part would be a waitress who joins with the Doctor to escape the wreckage. You think that she's going to be the new companion, but then she does something towards the end, to defend the Doctor, but something rash – she picks up a laser-gun and kills someone – in a situation that the Doctor could have talked his way out of, so effectively she fails Companion Academy. He's disappointed in her. She's left behind at the end, because she's Good But Not Good Enough. For the record, I said, 'I don't know this character's name. Maybe something like Chrissie.' What?! Bollocks to that. *Chrissie?!* What a terrible name. The ship is staffed by aliens – although they'll look exceedingly human – so she should have a nice, simple, sci-fi name.

FROM: RUSSELL T DAVIES TO: BENJAMIN COOK, TUESDAY 27 MARCH 2007 11:19:44 GMT

RE: THE PRESS LAUNCH

I met Kylie! Ha ha ha ha. Fell asleep laughing, woke up laughing. But I'd sooner pull McFly, so you win. Of course, if I met McFly, then I would. This is a fact.

FROM: RUSSELL T DAVIES TO: BENJAMIN COOK, WEDNESDAY 28 MARCH 2007 23:14:25 GMT

RE: THE PRESS LAUNCH

Stray thoughts today. In 4.2 or 4.3, the Doctor should be in the TARDIS, talking away quietly, 'I lost my people in the Time War…' He's wandering around the console, all introspective. And then Donna says, 'How d'you spell Dalek?' He looks up – and she's taking notes! Little pad and pencil! He'd hate that. 'You're taking notes?!' 'Well, you talk all the time.' 'I don't have people on board to take notes!' 'Oh, are there rules, then?' 'In this case, yes.' 'Well, I'd better write them down.' These two characters write themselves. But they mustn't bicker for too long. 'I'd better write them down' would be followed by a pause, then a *smile* from the Doctor. He likes her. Without a word, she puts down the notebook and asks him something real. That's how I write – little flashes of dialogue. In fact, 'dialogue' doesn't cover it; that's *them*, that's the dynamic, that's how they are. And then if you use that notebook somewhere vital later in the plot…

Talking of something real, it's about time that someone asked the Doctor, if the Time Lords are dead, why he can't go back in time to find/save them. No one's done that yet. Also, that's a nod to the series finale: Dalek Caan, the last surviving Dalek, will have voyaged into the Time War itself (forbidden! Impossible!) to pull out Davros. It will have sent Caan insane – a weird, broken, strangely holy Dalek, on a plinth, spotlit, revered, talking strangely un-Dalek-ly, more like a mad oracle or prophet. Caan could be a hero in the end. Funny how all these stories flow into each other.

I'm so excited about seeing Donna again, and everything that she can do, the sheer energy she brings to it, so the opening of 4.1 is really taking shape. Oh, the moment that Donna sees the Doctor! The moment that he sees her! (It should absolutely coincide with the appearance of the Big Snarling Beast.) My worry, though, is that 4.1 starts as very Donna-heavy – do we see the Doctor at all, until she does? – which could, given the size of this star casting, make it feel like *The Catherine Tate Show*. I must write up the Doctor more than I usually would when introducing a new companion. Interesting, that sort of worry, because it's only half a script-worry; the other half is an external, how-this-episode-will-be-perceived worry. That's an equal part of my job, let's not pretend otherwise.

A lot of knives will be out for Donna/Catherine, in that tabloid world. They always are, for successful women. I must, in the script, account for that '*Doctor Who* Becomes Comedy' backlash – give Catherine good, strong, emotional stuff to balance it. This how-the-programme-is-perceived thing is more of a factor on *Doctor Who* than any other show I've ever written. The purist writer in me says that this is wrong, that the story is the thing, that it's not the writer's job to think of external issues – I'm a writer, not a salesman. But also this is the most successful and popular thing that I've ever written, so who says those external worries are bad? Maybe they've *helped*?

Also, since Donna has seen the Empress and the creation of the Earth in *The Runaway Bride*, 4.1 has to be bigger.[4] It has to amaze her. I'm wondering about a portal, through which these Big Snarling CGI Beasts come. Yes, they've become plural. I want size. I think seeing 3.1 at last week's press launch, seeing the Judoon stomp across the Moon on the big screen, has put that thought in my head. I want packs of monsters in 4.1.

Big worry about 4.X today: the *Titanic*'s forcefields are deactivated by saboteurs, because someone wants someone dead, so the ship is hit by meteorites; once wrecked, murderous creatures should break out of the hold – but is that the same plan? The same saboteurs? It should be a different plan, surely? Saboteurs upon assassins

---

4 The Empress is a half-arachnid, half-human creature – a member of the alien Racnoss.

upon terrorists? Or are the meteorites a coincidence? Maybe the saboteurs should, um, magnetise the hull to attract them? The murderous creatures should be really slim, tight metal. Sexy! Like Kylie's stage-show Cybermen.[5] Or maybe, since this is a Christmas Cruise, the ship could have Robot Angel staff – beautiful golden faces, smiling cherub masks. Polite voices, great for killers. Like butlers. White tunics. Metal wings. Ooh, haloes! Deadly haloes! Maybe they're programmed to go murderous once the ship is hit? Ah, if they're programmed to go mad once the ship is hit, it is the same plan. It's part of the sabotage. I'm loving the sound of Robot Angels.

It all feels nice and creative, this. That good mood is persisting. I'm genuinely excited/scared about Saturday's transmission of *Smith and Jones*. That helps. Even seeing the *Radio Times* this week was thrilling. I'm a fanboy at heart.

FROM: BENJAMIN COOK TO: RUSSELL T DAVIES, THURSDAY 29 MARCH 2007 02:41:28 GMT

RE: THE PRESS LAUNCH

I spent three hours this afternoon re-entering numbers into my new mobile phone. My old one was stolen on Saturday. I'm still receiving text messages that were sent to me days ago, but were delayed by the bar on my stolen phone. There's one from you that reads, 'Oh, I hope you've got a new phone to receive texts…' I hadn't. 'I'm on the train to London TO MEET KYLIE!!!'

A question: you know the ending to 4.X already (the *Titanic* destroys Buckingham Palace, Kylie is left behind, etc), but do you always start writing stories with endings in sight? Isn't a leap into the dark ever more thrilling?

FROM: RUSSELL T DAVIES TO: BENJAMIN COOK, THURSDAY 29 MARCH 2007 23:12:14 GMT

RE: THE PRESS LAUNCH

I always know the ending. Well, usually. Emotionally. I know how it *feels*. I knew, from the first moment, that *The Runaway Bride* would end with the Doctor saying, 'Her name was Rose,' and more particularly that it would end with the Doctor and Donna in an ordinary street, with snow. I knew that *Casanova* would end with Old Casanova dying, and Young Casanova dancing into darkness. Right from the moment that *Queer as Folk* was conceived, I knew that it would end with Stuart and Vince dancing on a podium – and I knew *why*. Everything else – that poor, dumped boyfriend of Vince's, Stuart's loneliness, the circling drug-killer in the club – came later. But the central image – two men, eternally happy in a state of unrequited love – was a given. That was why I was writing the whole drama, right from the start, to reach that moment of happiness. It's as crucial as the first moment of thinking of the story. An ending is what the story *is*. For me, anyway.

I know that 4.1 will end with… well, it's a no-brainer, that one: the Doctor and

---

5 Kylie's 2005 *Showgirl* tour featured dancers in costumes inspired by the design of the Cybermen.

Donna spinning off into space, in the TARDIS, and happy. And 4.13 will end with the TARDIS circling above the Earth, and the Doctor making an address to the entire planet, welcoming them back home, promising to protect them for ever. Sometimes, I swear, I could write those scenes first. Except I couldn't, because I can never write scenes out of order. I physically cannot do it. Lots of writers do. Paul Abbott does, happily. If he gets stuck on a scene, he skips to a later one. If I get stuck, I sit there, stuck, until it's resolved, because the scenes that come later can't exist if they aren't informed by where they've come from.

I read an interview with Charlie Kaufman, the man who wrote *Being John Malkovich* and *Eternal Sunshine of the Spotless Mind* (both staggeringly brilliant movies), in which he said, *so* forcefully, that any writer who starts a script knowing where it's going to end is morally bankrupt, that they had forfeited their right to stand as a dramatist, because they weren't open to the infinite possibilities of storytelling. I thought, sod off! Firstly, any writer telling another writer how they *must* work can always sod off, no matter how brilliant they are. (That's why I'd never want any of these musings to be taken as a template for How To Write. It happens to be How *I* Write, that's all.) But also I disagree so strongly with Kaufman, I even think he's lying, even lying to himself. If you take away his dictatorial side, it's a fascinating thought; it did make me want to start writing something with no idea of where it's going, just to see what happens. Maybe it would be the best thing I've ever written. But the problem is, I'm not Charlie Kaufman, only he is. Three pages in, I'd have got interested in something, so I'd see the story, my story, the through-line, and immediately that would suggest its ending. I couldn't stop that happening.

It's fascinating how many successful writers start talking like censors – saying, 'You *must* write like this, you must *not* write like that.' The very people that should embrace freedom, and the right to make mistakes, become the people laying down laws. That Bonfire of the Vanities goes on and on. Stoked by writers! Don't they realise that they're becoming dictators?

FROM: RUSSELL T DAVIES TO: BENJAMIN COOK, SATURDAY 31 MARCH 2007 16:26:44 GMT
AND NOW ON BBC ONE...
I've been praying for rain, to increase our *Smith and Jones* viewing figures, and I just got back to the flat... and there's a *violent storm* blowing across Cardiff Bay! I am now wondering about the extent of my supernatural powers. I am going to wish for a billion quid and Freddie Ljungberg, and see what happens. Fingers crossed.

FROM: BENJAMIN COOK TO: RUSSELL T DAVIES, SATURDAY 31 MARCH 2007 17:29:54 GMT
RE: AND NOW ON BBC ONE...
It's sunshine here in Chiswick. I might start praying, too. If it gets to 6pm and there's still no sign of rain, I'll offer up my *Mine All Mine* DVD as a sacrifice to Tlaloc. But

will he be appeased?

FROM: RUSSELL T DAVIES TO: BENJAMIN COOK, SATURDAY 31 MARCH 2007 18:07:05 GMT

RE: AND NOW ON BBC ONE...

So *you're* the one who bought the *Mine All Mine* DVD? I knew we'd find that mystery shopper in the end. Actually, it's turned sunny again here. My supernatural powers are on the wane. I knew I should have wished for Freddie first.

The Hour Before *Doctor Who*! Exciting!

FROM: BENJAMIN COOK TO: RUSSELL T DAVIES, SATURDAY 31 MARCH 2007 18:16:13 GMT

RE: AND NOW ON BBC ONE...

Don't you ever wish that you *didn't* know what happens next? Isn't this the hour when you wish that you were 'just' a viewer? What are the Judoon? How does a London hospital end up on the Moon? What persuades the Doctor to invite Martha Jones aboard the TARDIS? Right now, aren't you wishing that you didn't know?

FROM: RUSSELL T DAVIES TO: BENJAMIN COOK, SATURDAY 31 MARCH 2007 18:23:47 GMT

RE: AND NOW ON BBC ONE...

Equally, what I don't get is the worry. Will it be crap? Will I be ashamed? Will it let me down? Gareth Roberts called it, marvellously, that sense of 'anticipointment' – all too ready for an episode of *Doctor Who* to be rubbish. That first episode of *Time and the Rani*, that was a deep, dark trough...[6]

> **Text message from: Ben**
> Sent: 31-Mar-2007 22:02
> Full Moon tonight. Dazzlingly bright over Chiswick. How perfect. How many kids must be looking up at the Moon right now, as they draw the curtains before bed, thinking of spaceships and Time Lords and Judoon?

> **Text message from: Russell**
> Sent: 31-Mar-2007 22:04
> That's funny, I just stood on my balcony ten minutes ago and thought the same thing. The Moon is bright and clear over the Bay. It was meant to be.

FROM: RUSSELL T DAVIES TO: BENJAMIN COOK, SUNDAY 1 APRIL 2007 10:30:02 GMT

RE: AND NOW ON BBC ONE...

8.2 million viewers! With a peak of 8.9 million! And a 39.5 per cent audience share! By

---

6 Broadcast in 1987, *Time and the Rani* was Sylvester McCoy's début serial as the Seventh Doctor.

the time that's consolidated, it'll be higher than last year's series opener. Oh Lordy.

FROM: BENJAMIN COOK TO: RUSSELL T DAVIES, SUNDAY 1 APRIL 2007 14:45:20 GMT

RE: AND NOW ON BBC ONE...

Amazing figures! Tlaloc must have appreciated *Mine All Mine*.

FROM: RUSSELL T DAVIES TO: BENJAMIN COOK, SUNDAY 1 APRIL 2007 19:27:08 GMT

RE: AND NOW ON BBC ONE...

I had some 4.1 thoughts last night. It was one of those nights when I thought, right, I'm going to go out and get rat-arsed in some club and end up in a Bute Town gutter. But this town is so bloody small. After an hour in one of the two gay clubs in the whole of Cardiff, I was besieged by *Doctor Who* staff, most of whom I don't even know ('Hello, I'm the man who's building *The Sarah Jane Adventures* website') or, bless 'em, friendly Cardiff gays who'd seen *Smith and Jones* – but *dozens* of them. It was doing my head in, so I left after a few drinks. But Cardiff on a Saturday night is like Beirut, so I had to walk all the way back to the Bay. I wasn't consciously thinking about scripts at all. I was too fed up. But by the time I got to the Bay, lovely and cold and desolate, at about 2.30am, and sat down on the seafront for a cigarette, a few things clicked into place. That often happens. You go for a walk and it's not the walk that clicks things into place, but the *end* of the walk –

I like the idea of the portal – a shimmering circle that you'd step through – to another world. I keep calling the portal the 'Venting'. It's not a good word or particularly appropriate, but that's what my head is saying right now. An alien world beyond the Venting. Nice alien vistas, a bit of a temple, where we discover the last survivors of that world. They've been overrun by these wild dog things. The rest of the population has been eaten. (The wild dogs should be called Vor-something. Vorlax? Vorleen? No, Vorlax is nice.) The survivors have opened the Venting to, literally, vent their world, to give the Vorlax a taste of fresh meat, and so saving their planet. Oh, the Doctor's anger! 'You've got a problem and what do you do? You PASS IT ON!' At the end, he seals the portal, leaving these wise old dying bastards to their fate. That's harsh. But good.

A great image came to me today. In fighting just the one Vorlax, the Doctor is wondering where it came from, and someone points out that the first sightings were in a boarded-up house. The Welsh valleys are full of boarded-up houses. There's something automatically spooky about them. The Doctor and Donna are approaching the house. As they get closer, they realise that the wooden boards over the windows are *straining...* moving... buckling... with a scratching and a scrabbling. In that moment, the boards rip off – and hundreds of Vorlax pour out, chasing and killing! There are people running and screaming. Huge pictures. An ordinary one-monster episode explodes, suddenly, into an epic. On the alien world, an image of an even greater threat to come: wooden gates to the city, behind which there are *millions* of Vorlax, snarling and snapping,

threatening to break through any second. Beyond that, huge *plains* of Vorlax. Can we make pictures that big? This is expensive. And how the hell do the Doctor and Donna survive that? Even if the Doctor seals off the alien world, what about the hundreds of Vorlax on the loose on Earth? Does he find a way to kill them? If so, he'd give that solution to the alien world; he wouldn't just seal them off. But I want him to seal them off. I'll think on. Great image, though.

FROM: BENJAMIN COOK TO: RUSSELL T DAVIES, MONDAY 2 APRIL 2007 10:31:53 GMT

RE: AND NOW ON BBC ONE...

How do you know when to start writing? All these images only exist in your head right now, yes? (Pretending for a moment that these e-mails hadn't happened!) At what point do you begin to write the actual script?

FROM: RUSSELL T DAVIES TO: BENJAMIN COOK, TUESDAY 3 APRIL 2007 02:34:17 GMT

RE: AND NOW ON BBC ONE...

How do I know when to start writing? I leave it till the last minute. And then I leave it some more. Eventually, I leave it till I'm desperate. That's really the word, desperate. I always think, I'm not ready to write it, I don't know what I'm doing, it's just a jumble of thoughts in a state of flux, there's no story, I don't know how A connects to B, I don't know anything! I get myself into a genuine state of panic. Except panic sounds exciting. It sounds all running-around and adrenalised. This is more like a black cloud of fear and failure. Normally, I'll leave it till the deadline, and I haven't even started writing. This has become, over the years, a week beyond the deadline, or even more. It can be a week – or weeks – past the delivery date, and *I haven't started writing*. In fact, I don't have delivery dates any more. I go by the start-of-preproduction date. I consider that to be my real deadline. And then I miss that. It's a cycle that I cannot break. I simply can't help it. It makes my life miserable.

My inability to start on time is crippling. Any social event – people's birthdays, drinks with friends, family dos, anything – gets swept aside and cancelled, because there's this voice inside my head screaming, 'I HAVEN'T STARTED WRITING!' I wake up, shower, have a coffee, watch telly, go to town, buy some food, potter about, buy a magazine, come home, e-mail, make phone calls, watch more telly, and it goes on and on and on until I go to bed again, and a whole day has gone. It's just vanished. Every single minute of the day, every single sodding minute, is labelled with this depressing, lifeless, dull thought: I'm not writing. I *make* the time vanish. I don't know why I do this. I even set myself little targets. At 10am, I think, I'll start at noon. At noon, I think, I'll make it 4pm. At 4pm, I think, too late now, I'll wait for tonight and work till late. And then I'll use TV programmes as crutches – ooh, must watch this, must watch that – and then it's 10pm and I think, well, start at midnight, that's a good time. *A good time?!* A nice round number! At midnight, I despair and reckon it's too late, and stay up despairing. I'll stay that way till 2 or 3am, and then go to bed in a tight knot of frustration. The next day, the same thing. Weeks can pass like that. I'm wondering if describing it to you might break the cycle. Probably not.

I've got this *Torchwood* script to write. Although it's a vague mess in my head, I know exactly, very exactly, the first five pages. You'd think, to make my life easier, I'd type out those five pages at least. I could open a file now, right now, and bash them out in about three hours. I'd wake up tomorrow morning so much happier, because a file labelled 'Torchwood 2.1' would exist. But no, I spend all day thinking, start, start, start. But I don't. It's gone 2am now, and I still haven't started. I go to bed in a state of despair, and wake up the same way. Literally, my very first thought when I wake up is a rush of fear and, well, I suppose self-hatred for being so stupid and slow. It's a lousy way to write. Or not write. It wrecks my life. I see my sisters about twice a year, my dad about three times, my best friend Tracy about five times, I might see you socially – what? – twice a year, and it's not like there's a long list of friends who might be taking up other evenings, because this lifestyle has excluded them, slowly, over the years. All the rest of the time, I cancel or simply don't appear. They all think I'm writing. The truth is, I'm more likely to be *not* writing, just sitting on my own, panicking. My boyfriend has the patience of a saint. Or he's a sap to put up with me. No, I'll go for saint.

It's ridiculous, because I can prove, conclusively, that the solutions start to appear every time I *do* start writing. A straightforward example: I spent ages not writing *Doctor Who* 3.11, *Utopia*, just sitting in a black cloud. There was a concrete problem: I had no idea why the TARDIS would end up at the end of the universe. Even though that's where this episode had to be set. Now, with hindsight, it's easy: the Doctor reacts badly to the arrival of Captain Jack, because Jack is an immortal, a fixed point in time, the Doctor can barely look at him, feels it in his guts, *and the TARDIS feels the same*. But imagine that you don't know those words in italics, that they haven't been imagined yet. Without them, the sheer coincidence of a) Jack arrives, and b) at the same time, the TARDIS is thrown to the end of the universe, is an awful, crippling, terrible, un-writable coincidence. The trouble is, because I'm telling you this in hindsight, the solution seems obvious. In fact, the words 'at the same time' spell out the answer. But it wasn't that clear when it was all in a state of flux – where everything is up for grabs and nothing is definite. It wasn't so much a question of how does the TARDIS get to the end of the universe; it was more one of should it? Why? Is that rubbish? Does it need to be connected to Jack? And these doubts were underscored by much bigger ones: is it right to bring back Captain Jack in Series Three? Will he work with David's Doctor? What does Martha do? Have I really got to set this in a lame quarry? How late am I going to be with 3.12/3.13 if *Utopia* is already so late? Does the Master work in this day and age? Can we delay production because I'm so late? Every question was jostling for space.

Eventually, the script was so late that I *had* to start work. Two pages in – two bloody pages – it just clicked: Captain Jack arrives, *therefore* the TARDIS goes to the end of the universe. That sounds so simple now, but it was the key to the whole episode. You'd think I'd learn from that example. You'd think that would tell me: start writing and it will begin to make sense. But I never learn. Next script, I'll go through the same process all over again. To make it worse, my career is as successful as it can possibly be, and I'm probably writing scripts to the height of my ability at the moment, so I can only conclude that I've lumbered myself with a painful system *that works*. Is that it? Is it like a superstition that I have to panic in order to write well? It drives me mad.

When I'm out and about and with people, at a production meeting or just bumping into someone and saying hello, I know I'm a funny guy – and I think that's *deliberate*. I am consciously having a laugh, because it's an escape, it's a relief from the cloud bearing down. Truth is, this e-mail isn't scratching the surface. It's worse than I'm describing. I'm not revelling in it; I'm sitting here thinking what a stupid idiot I am, and what a better life I could have, what a good, successful, happy life, and it's all my own fault. What the hell do my family and friends really think of me? I did begin to get slight warning bells at the last *Radio Times* Cover Party, by the sheer number of people – about eight separate people, five of whom I hardly knew – who came up to me with an opening gambit of 'Are you all right?' I thought, bloody hell, do I look like a corpse?! But I didn't really, which made me think: how am I spoken of? Like a lunatic?

Well, you did ask.

FROM: BENJAMIN COOK TO: RUSSELL T DAVIES, TUESDAY 3 APRIL 2007 11:42:18 GMT

RE: AND NOW ON BBC ONE...

I recognise – as I think most people would, especially writers – aspects of my own behaviour in what you describe in that e-mail. But would you call it writer's block? It doesn't sound entirely like writer's block, it's more self imposed than that, and you don't use that term, but I'm interested in how – or whether – you would define writer's block? Some people say that it's a fallacy...

FROM: RUSSELL T DAVIES TO: BENJAMIN COOK, TUESDAY 3 APRIL 2007 22:11:42 GMT

RE: AND NOW ON BBC ONE...

I couldn't help thinking that you might read that e-mail and think, sod off, you self-indulgent tosspot. It's all so me, me, me that I forget, everyone must feel like that. You're right. Well, not everyone. I read an interview with Jeanette Winterson once, in which she spoke about writing with such certainty that she made the process sound so wonderful, clear, pure, confident. It was so beautiful that I cut it out and kept it by my computer. It's now been swept away somewhere. That was stupid. But I remember that she described writing as being like flying. That must be nice. Feels more like falling to me.

I never call it writer's block, though. I don't know why, but I sort of react with revulsion to that phrase. I imagine it to mean sitting there with No Ideas At All. For me, it feels more like the ideas just won't take the right shape or form. Do writers ever run out of ideas? Doesn't the block say that something *else* is wrong? Something bigger? I don't know.

FROM: RUSSELL T DAVIES TO: BENJAMIN COOK, FRIDAY 6 APRIL 2007 10:34:13 GMT

RE: AND NOW ON BBC ONE...

There has been a lot of good, practical work over the past few days – not Maybe thinking, but actual sitting in meetings with writers and sorting out plots. A lot of *Torchwood* and *Sarah Jane*, and a great meeting with Gareth about the Agatha Christie episode. I adore those meetings. I'm in my element.

But in the 4.1 Maybe... I've found that I vividly and profoundly hate the estate, the Vorlax, and the alien planet. I think it's crap. It's very *Primeval*. Too *Primeval*. I like *Primeval*, but I don't want to copy it. Now, lodged in my head, is a simple image of how *funny* it is that Donna is actively looking for the Doctor, that in, say, a new plot there's something going on in an office block (boring setting, but bear with me), something alien, so Donna is investigating, partly in the hope that she'll meet the Doctor, and partly because that's what people who have met the Doctor *do*. They carry on the good work. And the Doctor is investigating too, but separately. This is the crucial image: you play a good 15 minutes at the top of the episode with the Doctor and Donna *not* meeting. She walks out of one door, he walks in another, neither knowing that the other is there. It's got all the fun that the housing estate idea didn't have. And doors! That's why I'm saying an office block – because it needs doors. And lifts. Donna gets in the left-hand lift, doors close, the right-hand lift opens, the Doctor steps out. This story isn't a farce, but it uses the shapes of a farce. That's the starting point, the inspiration, the heart of it. Of course, it leaves me with no story and no enemy, but there we go. Back to square one. Except –

Imagine a moment when the villain is unveiling, unmasking in some swanky office at night, and Donna has been investigating, and so has the Doctor, separately, but with both working out that something crucial is happening in this office. The Doctor has lowered himself down on a window-cleaner's cradle to look into the room (I'm determined to get that cradle back in, the one that was cut from *Smith and Jones*), and Donna is inside the building, outside the office, looking through a glass window. At the moment of the Big Reveal, where the Sinister Boss is revealing himself as a monster, what's *really* happening is: the Doctor and Donna are looking across the room and seeing each other on the other side! Her reaction! His reaction! Upstaging the monster! That makes me laugh, and that's good. It feels more like *Doctor Who* than anything else I've thought up. It's in character for both the Doctor and Donna. The fun of these scenes feels stronger than anything.

FROM: RUSSELL T DAVIES TO: BENJAMIN COOK, WEDNESDAY 11 APRIL 2007 23:48:42 GMT

TAKING THE FIFTH?

Lordy, what a night! Jane Tranter came to Cardiff this afternoon for a *Sarah Jane* read-through, but then she asked if she could come round my flat tonight, with Julie, for 'a chat', which they did. The chat was to formally convey from the Sixth Floor of the BBC that they want me to stay for a fifth series of *Doctor Who*. The three of us have talked about this before, loads of times, but Jane felt that she'd never really been 'official' about it. I still said no. It's not about the money, and Jane and Julie both know that. They knew my reply even before they'd walked in, and agreed with me, but professionally they had to come and represent the formal BBC point of view.

That's today's news. Hey ho. Turning down a fifth series. The thing is, Ben... a *fifth series!* Did you ever, ever, *ever* think that *Doctor Who* would be this important to the

BBC? That's the maddest thing of all, and the best thing of all.

FROM: BENJAMIN COOK TO: RUSSELL T DAVIES, THURSDAY 12 APRIL 2007 02:40:08 GMT

RE: TAKING THE FIFTH?

Tell 'em that you'll stay on for three million quid and Freddie Ljungberg on a serving dish! Go on, just for a laugh. See what they say. You're probably right to decline, but were you tempted? Just a little bit tempted? A teensy bit tempted? Not because of Freddie on a plate (was that even in the offing? It's late and I'm confused), but just because the BBC really does seem to want you to stay? That must be flattering, at least.

FROM: RUSSELL T DAVIES TO: BENJAMIN COOK, THURSDAY 12 APRIL 2007 03:19:05 GMT

RE: TAKING THE FIFTH?

Tempted? To do a fifth series? Not for a second. Weird, isn't it? I'm going to go to bed and think that through, and wonder why that is exactly. I'm not sure. I think, really, it's because the option is untenable, because way back, around the time that we filmed *Doomsday*, we promised this course of action to David. And to each other.

We decided that we'd have a fourth series (David's third), with a big ending, after which we'd take the show off air, just for a short while, apart from the odd Special, so that we could have a breather, and a new production team could settle in, find its feet, and prepare for Series Five. And there's all sorts of other plans, for the future, but... I'm almost superstitious about putting things into print. Julie, Phil, Jane and I committed to that initial promise, and we're sticking to our word. That promise means that the fifth series option does not exist for me. They *might as well* talk about buying me Freddie Ljungberg. It's flattering and all that, but it ain't gonna happen.

FROM: RUSSELL T DAVIES TO: BENJAMIN COOK, SATURDAY 14 APRIL 2007 16:20:20 GMT

RE: TAKING THE FIFTH?

The past few days have been so busy. I know that thinking of stories is a constant background beat, but sometimes the sheer volume of work can do a pretty good job at drowning it out. It's like the work *triples* when we're not filming. February and March are sort of my months off from writing, but now it's heading towards Writing Time for the rest of the year. This week, I've been feeling myself sort of withdraw. I'm alone in Cardiff this weekend and next week – very few meetings, just me, locked away. I'm becoming bad at replying to e-mails (I've been telling you less stuff, and I'm making an *effort* to write, though I do still want to), phone calls and messages are going ignored... and I *want* to be like that. I want everyone and everything to sod off.

That Series Five offer didn't help, in a weird way. The next day, I started smoking again (I've been off them for a while), eating really bad food, just sort of guzzling rubbish.

I've been browsing Outpost Gallifrey to read how crap I am.[7] I've been watching some of Series Three – not for work, but with a state of mind that says, deliberately, this isn't as good as I thought it was. In fact, it's crap. I've failed. I'm rubbish. I'm lucky. I'm a fraud. I've lost it, and this next script is the script that will expose that. Etc. I am, I realise, making myself miserable. That's the old dark streak of You Don't Deserve This ticking away, like I punish myself for being successful. Plots and stories in the Maybe are taking a back seat. Instead, I'm focusing on the schedule, because that's already a nightmare. My mind is going 'April, May, June' all the time, because those three months are going to require a script a month, and I never manage to complete a script a month. Why-oh-why can't I be happy? Why can't I just love this work? Why can't I feel like Jeanette Winterson in that quote I lost, where writing feels like flying? It's not even falling at the moment; it's sinking. Why do I get like this?

In the real world… yesterday, we said no to Dennis Hopper. He was available for only four days. I was weak and promised to make it work, then came home and realised that I'd lumbered myself with a cameo that doesn't fit 4.X at all. I wouldn't be able to do anything proper with that character because of the limitations. That's where Phil is marvellous. He knows me so well. He phoned on Thursday night and said, 'Between you and me, I'm worried about the pressure that this is putting you under. Should we withdraw?' He was voicing my every worry. So we nixed that. Good. What does Dennis Hopper mean to an eight-year-old anyway?

It's weird, not knowing if *Gridlock* is on tonight.[8] I'm quite excited.

FROM: BENJAMIN COOK TO: RUSSELL T DAVIES, SATURDAY 14 APRIL 2007 21:51:18 GMT

RE: TAKING THE FIFTH?

Three cheers for the football not overrunning! It *was* exciting, wasn't it, waiting to see whether *Doctor Who* would be on tonight or not? I wonder what effect the football and 7.40pm start had on the ratings. Well, we'll find out tomorrow.

>>That's the old dark streak of You Don't Deserve This ticking away, like I punish myself for being successful.<<

You make it sound conscious. Not like, 'Right, I'll piss myself off now,' but like the misery comes first, and then goes in search of stuff that'll encourage it. Is depression too strong a word? Self-induced or otherwise, depression is an affliction with a roll call of writers, poets, musicians and so on. Edgar Allan Poe wondered:

> *whether all that is profound, does not spring from disease of thought, from moods of mind exalted at the expense of the general intellect. They who dream by day are cognizant of many things which escape those who dream only by night.*

I love that. It's from his short story 'Eleonora', which is thought to be semi-

---

7 Outpost Gallifrey was a fan-run *Doctor Who* website and discussion forum with over 40,000 registered members, which spawned the Doctor Who Forum.
8 Had 14 April's FA Cup Semi-Final between Manchester United and Watford gone into extra time, *Gridlock* would have been postponed for a week.

autobiographical. Do you reckon this fear that your scripts won't be good enough actually makes them better, ultimately? Does it vanquish complacency? Or would your work be better, do you think, if you didn't harbour such glaring doubts?

FROM: RUSSELL T DAVIES TO: BENJAMIN COOK, SUNDAY 15 APRIL 2007 14:30:35 GMT

RE: TAKING THE FIFTH?

That's a great quote. But more important than even Edgar Allan Poe: we got EIGHT MILLION VIEWERS last night! This is a strange and lovely time. That's cheered me up. Talking of which…

The depression thing. I fight shy of the word depression, because real depression is so debilitating and awful that I feel a bit arrogant even to assume that I've touched upon it. Although I go into awful slumps, I do deliver scripts in the end, and I stay on top of work, just about, and I don't think Depression with a capital D has any such luxury. And yet… and yet… I'm well aware of those depression/creativity theories, and certainly I've watched it at work in other writers. Paul Abbott is genuinely bipolar, and that's a frightening and sometimes brilliant thing to behold. I'm nowhere near that. I even envy it, that's the killer. Suffering can seem so admirable and important. There is a widespread theory, propagated by the media and hugely by writers themselves, that writing and suffering are synonymous. With Jimmy McGovern, that seems to be a genuine, heartfelt philosophy – if you haven't suffered, you can't write. But that philosophy actually excludes certain people from the right to write, and that *has* to be wrong. That's a step away from book-burning. You can't have a list of who's entitled to write and who isn't.

When I was starting out, I felt that tyranny. You Must Suffer! It didn't help that one of the first writers I knew well was Paul, because the history of his childhood is so genuinely awful. It looms over his reputation like a monolith, and threatens to become the template for others. In the early 1990s, I used to think I'd never reach his level, because I haven't suffered. That's why *Queer as Folk* was such a breakthrough for me. It took me that long to realise that I had experience of a whole world that no one else was writing. I'm not equating gay with suffering there; I just mean *experience*. Everyone has fallen in love. Everyone has been bullied. Everyone has lost someone, somehow. Everyone has been ecstatic. Everyone has been suicidal, even if only slightly. That 'slightly' is the important thing. You don't need to have had your head shoved in the dirt; you only need to be able to imagine it. 'A moment's imagination is equal to a lifetime of experience.' I read that somewhere once, and it's so true. If those sorts of doubts – I'm not important, I haven't suffered, I'm too young/happy/middle-class to be experienced – are ever holding you back from writing, DON'T LISTEN TO THEM! It really is a tyranny, and it's bollocks.

I often get asked to give masterclasses in scriptwriting. I usually turn them down, but once, just once, I gave a great one. If I say so myself! I think I was angry about some recent interview with a 'suffering artist', and it inspired me. It was for the Fast Track people at the Edinburgh TV Festival, the eager ones who *really* want to get into telly, all about 18, 19, 20 years old. I challenged them to admit that they feel, at their age, that they haven't lived, that they don't know enough about the world to write about it. Gradually, reluctantly, lots of nodding heads. And then I played them two clips: one from an episode of *Buffy the Vampire Slayer* (*Out of Mind, Out of Sight*), where a girl has been so ignored that she becomes invisible, and another from *I, Claudius*, where young Claudius is being so ignored that he might as well be invisible. I pointed out that both those scenes are the same thing. One popular culture, one high art, but the same drama. More importantly, who *hasn't* felt like that? Especially at 18, 19, 20, you probably feel more ignored and left out than at any other time in your life. Of *course* you've lived. That's *you!* Which means that you can write *I, Claudius*, and you can write *Buffy the Vampire Slayer*. There's no limit to what you can write. I swear, it was like you could see light bulbs switching on over their heads. I was quite proud of that.

Queer as Folk was ten years of my life put on screen. Just about everything in that happened to me in some shape or form. Except having the baby, and he hardly features! But the best thing I ever did was write *Bob & Rose* next, which had never happened to me, ever, in any way. I've never even slept with a woman. Not once. Well, a bit of rubbing with Beverley Jacobs when I was 15, but that's only because she used to go out with a boy I fancied, and still fancy to this day, so I had my eyes closed, imagining him. Poor Beverley. Of course, in writing *Bob & Rose*, I did go through a long process of imagining the women in my life that I *do* love, the ones that maybe I'd be with if I were straight, and how I'd feel. A lot of that was based on my friend Tracy. When Julie met Tracy a few years ago, she said, 'My God, she's Rose Cooper! She talks like her!' You see, it all comes from somewhere. Every time you think, no, I haven't experienced that emotion, YES, YOU HAVE! In tiny ways. But that's all you need. You imagine and extrapolate from that. Most writers aren't murderers, but an awful lot of them write murders. Who hasn't *wanted* to murder someone? That's what they're tapping into, just that spark. But you certainly don't need to be steeped in blood to write it well.

You asked if the fear makes the scripts better. Well, I have no choice but to think that it helps, or it would be unbearable. To write without that fear is not an option – not yet, not for me – so I have to rationalise it, hope that it helps, or I'd go nuts. I can't imagine writing and thinking, this is easy. I'm marvelling at those words. This. Is. Easy. They're impossible. I might as well say, 'I'm a Martian.'

There I go again, saying that you don't have to suffer, while admitting that the process *is* an act of suffering. Still. No one said that this had to be logical.

Right. I've got to write a synopsis of 4.X for Kylie Minogue's agent. I never write treatments, but I have to this time, because they want to know what they're getting into. Once again, I think the word is 'busk'…

CHAPTER THREE

BASTARDS

In which *The People's Quiz* is shunted,
the internet is slated, and one beautiful day
with Wynnie la Freak makes everything worthwhile

FROM: RUSSELL T DAVIES TO: BENJAMIN COOK, TUESDAY 17 APRIL 2007 01:48:30 GMT

CHRISTMAS IS COMING

Here you go, Keeper of the Matrix. Not a bad read. I hate treatments, but they do make me concentrate. I'm going to bed now, *terrified* about the budget. How the hell are we going to afford this?

DOCTOR WHO CHRISTMAS SPECIAL 2007
STARSHIP TITANIC

The *Starship Titanic* sails above the Earth on its Christmas Cruise. Half original *Titanic*, half floating hotel, it's a luxury spaceship with holidaymakers on board, all decked out for the festive season.

The Doctor comes on board as a curious visitor, and soon makes friends with one of the ship's staff, Peth, a waitress. While everyone wines and dines around her, Peth has to clean up after them. But she's dreaming of a better life. And the Doctor is travelling alone for once – the lonely Time Lord. As he strikes up a friendship with Peth, liking her feistiness, her sense of humour, he wonders... could she join him on his travels in Time and Space, as his new companion...?

Disaster strikes! Meteorites hit the *Titanic* – and it's more like *The Poseidon*

Adventure In Space, as the ship is crippled, with oxygen running out. Worse, if the Doctor can't get to the Flight Deck in time, the ship might fall onto the Earth below, with its nuclear engines threatening to explode...

The Doctor joins with Peth to lead a small, brave band of survivors through the wreckage – and in true disaster movie tradition, they're picked off, one by one. But the Doctor soon realises that the meteorites weren't an accident: a saboteur is on board who wants them all dead. But why? What secrets are certain passengers keeping? And the saboteur hasn't finished yet: the ship's robot staff – frightening, blank-faced, golden Christmas Angels – have been reprogrammed to hunt down the living.

It's a race against time, as the Doctor and Peth battle through the ruins of the devastated ship, fighting flying Angels and the ticking clock, to save both the *Titanic* and the planet below. But as the Doctor and Peth are thrown together, can they truly trust each other...?

The *Doctor Who* Christmas Special for BBC One is a fun, scary, full-blooded 60-minute drama, complete with monsters, thrills, chases and terrible deaths, as the Time Lord and his friends battle against the odds to save the day. And they succeed – just in time for Christmas!

FROM: BENJAMIN COOK TO: RUSSELL T DAVIES, TUESDAY 17 APRIL 2007 16:45:14 GMT

RE: CHRISTMAS IS COMING

It's a sci-fi-murder-mystery-Christmas-disaster-movie-epic! With echoes of *The Poseidon Adventure*, *The Robots of Death*, and Kylie's 2001 *On a Night Like This* tour![1] What more could you ask for at Christmas? Good busk. I think it should end on a song, though.

Do you need to appreciate the costs involved in making television drama in order to write it? Or can understanding the expense inhibit invention?

FROM: RUSSELL T DAVIES TO: BENJAMIN COOK, WEDNESDAY 18 APRIL 2007 22:03:50 GMT

RE: CHRISTMAS IS COMING

Did you imagine that there wouldn't be a song? *The Poseidon Adventure* won an Oscar for Best Song for 'The Morning After'. '*There's got to be a morning after / If we can hold on through the night.*' I often sing it at 3am when I'm only on Page 22.

Yes, knowing the cost of television could inhibit invention, but I think writing is a stronger impulse than that; it overrides such plain little worries. Understanding budget isn't strictly necessary for a writer. You're there for the ideas; the production team is there for the making-of. At the same time, the writer-as-producer model is wonderful.

---

1 *The Robots of Death* is a *Doctor Who* serial first broadcast in 1977.

The more you do know, the more involved you are, the better the product gets. But getting that production experience in the first place is hard. I was a producer before I was a full-time writer, so I knew all that stuff first. To have a rough understanding of the costs – and, more importantly, the practicalities – has to help.

A lot of budget stuff is common sense. Write an army of 5,000, and it's going to cost. Write a great script set in one kitchen, and producers will love you for ever. *Doctor Who* is expensive to make, but that's because of our ambition. We could have aimed lower. Thankfully, we didn't. But we never relax and throw money around. We're so trusted. I like to think we respect that trust. That's why I went to bed shivering with fear the other night. I was genuinely scared by that 4.X synopsis, and felt a massive responsibility for it. I told Julie, 'I'm deeply worried that my imagination is flying into big-bucks movie territory. If I should pull back, now is the time to say so.' That's a bit disingenuous: I suspected that by offering Julie the chance to cut down, she'd respond by moving Heaven and Earth to get the money that we need so that I wouldn't be compromised. It's all politics. I'm not daft. But neither is she. Julie knows me too well. If she *did* say to pull back, I'd know that she meant it, that she'd reached her limits.

Getting out before Series Five is so wise. It'll leave the show at the height of production so that the next, future version *cannot* come back cheaper. Honestly, that's part of the strategy.

FROM: RUSSELL T DAVIES TO: BENJAMIN COOK, SUNDAY 22 APRIL 2007 01:09:17 GMT

RE: CHRISTMAS IS COMING
I keep worrying about 4.1. What the hell is Donna doing? Investigating? What is this high-rise office block? Beauty? Plastic surgery? Cosmetic surgery? The ultimate industrial beauty parlour? Big business, with aliens? In the car on the way up to Manchester (I'm back up north now), I spent a lot of time thinking about Botox. I mean Botox as in an alien spore that bursts out and transforms you. We've never done that creepy green transformation thing – humans turning horribly into aliens. If those humans are 40-something-year-old women who've been Botoxed to the hilt, so much the better. Imagine a scene in a wine bar where they transform, then lurch out into the street. Deadly Ladies Who Lunch! Not camp at all. It's sort of obvious and fun, which is good for a series opener. I'm amazed that we haven't done it before. I think, in my mind, all that 'beauty' stuff had become the sole province of Cassandra, but actually there's so much more that you can do with it.[2]

FROM: BENJAMIN COOK TO: RUSSELL T DAVIES, SUNDAY 22 APRIL 2007 22:08:45 GMT

RE: CHRISTMAS IS COMING
With the investigation of a high-rise city office at night, and the Doctor and companion-

---

2 'Last human' Cassandra, who débuted in *Doctor Who* 1.2, underwent over 700 plastic surgery operations until she was nothing but a piece of skin stretched onto a metal frame, with eyes and a mouth, connected to a brain in a jar.

to-be criss-crossing but taking time to meet, 4.1 is reverting to the template of that opening episode that you'd planned, all those years ago, were the call ever to come asking you to revive *Doctor Who*. The one with the escape-by-window-cleaner's-cradle sequence, and the grandad who plays in a skiffle band. You've come full circle.

Anyway, I see the *News of the World* is reporting that Kylie has been cast in this year's Christmas Special… as a Cyberwoman! A show spokesman has said: 'Russell is just putting the finishing touches to the episode and it will be TV dynamite.' Well, he's *half* right.

FROM: RUSSELL T DAVIES TO: BENJAMIN COOK, WEDNESDAY 25 APRIL 2007 22:37:42 GMT

RE: CHRISTMAS IS COMING

I've been silent, I know. I've been glum. Bloody glum. Script glum. It occurred to me – because this was *Torchwood* script glum, not *Doctor Who* glum yet – that it's going to be hard to write to you when I'm glum. I'm not saying that I don't want to; it's just that I'm really going to have to try hard. For one thing, it feels so indulgent. You can't stop that voice in the back of your head saying, 'Miserable? A writer? There are people out there desperately ill, in despair, in genuine, proper, medical Depression – and you dare to be miserable over a deadline? You actually *want* some of that?' Equally, when I'm in the middle of that worry, I reckon I could wrestle any of those bleeding hearts to the floor and beat them in the unhappiness stakes. Also, there's a fear, a natural fear, of appearing to be an idiot. I don't want to appear to be an idiot to you. And that multiplies because I'm a gay man, and you're handsome and young, so I want to look good anyway. Of course I do. But the fact that this correspondence is scary is a good reason to keep going. Always do what scares you. I'm not flagging this as a call to halt; I'm just trying to explain what I'm thinking.

On Saturday night/Sunday morning, I went to bed at 2am, lay awake, worrying – no, panicking, to be honest – and got up at 3am to work for an hour. And that wasn't typing work. I did anything rather than type. I trawled websites in search of stuff that I could vaguely call research, stared at old scripts, and just sat there doing nothing. Getting up in the middle of the night? I have *never* done that before, which made me realise that this script-panic is something extraordinary. So I took action –

I pulled out of that *Torchwood* script. I'm not doing it.

Poor Julie. She bears the brunt of all this and protects me from the consequences. It's easy for me in some ways, because with my status as a writer, frankly, I can get away with anything. That's awful, isn't it? No one shouting, no one berating me, no contracts being waved, just everyone running around making that decision easy for me. You could go power mad. Mind you, I'm mild and lovely compared to some of the stuff you hear about other writers. Or maybe this is the start of me getting worse. The truth is, I wasn't not-writing because I couldn't think of anything, but because I'm sick of fixing other people's problems. I sat there at 4am and thought: what am *I* getting out of this? Nothing. Just misery. So sod it, I'm off.

That was severe. First time I've ever done that. As a result, I'm quite cheery again. Nightmare welcome-back-to-Cardiff dinner with the *Torchwood* cast tonight, just when I feel I've abandoned them. (I haven't. I'll try to script-edit more.) Eve Myles got drunk, which was lively. Gareth David-Lloyd is just the sexiest bastard on this Earth. And Johnny Barrowman regaled us with stories of how many Josephs he'd like to sleep with, so it was a bit of a laugh.[3] The panic has abated. Now I'll have to wait for the 4.X panic…

The other thing is, when I do get in that pits-of-darkness mood, it's not quite true that I lock myself away; I can *use* a bad mood. I can use it to say things that I wouldn't otherwise. There's always a game being played, somewhere, somehow, isn't there? So I used that depression to make it very clear that shifting the *Doctor Who* timeslot every week, as has happened this year, is bloody stupid. Squandering, that was the word I used. Good word. So then Julie and Phil told Peter Fincham, using their own glumness too – and it worked! He's shifted *The National Lottery People's Quiz,* and we should go back to 7pm from Episode 6 onwards. The BBC is changing the format of a primetime Saturday-night quiz show just for us. What's more, suddenly, yes, maybe the *Doctor Who* budget can allow us to go abroad for the Pompeii episode. (For all of two days, but hey!) And what's this? Extra FX money for 4.12/4.13. The BBC has jumped through hoops to make me happy. That's how it works – and I know it.

FROM: BENJAMIN COOK TO: RUSSELL T DAVIES, THURSDAY 26 APRIL 2007 00:33:23 GMT

RE: CHRISTMAS IS COMING

I'm glad you're okay. You hadn't replied for a few days. I was a bit worried. Not worried about the correspondence (that's like a cockroach: it'd survive nuclear fallout), but worried that you'd thrown yourself into the Bay. I'm glad you haven't. Nonetheless, never feel that you *must* write to me when you're in Script Hell. I'd always prefer that you did, but I wouldn't want these e-mails to make a bad day ten times worse, forcing you to write it all down, to explain yourself.

Having said that (!), can I ask, did you ever feel, even in your darkest moments, that fixing *Torchwood*, that writing a 2.1 that would rejuvenate the concept, was actually beyond you? That you *couldn't* do it? Or was it a dawning realisation that you just didn't want to do it, and that you didn't really have to?

>>Now I'll have to wait for the 4.X panic<<

Of course, you could start writing 4.X now…?

>>They've jumped through hoops to make me happy. That's how it works – and I know it.<<

And that makes you feel… how? Relieved? Disgusted? Humbled?

---

3 Barrowman was, at the time, a judge on BBC One's *Any Dream Will Do*, a talent show that searched for a new lead to play Joseph in a West End revival of Andrew Lloyd Webber's musical *Joseph and the Amazing Technicolor Dreamcoat.*

FROM: RUSSELL T DAVIES TO: BENJAMIN COOK, THURSDAY 26 APRIL 2007 00:57:16 GMT

RE: CHRISTMAS IS COMING

I love that image of this correspondence surviving a nuclear war. The last remnant of civilisation. 'It's... glowing!'

>>did you ever feel, even in your darkest moments, that fixing *Torchwood*, that writing a 2.1 that would rejuvenate the concept, was actually beyond you?<<

Not for a second. Beyond me? Absolutely not. I do feel kind of sad, because I love that cast and I love that show's potential, but really it was eating into *Doctor Who* scripting time. The addition of *The Sarah Jane Adventures* to our schedules has just made me run out of days.

>>Of course, you could start writing 4.X now...?<<

Ha ha ha ha ha ha.

>>And that makes you feel... how? Relieved? Disgusted? Humbled?<<

I don't know. Does that make it more honest or less honest? When did I last do something for one honest, pure reason, instead of calculating how I can *use* it? Then again, *Doctor Who* benefits, so that's worth it.

FROM: BENJAMIN COOK TO: RUSSELL T DAVIES, THURSDAY 26 APRIL 2007 11:57:09 GMT

RE: CHRISTMAS IS COMING

Tell me, then – a serious question – do you have to be a bit of a bastard to succeed in this industry? Some people say that you do. Let's face it, you can afford to be, Russell, because you've achieved a certain status... but have you got where you are today by being nice to the people around you? Similarly, everyone always says how nice Julie is, but... but... I bet she can be a right monster when she needs to be.

FROM: RUSSELL T DAVIES TO: BENJAMIN COOK, FRIDAY 27 APRIL 2007 00:19:27 GMT

RE: CHRISTMAS IS COMING

It's gone midnight! It's my birthday! Do you know, once you're in your forties, you genuinely forget which birthday it is. I used to laugh at old folk and find that impossible. And here I am. Anyway...

Bastards. (Now, that's a chapter title!) No, I don't think you have to be a bastard. Not at all. In fact, people who are bastards – real, genuine, complete bastards – are few and far between, and I've never seen them succeed in TV. They might burn for a year or two, but it doesn't last. Like... hmm... one director, who's long since been reduced to game shows. God, I hated him. And a producer – bloody weird woman – who was put in charge of a very big show, swiftly got sacked, and has never been heard of since. But of course there are thousands of people on a lower level of Bastardom – the pains-in-the-arses, the shouters, the hysterics – and they do all right, because a lot of the industry thinks that's an acceptable way to behave. But why are they bastards? Insecurity, weakness, over-promotion... well, I could just go back and repeat the word 'insecurity' five-dozen times. That's always the problem, isn't it?

If I've learnt one thing, and I keep learning it, it's to be honest. That's seen me through my career. (But not sociopathically honest. There's no point walking into work and saying, 'Christ, Lynda, you're hideous!') If you don't say what you think, what's the bloody point? Nicola Shindler, who founded Red Production Company, always says that she and I are successful because we know our own opinions, and we say those opinions out loud, immediately.[4] But 99 per cent of TV folk are slow, unsure, don't speak up, or wait for someone else to speak up first. I remember my first meeting as a storyliner, on a Granada daytime soap called *Families*. I was young then, and terrified of this fabled job that I'd always wanted to do, not having a clue what it actually entailed. I felt out of my depth. I wore a leather biker's jacket, just because I needed armour, I needed to look tough, because I was so scared. The writers were devising the murder of a character, Don McLeod, and they'd cooked up this ridiculous story where – deep breath – the man whose baby had been kidnapped by the pub landlord's wife came into the pub, looking for revenge, and started a fight, and Don joined in, just because he was there, and he got punched and hit his head on the table and died. He was killed by a complete stranger. Despite my fear, I could not stop myself saying, 'No! If Don is going to be killed, it should be by someone who hates him, not some one-episode passer-by.' That sounds like such a small story, but it was huge to me. It was a pivotal moment. I knew that I was in the right job.

Then again, there are plenty of people who think I'm a bastard. Plenty. But I try not to work with them. I hope that's not me surrounding myself with yes-men. I can play the nice guy, and of course I want the world to think I'm nice, but to be honest and tough is going to earn you enemies. Once, I remember, we had to sack a 12-year-old girl from a children's show, because she wasn't good enough. I remember being amazed that people in the office were reeling, horrified, despairing, saying that we couldn't sack a kid... because I absolutely didn't care. It was for the good of the show. I insisted, she went, and the programme got better. I lost no sleep at all over that. Not one second. Seeing people's horror was one of those chilling moments when I thought, everyone else sees this differently – am I a bit odd? But it wasn't chilling enough to stop me.

I'm at the high end of the most expensive area of one of the most insecure, public, high-flown, backstabbing industries in the UK, so I suppose it's kind of disingenuous to say that I'm a nice man. And yet I think I am. (But I can't be.) I think about that a lot, not just prompted by your question. I do wonder. Julie, though... oh, Julie... now that's really, truly, gobsmackingly pure niceness. One in a million.

FROM: BENJAMIN COOK TO: RUSSELL T DAVIES, FRIDAY 27 APRIL 2007 15:34:30 GMT

RE: CHRISTMAS IS COMING

Happy birthday, Russell! You share it with Darcey Bussell, Patrick Stump from Fall

---

4 Red is a Manchester-based, independent production company, formed in 1998 by Shindler, a successful TV producer. Red's first production was *Queer as Folk*; later dramas include *Bob & Rose*, *The Second Coming*, *Mine All Mine* and *Casanova*.

Out Boy, and Prince Willem-Alexander of the Netherlands, which means… I don't know what it means. You're by far the tallest?

It's interesting what you say about being surrounded by yes-men. During their interview for *Doctor Who Magazine* the other month, the one where their *Doctor Who* colleagues posed the questions, I asked Julie and Phil *your* killer query: what is it that they like least about your writing? But they wouldn't answer it. Even though they knew how much you wanted them to. That's the drawback, I suppose, of being at the top of your game. Who's going to challenge you? Who can you rely on to be brutally honest with you? Who'll stop you from going too far? Anyone? No one? Doesn't that bug you, Russell? (Look, I've sent you some killer questions of my own, on your birthday. Now who's a bastard?)

FROM: RUSSELL T DAVIES TO: BENJAMIN COOK, SATURDAY 28 APRIL 2007 16:10:47 GMT

RE: CHRISTMAS IS COMING

Julie and Phil do still talk about that question. You're not forgotten, just unanswered, although Phil says, no, he can't think of anything. Julie *gets* the question, she knows what you mean (or what *I* mean – it was my question!), and she's still thinking, I swear to you. Maybe she's worried about saying something that would destabilise me, but I don't think so. She knows me better than that, and she knows it would do me good. It might be a long wait, but I think she'll get there in the end.

I do worry about being surrounded by yes-men. You're right, it happens. But the more able you are to surround yourself with people that you trust, the more likely it is to happen. Not because you want yes-men, but because people that you trust, whose judgement is sound, tend to be people whose judgement is close to your own. That becomes, naturally, a closed circle. I don't think it's happened to me yet. In the end, just as good writers are hard to find, so are good script editors, good producers and good execs. When you find good people like Julie and Phil, their sheer talent cancels out the risk of them yes-ing. I suppose the danger is not RTD And The Yes-Men, but a triumvirate of people who are so similar that contrary opinions don't get enough of a look-in. Then again, plenty of shows lack any sort of voice, so maybe our similarities make for a strong show.

But! The fact that Julie and Phil trust me is an equally great pressure. That can be worse than working for someone who thinks you're crap. Julie and Phil give every hour to this show, as do Ed Thomas, Louise Page, Jane Tranter, the gaffers, bloody everyone. That's what's pushing us into Pompeii, the thought of taking the show further, making it better, trying something that's really, *really* difficult. I got a great e-mail from Ed the other day, full of the impossibilities and impracticalities of realising Ancient Rome, ending with the words, 'Let's do it!' That brilliant man. He's the best production designer in the business. The thought of them having to work like dogs on a script that isn't quite good enough is awful. That pushes and challenges me. I'm not just being nice; their trust is a great pressure on me, to do well.

But I can't stop wondering – am I a bastard? I haven't been able to shake off that thought. After I activated those couple of anecdotes the other day about sackings and things, it sort of opened a little door onto similar tales, and the list of people I've sacked – well, you don't often get to sack people, but the people I've replaced, or excluded, or had removed, or plainly cut off is, well, it's more than a few. Blimey! Last night, I was on the phone to Julie, and I suggested a new *Torchwood* writer called James Moran to write the Pompeii script, because he's fast and good and new enough to be rewritten by me with no complaints. Julie said, 'Well, give me a few days to sort that out.' I said, 'Why? I could meet him tomorrow.' She said, 'I'll have to talk to Mark Gatiss.' 'Why?' 'Because this script would replace his World War II one,' she said, 'and he's been working on that for over a year.' I went, 'Oh,' and I actually got annoyed with Julie for worrying over something that I thought was trivial. Thing is, I didn't care. And this isn't some stranger; this is Mark! Lovely Mark! Brilliant Mark! A gentleman, and truly a gentle man. He's got one of the wittiest, wildest imaginations in this whole bloody country. I like Mark tremendously, I think he's wonderful, but this is for the good of the show.

I reckon I've got some sort of cut-off point, beyond which I just don't care. In the course of my career, I've faced sacked actors, rewritten writers and banished directors. While I sort of sympathise on a superficial level, it doesn't really touch me. Not at all. God knows what they say about me behind my back! I know of one script editor, who I had booted off a show years ago, who still calls me the Devil incarnate. But he was rubbish. So he was removed. Good. No matter how upset someone is, if it makes the programme better, then tough. That's being a bastard, I suppose. Is the word 'ruthless'? Except 'ruthless' implies a deliberate cutting-off of feelings, doesn't it? I just don't feel them. I do not notice when I've hurt someone. I've spent more time worrying about it in these paragraphs than I do in everyday life.

I've just remembered something. It was 1997, and I copped off with a bloke called Toby. I'll spare you the details. Let's just say it was a great night. But he only had a single bed, because he was a student, and it was a bit uncomfortable, sleeping there, and I'd tons of work to do… so I got up at 5am, got dressed, walked back home. A couple of weeks later, a friend of mine said that this Toby was being all bitchy and calling me stuff. That's a shame, I thought, he seemed really nice. About six years later – it took six years for this little thought to trickle down – I thought, hold on, I got up at 5am after a really great night, got dressed, and just left. Not a word. Not a note. I didn't leave my number. I just went. AND I WONDER WHY HE CALLED ME A BASTARD!!! I didn't think what the whole thing looked like from his perspective, not for one second. I couldn't see what I'd done. Six years it took me to see that. I am blind. I suppose we all do things like that, every day, but it does make me laugh, considering my whole job is based on how people see things.

I just Googled that Toby… and there's nothing. Every name is on Google somewhere. There can't be nothing. Did I make him up? Was I drugged?!

FROM: BENJAMIN COOK TO: RUSSELL T DAVIES, SUNDAY 29 APRIL 2007 12:08:52 GMT

RE: CHRISTMAS IS COMING

>>Is the word 'ruthless'? Except 'ruthless' implies a deliberate cutting-off of feelings, doesn't it? I just don't feel them.<<

You. Would. Make. A. Good. Dalek.

>>I suppose we all do things like that, every day, but it does make me laugh, considering my whole job is based on how people see things.<<

Logically, I suppose, artists should understand us better than anyone – better even than our families, our workmates, our closest friends. Artists are supposed to see us for who we really are. But then art isn't rational, is it? Here is something that Caitlin Moran once wrote in *The Times*. I liked it so much that I cut it out and kept it:

> By and large, there is a single reason why any artist gains an audience: he talks about us. He explains us to ourselves. While our friends, partners, children, bosses and colleagues will, as a rule of thumb, widely eschew embarking on penetrating analyses of our truest thoughts, or the deepest workings of our hearts, artists wade in there and write whole albums, or fill entire art galleries, or improvise 90 minutes of stand-up comedy about us, and what we're like, and what we think. And this is why we, on many occasions, do things that show we love our artists more than our loved ones. At least they notice us. At least they start conversations.

I'm not sure I agree with Caitlin completely, but it does sound like the beginning of a theory that's heading somewhere interesting. What do you reckon, Russell? Do artists understand us better? If that's true, why do they, by and large, make just as almighty a hash of real life as the rest of us?

FROM: RUSSELL T DAVIES TO: BENJAMIN COOK, SUNDAY 29 APRIL 2007 14:49:26 GMT

RE: CHRISTMAS IS COMING

I was at the Welsh BAFTAs last night. *Torchwood* beat *Doctor Who* as Best Drama! And Graeme Harper won Best Director. Oh, it was lovely. He's 60 years old and that's the first thing he's ever won in his whole hard-working life. Just to see him, all smiling and Sontaran-sized under the spotlight, holding a BAFTA mask, it was actually very moving.

Anyway, I love that Caitlin Moran quote. I'm not sure I agree with it either, but I love the way she wades in, never scared of showing her workings in the margin. God, she's clever. Though maybe she makes the whole process sound more generous and beneficent by saying that an artist 'talks about us'. How kind. But maybe it's 'talks about himself'. He just does it so well that everyone recognises it.

Then again, good writing is basically a good understanding of people. Never mind structure and character and that; just have a good, fundamental understanding of psychology. Not in a psychology-degree sort of way, but in a plain, accurate, human, down-to-earth sort of way. If your friend turns out to be having an affair, there's no point in standing around going, 'No! Never! I don't believe it! That can't be true!' The writer stands there thinking, that's *fascinating!* And even, oh, *of course!* That's not to say that a writer is all-forgiving or non-judgemental, but they're much more interested in *understanding* it, I think. (They? Me? We? Pronoun crisis here! Caitlin's use of the word 'artist' threw me – too scary a word.) The danger is to assume a generosity behind that, like, oh, the writer understands pain, wrongdoing, frailty, the-whole-of-bloody-humanity, therefore the writer must be lovely. In fact, the process is as selfish as… well, as anything else anyone ever does. You might have great insight into your mate's actions, but there's a lot of glee in that understanding, and self-satisfaction, even a feeling of superiority. Actually, are you more interested in your friend in that moment of crisis than on an ordinary day when everything's fine?

The solipsistic, uncaring bastard stands back, studying people and using them. Is that it? Is that what being a writer is?

FROM: RUSSELL T DAVIES TO: BENJAMIN COOK, MONDAY 30 APRIL 2007 15:13:46 GMT
RE: CHRISTMAS IS COMING
I tested the word 'Botox' on Phil earlier. He went, 'Ooh!' – so that's a good sign. I keep thinking of those Ladies Who Lunch, lurching down the High Street, with their Botox lines erupting into green frond-ish stuff. Monsters in fake Chanel suits! And a strong, hard, female villain, head of the Beauty Technique, played by someone like Amanda Redman.

I've spent a lot of time thinking about Pompeii, too. The Doctor and Donna arrive… but why do they leave the TARDIS if they know where they are? A quick bit of sightseeing, perhaps, and then they scarper back to the TARDIS – only to see it in the distance, on the back of a horse and cart! It's being taken into Pompeii, so they have to follow. If we can get exterior locations abroad, the Doctor and Donna have to wander through the city in pursuit. The TARDIS will be taken to a villa – our studio-build – and that's where I want a bit of *Asterix*. Roman families on TV are always standing around pontificating, but I want a nice, funny family, like the one in *Asterix and the Laurel Wreath*. A likeable, ineffectual dad, a hapless son, a strong wife, cheeky slaves. Plus, in the villa, to stop the Doctor just hopping into the TARDIS and leaving – Household Gods! I love the idea of Household Gods, like the Romans used to have, God of the Hearth, God of the Atrium… what were they called? Lares? But we can have real 'gods' speaking, issuing forth in flames… which are, of course, the aliens under the volcano. Fire People. (Why are they there?) Somehow, we've got to end up *inside* the volcano, or under it. When it goes off, the Doctor and Donna have to be hiding in a capsule of some sort – maybe a big white ceramic bubble, big enough for two (we might need Sontaran globe-ships later on, so it could double-up) – so they're literally blasted out of the volcano, in the bubble, like a cork from a bottle. That makes me laugh. Christ, the CGI costs…!

Oh, *soothsayer!* I thought of that this morning. You can't go to Roman times without a soothsayer. And what if the soothsayer is right? (And how?) That brings me to the crux of this episode, the interesting new slant: if the Doctor goes to Pompeii and he knows what's going to happen, why doesn't he help? He saves the world, so why not this one? What makes history established? Lord knows, there's never been a good answer to this in the history of the programme, but we could think of some fascinating dialogue – and it's a great attitude for Donna, marks her out as a new companion. None of the others has asked this essential stuff. The sadness of the end, as they have to leave everyone to die! (Everyone? There isn't exactly a list of the dead at Pompeii, so surely the Doctor can nudge someone to safety?)

Also, I keep thinking about 4.12/4.13. That's why, when I get to the end of a series, I can – fingers crossed – write them quickly, because I've had so long to think about them. I wrote 3.13 in four days. *Four days!* Saturday night to Tuesday night. Four days of hell, but all the same…! I'm thinking about Donna, Martha, Rose, Jack, Sarah Jane and Mickey as a team, and the tagline: 'ONE OF THEM WILL DIE!' I'd watch that! Trouble is, I don't want to kill any of them. Rose Tyler was never created to die. None of them was. They were all created to show off *Doctor Who*'s central premise: the world and the universe is wonderful, ordinary people can do great things, and the human race survives. At a cost, yes, but a cost to the *supporting* characters. I mean, really, imagine Martha's death. Or Donna's. Or even Jackie's. It's just wrong. Tonally, wrong.

Maybe Mickey could die? 'Noooo!' said Phil. But Mickey is the only one who seems killable, because he's not quite central, he's unlucky, he's the odd one out. It's inbuilt in Mickey's character. But then I get shivers, because it's always the black guy who cops it. Maybe that's politically correct of me, but political correctness can be political *and* correct. But how do I keep that tagline without delivering? Maybe one of them dies and Martha is on hand with a bit of CPR…? The repercussions of death are so complicated and wonderful to write, but really 4.12/4.13 is about fighting Daleks, not mourning. 4.13 has to have the happiest ending ever. I'm bringing them all back because I want to see six people standing around that six-sided TARDIS console, flying the Earth back home. It's *happy*. You can't mess with that. Then again, I'm perverse and more than capable of ignoring everything I've just said.

I've a great image of Sarah Jane surrounded by Daleks, all shouting 'Exterminate!' That would be thrilling! (Yes, it's fannish, but I reckon I'm allowed to be in my last proper episode.) And then Mickey dimension-jumps in, blasts them with his big gun, and says, 'No one kills a Smith!' Ha ha ha. Also, this thought blazed into my head the other day, as I was walking past Techniquest on the way to Tesco: DAVROS WOULD RECOGNISE SARAH JANE![5] How exciting! And Davros should be the Daleks'

---

5 Davros and Sarah Jane Smith both featured in 1975 *Doctor Who* serial *Genesis of the Daleks*.

slave, because I hate it when he comes in and takes control and reduces the Daleks to soldiers. You could even feel sorry for him.

Have I told you this next bit already? I've put the Doctor's bubbling hand on board the TARDIS so that when David regenerates, one day, he'll grow another self and send it off into the parallel universe, so Rose has a Doctor of her own.[6] Ahh! But then today I thought, why delay? His duplicate will now do this at the end of 4.13, which will be gorgeous, and close off the Rose story for ever. That way, the Specials in 2009 will really be special – no companions, almost no back-references at all. Nice and clean. Never delay gratification if you can have it now. As I said to Freddie Ljungberg last night.

FROM: BENJAMIN COOK TO: RUSSELL T DAVIES, TUESDAY 1 MAY 2007 00:40:40 GMT

RE: CHRISTMAS IS COMING

I saw a book in Waterstone's today called *How I Write: The Secret Lives of Authors*. It looked interesting enough, but had hardly any text in it. It wouldn't survive a nuclear war! Is the world ready for *The Secret Life of Russell T Davies*, do you think?

FROM: RUSSELL T DAVIES TO: BENJAMIN COOK, TUESDAY 1 MAY 2007 01:36:14 GMT

RE: CHRISTMAS IS COMING

I've heard about that *Secret Lives* book. It seems a bit intimidating. There was an excerpt in *The Guardian* the other day. Apparently, Alan Hollinghurst has 'a large Piranesi engraving of the ruins of the Baths of Diocletian in Rome' by his desk, while Jay McInerney has 'an Acheulian hand axe, crafted by Homo erectus half a million years ago'. Christ Almighty! I've got a Cassandra action figure on my desk. Still, that's novelists for you.

Did I ever tell you that Zadie Smith once wrote to me to say that *Bob & Rose* is her favourite drama ever, and she watches an episode once a week – and this was years after its transmission – in the hope that she'll create a character as real as Rose one day? *Zadie Smith!!!*

Anyway. I caused havoc on *Torchwood* last night. In 2.6, Ianto is killed, gets revived in 2.7 as the Living Dead – pale, but still sexy – and that strand runs throughout the rest of the series. Last night, I suddenly realised, wrong character. It should be Owen.[7] Seven scripts are now being rewritten, including scenes that are actually being filmed today! Lines handed to the cast on the spot. Someone said, 'We can't do it. It's too late.' I said, 'I'd make you do this at your mother's deathbed on Christmas Day if it makes the show better.' And it does. See, power mad! Still, it meant I had a meeting with Gareth David-Lloyd to explain it all. Christ, he's hot.

I'm talking about sex a lot. That means I'll start writing soon.

---

6 The Doctor's hand was cut off in 2.X, though he grew another. The original, severed hand, kept in a bubbling jar, appeared in *Torchwood* Series One, the final three episode of *Doctor Who* Series Three, and remains in the TARDIS throughout Series Four.
7 Medical man Owen Harper (played by Burn Gorman) appears throughout *Torchwood* Series One and Two.

FROM: BENJAMIN COOK TO: RUSSELL T DAVIES, WEDNESDAY 2 MAY 2007 10:10:51 GMT

RE: CHRISTMAS IS COMING

I couldn't sleep last night, so I sat in bed and watched *Bob & Rose* on DVD. I've been meaning to for absolutely ages, but never have. That's terrible, isn't it? But I thought I'd find out why Zadie Smith loves it with a passion that borders on insanity. I started watching at 4am, just one episode. Well, I still haven't slept! I ended up watching all six in succession. The whole lot. I cried when Penelope Wilton made that speech at the end of Episode 4 and handcuffed herself to a bus. And then I rewound, re-watched that bit, and cried again.

I'm going to get some sleep now. Slightly embarrassed.

FROM: RUSSELL T DAVIES TO: BENJAMIN COOK, WEDNESDAY 2 MAY 2007 17:01:41 GMT

RE: CHRISTMAS IS COMING

That e-mail means the world to me. Thank you. That scene in Episode 4 is extraordinary, isn't it? I'm going to tell you about that scene. One Sunday, many years ago, I went to a Stonewall Section 28 rally in that same Manchester square. Poor turnout. Bad speeches. But then a glorious drag queen called Wynnie la Freak decided to take action and stood in front of a passing Stagecoach bus. (Stagecoach's founder had sponsored a lot of anti-gay legislation in Scotland. Marvellously, by accident, it's a Stagecoach bus that Nathan gets on in *Queer as Folk* for his 'I'm doing it!' speech. You can see the Stagecoach logo clearly!) A few camp old things joined Wynnie in the road, everyone danced, the driver shouted, then it cleared and the bus went on. However, during that moment, every political speaker on stage turned their back and pretended it wasn't happening. I just stood there, too, and didn't join in. And then everyone went home – because what do rallies do? Nothing, I suspect. But then, I thought, I can use that…

When we came to film that scene, we ended up in the same square, with a lot of the same people in the crowd – casting went and trawled the Village for the genuine articles – and with Wynnie herself recreating that moment. In full costume. But better! With results! It was a bizarre day. A beautiful day. My favourite day's filming ever. That's not because of the sheer act of recreation, although that was a nice by-product, but because it's Bob and his mum and Holly (oh, poor Holly) who make it work.[8] We went to rehearse that speech, Penelope Wilton on stage, her voice rising… and everyone listened. Even the drag queens were silent. Passers-by were stopping to listen. It was real. It was like Monica Gossage's speech was real. And then Jessica Stevenson began to cry. And so did I. Actually, I'm sort of tearful just typing this, no kidding. It was so wonderful. People in the crowd were crying and hugging me, and saying, 'Why can't it really be like this?' Everyone became devoted to that scene and gave everything in every take. Christ, I know I exaggerate, but that's word for word how it happened.

---

8 Bob Gossage (Alan Davies), his mum Monica (Penelope Wilton) and his best friend Holly Vance (Jessica Stevenson), who's madly in love with him.

Best. Day. Ever.

When it was transmitted six months later, my mum was dying, and that episode was the last thing of mine she ever saw. 'I loved that bit with the mothers,' she said on the phone – and that was the last proper conversation we ever had, because she became insensible after that. The next Monday night, I was pacing up and down in a hospital corridor, just waiting for her to die (the hospital that the Judoon invaded, many years later – how mad is that?), and there in the background was Episode 5 playing out in the patients' lounge, and it just seemed so hugely unimportant. That soured *Bob & Rose* for me for a long time. But do you know what? Not any more.

That was shown at a gay festival thing in LA once, and I held this symposium on scriptwriting afterwards. Some lovely young writer stood up and asked, 'Why did that scene make me cry so much? I described it to my boyfriend afterwards, and I started crying all over again – and I don't know why!' We talked about that for a long time. You could pontificate with 57 theories, but I'm still not sure why. I don't know if I want to know. Other than the simple fact that, in that moment, Monica Gossage is *right*.

Of course, that poor old show died on air. Episode 1 went out on 9 September 2001. Two days later, New York exploded, the world went mad, and so did the TV schedules (the least important thing, I admit), so its timeslot was shifted left, right and centre. The last episode was shown at 11.30pm. But then, a few months later, I won Comedy Writer of the Year at the British Comedy Awards! For *Bob & Rose*! Live on ITV! I thanked my mum, which was nice. Bear in mind, *Bob & Rose* was in competition against the first years of *The Office* and Peter Kay's *Phoenix Nights*. I didn't even think *Bob & Rose* was a comedy, really. For a long time, I thought that award was a sort of 9/11 reaction – the championing of a sweet romance in the middle of what felt like World War III. Or it was a protest vote against bad scheduling. Or it was a gay thing. It's only in the past year or so – you really do spend that long thinking about things that you wrote – that it's begun to occur to me why it won. Maybe it was brilliant. That's why. Yeah.

'You there! Gorgeous creature!' Some things are just perfect, and that's one of them.

FROM: BENJAMIN COOK TO: RUSSELL T DAVIES, SUNDAY 6 MAY 2007 05:48:05 GMT

RE: CHRISTMAS IS COMING

Russell! You've topped *The Independent*'s Pink List! You're the UK's Number One Gay! Do you get an actual award? Sir Ian McKellen won it last year. I bet he got an award. Mind you, Peter Mandelson came fifth. *Fifth!* Who'd put Peter Mandelson on a Top 101 list of anything?

FROM: RUSSELL T DAVIES TO: BENJAMIN COOK, SUNDAY 6 MAY 2007 23:37:26 GMT

RE: CHRISTMAS IS COMING

The Number One most… er, most what? I'm not sure. Most influential? Most powerful?

Most sexy? Er, no! Still, it's the *most* in the land, and I'm Number One. Ahead of all the other homos in the UK.

On Thursday, I wrote a five-page pre-titles sequence for *Torchwood* 2.1. It's all I can contribute, a five-minute opener. But I love it. That's the blowfish in a sports car. It felt good, and then I felt sad that I'm not writing a full *Torchwood* script. Ups and downs. And I spent the weekend rewriting *Sarah Jane* 1.7/1.8, all of which was ignoring the fact that I've about four weeks to deliver 4.X. Except I haven't. At midday yesterday, I realised I'd miscalculated: it turns out that I've three weeks. Bollocks. I read my diary wrong. I'm a bloody idiot. Yesterday just dissolved into panic. I was going to write to you, because I thought it'd be a good thing to describe, but I couldn't even do that. I was sort of numb.

Sometimes I look at all these scripts piling up, and it defeats me. I love script-editing sessions with writers, but I hate the hours of reading that you have to do beforehand. And I'll tell you what pisses me off most of all: a meeting with a writer has to negotiate a hundred tricky things – the writer's mood, their passion, their style, their ambition, their failures, their idiosyncrasies – but now there's a new element entering the room: writers wondering, 'What will they say about me?' Meaning, online. More and more, with every writer. It's those internet message boards. The forums. They destroy writers. This job is full of doubts already, but now there's a whole new level of fear, shouting at us. It is now a writer's job, like it or not, to put up with it. It's like when Helen Raynor went on Outpost Gallifrey last month and read the reviews of her two Dalek episodes. She said that she was, literally, shaking afterwards. Like she'd been physically assaulted. I'm not exaggerating. She said it was like being in a pub when a fight breaks out next to you. I had to spend two hours on the phone to her, talking her out of it, convincing her that of course she can write, that we do need her and want her. That bastard internet voice gets into writers' heads and destabilises them massively.

The stupidest thing you can say is 'Ignore it', because no one can. Who can resist going in search of their own name on the internet? Coming to terms with it is the key. Helen knows that now. It was the same with Murray Gold during Series One: a massive loss of faith after the first episode leaked onto the internet, because he read the Outpost Gallifrey comments about his music. He was saying, 'I don't know how to do my job any more.' Noel Clarke read the online reviews of his portrayal of Mickey, but at least he got *angry*. Yet none of them has been attacked as viciously as I've been. I always thought I was a big old poof (albeit Number One Poof!), but sometimes I think I must be made of some sort of steel. I read that stuff and it doesn't stop me, not ever. I've got quite high-flown and fancy beliefs about art that maybe put it all into perspective. Principally: it is not a democracy. Creating something is not a democracy. The people have no say. The artist does. It doesn't matter what the people witter on about; they and their response come after. They're not there for the creation.

This is becoming one of the great arguments of the day, for populist writers especially. It taps into the whole debate across journalism about the democratisation of the critic.

It was summed up best by Rachel Cooke in *The Observer* recently, where she said that the online voice writes with a deep sense of exclusion. She wrote about that with some anger, but also with a lot of sadness. I don't see the sadness myself. I think it's *right* that they're excluded. Of course, it's always been that way, people have always carped on, but the internet means that we can all read it now. We're taught from childhood that the printed word has authority. If something is typed, it seems official. (History will look back on this as the maddest time – a period of ten years or so in which we all *typed* at each other!) So it can mess up writers when they read that endlessly critical voice. It's completely, *completely* destructive. I cannot see one iota of it that's helpful, except maybe in the toughening up. Helen is in a delicate position in that she's only just started, and she's on the verge of being really very good – and now she finds herself ruined by this wall of hostility. It makes me furious.

FROM: BENJAMIN COOK TO: RUSSELL T DAVIES, MONDAY 7 MAY 2007 04:40:59 GMT

RE: CHRISTMAS IS COMING

Dear Number One,

>>I read that stuff and it doesn't stop me, not ever.<<

But has it ever? Does your resolve not to let the critics affect you come from experience?

FROM: RUSSELL T DAVIES TO: BENJAMIN COOK, MONDAY 7 MAY 2007 10:47:02 GMT

RE: CHRISTMAS IS COMING

It doesn't feel like a conscious resolve; it's just the way I am, I suppose. Only one word makes me furious, and that's 'lazy'. If someone calls me that, I want to rip their head off. Honestly, it's the gap in my armour. It makes me vicious. Writers spend vast amounts of their lives being modest, crippled by doubt, insecure, self-deprecating. Somewhere that has to stop.

It must be experience, though. That experience was *Queer as Folk*. The first three weeks when it was on air, it was like I lived on the radio. I'd sit in my office with calls booked for every half hour, sometimes for the whole day, talking to every Radio Back Yard in the country. I remember not having time to make a coffee. I considered moving a kettle into my office. Some of those were shock-jock radio stations, like the old Talk Radio, where they'd be vile. Much to my surprise, I loved it. I'd weigh in and have a fine old time. I made the Talk Radio Breakfast DJs admit to not even having watched *Queer as Folk*. Later on, sitting in the BBC 5 Live studio, facing Nicky Campbell while he complained about the Jill Dando joke in *Queer as Folk 2*, I was defending even that honestly.[9] It toughens you up. There was one caller to that show, a retired teacher from an all-girls school, who said that she'd never taught a lesbian in

9 Dialogue in *Queer as Folk 2* mentions a lethal drink named after murdered TV host Jill Dando – 'one shot goes straight to your head'.

all her born days. I told her that not only was she a bad teacher, but she'd let down every girl that she'd ever taught – that she wasn't just retired, she was forgotten! The key to get through that whole time was not to defend the work, because I always think defence sounds like an apology, but to go on the attack. It was exciting.

FROM: RUSSELL T DAVIES TO: BENJAMIN COOK, MONDAY 7 MAY 2007 21:31:25 GMT

RE: CHRISTMAS IS COMING

Having wittered on this morning, I've just found an interview with AA Gill in today's *Media Guardian*, and he says, of being a critic:

> *Can anyone do it? Is everyone's opinion worth the same? No. My opinion is worth more than other people's. Of course that's a horrendously arrogant thing to say, but that is the nature and basis of criticism. If you are sticking your opinions in front of two million readers every Sunday, then you have to believe that your opinion is worth more.*

So that's a) hooray, and b) oh Christ, I'm turning into bloody AA Gill!

Mind you, later on in the paper, talking about some drama, it says: 'In the most inappropriate piece of casting since Alan Davies was plonked into *Bob & Rose...*' Hmph! You see? You've got to be made of steel or you're flayed alive.

FROM: BENJAMIN COOK TO: RUSSELL T DAVIES, MONDAY 7 MAY 2007 23:07:27 GMT

RE: CHRISTMAS IS COMING

I've found the Independent Television Commission's Programme Complaints and Interventions Report on *Queer as Folk 2*. Apparently, 15 viewers (I know! That many!) complained about your Jill Dando joke:

> *The ITC recognised that some viewers had been very upset by this remark and was sorry for the distress caused. However, given the dramatic context with its serious intent, the ITC concluded that this 'joke' was not in breach of the Programme Code.*

I especially like the bit where they put the word 'joke' in inverted commas.

FROM: RUSSELL T DAVIES TO: BENJAMIN COOK, MONDAY 7 MAY 2007 23:30:18 GMT

RE: CHRISTMAS IS COMING

My favourite complaint was on Channel 4's daily log after Episode 1 of *Queer as Folk* was broadcast: 'My cleaner was so upset, I had to send her home!' Ha ha ha. I swear to God that's true.

FROM: RUSSELL T DAVIES TO: BENJAMIN COOK, TUESDAY 8 MAY 2007 18:11:06 GMT

RE: CHRISTMAS IS COMING

An update: Julie and Phil don't even have to ask how I'm getting on, they know my moods, so they're planning to shift the start of filming back a week. Good. But then they ask me, 'Is that what you want to do?' And I say, 'Don't make it my decision!'

I spent a long time wondering today, as I always do, *why don't I just start?!* I know the

4.X pre-titles: the Doctor pulls the TARDIS off the prow of the *Titanic* (resolving the 3.13 cliffhanger, where the *Titanic* crashes through the walls of the TARDIS control room), the TARDIS materialises in a cupboard on board, he steps out into Reception, wanders through, seeing a lot of our supporting cast, goes out on deck, and the camera pulls out to see the *Titanic* flying above the Earth. Over the ship's Tannoy, we hear: 'Welcome aboard the *Starship Titanic*!' I know that pre-titles. SO WHY DON'T I WRITE IT?

Maybe it's a dreadful decision to cross *Doctor Who* with a disaster movie. A lot of *Doctor Who* is to do with *why* and *who* (why's the *Titanic* been hit? Who turned off the shields?), whereas the narrative of a disaster movie is more about *how* they survive. It's difficult for the Doctor to investigate when he has to follow quite a linear path, simply surviving. It suggests that one of the main characters is involved with the villainy ('Yes, Doctor, it was me! I took down the shields!'), which is a hell of a coincidence, because by definition, to get screen time, that character has to be one of the survivors who happens to be with the Doctor. It doesn't fit. Formats are clashing. And why would he (or she?) be on board a ship that he's sabotaged?

But I've decided that 4.X should have an alien called Bannakaffalatta. We've budgeted for one spiky alien – I'd hate everyone on board the *Titanic* to be humanoid – so that's a good name. And I'm hung up on the idea that everyone should be in black tie. Maybe the Doctor, too. And should the Angels use their haloes as weapons? Like killer Frisbees? A nice scene with the Doctor and survivors fighting off flying Frisbees with… well, with anything, with sticks of metal, swinging at them. But how do haloes kill? They can't slice off your head, not at 7pm on Christmas Day! Also, I'm thinking that the Captain is part of the scheme. He's the saboteur – which is revealed early on. He has a young, sexy Midshipman (is that the word, Midshipman?) with him, who discovers the truth and survives. Maybe he's trapped on the damaged Flight Deck trying to control things, while the Doctor is fighting to reach him.

Also, I spent ten minutes panicking that the 2008 Christmas Special is a lot closer than I think. Apart from 'Period drama, Cybermen in the snow,' it's blank. Christ!

FROM: BENJAMIN COOK TO: RUSSELL T DAVIES, TUESDAY 8 MAY 2007 21:38:13 GMT

RE: CHRISTMAS IS COMING
Heard anything from Kylie yet? It's been a while, but the tabloid rumours persist…

FROM: RUSSELL T DAVIES TO: BENJAMIN COOK, WEDNESDAY 9 MAY 2007 01:41:17 GMT

RE: CHRISTMAS IS COMING
That'll be Will Baker in the papers. Apparently, Kylie *is* still interested, but it's so difficult to get through her layers of agents and managers. It's like that with big stars. Her agent has the synopsis, and then you hear sod all for weeks. But David did go for dinner with her – and to the theatre, to see *The Sound of Music*. How that didn't make the tabloids, I'll never know.

MIDSHIPMAN FRAM

CHAPTER FOUR

INT. SPACESHIP

In which George Lucas is snubbed,
Charlie Hunnam's arse is discussed, and the
Controller of BBC One puts his foot in it

FROM: RUSSELL T DAVIES TO: BENJAMIN COOK, FRIDAY 11 MAY 2007 15:20:45 GMT

RE: CHRISTMAS IS COMING

I thought I should write to you, because I had a rush of ideas just now. I'd gone out to town to buy some food. It's always when I leave this desk, things start clicking. Literally, walking through Marks & Spencer. I know I'm talking to myself. I must look like a nutter. I thought, what if it's an insurance claim? It's the people who own the *Titanic* who have magnetised the hull to attract the meteorites. No, I don't mean insurance – insurance would be insane, since your shares would plummet if your ship crashed. I mean that the Big Boss is on board, he has set it up, he has himself a nice stasis pod, protecting him from harm, so his people can pluck him from the wreckage and he'll be declared dead. Or something. The Angels are pre-programmed to kill the survivors so that no one's left. The ship falling onto the Earth is a by-product, not part of the overall plan. And only the Doctor cares; to everyone else it's just a primitive planet below.

But why not fake a car crash? Why would the Big Boss take everyone with him? In fact, if the ship is going to crash into the Earth, why do the Angels need to kill the survivors at all? They're going to die anyway. But that sort of thing shouldn't stop me. Let it ride. I mustn't bore myself with reasons why not. There are always a million dull reasons why not. Go for the images, the feel of it, the potential, the dynamic. Details come later. I'll think on.

Oh, and Kylie Minogue should die. That struck me like a thunderbolt in the taxi back from town. *Wham!* Disaster movies should always have deaths of people that you don't want to die. She should be the next potential companion, but cops it. I'd never considered that before. That feels good. It's not so much the ideas; it's the fact I'm *having* ideas. That's what feels good.

FROM: BENJAMIN COOK TO: RUSSELL T DAVIES, FRIDAY 11 MAY 2007 17:55:52 GMT

RE: CHRISTMAS IS COMING
So... okay, really, honestly, why don't you start writing now?

FROM: RUSSELL T DAVIES TO: BENJAMIN COOK, FRIDAY 11 MAY 2007 18:30:02 GMT

RE: CHRISTMAS IS COMING
I don't know. Honestly. I'm just sitting here like an idiot. Like a bloody idiot. All day. I'm eating badly, smoking heavily... but that seems to be part of the getting-ready-to-write crap. I worked my way through about 50 cigarettes with the *Sarah Jane* rewrite earlier this week. That's just absurd, even for me. I'm killing myself. I'm looking scruffy, because I'm not bothering to iron shirts. (The Number One Gay!) My VAT needs doing, but I'm ignoring it. I missed my nieces' birthdays last week. I haven't even sent a card. I *still* haven't sent a card. And I'm as horny as hell. Like a stupid teenager. That's more like it, though. That's a better description of what this process actually *feels* like.

FROM: RUSSELL T DAVIES TO: BENJAMIN COOK, TUESDAY 15 MAY 2007 19:01:40 GMT

RE: CHRISTMAS IS COMING
I'm in a stinking mood. Panic, panic, panic. Everyone is giving me a wide berth, because I'm just being vicious to them. They recognise the signs. I suppose I should write it all down properly, but even this correspondence can sod off –

No, it shouldn't. It won't. But that's how it feels. Just bad. I keep telling myself to start work at 9pm, to start typing. That's my latest target.

FROM: RUSSELL T DAVIES TO: BENJAMIN COOK, WEDNESDAY 16 MAY 2007 02:51:27 GMT

RE: CHRISTMAS IS COMING
Hmm, look, I started. Not at 9pm, at midnight. Sheer panic. It'll do me good, waking up tomorrow knowing that a 4.X file exists. That's better than nothing.

```
1. INT. TARDIS - DAY

REPEAT OF 3.13 SC.92. THE TARDIS in flight. THE DOCTOR walks around
the console. Deep in thought. And then...

EXPLOSION! The Doctor's showered with debris!
```

He's on the floor. Coughing. Smoke in the air. He waves his hand to
clear the air, looking up. Gobsmacked.

                    THE DOCTOR
     What? But… what??

FX: WIDE SHOT, the PROW OF A SHIP, an old-fashioned liner, now
sticking through the whole of the right-hand wall of the Tardis,
filling half the space.

The Doctor finds in the debris, a lifebelt. He flips it over. It
says: TITANIC.

                    THE DOCTOR (CONT'D)
     What??!

(End repeat, new material.) He leaps to his feet, slams away at
the Tardis console.

FX: the prow of the ship withdraws through the hole.
He slams more switches, the Time Rotor rising and falling, the
sound of materialisation filling the air…

                                              CUT TO:

2. INT. SMALL CUPBOARD – NIGHT

Tiny, dark linen cupboard, just big enough for…

FX: the TARDIS materialises.

THE DOCTOR steps out, still brushing himself down. Opens the
cupboard door, steps out –

                                              CUT TO:

3. INT. TITANIC RECEPTION – CONTINUOUS

THE DOCTOR steps out.
Large space, reception desk, all wood & marble, more TITANIC
signage, STEWARDS passing to and fro, and GUESTS in their finery,
chatting, laughing. It all looks very 1912. Almost. And it's
decked out for Christmas, though nothing gaudy, all very classy.
The Doctor walks through…

Men in black tie. Ladies in posh dresses. Staff looking
immaculate. A WAITRESS in uniform – PETH, young, feisty – walks
past the Doctor, carrying a tray. Then he sees –

Two GOLDEN ANGELS, guarding a set of internal doors. THE HEAVENLY
HOST. They look like metal statues – tall, with beautiful gold,
blank faces, simple tunics, hands locked in a prayer gesture,
folded wings, haloes suspended above their metal hair by thin
struts. But as the Doctor stares, one of them slowly turns his
head. Looks at the Doctor.

Black eyes in a gold face.

The Doctor creeped out, then distracted by seeing –

An alien – BANNAKAFFALATTA – strolling past, in black tie; three foot tall, head like a spiky blue football.

And the Doctor's getting the hang of this now, keeps walking, goes to a metal ship-type door in the wall, marked DECK 15, spins the wheel, opens it –

                                                              CUT TO:

4. EXT. DECK 15 – CONTINUOUS

THE DOCTOR steps out. Traditional deck, wooden floor, bronze railing, Titanic lifebelts on display, GUESTS standing with cocktails, enjoying the view. To the left, to the right, all very traditional. But in front…

FX: the Doctor walks to the railing, the night beyond. Revealing that the blackness is not just night, it's SPACE, and below him: THE EARTH.

CU The Doctor – he gets it!

                          THE DOCTOR
    Riiight…

FX: LONG HERO FX SHOT, ZOOM OUT from the Doctor on the deck, pulling back to see the whole ship – A STARSHIP, exactly like the Titanic, but with mighty antigravity engines underneath – keep pulling out wider, to see the vessel sailing majestically above the Earth. Over this:

                          TANNOY
    Starship Titanic is now in orbit above Sol 3, also known
    as Earth. Population: Human. And in accordance with local
    customs: Merry Christmas!

                              CUT TO OPENING TITLES

5. EXT. FX SHOT

NEW ANGLE on THE TITANIC, its sheer beauty.

                                                              CUT TO:

6. INT. BRIDGE – NIGHT

Quiet and dark. A long room, rather than deep, the only place with futuristic technology on display, computer banks, etc, though at the centre there's still a big old-fashioned wooden SHIP'S WHEEL. Facing windows, which look out onto BLACKNESS (the view will be GREENSCREEN later).

CREW in smart 1912-ish uniform – NB, everything on board is only an approximation of the period. CAPTAIN HARDAKER stands centre – 60, wise, calm.

                          CAPTAIN HARDAKER
    Orbit nice and steady. Good work, Mr Cavill. And maintain
    position.

Crew operate controls, the sound of engines slowing. The Captain relaxes a little:

                    CAPTAIN HARDAKER (CONT'D)
    Now then, gentlemen. According to the traditions of the planet
    below, Christmas is a time of celebration. I think you might
    be entitled to a tot of rum. Just the one! Off you go, I'll
    keep watch.

Smiles, salutes, 'Sir!', and the men head off… Except the
youngest, MIDSHIPMAN BLANE, young, nervous.

                    CAPTAIN HARDAKER
    And you, what was it…?

                    MIDSHIPMAN BLANE
    Blane, sir, Midshipman Blane.

                    CAPTAIN HARDAKER
    You're new, I take it?

                    MIDSHIPMAN BLANE
    Only just qualified, sir. First trip out!

                    CAPTAIN HARDAKER
    Then you can stand down, Midshipman. Go and enjoy yourself.

                    MIDSHIPMAN BLANE
    I would, sir, but, um… Regulations say the Bridge has to be
    staffed by two crewmembers at any one time, sir.

                    CAPTAIN HARDAKER
    Well said. Very good! Just you and me, then. It's only a
    Level Three planet down below, fairly primitive, they don't
    even know we're here. Should be a quiet night.

                    MIDSHIPMAN BLANE
    Yes, sir.

                                                        CUT TO:
7. INT. BALLROOM – NIGHT

THE DOCTOR, now adjusting his black tie, walks in.

More of a LOUNGE than a ballroom, tables and booths with GUESTS,
drinking, milling about; dotted about, more HEAVENLY HOST,
standing perfectly still; then a dance floor, and a stage, on which
the SINGER & BAND are performing a lounge-music-version of I Wish
It Could Be Christmas Every Day.

All normal, until the Doctor looks up…

FX WIDE SHOT: VAST ROOM, levels of seating rising up into a
vaulted roof, GUESTS milling about.

The Doctor strolls through, looking around…

His POV: BANNAKAFFALATTA, with some ordinary GUESTS, at a table,
all laughing.

His POV: another table, MORVIN (male) & STRUZIE (female), a large

```
pair, tucking into a buffet; they like their food. For some
reason, they're dressed as cowboy & cowgirl.

The Doctor then distracted by loud voices -
```

This is weird, showing it to someone at this stage. It feels so odd. But I'd better get used to it. Do you want to read this stuff? I've no idea. So far, I'm thinking… is it a bit dull? The Doctor wandering is deadly dull. The Doctor is best under pressure. But it's hard to generate plot until the meteorites hit. Then again, with all the on-air trailers in December, everyone will know that it's a disaster movie, so there's a pleasure in just meeting the characters. I want to hit the disaster by Page 15 – about 11 minutes in. That feels right.

Other thoughts: Midshipman Blane should be sexy as hell. I don't often think of specific actors, but maybe Russell Tovey. Or posh like Lee Williams. Blane is not a sexy name, though. I'll change it. Struzie should be Debbie Chazen, who played Big Claire in *Mine All Mine*. We offered her a Slitheen in *The Sarah Jane Adventures*, but she begged to be in *Doctor Who* proper. A disaster movie needs a larger woman, and she's a hoot. And Bannakaffalatta? Jimmy Vee. Oh, the thought of little Jimmy and Kylie in a scene together!

FROM: BENJAMIN COOK TO: RUSSELL T DAVIES, WEDNESDAY 16 MAY 2007 03:10:44 GMT

RE: CHRISTMAS IS COMING

How does it feel to have started, Russell? Good, surely? Apart from the strangeness of sending what you've written to me already…

I'm privileged to be the first person to read this. Of course I want to! How could you even ask? But I'll try to resist the temptation to be all subjective and say nice things – or horrible things (you never know) – about what you're sending me. If you decided that something worked because I'd said I think it's great, or that something didn't because I'd questioned it, I'm worried that this project would come crashing down around our ears. At the very least, the world would stop turning. Let's see how long I can remain an impartial observer. Invisible Ben! I will, however, be asking questions. For example –

It's technical, this one, but worth asking before we go on… you talk about WIDE SHOTS, CUs, FX shots, camera angles and so on, but really who should determine this: the writer or the director? Do you, literally, write each shot into your script? Or do you plan them in your mind's eye but let the director decide?

FROM: RUSSELL T DAVIES TO: BENJAMIN COOK, WEDNESDAY 16 MAY 2007 03:44:51 GMT

RE: CHRISTMAS IS COMING

How do I feel? Scared, because I should have started ages ago. Scared sick. Sick because I gave up smoking again on Saturday, but then I reached Page 2 and went scrabbling through bags and coats, like a teenager at a party, until I found an old pack with four fags left. The script just felt so slow and dead without them. I only stopped writing for tonight because those four have gone. I'm feeling desperate that I'll never write without smoking again. Series One and Two were written without fags, but that feels like five million years ago now.

But I haven't gone to bed yet. I'm too wired by cigarettes and the nicotine patch that I ripped off.

>>you talk about WIDE SHOTS, CUs, FX shots, camera angles and so on, but really who should determine this: the writer or the director?<<

I like to give some camera directions, but not too many, not so many that it reads like a list. When someone is reading a script – principally, the director – they should *feel* it, the pace, the speed, the atmosphere, the mood, the gags, the dread. I'll give camera directions that enhance the mood: WIDE SHOT if something is barren, lost, empty (or huge, busy, epic, if you've the budget), and CU (close-up) when it's focused, intense, when someone's whispering 'I love you'. I never bother with the more ordinary technical shots like MCU (medium close-up) or LONG SHOT (you can see the whole body, but not as wide as a WIDE SHOT), because they don't *feel* like anything, do they? But I'll describe a crane shot, rising up or rising down, if the moment is epic, if you need to feel that huge sweep of events. Also, frankly, then you stand a good chance of the producer setting aside money for a crane, right from the start, for that scene. Cranes are expensive. But it's all emotion, in the end. Scripts can be so dry. *Feel* them. A lot of the time, new writers are told specifically – and strongly – not to write camera angles, because it's the director's choice, but I reckon that's just power games. I've never heard of a director objecting, only power-broking producers and script editors talking on their behalf without consultation.

Stage directions, as opposed to camera directions, are a whole art in themselves. The classic mistake that we get from newer writers, or writers not used to writing action, is something like this:

```
The Doctor runs up the stairs, explosions all around him, and
soldiers appear, but he runs into a huge white space, with a
glowing blue column rising up into the sky, and it's crackling
like electricity, and a white halo surrounds him.
```

Eh? What? *What?!* Calm down. Break it down. Tell me exactly what's happening. I spend huge amounts of time making sure that stage directions match the tone and rhythm of the scene – like in an action scene, where I use dashes instead of full stops to make sure that everything is moving fast:

```
BEN walks into the room, invisibly. He looks around. Sees the
wallet by the bed.

He walks towards the wallet –
```

```
- but it explodes! -

- and he's running, running, running -
```

Do you see, you *read* it fast? It feels energised. If that gets into the director's head, then you stand a good chance of it working. Funnily enough, a semicolon always looks considered and classy; it slows things down, makes you read more closely:

```
- BEN keeps running -

- and stops. He's in a huge, beautiful, empty amphitheatre;
classical columns, white marble.
```

Another example: to put 'Pause' on a line of its own makes it *feel* like a pause:

```
BEN looks around. He can hear singing.

Pause.

Then he moves on…
```

That's much more effective than:

```
BEN looks around. He can hear singing. Pause. Then he moves on.
```

The first version *feels* the same as what Ben is feeling. I think that's vital. And I strip out adverbs like crazy, because they don't sound dynamic. (This is really personal stuff now. Other writers would be guffawing.) I prefer to write:

```
BEN runs across the amphitheatre, fast -
```

Instead of:

```
BEN runs across the amphitheatre quickly.
```

The first one feels faster, whereas the second is too considered. It's not a novel; it's a script and it has to flow. It has to feel like pictures. (I like this new script, by the way. Your wallet exploded and you ran into an amphitheatre. I might add some gladiators in a minute. Be warned!)

I avoid the word 'we', too. It's a real pain to eliminate it – along with 'our' and 'us' – and other writers seem to use it with no ill effects, but it feels wrong to me. 'We see BEN running.' I prefer 'BEN is running', because there is no 'we' inside the script; there's just Ben. Steven Moffat is a good example of the opposite: he's all 'we' and gags in the stage directions, self-referential statements about the actors and stuff. He personally is very present in his stage directions, and it works brilliantly.

Incidentally, we're the only people I've seen who do that FX line break:

```
FX: the prow of the ship withdraws through the hole.
```

It's a great system, though I'd beware of using it outside of *Doctor Who* circles. People might not get it, because it's unique. I say unique, but I'll probably discover that the whole of Hollywood does it now and always did.

FROM: BENJAMIN COOK TO: RUSSELL T DAVIES, WEDNESDAY 16 MAY 2007 11:02:51 GMT

RE: CHRISTMAS IS COMING

One more anal question (for now): when writing stage and camera directions, which words should you capitalise? Once you've capitalised a word once, should you refrain from doing so for the rest of that scene?

FROM: RUSSELL T DAVIES TO: BENJAMIN COOK, WEDNESDAY 16 MAY 2007 12:29:12 GMT

RE: CHRISTMAS IS COMING

I capitalise every character's name when they first appear, but this is partly a production thing, so that the person drawing up the shooting schedule can spot the name easily in order to break down who's in which scene. That's why, if a character is referred to but they're not in the scene, they're not capitalised:

```
CU THE DOCTOR. He's thinking of Rose.
```

I used to capitalise names all the way through. A lot of people do. But then I noticed that Paul Abbott changed his system, that he only capitalised them the first time they appear. At about the same time, Nick Elliott (Controller of Drama) at ITV said to me, 'Why do people use all these capitals? Why are they shouting at me?' So I changed, too.

As for other words, it's very indiscriminate, but I tend to do it when it's important:

```
Ben pulls out a LASER GUN.

Then he RUNS!
```

It's kind of telling the director: show this! But a lot of people don't do it at all. If it's worrying you, don't do it. But I do think it gives the script energy, sometimes.

FROM: RUSSELL T DAVIES TO: BENJAMIN COOK, WEDNESDAY 16 MAY 2007 18:48:18 GMT

RE: CHRISTMAS IS COMING

Here's more. I tend to do this, work all day in a panic, then stop at 6pm-ish, catch up with rushes and e-mails, then return to writing at about 9pm or 10pm, depending on what's on telly. But I thought I'd show you this now. I keep changing as I go along, too fast for you to note. For instance, I realised while writing earlier today that I didn't have the Host malfunction at any point – and I was lacking spookiness – so I went back and wrote that into the middle of Scene 7. There's a rewrite that no one ever saw.

My thoughts on it so far: I like the Doctor and Peth; they feel good, nice dialogue. It makes it all feel more real. It's very, *very* strange writing dialogue that might be said by Kylie! Morvin and Foon (I thought Struzie was sayable in too many different ways, so I changed it to Foon) are sweet. Too sweet? These Christmas Specials are so direct, so plain, so on-the-nose. But so they should be. It's Christmas. It's not the time for *The Girl in the Fireplace* or *Human Nature*. But I really should have started weeks ago. Oh Christ! What I'm really thinking is: it's crap, I'm rubbish, this will be a public debacle. Christmas Day, with everyone watching – what a way to fail! That's public execution. But I suppose we can take this insecure crap as read from now on.

FROM: BENJAMIN COOK TO: RUSSELL T DAVIES, WEDNESDAY 16 MAY 2007 20:37:42 GMT

RE: CHRISTMAS IS COMING

I've just been to Sainsbury's. They're selling *Doctor Who* Petits Filous Frubes. Cyber-Strawberry flavour. Slogan: 'I'm f... f... f... frozen in time!' Is your fridge full of this stuff, Russell?

Thanks for the f... f... f... further instalment of script. A couple of months back, we considered whether lead characters have to be sympathetic, and it's a disaster movie convention that the headlining catastrophe is made more comprehensible by showing it impacting on characters that we care for. But *how* do you make an audience care about your characters? And quickly? Movies in this genre often present 'stock' figures – the star-crossed lovers, the courageous-but-doomed hero – so is that it? Is it identifiability that makes us care? Or universal traits? Must we find aspects of Bannakaffalatta with which we identify? (We're all a bit spiky from time to time!) Or furnish your characters with a rich spectrum of personal details? The more they reveal about themselves, the more we care? Or do you focus on their vulnerability? To offer another example, at what point in *Bob & Rose* do we start to care about Bob and Rose? And why? We care about Nathan in *Queer as Folk* within two minutes flat – but is that just down to Charlie Hunnam's lost-puppy-dog eyes?

Right. I'm off. My f... f... f... flatmate, Matt, is eating Martha Jones, and I'm enjoying the Moxx of Balhoon. And later I might try a Frube. Boom boom! Mmm... Cyber-Strawberry!

FROM: RUSSELL T DAVIES TO: BENJAMIN COOK, WEDNESDAY 16 MAY 2007 20:52:44 GMT

RE: CHRISTMAS IS COMING

>>We care about Nathan in *Queer as Folk* within two minutes flat – but is that just down to Charlie Hunnam's lost-puppy-dog eyes?<<

Charlie Hunnam's arse, I'd say. Lovely man, Charlie. He's really clever. At his audition, we asked him his favourite actor. He said, 'Christopher Walken,' which is just about the most intelligent reply I've ever heard to that question. Plus, *the arse!*

I am hooting at those Frubes. They're the only licensed product that Julie and I were ever unsure about, but that sort of thing can be worth a fortune for BBC Worldwide.

The how-to-make-an-audience-care thing is hard. I'll come back to that, I promise.

FROM: BENJAMIN COOK TO: RUSSELL T DAVIES, WEDNESDAY 16 MAY 2007 22:55:06 GMT

CHARLIE HUNNAM'S ARSE

You're mentioned in the new *Radio Times*. TV reviewer Alison Graham says that you and your team 'must be hurt' not to have received BAFTA nominations this year. She has a point. It's an odd list, isn't it? Notable omissions.

FROM: RUSSELL T DAVIES TO: BENJAMIN COOK, WEDNESDAY 16 MAY 2007 23:03:34 GMT

RE: CHARLIE HUNNAM'S ARSE

Let us never change that subject line. Ever. Mmm.

I'm not bothered about the BAFTAs, to be honest. Last year was so extraordinary, it can never be topped.[1] Besides, history decides in the end. Everyone thinks that *Queer as Folk* won a BAFTA, when it wasn't even nominated. Now, that was shocking. And the last thing that I need is a night in London. I'm mad and script-obsessed at the moment, therefore a bit destructive. The other day (I didn't tell you this), my agent got a call from George Lucas' people. Apparently, Lucas is in London and he wants to meet me about writing for his new *Star Wars* TV series! But I said no. Well, I can't go to London, I haven't the time, and Lucas didn't exactly beat a path to Cardiff, so he can't be that interested. Mind you, they really want a UK writer, apparently. When I find out who it is, I won't be so snooty; I'll just be jealous.

FROM: RUSSELL T DAVIES TO: BENJAMIN COOK, THURSDAY 17 MAY 2007 02:23:36 GMT

RE: CHARLIE HUNNAM'S ARSE

Phew, 12 pages, almost! That's a good day. It doesn't feel *quite* as terrifying as normal, maybe because a disaster movie has an inbuilt shape: arrive, disaster, climb, safety. That shape helps.

I'm on Page 16, and we're close to the disaster. I keep page-counting. It's a constant tick. I can't help it. The script was 17-and-a-half pages, but I edited it down by cutting

----

1 At the 2006 British Academy Television Awards, *Doctor Who* won the Best Drama Series category, as well as the Pioneer Audience Award voted for by TV viewers.

MR. MAXITANE!

lines and shifting stage directions. Can the trip to Earth be cut, too?[2] Is it a diversion? It's only there for the Buckingham Palace gag at the end. Then again, that gag is brilliant. It keeps making me laugh, even now. I love a gag. Oh, and I went back and changed Midshipman Blane to Midshipman *Frame*. Much sexier! Of course, they'll all start dying soon. I'm worried that the dying, though necessary, might be too horrible. Also, I'm thinking it's kind of obvious that Mr Maxitane is behind the whole thing.[3] Good thought tonight, though: the Host are programmed to kill surviving passengers… but the Doctor is not a passenger! I like that. Nice.

FROM: BENJAMIN COOK TO: RUSSELL T DAVIES, THURSDAY 17 MAY 2007 08:34:20 GMT

RE: CHARLIE HUNNAM'S ARSE

Hang on… *Prince Charles?!*[4] Kylie Minogue I can believe, but the Prince of Wales?

---

2 A group of passengers from the *Titanic* – including the Doctor and 'Peth' – led by the ship's historian, Mr Copper, teleport down to Earth for some sightseeing… to find London almost deserted. A lone newspaper seller, Stan, explains that 'everyone's scarpered, 'cept me and her Majesty,' in the light of the previous two Christmases' alien invasion attempts (2.X and 3.X).
3 'Mr Maxitane' (Max Capricorn in later drafts) is the boss of the *Titanic* – a fat mogul with a cigar and bodyguards.
4 In this original draft of 4.X, a BBC news programme on newspaperman Stan's portable TV shows Charles, Prince of Wales, being interviewed: 'My mother will be staying in Buckingham Palace throughout the festive season, to show the people of London, and the world, that there is nothing to fear.'

He'll *never* do it.

FROM: RUSSELL T DAVIES TO: BENJAMIN COOK, FRIDAY 18 MAY 2007 19:07:02 GMT

RE: CHARLIE HUNNAM'S ARSE

The meteorite has hit! Also, there are some changes to the scene order earlier on, and I've tweaked a few lines. I got that Tannoy speech in Scene 4 right:

```
                        TANNOY
     Starship Titanic is now in orbit above Sol 3, also known
     as Earth. Population: Human. Ladies and gentlemen,
     welcome to Christmas!
```

That's better, isn't it? And I've made Bannakaffalatta red, not blue, because he was too Moxx-like.

I've solved the coincidence of the Doctor knowing all the survivors, by making him to blame for all the survivors being together at the time of the accident. It's a lot of effort and page count to get them all together in that corridor, but it'll save

time later. On the whole, I think it works by being really obvious. Also, I spent a long time thinking that the meteorites wouldn't be burning. They'd be rocks. They'd only burn on entering the atmosphere. But they *need* to be burning, because it looks better, so I gave Frame and the Captain a bit of dialogue saying they were composed of 'flammable nitrofine rock'... and then cut it, because that's dull and I don't care. They're gonna burn!

FROM: RUSSELL T DAVIES TO: BENJAMIN COOK, SATURDAY 19 MAY 2007 00:48:06 GMT

RE: CHARLIE HUNNAM'S ARSE

I'm back in Manchester. I doubt I'll be able to work on the script this weekend, because I have to write up my notes on those seven bloody scripts – which are now nine – and watch an edit of 3.12, and... and... oh it's absurd! At least that'll leave next week free to write all the time.

A few notes about that latest draft: in the rush towards the meteorites, I completely forgot to write any more Mr Maxitane. I remembered him in the car on the way up. Whoops! But I love Midshipman Frame. I can't decide if he should live or die, though he'll certainly survive a lot longer. The Captain, too, is quite good and grave – well, again, he's far from subtle, but this isn't about character portraits; it's all about one

Big Bloody Smash. It's strong, bold and punchy on Christmas Day. Very blockbuster. Also, in the car, I wondered if the Host should start each speech with 'Information'…? 'Information: you are on board the *Titanic*.' 'Information: you are all going to die.' Nice verbal tic. It makes them 'imitatable'. Kids in the playground and all that. And it helps to keep explaining what they are – information points – because their function isn't really clear. I might try it.

FROM: RUSSELL T DAVIES TO: BENJAMIN COOK, MONDAY 21 MAY 2007 23:40:21 GMT

RE: CHARLIE HUNNAM'S ARSE

Some nights, I'm just wasting my time. I've spent hours sitting here (I'm back in Cardiff now), making poxy little changes to 4.X, but not getting anything more written. For instance, I took out the Doctor showing his psychic paper to the Host, because I'm not sure that psychic paper works on robots.[5] I didn't have a day to lose, but I've lost it. Bollocks. I don't have the energy to write the rest of the meteorites-hitting stuff. I'm scared by the gaping holes, the blank paper, to come.

FROM: RUSSELL T DAVIES TO: BENJAMIN COOK, TUESDAY 22 MAY 2007 19:16:24 GMT

RE: CHARLIE HUNNAM'S ARSE

Kylie Minogue just phoned me!!!

FROM: BENJAMIN COOK TO: RUSSELL T DAVIES, TUESDAY 22 MAY 2007 19:20:40 GMT

RE: CHARLIE HUNNAM'S ARSE

I hope you told her you were busy.

She should go through your agent like everyone else.

FROM: RUSSELL T DAVIES TO: BENJAMIN COOK, TUESDAY 22 MAY 2007 19:25:00 GMT

RE: CHARLIE HUNNAM'S ARSE

I told her we were going for Dannii.[6]

No, I didn't recognise the number, so I didn't answer. *D'oh!* But that means she's on my answerphone, which is better. And now I'm on hers. She wants to chat about Peth – actor-y stuff, I think. She's talking about getting a drama coach. My God, this is really, *really* real! (I still won't believe it until she's in Upper Boat.)[7]

FROM: RUSSELL T DAVIES TO: BENJAMIN COOK, WEDNESDAY 23 MAY 2007 23:47:18 GMT

RE: CHARLIE HUNNAM'S ARSE

Lordy God. No script, again. I spent all day sorting out other people's scripts. I woke

---

5 The Doctor's psychic paper, an apparently blank piece of card in a small leather wallet, débuted in 1.2. It allows whoever is holding it to show people whatever they want them to see on the card.
6 Dannii Minogue, Kylie's sister.
7 Upper Boat is the Cardiff-based studio complex where *Doctor Who*, *Torchwood*, and *The Sarah Jane Adventures* are filmed. Standing sets such as the TARDIS control room, the Torchwood Hub, and Sarah Jane's attic are stored here.

up, saw the sunshine, and refused to go into the BBC, so I set up shop outside the Starbucks in Cardiff Bay – and all the Series Four writers came to me, one by one. Me, Julie and Phil, sitting outside, like Starbucks shareholders. It was brilliant. But I spent a total of *nine hours* talking. Talking, talking, talking. Nine bloody hours. It's broken the back of a lot of stories, so it'll pay off. Now, finally, I can get back to work. I haven't written anything new since Friday. Julie said, 'You keep forgetting, it's like this every year.'

Yes, I forget.

FROM: RUSSELL T DAVIES TO: BENJAMIN COOK, FRIDAY 25 MAY 2007 02:22:21 GMT

RE: CHARLIE HUNNAM'S ARSE

More script. Nice stuff. I think. It's hard to negotiate eight people in one scene. I can't wait to start killing off the bastards. I wonder, who do you think is going to die?

FROM: BENJAMIN COOK TO: RUSSELL T DAVIES, FRIDAY 25 MAY 2007 15:26:57 GMT

RE: CHARLIE HUNNAM'S ARSE

You've said that Kylie should die, but I'm not convinced you'll go through with it. I reckon Rickston will die, because he's young and ruthless.[8] But then maybe that's what you want us to think. Mr Copper is too sweet to snuff it. But the same could be said of Bannakaffalatta, and I'm sure you'll relish giving the conker a *horrible* death. And Morvin and Foon are fat, so they've no chance. Midshipman Frame might die, too. Probably from hypothermia after he accidentally loses all his clothes.

My favourite stage direction so far is: 'STUNT as a HANDSOME MAN falls off the balcony, plunges down.' You introduce and kill off a man in the very same line, but make him handsome – what, to rub it in? Poor Handsome.

FROM: RUSSELL T DAVIES TO: BENJAMIN COOK, FRIDAY 25 MAY 2007 17:18:24 GMT

RE: CHARLIE HUNNAM'S ARSE

Yes, I'll try to take off the Midshipman's clothes. Well, maybe his jacket. Oh God, I think I fancy Midshipman Frame! That's weird, isn't it? It's like fancying a cartoon character – which is entirely possible. Oh, it's all sex. I can never say that enough. Do I only write in handsome men because I think, I honestly think, that we'll cast someone gorgeous, he'll fancy me like mad, and maybe even fall madly in love with me? This has never happened. I'm still thinking of Russell Tovey for Frame, because a) he's brilliant (one of the best young actors in the country), b) he's strangely sexy, and c) he's gay, and therefore d) the above plan will finally happen.

In other news, Dennis Hopper *still* wants to be in it. He's offered to clear three weeks for us. But the only character he could play is Mr Copper, which is hardly a big enough

---

8 Sharp young businessman Rickston Slade.

part for him. Oh! Unless he could do a cameo as the Captain? And Kylie is now leaving me texts: 'Sorry I haven't phoned back. I'm in Cannes and it's crazy.' This is surreal.

And I am thinking about your how-to-make-an-audience-care question…

FROM: RUSSELL T DAVIES TO: BENJAMIN COOK, SATURDAY 26 MAY 2007 03:12:39 GMT

RE: CHARLIE HUNNAM'S ARSE

Just under four pages today. That's poor. It really is a challenge to marshal this many characters in a group, within scenes…

I know in rough blocks what comes next: the Shattered Room, where people can pause and have a chat (and make this episode affordable); then the Canyon, where there are Terrible Deaths and a Host Attack; then up to the Bridge, while the Doctor goes to Host Containment; then the plummet down towards Earth, and the ending. Now, though, I start to worry that it's too long, that it'll end up at a hundred pages. It should be 80 pages for 60 minutes. And the expense is beginning to freak me out. Maybe I could make it cheaper by having Midshipman Frame tie a rope out of all his clothes and haul up the survivors. Yes, that'll do.

It *feels* all right, though. Worry, fear, deadline, late, budget, all of that, but I've felt much worse at this midway stage. I might keep moaning about the disaster movie format, but I can use it to pull myself along. I think, in the end, it helps. It's a funny old format. It doesn't exactly make room for subtext, which is fine, it's Christmas Day entertainment –

But then, the other night, I saw a repeat of *Longford*, that Channel 4 drama about the Moors Murders, and it did me no good at all. I sunk into a proper old gloom. I didn't even tell you about it, because it was foul. Peter Morgan is such a fine writer, damn him. All writers hate other writers. It *is* a competition. His *Longford* script was so fine and subtle, so deceptively simple, heartbreaking and true, and I was so powerfully jealous. I thought, I'm sitting here typing 'INT. SPACESHIP'! What am I doing with my career?! The answer is, having a wonderful time, with absolute freedom, I know, I know. All the same, looking at *Longford*, the real tick and beat and pulse that goes on between people, the sheer epic quality of ordinary life, even the lives of Lords and murderers, made me ache.

I'm not knocking *Doctor Who* here, or my love of it. This show *should* be different. But I do wonder – to be sort of snotty about it, I suppose – whether I'm coarsening myself; when I go back to regular drama, it'll be like starting again from scratch. That's why I turned down the opportunity to meet George Lucas the other day. The thought of more years typing 'INT. SPACESHIP' and playing with other people's toys… I mean, no matter how much I love *Doctor Who*, it's not *mine*. I didn't create this show.

Ah well. Lucas might not have liked me anyway. And I can always tell people that I turned him down.

FROM: BENJAMIN COOK TO: RUSSELL T DAVIES, SATURDAY 26 MAY 2007 21:11:52 GMT

RE: CHARLIE HUNNAM'S ARSE

So. You know in rough blocks what comes next. But do you often change your mind as you write? About big things? Literally, midway through a script? Like whether or not to kill off a character? Originally, in *New Earth*, the Face of Boe bit the dust, but got a reprieve in later drafts.[9] Even JK Rowling, who's had the final *Harry Potter* book (I can't wait!) planned for years now, has said that she's decided to save one key character from certain death, but kill off two others that she'd planned to keep alive...[10]

FROM: RUSSELL T DAVIES TO: BENJAMIN COOK, SATURDAY 26 MAY 2007 22:42:12 GMT

RE: CHARLIE HUNNAM'S ARSE

Old Boe's demise shifted from *New Earth* because that was in the draft in which *everyone* dies, even the patients, and it was miserable as hell for an Episode 1. At the same time, we'd just been commissioned for Series Three, and I realised how huge that 'You are not alone' could be if held back till *Gridlock*. But I don't often change really big things like that as I write. I'd say things *develop*, rather than change...

Holly in *Bob & Rose* was written, in her first scenes, as just The Gay Man's Best Friend. She was the comedy support, nothing more. During Episode 1, Holly went on that date with Bob and the schoolteacher, as best friend and fag hag, and all the way through, literally as I was typing, I was thinking, this character's dull – and how do I make this story last six episodes? And then... you know how annoyed I get when writers bang on about characters having lives of their own? Well, this is the closest I can ever remember to feeling like that, because Bob, Holly and the teacher were out on that date, and Holly found herself alone with the teacher, and then all of a sudden... she was lying. She was saying things that would split up Bob and the teacher. I can remember that like an explosion in my head – it was as though she started lying in front of me. (I love writing liars. Everyone lies.) Suddenly, on the spot, the show had three lead characters – and, more importantly, I'd enough story for six episodes.

I know exactly who lives and who dies in 4.X, except for Midshipman Frame, although I keep playing with it in my head – because that's the same game that the audience will be playing. (Your list of survivors was interesting, because I've fooled you a *little* bit, which is good for this format.) Actually, Frame is the most interesting one. I love him for not telling the Doctor that he's injured (see, lying again), because that's so selfless and professional – so I swing wildly between thinking, he's so good, he should survive, he's so good, he should die. Poor soul. In fact, I think the character that I've most enjoyed writing in 4.X is the Captain – again, because he's lying. That gives him

---

9 The Face of Boe, a gigantic face in a case, débuted in *Doctor Who* 1.2. Russell intended the Face to die in 2.1, in a hospital on New Earth, after revealing his greatest secret – 'You are not alone' – to the Doctor, but this was removed from later drafts. Instead, the Face died – and imparted his words of wisdom – in 3.3.
10 *Harry Potter and the Deathly Hallows*, released on 21 July 2007, is the final book in Rowling's heptalogy of *Harry Potter* novels.

weight. When he describes the *Titanic* as 'an old ship, full of aches and pains', he's talking about himself, really.

FROM: BENJAMIN COOK TO: RUSSELL T DAVIES, SUNDAY 27 MAY 2007 01:09:47 GMT

RE: CHARLIE HUNNAM'S ARSE

>>I swing wildly between thinking, he's so good, he should survive, he's so good, he should die.<<

And what decides? Well, you do. Obviously. But what's stopping you deciding right now? Or will it come down to how you're feeling on the day? The mood that you're in when you sit down to write his final scene? Or whether there's room in the story for another death? Or are you putting off making a decision because you've become attached? Do you – whisper the word – *care* about La Frame?

FROM: RUSSELL T DAVIES TO: BENJAMIN COOK, SUNDAY 27 MAY 2007 11:25:49 GMT

RE: CHARLIE HUNNAM'S ARSE

Oh, I'm loving La Frame, but the script will decide – the tone of it, the feel of it, the shape of it. Actually, to be blunt, I think Christmas Day will be the eventual decider. Frame's death would be towards the end of the Special, and that would be such a downer. Then again, I *love* writing a good death.

>>Do you – whisper the word – *care* about La Frame?<<

How do you make an audience care about your characters? I've been struggling with that question. 4.X is full of what Hollywood calls 'pat the dog scenes' (an old phrase meaning that if a character pats a dog, that character must be good), and that's because of the disaster movie set-up – or maybe the speed with which you have to introduce any supporting character in *Doctor Who*, given that they're components of a much bigger, much odder format. Frame is young and dutiful, so we like him; Morvin and Foon have won their tickets because they like TV, so we like them; Peth is shining with sheer 'I love the Doctor', so we like her. We like waitresses anyway, because we empathise towards the working classes. That's a whole discussion in itself. In the end, though, I think what you're talking about is *story*, not character. You care about a character *because they're in the story*. You've chosen this story, you've switched on this programme, you've picked up this book, you've paid to see this film, and that's where the caring comes from. Your choice. Your investment. From thereon in, it's up to the story. (That's where it can go wrong: if the story doesn't work, the characters aren't served.) It goes way beyond pat-the-dog moments; it's the space that characters occupy in the story, the role that they fulfil, the *reason* that they're on screen that attracts you…

How can I explain this better? It's pictorial. This is a visual medium, but visuals don't have to mean landscapes, long lenses, stunts, hundreds of extras; it's the ordinary pictures, the sheer existence of people on screen, the fact that I've chosen to put them there and that you've chosen to watch. I realised this on *The Second Coming*, when we spent a million drafts on Steve and Judith's backstory – the fact that they'd always known each other, always sort of fancied each other, she'd got married and divorced, and these two inarticulate idiots were still dancing around each other.[11] An awful lot of thought and script meetings went into that, all of it compressed into their conversation out on the pavement at the beginning, before their first kiss and Steve's awakening as the Son of God. All of that work was to establish, simply and fundamentally, an attraction between them. When I watched it back – well, after I'd watched it many times – I realised the most crucial thing: none of that was necessary. The fact that Lesley Sharp and Christopher Eccleston were on screen, at the same time, together – especially late at night, outside a city-centre club – did all the work. You could lose the sound and still realise what was happening between those two. Put a man and a woman of roughly the same age on screen and you're telling a story. That's a love story. (Storytelling is very heterosexual in that sense. But that's why gay storytelling is exciting, because the images are still new.) The *choice* to put those two characters together on screen, in a story, is the crucial thing. Everything else is just detail. And luck. That's what makes you care. The archetypes. They run deep.

Back to basics: the most important thing is honesty. That's where Tony from *Skins* – your favourite – is interesting, because he's undoubtedly meant to be a Stuart from *Queer as Folk*, but he doesn't connect with us so easily, because there's barely any recognition. Tony isn't believable. (Perhaps the kids *do* like Tony, but maybe that's wish-fulfilment; they want to be like him, therefore they admire him. But you have to be younger, I think, for that to work. Plus, he did look good in his pants – and there we're back to pictures again!) You can see what they were trying to do on *Skins*, because the plan for Series One, as we now know, was to bring down Tony, to make him suffer, make him realise that he's wrong, and therefore ascend to sympathy. They almost got there by the end, but only by having Tony pat a dog – more specifically, hit a bus! (They had to mow him down in the finale in order to make us care!) I love the fact that everyone expected Stuart to follow that path. So many people wanted him to be brought down. Or run over. Except I never did that. He survived anything thrown at him.

I've gone from dogs, to waitresses, to pavements, to Tony in his pants, all to answer your caring question, when, if I were giving advice to you about your very first script, I'd just say: don't think about it. Ever. Don't sit there thinking, will anyone care about my characters? Put your energy into making the characters real, and honest, and true, and interesting, and three-dimensional – and the caring should follow. Like a dog.

FROM: BENJAMIN COOK TO: RUSSELL T DAVIES, SUNDAY 27 MAY 2007 18:23:35 GMT

RE: CHARLIE HUNNAM'S ARSE

>>Put a man and a woman of roughly the same age on screen and you're telling a story.

---

11 Video-shop worker Steve Baxter (played by Christopher Eccleston) and schoolteacher Judith Roach (Lesley Sharp).

That's a love story.<<

This, I suppose, is why we warm to the idea of the Doctor and Rose in love. But that's pictorial, really. That's all about images. It's because they look right together. If we thought about it reasonably, we'd realise that he's 900-odd years old and she's barely out of her teens, and then it's just *wrong!*

FROM: RUSSELL T DAVIES TO: BENJAMIN COOK, SUNDAY 27 MAY 2007 19:01:58 GMT

RE: CHARLIE HUNNAM'S ARSE

That's so true. How many 'love' lines are there between the Doctor and Rose? About six! And yet it's talked about as the central spine of the series. Well, that's a bit disingenuous, because that's what I wanted, but we didn't really have to try. Man, woman, on screen = love story. Very little work necessary.

I hooked onto that visual thing with the transmission of *The Second Coming*, because ITV was braced for an absolute storm of protest… which never really came. Lots of mad phone calls, a couple of death threats, but all very normal. Quite apart from the theory that maybe it was crap and no one was bothered (that doesn't usually stop the religious hardcore), I think the key was that it didn't disrupt or criticise – or even *use* – the classic religious iconography. No classic pictures. No crucifixes. No angels. That's what people get upset about, when the pictures are played with, especially when the pictures have been there since childhood. If they're that deeply embedded, then they're sacrosanct.

That simple image thing is right at the root of homophobia, too. The fundamental image of life, of family, of childhood, of survival, is man and woman. Every story, every myth, every image reinforces that. Even the images of the real world reinforce that, because statistically heterosexuality is the norm. It's the default. It's the icon. Man/man or woman/woman disrupts a fundamental childhood image. Homophobia does seem to come from some gut instinct that's beyond the religious or the physical act or whatever. It's primal, and I think that's from the pictures. It's from what we see and what we're shown. That's why, in this gay lark, I stress visibility. Change the law, have education classes, do whatever you want, just be *seen*. I don't just mean on Pride Marches, because they're shoved away in an alcove, but I mean everywhere, all the time. I barely ever do an interview without mentioning being gay, and that's deliberate. We have to become visible, especially to the young, as part of the norm, then the picture starts to develop and widen.

FROM: RUSSELL T DAVIES TO: BENJAMIN COOK, SUNDAY 27 MAY 2007 23:37:06 GMT

RE: CHARLIE HUNNAM'S ARSE

I've done little work today. The only things I've changed are… I've renamed the Ballroom the 'Entertainment Lounge', which is more accurate; it's more of a hotel/bar. If I say Ballroom, the Locations Department will look for ballrooms to film in, no matter what the stage directions say. What's more, and rather annoyingly, I've looked it up and strictly those are *meteoroids*, not meteorites. Meteoroids only become meteors when they hit the atmosphere, and meteorites are the rocks left behind. Damn it, 'meteorites' sounds so much better! I wrestled with that for a while. I don't normally get so hung up on scientific detail – but I tend to think, if something is bugging my non-scientific mind, then it's indeed a buggable offence and should be corrected.

But I'm still ignoring the fact that the meteoroids wouldn't be burning since they're not in an atmosphere. Burning looks brilliant.

FROM: RUSSELL T DAVIES TO: BENJAMIN COOK, MONDAY 28 MAY 2007 23:49:21 GMT

RE: CHARLIE HUNNAM'S ARSE

I've written nothing today. I know exactly what the next scene is. I'm just feeling sour. Hey ho.

FROM: BENJAMIN COOK TO: RUSSELL T DAVIES, MONDAY 28 MAY 2007 23:52:27 GMT

RE: CHARLIE HUNNAM'S ARSE

But which came first: the feeling sour, or the not writing?

FROM: RUSSELL T DAVIES TO: BENJAMIN COOK, TUESDAY 29 MAY 2007 00:12:24 GMT

RE: CHARLIE HUNNAM'S ARSE

One feeds into the other. It drives me mental. I *think* the feeling sour comes first, though equally it comes from the script, all those voices at the back of my head saying, 'Is this a waste of BBC money?' And then an external trigger allows them dominance. That *Longford* last week really didn't help. Neither did the broadcast of *Human Nature* on Saturday, to be honest – in a really, really selfish way. I had a whole Sunday of people saying, 'That was brilliant,' and specifically, 'What a brilliant script. Paul Cornell is a genius.' Which he is. But I'm thinking, if only you knew how much of that I wrote! But I stifle myself, so it all goes inwards. It festers. People know that I polish stuff, but they think that polishing means adding a gag or an epigram, not writing half the script. I know it shouldn't, but it drives me mad. How selfish. But tiny things like that gang up on me.

FROM: RUSSELL T DAVIES TO: BENJAMIN COOK, WEDNESDAY 30 MAY 2007 03:45:29 GMT

RE: CHARLIE HUNNAM'S ARSE

Back in action! Well, eight pages. They're eminently cuttable – it's the backstory stuff – but that's the way to afford this, lots of chat. If the page count is too long, then these pages will be cut, but it's good to write *anything* to get me over that hump.

FROM: RUSSELL T DAVIES TO: BENJAMIN COOK, WEDNESDAY 30 MAY 2007 23:45:39 GMT

RE: CHARLIE HUNNAM'S ARSE

Bit more. Poxy, really. I thought the Stairwell was going to be a short sequence, but it turned out to be long and bothersome, so I'm up to Page 47 already.

I spent a lot of time going back through the rest of the script, tidying up nouns and things: sometimes it's called COMMS BOARD, sometimes COMMS PANEL, so I've standardised that. (You'd be amazed how many finished scripts come through – even shooting scripts – that say DINING ROOM, then LIVING ROOM, then LOUNGE, when in fact it's all the same room; the writer has just been careless and given it a different name each time. The Design Department will go out and look for three different rooms!) And I went back and put a forklift truck into the Host Containment Cells, because I might need it later. It's introduced in Scene 8:

```
An ENGINEER is driving up in a small FORKLIFT TRUCK, which has
three deactivated HOST stacked up on its scoop, horizontally, like
dummies. Engineer brakes, gets out:

                          ENGINEER
      That's four of them now, four of them on the blink.
```

The forklift's eventual fate is horribly expensive, so that's a worry. It might get cut.

Oh! Forgot to tell you – looking up the real *Titanic* online today, what did I find? A computer game, released in 1998, called – wait for it – *Starship Titanic*! By Douglas Adams! I got straight onto BBC Editorial Policy to see if we're all right copyright-wise. If we're not… oh, damn! I *must* have heard of it, and yet this feels brand new. I got the title *Starship Titanic* off of Peter McKinstry's design sketch for the 4.X vessel. I thought, ooh, nice title. The funny thing is, you can't copyright titles. I could call 4.X *Oklahoma!* if I wanted to, though that would be odd. I've suggested *Voyage of the Damned* instead. Strangely, this does have one benefit: we always end Episode 13 with the graphic 'DOCTOR WHO WILL RETURN AT CHRISTMAS IN…', plus the title, and the word 'Starship' would have given away that it's not the real *Titanic* crashing through the TARDIS at the end of 3.13. The new title might help… if the secret isn't blown by then anyway.

Talking of secrets blown, tomorrow's *Sun* is running our plan to take *Doctor Who* off air after 2008. Bollocks! God knows how they got hold of that. Their contacts are good. With any luck, no one will believe them – or we'll be facing a media storm. It's a nightmare. It's way too soon for this information to be released. Peter Fincham is now talking about overruling Jane Tranter, and doing only one Special for Christmas 2008, then getting a whole new team in place for a full series in 2009, or something. Good luck to 'em. I'll be gone.

All things considered, it's not been a great day.

FROM: BENJAMIN COOK TO: RUSSELL T DAVIES, THURSDAY 31 MAY 2007 12:31:56 GMT

RE: CHARLIE HUNNAM'S ARSE

It's a computer game! Did I know that? I must have heard about Douglas Adams'

Starship Titanic before now, so why didn't it ring any bells? Couldn't you say that it's a 'homage'? Maybe not. Or give it a subtitle? *Starship Titanic: At World's End...*? Definitely not.

You're right, *The Sun* is reporting that *Doctor Who* is ending after 2008. How that corresponds with the same paper's reports that David is leaving halfway through Series Four, I don't know. What does *The Sun* think will happen for the second half of Series Four? A different guest presenter will play the Doctor each week? (Hey, there's an idea! Copyright Benjamin Cook!) If you know in advance that a story like this is going to appear in the tabloids, isn't there any way that you can spike it? Isn't it in *The Sun*'s interest to keep you guys on side?

As things stand, what *is* the plan for 2009 and beyond? You talk of the BBC taking the show off air for a while, but how long is a while? How long will we be waiting for a Series Five? Couldn't a new production team prep their episodes while you are still in production? Why can't the show just keep going? Wouldn't that be safer for *Doctor Who*'s long-term future?

FROM: RUSSELL T DAVIES TO: BENJAMIN COOK, THURSDAY 31 MAY 2007 18:42:10 GMT

RE: CHARLIE HUNNAM'S ARSE

The BBC is powerless with the press. No one can control the papers, they'll print what they want, and we need them, so threatening to withhold or punish simply doesn't work. We'll just go crawling back, cap in hand. But the central problem is that the BBC is a public service broadcaster, funded by the public, so we are Not Allowed To Lie – and we end up craven and apologetic. That's why the leak about Christopher Eccleston leaving could not be plugged. Once asked by *The Mirror*, Jane Tranter could not deny it. Even though it ruined the surprise cliffhanger to Series One. How incredible would it have been to keep the Ninth Doctor's regeneration a surprise? But we had to be scrupulously honest. It's all still the consequences of the Hutton Inquiry.[12] But *Doctor Who* is hardly Hutton! This is fiction! I don't give a damn, I'll lie all I like if it safeguards the stories that we're telling. They can't stop me. But there's little point while Peter Fincham has to tell the truth. Madness.

The plan for 2009 and beyond? Well... we'll transmit Series Four next year, then a 2008 Christmas Special, and then two hour-long Specials in 2009, most likely Easter and Christmas Day. Then a third Special in 2010 should segue into a brand new Series Five, with a new production team. We've planned this for ages. I remember discussing it with Julie and David, in Woods Restaurant in Cardiff Bay, a few days before filming began on *The Runaway Bride*. The show, by 2009, will simply need a rest. We need to

---

12 The Hutton Inquiry was a 2003–2004 judicial inquiry, chaired by Lord Hutton, into the circumstances surrounding the death of Dr David Kelly, an employee of the Ministry of Defence, in July 2003. Kelly had been named as the source of quotes used by BBC journalist Andrew Gilligan, forming the basis of media reports that Tony Blair's Labour government had knowingly 'sexed up' a dossier on Iraq and weapons of mass destruction. The inquiry cleared the government of wrongdoing, but the BBC was strongly criticised, leading to the resignation of both the Chairman and the Director-General of the BBC.

starve people a bit. We're producing 14 movie-sized episodes a year, which are then repeated ad infinitum, and ratings are bound to decline, even just a little. *Doctor Who* is a phenomenon right now, but nothing stays a phenomenon. Not without careful management. People need to be begging for new *Doctor Who*, instead of just expecting it. That's fine for kids, too. They can wait a few years between *Harry Potter* books and *Star Wars* films. If anything, the wait *increases* the legend.

Meanwhile, a new production team can move in. Hopefully, they can start sniffing around even earlier than 2009, to see us at work on Series Four this year and next, but that's a lot less essential than you'd think. No matter how much we complain that this show is hard to make, it's still a UK drama, with scripts and crews and actors, like any show. The best thing that a new team can do is move in, trample over the way that we did things, and find new ways for themselves. While I'm sure that we'll all be around to help and support the newcomers, they'd be better off packing up our stuff and throwing our boxes into the street. New show! New team! New start! The most complicated advice that needs to be passed on is nothing to do with the drama; it's to do with negotiating the BBC. Publicity, funding, merchandising, BBC Wales overheads, all those complicated areas. (Julie's speciality!) You can't really see that in action, but it can be explained over 57 coffees.

But *Doctor Who* can run and run. Definitely. If it's managed this carefully. One day, of course, something will go wrong by accident, and people will look elsewhere, and some mean BBC Controller will take it off air... but only for it to come back blazing a few years later. That, now, is the definition of *Doctor Who*. It's the show that comes back. To the extent that we're building this Glorious Return into the 2010 schedules ourselves. It's not quite like any other show – which has always been *Doctor Who*'s outstanding feature, don't you think?

FROM: RUSSELL T DAVIES TO: BENJAMIN COOK, SATURDAY 2 JUNE 2007 02:35:42 GMT

RE: CHARLIE HUNNAM'S ARSE

Just rewrites today. A thousand fiddles on a thousand lines. Every day, when I reopen the file, I start right on Page 1 and go through it all again. I never go straight to where I left off last night. I went back to that scene on Earth, in the city street, and gave Mr Copper a credit card. It's handy to place props that you might use later, like the credit card, like the forklift; it's easy to cut them if I don't use them, but their existence sort of seeds them, and I start to play with their potential.

I set myself two new targets today: to get the meteoroids hitting by Page 23 – done! – and to reduce the whole script down from 50 pages. I got to 48. But preproduction starts on Monday. IN TWO DAYS' TIME! The director – it's James Strong – needs to start work. I have to work like hell this weekend.

FROM: RUSSELL T DAVIES TO: BENJAMIN COOK, SUNDAY 3 JUNE 2007 02:24:48 GMT

RE: CHARLIE HUNNAM'S ARSE

More! Lots! About 11 pages! I've been building up to this Canyon sequence for days. Christ, that's tiring. Writing action sequences is exhausting.

FROM: RUSSELL T DAVIES TO: BENJAMIN COOK, MONDAY 4 JUNE 2007 02:14:51 GMT

RE: CHARLIE HUNNAM'S ARSE

Here's more. Not as many pages as I'd hoped. But I went back and seeded in Mr Maxitane – now called Max Callisto – throughout. No longer sat in his posh roped-off area in the Entertainment Lounge at the beginning, I've put him instead onthe comms panels and wall-screens all over the ship, in a commercial for Max Callisto Cruiseliners, playing on permanent loop. And I changed Peth's name to Astrid. Peth is her surname now. I never liked the name Peth, I only came up with it quickly for that treatment, and it's bugged me every day since. 'Astrid' sounds more spacey, more like a futuristic Doctor's companion. Astra was too obvious, I thought.

FROM: RUSSELL T DAVIES TO: BENJAMIN COOK, TUESDAY 5 JUNE 2007 02:42:56 GMT

RE: CHARLIE HUNNAM'S ARSE

Almost finished. About 13 pages today. That's good. All those random props are paying off – the forklift truck, the teleport bracelets, the commercial. And Midshipman Frame's first name is Alonso, not Bosworth. But this is still so expensive, there might have to be major cuts. Anyway, you're not alone now, because I handed in these first 61 pages to the production team today, to start prep. Lordy God, it's real…

I was going to bring in the Judoon at the end, wasn't I? Not enough time. Also, it'd just feel odd now, like they've walked in from another adventure. Too big. Too comic. The allocated Judoon costumes refurbishment money can go into some prosthetics for Max. We've allowed for ten Host, too, but I don't think we need more than six. That's good.

In other news… Peter Fincham walked into a meeting with Catherine Tate today, with loads of executives from Tiger Aspect Productions (a huge London indie) and said, 'So you're going to be the new *Doctor Who* companion?' *Noooo!* Jaws dropped. Secret out, all round London. Christ!

The real reason this is bad is that the tabloid reports are going to be 'FREEMA SACKED!' with a vengeance, which isn't true; we've so many plans for her. I can't believe it. After all these months of secrecy. Catherine is gutted. She'd told *no one*. Damn.

FROM: BENJAMIN COOK TO: RUSSELL T DAVIES, TUESDAY 5 JUNE 2007 10:32:10 GMT

RE: CHARLIE HUNNAM'S ARSE

YOU *DO* KILL KYLIE!!! And oh – you saved the Queen.[13] Well, you couldn't kill her

---

13 In this draft, Buckingham Palace is destroyed when the plummeting *Titanic* crashes to Earth, but the Queen escapes in the nick of time.

on Christmas Day. I'm sure it says so somewhere in the BBC Charter.

Here's a curious thing: Astrid plummets to her death; two pages later, the Doctor is joshing about Midshipman Frame's first name; another two pages, and the Queen is in a nightie and curlers, running downstairs with two courtiers and a corgi! Back in March, you said with regards to E4's *Skins*: 'It's the oddest hybrid of a drama and broad sitcom. Mind you, people say that about my stuff.' Comedy and Drama (or Comedy and Tragedy – the more traditional division) are common bedfellows in a Russell T Davies script, but is it a mistake to think of them as diametric opposites? Does the genre 'comedy-drama' (or 'dramedy', I've heard it called) really exist outside of BBC press releases and whatnot? Are there occasions when you'd consider it unworkable to blur the line between Comedy and Drama in this way? I mean, if you can progress suddenly and speedily from heartbreak as Astrid is killed, to a deliberately daft, tangential cutaway gag… what *won't* you do, Russell?

FROM: RUSSELL T DAVIES TO: BENJAMIN COOK, TUESDAY 5 JUNE 2007 13:09:56 GMT

RE: CHARLIE HUNNAM'S ARSE

Yes, I hate saying Comedy and Drama, because it automatically assumes that Drama = Tragedy. Big, big mistake. Drama encompasses the whole range. But I believe passionately that Comedy and Tragedy exist alongside each other. No way are they diametric opposites; they're right next to each other, and they overlap in a thousand different ways. *Queer as Folk* Episode 3 is like a thesis on that. There's a huge comedy sex scene, which results in a slapstick fall off a window ledge, intercut with the horniest threesome in the world, intercut with a drugs overdose in which a man dies. I chose to intercut Tragedy with Comedy and Sex. The whole world is compressed into that; the coexistence of all those things.

Pause for a weird story. That overdose scene really happened to me, in my kitchen, with a man like that – and I wrote it into the script. The existence of that scene was one of the great engines of *Queer as Folk*. A week before filming, the location fell through, and the production team said, 'Can we use your house?' Honest to God. So there's a man, acting out what could have happened to me, but dying, in the place where it actually happened. I can't tell you how that makes my head explode. Funny thing is, I believed that coincidence until about a year ago, when I realised that the director, Charles McDougall, who was a truly mad genius, was so intent on accuracy that he must have changed locations on purpose. I bet there was no 'other location'. It took me eight years to realise that. (They painted my house and redecorated, by the way. It's not really that awful hippy colour.)

But I have to write like that. Funny, sad, all at once. That's how life is. You can have a pratfall at a funeral. You can laugh so much that you choke to death. The Master is dark and genuinely, drum-beatingly insane, and therefore can be funny as hell. Jackie Tyler makes us laugh, but I knew that I'd uncover something sad at the heart of her. Her sadness over her absent daughter is there as early as *Aliens of London*, but you don't really get to see it properly until *Love & Monsters*. Idiots will say, 'Ah, that character is developing now' – what, like you were going to play it all in the first 30 seconds?! – but that capacity was always there. It had to be. Even in *Rose*, when Jackie is ostensibly 'funny', telling her daughter to get a job in the butcher's, Jackie is one of the things that's holding Rose back – and that's quite dark, at its heart. 'Funny' is hiding a lot of other stuff.

Many people hate that in my writing. Not just the fans, but also commissioners. Tessa Ross at Channel 4, who axed the greenlit *The Second Coming* before it was picked up by ITV, did so because she thought that my writing is essentially lightweight. Nicola Shindler has warned me about that: she says there are a lot of people who don't take my scripts seriously, because of the level of comedy. But I don't worry about that. It's how I write, it's me, and I'm not changing it. I think having a sense of humour is a powerful and human thing, it's one of our survival mechanisms, and it's never destroyed. Equally, a sense of humour can be cold, almost ruthless, but I've never found a single situation – not my mother's death, not my overdose, not anything – in which something funny hasn't happened. That's why I think it's so, *so* wrong to write with a Comedy or Tragedy label in your head. Life isn't like that. Indeed, I think *Mine All Mine* went wrong because I actually thought, I'll make this funny. Conversely, I took *Bob & Rose* incredibly seriously, and won Comedy Writer of the Year for it!

Anyway, more script. I've finished. It feels okay.

I'm off to London now. It's the *Jekyll* launch. It's Steven Moffat's new drama for the BBC. I can't wait to see it. I had to get up early and work like hell to finish this script, all so I can have a night out. In London Town!

FROM: BENJAMIN COOK TO: RUSSELL T DAVIES, THURSDAY 7 JUNE 2007 22:30:36 GMT

RE: CHARLIE HUNNAM'S ARSE

You've finished! What's been the early feedback? Do you even get feedback? From Julie? From Phil? Do you take notice of it? Are you back in Cardiff now? How was London? How was *Jekyll*? Any good? All these questions!

FROM: RUSSELL T DAVIES TO: BENJAMIN COOK, FRIDAY 8 JUNE 2007 01:26:56 GMT

RE: CHARLIE HUNNAM'S ARSE

I'm back in Cardiff. In fact, I've just got in from the BBC Worldwide Licensees' Dinner, at the St David's Hotel. I can see them all from my window, still dancing. It's a jamboree junket for all the *Doctor Who*, *Torchwood* and *Sarah Jane* merchandise licensees – over 200 of them! I had to talk to the man who makes the Frubes. I wanted to say, 'My friend said his flatmate was eating Martha Jones!' But I didn't. Frubes Man said they're a resounding success. Flying off the shelves, he said. Imagine being Frubes Man! I'm knackered from smiling. Christ, it's exhausting.

Now, *Jekyll* was wonderful. I loved it. It's well worth watching. I fear that the BBC might neglect it a bit, because it's a tricky one to sell, but of course it's *so* clever. Steven is over at the St David's now, pissed. Paul Cornell is there, too, and said that he'd heard from Kate Bush, because she loved his two Series Three episodes so much! *Kate Bush!* How funny.

Anyway, I've no time off, because *Torchwood* is in crisis – one script down, blah, blah, blah. That poor show lives in a state of crisis. But *Voyage of the Damned* has been well received, thank God. Julie loves it. Phil loves it. I think. I'm never sure, because they're just glad to get a working script. Of course I get feedback, I'll have any note going, although there hasn't been time for a proper notes session yet. But *I'm* happy with it. It's a sort of 7/10 script at the moment. It's kind of lame having Max as the villain, I suppose, but it's the only possible solution. It's not credible that one of the survivors could go 'ha ha!' in a sudden reveal, and turn out to be part of the evil plot. That's why I had to turn Max into a cyborg box, because the dramatic reveal of... *a businessman!* was too rubbish for words. Also, I loved the forklift once I'd planted it on, ooh, whichever draft, but to have Astrid use that against a human Max would have been ridiculously violent.

The real editing will come with the expense. It's a nightmare. Ed Thomas has about, I don't know, £20,000 to £30,000 to spend on a Christmas Special. I saw him just now at the licensees' dinner. He said, 'I've costed up to Page 66, and it's already £87,000!' That's just what I didn't want to hear. Oh well, we'll think of something.

IL DOCTORE!

CHAPTER FIVE

THE REWRITER'S TALE

In which Buckingham Palace is saved,
Kylie plays gooseberry, and Kasabian
narrowly avoid sex in a tent

FROM: RUSSELL T DAVIES TO: BENJAMIN COOK, FRIDAY 15 JUNE 2007 17:19:55 GMT

FW: MEETING NOTES

We had a 4.X script meeting today. Here, for the record, are the notes from the script editor, Brian Minchin:

DOCTOR WHO 4.X DRAFT ONE: NOTES

Dear Russell,

Thank you again for such a lovely meeting. There are very few notes on such a wonderful script. I've summarised this morning's discussion below:

BUILDING UP THE ROLE OF ASTRID

Finding more time with Astrid and the Doctor. We should almost believe that she could be the next companion. If possible, more moments when we learn more about Astrid: her history, her family, her perception of the Doctor.

Astrid kissing the Doctor.

We talked about everyone being a bit in love with Astrid, and that it would be great to have a moment between her and Mr Copper.

Making more of the moment when Astrid decides to follow the Doctor to

Deck 31.[1]

Spelling out her sacrifice at the end: she's doing something that the Doctor wouldn't do in killing Max.[2] Pushing her heroism: Astrid doesn't want to go over the edge with Max, but she needs to keep her foot on the pedal/hold onto the gear stick. Making this sequence explicit so that we understand why she can't leap off the forklift before it propels her into space.

MAX CAPRICORN

Should the Doctor have a plan in mind when he's confronting Max?

Also, we discussed whether there is a way to build up Max before we see him, but didn't have any useful thoughts.

LOCATION CHANGES

The Titanic Reception is CUT. All action from these scenes will be relocated to the Entertainment Lounge, corridors, and Deck.

Please note that ALL corridors should be shot in ONE corridor location, but redressed/with different lighting.

COSTUME AND MAKE-UP

In order to signify that all the guests on board are 'alien', each character has a small bindi on their forehead.

The Stewards will be in naval costumes.

FROM: BENJAMIN COOK TO: RUSSELL T DAVIES, SATURDAY 16 JUNE 2007 12:50:34 GMT

RE: FW: MEETING NOTES

Are you nodding in agreement at the meeting notes, or shaking your head in disgust? Or did you kick out any note that you didn't agree with during the meeting? (And Brian's opening paragraph – is that how *all* notes from script editors begin? Are they told to do that? Or do some notes to writers start with: 'Thanks for nothing, you talentless bastard. Your script was a terrible piece of rubbish. Here is the first instalment of notes'...?) Also, Ed must have costed the whole script by now, so what's the damage?

FROM: RUSSELL T DAVIES TO: BENJAMIN COOK, MONDAY 18 JUNE 2007 14:21:53 GMT

RE: FW: MEETING NOTES

Script editors are *trained* to write an opening paragraph like that, with compliments, on any set of notes, on any show. It's polite and gets things off to an agreeable start. Of

---

1 The Host Containment Cells are on Deck 31. This is where the Doctor discovers an indestructible 'Omnistate Impact Chamber' hiding Max Capricorn, now a cyborg – a severed head sticking out of a metal box (five feet tall, three feet wide), laced with tubes and blinking with computer panels, but driven by big industrial wheels; it's a mobile life-support system.

2 Astrid kills the 'Max-Box' – and herself – by ramming it with the forklift truck, and pushing it down a shaft into the *Titanic*'s engines.

course, if you know that, the compliments are useless. But they're good notes. Though, as you say, I kicked out any that weren't good. I'm trying to think of an example… oh, I remember, a tiny thing: someone suggested that the Doctor and Astrid, in Scene 3, should look at each other as they pass for the first time. *Duh!* Stupid note. The whole joy of that passing is that they don't acknowledge each other; the audience knows more than the characters do.

In a way, with Kylie cast (provisionally), I relaxed slightly with Astrid and didn't work hard enough at her, because I thought that the sheer iconic imagery of her casting was enough. I'm a fool. I can see that now, and I'm happy to bump up her part. Also, if you know how a character is going to end, sometimes that can rob them of energy. I tell off other writers for this, then go and make the same mistake myself. Since I knew from the start that Astrid would die, there's an ever so slight indifference towards her. It feels as though any Astrid Could Be A Companion scene is *false*. I've got to fight that. Making Astrid more of a hero, though? Unfortunately, that's buggered – because now we *are* offering Mr Copper to Dennis Hopper. If Dennis Hopper should, in a mad world, accept the part, we'll have a similar set of notes – doubtless from his agent – asking for Mr Copper to be bumped up further in the heroic stakes. This is one of the problems of casting before writing: it starts to affect the production. In fact, when I explained this to Julie, she said, 'I wish you'd told me, because then we wouldn't have sent the bloody script to Dennis!' Julie wants Astrid absolutely central, quite rightly.

Should the Doctor have a plan in mind when confronting Max? That's a great idea, but I can't imagine what it is. The Doctor is weak in those scenes, I've compensated with verbiage, and I've no idea how to fix it. But I'm confident I'll think of something. And building up Max before we see him? That's tricky. It's a slight disappointment as Max unveils himself, I admitted as much in my e-mails to you, but the Big Reveal *can't* be anyone else in the cast. If that scene were the absolute climax, I'd have to rethink, but we still have the plunging *Titanic* – the proper, adrenalin-filled climax – to come. I think we have to live with it. But I'll keep thinking. Often, with things like that, you realise the solution… in 12 months' time!

Also, Phil tapped into something that I've worried about from the start: the passengers on the *Titanic* are going to look human, like the *Titanic* has time-travelled from 1912 or something, or like humans from the future have time-travelled back for a laugh. It doesn't matter how many times you say that they're from the planet Sto; it's the *pictures* that matter, and this looks like a bunch of humans partying. I suggested that everyone wears bindis. It's all that I could think of. We can't afford alien prosthetics on every single extra. I'll try to write it into the dialogue somehow. If we'd a huge budget, everyone would have gills.

The script has been costed – and Ed reckons that we're £45,000 over budget! This is terrifying. This is major. Cutting the Reception will only lose us about £10,000, so another £35,000 has to be found. We won't have all the answers for the next draft, so

I'll just rewrite as is and we'll come back to it. We've about three weeks to sort it all out, but we've never been faced with such an overspend from the Design Department. This is serious.

FROM: RUSSELL T DAVIES TO: BENJAMIN COOK, MONDAY 18 JUNE 2007 23:42:15 GMT

RE: FW: MEETING NOTES

Tonight, I got told that 4.X has 197 days of CGI FX too many![3] It's only supposed to have about 350 in total – and that's big – so I'm more than 50 per cent over. Problem is, The Mill is so busy, they've taken a *fortnight* to work this out. But I have to move on fast, not wait for number-crunching. I'm frozen with terror at the amount of time I have to write 4.1, and polish Gareth Roberts' Agatha Christie script, Keith Temple's Ood script and James Moran's Pompeii script. It looks like I have about four weeks to do all that!

So. Big cuts to 4.X. Poor old Buckingham Palace has to go. We need to convert the cost of building – and destroying – a scale model into money for The Mill. I might keep the flagpole smashing through the window of the *Titanic*, because that makes me laugh, though Ed's department is £45,000 over, so, um, I might not. Plus, I've just worked out a new end sequence for Astrid – her death isn't very sad at the moment, is it? – which requires even more FX, at least another eight shots or so. When I described the new ending to Julie – it's lovely, sentimental, Christmassy – she said, 'Well, we've got to keep that!' But how are we going to find the money?

FROM: BENJAMIN COOK TO: RUSSELL T DAVIES, WEDNESDAY 20 JUNE 2007 06:38:12 GMT

RE: FW: MEETING NOTES

I'm off to the Glastonbury Festival this afternoon, so I'll be without e-mail access for a few days. (Five nights in a tent – bliss!) Best of luck with the FX cuts and Astrid's new death. Can I ask, before I go, is it preferable for a writer to edit his or her own work, do you think, or for a script editor to do it? A writer knows their script better than anyone, but a script editor provides an alternative eye and a fresh perspective.

FROM: RUSSELL T DAVIES TO: BENJAMIN COOK, WEDNESDAY 20 JUNE 2007 08:45:14 GMT

RE: FW: MEETING NOTES

Script editing. An editor is *vital*. Everyone should have one. You can't always edit something yourself; you need that fresh pair of eyes. (Not a friend. Or your mum. That's no good.) The 'second death' that I'm about to write for Astrid seems absolutely intrinsic, and it's weird to think that I didn't put it there in the first place. I felt dissatisfied with the original, but only in a vague, shoulder-shrugging way. I could ignore that nagging

---

3 Post-production company The Mill is responsible for the (computer-generated) visual effects on *Doctor Who*, *Torchwood* and *The Sarah Jane Adventures*. An FX day equals a day's work for one person at The Mill. 'Theoretically, if The Mill had 350 FX days allocated and 350 people working on *Doctor Who*, they could finish an episode in a day,' explains Russell. 'Except it's not quite literal. The Mill's definition of a day must include... well, payment for talent, genius, planning and all that.'

DESIGN CUTBACKS

This is Russell's reply to Phil Collinson's e-mail about the Design Department's cutbacks. 'I was officially sulking,' recalls Russell, 'because I had to make so many cuts. Every time Julie or Phil phoned me up, I was all monosyllabic and clipped. "Yeah. Fine. Okay. Bye." What a child! But I couldn't help it. And then I e-mailed them, and was all agreeable and full of exclamations! Like! This! That reinforces the sulking, because they know those exclamations ring false. How ridiculous – especially since I know full well that they're out there, banging the phones, scrimping and saving every last penny for me...'

FROM: RUSSELL T DAVIES TO: PHIL COLLINSON, DATE: TUESDAY 19 JUNE 2007 18:08:44 GMT

RE: EP. X

>> Hi Russell,

Sorry to bombard you, but I've just had a budget meeting with Ed. We have our work cut out, and all of these are just suggestions, but I wonder if we could make some cuts and trims, and we discussed the following possibilities: <<

Don't worry, Phil, it must be done.

>> Deck 22 has gone altogether, which is a good saving.[1] We left some money to build windows into the Entertainment Lounge, but how many do you think we need? <<

I could make do with a single porthole.

>> The Bridge. At the moment, this set is budgeted to be built on a rostrum. A good saving could be had if we build the main set on the ground instead, but then build a small section – say, a six-foot-square corner – on a rostrum, and shoot the Host/Doctor breakthrough, in medium close-up, on that.[2] We could cheat a way of getting a shot with Frame and the ship's wheel in the foreground, so that it feels like the same set, and then close-up shots of the Doctor climbing out. We'd build both sets side by side, and match the main set to the breakaway one for all action after the breakthrough. It'll save us a good few grand. <<

Of course that'll work. Simple!

>> Host Containment Cells. That's a big build, to construct individual cells as scripted. Could we rethink this and have a kind of robot deactivation area – an industrial space, a big console, some kind of operating table in the centre, with a robot on, and other

1 The setting for Scene 4, Deck 22 was 'Deck 15' in the original draft.
2 Midshipman Frame is trapped on the Bridge. From Deck 31, the Doctor flies up through the gutted *Titanic*, carried by two Host, soaring higher and higher... as both Host raise their arms, fists clenched, and punch through the floor of the Bridge.

robots standing against the wall but 'plumbed in'? This would mean we could find an industrial-type location, and avoid big construction costs. The console – or one of the walls – could part to reveal Max. <<

Lovely!

>> Do we ever go back to the Entertainment Lounge after the meteoroid crash? It'll save us money if we don't have to redress this room. If you cut the big shot as the meteoroid rips through, will you still keep Sc.44/2 (people consumed by flame), Sc.46/1 (stuntman falling over balcony), Sc.46/2 and Sc.46/3 (handsome man and woman's death), and Sc.51/1 (man tumbles through space)?[3]<<

44/2 is gone. 46/1 is gone. 46/2 and 46/3 are gone. In fact, I'd better cut 51/1, too. This does mean I have to keep the Chief Steward's death in full, or the meteoroids hit the *Titanic* and we see no one die. *No one!*

---

3 Scene designations are from The Mill's FX list, so 44/2 means Scene 44, FX Shot 2, and so forth.

voice. All writers do. It took a proper meeting with others to express that dissatisfaction. Even a stray remark can make all the difference: just chatting before the meeting, Brian Minchin said, 'I didn't expect Astrid to die. I thought the teleport bracelet would save her.'[4] I thought, ah ha! I'd forgotten that she was even wearing it. Instantly, I knew what to do. I didn't say anything during the meeting, I just agreed with the general dissatisfaction and promised to fix it, knowing full well what I was going to do...

You're dealing here with a script that works, essentially, but the process of writing isn't an exact science. It's imprecise, moody and instinctive, so you need people to keep you on track and remind you why you're writing in the first place. Of course, finding the right people is key. The industry is full of rubbish script editors. The bad ones are vandals. They don't just destroy scripts; they destroy writers. It takes a lot of work when you're young, or starting out, to survive those people. Well, to even recognise them in the first place. That's hard work.

FROM: RUSSELL T DAVIES TO: BENJAMIN COOK, FRIDAY 22 JUNE 2007 23:48:54 GMT

4.X DRAFT TWO

I've been watching the Glastonbury coverage on BBC Three. Isn't Amy Winehouse stunning? I hope you're having a good time. I eagerly await tales of drugs and sex. In a tent. With Kasabian. I just got a text off John Simm – he's there, too. And so is Freema. Have you met up? The Master could have hunted down Martha Jones at Glastonbury! With you watching!

---

4 Astrid uses one of the ship's teleport bracelets to follow the Doctor down to Deck 31. She's still wearing it when she plummets to her death.

Here's the revised 4.X for you to read on your return. It's still over-budget. I haven't cut enough FX shots. More changes to come, I suspect. Maybe we'll have to reconsider that whole forklift death, because that's eating into our budget hugely. Still, I'm pleased with the new Buckingham Palace sequence and Astrid's second farewell…[5]

FROM: BENJAMIN COOK TO: RUSSELL T DAVIES, TUESDAY 26 JUNE 2007 18:20:55 GMT

RE: 4.X DRAFT TWO

I'm back from Glastonbury. I spent most of it stuck in the mud (I think some folk are still there, stuck fast), but I had the most awesome time. You'll be saddened to hear that I didn't have sex with Kasabian. (Would you, though? *Really?!* It'd be like making out with Topman's entire autumn range. Plus, you'd get stubble rash.)

I returned from The Mudbath to find an invite to the 4.X read-through next Monday, in London. Cheers for that, Russell, since I'm sure you had something to do with it. I've just read the revised 4.X, and I almost prefer the new version of the Buckingham Palace gag, though not quite. But Astrid's second death is stunning. (Invisible Ben isn't supposed to tell you things like that, is he? Oh well!)

Once you'd started, you wrote 4.X at a fair lick. Barring the occasional day or so when not much happened, you rattled off the thing pretty damn fast. You started at midnight on 15 May and finished Draft One on 5 June, just three weeks later. That's speedy. Is that a necessity of your workload? Would you have liked longer? If you'd had an extra week, or a month, would you have filled it constructively, do you think? And have you always written that quickly?

FROM: RUSSELL T DAVIES TO: BENJAMIN COOK, TUESDAY 26 JUNE 2007 23:13:50 GMT

RE: 4.X DRAFT TWO

A read-through with Kylie Minogue! Marvellous, isn't it? She's going to watch *Last of the Time Lords* on Saturday with David. Madder and madder! And we've cast Clive Swift as Mr Copper. That's brilliant! (Dennis Hopper, it turned out, isn't available for *that* many days.) And Geoffrey Palmer is Captain Hardaker, which is glorious. Also, Russell Tovey as Midshipman Frame, which is my favourite casting of the lot, because he's going to be huge, that man. He's amazing. I think I'd make him the Eleventh Doctor.

I love that new Astrid ending. Pure sentiment. Pure Disney. It would be way too sentimental if she weren't dead, but since she still cops it, well, I reckon it's grand. I'm gutted about Buckingham Palace, though. Always will be. It's a big set-up for a gag that never happens. We've almost reached an FX compromise: lost a few more shots, but kept Astrid's death and all the major stuff. I think we've about 40 more FX days to

---

5 In this new version, the *Titanic* misses Buckingham Palace by an inch, sailing overhead and back into space. The Doctor uses the emergency settings on the ship's teleport to bring back Astrid – for her 'second farewell – but the system is too damaged, and she returns as just 'an echo, with the ghost of consciousness'. They kiss, then the Doctor lets Astrid go; she turns to stardust and spirals away into space.

lose, but that's doable. Phil came over tonight, and we found a possible 40 days or so. He'll take that back to The Mill tomorrow and I'll get sent a report tomorrow evening so that I can do the final rewrites overnight.

Would I have liked longer to write 4.X? Well, I've always written fast. The second drama script I ever wrote, *Dark Season* Episode 2, I completed in two days flat – which makes it sound like a piece of piss, but I hope this correspondence is making it clear that it's the thinking beforehand, not the typing, that takes up my time. You're right, though, give me more time and I'd waste it – not consciously, but just because the adrenalin isn't there. In the old days, I had so little faith and so much fear, I used to write out the entire episode in longhand first, on one sheet of A4. Well, it was 'tiny hand', not longhand. I can write very small. Microscopic writing. It's a handy skill. (In wartime.) I loved those pages, but they were a crutch. As the years went by, they became just scribbled headlines, then a few words and maybe a drawing, until slowly, over about ten years, I abandoned the paper and wrote straight onto the screen. I can't remember that transition actually happening – there was no great Paper-Less Ceremony – because it just evolved. But today the notion of writing a line, pausing, taking a walk, in mystic contemplation, feels alien to me. Once I'm into a script, I hurl myself into it and stay there. The quiet days in the middle are more tiredness than anything.

The fear of screwing it up wastes time, too.

FROM: RUSSELL T DAVIES TO: BENJAMIN COOK, WEDNESDAY 27 JUNE 2007 22:39:01 GMT

RE: 4.X DRAFT TWO

It's been another bastard of a day. We realised… well, to fill you in, when David finishes Series Four, he's off to the Royal Shakespeare Company to play Hamlet. *Wow!* (Equally, *bah!* I've never been able to sit through *Hamlet*. Have you?) Oh, and that's very, *very* top secret. Don't even let David know that you know. Anyway, we realised today that the RSC needs to announce David's casting in September, which, because of the dates, will immediately make it obvious that there won't be a Series Five with him in 2009. The secret will be out. Heaven knows what we're going to do.

FROM: BENJAMIN COOK TO: RUSSELL T DAVIES, FRIDAY 29 JUNE 2007 22:55:31 GMT

RE: 4.X DRAFT TWO

David's doing *Hamlet*? Wow indeed. No *bah!* from me. He'll be magnificent.

FROM: BENJAMIN COOK TO: RUSSELL T DAVIES, MONDAY 2 JULY 2007 21:33:01 GMT

THE READ-THROUGH

Wasn't today's read-through AMAZING? Can you believe Kylie, walking around, introducing herself to everyone?

I always thought, in my naivety, that read-throughs were for the actors' and director's benefit, primarily, so that they can get a feel for the script as a whole before shooting it all out of order? But afterwards, once the cast had left, you, Julie, Phil and James got together for script notes. Do you often rewrite the script as a result of the read-through? Heavily, ever? Do you amend scripts based on each actor's performance? Their portrayal? Their delivery? Or is it just for technical stuff, like the timing of an episode? This is a question of the actor's relationship with the script: should the script shift to fit the actor, or is it the actor's job to fit the script?

FROM: RUSSELL T DAVIES TO: BENJAMIN COOK, MONDAY 2 JULY 2007 22:04:28 GMT

RE: THE READ-THROUGH

It was an INCREDIBLE read-through. Best of all, *Kylie can act!* I always knew she could – I was a faithful viewer for all those years of *Neighbours*, and she never delivered a duff performance – but she really nailed Astrid, didn't she?

Tell you what, though, there was an even greater revelation for me: I love that 4.X script. Really, properly love it. I'd been a bit unsure about it till now – I always am, I suppose – but I felt the format clicking into place. That was magical. It's so obviously a disaster movie that I'd got used to the idea, way back, and even got over it. I'd forgotten its impact. The thrill of it was overwhelmed and absorbed into all the problems of writing it. Yesterday, it was like seeing it as new. All that moaning to you about the disaster movie format... and I was forgetting that I love them.

>>Do you often rewrite the script as a result of the read-through?<<

That's what they're for – for performance and timing, but also to make the script better. That's why a Pink Draft is issued after a read-through. The pink pages are any pages that have been revised at all. At a *Doctor Who* read-through, we all scribble down notes. Small performance things – tone and pitch, don't shout this, be quiet with that, emphasise that gag – but also proper drama notes. Why is she so cross? Can we explain why he runs? Do we even need that scene? Etc.

>>Heavily, ever?<<

If need be. I sat in the read-through of *The Grand* Series Two, Episode 1, and realised I'd got a major plot wrong. We were axing two main characters, so I wrote them having an affair that would lead to their exit in Episode 4. But I realised, sitting in the read-through, that it was just crap. Wrong actors, wrong characters, wrong story. In the meeting afterwards, I chucked it out – and it was about 50 per cent of the script. Not only that, but the next three scripts, with the characters in mid-affair, were lined up to be shot. They all had to be rewritten. It had to be done, overnight! It doesn't matter how much work it is; there's no point in filming a mistake.

>>should the script shift to fit the actor, or is it the actor's job to fit the script?<<

You cast someone to fit the script; lines and emphasis can change. Unfortunately, a lot of scripts are loose and vague, therefore the actor has too many options, or no options, so the performance swings away from the script, the director swings away from the actors, and… oh, a mess. That's bad TV drama. Actually, that's just ordinary TV drama. The sheer not-quite-ness of it all.

FROM: BENJAMIN COOK TO: RUSSELL T DAVIES, WEDNESDAY 4 JULY 2007 00:21:34 GMT

RE: THE READ-THROUGH

The BBC has just announced Catherine Tate's casting in Series Four, in a press release issued at midnight. Eh?! Why announce it this soon? Mind you, the internet is going into meltdown.

```
PRAC FX: SPARKS & SMOKE from BEN's computer.
```

FROM: RUSSELL T DAVIES TO: BENJAMIN COOK, WEDNESDAY 4 JULY 2007 01:52:45 GMT

RE: THE READ-THROUGH

The Sun got wind of Catherine Tate, so we've fought back, for once, and spiked their exclusive by releasing Catherine's name to everyone. Ha! But there's worse to come. The *Daily Mail* has got wind of David's booking as Hamlet. We're battening down the hatches. None of us is quite sure what to say. In amongst all this, Julie and I reflected with horror today that we haven't been able to tell the staff what's going to happen after Series Four. People who have moved to Cardiff, with mortgages and everything. It's a bloody hurricane. Of our own making. I can't imagine another show with this trajectory or adrenalin.

Here's a quick update on everything else: in the next 17 days, I have to rewrite Keith's script, plus Gareth's, plus James's, which then gives me eight days to write 4.1. This is impossible. It's a bloody mess this year; we are *so* behind. I don't know why that is. Maybe I'm slowing down. Being ground down? I feel sick with worry. When I slow down, the whole engine slows down, the whole *Doctor Who* factory. I know, for example, that I'm not bullying anyone about the other writers' deadlines, when I should be. It's all my fault. Realising that makes me feel *more* sick, which then, I suspect, slows me down further. Vicious circle.

On a more positive note, I had a script meeting with Gareth after the read-through, so he can rewrite as much of his episode as possible while I'm rewriting Keith's – and Gareth was *brilliant*. He learns, and learns, and learns. We went in with the biggest problem: why is Agatha Christie caught up in a murder mystery? Isn't that a bit of a coincidence? Agatha's sheer presence had to become part of the plot. I said, 'We're not leaving this room until we solve this, even if we're here for ever.' We'd cracked it within ten minutes. 'Hang on,' we said, 'if we make one of the characters a Christie fan and they're reading a Christie novel as the alien activates… then the alien mentally inherits the murder mystery as a template and bases its actions on that!' Problem solved.

And then Helen Raynor came in to discuss her two-part Sontaran adventure. I had to give away one of my favourite ideas ever: Evil Cars! With Evil Sat Nav! I've been dying to write that for years. In fact, Evil Sat Nav was in the first draft of *The Runaway Bride*, on board the speeding taxi, with the Empress of Racnoss using it as her eyes and ears on Earth – though I junked that idea before I even delivered the script. Now someone else gets it. Damn.

Also, we cast Max today: George Costigan. It was almost on the cards for Dennis Hopper to be Max, because it's fewer days on set than Mr Copper, but we just ran out of time. He had the script and apparently was willing, he's even in the country now, but we didn't hear back (it's hard to nag American agents), and we needed Max for a prosthetic fitting on Wednesday, so it all fell through. But George Costigan is perfect.

That's about it, update-wise. Oh, except I e-mailed Julie today saying:

> It almost goes without saying, but… in the climax to Series Four, with Donna, and Martha, and Rose, and Sarah Jane, and Captain Jack, all battling away to save the Doctor… I suppose you'd want a mysterious shimmer of blue stardust to make an appearance at some point, wouldn't you?

She e-mailed back with an 'OH YES!' So that's a laugh.

FROM: RUSSELL T DAVIES TO: BENJAMIN COOK, SUNDAY 8 JULY 2007 21:30:00 GMT

JAMES MARSTERS' ARSE

It's not often that I'm sat in a Cardiff bar with Spike from *Buffy*, and Kylie Minogue walks in![6] This city is now, officially, insane. And James Marsters is the sexiest bastard alive, much more so than he is on screen. As straight as the day is long, and yet every single conversation came back to sex with him. I wasn't complaining.

For all that, I'm back in the flat now, rewriting *Planet of the Ood*…

FROM: BENJAMIN COOK TO: RUSSELL T DAVIES, SUNDAY 8 JULY 2007 21:59:33 GMT

RE: JAMES MARSTERS' ARSE

Kylie Minogue playing gooseberry. Who'd have thought it?

How are the Ood coming along?

FROM: RUSSELL T DAVIES TO: BENJAMIN COOK, SUNDAY 8 JULY 2007 22:34:07 GMT

RE: JAMES MARSTERS' ARSE

The Ood are… late. Bloody Ood. Must keep going, though, because I'm rewriting Agatha next week. She's fighting a giant wasp. We really couldn't think what sort of enemy she should fight. Dickens? Ghosts. Shakespeare? Witches. But Agatha…? Then Gareth came up with a wasp – and I remembered the old paperback cover of *Death in the Clouds*, which has a plane being attacked by a symbolically giant wasp. 'That'll do,' we said. Our most tenuous link yet.

---

6 American actor James Marsters, best known as Spike in *Buffy the Vampire Slayer* and its spin-off series *Angel*, was in Cardiff to film three episodes of *Torchwood* Series Two, in which he plays Captain John Hart, a rogue Time Agent.

FROM: BENJAMIN COOK TO: RUSSELL T DAVIES, SUNDAY 8 JULY 2007 22:49:04 GMT

RE: JAMES MARSTERS' ARSE

A Giant Wasp? I'll be happy so long as you've a posh butler, a country house, and someone murdered by a poisoned dart. Oh, and Agatha should be played by Madonna.

When you get a moment, can you explain the 'rewriting' process on *Doctor Who*? Do you ever worry about treading on other writers' toes?

FROM: RUSSELL T DAVIES TO: BENJAMIN COOK, SUNDAY 8 JULY 2007 23:05:56 GMT

RE: JAMES MARSTERS' ARSE

No dart, damn it. But a poisoned sting – that's close! And death by lead piping, just because that's so irresistible. (Donna: 'Who uses lead piping?!') How we're going to get a Giant Wasp – a Vespiform, to be precise – to wield a piece of lead piping is going to make for a fun Tone Meeting.[7]

Rewriting? I write the final draft of almost all scripts – except Steven Moffat's, Matthew Graham's, Chris Chibnall's and Stephen Greenhorn's – and that draft becomes the Shooting Script. I might change at least 30 per cent of the material, often 60 per cent, sometimes almost 100 per cent. I go over every line of dialogue, either adding new stuff or refining what's there; sometimes that means enhancing a line that the original writer hasn't realised is good. I'll bring out themes, punch up moments, add signature dialogue, clarify stage directions and make cuts. To every single scene, if need be. Usually, the basic shape remains intact, but sometimes I'll invent brand new characters and subplots… while at the same time remaining faithful to the original writer. I'll even impersonate them.

Sometimes, yes, this does mean treading on other writers' toes. I'm sure some of them think of it as vandalism. Equally, to be fair, others are very grateful. But my job is to get the Best Possible Script on screen, even if that means stampeding over someone. The viewer at home doesn't care who wrote it; they just want it to be good. My job is to make it as good as it can be. Take no prisoners! And it's got to be done fast, so I haven't time to pussyfoot around, transplanting lines of dialogue, delicately. Even interesting stuff has to go sometimes, because I can only find room for myself by shifting back all the furniture, making it my own. This is a multi-million quid show that has to be the absolute best it can be.

Hey, filming on 4.X starts tomorrow. The first of three days on the Strut.[8] That's in at the deep end.

---

7 Tone Meetings are where the heads of departments, the producers and the director, gather to work out, scene by scene, how the episode can be made.

8 The Strut is a jagged and broken bridge across a huge canyon, where many of the *Titanic*'s floors have fallen through as a result of the meteoroid collision. The Doctor, Astrid, Rickston, Bannakaffalatta, Morvin and Foon must make their way across; the last three don't make it.

FROM: BENJAMIN COOK TO: RUSSELL T DAVIES, MONDAY 9 JULY 2007 07:49:44 GMT

RE: JAMES MARSTERS' ARSE

Today's *Guardian* says you're the fifteenth most powerful player in the media industry. (You have to question the choice of the word 'player', don't you?) You're up from Number 28 last year. You're the highest-ranking TV producer on the list. Well done! Again! You're making a habit of these polls, aren't you?

FROM: RUSSELL T DAVIES TO: BENJAMIN COOK, MONDAY 9 JULY 2007 08:30:09 GMT

RE: JAMES MARSTERS' ARSE

That gives me a year to murder 14 people. It can be done.

FROM: BENJAMIN COOK TO: RUSSELL T DAVIES, MONDAY 9 JULY 2007 08:45:55 GMT

RE: JAMES MARSTERS' ARSE

I wondered why you were so hung up on lead piping the other night.

FROM: BENJAMIN COOK TO: RUSSELL T DAVIES, TUESDAY 10 JULY 2007 10:20:48 GMT

RE: JAMES MARSTERS' ARSE

Have you seen yesterday's rushes yet? How's the Strut looking? Can you explain why it's important, as showrunner, that you view each day's rushes?

FROM: RUSSELL T DAVIES TO: BENJAMIN COOK, TUESDAY 10 JULY 2007 11:30:24 GMT

RE: JAMES MARSTERS' ARSE

The rushes are wonderful. The Strut is an amazing set. I watch the rushes to correct things, if they can be corrected in time; sometimes it's too late. For example, Foon has a daft hairstyle – but it's too late to change, because of continuity, so there it is. In extreme circumstances (if she were the lead), I could demand for it to be re-shot, but not in this instance. It can be toned down, though. Babs Southcott can do anything! We can get away with it, because Foon is a big, funny character. She can support big hair. You can even argue, when Morvin dies, the funny hair is marvellously contradictory; she's a tragedy in clown's clothes, which has a nice sort of resonance.

Mainly, I'm looking at the rushes for tone. The pitch of it. The height. The broadness. The speed. The precision. For example, the moment they arrive on the Strut is too hysterical. 'Look! Big drop! Eek! Oh no!' It's all full-pitch. When Morvin falls to his death, the pitch has nowhere to go. They're already squealing, so there's no contrast. That led me to a note that I'd never given James until now, because it hadn't occurred to me: don't make it too hysterical. Disaster movies thrive on that grim tone, that quiet fear, that bravery in the face of death, small people in big events, not screaming and shouting. There are blunter notes, too. Debbie Chazen is wonderful. More of her, please. Favour her. Gray O'Brien (Rickston)'s accent is brilliant. He's Scottish playing posh. Design, Wardrobe and Make-Up have done a brilliant job… so I pass on the praise. Those teams work so hard and they love to hear that we're happy. Everyone is overworked – and people like Louise Page worry so much, she *needs* that text to say thank you. And me and Julie text all the lead actors – they need it and deserve it. It's a blizzard of texts from midday onwards.

Best of all, watching rushes does *me* good, because when I see them standing there, dirty, grimy, scared, the Time Lord, the pop star, the fat couple, the old man, the businessman, the red conker, all looking down at the terrible drop, with the viewer knowing – oh, just knowing – that some of them will die, it makes me think, really, powerfully: I love this episode. My confidence in this script is growing.

FROM: BENJAMIN COOK TO: RUSSELL T DAVIES, TUESDAY 10 JULY 2007 12:01:07 GMT

RE: JAMES MARSTERS' ARSE
So is it only during filming – and afterwards – that tone can be assessed properly? How far, really, can tone be established at the scripting stage? Or at the Tone Meeting? And how does a TV show, as opposed to any individual episode, find its overarching tone? Its voice? New *Doctor Who* found it within five minutes, whereas *Torchwood*… well, that show may have found its voice, but it's hard to tell, because it keeps losing it. In the opening five minutes of your *Torchwood* episode, the Series One opener, a character uses the f-word – and it really jarred, I thought. It stuck out, sorely. It felt wrong. Like watching K-9 hump a lamppost.[9]

FROM: RUSSELL T DAVIES TO: BENJAMIN COOK, TUESDAY 10 JULY 2007 13:11:24 GMT

RE: JAMES MARSTERS' ARSE
Above all, tone comes from the script. (I would say that!) You get 57 dozen people working on a drama, at key stages, and they all wander off. No, it's not fair to call it wandering, because they're creative people, they're employed to use their imaginations, but everyone creates in a slightly different way, sometimes in a radically different way. The director, the producer, the design teams, etc, should be interpreting the show in the *same* way, so the script should convey the tone in every adjective, in the layout of its pages, in the names of its characters; everything should transmit the tone. I mean, if Rose Tyler had been called 'Ace', what would the design teams have thought? Street-smart, tough, DMs, rough mother, nasty flat, etc. From one word, the tone starts to go wrong. All the smaller stuff – the words, the names, the style – conspire together to make a show that works, or a show that doesn't.

Even then, it's amazing how often the script is forgotten. *The Second Coming* had devil-possessed people and the script said, specifically, that they have 'tiny white glints of light in their eyes'. Then you bring 57 dozen more imaginations on board, and everyone but everyone who read that script – the producer, the exec, the channel, everyone – said

9 The Doctor's robot dog K-9 débuted in 1977 *Doctor Who* serial *The Invisible Enemy*, remained with the show until 1981, and returned, alongside Sarah Jane Smith, in *Doctor Who* 2.3.

PLANET OF THE OOD

This is Russell's e-mail to his fellow producers (including Susie Liggat, overseeing five episodes of Series Four, with Phil Collinson becoming exec for those episodes) and script editor Lindsey Alford, accompanying his completed rewrite of *Planet of the Ood*...

FROM: RUSSELL T DAVIES, TO: SUSIE LIGGAT; PHIL COLLINSON; JULIE GARDNER; LINDSEY ALFORD
CC: BENJAMIN COOK, TUESDAY 10 JULY 2007 04:09:40 GMT

EP 4.2

Here we go. Finished. I haven't had time to check for typos and stuff, but...

Remember I promised you no new locations, Susie? But then Mr Halpen had to go and mention a cinema... so now there's a cinema, and an Ood attack within the cinema.[1] Ideally, it's one of those posh press-launch cinemas, but do they even exist in Cardiff? It could always be a real cinema, one of the smaller ones, but I worry that it's going to look like we filmed in the local Odeon. Not very Forty-Second Century! But it's worth trying. We've the same old sets revolving around this story, so it makes a nice change – and great for kids, to imagine monsters romping through a cinema.

1 Mr Halpen is Chief Executive of the Ood-Sphere, which markets and sells Ood to the galaxy in the Forty-Second Century. The cinema is the setting for a scene where Ood kill a visiting party of sales reps. Although this scene makes the transmitted episode, the location has been altered to a less costly Sales Reception Room.

to me, 'How are we going to do the red eyes?' Red? *Red?!* I spent months going, '*Red?!*' The script never said red, anywhere, but people thought instinctively that devil = red. A natural assumption, but wrong. Even having hammered home 'white', the FX guys went off and came back with... green cats-eyes! I had to keep saying, 'No, no, no,' until I sat down with a pen and paper and drew exactly what we needed. It worked. It was a fantasy element, and I was the only person on that team who really knew his fantasy, from TV sci-fi to B Movies to the best that cinema has to offer. I know what looks tacky and what looks creepy. All those years of watching sci-fi pay off. And deciding that fine line, deciding why red and green are bad and white is good, that's a judgement call. That's tone.

Of course, that's a tiny example, but that's what we're talking about, a whole string of tiny examples, which gather together to form the whole. If it's not controlled, you end up with a mess. To take *Skins* as another example – they did get the tone right, bang on, spectacularly right... in their trailers. They were fantastic, weren't they? You've said so yourself. It looked like it was going to be the most mind-blowing drama, because of those images – wild, feral, sexy, *new*. If the drama had looked like the trails, it would have been magnificent. A lot of people worked very hard on that series, I'm sure, but I don't think the tone was controlled enough. I'm lucky in that I'm given the authority to control. I'm 6'6", loud, compulsive, pedantic, deliberately gregarious, and I get my point across. I describe my job as 'transmitting'. You have to transmit all the time what this show is. To do that, you can't talk too much about the vague concept of the show; you have to talk about the cutlery, the sound effects, the colour of that light in the background, and what sort of jeans Martha is wearing.

Then again… my first *Torchwood*? Yes, I agree, I'd take out that f-word now. It was trying to set a tone. It was saying, 'Go away kids' – as if that ever works! Swearing rarely feels natural on TV. There's still so little of it on that the words stand out artificially. When I hear a swear word on telly, I look at my watch. I think, oh, 20-past-nine. It takes me right out of the scene. It needs to be judged carefully. It's hard to imagine *Queer as Folk* without it – it's part of the energy – but I won't do it again on *Torchwood*. I don't think it sits well with sci-fi. (Why didn't I remember that when I was *Torchwood*ing? Trying too hard, I suppose.) Someone used the f-word in the first episode of *Bob & Rose*, and Paul Abbott told me to take it out. He was so right. Such a delicate word, it jarred.

See? You never learn.

FROM: RUSSELL T DAVIES TO: BENJAMIN COOK, TUESDAY 10 JULY 2007 13:43:20 GMT

RE: JAMES MARSTERS' ARSE

I've been thinking. That last e-mail – a lot of it was crap, the tone stuff. It was based on the assumption that the script is good, and then gets ballsed up by various levels of creativity. It was written too much from the writer's point of view. Truth is, tone goes astray not because of interference, but because, simply, most scripts don't work. That doesn't mean it's anyone's fault. Many scripts don't work because… well, because they're scripts. They're not an exact science. Just as most things in life don't work – machines, marriages, friendships, paper planes, everything. It's so easy, with hindsight, to say what went astray, much harder to pinpoint it at the start; otherwise 99 per cent of dramas would be brilliant. In fact, 99 per cent of life would be brilliant! And that's never going to happen. Everyone should have permission to fail and to try again.

If you listen to Bryan Elsley, the co-creator and driving force behind *Skins*, talking about the future of drama and the need for a narrative for a young audience, he is absolutely fascinating – and maybe absolutely right. He did the most brilliant interview about this, maybe two or three years ago, I think for the *Sunday Times*. That interview was so memorable because it *frightened* me. It said that the people running TV now are of the generation that grew up with it – we know it, we know TV, its forms and potential – but for the generation coming up, those brought up not so much on TV but on video gaming and user content, etc, TV is archaic. Soon, Bryan said, we – meaning me and him, and all of us of a certain age – would be as redundant as the generation before us. It was a real call to arms, to say that new forms of storytelling were on their way. Maybe we won't like it, but that change, that shift, will and must happen. (Will it? Aren't certain rules about drama, about storytelling, as old as the hills? Aren't there some truly fundamental needs that will never change?) Looking back, that was the path that led Bryan to *Skins*. He really is amazing, and *Skins'* uncertain tone just means that he's stumbled slightly on the first step. And stumbled bravely. Like you, I am looking forward to Series Two, despite Series One's shortcomings – so *Skins* is far from a failure.

But hey, I loved your *Torchwood* criticism. Invisible Ben does make me laugh: I'm telling you all sorts of things and you might be thinking, *blimey*, or *yeuch*, or *you bastard*, and yet you have to stay invisible. You're like Rose and her dad sneaking into the Cyberfactory in *The Age of Steel*: give yourself away and… well, you'll be taken to the Cybercontroller and given plenty of time to destroy him. Never got that quite right, did we? But when you describe *Torchwood's* failure of voice – which is my fault, I suppose, though they're all working hard to fix it for Series Two – then I sort of know where we stand, and can go further.

CHAPTER SIX

FIRE AND BRIMSTONE

In which JK Rowling is offered a part in *Doctor Who*,
Russell begins the search for his successor,
and Emergency Protocol One is activated

FROM: RUSSELL T DAVIES TO: BENJAMIN COOK, TUESDAY 10 JULY 2007 22:49:33 GMT

SAD NEWS...

I just heard that David's mum is very ill. He's left the set and driven north, heading home to Scotland. Oh, bless the man. Filming in ruins, schedule buggered, and no insurance, because you can't insure against that sort of thing, but never mind that – poor David. Poor mum.

FROM: BENJAMIN COOK TO: RUSSELL T DAVIES, WEDNESDAY 11 JULY 2007 13:34:12 GMT

RE: SAD NEWS...

When you hear the news that David has to dash off, when Phil or whoever breaks it to you, and you realise that the making of one of your scripts is, unavoidably, compromised – what do you do? Do you shrug and move on? Are you too busy worrying about writing to get caught up in such production problems? Is that Phil's job? Or do you have a moment, however brief, of sinking your head into your hands and weeping uncontrollably?!

FROM: RUSSELL T DAVIES TO: BENJAMIN COOK, THURSDAY 12 JULY 2007 21:35:06 GMT

RE: SAD NEWS...

Still no news on David's mum. We've managed to rearrange stuff so far, to fill in with non-Doctor material, but tomorrow we run out! The whole set – Kylie, too – on

157

standby. But imagine David, with his work ethic, *knowing* that. Poor bastard.

Production crises are a world apart from plain old script worries, probably because a production crisis is shared. There's almost no problem that you can't write your way out of. Location falls through? Lose a cast member? Camera fault? They can all be written around. That training comes from working on the soaps, I think. I was on *Coronation Street* when Lynne Perrie (who played Ivy Tilsley) was forever falling sick or off the wagon, and always at least one actor, in an ageing cast, needed a sudden day off. Soaps are great big ruthless machines that simply can't stop, so you have to find a way to cope. The only *Doctor Who* example I can think of is *The Shakespeare Code*, when the Doctor and Lilith were meant to have a sword fight. On the day of filming, the stuntwoman hit the stuntman's eye with her sword – yikes, his eye! – and filming had to stop on the spot. But while the ambulance came in, and he was taken away (and it was horrific – the whole crew was shaken up), Phil phoned me up, explained the situation, and I started typing away with a new version, as transmitted, replacing the sword fight completely; Lilith tries to seduce the Doctor instead. It only took me 20 minutes. A few hours later, we were filming the alternative version. Horrible and awful, but the show must go on.

That can happen, in a small way, all the way through production. Constant rewriting. Normally, it's because a scene has been dropped at the end of a day; they simply ran out of time. If it can't be rescheduled, I'll type away to adjust yet-to-be-filmed scenes, to remove the original scene from existence. But it's never face-in-hands weeping time. Even now, I'm half-thinking of a version of 4.1 that would be *very* Donna-heavy, in order to give David a fortnight off. He's not asking for that, but I think it's our responsibility to at least offer it. He has nine months ahead of him of being the leading man, and he won't get a proper break until Christmas now, so we have to consider practical ways of helping him cope. A Donna-heavy episode would be completely wrong for the show, but we could make it work. To hell with art.

Anyway… I go on a month's holiday next Friday, in Italy, which is obviously buggered because I'll still be rewriting James Moran's Pompeii episode. I've said to my boyfriend, 'I'll have to work a bit on the laptop,' but I haven't admitted that I'll have to work about 12 hours a day, every day, no weekends. That's not going to go down well. Truth be told, if it's a nightmare, I'll just come home. I've worked on holiday before – Episode 5 of *Mine All Mine* was written in France – and it was truly awful. Typing in that heat. Typing while your mates are frolicking in the pool. That episode of *Mine All Mine* is easily the worst, and that fact is haunting me now.

When I get back, I now have a fortnight to write 4.1. I'm looking at it with terror, especially because it should be a fast, dynamic, funny episode, and this bad mood is the worst to be in when writing in that style. I'm not saying you have to *be* happy to *write* happy – I don't think writing is ever happy – but you do need energy. You need to be galvanised. I feel a long way from that. I feel old, and fat, and slow. If I knew what

DR. REGENERATES!!

happened in 4.1, that would help. I have some ideas, like the first two scenes:

Sc.1. Donna leaves her house, locks the door.

Sc.2. The Doctor leaves the TARDIS, locks the door.

I know that sounds small, but it took a long time for it to arrive in my head. It sets up the crux of the episode: the symmetry of them both on the same mission, neither knowing that the other is there, and the fact that they're destined to meet. Apart from that, I've a nice image of Donna going to visit someone who's been Botoxed (I still like the Alien Botox idea), having stolen something – say, a vial – from Alien Botox Inc. Donna talking to this other woman and fiddling with the vial, which activates the alien inside the woman! Donna chases the alien into the street, but it's whisked away by an Alien Botox van (alerted by Vial Activation), which races along... past the Doctor, who's also running to the crime scene! High shot: the Doctor and Donna, standing in parallel streets, literally, both giving up and walking away, not realising that the other is there. That's good. It's still not a story, though.

I had another idea this morning. You know how, in 4.13, I'm going to regenerate the Doctor's hand-in-a-jar into a second Doctor, which can then travel off into the parallel universe – in the blue suit! – to live with Rose for ever? This morning, I suddenly thought, well, if you've two Doctors in 4.13, why not use them both? Properly? You've fleets of Daleks, and a red Dalek (I fancy a red Dalek – might look good), and Davros, and the End Of All Life In The Universe… so what can possibly save the day? *Two Doctors!* 'This situation needs two of us.' One in brown, one in blue, sparring off one another. It's so irresistible to end 4.12 with the Doctor, shot by a Dalek bolt, saying, 'I'm regenerating!' All that regenerative energy shoots out, but he channels it into the hand-in-a-jar, so his original self is healed, not changed, and the regeneration power creates a whole new Doctor around the hand. (Hmm, the new Doctor would be naked. I'll have to be clever with that. I'm all in favour of nudity… but not the Doctor!)

Other thoughts… Christmas 2008: Cybermen rising from the grave. We haven't really done rising from the grave before. Not fully. A Victorian funeral, in the snow, all the mourners and headstones, when hands start reaching up from the graves. Cyberhands! The humans are pulled into the earth. End on a silent graveyard, snow falling. That could be the pre-titles sequence.

FROM: BENJAMIN COOK TO: RUSSELL T DAVIES, FRIDAY 13 JULY 2007 11:58:01 GMT

RE: SAD NEWS…

Whereabouts in Italy is your 'holiday'? Aren't you just a little bit tempted to say, 'Screw this, I'm not flying back for anyone. Somebody else can sort out this mess'…? Or are you too much of a control-freak?

>>I don't think writing is ever happy<<

Do you really believe that?

FROM: RUSSELL T DAVIES TO: BENJAMIN COOK, FRIDAY 13 JULY 2007 20:12:54 GMT

RE: SAD NEWS…

The holiday villa is in Sorrento. Frankly, it's palatial. But today I made the terrible decision: I booked myself a flight home after just seven days out there. I simply can't stay away. That's not control-freakery; that's genuine panic. The rest of the team is brilliant at sorting out problems, but I'm the only one who can rewrite an entire episode. I need to be here. I can holiday when all this is over.

Do I *really* believe that writing is never happy? (What a day to ask me!) Well, I think that was a grandiose thing for me to say. I must have been in martyr-mode. It can be unhappy, certainly. Writing can be a hell of a load of misery. It's such a hard job. Writers never talk about how hard it is, out of the fear of being pretentious. 'Try being a nurse or a teacher,' people say. No, sod you – try being a writer! Try sitting with every doubt and fear about yourself and everyone, all on your own, with no ending or help or conclusion. I know I'm sort of a happy man and love a laugh, but I think that's because the job is so hard. At the same time, writing can be the most wonderful job in the world. When I'm happy with a script, I'm happier than you can ever imagine. Delirious! I think what I mean is, writing is never *easy*. Yes, that's what I meant. Moffat sent me a great e-mail about this the other day, in which he wrote:

John Cleese once said (at the time of Fawlty Towers, *when he* owned *comedy) that he thought*

his main advantage as a writer was that he knew how hard it was supposed to be. That's what
I mainly think when I read scripts – I think, you have no idea how hard this is.

'You have no idea how hard this is.' I could have that as a tattoo.

FROM: RUSSELL T DAVIES TO: BENJAMIN COOK, SUNDAY 15 JULY 2007 23:23:52 GMT

RE: SAD NEWS...

David's mum died at noon today. So sad. He's back at work tomorrow – because he wants to be – and will stay until the funeral, which is Saturday. I can see what he means, he'd rather be working, although I worry that – having been through it myself – he doesn't know how huge and never-ending it is, the death of a parent. To be going through that with a bloody great camera shoved in your face...

FROM: BENJAMIN COOK TO: RUSSELL T DAVIES, MONDAY 16 JULY 2007 00:49:27 GMT

RE: SAD NEWS...

I hope David is all right. It's easier to throw yourself into work, I suppose, but all the same a brave decision to continue working.

She must have been so incredibly proud of him.

FROM: RUSSELL T DAVIES TO: BENJAMIN COOK, TUESDAY 17 JULY 2007 12:25:49 GMT

RE: SAD NEWS...

David says the hardest thing is having to learn lines at night. Poor bastard.

I told Julie today that I was cancelling most of my holiday. She just said, 'Well, yes.' Hmph. I was expecting some protestations, even if they were faked, but I think, in her head, she's been assuming for ages that the holiday is cancelled. Still, this does mean I'll be in Cardiff for Russell Tovey's Midshipman Frame scenes. How is a man with sticky-out ears so completely beautiful? And he's gay – I can't bear it! Matt Jones said to me yesterday, 'You're the only exec I've ever met who talks openly about fancying his cast.' I said, 'Yes, but I'm the only one who's not actually shagging them.' I'm all talk.

I could bring back Midshipman Frame in 4.12/4.13, actually. I have been wondering, but the cast list is already so huge that Russell would only have time for six lines. Well, we'll see...

Oh, and for the record, I just e-mailed Moffat and finally spoke about the Elephant in the Room. I asked him: is he interested in the job? I'm fascinated to know what his reply will be. As is the whole *Doctor Who*-loving world.

FROM: BENJAMIN COOK TO: RUSSELL T DAVIES, TUESDAY 17 JULY 2007 12:51:37 GMT

RE: SAD NEWS...

Wow. Okay. Who actually chooses your successor, then? Do you really have a say?

FROM: RUSSELL T DAVIES TO: BENJAMIN COOK, TUESDAY 17 JULY 2007 13:11:02 GMT

RE: SAD NEWS...

It's not like I've got a say; it's just that I'm here, now, in the job, so of course I'm part of it.

Silence from the Moff, though. He usually writes back straight away. It's a cliffhanger!

STEVEN MOFFAT

This is Steven Moffat's reply to Russell's 'Elephant in the Room' e-mail. It would be a couple of months before either Russell or Steven had a chance to follow this up...

FROM: STEVEN MOFFAT TO: RUSSELL T DAVIES, THURSDAY 19 JULY 2007 11:59:42 GMT

RE: HELLO

I hope you don't think I'm being weirdly reticent here. I am, of course, thrilled to my socks. It's not only a dream job; it's *my* specific dream job since I was about seven. But there's so much to process – kids, Hartswood, Cardiff, other projects, that giddy mountain of Things I'm Never Going To Write And I'm 45 Already, and Sue and I haven't worked together since *Coupling* stopped, and we're keen to.[1]

But I love *Doctor Who* to tiny bits, I know I'm good at writing it, and I *so* want it to continue. And if there were a way to make this work, I know it would be – to coin a phrase – the trip of a lifetime. So, total turmoil in my head. Probably something you're not unfamiliar with.

Of *course* I'm going to talk about it, and hear what the offer is (assuming there *is* an offer, which I won't until there is), and add that to the general confusion. If you don't mind, I'd need to talk to you too, so I can hear the Horrid Truth and the Hidden Wonders. And listen – don't get reticent on advice. You get stuck right in.

But never mind that for the moment. Russell, seriously, it's a *huge* honour even to be in the frame as the guy who follows you. Bloody terrifying, but a huge honour. Thing is, you've really got big shoes. It's not a metaphor – you've actually got enormous shoes. They may haunt my dreams.

Reproduced with kind permission

1 Hartswood Films is an independent production company founded by Steven Moffat's mother-in-law. Moffat's wife, Sue Vertue, is a producer and board director at Hartswood. Her producing credits include BBC sitcom *Coupling*, which Moffat created and wrote.

Text message from: **Ben**
Sent: 18-Jul-2007 16:52
I'm on set with Kylie Minogue! In Cardiff's old Coal Exchange building! Ha ha ha! Mind you, on such a sunny day, trust us to be filming inside.

> **Text message from: Russell**
> Sent: 18-Jul-2007 17:56
> Kylie just asked me if I wanted dinner in the hotel tonight. I turned her down, because I'm rewriting Agatha bloody Christie. I'm telling you this just so you can make a note of my pain in The Great Correspondence. Oh, my life!

> **Text message from: Ben**
> Sent: 18-Jul-2007 20:31
> You chose Agatha over Kylie? Are you sure you're gay?

> **Text message from: Russell**
> Sent: 18-Jul-2007 20:45
> I think choosing Agatha over Kylie is a whole new level of gay. Gay Mark II.

FROM: RUSSELL T DAVIES TO: BENJAMIN COOK, WEDNESDAY 18 JULY 2007 22:07:16 GMT

AGATHA CHRISTIE

I'm now amusing myself by trying to get as many Agatha Christie titles into the dialogue as possible.

FROM: BENJAMIN COOK TO: RUSSELL T DAVIES, WEDNESDAY 18 JULY 2007 22:25:56 GMT

RE: AGATHA CHRISTIE

I'll give you £20 if you can slip in *Ten Little Niggers*.

FROM: RUSSELL T DAVIES TO: BENJAMIN COOK, WEDNESDAY 18 JULY 2007 22:33:43 GMT

RE: AGATHA CHRISTIE

Actually, I did try:

```
                        DONNA
     It's like Ten Little –

                        THE DOCTOR
     Niggles aside, let's look in the library.
```

But I thought it was too risky, so cut it.

FROM: RUSSELL T DAVIES TO: BENJAMIN COOK, THURSDAY 19 JULY 2007 17:24:18 GMT

RE: AGATHA CHRISTIE

Well, I've finished 4.7. That was hard. Bloody hard. Gareth's version is much more intricate than it would first appear, so I had to be really, really careful, filtering through it. I couldn't just blunder in, adding explosions and monsters. I had to keep the lightness and the cleverness of Gareth's original. That's exhausted me. *(cont p166)*

THE ADIPOSE

This e-mail exchange, on 18 July, between Russell and visual FX producer Will Cohen, from The Mill, regards the monsters in 4.1. 'I blabbed to someone else,' Russell told Benjamin later that day. 'I feel unfaithful. I've been having various thoughts and worries about 4.1 for about three days now, and simply haven't had time to write to you about them all. But then Will came blundering in with a production question, and I sang like a canary...'

FROM: WILL COHEN TO: RUSSELL T DAVIES, WEDNESDAY 18 JULY 2007 11:47:43 GMT

EP. 1 – SERIES FOUR

I know you're insanely busy, but I'm just wondering, for my own advanced scheduling purposes, if you think there may be a CGI creature in Ep 1...?

FROM: RUSSELL T DAVIES TO: WILL COHEN, WEDNESDAY 18 JULY 2007 11:59:21 GMT

RE: EP. 1 – SERIES FOUR

I'm beginning to think there might be. I'd been thinking of a green vegetable/seaweedy monster, creeping over human skin... but that's been done to death, hasn't it? And now I'm quite excited by the idea of a different sort of CGI creature – depending on the cost. Have you seen that car advert with those sinister little puppets/knitted soft toys chasing after a car?[1] They're only a few inches tall. I think they're meant to be funny, but they creep me out. I was thinking along similar lines as that, but spongy creatures – almost cute, rudimentary, blank blobs, maybe eight inches tall, with stumpy arms and legs, and a mewling mouth. No lip-sync; they just mewl. They'd trot along, seemingly cute, like a kid's soft toy – but deadly! And they'd be white – or a sort of marbly white – because they're actually made out of fat. Don't laugh, they are! It's modern-day Earth, a sinister weight-loss plan. 'Your fat just walks away from you.' And it *does*! People take a pill, which turns out to be an egg, then, while you're sleeping, a little creature grows out of your fat, comes alive, separates away from you and walks off. Yikes. Horrible.

Trouble is, for some shots, we'd need hundreds of them. Trotting along the streets. Mewling. Clambering over people. We've never done that hordes-of-little-creatures shtick. I'm quite excited by this idea. I'm worried that we might, in our fourth year, start to repeat ourselves with CGI Big Monsters, whereas little, scuttling, cute-but-horrible white blobs, with stumpy legs and mewling mouths... well, it feels new. But also it feels difficult, problematic, expensive, and a nightmare. I rather like that!

---

1 The C.M.O.N.S., a band of woven hand puppets, featured in adverts for the 2007 model Vauxhall Corsa.

FROM: WILL COHEN TO: RUSSELL T DAVIES, WEDNESDAY 18 JULY 2007 12:06:01 GMT

RE: EP. 1 – SERIES FOUR

I absolutely love this idea. It's fresh, exciting, scary and fun. We want to blow everyone away with the series opener. Heading outside the comfort zone – exactly where we want to be! If we keep the amount of FX shots to a minimum, we may be able to use this crowd software, Massive. We have an exclusive western-hemisphere license for Massive, which uses AI to tell the models what to do, to step over or move around things in an environment. I'll get to thinking about time, costs, etc, and e-mail you back later.

FROM: WILL COHEN TO: RUSSELL T DAVIES, WEDNESDAY 18 JULY 2007 12:29:33 GMT

RE: EP. 1 – SERIES FOUR

Sorry to bombard you, Russell, but we're having chats. How about if the fat doesn't take any one shape, but can change to a multitude of forms? When the creatures attack people, they can transform into a head, mirror people screaming or laughing, etc? My worry about a white blob is how it would look, a few pixels in size, in a daylight street scene…? Check out on YouTube our Tooheys Extra Dry commercial – I'll send you the link – where someone's tongue leaves their body while they're sleeping and heads off to a party.

FROM: RUSSELL T DAVIES TO: WILL COHEN, WEDNESDAY 18 JULY 2007 12:46:15 GMT

RE: EP. 1 – SERIES FOUR

OH MY GOD, THAT TONGUE! That's brilliant. That's what the Adipose – yes, they're called Adipose (I remember from O Level Biology, 'adipose' is a posh word for fat) – will do. They'll separate off from someone when they're sleeping. They distend out of the stomach, the stomach skin stre-e-e-etching, and then *plop!* – divide off into separate little creatures. I'd like them to be expressive, but I think they might start to lose their identity if they morph into any shape. I think the sheer, weird, freaky *cuteness* of these things is the key.

Back when we very first started, in 2004, I wanted to use the best imagery from current adverts and pop videos. Like Cassandra, inspired by stick-thin celebrities, etc! But ever since her, I think I've become a bit traditional, and it's time to remember core values, to remind myself of why I'm doing this, and to push things further than Yet Another Monster.

I'm off on my holidays in half an hour. I'll have my mobile on me in Italy, but only my BBC e-mail while I'm away. I've never used that account before. You get given it when you join the BBC. A lot of people have presumed that it's working all the time. The IT man opened it up yesterday, for the first time, and there were 24,000 e-mails waiting for me! I told him: 'Delete.'

> **Text message from: Russell**
> Sent: 25-Jul-2007 10:13
> Nice and hot here. Very hard to work. I have to lock myself away to write. Bah! But I'm 70 pages into the new *Harry Potter* book. Blimey, what a return to form. Good old JK! I can't read fast enough.

> **Text message from: Ben**
> Sent: 25-Jul-2007 12:33
> I finished it in 24 hours. Just wait till you reach Chapter 36!

> **Text message from: Russell**
> Sent: 26-Jul-2007 17:37
> Dobby just died! I am RIDICULOUSLY sad. It's turning into a bloodbath. But so exciting! I'm abandoning Pompeii. Blame JK.

> **Text message from: Russell**
> Sent: 27-Jul-2007 11:53
> I finished it last night. What a book! Mrs Weasley fighting Bellatrix! 'NOT MY DAUGHTER, YOU BITCH!' Ha ha ha.

FROM: BENJAMIN COOK TO: RUSSELL T DAVIES, SUNDAY 29 JULY 2007 18:13:16 GMT

HOLIDAY!

Good holiday?

FROM: RUSSELL T DAVIES TO: BENJAMIN COOK, SUNDAY 29 JULY 2007 20:21:48 GMT

RE: HOLIDAY!

Holiday fine, yes. Gone now. Mind you, I was even recognised in a tiny restaurant on a godforsaken cliff top on the Amalfi Coast, by a little girl called Molly. One of these days, I'm going tell 'em to sod off, just to see the look on mum and dad's face!

No, I won't. But I dream of it.

I was back in this flat for five minutes – *five bloody minutes* – before Julie was at the door. Lovely to see her and all that, but *c'mon!* It's like walking into a blizzard. I've a mountain of work. I have to rewrite the end of 4.7, because David thinks – quite fairly

– that ramming a car into the Vespiform is the Doctor committing murder.[1] Good point, but… any ideas?

But! I had an idea on holiday. Such a mad idea that I phoned Julie, to start setting it in motion. I was in the shower on Saturday morning (you may avert your eyes), thinking about how much I'd enjoyed that last *Harry Potter* book, how I'd love to write something like that, remembering that, back in 2004, I asked JK Rowling to write an episode of *Doctor Who*, though she politely declined, and reflecting that we can't possibly get someone to star in next year's Christmas Special who's as famous as Kylie… when all those things coalesced. *BAM!* I thought, don't ask JK to write a *Doctor Who*, ask her to *be in* a *Doctor Who*! We've done Dickens, Shakespeare, Agatha Christie… why should kids think that all great authors are dead?

Imagine it. A cold Edinburgh Christmas Eve. JK Rowling walking through the snow, pursued by a journalist. 'What are you going to write after *Harry Potter*? The difficult second album…' Later, JK sits down to write. At the same time, a Space Bug (maybe the same as Donna's time-psych creature in 4.11), probably put there by the Rita Skeeter-type journalist, leaps onto her back.[2] *ZAP!* JK's imagination becomes real! A world of Victorian magic replaces the present-day world. The Doctor arrives and has to battle through a world of witches and wizards, with wands and spells and CGI wonders, to reach JK Rowling at the heart of it all…

That's either brilliant or more like a *Blue Peter* crossover. But worth trying. It's different, certainly. So, Julie is trying to set up a meeting with JK. It's easier getting into Fort Knox at the moment, but that's Julie's skill. (Fort Knox? Is that still true? Or are my allusions getting old?) Imagine those opening titles: 'DAVID TENNANT' flying at you, then 'JK ROWLING'! She's the only name in the whole wide world who's bigger than Kylie right now. Imagine the Doctor in a world of magic made real – that would be glorious. So, there we go. That's under way.

FROM: BENJAMIN COOK TO: RUSSELL T DAVIES, MONDAY 30 JULY 2007 01:38:37 GMT

RE: HOLIDAY!
That would be – oh God.

Do you really think she'll consider it? Did you see her on *Blue Peter* the other week, a couple of days before *Deathly Hallows* was released? She was shown a clip from *The Shakespeare Code* – the bit where the Doctor tells Martha about crying when he read Book Seven. JK seemed tickled. But can she act?

FROM: RUSSELL T DAVIES TO: BENJAMIN COOK, MONDAY 30 JULY 2007 02:15:24 GMT

RE: HOLIDAY!
That was Julie's first question. After she stopped laughing. I said I'd write around it.

---

1 The script had the Doctor driving an open-top tourer into the Vespiform, which falls into a lake, where it drowns.
2 Rita Skeeter is a reporter of dubious repute in the *Harry Potter* novels.

Besides, did you see JK being interviewed by Jeremy Paxman on *Newsnight* before the release of Book Five? She's the only person I've ever seen run rings around him. That woman is ineffably cool and self-assured. Anyone who can do that can act. (I just made up that rule, but I'm sticking to it.) Even if it never happens, it's enough to keep me going through the dark hours. Well, that and Bel Ami porn.

FROM: RUSSELL T DAVIES TO: BENJAMIN COOK, MONDAY 30 JULY 2007 23:51:51 GMT

RE: HOLIDAY!

I've just been for drinks with Kylie and cast and crew. Everyone's excited about Bernard Cribbins' day on set tomorrow. It's a pity, really, that Stan the newsvendor is just a cameo. Kylie had never heard of Bernard, until we told her that he was the voice of the Wombles! I'm tempted to come on set with you all tomorrow, except I'm so short of time. Not a word of Pompeii rewritten. I haven't even opened the file. But I'm getting interested in soothsayers, in a sort of Sisterhood of Karn way, or the Seeker in *The Ribos Operation*, or that wonderful Fortune Teller in *Snakedance*.[3] Thank Christ for *Doctor Who*'s rich history! There's a wealth of ideas to draw from in a crisis.

FROM: BENJAMIN COOK TO: RUSSELL T DAVIES, TUESDAY 31 JULY 2007 08:45:45 GMT

RE: HOLIDAY!

You really should come on set tonight. You might never again get the chance to see Kylie Minogue on the streets of Cardiff. Unless her career takes a real turn for the worse.

FROM: RUSSELL T DAVIES TO: BENJAMIN COOK, TUESDAY 31 JULY 2007 15:16:25 GMT

RE: HOLIDAY!

Oh, all right, I am coming tonight. I couldn't resist. Pompeii can burn.

FROM: RUSSELL T DAVIES TO: BENJAMIN COOK, FRIDAY 3 AUGUST 2007 12:38:55 GMT

RE: HOLIDAY!

Christ and damn and bollocks. It's August.

This is a new low: I'm resorting to going into a Tone Meeting on Monday – it's for Block Three – with a few paltry pages (I hope) of 4.3, and a three-page synopsis of 4.1.[4] This is bad. It's bordering on an emergency. It feels awful – literally, makes me feel sick. I've just flagged up to Julie that we could abandon Pompeii, and bring in Mark Gatiss' World War II/Natural History Museum script instead.

---

3 The Sisterhood of Karn appeared in 1976 *Doctor Who* serial *The Brain of Morbius*; the Seeker in 1978's *The Ribos Operation*; the Fortune Teller in 1983's *Snakedance*.
4 Each series is split into filming blocks of one, two or three episodes, overseen by the same director. Block One of Series Four comprised 4.X only (directed by James Strong), Block Two comprised 4.7 and 4.2 (Graeme Harper), and Block Three comprised – at this stage – 4.3 and 4.1 (Colin Teague).

FROM: RUSSELL T DAVIES TO: BENJAMIN COOK, FRIDAY 3 AUGUST 2007 21:45:41 GMT

RE: HOLIDAY!

Emergency Protocol One has been activated! Block Three has been split in two. Colin Teague will now direct 4.3 on its own (instead of 4.1 and 4.3 together), and James Strong will come back to direct 4.1 in a brand new Block Four. In other words, while Colin is shooting the Pompeii episode, that's the prep time for James on the Adipose one.

This takes the pressure off scripts, because now 4.1 doesn't have to be ready until the beginning of September. This is a huge relief for me, but also chronic; it means paying off Colin and his editor for the work that they'd have done on 4.1, plus finding a new chunk of money to pay James. That's money that won't be seen on screen. Technically, that's terrible. In practice, it's the only way that we're going to get on air. Bloody hell.

FROM: RUSSELL T DAVIES TO: BENJAMIN COOK, SATURDAY 4 AUGUST 2007 14:17:53 GMT

POMPEII

Finally, I've started on Pompeii. Five pages in. That's five pages better than this morning. (I woke up in abject terror.) But what do these bloody soothsayers want? What and why and how? I think by breathing in the gases from the hypocaust, people in Pompeii are turning into stone… because the Stone Aliens (yes, really!) aren't really stone, they're *dust*, and they need to be inhaled to become, gradually, their stone selves. Well, that's my idea for now, but it still doesn't decide what the soothsayers do. I just like soothsayers.

FROM: BENJAMIN COOK TO: RUSSELL T DAVIES, SATURDAY 4 AUGUST 2007 15:33:41 GMT

RE: POMPEII

Who has the horrible job of telling the writers that you're taking over their scripts?

FROM: RUSSELL T DAVIES TO: BENJAMIN COOK, SATURDAY 4 AUGUST 2007 15:56:23 GMT

RE: POMPEII

That's always Julie's job. The writers are told in advance that it *might* happen. It's a condition of the contract. They've all got my number and e-mail address, if they want to have a pop at me. Once it's done, I do phone them up to explain how and why and wherefore. Keith Temple was absolutely delightful about my rewrites on his Ood script. Such a nice bloke.

FROM: RUSSELL T DAVIES TO: BENJAMIN COOK, TUESDAY 7 AUGUST 2007 23:31:10 GMT

RE: POMPEII

Donna Noble arrived today! She was glorious. We had the read-through for 4.2 and 4.7, Catherine sat right next to David, and she was dazzling. After all that Penny/Donna development, I just sat there and thought, this is *exactly* what I wanted. All that work, all that thinking, all those e-mails to you, actually had a result. She's an equal to the Doctor, a friend, a mate, a challenge. It struck me – this is how Barbara Wright would be written, if she were a 2007/8 character.[5] That feels good. Catherine takes a funny line, makes it five times funnier, and aims it like a dart – which makes David raise his game. He throws back a javelin! I'm so happy. I realised how scared I'd been all this time, because you never really know if something is going to work.

Anyway, this has all interrupted the writing of Pompeii. It's annoying, when writing gets interrupted, because you lose the energy, the drive, the flow. It's hard to summon it back. I'll have to smoke-and-coffee myself back into that state tomorrow. I sat here for hours today – all day, really – and managed little more than reducing the length from 33 pages to 32, then I wrote one new page, which is all right-ish, and added a joke for Donna about going to the shops in Pompeii ('T K Maximus')… but I promised to deliver the script tomorrow! Especially with Colin and Phil heading off to Cinecittà Studios on a recce this week.[6] (It looks as though filming in Rome really will happen!) Not the best time for me to slow down. But I'll have to panic tomorrow. Of course, while I pause, the problems and worries are stirring. How come the Stone Aliens' presence in Pompeii is allowing the city's soothsayers to tell the future? In *Doctor Who* terms, there must be a scientific explanation, even if it's not *real* science. Is Pompeii on a Time Rift? Don't laugh, it's a quick solution.

FROM: BENJAMIN COOK TO: RUSSELL T DAVIES, WEDNESDAY 8 AUGUST 2007 00:10:26 GMT

RE: POMPEII

So what does a normal day consist of, to stop you writing? What's a typical day, in your role as showrunner?

FROM: RUSSELL T DAVIES TO: BENJAMIN COOK, WEDNESDAY 8 AUGUST 2007 00:38:34 GMT

RE: POMPEII

Well, there's no such thing as a typical day. But today? Um… a read-through. Plus, talking Catherine and Phil through what will happen in 4.1 so that everyone knows where Donna is coming from. (I enjoyed describing it – it sounds fun and weird – but I'm acutely aware that it has no ending.) I sorted out *Sarah Jane* Dub dates with Julie. A compulsory set visit, if only to see Russell T. Ovey. (He told me that *Bob & Rose* is one of his favourite shows ever, and actually *quoted lines* from Episode 6. He loves me. It's official.) I had to sort out the end of *Doctor Who* 4.7, because of David's worry about killing the Vespiform. (David T. Ennant: clever, sexy *and* good on scripts. Why don't I hate him?) I had to come home and do that rewrite, as well as some further rewrites

---

5 Barbara Wright (played by Jacqueline Hill) was one of the original *Doctor Who* companions, joining the show at its inception in 1963 and staying until 1965.
6 Rome's legendary Cinecittà Studios is where HBO/BBC series *Rome* was filmed, on five acres of outdoor sets comprising elaborate reconstructions of Ancient Rome.

on 4.2. I had to clear the press release for Friday – we're releasing a photo of David and Catherine on set for 4.7. This involved 20 e-mails. I noticed that the BBC *Doctor Who* website has a new page of artwork, which we'd promised exclusively to Worldwide for books and magazines, so I alerted Julie – that's a major storm on the way.

What else? I decided to swap 4.2 and 4.3 in the transmission order – Pompeii first, then Ood – so I set that in motion. Since the Ood tale is surprisingly dark, I'd thought that it would undercut people's comedy expectations of Life With Donna, but then, at the read-through, I thought that the Ood episode was dark to the point of grim. It's a very macho, testosterone-fuelled script, and they're never my favourites, so, yes, it's better as the third episode. Also today – I watched rushes, *Doctor Who* and *Torchwood*, all good, no notes, and the online edit (the finished picture with FX added) of *Sarah Jane* 1.3/1.4. I worried about the decision to kill Tosh and Owen at the end of this year's *Torchwood* (I'm happy to kill the characters, not happy to lose the actors – but that show needs a shock), so I sent concerned e-mails to Julie. Also, I'm still debating with Julie whether to leave Mickey Smith in this universe at the end of 4.13, so he can guest in *Torchwood* and *Sarah Jane* as a sort of roving character – and in *Doctor Who*, if the next production team fancy a link with the past. Yes, I think we're going to do it.

Also, and this is top secret (do not tell anyone), Phil has been offered the job as producer of *Coronation Street*! I'm so happy for him. He loves *Coronation Street*. It's possibly the only job in the UK that could replace *Doctor Who* in his heart. He'd be the king of Manchester! And it wouldn't be till the beginning of next year, so he'd only miss the filming of the final two episodes of Series Four. But... but... Jane Tranter wants him to stay at the BBC (of course she does – he's brilliant), so she's throwing a brand new North-West Drama job at him. He'd be based in Manchester, as Head of Drama for the entire region. Well, Phil doesn't know what to do. What a dilemma! Today was talking him through that. Russell T Counsellor.

And then more work – I disagreed with Peter McKinstry's design of Ood Sigma's hip flask.[7] It's too tricky for a blind and gloved actor. Lovely design, though. I ate a lasagne, cold, because I didn't have time to heat it up. That's bad, isn't it? I saw a second hip-flask design, and approved it. I was asked to sign off on the Series Three DVD boxset cover, but didn't, because it's terrible. I texted Russell Tovey, just... because. I read and approved three BBC Novel proposals and one BBC Audiobook proposal. I suggested a commission for Joe Lidster for a *Torchwood* radio play. I e-mailed Ben –

Oh. That's you.

Bloody hell. And this is a normal day. It's barmy. Mind you, every time I say to myself, 'I can't wait for it all to end,' something grabs me. Julie and I spent the car journey to Upper Boat today talking about the New Studio. They're thinking of building it from scratch next to the St David's Hotel. Near my flat! To house *Doctor*

---

7 In *Doctor Who* 4.2, Ood Sigma (played by Paul Kasey) is the personal servant of Klineman Halpen, the manager of Ood Operations.

Who, Torchwood, Sarah Jane, and various other BBC shows. That's vast. They're even talking about having Universal Tours-style visits! Just as I contemplate leaving, they go and make the empire bloody tangible, right on my doorstep. Oh, so tempting, to stay and help set that up. That's *thousands* of jobs, literally. It's only a plan at the moment, but a plan that's hastening every day. Ed Thomas is drawing up designs. It would be his masterpiece. And I'll miss it. Well, I'm going to keep this flat on, so I can press my nose up against the windows and cry.

I really can't keep working at this rate. It'll kill me. It has to stop.

FROM: RUSSELL T DAVIES TO: BENJAMIN COOK, FRIDAY 10 AUGUST 2007 02:14:55 GMT

RE: POMPEII

I'm on Page 43 of Pompeii. Not enough. Colin and company are in Rome right now, screaming for pages. Well, tough. It took all day to think of the water pistol. The Doctor uses it to face off the alien-possessed High Priestess, the head of the Sibylline Sisterhood in Pompeii. That's where the time goes. Or rather – I thought of the water pistol at about midday (in the middle of a *Sarah Jane* Edit), and it took the rest of the day to *convince myself* it can work. A lot of doubt. Eventually, I realised it's a great scene; it's very Doctor to face an alien with a water pistol. His character allows you to get away with murder. Sometimes.

FROM: BENJAMIN COOK TO: RUSSELL T DAVIES, FRIDAY 10 AUGUST 2007 22:51:04 GMT

RE: POMPEII

There are reports on the news that a fire last night destroyed part of the Cinecittà Studios in Rome. Isn't that where Colin and Phil and the team are at the moment, on the recce? According to BBC News:

> *Flames leapt 40m (130ft) into the air at one point before the blaze was brought under control. The fire engulfed about 3,000sq m (32,000sq ft), firefighters said. There were no reported deaths or injuries. Firefighters fought the blaze all night and prevented the fire spreading to the densely populated urban area around the film studios. The fire began in a store for film sets, destroying sets used in a television series about ancient Rome, produced by HBO and the BBC.*

Phil didn't nip outside for a smoke, did he, and drop his cigarette? Will *Doctor Who* still be able to film at Cinecittà?

FROM: RUSSELL T DAVIES TO: BENJAMIN COOK, SATURDAY 11 AUGUST 2007 02:50:16 GMT

RE: POMPEII

The fire! Yes, bloody hell. The reports from Rome are that there's still enough of the set left standing for us to film on. Of course, I did ask if they had footage of the burning, because that could look brilliant for us! Phil harrumphed at me. Well, it's an idea. How mad, though. And thank God, otherwise we'd have to go to Malta instead.

In fact, I've just finished the 4.3 script. I'm knackered. I need sleep.

(RE)WRITING POMPEII

In this extract from James Moran's original script for 4.3, the Doctor and Donna have just arrived in Pompeii (which they've mistaken for Rome) in AD 79, in a bustling Pompeian marketplace...

                              DONNA
            This is - this is not today.

                              DOCTOR
            Course it's today. Every day is today, as long as it's
            today. Basic time theory, that.

He strides off, exploring. Donna has trouble speaking.

                              DONNA
            No, it's not 'today'-today. It's before today. Not present
            day. The past. We're in… the past.

A market trader holds out a gourd to Donna.

                              MARKET TRADER 1
            Gourd, madam? Very reasonable.

                              DONNA
            No, thanks, I… I've already got one. Doctor!

                                                            CUT TO:

4. EXT. SIDE STREET OF MARKET

An offshoot of the market, filled with interesting fruits and
foods. Donna struggles to keep up with the Doctor.

                              DONNA
            We're in the past!

                              DOCTOR
            You don't want to see the boring old present, do you? We
            want to see what it was really like. In the past. Soak up
            all that past-y goodness. Look at it.

Donna touches a wall, picks up a vase. Tears in her eyes.

                              DOCTOR (CONT'D)
            Ah, good old Rome! The Colosseum! The Pantheon! The Circus
            Maximus!

He looks around at the surrounding area, standing on a box to
get a better view. It's obvious that none of the things he just
mentioned are anywhere in sight. He frowns.

                              DOCTOR (CONT'D)
            Well, somewhere around here, I'm sure. Might be a tad off
            course.

                              DONNA
            And it's safe? You've been here before?

>   DOCTOR
> Once, yes. Didn't go very well, had to leave in a bit of
> a hurry… And I had NOTHING to do with Rome burning down,
> before you ask, that was entirely not my fault at all.
> Mostly. Anyway, it's all been rebuilt now.
>
>   DONNA
> Simple 'yes' would be fine. Hold on — I spoke to that man.
> You! Can you understand me?
>
> She addresses another trader.
>
>   MARKET TRADER 2
> Course I can.
>
>   DONNA
> Doctor! I'm speaking Latin! I must be one of those language
> geniuses. You know, like how Einstein was rubbish at school,
> but then it turned out —
>
>   DOCTOR
> No, that's the TARDIS. Translation thingy, gets inside your
> head.
>
>   DONNA
> Oh. I'm not a genius, then?
>
>   DOCTOR
> Not as far as I know. Where _is_ everything?
>
> He's still trying to get his bearings, nothing looks familiar.
> Donna is still staring at everything, taking in the sights,
> sounds, smells, madness.
>
>   DONNA
> Okay, so we're in ancient Rome. I can handle this. I can do
> this.

Reproduced with kind permission

This is Russell's rewrite (on 4 August 2007) of that section…

>   DONNA
> I'm here, in Rome, Donna Noble, in Rome! Me! This is just
> weird. I mean, everyone here's dead!
>
>   THE DOCTOR
> I wouldn't go telling them that.
>
>   DONNA
> No, but… Hold on a minute, that sign over there's in
> English. You having me on, are we in Epcot?
>
> Hand-painted stall-sign, _Two amphoras for the price of one._
>
>   THE DOCTOR
> No, that's the Tardis translation circuits, just makes it
> look like English. Speech as well, you're talking Latin,
> right now.

                                        DONNA
Seriously? I just said 'seriously' in Latin? But… what if
I said something in actual Latin? Like, 'veni vidi vici',
my Dad says that when he comes back from the football, if I
said 'veni vidi vici' to that lot, what would it sound like?

                                 THE DOCTOR
Um… I'm not sure. Have to think of difficult questions, don't
you?

                                          DONNA
I'm gonna try it…

Goes up to a STALLHOLDER, a cheery Cockney, selling fruit.

                                  STALLHOLDER
Afternoon sweetheart, what can I get you, my love?

                                          DONNA
Veni vidi vici!

                                  STALLHOLDER
                                    (like she's dumb)
Ah. Sorry. Me no speak Celtic. No can do, missy.

                                          DONNA
Yeah…
                                   (back to the Doctor)
How's he mean, Celtic?

                                   THE DOCTOR
Welsh. You sound Welsh. There we are, I've learnt something.

As they stroll away –

CUT TO A SOOTHSAYER, good distance away. Woman, 20s, in robes,
face painted white, with strange patterns. Part-witch, part-
priestess. She's hiding in the shadows of a doorway, staring at
the new arrivals.

And she keeps to the shadows, as she follows them…

                                                        CUT TO:

2. EXT. POMPEII STREET – DAY

THE DOCTOR & DONNA walking along.

Throughout: a good distance away, the SOOTHSAYER follows.

                                          DONNA
Don't our clothes look a bit odd?

                                   THE DOCTOR
Naaah, Ancient Rome, anything goes. It's like Soho, but
bigger.

                                          DONNA
Have you been here before, then?

```
                          THE DOCTOR
        Ages ago. And before you ask, that fire had nothing to do
        with me, well, not very much, well, a little bit, well...
        But I never got the chance to look around properly! The
        Colosseum! The Pantheon! The Circus Maximus! Although... you'd
        expect them to be looming by now, where is everything? Let's
        try this way...
```

JAMES MORAN

After reading Russell's rewrite of his Pompeii episode, James Moran
e-mailed script editor Brian Minchin...

FROM: JAMES MORAN TO: BRIAN MINCHIN, MONDAY 13 AUGUST 2007 11:20:15 GMT

RE: 4.3

Had a quick read, through half-closed fingers – such a strange feeling, I knew
it would be different, because it's always weird being rewritten. But it's bloody
brilliant! Once I got used to reading it – by Page 20, I was just enjoying the story. It
belts along, it's funny, it's clever, some of my jokes are still there, some are Russell's
new ones, and I nearly wet myself at the water pistol gag. I wish I'd thought of that.

Normally, being rewritten is a horrible experience, but in this case, while it
feels slightly odd (which it *always* will – it can't be helped), every single change is
right, right for the story, makes it feel more part of New *Who*, and is done to make
for a better episode, instead of competing for lines. (I had a few bad months on
a different project, where it felt like the other guy was changing stuff just to try
to stamp himself on it, rather than to make it better – and some stuff suffered.)
Everything in RTD's rewrite serves the story and builds on the stuff that I set down,
instead of throwing it out. I can see *why* everything has been done, rather than
'what the hell are you thinking?!' – which has happened to me on other things.

I've learned a lot from seeing my version magically transformed into a proper *Who*
TV episode. It's really bizarre, and quite fantastic, and I don't know how RTD has
managed to do a rewrite where I feel enriched, and educated, and happy. Clearly, he
has evil mind-melding powers.

Reproduced with kind permission

FROM: BENJAMIN COOK TO: RUSSELL T DAVIES, SATURDAY 11 AUGUST 2007 03:58:19 GMT

RE: POMPEII

Why exactly don't you insist on a co-writer's credit for 4.3?

FROM: RUSSELL T DAVIES TO: BENJAMIN COOK, SUNDAY 12 AUGUST 2007 18:33:52 GMT

RE: POMPEII

I know, I know, that credit thing… but it just crept up on us, really, until it became a sort of policy. It was never planned that way. Back in 2004, we'd always talked about my rewriting as a possibility ('polishing' we called it, when we were young and naive, before we actually had scripts in our hands, and I'd never rewritten anyone before, ever), but Andy Pryor kick-started the whole process when we wanted to offer the part of Charles Dickens to Simon Callow. We really *needed* Simon Callow for that part – but Mark's script for *The Unquiet Dead* wasn't ready.

After that, in some ways, it became a trap. I'd be rewriting an episode and I'd be thinking, well, if I didn't get a credit for the last script that I rewrote, why should I single out this one? And I have to be fair to the original writers: they work so hard and deserve that credit. It's partly arrogance as well, because I don't think my rewrites are as good as my actual scripts. (With the exception of *The Impossible Planet/ The Satan Pit*. God, I love that story!) For instance, I think the Pompeii episode works now, though it's curious how it's still inherited the linear shape of James's original. I reckon I'd have written it better had it been mine from the start. Instead of all those months of thinking and consideration, rewriting somebody else's script is more like plate-spinning – keeping lots of things in the air, making them look pretty, hoping that they won't crash. In an emergency, I throw lots of things in there – soothsayers, psychic powers, prophecies, funny squares of marble – and hope that I can make a story out of them as I go along, like an improvisation game. When you've a big, central conceit like a volcano, as long as you make sure everything streamlines into that (it's not plate-spinning; it's a maypole – it's a multi-metaphor!), then it should hang together. The psychic powers are caused by the dust, which is the aliens, and the aliens are thwarted by the volcano erupting, etc, etc, etc. Ram them all into each other. It's not a maypole; it's a car crash! Fun, though.

FROM: RUSSELL T DAVIES TO: BENJAMIN COOK, SATURDAY 18 AUGUST 2007 00:29:47 GMT

RE: POMPEII

I was doing further production rewrites on Pompeii today, and thinking about our e-mails earlier in the year, and what I said about characters, that you should keep turning them, keep seeing them in new lights, so they live a bit more. Now, James didn't have time to get his Pompeii script to that stage of finessing, so he only got the Caecilius family to first base – the father was henpecked, Metella was a nag, Quintus was sullen, Evelina was girlish.[8] Fine, good starting point, and James made them much more distinct than a lot of writers would have done. But then the turning must start. Take Quintus (who only has 25 or so lines, so theoretically a small part, but it's true that no parts are small) – a lot of my rewrite consisted of turning him, like a barbecue, making sure that he's cooked all the way through. Metaphor heaven! In my rewrite, he's sullen and hung over when he first appears, but then he deepens as he defends his sister before his parents ('But she's sick!'), then greedy when the Doctor offers him money

---

8 The Roman family in 4.3 consists of a father (Lobus, listed as Caecilius in the script), mother (Metella), son (Quintus) and daughter (Evelina).

to take him to where Lucius lives, then as scared as a little kid when they break into Lucius' quarters ('Don't tell my dad!'), then brave when he throws the burning torch at the soldiers to escape Lucius, then magnificent back at the Caecilius' villa when he kills the Pyrovile with the bucket of water.[9] And then he's transformed at the end: the sullen youth has become a doctor himself, the image of his hero.[10] That's what I mean by turning. No one is fixed. They're all capable of change – not just once in some plot-reveal, but all the time. They become more distinct by allowing them a fuller life. Quintus goes through a lot of stuff, but there's still an essential Quintus-ness to him, which only gets richer as he turns.

In other news… Peter Capaldi agreed to play Caecilius today. Brilliant casting! And with the most handsome Quintus you could imagine: a young actor called Francois Pandolfo. Julie said, 'Does his skin-tone match the rest of the family?' Me, Phil and Andy: 'Shut up! Who cares?'

FROM: RUSSELL T DAVIES TO: BENJAMIN COOK, TUESDAY 21 AUGUST 2007 23:04:21 GMT

RE: POMPEII

It's dawning on me that 4.11 and 4.12/4.13, which once felt nice and distant, are approaching at the rate of knots. It all has to be done by Christmas! Judging by my work rate this year, that's impossible. A bed of panic is building up, which is a shame, because the past few days have seen good 4.11 thoughts. For example, just how much should this alt-world of Donna's change? It really should be a World Descending Into Anarchy. I've been thinking that we should bring back Chipo Chung (Chantho in *Utopia*), without her alien prosthetics, as one of Donna's real-world mates. Donna could find her being carted off in a truck, by soldiers, to the internment camps, because she's 'not British'. That sort of world. 'It'll be the redheads next,' says Rose to Donna. Is that going too far? For a world without the Doctor? No.

For 4.13, I keep playing 'Live and Let Die'. That's how exciting the finale should be. Not the lyrical bits; the fast bits where that song is so epic and dynamic. It sort of makes me want to stand up. Sometimes, I do. I'm listening to it right now, on repeat. It's exhausting. Noisy old song. End of 4.13, the whole place exploding, everyone running for the TARDIS – Donna, Martha, Rose, Captain Jack, Sarah Jane, Mickey, Jackie, everyone – and the Doctor shoving them through the TARDIS door. He counted them out; he counts them back in again. He saves *all of them*. Yes, we're back to that 'One of them will die' prophecy, but I'm sorry, Ben, I can't. I just can't. I can't kill any of them. There's no room for anyone to die. That's why it's worth bringing back Midshipman Frame, because he can die, and they'd be sad for, ooh, a minute, but that's all.

And Christmas 2008 is steaming up on the horizon! I should be writing that in

---

9 Lucius Petrus Dextrus is Chief Augur of the City Government. He serves the alien Pyroviles, rock creatures born out of magma.
10 At the end of 4.3, set some time after the eruption of Pompeii, Quintus is training to be a doctor.

January. That's like *tomorrow!* That could be JK Rowling, or Cybermen in Victorian London. David doesn't like the JK idea, he thinks it sounds like a spoof, so we've paused slightly, wondering whether to win him round or just abandon something that he's not going to be happy with. We've got to keep him happy. He keeps *us* happy. (You should see the rushes of him and Catherine chasing Agatha Christie in vintage cars – it's a hoot!) Plus, he might be right. So that idea has parked itself, while Julie tries to find ways to approach JK anyway. And I doubt we'd ever get JK – she doesn't *need* to do it – so Cybermen in the snow are hauling themselves back into my head. Workhouses. Starving children. At Christmas. The Little Match Girl. That's the companion, the Little Match Girl. Well, maybe a bit older and foxier. The Foxy Match Girl.

But we've production problems already: we worked out – no, Julie worked out – that we've only really time to shoot *two* Specials after Christmas 2008. We wanted three: Christmas 2009, New Year's Day 2010 (instead of Easter 2009, which was the original plan) and Easter 2010, which then would lead directly into Steven's (or whoever's) Brand New Series. Except that doesn't work, does it? The Brand New Series needs a brand new start. Clean sheet. Not following on seven days after us. So what if we only do Christmas 2009 and New Year's Day 2010? But! We're all geared up for three Specials. We don't want to drop one. I did suggest Halloween 2009, which lands on a Saturday, but then I realised that it would transmit in the middle of *The X Factor*, which is way too scary. Even if we reverted to the original plan of an Easter 2009 Special, there's no time to film it, what with David going off to do *Hamlet* next summer. I mean, if we added it onto the end of this Series Four production run, that'd only give David a week off in between *Doctor Who* and *Hamlet*. That's inhuman. After that, he won't be free until January 2009. We wouldn't be able to complete post-production in time for Easter on a Special filmed in January and February 2009.

So now – and this is mad – Julie is suggesting that we film an Easter 2009 Special in two halves: two weeks at the end of this Series Four production run, following straight on from the Christmas Special 2008 (and shooting all the FX stuff first, if we can), then picking up the rest of the story in January 2009. I think that's *insane*, but I love Julie's nerve. Really, though! I mean, cast availability and all that. That's asking for trouble. Let alone David's hair! If he filmed in January 2009, immediately after *Hamlet*, that'd mean his Hamlet would have to have Doctor-length hair, and I bet you a million quid he's going to want to look very different. But Julie keeps saying, 'We'd be ahead! Imagine being ahead! I love being ahead!' And that, Ben, is how she builds empires. It's not just money and schedules; she loves introducing *risk*.

And so it goes, round and round and round… with no idea what these stories actually are, by the way. I'd better start thinking!

Meanwhile, 4.1 is forging its way to the front of my head. But I can't think of an ending. I can think of a *story* ending, that's Donna joining up, but I can't think of a straightforward *plot* ending, the defeat-the-aliens ending. That's normally in place by now. And do I or do I not have Rose appear towards the end of 4.1? Yes, it's irresistible, but I'm worried that Rose might upstage our This Is Catherine Tate publicity. It'd be brilliant, just brilliant, to have two edits: one a false scene, where Donna hands over her car keys to any old woman, and that's the version we issue to the press and show at the launch, so no one, but no one, knows about the real, second version *until it's actually transmitted!* I love that idea.

FROM: BENJAMIN COOK TO: RUSSELL T DAVIES, TUESDAY 21 AUGUST 2007 23:23:17 GMT

RE: POMPEII
A false scene for publicity purposes? Wouldn't The All-New We Never Lie BBC consider that deceitful?

FROM: RUSSELL T DAVIES TO: BENJAMIN COOK, TUESDAY 21 AUGUST 2007 23:48:41 GMT

RE: POMPEII
Well, stories *are* deceitful. That's my answer. Having two versions of a show is expensive and ridiculously paperwork-heavy, but I think we can cope. Very tempting.

CHAPTER SEVEN

STRUCTURE & COSMETICS

In which Billie Piper's honeymoon causes problems,
Ken Barlow's death is anticipated, and Russell
contemplates a *Doctor Who* movie

FROM: RUSSELL T DAVIES TO: BENJAMIN COOK, WEDNESDAY 22 AUGUST 2007 22:07:19 GMT

TIME-CHECK

I went out for a walk this afternoon. I passed a woman and heard her say to her
husband, 'What time-check is it?' He said, 'Half-past-five.' I thought, *time-check?!*
That's a word now? Is it hyphenated? Whatever happened to 'What's the time?' But
instantly that rattled off into dialogue, in my head, as I was walking along...

                              MAN 1
        What's the time-check?

                              MAN 2
        Um... Half past five.

                              MAN 1
        Right. We'd better get going.

    Pause.

                              MAN 2
        What did you say, time-check?

                              MAN 1
        Yeah.

```
                        MAN 2
Where's that from?

                        MAN 1
Why, what's wrong with it?

                        MAN 2
Everyone else says 'time'.

                        MAN 1
Oh, do they? Well, I apologise. Is there a list of words
I can and can't use?
```

And off they go, straight into an argument! The term 'time-check' is irrelevant, it's just a hinge; it's the relationship that matters. It could be a man and a woman, any combination, but they sound like either a couple who have been going out for a few months, so the initial shine has rubbed off and now they're *really* getting to know each other, or a couple who have been together for far too many years and are now disintegrating. The former, I think. The latter would be more stark. But I like the fact that they're heading out somewhere. It's about 6.30pm, 7pm, they're putting on ties, like they're going somewhere posh. Dialogue, mood, location, all there, all vague, but at the same time precise. I might use that exchange in a script one day. I might not. But I bet I will. The opening family dialogue in *Mine All Mine* ('What colour is linen?') was overheard and stayed in my head for about 15 years before I used it.

Anyway, I thought I'd write and tell you that, because after tens of thousands of words, trying to tell you what writing is like, it struck me: *that's* what it's like. All the time, in my head. Writing!

FROM: BENJAMIN COOK TO: RUSSELL T DAVIES, WEDNESDAY 22 AUGUST 2007 22:16:30 GMT

RE: TIME-CHECK

Maybe the woman was from up north and you misheard her say, 'What's the time, *chuck*?' Ho ho. Interesting that the dialogue in your head changes, immediately, to Man 1 and Man 2, rather than Man and Woman as per the original. You're so gay.

When you're writing dialogue, do you say the lines out loud to yourself? How do you develop an ear for certain speech rhythms, dialogue patterns and accents? Could you hear Kylie's Australian twang when you were writing Astrid's lines?

FROM: RUSSELL T DAVIES TO: BENJAMIN COOK, WEDNESDAY 22 AUGUST 2007 22:32:11 GMT

RE: TIME-CHECK

I couldn't hear Kylie's Australian twang, but I could hear *Astrid* – young, innocent, inquisitive. If I tried to write Australian, I think we'd end up with cod nonsense. I think all my characters speak with the same rhythm, essentially. My rhythm. Sarah Harding, who directed the second half of *Queer as Folk* and who's very knowledgeable about music, used to say that she could sing my scripts. The loon. Some people say it's a Welsh thing. I don't know.

I do say the lines out loud, but I don't *stop* and do it. I don't finish a scene and give it a reading. You'd find me muttering away constantly, sitting here. All night. Always testing for the rhythm, to make it sound right, to find a better way of saying it. It's good to read stuff out loud. You can find all sorts of problems. The tiny details that make dialogue better. My favourite pet hate (can you have a favourite?) is the list of three adjectives: just watch a week's telly and see how often it crops up, dialogue that goes 'I felt hurt, angry, betrayed'. It's just the writer listing, showing off his so-called understanding of motive. It doesn't exist in real life. People don't talk like that. It's much more accurate, more believable, more sayable, if you make the simplest rephrasing: 'I felt angry. God, I was so hurt. You betrayed me!' Much better. Instant polish. Even then, I bet the scene would be more interesting without it. Whatever's going on, you can pretty much assume those emotions.

FROM: BENJAMIN COOK TO: RUSSELL T DAVIES, WEDNESDAY 22 AUGUST 2007 22:39:45 GMT

RE: TIME-CHECK

Would you agree, though, that every character is always talking about him- or herself? Every character has their own agenda and it's the centre of their world, especially in dialogue with other characters. Is that true?

FROM: RUSSELL T DAVIES TO: BENJAMIN COOK, WEDNESDAY 22 AUGUST 2007 23:14:21 GMT

RE: TIME-CHECK

Yes, absolutely true. Remember what we were saying about Captain Hardaker in *Voyage of the Damned*, 'full of aches and pains'? Thing is, to think about yourself all the time isn't necessarily selfish; the self is all we've got. We might touch on other people, glance off them, and sometimes, maybe once in a while, *maybe*, see deeply into them. But the other 99 per cent of the time? It's just yourself. There's no other option.

Dialogue is just two monologues clashing. That's my Big Theory. It's true in life, never mind drama! Everyone is always, *always* thinking about themselves. It's kind of impossible to do otherwise. I just hate dialogue that goes:

```
                    RUSSELL
      I went to town.


                       BEN
      Why?


                    RUSSELL
      Because I needed to see Stan.


                       BEN
      And what did he say?
```

```
                              RUSSELL
         He said you knew the truth.

                              BEN
         Yes, I do.

                              RUSSELL
         Why didn't you tell me?

                              BEN
         Because I was scared.
```

It's like they're both *listening* to each other. Rubbish! Appalling amounts of TV dialogue is like that, especially on the soaps, whereas in reality we're all waiting to say the next thing that we want to say. Truest phrase ever: 'The opposite of talking isn't listening. The opposite of talking is waiting.' Fran Lebowitz said that, and I bloody love it.

FROM: BENJAMIN COOK TO: RUSSELL T DAVIES, WEDNESDAY 22 AUGUST 2007 23:25:49 GMT

RE: TIME-CHECK

We're all talking about ourselves... and yet our instinct is to *guard* our inner selves, sometimes even from those we love. Wouldn't you have thought those two ideas are mutually exclusive?

FROM: RUSSELL T DAVIES TO: BENJAMIN COOK, WEDNESDAY 22 AUGUST 2007 23:47:32 GMT

RE: TIME-CHECK

The opposite of exclusive: they're the same thing, in a way. We think of ourselves, but reveal ourselves through what we say. I think 'reveal' is the crucial word there. We don't actually *say* what we're thinking, not deliberately, not consciously. We're revealing and guarding at the same time. You hear it, every day, in the way people say other people's names. If someone fancies someone, but hasn't said so out loud – and might not even be hugely conscious of it themselves – the way that they say that person's name just gives it away. More importantly, the number of times they say that person's name, every day. Oh, don't you just *love* people, for all their transparency and hopelessness?

That's what dialogue is: it's tapping into those tides and urges, revealing glimpses of it, though never revealing any one final truth, because there isn't any one final truth; we're many things, to many people, and a great unknown to ourselves. I love that bit where you say that we guard ourselves 'sometimes even from those we love'. I think it's *especially* from them. All the time. Or maybe I'm a cynic. But I don't think 'love' is the cure-all, the great honesty; it's the most complicated area of the lot. Hence, thousands of years of love stories. It's the centre of fiction, with no sign of exhaustion.

It really is crass to use Captain Hardaker as an example, because he's hardly the finest fictional creation ever (though I look forward to presenting the annual Hardaker Award), but he *is* doing what we're talking about. 'It's an old ship, full of aches and pains' is talking about himself both physically and – if you want to get wanky – morally. But he's not saying, 'Actually, I'm going to kill myself.' Revealing and guarding at the same time – don't we always? I don't actually imagine that Hardaker is thinking, aha, I'll talk about myself metaphorically. It's more of a mood than that.

FROM: BENJAMIN COOK TO: RUSSELL T DAVIES, THURSDAY 23 AUGUST 2007 00:04:07 GMT

RE: TIME-CHECK

Dialogue should be character-driven, but how naturalistic should it be, do you think? It depends on the show, I suppose, and *Doctor Who*'s dialogue is often heightened, but completely naturalistic dialogue would be so clotted with 'ums' and 'ers' and clichés and 'at the end of the days' and 'oh my Gods' that it'd be unbearable to read or listen to. Should dialogue in TV drama reflect day-to-day speech?

FROM: RUSSELL T DAVIES TO: BENJAMIN COOK, THURSDAY 23 AUGUST 2007 00:41:51 GMT

RE: TIME-CHECK

How you want your dialogue to sound is entirely personal. That's one of the things that defines a writer. I think the strongest writers in the land write dialogue that sounds like themselves. Paul Abbott's characters sound like Paul. Kay Mellor's sound like Kay. Alan Bennett's sound like him. Within that, they might be writing posh lords or checkout girls or mystic swamis or cruel murderers, and each of those characters would be distinct, with their own speech patterns, rhythms, habits… and yet there's a fundamental Abbott/Mellor/Bennett that creeps through.

I'd always aim for naturalism, within reason. I mean, let's not pretend, all the speeches in a script are chosen, honed, shaped, edited, so it's always going to be a faux-realism. (If only your real-life-blather could go through that process. We'd sound wonderful!) It just depends which faux you fancy and how you use it. It depends on the drama. The dialogue in *The Second Coming* was unusually stripped down for me – sparse, blunt, few jokes – because it was a cold world. *Queer as Folk* was foul, savage, funny – very gay! *Doctor Who* has much more bantering, a witty tone, because that fits the Doctor. That's how he survives. And so on. But –

I'm not answering this too well, because I don't think about it much. And yet I sit here all day trying to choose the right words, so I think about it all the time, I suppose. Hmm. I just think that dialogue has to be sayable. It has to sound real, while being highly artificial. Blimey! No one said it was easy.

On a practical level… avoid repeating words. That's the simplest advice, and yet it's what I must spend 50 per cent of my time doing. Like the word 'just'. I can use that word night and day. I just fall into it. 'I just thought I'd pop in and say hello, cos I was just thinking about you, just the other day.' Cut the 'justs'! How many months of my life have I spent cutting 'justs'?! But word repetition – and those clichés that you mentioned – can be dangerous. Make sure that every speech doesn't start with 'Well' or 'So' or 'Right'. 'Well, I think we should go to town.' 'Well, I don't.' 'Well, you would.' Easy trap to fall into. And watch out for the repetition of words across scene divides. It's really easy to end a scene with 'I hope you find him', and then you go and make a cuppa, come back and start the next scene with 'I hope you find the room comfortable'. When that runs as one, you go ouch!

The second thing I do is trim dialogue down into blocks. Discrete sentences. What I mean is, when I started writing – and was a lot more florid – I would have had the Doctor saying, 'I'm gonna go back to the TARDIS, and find the Daleks, and then I'll stop them, and then have a cup of tea.' Nowadays, I'm more likely to write, 'I'm gonna go back to the TARDIS. Find the Daleks. Stop them. And then, tea.' I spend a lot of time trimming down like that. Although, evidently not as much as I'd like to think. I remember Peter Kay phoning me from the set of *Love & Monsters* and saying, 'Did you buy a job lot of commas somewhere? It's all bloody commas! How am I supposed to learn this? Never seen so many bloody commas in my life!' (Mind you, then I read his autobiography and realised that I could have sold him some. Ha ha.) But even the commas are a way of breaking down dialogue into blocks. I wouldn't have a character say, 'I'm going to Deck 31 to find whoever's behind all this.' I'd have them say, 'I'm going to Deck 31, to find whoever's behind all this.' Better or worse? I don't know, but I can't stop myself doing it. Comma mad. But what the commas and full stops are doing is imposing a rhythm, my rhythm, on the words, deciding when they're fast, when they're slow, when they stop. That's not the quest for naturalism; that's the quest for the drama, to decide when it's hard, when it's witty, when it's throwaway, when it's stark, how a scene rises and falls and builds and declines. That's rhythm.

I do put in 'ums' and 'ers', to an extent. An 'um' or an 'er' indicates that the character is hesitant, scared, out of their depth, whatever. But do it constantly and it drives people nuts. Never make a script annoying to read. I gather 'ums' are unpopular and frowned on now, particularly in the US. I think it's seen as a bad habit. I've even seen it argued that you shouldn't start speeches with filler words like 'Right' or 'Well' or 'So', that you should let the actors add that sort of thing, to naturalise it themselves. I find that ridiculous. If no one is regulating it, that's just asking for every speech to start with 'Well'. That's why you can't leave it to the actor. They don't have an overview of the whole script and its rhythms. If an actor adds a 'Well' to the last line of a scene, they won't necessarily have realised that the first line of the next scene starts with a 'Well', particularly if they're not in that scene. Besides, those words are important. In fact, they aren't just filler. 'Right' is decisive. 'Well' is calmer. 'Well!' is flouncy. 'So' is deliberate. Every word says a lot.

I am at that stage of my career when the script editor or producer will phone me up for approval if an actor wants to swap something as tiny as an 'and' for a 'but'. This means that I'm a despot and will soon fall.

FROM: RUSSELL T DAVIES TO: BENJAMIN COOK, THURSDAY 23 AUGUST 2007 21:26:22 GMT

BILLIE

Bad news. Billie's agent phoned yesterday. Now, this is a hugely powerful man, but he called in a genuinely regretful voice. I didn't think he had a genuinely regretful voice. Billie is getting married on New Year's Eve… and wants to go on honeymoon for the whole of January! That's when we film 4.12/4.13! That's when Freema, and John, and Lis Sladen, and Euros Lyn (who's going to direct) have all been booked for. *Nooooo!!!* The whole series finale is lying in disarray. Further updates to follow…

FROM: BENJAMIN COOK TO: RUSSELL T DAVIES, THURSDAY 23 AUGUST 2007 21:39:45 GMT

RE: BILLIE

Oh no! How can you get around that one? Write her out? Change the filming dates? What are your initial thoughts? This time, surely, you're sinking your head into your hands and weeping uncontrollably? No? You *must* be!

FROM: RUSSELL T DAVIES TO: BENJAMIN COOK, THURSDAY 23 AUGUST 2007 22:29:31 GMT

RE: BILLIE

For about ten seconds, I was just sad. Really sad. Mourning for a lovely story that's gone. It'll never be seen. Not angry, though. That's a waste of time. Leads nowhere. But that deep keening feeling lasts ten seconds, and then I get on with fixing it. Immediately. Within about ten minutes last night, I'd thought, right, move the story where the Doctor's hand-in-a-jar grows another Doctor and he sends it to Rose in the parallel world to David's very last episode. Even if it means only seeing Billie on Bad Wolf Bay, we can always manage *one* day's filming with her. It wraps up a whole era nicely. And less people in 4.12/13 will make life easier for me. It's one hell of a cast list. In a way, it makes Rose being lost for ever even more poignant, because she can't even be there for the grand reunion.

Julie greeted me today with a sad 'How are you?' She thought I'd be glum, but really I'm not. I'm not just putting on a brave face. In fact, my greatest sadness is for Mickey Smith/Noel Clarke, because now there's no way to bring him back. That's a shame. But it could all change tomorrow. That's the other thing I've learnt. Like with all that Penny/Donna stuff. Keep on your toes. Julie is on red alert. If anyone can solve this, it's her. I think about the only problem we couldn't cope with is if David disappeared off to Guatemala tomorrow. But then we'd have to close down, so it wouldn't even be my problem –

Ahh, bollocks, what am I saying? I'd even find a way around that.

Funny thing is, Julie, Phil and I have all been invited to the wedding. We'd just stand there glowering. Good old Billie, though – I do love her. She's a phenomenon, and this is what dealing with phenomena is like.

FROM: BENJAMIN COOK TO: RUSSELL T DAVIES, THURSDAY 23 AUGUST 2007 22:38:14 GMT

RE: BILLIE

You say that absolutely anything can be written around. If you wanted Mickey to come back, but you can't feature Rose, well, why can't you write around that? What's stopping you?

FROM: RUSSELL T DAVIES TO: BENJAMIN COOK, THURSDAY 23 AUGUST 2007 23:29:47 GMT

RE: BILLIE

Hmm, anything can be written around... with integrity. You have to be ruthless with the logic of it. If Mickey came back, it would mean that travel between universes is possible – so where the hell is Rose? Why hasn't she come back for the Doctor? You start to think of dialogue like Mickey saying, 'We invented a universe-hopping machine, and I was the first one to try it, but it turns out it could only work once – and here I am!' Do you see, it's just getting silly? That dialogue is lame. Not one word of that is interesting or heartfelt. It's bending the rules too far. And that integrity is what makes the story good.

FROM: RUSSELL T DAVIES TO: BENJAMIN COOK, FRIDAY 24 AUGUST 2007 14:21:39 GMT

RE: BILLIE

First viewing of 4.X today. Interesting. Let's shove in the caveats first: it's an early viewing, there's much more work to be done, it's running at 78 minutes and really should be reduced to 65-ish, and first viewings are often a bit unnerving and off-putting. Every edit after that is dedicated to lifting the programme to what it should be, what it deserves to be, and we always get there. But beyond the cut-this, cut-that, tighten-the-whole-thing-up-and-give-me-more-Frame notes, I'm sitting there, as writer, wondering what the hell I've done and why I did it.

A great sense of dismay at watching the disaster movie format fight the *Doctor Who* format. Yes, the very thing that I worried about as I wrote it. Do you remember, at the end, I was really proud that I'd combined them? The funny thing is – and I learn this lesson every time, yet forget it – if a fault is fundamental, any problem-solving is only papering over the cracks. The cracks always show. Faults persist. They always do. The disaster movie fights the essential nature of the Doctor, because he becomes just Any Old Survivor – a clever one, the leader, yes, but a hapless victim of events. He's *lacking*. Now, when the plot turns and he changes ('No more!' he says), then he's in charge again and good old *Doctor Who* kicks in; next thing you know, he's outwitting Host, battling the Max-Box, saving the ship, and he's the hero. Everything feels right. But that's a good 50 minutes in.

The Edits next week will go back to papering over the cracks. The fight goes on, long after it's been shot. Maybe none of this will be too evident by the time we're finished. (It will, though. I'll see it.) But... what do I think now? If a fault is fundamental, if it's in the *concept*, you can never fix it? Not without a *complete* rewrite, which has the Doctor on board for very different reasons? In the end, I think you're left facing the fact: there's no such thing as a perfect script. But is that just giving up?

I'm skipping all the excellent stuff, too. Kylie driving a forklift truck, fighting the Max-Box, is insanely fantastic. Her death is wonderful (and what a performance – she's amazing). Lots of good laughs with Morvin and Foon. And loads of sequences, like the Strut, that won't truly work until the FX are in place. And pace is the key – at the moment, it's leisurely, so you've time to dwell on the faults. Phil came up with a wonderful phrase: 'Edit it like you're ashamed of it.' We were hooting at that, but he's right. Don't dwell, don't luxuriate, don't show off, don't rely on FX, or Kylie or David. Be blunt, be fast, be ruthless. We had the same problem with *Tooth and Claw*: it ran at 55 minutes, and we made them cut it down, without losing a single line or scene, to 45 minutes, just by taking out every pause, every pan, every relax, until it moved like lightning. And it was magnificent. So we'll get there.

FROM: BENJAMIN COOK TO: RUSSELL T DAVIES, SATURDAY 25 AUGUST 2007 22:49:14 GMT

RE: BILLIE

I interviewed Catherine yesterday, on location for the Ood episode, at Twin Peaks Hangar (honestly, that's what it's called) at RAF St Athan, in the Vale of Glamorgan. There were soldiers with guns on the gate. We weren't allowed to use our mobile phones inside or we'd be shot at. 'I genuinely couldn't believe they'd asked me,' she said about being asked to come back as Donna. 'Even now, I just can't believe it.' Apparently, she didn't have to think twice about signing up for Series Four: 'It was a bit of a no-brainer for me, really.' Bless her.

And then – blimey – I spent this morning in a London photo studio with Kylie Minogue, posing and pouting with a Dalek (her, not me) for her exclusive *DWM* cover shoot. 'I've had to gracefully accept second billing today,' she said of the Dalek, adding: 'Well, at least I'm younger!' She was full of praise for you and Julie, too. Apparently, she fell in love with the two of you after that first meeting in London. It must have been your Muppet duet, Russell. (She said it was your 'humour, talent and passion for the show', but I still reckon it's the duet.) What a couple of days! Oh, and I had my photo taken with Kylie. It was obligatory.

How's your day been? Have you started 4.1 yet? I'm surprised at your latest assessment of *Voyage of the Damned*. 'Any problem-solving is only papering over the cracks.' Well, isn't that true of the storytelling process full stop? If you're inventing something artificial, something false, and yet you're wanting to convince people that's it's real so that they can suspend their disbelief sufficiently, surely you're 'papering over the cracks' from the moment that you start writing?

FROM: RUSSELL T DAVIES TO: BENJAMIN COOK, SATURDAY 25 AUGUST 2007 23:26:25 GMT

RE: BILLIE

I like your version of papering over the cracks. I'm going to cling to that. Maybe the cracks are more evident with 4.X because it's so clearly a hybrid. You're right, most stories require the writer to wallpaper like crazy, especially those stories that demand so many suspensions of disbelief. Often the wallpapering is sleight of hand – like in *Tooth and Claw*, taking the incredible coincidences of Queen Victoria, the Koh-I-Noor, and a werewolf all being in the same place, at the same time, and fighting hard to make that *essential*, rather than just an accident. I am a wallpaperer. Yes, that's what I am.

I'm so glad you interviewed Catherine. That Ood stuff is looking wonderful, isn't it? A quarry in the snow! And I'm loving the thought of Kylie's photo shoot. My God, if that isn't the best-selling *DWM* ever, I don't know what is… though I'd buy a few copies more if it were Midshipman Frame posing with a Dalek.

I'm making a promise, here and now, to start 4.1 on Monday night. Hold me to it! Mind you, I went and saw *The Simpsons Movie* this afternoon (not bad, not brilliant), and thank God I dropped that original 4.1 plot, the inverted-bowl-over-the-Estate plot, because that's what happens to Springfield!

FROM: BENJAMIN COOK TO: RUSSELL T DAVIES, MONDAY 27 AUGUST 2007 20:31:09 GMT

RE: BILLIE

So. Have you started yet?

FROM: RUSSELL T DAVIES TO: BENJAMIN COOK, WEDNESDAY 29 AUGUST 2007 23:54:48 GMT

RE: BILLIE

No, I haven't started. Problems with *Torchwood* have sort of got in the way. The future of the show's looking a bit scary. Chris Chibnall isn't doing a third series – and I don't blame him, he's brilliant, he should fly free! – but I don't know how we'd make it without him. He's just delivered 2.12. Best. *Torchwood*. Ever. I swear, it's wonderful. And he puts in the hours, which few do. So, Julie has a series with no lead writer. That puts me in a tricky position, because I love Julie, and I did invent the bloody show, so how can I *not* help? This is really beginning to bug me. I lay in bed last night, thinking, I'll never be rid of this bloody place. What do I do? Oh, there are worse problems to have.

Even while I'm scared and terrified, and berating myself for not having started 4.1, my head is filling up with all sorts of 4.1 scenes. Have I told you the bit where the Doctor admits that he wants a travelling companion, but with no strings, no Martha-fancying stuff, and he sighs, 'I just want a mate'…? And Donna says, horrified, 'You want *to mate?*' He says, 'No, I said *a mate!*' Ha ha. Dialogue like that keeps me going. That won't be said until right at the end, but it's something to look forward to.

Top: The Three Who Rule! L–R: Russell T Davies (Head Writer and Executive Producer), Phil Collinson (Producer) and Julie Gardner (Executive Producer).

Right: July 2004, and the first series of the revived *Doctor Who* begins shooting in Vauxhall, London...

Above: ... with Christopher Eccleston as the Ninth Doctor and Billie Piper as his companion Rose Tyler.

Above: David Tennant makes his entrance proper as the Tenth Doctor in the 2005 Christmas Special *The Christmas Invasion*.

Left: David in a quarry on Barry Island during the summer shooting of *The Christmas Invasion*.

Below: The first battle between David's Doctor and John Simm's Master took place during the Series Three finale.

Top: The Doctor first encountered Donna Noble (Catherine Tate) in the 2006 Christmas Special, *The Runaway Bride*.

Above left: Elisabeth Sladen returned as legendary companion Sarah Jane Smith both in *Doctor Who* and in her own spin-off series for CBBC.

Above right: Freema Agyeman, who played Martha Jones in Series Three and Four, with Russell.

Left: David Tennant and Kylie Minogue at the read-through for 2007 Christmas Special *Voyage of the Damned*.

Top: Kylie explores the TARDIS set.

Above left: A Dalek meets Kylie Minogue – and Benjamin Cook – during a *Doctor Who Magazine* cover shoot.

Above right: Russell T Davies, Debbie Chazen (Foon) and Kylie Minogue during filming of *Voyage of the Damned*.

Left: David Tennant in festive mood!

Above: 2010 showrunner Steven Moffat on set for the 2007 *Children in Need* mini-episode *Time Crash*, along with Fifth Doctor Peter Davison.

Left: Russell Tovey as Alonso Frame.

Below: The Adipose from *Partners in Crime* in all their CGI glory!

This page: Fun in Rome for the filming of *The Fires of Pompeii*.

Top: The cast and crew enjoy the Italian nightlife. L–R: David Tennant, Colin Teague, Steve Smith, Benjamin Cook, Phil Collinson, Tracie Simpson, an Italian waitress (!), Sarah Davies, Andy Newbery, Ernie Vincze and Catherine Tate.

Above left: Producer Phil Collinson leaps athletically onto a table because of a deadly, slavering Roman rat! Eeeek!

Above right: David Tennant samples the local cuisine.

Right: The night shoot for *The Fires of Pompeii* at Rome's legendary Cinecittà Studios.

Above: Davros (Julian Bleach) and the Daleks return for the 2008 season finale.

Right: Cast and crew gather on the set of *Journey's End*.

Below left: Together at last – Rose and Doctor #2 at Bad Wolf Bay.

Below right: Scaremongering from the newspapers as David Tennant injures his back.

Overleaf: David Tennant, Russell T Davies and John Simm during the cover shoot for *The Writer's Tale: The Final Chapter.*

FROM: RUSSELL T DAVIES TO: BENJAMIN COOK, FRIDAY 31 AUGUST 2007 01:44:09 GMT

4.1

Look! I've started! Penny Carter lives![1] She's in there! And destined to die horribly, I suspect. A bit like she could have been the companion, but gets murdered instead. I like that.

Weird, actually, because I'd promised myself I'd start at 8pm, and then, at 7.55pm, I was clicking through the channels, desperate to find anything that I could watch so that I could put it off until, oh, 10pm or so... and there on BBC Three was the final scene of *The Runaway Bride*. Donna in the snow. Like a sign! At the end, she turns away, walks back into her house, and I went to the computer and started typing.

It feels... okay, at the moment. Only okay. This opening sequence is funny, I hope, but it's been in my head for weeks now (the whole shtick of the Doctor and Donna crossing paths, but not meeting), so I just don't find it so funny any more. It stopped amusing me way back. So is it still funny? I just don't know. Also, I'm still a good few pages off seeing a monster. That feels bad. I could have a pre-titles sequence of someone being horribly murdered by an Adipose, but the pre-titles murder is wearing a bit thin now, and I loved the energy of starting Series Three with no pre-titles. Last year's opener went straight from the continuity announcer into the titles into Martha, and that had a real welcome-back energy to it.

Still, thank God I've begun – this script that we've been talking about since February!

FROM: BENJAMIN COOK TO: RUSSELL T DAVIES, FRIDAY 31 AUGUST 2007 13:25:58 GMT

RE: 4.1

YOU'VE STARTED! I want to ask you about beginnings. I'm wondering about when to start a narrative. At what point should the story begin? Is the answer, simply, just as it's about to get interesting? Backstory can be filled in later, right?

FROM: RUSSELL T DAVIES TO: BENJAMIN COOK, FRIDAY 31 AUGUST 2007 21:23:02 GMT

RE: 4.1

The job of a first scene is to make you watch, and to keep you watching. My friend Patrea, a lovely writer, argues the opposite: she says that first scenes are bums-on-seats time, that they should give you time to come in from the kitchen and settle down. Nothing too vital. Mind you, she said that to me 15 years ago. I wonder if she's changed her mind now that TV is faster and louder and there's much more choice.

If the first scene grabs you, it shouldn't do so by lying or creating a false premise. Any old script could start with an explosion, but the explosion has to be integral. The real

---

1 In 4.1, Penny Carter is the name of a journalist, working as science correspondent for *The Observer*, who's investigating Adipose Industries, a London-based company, run by Miss Rattigan (renamed Miss Foster in later drafts), which sells 'miracle' diet pills.

reason that 4.1 can't open with a murder by an Adipose is that I'm not yet convinced they *do* murder. Well, they will do later on, when they're ordered to, but their first appearance will be more weird and unnerving than murderous. Instead, the opening of 4.1 is setting out the stall for the whole episode: the Doctor and Donna meeting again. That's the story. The aliens are just the plot that gets in the way. The cutting between the Doctor and Donna is played as a sort of cute conceit, but that's dressing up on the surface; underneath that, it's absolutely fundamental.

In *Queer as Folk*, the meeting of key characters marks the start of the story, I suppose – Stuart and Nathan, with the third part of that eternal threesome, Vince, watching them. Of course, if you mean *literal* start, then that's Vince talking direct to camera. Unusual technique. I was experimenting – and I never intended that to go past Episode 1. I did that because… well, I was younger, and that's when you try out the tricks. You learn to lose them, I think, as you go on. You'd think that narrative tricks were the domain of the experienced scriptwriter, but I tend to find that they're used by the newcomer, thrilled with all these brand new toys, mastering them. As you get older, you learn to trust the story a bit more, just tell it. Maybe. But since the drama was throwing you head first into The Gay Scene, I wanted those pieces to camera so that you'd connect with those boys and get the humour of the piece –

Ah, but crucially, although the bits to camera came first, they existed for the ending. It was impossible to get a proper cliffhanger out of Episode 1's story. Stuart and Vince drop Nathan off at school. It's hard to imagine that they'd ever see him again, because he's just a kid. It could have looked like the end of the story, so the pieces to camera bookending the episode allowed me to drop in Nathan, at the end, saying (of Stuart), 'Six months later, he was *begging* me to stay.' And that worked. People were intrigued. In that instance, the ending of Episode 1 decided the start.

In fact, there's a second start to Episode 1: after Vince's piece direct to camera, we cut to Stuart, Vince and Phil hitting the streets, copping off, funny dialogue, something I very much wanted to show.[2] All bloody gay dramas have scenes inside clubs – we had surprisingly few – and so I wanted to show something new, that extraordinary street life when the clubs shut (in the days when clubs did shut), when the streets would come alive with a whole different sort of gay life. I suppose that's an anthropological choice, not a story choice – except the anthropology is laying out the whole style and intent of the show, and it's that Walking The Gay Streets that leads Stuart to Nathan. Plus, it looks good. Then there's start number three: Nathan on Canal Street, asking Bernie what's the best place to go, and Bernie's foulmouthed reaction.[3] That was absolutely laying out my other agenda: in contrast to Vince's funny piece to camera, you get a virtuoso destruction of the entire gay scene from a bitter old man. Not like me at all, ha ha! Finally, start number four (*four!*): Stuart spotting Nathan, Vince seeing this…

---

2 Phil Delaney (played by Jason Merrells), friend of Stuart and Vince.
3 Bernard Thomas (played by Andy Devine), a cynical veteran of the gay scene, in *Queer as Folk* and *Queer as Folk 2*.

and off we go for eight weeks!

It's funny, that list, because it makes you ask – so what *is* the start? Where does the story start? It doesn't have to be the first scene. But should it be? I can imagine a *Queer as Folk* that begins with that fourth start, with Stuart strolling past Nathan, stopping, going back. I could make that work, although I'd worry that I wasn't invested in any of the characters. So, starting where the story starts isn't as obvious as it sounds. A lot of the story revolves around Stuart and Nathan, but also the story of *Queer as Folk* is the story of that whole world, so that's what I laid out first.

Oh! I was just reading back this e-mail, and I'd completely forgotten that there *was* a different start. Long since lost. *Queer as Folk* Episode 1, Draft One, started with Nathan and Donna (I've used the name Donna before – I didn't even realise that until now) in an ordinary teenage party – drink, snogging, vomit, etc – and Nathan watching while everyone around him cops off, but he has to stay quiet and closeted.[4] The turning point comes when he sees someone's 12-year-old brother snogging a girl in the alley outside – like, 12-year-olds are getting some and he isn't! Nathan makes his mind up on the spot, goes to the room where everyone has dumped their coats, ransacks them until he finds £20, and just walks out – abandoning poor Donna – and gets the bus to Canal Street. (My favourite bit in that is the stealing the money. There was always a danger that Nathan would be the sweet, innocent victim of *Queer as Folk*, but actually he was fabulously selfish and ruthless, and the theft set that up, right from the start.) I think, in that version, he'd come out to Donna already, so he got on the bus saying where he was going in a scene that then must have become, in the transmitted version, Episode 2's 'I'm *doing* it! I'm really doing it!' scene. That Draft One opening was a good start. It was great. But Nicola Shindler said, quite rightly, 'Cut it. Get on with it.' All the scene is doing is saying that Nathan is young, closeted, a virgin. But when you see him sitting on his own, on Canal Street, when he approaches Bernie and is spotted by Stuart... well, Nathan looks young, closeted, a virgin, so there's no need for any establishers. You can't say that dropped opening scene was *wrong* exactly, but the main imperative was: get on with the story.

Similarly, *The Second Coming* had to start before Steve's revelation... though we did always wonder, even sitting in the Edit, whether it would have been better to start with a bedraggled man, a stranger, running over the moors, gasping, panting, collapsing in front of a car and proclaiming that he's the Son of God. That was tempting. I think the big-screen version would start there, but again, on TV, I wanted a bit of backstory, a bit of real life, and the kiss from Judith, which is *really* when Steve's life changes. Then again, when *The Second Coming* was adapted for HBO (they commissioned a trial script for a potential series, never made), they had a good 30 minutes of backstory at the top, the revelation came right towards the end of the first episode, and it worked.

---

4 Donna Clarke (played by Carla Henry), Nathan's best friend.

In fact, I did wonder if it was better. It was a very good adaptation.

And new *Doctor Who*... well, it had to start with Rose Tyler. Except it didn't, actually. It started in outer space, zooming in on her flat. We needed that. It gave her whole world an outer-space context, with the promise of weird things to come. I drilled into the production team that the whole montage of Rose's life had to last only two minutes (we failed with the two minutes, I think, but we came close) before things turned sinister, with shop window dummies coming to life in the basement. That's when the world of *Doctor Who* arrived. That was the real start.

In the end, I think what I'm saying is, start with the story *and its context*. Its surrounding world. But that's just me. Maybe I worry about context too much.

In other news... we spent all day hammering 4.X into place. I like it much more now. We took out all the flab and the pauses, so it's ten minutes shorter now – 71 minutes – and much better. Also, right now, David and Julie are being police-escorted down the motorway to get to the Blackpool Illuminations! David is switching on the lights. The traffic was so bad that they've got outriders clearing the way. I wish I could have been there. Meanwhile, I texted Russell Tovey, to tell him how good 4.X was, and he replied: 'I'm in Ibiza with my boyfriend.' I'm in Cardiff. Life is a bitch.

FROM: RUSSELL T DAVIES TO: BENJAMIN COOK, SATURDAY 1 SEPTEMBER 2007 02:39:37 GMT

RE: 4.1

That's enough work for tonight. I'm too tired. The monster is about to appear, and then the action starts, but that needs a lot of energy to write. Monster on Page 13! That's late. Bollocks. I'll try to trim it down. There's a lot of adult chat so far, which doesn't feel very *Doctor Who*-ey at all. It's more like a detective yarn. Still, that's the story. Follow the story. But I'm worried that it's a bit dull for kids. Mind you, the monster is revolting, so that'll make up for it.

I needed a gizmo inside every customer's house, to activate the Adipose. I couldn't think what it could be. That's why I stopped last night, because I was stuck. I spent all day trying to invent something. Sitting in the 4.X Edit, just thinking, what activates the Adipose? What gizmo? Originally, I'd thought of mobile phone signals – something about banning digital signals from Adipose HQ, because they needed one, clear signal to activate all the Adipose at once. But that's rubbish, isn't it? Like other digital signals would interfere! Like a big, modern building with computers and sales floors would be digital-free! But I had no better idea. I delayed writing tonight until 10pm – still no idea, but I sat down to write anyway. The moment I started writing, I just thought, oh, it's a free gift! It's a pendant. You always get free gifts with these mail-order things.

Right, to bed! I must write loads tomorrow, but it's Cardiff Mardi Gras. I'm the patron, so I've got to go. Charlotte Church is the other patron, but she's too pregnant.

FROM: RUSSELL T DAVIES TO: BENJAMIN COOK, SATURDAY 1 SEPTEMBER 2007 16:06:48 GMT

RE: 4.1

Here's this afternoon's work. This is revolting! The Adipose are disgusting. For the first time ever on this show, I'm typing something wondering what Editorial Policy will make of it. In fact, I went back through it and took out most of Stacy's pain.[5] Originally, I had her writhing and suffering and stuff, and it was too horrible to watch.

Now I must go and address the gays at Cardiff Mardi Gras. I'll come back and continue tonight.

FROM: BENJAMIN COOK TO: RUSSELL T DAVIES, SATURDAY 1 SEPTEMBER 2007 16:32:07 GMT

RE: 4.1

Browsing the BBC Writersroom website the other day, I found some guidelines – on Situation Comedy, but I wonder whether the same rules apply to Drama – that state:

> *It is useful to think of organising a story in three acts. The first act [...] sets up the major story of the episode, and introduces the major sub-plot. The final act [...] resolves both main plot and sub-plot. The middle act [...] develops the narrative but, around halfway through the script, pushes things off into an unexpected direction.*

Do you agree? Is there a formula for determining what happens when? Do all self-contained stories follow a three-act structure? I'm trying to think of exceptions, but it's difficult, because three-act structure is, in effect, Beginning, Middle and End. All stories have that, don't they? (But not necessarily in that order?) I ask because the end of Scene 43 in your latest instalment... well, that's the end of Act One, isn't it?[6] It's an advert break, if the BBC were a commercial station. I'm not saying that you thought, right, this is the end of Act One. But perhaps an experienced scriptwriter organises his story in such a way without even thinking?

FROM: RUSSELL T DAVIES TO: BENJAMIN COOK, SATURDAY 1 SEPTEMBER 2007 22:41:28 GMT

RE: 4.1

That's funny, I just opened the script again for the first time in hours, and that bit you mention – the Doctor and Donna in the street, alone – is on Page 20, exactly a third of the way through a 60-page-ish script! It *is* the end of Act One! I hadn't realised. Oh, that's weird. I wonder if I like knowing that.

The language of scripts has now become so formalised, it's losing its mystique (and that's good – there shouldn't be mystique), but along with that comes all the deconstruction, and then the textbooks, the experts, the catchphrases. I've never read

---

5 Investigating Adipose Industries, Donna visits one of their customers, Stacy, at home. However, Donna activates an Adipose pendant, inadvertently, causing Stacy's body to divide into several Adipose creatures, killing her outright. The Adipose escape.
6 The Doctor and Donna are, separately, pursuing the escaped Adipose – but lose them. The final image of Scene 43 is a high shot, from above the houses, of Donna standing in the middle of Stacy's street, and parallel to her, in the next street along, the Doctor standing in the middle of the road, each unaware of the other being there. Then Donna walks off one way, the Doctor the other, into the night...

any of those how-to-write books. They scare me. I was once bought a copy of Robert McKee's stuff. I opened it at a stray paragraph, flinched at what I read, and closed it. I've never opened it again. But not because I disagreed with it. Rather, the paragraph that I read was so accurate that it sort of shocked me. I thought, I don't want to know! I'd rather think about that stuff myself than be taught it. I don't want some tutor's voice intruding into my head when I'm trying to write. I've enough voices already, thank you.

And here I am, talking about how to write. So sue me.

This script language wasn't really around when I was starting out, certainly not in TV, so I'm not versed in it. It's not how I think about scripts. I don't think, Act One, Act Two, Act Three. It's just not wired into my head. (But I'm 44. If I were 18, maybe I'd be rattling off Third-Act-B-Plot-Denouement theories like a good 'un.) I do think about shape and rhythm, though, and the direction and velocity of a script – and, crucially, I do think of Beginning, Middle and End. As you said, that's the same thing as Act One, Act Two, Act Three, but in a different language. Every story ever told has a Beginning, a Middle and an End. It's fundamental. But this is where I'm wary of a formula, because I don't think of the Beginning, *then* the Middle, *then* the End. They're all connected, they're all the same thing, each dictates what the other is. It's back to that big soup of Maybe in my head. Soup is shapeless.

Julie and I argue about this. When she reads 4.1, she'll say what you said: the Doctor and Donna in the street, walking off into the night, in opposite directions, that's the end of Act One. And I suppose you're both right. There's a clear break, we shift location, we shift mood. But *I* never think of it like that. I just know that the story has to pause there. It has to earth itself and get a bit more real and heartfelt. That's when Donna will go and visit her dad on the hillside (we're inviting back Howard Attfield, who played Geoff Noble in *The Runaway Bride* – along with Jacqueline King, who played Donna's mum, Sylvia), where he sits with his telescope. After that, Donna goes back to Adipose Industries. Whatever her dad says on that hillside has consequences, pushes Donna onwards. Every scene should advance the story, even if the advance is tiny. (People often mistake this for 'every scene should *change* the story', so you get labyrinthine scripts full of plot twists and sudden shocks and reveals, which is the path to nonsense.) The scene must change Donna's mind – so she goes to work, meets the Doctor, and then it's a hell-for-leather race to the finishing line. But I don't sit with diagrams or cards or a sheet of A4, working that out. I just feel it. Maybe it's inbuilt. Maybe I'm more disciplined than I realise. Maybe that's why I run away from a single Robert McKee paragraph, because I like the arrogance of imagining that I've worked it all out for myself... when, in fact, it's commonplace.

I worry a lot about that formal structure language, because it's the one thing that the inexperienced cling to. A learnt language. Like a set of crutches. Meetings throughout the industry now consist of script editors and producers sitting there saying, 'Where's the Second-Act Reversal?' Idiots. Really, they should be saying, 'Who is this man? Why is he scared? Does his wife really love him? Can he really kill her?' They talk about the shape, not the essence, obscuring valid discussion of the actual story – and story is far more important. In fairness, as I've said from the start, it's hard to talk about actual writing – the ideas, the scariness, the exhilaration – so I shouldn't be surprised if the formal language is a substitute, but I really do start to react violently when the substitute begins to take control…

It's easy to mock something that a lot of writers find useful, but those BBC guidelines that you quoted say 'halfway through the script, [the narrative] pushes things off into an unexpected direction.' Really? Must it? Things like that start to become rules, not suggestions. But *Goldilocks and the Three Bears* doesn't do that. (And I'm not using a fairytale lightly; that's a classic story that will outlast us all.) The bit where Goldilocks eats the bears' food and tries out their beds and goes to sleep (the 'middle act') doesn't surprise us; it's clearly setting us up for a 'final act' in which the three bears return home. And we bloody love it, because we just know what's going to happen. Equally, who's to say that you can't spin off in an unexpected direction a few minutes into the 'first act'? That's what great, modern films do, like the Charlie Kaufman stuff, like *Being John Malkovich* or *Eternal Sunshine of the Spotless Mind*. (I'm sure someone could draw up a list showing how those stories do, in fact, conform to absolute rules, but to hell with 'em. I'm not listening.) If you're a writer, don't fret away the hours worrying about this structure stuff. All the joy and fear and fun and despair is in the writing, not in the flowchart.

P.S. Cardiff Mardi Gras was barmy. I ended up on stage with Lisa from *Big Brother 4* and Faye from Steps.[7] Oh, and a Dalek. Then I got mobbed outside the park. One person, then five, then ten, then 20, and they were all drunk, and I was getting pushed onto the road and grabbed by short drunk Welsh men. Ever so slightly scary. Imagine being David Tennant!

FROM: BENJAMIN COOK TO: RUSSELL T DAVIES, SATURDAY 1 SEPTEMBER 2007 23:21:51 GMT

RE: 4.1

You met Lisa from *Big Brother 4*?! OH! MY! GOD! So jealous!

End irony.

A question: how do you think the structure of a story written for TV differs from that of, say, a movie? The shape must vary depending on the length of the story being told, even within TV formats? Is it a 25-minutes-a-day serial drama, a 13-week run of 45-minute episodes, a 60-minute Christmas special, or two 90-minute episodes shown over a bank holiday weekend, probably starring Robson Green as an ordinary man with a mildly interesting job, who's pushed to the limit when his child, wife or girlfriend is murdered, kidnapped or involved in a car crash? But does the narrative

---

7 Lisa Jeynes was a contestant in the fourth series of Channel Four game show *Big Brother*; Faye Tozer is a former member of pop group Steps (1997-2001).

structure of television drama, regardless of length, stand distinct from other storytelling mediums? If you're watching a movie, the chances are that you're sat in a cinema or you've purchased a DVD or… well, you're less likely to walk out or turn off. This must make a difference.

Also, what is it that attracts you, Russell, to telling stories on television as opposed to writing a novel or film script or radio play?

FROM: RUSSELL T DAVIES TO: BENJAMIN COOK, SUNDAY 2 SEPTEMBER 2007 03:52:10 GMT

RE: 4.1

Films are a whole different world. I'm often asked to write films, and it scares me a lot, because it's a whole new regime. That's why I *will* write one eventually; scary and new is good. I was thinking today about a *Doctor Who* movie, should it ever happen, because suddenly it occurred to me that something that we take for granted about the Doctor becomes a huge selling point in a movie: the fact that he doesn't use weapons. That's just a given on TV (well, bar the odd moment where he has to blow everyone up!), but in the cinema, a cinema full of action heroes with Uzis and blades and bullwhips, the Doctor becomes a truly extraordinary figure. You'd actually centrepiece that, rather than assume it. There's something of some sort of Film Theory at work in there; that movies have more focus, less sprawl, more of a centre; a simple characteristic can become a movie's entire purpose.

This whole formality about structure in storytelling has really evolved from the movies, and sometimes, I suspect, it just doesn't fit television. Television can ramble, and pause, and deviate, and accelerate. It really is a different art form. With the soap opera, we've a brand new form, which is still evolving. We've had 47 years of Ken Barlow's life.[8] *Forty-seven years!* Like it or not, no fictional character has ever existed in such everyday detail. Not ever. Brand new form of fiction! And utterly shapeless – a couple of dozen different production teams, with different agendas, over all those years, with no overall plan – and yet time is going to impose on Ken Barlow a Beginning, a Middle and an End, as we move from his youth, through his adult life, to his death one day. Fascinating, isn't it? Structure imposes itself, just through the passage of time. There has never been a fictional form like the soap opera before. It's hugely underrated and unconsidered.

As for whether structure differs depending on the length of the story – well, again, every script is different, and every show is different. That's another reason for my distrust of blanket rules. Look at the rambling shape of *The Royle Family* or *Early Doors* – idiosyncratic, shambling, eccentric and genius. I think standard sitcom rules would decree that those shows shouldn't exist. At the opposite end of the scale, there's Steven Moffat's *Coupling*, which is plotted as tight as a drum, with the precision of a Swiss watch. All different. Again, though, they all have some sort of Beginning, Middle and

8 Ken Barlow (played by William Roache) is the only surviving character from the first episode of *Coronation Street* in 1960.

End. Every story does, just in the telling of it.

The worst thing that happens these days is that channels and commissioners think that a shape is flexible. They take a two-hour drama and split it into two one-hours. That's a profoundly different shape. It happened with *Casanova*. That was written as two 90-minute episodes for ITV, but when it shifted to the BBC, who don't really have 90-minute slots, it became three 60-minute episodes. I rewrote it to a certain extent, but there wasn't time to rewrite from scratch, so the 90-minute shape remained inbuilt – and the finished drama staggered a bit as a result. (It's still two 90-minute episodes on the DVD, for boring overseas-licensing reasons, which *almost* restores it.) Very often, shows are written, or at least conceived in detail, or even completely shot, but then a new duration or slot is imposed – and it really can ruin something. That script has been through a writer's head, he's forged his way through his own personal Beginning, Middle and End, and then the whole thing is fractured and pasted back together. Terrible.

>>what is it that attracts you, Russell, to telling stories on television as opposed to writing a novel or film script or radio play?<<

I watch TV. I love TV. If there's a big movie on TV tonight, I'm still much more likely to be hopping my way between *The X Factor*, *Casualty* and *Smallville*. TV is my first choice. Always. Therefore, I *think* TV. When I think of *More Gay Men*, I don't think of a one-off story; I think of a six-part TV series, immediately. That's instinctive. I like looking at new televisual shapes, too. I'd love to write a drama in 52 episodes. Once a week, half an hour, on BBC Three or Four, just the simple story of a man and his life, so you can see how character and story develop over a whole year. That idea sprang out of the conversations we're having here. (No, you can't have ten per cent!) I'd call it *365*. Or maybe *Happy Birthday*, if you started and ended on the man's birthday. I like that, because I think a lot of telly still apes film, and not enough says, look, here's a sprawling, constant, available-to-all art form that doesn't often take advantage of its uniqueness. A story can last a year. Literally. I find that exhilarating – and knackering, because I'd have to write them all, God help me. Imagine having to write a half-hour script every week! I'm interested in what would happen to *me*.

Anyway, here's a bit more of 4.1. Nice last scene. Sentimental. But it's meant to be. It's funny, you defining that street scene as the 'end of Act One', because then I thought of the next scene as the 'start of Act Two' – and wrote it accordingly! This e-mail correspondence is having a direct effect on the actual script. Is that weird? I think it's good. And now it means that posters on Outpost Gallifrey will be allowed to blame *you* for the downfall of western civilisation, too!

44. INT. NOBLES' HOUSE - NIGHT

DONNA comes in, still shaken. A pause. She gathers herself, exhausted, then...

Real life slams back in! Mum, SYLVIA, in the kitchen -

> SYLVIA
> And what time's this?

> DONNA
> How old am I?!

> SYLVIA
> Not old enough to use a phone!

                                                  CUT TO:

45. INT. TARDIS - NIGHT

THE DOCTOR hurries in, goes to the console, fast, starts
pressing buttons, preparing a scan. Then, carefully, he gets
out, dangling on its chain…

The GOLD ADIPOSE CAPSULE.

                                                  CUT TO:

46. INT. NOBLES' HOUSE - NIGHT

SLOW TRACK IN ON DONNA, just sitting there, as SYLVIA busies
herself all around her, passing to and fro.

> SYLVIA
> …I thought you were only moving back for a couple of
> weeks, but look at you! You're never gonna find a flat
> while you're on the dole! I mean, it's not the 1980s, no
> one's unemployed these days. Except you! How long did
> that job with Health and Safety last, two days? Then you
> walk out! 'I have other plans.' Well, I've not seen 'em!
> And it's no good sitting there dreaming, no one's gonna
> come along with a magic wand and make your life all
> better -

> DONNA
> Where's Dad?

> SYLVIA
> Where d'you think he is? Up the hill! Where he always
> is!

                                                  CUT TO:

47. EXT. HILLSIDE - NIGHT

DONNA trudging up a lonely hillside.

FX: beyond her, the lights of London, glittering.

But she's not here for the view. There's her dad, GEOFF,
sitting on a little camping chair, with a telescope - nothing

too expensive, the amateur astronomer. All nice and quiet; she
loves her dad.

> GEOFF
> Aye aye. Here comes trouble.

> DONNA
> Permission to board ship, sir.

> GEOFF
> Was she nagging you?

> DONNA
> Big time. Brought you a thermos. And a Mars Bar.
> Seen anything?

> GEOFF
> I've got Venus, with an apparent magnitude of minus 3.5.
> At least, that's what it says in my book. Come and see.
> There you go…

She puts her eye to the telescope.

(FX?) Her POV through TELESCOPE. Venus just a dot.

> GEOFF (CONT'D)
> The only planet in the solar system named after a woman.

> DONNA
> Good for her.

Donna leaves the telescope, looks up into the night sky.

> DONNA (CONT'D)
> Imagine if you could go out there.

> GEOFF
> We will. One day. Bit late for me, I suppose. But a
> hundred years' time, there's gonna be people like you
> and me, striding out amongst the stars.

> DONNA
> Don't suppose you've seen a little blue box?

> GEOFF
> Is that slang for something?

And she sits on the grass, next to him.

> DONNA
> No, I mean it… If you ever see a little blue box, flying
> up there in the sky… You shout for me, Dad. Oh, you just
> shout.

                    GEOFF
                (smiles, kind)
    I don't understand half the things you say, these days.

                    DONNA
        Nor me.

    Pause.

                    GEOFF
        Fair dos. You've had a funny old time of it, lately.

                    DONNA
        You can talk.

                    GEOFF
        Oh, I'm on the mend. But you had poor old Lance, bless
        him.[9] That mad old Christmas.

                    DONNA
        S'not the half of it. You wouldn't believe the things
        I've seen.

                    GEOFF
        Then tell me.

                    DONNA
        Just tonight, I was…
                (pause)
        Doesn't matter. Sometimes I think I'm going mad.

                    GEOFF
        Well, you're not yourself, I'll give you that. I dunno.
        You just seem to be drifting, sweetheart.

                    DONNA
        I'm not drifting. I'm waiting.

                    GEOFF
        What for?

                    DONNA
        The right man.

                    GEOFF
        Oh, it's always a man.

    HIGH SHOT, slowly pulling out, Donna & Dad looking up.

                    DONNA
        No, I don't mean like that. But he's out there

----

9 Donna's fiancé, Lance Bennett (played by Don Gilet), turned out to be working for the Empress of the Racnoss, who later murdered him.

```
          somewhere… And I mean for real, he exists, I've met
          him. And I just let him fly away. But I'm gonna meet him
          again, Dad. One day. If I have to wait a hundred years.
          I'll find him.

                                                              CUT TO:


     48. INT. TARDIS - NIGHT

     CU on THE DOCTOR with glasses & attachments like in 3.12,
     studying the opened CAPSULE, tiny wires trailing out.

                              THE DOCTOR
               Fascinating. Seems to be a bio-digital relay specifically
               for…

     Looks up, looks round, aware that he's talking to himself.

     WIDEST SHOT POSSIBLE of the Tardis. The ancient, slow creak of
     the vast, empty space.

     The Doctor alone.
```

It is an absolute nightmare explaining what Donna has been up to since *The Runaway Bride*. What did she tell everyone happened to Lance? I have a version worked out (London was attacked by the Empress' Webstar, so Donna would have said that he died because of that), but it's a five-page speech – no, worse, it's a fake speech, because she would have had that out with her parents long ago – and I just don't want to stop for that amount of exposition. No wonder the Doctor never went in for that Christmas dinner with her folks!

FROM: RUSSELL T DAVIES TO: BENJAMIN COOK, SUNDAY 2 SEPTEMBER 2007 15:48:45 GMT

RE: 4.1

I've been sitting here for two hours, fiddling over rewrites to Donna and Geoff's chat in Scene 47. I'm sending you the new version. I thought you might like to see what I'm up to…

FROM: BENJAMIN COOK TO: RUSSELL T DAVIES, SUNDAY 2 SEPTEMBER 2007 16:00:03 GMT

RE: 4.1

Cheers for that, Russell. If you've time to answer this, I'm interested in why you've made those changes to Scene 47. Despite all the thought processes that I keep asking you about, we haven't answered exactly what it is that you do, 'tweaking' and 'fine-tuning', when sat in front of your computer, with last night's script on the screen…

FROM: RUSSELL T DAVIES TO: BENJAMIN COOK, SUNDAY 2 SEPTEMBER 2007 17:17:12 GMT

RE: 4.1

Well… the opening to Scene 47 remains unchanged, as things stand, right up to Geoff telling Donna that Venus is the only planet in our solar system named after a woman. 'Good for her,' says Donna, and then she adds: 'Imagine if you could go out there.' When I went back to that today, I realised that last line of Donna's was *way* too on-the-nose. This is the new, subtler version:

```
                    DONNA
     Good for her.

  Donna leaves the telescope, looks up into the night sky.

                    DONNA (CONT'D)
     How far away is that...?
```

And then I spent about half an hour on the internet, trying to find the distance from Earth to Venus – in miles, because Geoff wouldn't use kilometres! I discovered that on the transmission date of this episode – say, roughly, early April 2008 – Venus is too far away, behind the Sun, so Geoff wouldn't be able to see it. Damn. So I changed Venus to Mars – and changed Donna's line about a Mars Bar to a Twix, or there's too much Martian talk, but I really hated cutting the 'only planet named after a woman' line. But then I realised that this is actually 2009, in story terms, since *The Runaway Bride* was set at Christmas 2007, and this episode takes place a little over a year later. I entered that April 2009 date – and Venus *is* close! Hoorah! The 'only planet named after a woman' line went back in. If I've got the calculations right...

```
                    GEOFF
     About 26 million miles. But we'll get there! One day.
     Hundred years' time, we'll be striding out amongst the
     stars. Just you wait.
```

You'll have noticed that I took out Geoff's 'Bit late for me, I suppose' line. That lovely actor, Howard Attfield, has been ill and had chemotherapy. That's why there's that reference later on in the scene to him having been ill ('Oh, I'm on the mend'), though even that makes me shiver, so I might take it out. But 'Bit late for me, I suppose' is equally grim, isn't it? Also, I had Geoff saying 'there's gonna be people like you and me, striding out amongst the stars', but I thought that was, again, a bit unsubtle, since we all know that Donna *will* be flying off into space by the end of this episode.

The scene continues unchanged until:

```
                    DONNA
     That's not the half of it. Things I've seen. Even
     tonight, I was...
                         (pause)
     Doesn't matter. Sometimes I think I'm going mad.
```

I took out a line of Geoff's – 'Then tell me' – interrupting Donna's speech. It was just fluff. No, it wasn't fluff, it was meant to be a little bit insistent, to suggest that there has been a lot that Donna hasn't been telling her dad since Christmas, but only a CSI forensic-style examination would get that amount of meaning from a simple line, so it's gone. And it saves space.

```
                    GEOFF
      Well, you're not yourself, I'll give you that. I dunno.
      You just seem to be drifting, sweetheart.

                    DONNA
      I'm not drifting. I'm waiting.
```

I keep worrying about that line. Is it too poetic? It's staying for now, but it's on a caution.

```
                    GEOFF
      What for?


                    DONNA
      The right man.


                    GEOFF
      Oh, it's always a man.


                    DONNA
      No, I don't mean like that. But he's out there
      somewhere… And I mean for real, he exists, I've met him.
      And then… I just let him fly away.

                    GEOFF
      Well then. Go and find him.
```

Now, that line of Geoff's is the biggest change. I made a mistake, because Donna came to this scene with a very fixed state of mind. She could have delivered her big 'I'll find him' speech from the moment that she arrived. I'd forgotten the point of the scene, which is that contact with her dad *changes* Donna. She's lost, upset over Stacy… so now, I hope, there's a slight sense that she's sort of given up, and then a quiet word from her dad puts her back on track. Funny thing is, I was rereading our e-mails and I saw that yesterday I said to you, 'Whatever her dad says on that hillside has consequences, pushes Donna onwards.' Clear as day. But when I came to write that scene… I forgot! Sometimes, I can get too close to a script and lose sight of why I'm there. I wander away from my original intention. Or maybe I've lived with that intention for so long that I take it for granted and forget to actually say it. That one, I forgot overnight! Thank God for these e-mails.

That's what rewriting is: discovering the point of a scene. If it has no point, cut it.

Unless it's got a great gag. Or a naked man. And you'll see that Donna's 'He's out there somewhere' line has been shifted from her earlier speech, because it sounds better here. And Donna's speech here needs to be longer, for the camera move and for the mood. The scene continues:

```
Donna lies back. HIGH SHOT, pulling out on the two of them,
both Donna and Dad looking up at the night sky.


                    DONNA
    Yeah. That's what I'm gonna do. If I have to wait a
    hundred years. I'll find him.


                    GEOFF
                  (laughing)
    God help him.


                    DONNA
    Oh yes!
```

I'm not sure about the last couple of lines. I thought Donna's big speech was a bit too 'written', so those two little grace-note lines take the edge off it. It's more natural now. Less pretentious. It was too Disney before, and now it's more me. Plus, it's nice to see them laughing. Laughing in the dark. But I still might go back to the original, because Disney is good and I'm worried that the throwaway laughter undercuts the drama of a woman dreaming of the Doctor. I don't know. Also, ticking away in my head: how upset is Donna over Stacy? Did she call the police? Did she leave the front door open?! It's a big problem. There are all sorts of scenes and lines that I could put in, but they don't lead anywhere. Nonetheless, it's bugging me.

FROM: RUSSELL T DAVIES TO: BENJAMIN COOK, MONDAY 3 SEPTEMBER 2007 03:43:03 GMT

RE: 4.1

I've done more. Lots of trims to what I'd already written, though. Also, I changed Miss Rattigan's name. I used it because Rattigan was the name of the family in *Revelations*, the old soap that I invented at Granada. It's kind of a lucky charm. But it kept making me think of the villain, Professor Ratigan, in Disney's *The Great Mouse Detective*! Plus, I thought of a nice gag for her new name, Miss Foster. Finally, she's getting a bit of life to her. She's a *mother*.

I'm very pleased with the Doctor and Donna's meeting. (Very pleased?! BLOODY DELIGHTED! If not ECSTATIC!) It's everything that I wanted it to be. It's so nice to write for such brilliant, skilful actors. And I revised – yes, further – the scene of Donna and Geoff on the hillside. After her line 'You can talk', it now goes:

```
                    GEOFF
    Oh, I'm on the mend. But you had poor old Lance, bless
    him. That mad old Christmas.
```

```
                          (beat)
     I wish you'd tell us what really happened.
```

Finally! *That's* the missing line. After all that wondering what Donna did or didn't tell her parents after *The Runaway Bride*, I realised this morning, walking to Tesco, that a lot of Donna's unhappiness comes from not being able to tell anyone about the Doctor. Geoff's line – 'I wish you'd tell us what really happened' – encompasses all that, and Donna's next speech flows a little better as a result:

```
                      DONNA
     I know. It's just… The things I've seen. Sometimes I
     think I'm going mad. Even tonight, I was…
                          (pause)
     Doesn't matter.


                      GEOFF
     Well, you're not yourself, I'll give you that. You just
     seem to be drifting, sweetheart.


                      DONNA
     I'm not drifting. I'm waiting.
```

And then the scene continues as before, until Geoff says, 'Well then. Go and find him.' To which Donna replies:

```
                      DONNA
     Ohh, I've tried. He's… nowhere.


                      GEOFF
     Oy! Since when did you give up? I remember you, six
     years old, I said, no holiday this year, so you
     toddled off, all on your own, and got on the bus! To
     Strathclyde! We had police and everything!
                          (both laughing)
     Where's she gone, then? Eh? Where's that girl?

Donna lies back. HIGH SHOT, pulling out on the two of them;
Donna and her Dad, looking up at the night sky.

                      DONNA
     You're right. I'll do it. Just you watch me! He's out
     there somewhere. And I'll find him, Dad. Even if I have
     to wait a hundred years… I'll find him.
```

In working and working through this scene, *that's* what it's all about. Dad changes Donna's mind by inspiring her. (Interestingly, didn't I once say that I didn't write funny dads? Because dads aren't funny? But here he is – Geoff is funny and sweet. This proves that I talk bollocks.) However, I cut the two grace-note lines (Geoff: 'God help him.' Donna: 'Oh yes!'), which hurt, because I loved them, but they distracted from this irresistible on-screen cut from 'I'll find him' straight into Scene 48 of the Doctor in the TARDIS.

Also, today, funnily enough... I worked out what David's last words could be, one day, before his regeneration. I've stored that away.

FROM: BENJAMIN COOK TO: RUSSELL T DAVIES, MONDAY 3 SEPTEMBER 2007 13:40:54 GMT

RE: 4.1

>>I worked out what David's last words could be, one day, before his regeneration.<<
What? What?! WHAT??!!!

FROM: RUSSELL T DAVIES TO: BENJAMIN COOK, MONDAY 3 SEPTEMBER 2007 14:01:40 GMT

RE: 4.1

I'm not telling you. Ha ha ha. You've got to have something to wait for.

CHAPTER EIGHT

STILL
FIGHTING IT

In which tight white pants are all the rage in Rome,
the producer of *Doctor Who* makes a scene in a restaurant,
and Steven Moffat says yes

FROM: BENJAMIN COOK TO: RUSSELL T DAVIES, MONDAY 3 SEPTEMBER 2007 15:33:52 GMT

TODAY'S ANNOUNCEMENT
'No *Doctor Who* return until 2010,' declares BBC News.

'*Doctor Who* to return for fifth series in 2010,' says the official *Doctor Who* website.

How's the *Doctor Who* crew taken the news that there will be no Series Five in 2009?

FROM: RUSSELL T DAVIES TO: BENJAMIN COOK, MONDAY 3 SEPTEMBER 2007 15:54:06 GMT

RE: TODAY'S ANNOUNCEMENT
The weeks of work that bloody press release has taken! The RSC was going to announce that David is doing *Hamlet*, at a press conference on 11 September, so everything was timed for then… until the RSC brochure was sent out last week, mentioning David! Clearly, their PR is as good as ours. Numbskulls. So the news of no *Doctor Who* series in 2009 has all been a bit rush-released. Phil and Julie were going to talk to all the staff and heads of departments calmly and properly, but then had to run around like idiots on Friday instead, blabbing to one and all.

I'm a bit locked away here, so I'm not sure how it's gone down, though Julie and Phil say not too bad. Everyone has been aware of the rumours for ages, so I don't think anyone is very surprised. A lot of people said, 'I thought so.' Many of the staff are freelance, and this is how the freelance world works. Jess in the office was immensely pragmatic:

she said she's been travelling about as a freelancer for ten years now, so she'll always get work.[1] The most worrying thing is for the crew, the regular crew on set every day, those that live in Cardiff. I haven't even time to ask those that I'm worried about – people like Lindsey Alford, who've moved lock, stock and barrel to Cardiff. I'm not sure where that leaves them. I can't leave this desk to find out. That's terrible. But there's the promise of work to come, the *Doctor Who* Specials, maybe *Torchwood*, maybe *Sarah Jane*, as well as bigger plans to move *Casualty* here when the new studio is built. Lindsey was in Bristol, on *Casualty*, before this, so she might stay, she might move on. A freelancer's life. I'm the same. I can't think when anyone last asked me how I feel having to spend all this time in Cardiff, away from Manchester. It's just assumed, that's what you do. It's the distorting *Doctor Who* prism that makes today's announcement seem inflated; this sort of thing is normal in this industry.

Exciting, though. I like change.

Besides, it's not as lengthy a filming break as it might have been, because the BBC is just desperate for a Series Five as soon as possible. And Julie is hitting problems: it's terribly hard to raise the money for these Specials if BBC Worldwide isn't getting much in return. When there's no surrounding series to ameliorate the cost of a Special, the budget becomes frighteningly small. So, we'll still make the 2008 Christmas Special at the end of Series Four, and then, it's been decided, come back in January 2009 to make three more Specials – probably for Christmas 2009, New Year's Day 2010, and an Easter 2010 Special. Then Series Five will have a new production team. The show really only goes off air for 2009. And that's summed up weeks of really delicate discussions. Though the plans still keep changing!

FROM: BENJAMIN COOK TO: RUSSELL T DAVIES, MONDAY 3 SEPTEMBER 2007 23:30:14 GMT

RE: TODAY'S ANNOUNCEMENT

On days like this, when the press/internet/schedule is going crazy, is writing an escape? From real life? It is an escape, quite often, for people who write in their spare time, but it's your job, your career, and what you write affects the lives and careers of lots of other people. Often, for you, writing is the very thing that you try to escape from (all those diversion techniques, etc), but was it the opposite today?

FROM: RUSSELL T DAVIES TO: BENJAMIN COOK, TUESDAY 4 SEPTEMBER 2007 01:53:57 GMT

RE: TODAY'S ANNOUNCEMENT

Tricky, that one, about escapism. Hard for me to judge, because the time I spend writing is to the detriment of my family and friends, so am I escaping them? Am I choosing to be like this? 'Escape' implies a choice. Would I be like this anyway if I worked in Greggs? Would I spend all my time getting the lattice pastry on the

---

1 Production co-ordinator Jess Van Niekerk.

chicken-and-ham pies correct? (The answer is yes.) To be honest, I have trouble with 'escapism' full stop. It's usually a derogatory term. Or condescending. At best, cute. Is the person who goes upstairs for a couple of hours a week to write a never-published work, or watch *Star Trek*, or play with a train set, actually escaping? It makes the pastime, whether it's a hobby or a job, seem tiny and silly, when it's a vital part of your life. It's best summed up by that encounter with the Time-Check Woman the other week. Writing is actually my way of engaging with the world, not escaping from it. I meet someone, I see something, and I'm breaking it all down into dialogue, and story, and rhythms. But that doesn't mean I'm escaping. It's not dreamland – clearly it's not, because I've built a multi-million-plus empire in South Wales out of it. Not that success is a measure of how real this is, although… well, it *is* a measure.

The very word 'fiction' implies another world, literally a different place, whereas no one claims that a dedicated sportsman is escaping his life, or a chef, or a nurse. But the poor writer – the sci-fi one especially – is seen as running away. Bollocks. This is real, for me, and it's tough, it's fun, it's practical, and it's very, very important.

I was in just the mood to answer that!

FROM: RUSSELL T DAVIES TO: BENJAMIN COOK, TUESDAY 4 SEPTEMBER 2007 17:14:42 GMT

RE: TODAY'S ANNOUNCEMENT
Here's more script. I've sent this to the office, too, so that they can start to prep – or just weep at – the window-cleaner's-cradle sequence.[2]

FROM: RUSSELL T DAVIES TO: BENJAMIN COOK, WEDNESDAY 5 SEPTEMBER 2007 01:24:20 GMT

FW: TEST AND DESIGN OF ADIPOSE
Look at the Adipose! The Mill sent me these to approve today. The one on the left, 'G', that's the one. Ha ha ha.

2 The Doctor and Donna try to escape Adipose Industries in a window-cleaner's cradle down the side of the building – but Miss Foster sabotages the cradle during its descent, and the Doctor and Donna are left hanging…

FROM: BENJAMIN COOK TO: RUSSELL T DAVIES, WEDNESDAY 5 SEPTEMBER 2007 01:28:28 GMT

RE: TEST AND DESIGN OF ADIPOSE

That is so cute! Am I the only one already thinking of the merchandising opportunities?

FROM: RUSSELL T DAVIES TO: BENJAMIN COOK, WEDNESDAY 5 SEPTEMBER 2007 01:39:29 GMT

RE: TEST AND DESIGN OF ADIPOSE

Yes, I'm thinking… well, that I've lost a bloody fortune by inventing these under a BBC contract! Talking of which…

It's all hitting the fan over Monday's press release. If I told you all the shenanigans, I'd have to type for 500 hours. Peter Fincham, having been talked through our plans for 2009 so many times, is reacting to the press release like it's brand new information. Seriously! Since this stupid Queen business, he's in siege mentality.[3] He's been phoning up Julie: 'Why are we doing this?! *Why?!*' Maybe I'm getting paranoid, but I reckon if it escalates one more notch, just one, then his next step is to overrule Jane Tranter, magic a new production team out of nowhere, and have a complete new series in 2009. That's how much of an emergency it is. Interesting times.

FROM: BENJAMIN COOK TO: RUSSELL T DAVIES, WEDNESDAY 5 SEPTEMBER 2007 01:58:10 GMT

RE: TEST AND DESIGN OF ADIPOSE

Scary times! What other programme in Britain has had its 2010 commission headlined in the newspapers? Does the media hoo-hah of the last couple of days not affect your writing of 4.1 at all?

FROM: RUSSELL T DAVIES TO: BENJAMIN COOK, WEDNESDAY 5 SEPTEMBER 2007 02:13:04 GMT

RE: TEST AND DESIGN OF ADIPOSE

Oh, it drives me mad. I don't know a lot of what's going on; Julie keeps it from me, to protect my writing time, but tonight she was so tired and worn down and disheartened by it all that it came out in a great big blurb. Julie's outpouring only came about because I happened to mention that I was worried that David personally was taking a lot of flak for the 'gap year', like we'd done it in order for him to do *Hamlet*. In fact, we'd decided to pause anyway, ages ago – a decision taken *with* him, yes, but the *Hamlet* offer came up afterwards, when he knew that he had free time; we decided first. I suggested to Julie, off the cuff, that I could mention this in my column in *Doctor Who Magazine*, and Julie blanched. And then the outpouring started, because she had to tell me how severe things were, in order to stop me saying anything to anyone. Not

---

3 In July 2007, at a press launch of the BBC's forthcoming autumn schedule, Fincham introduced a trailer for the documentary *A Year with the Queen*, and told journalists that the Monarch had walked out of a photo shoot 'in a huff', after being asked to remove her tiara by photographer Annie Leibovitz. However, unknown to Fincham, the footage in the trailer had been assembled in the wrong order by production company RDF Media; the Queen had actually been walking *in* to the photo shoot. Fincham admitted the error, and initially rejected calls that he should resign.

out of secrecy, but because the smallest word now becomes so inflammatory. Even to the BBC One Controller. Madness. *Doctor Who*! That little show. So bizarre.

But to answer your question… no, it doesn't affect my writing. Not one jot. Completely separate worlds. Doesn't intrude at all. Thankfully.

FROM: RUSSELL T DAVIES TO: BENJAMIN COOK, WEDNESDAY 5 SEPTEMBER 2007 23:57:56 GMT

MORE ADIPOSE

I'm going to keep going and see if I can finish tonight. There's a Tone Meeting tomorrow…

FROM: BENJAMIN COOK TO: RUSSELL T DAVIES, THURSDAY 6 SEPTEMBER 2007 00:27:57 GMT

RE: MORE ADIPOSE

This episode will be responsible for *so* many kids wetting the bed. I hope they make Adipose soft toys. Or sponges! (Or squeezy stress balls. Yeah.)

FROM: RUSSELL T DAVIES TO: BENJAMIN COOK, THURSDAY 6 SEPTEMBER 2007 00:51:37 GMT

FW: ADIPOSE SHARP FANG

The Adipose stress ball? I'd have that! Here's the final design for the Adipose. I asked The Mill to give it one little fang, off centre, because… well, that's what makes a monster. A sharpened tusk! Like there's a *tiny* bit of nastiness to them. And it's funnier off-centre.

FROM: BENJAMIN COOK TO: RUSSELL T DAVIES, THURSDAY 6 SEPTEMBER 2007 02:59:35 GMT

IT'S 3AM. ARSE.

Finished 4.1 yet? Or have you fallen asleep at the keyboard? How's it going?

FROM: RUSSELL T DAVIES TO: BENJAMIN COOK, THURSDAY 6 SEPTEMBER 2007 03:15:07 GMT

RE: IT'S 3AM. ARSE.

It's going *very* well, thank you. The final pages are near. I suddenly sped up. How marvellous that you've been following this script in every detail (remember when it started with a jilted Penny, walking down the street, past the TARDIS?), and now it feels as though you're here for the final pages, keeping vigil.

FROM: BENJAMIN COOK TO: RUSSELL T DAVIES, THURSDAY 6 SEPTEMBER 2007 03:27:40 GMT

RE: IT'S 3AM. ARSE.

I'm keeping vigil with a glass of red wine. I'm reading Nicola Shindler's brilliant Huw Weldon Memorial Lecture from 2002. Apparently, Jimmy McGovern once said to Nicola that though he hates scenes that he's written being cut, he'd prefer for an audience to be confused for ten minutes than bored for even ten seconds. I like that.

FROM: RUSSELL T DAVIES TO: BENJAMIN COOK, THURSDAY 6 SEPTEMBER 2007 03:35:18 GMT

RE: IT'S 3AM. ARSE.

That lecture was fantastic. You'd love Nicola. She's like Julie, but ruder – and every bit as lovely. I often quote that Jimmy McGovern thing in Edits. In fact, tonight, I've been slicing through earlier scenes in 4.1 like a man possessed, cutting and trimming, because the page count is seriously freaking me out now.

I'm sending you what I've written so far. Normally, I don't give a hoot about swinging from comedy to darkness, but even I'm surprised by the way that this script is ricocheting to and fro. Of course, I'm terrified about the budget. I've spent about £500 million, so it'll have to calm down. Or I might ask them to axe BBC Three.

FROM: RUSSELL T DAVIES TO: BENJAMIN COOK, THURSDAY 6 SEPTEMBER 2007 03:51:18 GMT

RE: IT'S 3AM. ARSE.

I have just typed the stage direction:

    It's ROSE TYLER.

FROM: BENJAMIN COOK TO: RUSSELL T DAVIES, THURSDAY 6 SEPTEMBER 2007 03:55:55 GMT

RE: IT'S 3AM. ARSE.

What?! She's made the cut?! I thought you didn't reckon on getting Billie back for more than one day's filming. This isn't her one day, is it?!

FROM: RUSSELL T DAVIES TO: BENJAMIN COOK, THURSDAY 6 SEPTEMBER 2007 04:00:24 GMT

IT'S 4AM. ARSE!

No, it's not her only day. But it's costing us. We've had to rearrange the schedule and pay people off. As ever, Julie sorted it all out.

One more scene to go! This is like a live transmission.

FROM: BENJAMIN COOK TO: RUSSELL T DAVIES, THURSDAY 6 SEPTEMBER 2007 04:03:02 GMT

RE: IT'S 4AM. ARSE!

A live transmission? Perhaps Graham Norton will bleed into our e-mails.[4] I can't go to bed now – it's the lethal cocktail of red wine, a speech by Nicola Shindler, and Rose Tyler. For God's sake, send, send, send!

FROM: RUSSELL T DAVIES TO: BENJAMIN COOK, THURSDAY 6 SEPTEMBER 2007 04:11:04 GMT

RE: IT'S 4AM. ARSE!

Graham Norton? Sound bleed? Oy, enough of that language!

Ahh, I just typed the last line. It's made me cry. How pathetic.

---

128. EXT. HILLSIDE - NIGHT

WIDE SHOT, GEOFF on his lonely mount.

He's pottering about with the TELESCOPE. Happy. A sip of tea. Gene Pitney on the earphones.

Then he looks through the eyepiece, focusing it…

Stops. Eh?! Looks up, without the telescope. But…?

Looks back through the eyepiece.

And then he's all excited!

FX: GEOFF'S POV. The night sky, with a LITTLE BLUE BOX spinning across the sky.

He calls off, as though she might come running -

                    GEOFF
    But… Donna! Donna! It's the flying blue box!!

Looks back through the eyepiece.

Stunned. Whispers.

                GEOFF (CONT'D)
    Whaaaat…?

HIS POV: CLOSER on the TARDIS. DONNA standing in the doorway. Waving at him! Behind her, THE DOCTOR, and he gives a little wave, too.

                GEOFF (CONT'D)
    But that's… that's…

---

4 In some regions, the first few minutes of the original BBC One broadcast of *Doctor Who* 1.1 were marred by the accidental mixing of several seconds of off-air sound from Graham Norton hosting *Strictly Dance Fever*.

> And he abandons the telescope. Waves up at the sky! With a
> great big *yahoo!*
>
> FX: THE TARDIS spins away into space…
>
> HIGH SHOT: on Geoff, on his little hillside, in the middle of
> the night, waving up at the sky and whooping with joy.

DONE! All 58 pages. Ahh, I'm glad you were here. That was nice.

Three more scripts to go before I can take a holiday. No, four. Maybe five. Oh bollocks.

FROM: BENJAMIN COOK TO: RUSSELL T DAVIES, THURSDAY 6 SEPTEMBER 2007 22:17:36 GMT

SO…

How did the Tone Meeting go? What does everyone think of the script? How shattered have you been today? I hope you're all right.

FROM: RUSSELL T DAVIES TO: BENJAMIN COOK, THURSDAY 6 SEPTEMBER 2007 23:18:24 GMT

RE: SO…

I'm fine. Knackered. Of course, at this time of night, I begin to wake up again. I've still got to read Helen Raynor's Sontaran two-parter tonight, which I'll have to start rewriting on Monday. We're going to cast Christopher Ryan (Mike from *The Young Ones*!) as the Chief Sontaran. And all the Sontaran extras will be the same height, because they're all really short and dumpy and angry. Sontarans *are* trolls. It makes sense.

The 4.1 script went down well, I think. Well, Julie said that she loved it, and so did Phil, though maybe they're just glad to see a script. But a Tone Meeting isn't really the time or place for opinions, just hard facts. (We'll have a proper script session soon, of course.) My God, that team is extraordinary. That script is impossible. The cradle sequence especially. Any other production team would chuck that out, but they just set about it, breaking it down, shot after shot, battling, wrestling, finding the right way to do it. It's a thousand times more difficult than it first seems, what with the Health and Safety implications. And all sorts of things you don't think of, like… with the cradle hanging vertically, plus a cable hanging down, which Donna is holding on to, the sheer height of that is about 30 feet, beyond anything our green-screen studio can manage. Or anyone's studio! Still, they battled on. Fighting. The best team in the world. I worry that there's going to come a nasty moment, when all the costs are added up. Big decisions to come, I fear.

As for me, I'll read the script back tomorrow night, in Manchester. But I think I love it. It feels good. I'm pleased that it's done. That feels miraculous. Most of all, though, I'm bothered by those two guards; the way that they get electrocuted in the doorway is so lame.[5] I hate that scene. But I'm stuck with them. I tried everything in my head. I mean, Miss Foster needs two guards or she'd look weak. (In one of those late-night drafts that I sent you, I upped it to eight guards, which I then got rid of the next day, because two were hard enough to deal with!) I suppose they could stay with Miss Foster and be beamed up with her, but then they'd have to fall to their deaths with her, and that's just not as good. It's such a great image, Miss Foster floating up with her children, all on her own. Two extras would spoil it. Plus, if they're with Miss Foster, that means she never sent them to go and stop the Doctor, which is a bit stupid. She must *try* to stop him. But what else to do? Trap them in a lift? I've done a million lift scenes. And no soldier would be so daft as to use a lift in any emergency. Could the Doctor lock the stairwells, so they're stuck inside? Equally lame. Maybe Donna could find a way to knock them unconscious? Nah, that's rubbish. Quite apart from the fact that I can't think of a way for her to do that, I really don't like that sort of physical violence from the companion. Four years in, and I've rarely resorted to the Doctor or companion having to clobber someone unconscious. I'm sort of proud of that, though it does write me into corners. When trapped with a guard, I much prefer to write some sort of distraction – then run! Idiots punch. And punches can kill. Oh, listen to me.

That's why I was writing till gone 4am. I could work out everything else, but I've two irrelevant bloody security guards going round and round and round in my head. I woke up today, worrying about them. I've tried to cover it with fluffy dialogue, tried to make it look inbuilt in the plot; the Doctor can only electrocute them from a distance because Miss Foster has mysteriously 'wired up' the building. Why's she done that? Turns out, she's turned it into a 'Levitation Post'. Which is bollocks. There's a bloody big spaceship above, perfectly capable of beaming up everyone, like spaceships do. But all that dialogue is there to excuse the electrocuting-the-guards moment, a sure sign that something has gone wrong with the plot. Adipose, Stacy, capsules, cradles, levitation… and the one thing that's bugging me is the sodding security guards! It's the one bit that I don't *believe*.

Also, I'm still wondering about a couple of lines that I cut, to get 59 pages to 58: at one point, as the whole of London heads towards Emergency Parthenogenesis and everyone's clothes are writhing, Donna said, 'Do they have to be wearing their pendants?' The Doctor said no – having introduced the pendant as a trigger, it's unlikely that anyone would actually wear such a cheap and rubbish free gift. Well, maybe Suzette. 'They only have to touch the capsule once,' explained the Doctor, 'and it biotunes into them.' Nonsense, but sort of believable nonsense. And yet, in the middle of a crisis, with all those Adipose about to burst out of Roger and Suzette and Nice Man and 497 others… who gives a damn about those dull explanatory speeches?

5 The Doctor electrocutes Miss Foster's two security guards, just enough to stun them, by rewiring Adipose Industries (Miss Foster has wired up the whole building, to convert it into a 'Levitation Post' so that she and her Adipose children can levitate up to the Adiposian spaceship)… and the guards fall to the ground unconscious.

It's that old problem: how much do you explain to the audience, when the characters wouldn't waste time chatting about it? So, I'm still wondering about that. (Did you wonder about it?)

Other than that – yes, I'm happy. I particularly love the litterbin. The fact that Donna would leave her mother's car keys in a bin, because she's rushing off to travel in time and space (and must worry that the Doctor will take off without her), is so mad that it's real! I absolutely believe the silliness of that scene. The daft things that people do.

FROM: BENJAMIN COOK TO: RUSSELL T DAVIES, FRIDAY 7 SEPTEMBER 2007 18:47:34 GMT

RE: SO...

I didn't wonder about the missing info-dump speech, but I did wonder whether you'd really get three people – Suzette, Nice Man and Young Woman – out of the 500 across London, all in the same wine bar at the same time. Bit of a coincidence.

FROM: RUSSELL T DAVIES TO: BENJAMIN COOK, MONDAY 10 SEPTEMBER 2007 16:56:14 GMT

RE: SO...

Sorry for being a bit quiet. I've spent three days going *clomp*. Those scripts don't half knacker you. My poor boyfriend, all he gets out of me on a weekend home is *clomp*. Still, I felt guilty, so I just went and bought him a car. Oh, but he so deserves it. If only for putting up with me and all this *Doctor Who* nonsense.

Phil is texting from Rome! How exciting. When do the rest of you get out there?

FROM: BENJAMIN COOK TO: RUSSELL T DAVIES, MONDAY 10 SEPTEMBER 2007 21:57:08 GMT

RE: SO...

I'm off to Rome on Tuesday. I hope the hotel has internet access.

FROM: RUSSELL T DAVIES TO: BENJAMIN COOK, TUESDAY 11 SEPTEMBER 2007 23:49:27 GMT

RE: SO...

It'd better have internet access. I want Roman Scandal!

I'm supposed to start rewriting the Sontaran episodes this week, but actually Helen deserves another crack at 4.4. Anyway, I'm still going *clomp*, so to hell with it.

> Text message from: **Ben**
> Sent: 13-Sep-2007 09:08
> 'And... action!' Filming in Rome has begun. It's looking fantastic. There's a mule on set, and chickens, and I'm standing on a replica Roman toilet to get a good view.

Text message from: Russell
Sent: 13-Sep-2007 09:46

A mule! Ha ha ha, how brilliant. Thanks for letting me know. Big kiss to Francois Pandolfo. In a strictly professional way.

Text message from: Russell
Sent: 13-Sep-2007 23:03

Hope all went well at Cinecittà today. It's very odd sitting here while everyone's abroad. I feel like the caretaker of a school.

Text message from: Ben
Sent: 13-Sep-2007 23:22

Filming went well. We're all on a night out in Rome. It's like St Trinian's on tour! Everyone has worked so hard today. How are things in the UK?

Text message from: Russell
Sent: 13-Sep-2007 23:43

It's all go here. We've just told Burn and Naoko that they won't be in the third series of *Torchwood*, because we're killing off Owen and Tosh. Madness in two countries simultaneously.

Text message from: Ben
Sent: 14-Sep-2007 00:24

There's a rat in our restaurant. Phil is standing on the table. The producer of *Doctor Who*! Oh, now he's asking for a discount. He says it's taken two years off his life.

Text message from: Russell
Sent: 14-Sep-2007 00:31

Tell him that makes him 41. That'll make him cross. Hey, if I were in a restaurant, scared of a rat, I'd cling to... ooh, Francois maybe?

Text message from: Ben
Sent: 14-Sep-2007 00:35

I'll suggest it to Phil.

Text message from: Russell
Sent: 14-Sep-2007 13:49

According to The Mill's list, we're 150 FX days over on 4.1. I have to suggest cuts. Damn.

Text message from: Ben

Sent: 15-Sep-2007 00:50

It's the night shoot at Cinecittà! Is Francois' tunic supposed to be so short?

Text message from: Russell

Sent: 15-Sep-2007 00:55

We spent a long time MAKING Louise Page shorten it. Oh, the power!

Text message from: Ben

Sent: 15-Sep-2007 01:02

Colin Teague is worried about the shot of Francois climbing through the window of Lucius' quarters. Um – we'll see everything! Have you done this on purpose? Louise is not happy. She's insisting that Francois wears underwear.

Text message from: Russell

Sent: 15-Sep-2007 01:09

Exactly as I planned. Who d'you think wrote the climbing-through-the-window scene? Ha ha ha. I'm sure the Pyroviles invented tight white pants. I'll issue a pink page to that effect.

FROM: RUSSELL T DAVIES TO: BENJAMIN COOK, TUESDAY 18 SEPTEMBER 2007 23:50:05 GMT

ROMAN HOLIDAY

Are you back from Rome? The rushes are amazing. Oh, but here's tonight's script problem (this one has me stumped)… the one thing that we can't afford to shoot on 4.1 is the Doctor and Donna and Miss Foster having their conversation on the rooftop, with the Doctor and Donna already in the stationary cradle. As soon as the cradle falls, we're fine, bizarrely. We can afford the stunt, the Adipose, the End Of The Sodding World, but not that confrontation scene. (The reasons are too dull to go into. It involves the number of nights – just one, apparently – for which we can afford a crane and an actual cradle, as opposed to the cradle that we'll build in the studio for the stunt sequence against green screen.) Of all the things that I expected to be cut (which included the entire cradle sequence), I never expected that. The Doctor's whole confrontation with the enemy! Where the plot is explained! Bollocks.

So… they escape to the roof, Miss Foster chasing, cut around the actual moment of descent to avoid the precise mechanism, so the Doctor and Donna are already heading down when Miss Foster nixes the equipment, and then we go into the stunt sequence as written, minimal changes. But then the Doctor and Donna run through the building, meet Miss Foster, and have that pivotal conversation… in a corridor? Or on a stairwell? That's a very flat, lame setting compared to a rooftop at night. It's just not good enough. And then what? The Doctor and Donna can't just run away. The Doctor would have to find some clever way to outfox Miss Foster and the guards, but then that raises the question: why didn't the Doctor do that in the first place, instead of trying to escape via the cradle? So, um…

FROM: BENJAMIN COOK TO: RUSSELL T DAVIES, WEDNESDAY 19 SEPTEMBER 2007 01:46:33 GMT

RE: ROMAN HOLIDAY

The rooftop dilemma! Don't you usually get around these things by having the Doctor talk to the villain over intercoms or TV screens?

FROM: RUSSELL T DAVIES TO: BENJAMIN COOK, WEDNESDAY 19 SEPTEMBER 2007 02:02:16 GMT

RE: ROMAN HOLIDAY

I just read the script again. I suppose the Doctor and Donna could meet Miss Foster and the guards for the vital dialogue in the darkened sales-cubicles room. That's quite a good setting. Bit of space. Better than a corridor. In some ways, the heart of Miss Foster's empire.

And how to escape? It just struck me: the Doctor has a sonic screwdriver *and* Miss Foster's sonic pen.[6] What happens when you hold two sonic devices together? I'll tell you what. You get wibbly-wobbly vibrations and guards clutch their ears for long enough to enable you to escape! That's what happens, because I say so. I hate using the sonic screwdriver as a solution, but that's what comes of making this an action-adventure series with a hero who doesn't carry a gun. Small price to pay. The episode has gone to great lengths to give the Doctor two sonic devices at the same time, so it'll look like I planned it all along.

FROM: RUSSELL T DAVIES TO: BENJAMIN COOK, FRIDAY 21 SEPTEMBER 2007 23:41:24 GMT

LATEST 4.1

We saw the half-finished FX on 4.X today. The *Titanic* sailing over Buckingham Palace is so brilliant, we stood up and clapped! Amazing. We also realised, for the first time, that since the BBC's trouble with the Queen, it's probably a very good thing that we didn't trash the Palace after all. Phew.

Also, I've been tweaking 4.1 today, to lose some more FX days and in the light of notes from Julie and… well, YOU, actually! One of them is your note. When you wondered about the coincidence of so many of the 500 victims being in such close proximity, I realised that I'd made it 500 because initially I'd planned to kill them all, have them all do a Stacy rip-apart, before I decided that was just gruesome and undeserved. And expensive. (I'd thought 500 was a reasonable massacre!) Now they

---

6 The sonic screwdriver is a tool used by the Doctor since 1968 serial *Fury from the Deep*. Its most common function is to operate virtually any door lock, mechanical or electronic, but it has also been used for everything from repairing equipment to detonating landmines. In 4.1, Miss Foster has a sonic pen… until the Doctor pinches it.

don't die, though, so I've upped it to 10,000 people, making the threat much bigger. So that little wonder of yours was brilliant. Thank you.

FROM: BENJAMIN COOK TO: RUSSELL T DAVIES, SATURDAY 22 SEPTEMBER 2007 00:57:00 GMT

RE: LATEST 4.1

Now, *that's* got to be worth ten per cent?

FROM: RUSSELL T DAVIES TO: BENJAMIN COOK, SATURDAY 22 SEPTEMBER 2007 01:03:52 GMT

RE: LATEST 4.1

Ha ha ha. No.

FROM: RUSSELL T DAVIES TO: BENJAMIN COOK, SATURDAY 22 SEPTEMBER 2007 13:26:21 GMT

RE: LATEST 4.1

I'm so behind with the 4.4 rewrites. I quite like what I'm thinking: lovely stuff with Donna returning home, having travelled in time and space; the Doctor's new attitude to UNIT (he doesn't like them – men with guns – he wouldn't); the Doctor knocking out a Sontaran with a tennis ball! It all feels good, but it's a lot of work.

Also, I forgot to tell you, I walked to Tesco yesterday, thinking about Gwen and Ianto defending the Torchwood Hub from advancing Daleks in 4.12! Daleks in the Hub! I was almost hyperventilating with excitement.

FROM: BENJAMIN COOK TO: RUSSELL T DAVIES, MONDAY 24 SEPTEMBER 2007 18:04:40 GMT

SARAH JANE

I've just seen Lis Sladen on the CBBC channel, being interviewed by a cactus.

FROM: RUSSELL T DAVIES TO: BENJAMIN COOK, MONDAY 24 SEPTEMBER 2007 18:26:40 GMT

RE: SARAH JANE

A Spanish cactus at that. Or was it Mexican? What happened to good-looking CBBC presenters?

Tonight, Jane Tranter and Julie Gardner are having dinner with Steven Moffat. The future starts here! Mind you, what if he says no? (He won't actually give an answer tonight. Months of negotiations, etc.) But Christ alive, what happens then? I can't even bear to think about it.

FROM: BENJAMIN COOK TO: RUSSELL T DAVIES, MONDAY 24 SEPTEMBER 2007 18:36:15 GMT

RE: SARAH JANE

Of course he won't say no. He won't, will he? Who'd say no? It's the best job in the world.

FROM: RUSSELL T DAVIES TO: BENJAMIN COOK, MONDAY 24 SEPTEMBER 2007 19:03:04 GMT

RE: SARAH JANE

He might say no. I wonder. For starters, he's got kids and a wife. He works with Hartswood, which is practically his company. And now he's writing stuff like *Tintin* for Spielberg, his agent might clobber him if he goes and does a TV show.[7] Plus, if someone else takes over from me, they'd be begging scripts off Steven anyway, so he'd still get to write *Doctor Who*. All the fun, none of the pain.

FROM: RUSSELL T DAVIES TO: BENJAMIN COOK, WEDNESDAY 26 SEPTEMBER 2007 00:54:36 GMT

RE: SARAH JANE

I just got a midnight e-mail from A. N. Other Writer. Having trouble with 'the basic linear causality' of an episode. *Basic linear causality?!* Do you see the crap that writers talk? Really, though, if you think of a script in terms like that, how the hell are you ever going to get anything written?

> Text message from: **Russell**
> Sent: 27-Sep-2007 09:05
> Guess who we've got for Miss Foster? Sarah Lancashire!

> Text message from: **Ben**
> Sent: 27-Sep-2007 09:15
> Brilliant casting! That's going to be one sexy mother foster!

FROM: RUSSELL T DAVIES TO: BENJAMIN COOK, THURSDAY 27 SEPTEMBER 2007 20:53:31 GMT

4.4 COMPLETED!

Another script done! Yes, I've finished 4.4. It's like a bloody production line. Well, it *is* a production line.

I admitted to Julie today that Tom MacRae's Episode 8 simply isn't right. Tom's script is good, and we could make it great, but I don't think it can ever be great enough. It's misconceived. This is entirely my fault: I don't like the concepts I gave him, and I don't like the overall tone of both 4.7 and 4.8 being comparatively light, fun episodes. Two in a row. I'm left with the prospect of having to write a replacement script myself. But I've no time. I'd have about three days! Even if I could do it in three days, I'd lose more time than that – for recovery. (Julie said today, 'This is the only job in writing where you actually talk about having Recovery Days!') We're going to wait a week, to get 4.5 dealt with, and then decide what to do about 4.8…

---

7 Moffat has scripted *The Adventures of Tintin: Secret of the Unicorn* (scheduled for a 2011 release) for directors Steven Spielberg and Peter Jackson.

FROM: RUSSELL T DAVIES TO: BENJAMIN COOK, FRIDAY 28 SEPTEMBER 2007 16:11:31 GMT

THE MOFF

Steven just e-mailed me. He admitted, in an unguarded moment, that YES, HE'S GOING TO DO *DOCTOR WHO*! So that's exciting.

FROM: BENJAMIN COOK TO: RUSSELL T DAVIES, FRIDAY 28 SEPTEMBER 2007 16:21:45 GMT

RE: THE MOFF

That's great news. He'll be brilliant. As of tonight, I shall start e-mailing Steven Moffat instead. Goodbye, Russell.

FROM: RUSSELL T DAVIES TO: BENJAMIN COOK, FRIDAY 28 SEPTEMBER 2007 16:30:37 GMT

RE: THE MOFF

Have you read Steven's *Children in Need* script?[8] It's a hoot and very lovely. Next Sunday, 7 October, that's when they're shooting it at Upper Boat. Peter Davison Day! Poor Louise Page, trying to find a pair of striped trousers like the Fifth Doctor's! Did they *ever* make trousers like that?

FROM: RUSSELL T DAVIES TO: BENJAMIN COOK, FRIDAY 5 OCTOBER 2007 11:32:10 GMT

PETER FINCHAM'S ARSE

Terrible rumours flying around the BBC right now. It looks like Peter Fincham is resigning any minute – along with his Head of Press, Jane Fletcher, who's done more to support *Doctor Who* than I can ever tell you. Wonderful woman. All over this stupid bloody Queen business! It makes me sick. Further reports to follow…

Sorry for my silence over the last week. I'm snowed under like you will not believe. 4.5 is requiring a lot of work. A Tone Meeting on Monday! Filming any day now! Bloody hell. It's doing my head in. I'll tell you what's really crippling me: all my emergency solutions end up nicking stuff from what I've planned for 4.12/4.13. I'm robbing my own scripts to make these ones work. That's pissing me off profoundly.

Oh, and I've submitted the absolute final draft of 4.1, with post-read-through changes – a bit more explanation of the capsules and a couple of lines rephrased to sound more elegant. Also, your note on the scale of Miss Foster's scheme went further (see, you were right), so it's gone from 500 people, to 10,000, and now it's a million!

FROM: BENJAMIN COOK TO: RUSSELL T DAVIES, FRIDAY 5 OCTOBER 2007 21:32:17 GMT

RE: PETER FINCHAM'S ARSE

'BBC ONE BOSS QUITS OVER QUEEN ROW!' say the news reports.

So it's happened. This is madness.

---

8 Moffat wrote *Time Crash*, an eight-minute mini-episode of *Doctor Who*, for the BBC's *Children in Need* telethon. Broadcast in November 2007, it depicted an encounter between the Tenth Doctor and his former, fifth incarnation, played by Peter Davison.

FROM: RUSSELL T DAVIES TO: BENJAMIN COOK, SATURDAY 6 OCTOBER 2007 00:14:06 GMT

RE: PETER FINCHAM'S ARSE

I swear, I'd resign from this stupid organisation. Except I love *Doctor Who*, so what would be the point? The loss of Jane Fletcher is scandalous. Never has a woman worked so hard. She was completely wonderful. Oh, it makes my blood boil.

> **Text message from: Russell**
> Sent: 7-Oct-2007 11:10
>
> Davison Day! And I'm sat in the flat rewriting the bloody Sontarans. Bah! Have fun.

> **Text message from: Ben**
> Sent: 7-Oct-2007 11:22
>
> You're not coming?! Your inner fanboy must be screaming a lament. Don't be daft. You've got to pop in. History in the making!

> **Text message from: Russell**
> Sent: 7-Oct-2007 11:45
>
> If the universe implodes because two Doctors meet, at least I'll be a distance away. Oh, maybe I'll come along for a bit this afternoon.

FROM: RUSSELL T DAVIES TO: BENJAMIN COOK, MONDAY 8 OCTOBER 2007 04:33:42 GMT

FINISHED 4.5!

I've finished 4.5! That's 24 pages today! Plus a visit to Upper Boat! I'm exhausted. And it's the bleedin' Tone Meeting in a few hours. But I really did love today, in studio. Sorry I had to leave before the end. I was quite sad for a bit afterwards, thinking how good Peter Davison looked. Proper lighting. Proper set. Brilliant dialogue. He should have been like that in the '80s. Never was.

If I keep up this rate of work, I could find the time to replace Tom MacRae's 4.8 with a completely new episode. It means writing two episodes, 4.8 and 4.11, in two weeks – yikes – but it can be done. Downside: it might kill me. Sooner or later, at this rate of work, a kidney is going to burst or something. Still. You can buy kidneys. I keep remembering that 4.8 is going to be our fiftieth episode. (Can you believe it? I still think the world has gone mad. For four years now. Four good years.) Tom's script is nice, it's clever, it's funny, but the truth is we can be more adventurous. Shame, to have an ordinary fiftieth episode, even if we're the only ones aware of the numbers.

FROM: BENJAMIN COOK TO: RUSSELL T DAVIES, MONDAY 8 OCTOBER 2007 12:59:42 GMT

RE: FINISHED 4.5!

>>Downside: it might kill me.<<

Upside: it might not.

How was the 4.4/4.5 Tone Meeting?

FROM: RUSSELL T DAVIES TO: BENJAMIN COOK, MONDAY 8 OCTOBER 2007 22:19:08 GMT

RE: FINISHED 4.5!

It might not? Yes, I like that. The thing is, it really could. Writing 24 pages yesterday took me 80 cigarettes. I will be able to say, honestly, that the Sontarans killed me.

The Tone Meeting was good, but I was so tired. I got a bit tetchy. Actually, I got a bit tetchy with good reason. One of the funny things about rewrites is, a lot of people aren't very good at deleting the old drafts from their heads. That's a particular problem when they're the producer or director! It's a really subtle, insidious thing that creeps in and makes scripts, or the production of scripts, indistinct. It drives me bananas when people start quoting from old drafts, in which the Sontarans had different motivations. It's more pernicious when it creeps into tiny, important details of character and backstory. Clarity and definition can go out of the window. That sort of creep and bleed is the reason – no, one of the reasons – why so much drama is neither here nor there. No definition. Drafts upon drafts. Muddling along.

Worth it in the end, though. For all its improvised, battling, freefall blundering, I think 4.5 is a rather marvellous episode. Best of all, it ends with a fantastic Doctor scene: that final confrontation with the Sontarans on their spaceship. I think that's bloody excellent. It's really hard to find new things for the Doctor, especially new climaxes, so I'm really chuffed with that. Hoo-bloody-ray.

FROM: BENJAMIN COOK TO: RUSSELL T DAVIES, TUESDAY 9 OCTOBER 2007 00:36:25 GMT

RE: FINISHED 4.5!

But haven't *we* both found it difficult to delete old drafts from our heads? Or you wouldn't have got tongue-tied when you bumped into [Miss X] in Oxford Street back in March, because you still had Penny-as-played-by-[Miss X] in your mind. And neither of us can read 4.1 without a certain pang when Penny pops up. That said, there's a difference, I know, between what we natter about in these e-mails and what's required from folk at Tone Meetings. When you're wearing your writer's hat (I imagine it's a beret, with pink tassels), old and new drafts are fluctuating in the quantum state of Maybe. However, in your executive producer's hat (a pith helmet, I reckon, with solar panels that power a miniature fan to keep you cool), you need to be more disciplined. Is that true? At this stage in production, is it easy enough to divorce your role as writer from your role as executive producer?

FROM: RUSSELL T DAVIES TO: BENJAMIN COOK, TUESDAY 9 OCTOBER 2007 22:00:36 GMT

RE: FINISHED 4.5!

I didn't mean that writers should delete old drafts from their minds; just producers and directors and anyone on the floor, hands-on making it. Maybe that sounds hypocritical, because I know it's easier said than done, but they have to concentrate on what they're making now, without confusing it.

I do find it easy to divorce my two roles. With my producer's hat on (it's lemon), if a scene becomes impossible or expensive or is simply dropped on the day because they ran out of time, then I can score a great big line through it. Even if I loved it. I won't moan or bleat or feel any substantial regret. It's something that writers in this country need to be trained in, like in the US. We still cling to that notion of the writer-eccentric (the slippers, the attic, the cardigan), which is a bloody nightmare on set. That sort of writer kicks up a fuss if a character is wearing a white shirt instead of a blue one. That sort of writer shouldn't be allowed near filming. Mind you, that writer-eccentric does allow you to get away with murder. Writers are allowed, professionally, to be stroppy, and weird, and angry, and demanding, and petulant, and oversexed, and drunk. As long as your writing is good, that behaviour is sort of revered. Even expected. We're allowed to misbehave, because it's seen as creative, like it's part of the job. Rubbish!

So many writers get credited as execs these days, because that's the goal, career-wise, for a writer. Half of them – most of them – don't know what exec'ing actually is, and couldn't do it, and don't want to. It cheapens the title. A while ago, a writer-friend of mine, a powerful writer – who shall remain nameless – was demanding an exec credit on a big ITV show of his, so he phoned me up, asking what jobs I did to earn that credit. I listed them all: casting actors, working with directors, production meetings with heads of department, rushes, Edits, Dubs, etc. He said, 'I don't do any of that.' I said, 'Sod off, then!' But he got his exec credit anyway, without taking on any of those duties. That's what pisses me off.

FROM: RUSSELL T DAVIES TO: BENJAMIN COOK, WEDNESDAY 10 OCTOBER 2007 12:51:53 GMT

MORE WORK, LESS MAYBE

I must update you on the Maybe, although it feels wrong calling it that now. 'Maybe' was nice and mystical back in February, when I was planning, not writing. Now I think the word is just 'Work'. It can't fluctuate so much any more. I have to make choices. Fix it. Write it.

One terrible thing is happening – and I can't stop it bleeding into my thoughts. Howard Attfield, who plays Donna's dad, has been ill. As you know, he's had cancer and chemo. The agent told us about it, but said that Howard was more than happy to do Series Four. And already I'm using that, in the story. That sounds terrible, but it's what happens; I start weaving it in. That, I think, has been part of the Donna and Geoff closeness that's crept into their scenes together in 4.1 and 4.4/4.5. (Look at me, absolving myself of blame by saying 'crept into', giving it a life of its own!) But now that we've started shooting 4.1 and Howard is on set... blimey, he's ill. He's not had chemotherapy; he's *having* it. Phil was talking to him about his scenes in 4.4/4.5, and

Howard said, lightly, 'That's if I'm still here.' He's dying. That lovely man is dying. And there it is feeding back into the scripts and onto screen. It can't not. That scene of Donna and Geoff on the hillside is utterly exquisite. Wonderfully shot. Beautifully acted by Catherine and Howard. Each draft and redraft over every little line of that scene was so worth it. It's one of best scenes that we've ever shot. But if you add this knowledge about Howard to what you're watching... well, it's heartbreaking. I watched the rushes and cried.

To be blunt: how do we plan ahead? What do we do? Talk about the Maybe being in a state of flux! I don't know what to do. Howard is supposed to be in 4.11 and 4.12/4.13, but... ouch. I'm writing his illness into the story (can I do that? Should I?), that Donna has to face the death of her father. That she always was. That she went looking for the Doctor on the day that Geoff was diagnosed. That she's running away – and will, one day, have to walk back and face it. And then Donna Noble grows up.

I can't talk about this too much more. I'm sorry, Ben. It feels obscene. It feels fascinating. It's sort of *too* fascinating. Does that make sense?

Elsewhere, this mysterious 4.8 that I haven't got time for has been building in my head. It had taken a fair old shape, when I happened to see *Jeepers Creepers 2* on ITV the other night... and it was exactly what I had in mind. Everyone trapped on a bus, with a monster outside. They stole my idea! Five years ago! Those time-travelling Hollywood bastards. My version is set on an alien planet. Donna is busy moonbathing, so the Doctor goes off on a tourist trip, in a tank-like bus thing. But we don't see the outside. No models, no CGI, apart from an establisher of the planet. This, literally, takes place on one set – inside the bus – which will have to seal off its windows, so let's say there's a big old powerful X-raying sun outside. So it's a box. It's a show set in a box. That'll help our budgets right now. The box sets off on its journey, with the Doctor and five or six other interesting people on board, but then it breaks down. There Is Something Outside. (Or is there?) They're trapped. Forty minutes of fear! Never leaving the box. God only knows how or what happens. I don't think we've the money for a monster, so it's sort of psychological terror.

At the heart of this, I've one idea that keeps nagging, because it feels so attractive, and unnerving, and plain terrifying. Whatever's outside the box, one woman inside becomes possessed by it – and she repeats everything that you say. She has no speech of her own; she just repeats everything. All the time. You know how it drives you mad when people repeat what you say? When kids do it? Imagine that *not stopping*. Forty minutes of it, inside a box, with the lights failing and the heat rising, and the paranoia building, and this woman (I like the name Sky), this woman with wild, staring eyes, *will not stop*. Worse than that – better than that – her repetition starts to synchronise! Her repeats get closer and closer to your words until they're overlapping. She's saying words at *exactly the same time as you!* Speeches would be laid out as:

THE DOCTOR & WOMAN
What are you doing, what's inside you, what is it…?

That's hard to shoot. That actress would have to learn the entire script. She wouldn't just say the Doctor's words, she'd say everyone's, no matter how fast it gets. Incredible moments where all the other characters are talking at once, and she sort of manages to say everyone's words at once, like talking in tongues. It's a real possession story. It's the tension of it that I love. The weirdness. Even the technical difficulty of shooting this becomes fascinating. All that production-tension creeping onto the screen. Also, it's key to the Doctor – or David's Doctor – because he uses words so well, and this is all about him losing his speech.

But how does it end? That, in truth, is why I'm a bit scared of commissioning myself here. Dragging those endings out of my head, that's what hurts, that's what makes me smoke and burn. Last week, when I was staring at 4.5 and had no idea how it ended, it was a great big raw screaming hole. It was a mindless panic. And it had to be fixed by Monday. It's horrible, looking into that. The blank space of an unknown ending. When I talk about being exhausted and recovering from a script, what I really mean is recovering, physically, from going through that fear. I'm not even going to qualify that with an 'Oh, how pretentious', though my fingers are dying to type a self-deprecating qualifier. No matter how difficult 4.11 and 4.12/4.13 are, I know how they end, so I've somewhere to head for. But I've no such luxury with 4.8. It's tempting me forward, but repelling me at the same time.

FROM: BENJAMIN COOK TO: RUSSELL T DAVIES, THURSDAY 11 OCTOBER 2007 15:10:56 GMT

RE: MORE WORK, LESS MAYBE
I hadn't realised that things were quite that serious for Howard. That's terrible. I only met him briefly on set for *The Runaway Bride*. He seemed to be having a good time. Very happy. Very twinkly. I really hope I see him again. It seems fitting that he should influence his character's path, and Donna's, to some extent.

Hey, I saw the report in the *Daily Star* the other day, that Billie and everyone is coming back for the series finale. How the hell do they find out this stuff?

FROM: RUSSELL T DAVIES TO: BENJAMIN COOK, THURSDAY 11 OCTOBER 2007 19:51:55 GMT

RE: MORE WORK, LESS MAYBE
Heaven knows! We're very worried about that. It's a top-level leak. Almost no one knows the full size of these plans. But what do we do? Suspect everyone? There's nothing we can do. Some sly little shit will have to be hot with their tiny victory. But talking to the *Daily Star*…! How dumb is that? At least *The Sun* has readers.

FROM: RUSSELL T DAVIES TO: BENJAMIN COOK, FRIDAY 12 OCTOBER 2007 20:54:46 GMT

RE: MORE WORK, LESS MAYBE

Poor Howard. It's looking bad. We're trying to bring his 4.4/4.5 scenes forward to film *next week*, plus any scenes from 4.11 that I can write in advance. It's that bad.

FROM: RUSSELL T DAVIES TO: BENJAMIN COOK, SATURDAY 13 OCTOBER 2007 03:33:46 GMT

RE: MORE WORK, LESS MAYBE

Oh well, I started 4.8. Like an idiot. I couldn't resist. I'm giving myself this weekend. If I can convince myself by Sunday night that there's a story in this Space Bus (I'm calling the Space Bus *Crusader Five*) – and a story that I can complete in time – then I'll keep going. Prep on 4.8 starts on Monday, so that's a handy deadline. If it doesn't work… well, I can keep it as a pet project; something will happen to it one day. Every idea gets used somewhere, eventually.

FROM: BENJAMIN COOK TO: RUSSELL T DAVIES, SATURDAY 13 OCTOBER 2007 12:31:17 GMT

RE: MORE WORK, LESS MAYBE

CRUSADER FIVE IS GO! I'm leaving for Newport in an hour, but I've just sat here and read what you've written of 4.8, so now I'm running late. Obviously, I'm Invisible Ben, so I can't tell you whether or not I enjoyed it. But I did enjoy it. More's the point, you sound as though *you're* enjoying this one. I'm on set tonight, through the night, for Miss Foster's confrontation with the Doctor and Donna, but send me more and I'll read it when I get back to the hotel at 6am.

FROM: RUSSELL T DAVIES TO: BENJAMIN COOK, SATURDAY 13 OCTOBER 2007 13:11:20 GMT

RE: MORE WORK, LESS MAYBE

I'm glad you enjoyed it. I'm still not sure. I've chosen the hardest thing to write, which is eight people all in one scene at the same time. That's why most drama consists of two-handers. Much easier. The sheer effort of keeping eight characters on the boil, while not forgetting anyone, but not delaying things by laboriously giving everyone their turn, is technically one of the hardest things to write.

Have fun on set. That episode is looking wonderful. I swear, the scene where the Doctor and Donna see each other through their respective windows is The Funniest Thing Ever. Certainly, the funniest thing that I've written for ages. You write and write and write, hoping to hit something *that* funny, and sometimes, rare times, you get there. Catherine plays a blinder. (She texted me afterwards to say, 'I'm petitioning them to bring back *Give Us a Clue*.') And then David raises his game and gets even funnier. Oh, I'm happy.

And Sarah Lancashire was born to play a villain.

Text message from: Russell

Sent: 13-Oct-2007 23:49

It's weird to think of everyone filming on a Saturday night. I don't think we've done this before. It robs me of my martyr status – I'm not alone! How goes it?

Text message from: Ben

Sent: 14-Oct-2007 00:30

I was interviewing Sarah Lancashire when you texted. She said that your scripts are 'non-negotiable' and 'uncompromising', and that she 'believes every single beat'. The bribe worked, then?

Text message from: Russell

Sent: 14-Oct-2007 02:04

Ah, that's nice of her. I've known her for years. Always wanted to work with her – now she's an evil alien Supernanny! Who'd have thought?

Text message from: Ben

Sent: 14-Oct-2007 02:07

How goes *Crusader Five*? You have to work the number 50 into the script somewhere. Couldn't it be *Crusader 50* instead?

Text message from: Russell

Sent: 14-Oct-2007 02:10

Oh, I forgot that! Right, the Space Bus is called *Crusader 50* now. Good call.

FROM: RUSSELL T DAVIES TO: BENJAMIN COOK, SUNDAY 14 OCTOBER 2007 03:50:33 GMT

RE: MORE WORK, LESS MAYBE

This is hard work. Just laying it out on the page, clearly explaining what's happening and timing it right. I think it works, it's scary, the concept is scary, but… I just don't know. My brain is bleeding. Good night.

FROM: BENJAMIN COOK TO: RUSSELL T DAVIES, SUNDAY 14 OCTOBER 2007 12:07:05 GMT

RE: MORE WORK, LESS MAYBE

Chatting to Phil on set last night, he mentioned Howard. He said that depending on how you write him into later episodes, it might be worth recasting – and reshooting the scene on the hillside – though Phil did stress that he really didn't want to. Is that an option, do you think?

I shared a car back to the hotel with Sarah. I hadn't realised that her dad was a writer,

Geoffrey Lancashire, who wrote episodes of *Coronation Street* years before Sarah was in it. She's another one fascinated by what makes writers tick. Her theory is that you have to be slightly unhinged to be a writer. 'All the best writers are mad,' she said. Then again, it was 5am, so she could have been talking in tongues and I'd have duly nodded.

FROM: RUSSELL T DAVIES TO: BENJAMIN COOK, SUNDAY 14 OCTOBER 2007 12:22:16 GMT

RE: MORE WORK, LESS MAYBE

My brain is buzzing. This Space Bus script is driving me mad. Perhaps in a good way. I woke up with it whirring and whizzing through my head. I wish I had a Dictaphone, so I could babble out all the ideas. I'll keep going till tonight, then decide whether to abandon it or keep going. Or maybe I'll send it to Julie and Phil to decide. It's about to turn into a Balloon Debate – who to throw out of *Crusader 50*? I used to love Balloon Debates in school. Some kid would stand there droning, 'I am Florence Nightingale and I saved lots of lives,' some other kid would come back with 'I am Winston Churchill and I won the war,' and I'd just be sitting there thinking, *we throw someone out of a balloon?! Brilliant!* (Am I showing my age? Do they still have Balloon Debates? Do you know what I'm on about?)

Bless Sarah Lancashire, she's always been dying to write herself – so tempted by it, after years of watching her dad, who's well remembered and much loved in Manchester – and I used to nag her to start, but maybe she's wise. Maybe it's better, staying away. Who needs it? But she really is clever, isn't she? Much underestimated. You don't get to that status in the industry without a keen mind.

Poor Howard. That's the final option, to recast and reshoot. Oh, but that would be terrible. (A lot easier for us, though.) It doesn't bear thinking about.

FROM: BENJAMIN COOK TO: RUSSELL T DAVIES, MONDAY 15 OCTOBER 2007 18:03:16 GMT

RE: MORE WORK, LESS MAYBE

What do Julie and Phil make of the Space Bus episode? Is it going to be yours or Tom MacRae's? And have you warned Tom yet?

FROM: RUSSELL T DAVIES TO: BENJAMIN COOK, TUESDAY 16 OCTOBER 2007 18:56:35 GMT

RE: MORE WORK, LESS MAYBE

They love it. Phew. However, in 4.1 news, Howard is so frail, he's broken his leg, so his wife, bless her, phoned up and admitted, 'I think we'd better stop.' He's definitely out. The terrible thing is, we couldn't claim insurance before for filming any replacement scenes, because we'd known that he was ill and took the risk. No insurance. But now that he's broken his leg, we have insurance money for a brand new hillside scene. That's weird. But we needed the money.

Yesterday, in the space of 12 hours, after deciding that Howard couldn't continue, I said that I wanted to rewrite it with Donna's grandad instead, so Howard and family won't have to see a new Geoff on screen – and Phil suggested Bernard Cribbins. Donna's grandad is the newspaperman from *Voyage of the Damned*! We phoned up Bernard's agent… and he's free! He loved his day with us, so he's on board. Well, not quite – money to sort out and all that – but technically the deal is done. Christ, this show can move fast sometimes. That was a blizzard of phone calls and e-mails. So, today, I've rewritten Geoff as Wilf. The newspaperman was Stan in 4.X, but I like Wilf better for a longer-running part. His name is never said on screen in 4.X, so all we have to do is change him to Wilf in the end credits.

It's spooky, though, because that hillside scene is one of the few that I obsessed over in our e-mails – and here it is cropping up again. Of course, we're faced with the outrageous coincidence of the Doctor meeting the grandfather of the woman with whom he fought the Racnoss, the same woman who's about to track him down. Phil suggested reshooting the Christmas scene so that Bernard didn't appear twice. I said, 'No, let's make it the same man.' It's sort of funny. I've just rewritten 4.4/4.5 as well (it's been a hell of a day), in order to change the dad to the grandad. At the Nobles' house, Wilf recognises the Doctor, the Doctor recognises him, Donna realises that the Doctor and Wilf have met before, and Sylvia still has to recognise the Doctor from the wedding in *The Runaway Bride*, while handily adding that Wilf wasn't there because he had Spanish flu! That's the maddest scene ever. We could just ignore all these links, but we've a dedicated audience – not the fan-audience, but the other 7.9 million – so I think this casting needs to be acknowledged. And the fact that it's not any old actor, it's Bernard bloody Cribbins, sort of allows the madness.

Nonetheless, that fanboy part of me does have his teeth slightly on edge, so I'm going to take care of it in 4.11. When Rose is trying to get Donna to put history back on course, she's going to say something like, 'You met the Doctor, then your grandfather did, then you found the Doctor for a second time. That's not just coincidence. It's like the universe was trying to bind you to the Doctor. To stop this [the parallel world] from happening.' That's a fair bit of nonsense, and posits the universe, or at least destiny, as a sentient force, but it's kind of spooky. I like that. At the very least, it's saying, 'We know this is barmy.' The only time I try to rule out huge coincidence is when it actually *changes* the plot. But here it doesn't. It's just detail.

Yesterday continued to be weird. If my favourite thing in 4.1 is the hillside scene, my least favourite is those bloody guards being electrocuted in the doorway, isn't it? I never could think of a solution. Well, at 3.36am – I noted the time – my phone rings. They're on a night shoot – oh God, red alert – so I grab my phone and, sure enough, it's James Strong. Oh no, what's wrong?

> JAMES
> Russell! David's asking, about these guards, the ones who get electrocuted. How does the Doctor know where

they are, to electrocute them?

> RUSSELL
>
> Well, he doesn't. He's discovered the wiring that Miss
> Foster's used to convert the building into a Levitation
> Post, and he uses that to electrocute all the doorways.

> JAMES
>
> Ah. Right.
> (pause)
> They aren't coming through a doorway.

> RUSSELL
>
> Right. Why not?

> JAMES
>
> The doorways here are rubbish.

> RUSSELL
>
> Oh-kaaay. So how do they get electrocuted? In your
> version?

> JAMES
>
> They come through a sort of archway.

> RUSSELL
>
> So the archway electrocutes them?

> JAMES
>
> Yes.

> RUSSELL
>
> But they don't actually touch anything?

> JAMES
>
> No.

> RUSSELL
>
> And you've already shot this?

> JAMES
>
> Yes.
> (pause)
> The doorways really are rubbish.

> RUSSELL
>
> So the Doctor electrified every single archway in the
> building, with such strong electricity that anyone
> passing through one would get electrocuted.

> JAMES
>
> Yes! That works!

> RUSSELL
>
> Good. Oh, and James? You tell David that's your version.
> Not mine.

                    JAMES
    Okay.

                    RUSSELL
    Night then.

                    JAMES
    Night.

And don't you love the way that I made myself sound good there? But it just proves something (poor James, it's not his fault at all): if something is a problem, it'll *always* be a problem unless you fix it. Like the best problems, it comes back to haunt you – on the page, on the shoot, in the Edit, on transmission. I failed to fix that. Clearly failed. It would always have gone wrong, somehow. It was wrong from the start. I bleated about it to you, but didn't actually do anything. Lesson learnt. Well, maybe.

FROM: RUSSELL T DAVIES TO: BENJAMIN COOK, WEDNESDAY 17 OCTOBER 2007 17:11:03 GMT

RE: MORE WORK, LESS MAYBE

No more Space Bus script yet. I sat with it last night and just couldn't get into it. If you're not into that script, if you're not devoted, and hooked, and scared, and passionate, it just reads like a bunch of boring people stuck in a box. Hopefully, this isn't true. I've just got to get in the mood and launch myself into it. I can finish it tonight, I reckon.

But now I've got to phone Bernard Cribbins. It turns out that he thought he was travelling *in* the TARDIS! As a companion! So it looks as though that's about to go bollocks-up.

FROM: RUSSELL T DAVIES TO: BENJAMIN COOK, THURSDAY 18 OCTOBER 2007 04:17:59 GMT

RE: MORE WORK, LESS MAYBE

It's finished! See 4.8 as a belated birthday present, Ben. (God, I'm cheap.) Happy birthday! (It is the 17th, isn't it?) You old man.

FROM: BENJAMIN COOK TO: RUSSELL T DAVIES, THURSDAY 18 OCTOBER 2007 13:43:38 GMT

RE: MORE WORK, LESS MAYBE

Thanks, Russell. That's one CREEPY episode! It scared the crap out of me. What's it going to do to the kids? Hey, I just thought – the monster knocking on the outside of the Space Bus *has no name*. Yes, that makes it creepier, but mightn't Gary Russell's head explode? How is he going to enter it into his Great Big Encyclopedia Of Everything In *Doctor Who* Ever? Won't somebody think of Gary Russell's mind?!

FROM: RUSSELL T DAVIES TO: BENJAMIN COOK, THURSDAY 18 OCTOBER 2007 21:02:29 GMT

RE: MORE WORK, LESS MAYBE

Your typing sounds somehow… older. Have you aged suddenly? Ha ha ha.

I'm coming down off that 4.8 rush. I keep saying things to people like 'I'm not tired', but I think that's bravado. Vanity, I suppose. I want to say 'I'm fine' and sound impressive, but this morning I found myself hobbling to the shops. Hobbling! And wheezing. My legs aching. My knee hurting. My ear's a bit deaf. I'm chronic. Bollocks I'm not tired. I watched old people walking past in the Bay, faster than me. Still, 4.8 seems to have gone down a treat. Ed Thomas is very excited about building the *Crusader 50* set. And I think I should call the episode *Midnight*.[9] What do you think? Or *Crossing Midnight*, but maybe that's pretentious. David has been sent the script tonight. I'm slightly dreading his response. All those lines! He's going to kill me.

It's the opposite of *Voyage of the Damned*, that script. In *Voyage*, a group of survivors are wonderful. In *Midnight*, they're awful. Humans at their worst. All paranoid and terrified. Much closer to the real world – or my view of the world. That's partly why it was so hard to write; the language is very stripped down, there are very few jokes or conversational riffs, all those things that I normally rely on. The characters haven't even got much backstory, which is odd, because Trapped People Dramas usually rely on that. But this one's about who they are now. Very bleak.

....
9 4.8 is set on a planet called Midnight.

242

CHAPTER NINE

STEVEN MOFFAT'S THIGHS

In which the Doctor gains a wife, Donna's fate is sealed,
and *The Guardian* portrays Russell as giggling,
primping and lipsticked

FROM: RUSSELL T DAVIES TO: BENJAMIN COOK, FRIDAY 19 OCTOBER 2007 01:16:49 GMT

RE: MORE WORK, LESS MAYBE

4.1 is cursed! Last night's filming had been rescheduled from its original date, because of the rain two nights ago, so we ended up shooting the Donna-goes-to-the-TARDIS-with-her-hatbox scene up against a nightclub, with *BAM BAM, BAM* music and crowds of drunk Welsh, literally, yelling. Very loud. On and on and on. The offstage noise is terrible. With David and Catherine soldiering on bravely. Take after take after take. Today, David sent Phil, Julie and me an e-mail, complaining – well, complaining is too strong a word for him. He was just genuinely sad, because it's a lovely scene and he thinks that their performances were constrained. Ideally, we'll have to reshoot.

This show is so well run that sometimes I forget that days like this are normal, if not inevitable. This is a walk in the park compared to most other shoots. On *Queer as Folk*, we had one day so bad that the police were called in. We were filming outside Stuart's flat, in a dead rough area, and the local pub turned its music up deliberately. When they discovered the show's name, they turned it up further still. It was blasting out. When we went in to ask them to turn it down, the crew was threatened with machetes!

Also last night, James called from the Nobles' kitchen, pointing out that Sylvia says that Donna is unemployed, though Donna is clearly in work clothes. Damn! Over the phone, I added a line: Sylvia saying, 'It's no good dressing up like you're job-hunting. You've got to *do* something.' I should have seen that one. It's terrible for

243

Jacqueline King. No actor likes having a line added on the spot. (But I'm delighted that Jacqueline is back as Sylvia. You just smile when you see her on the rushes. She's so clearly a descendant of Jackie Tyler, and that's really good.) And then tonight it was Phil phoning from the set, asking if there should be extras in the street as Miss Foster addresses the masses of Adipose and levitates. I said, 'No! What would extras do? Stand there and boggle badly?' That's what Phil had thought, but he wanted to check.

FROM: RUSSELL T DAVIES TO: BENJAMIN COOK, SATURDAY 20 OCTOBER 2007 15:57:05 GMT

RE: MORE WORK, LESS MAYBE

I'm interviewed in *The Guardian* today. Yet another interview in which I'm portrayed as giggling, primping and lipsticked. In this one, I keep squeezing the journalist's arm and practically burst into tears at one point. What a load of bollocks. As if. I've read so many of those camped-up interviews now. I'm almost beginning to suspect it's true. That's sobering. I was asked to do *The South Bank Show* once, but I turned it down, because it was being directed by the man who did Paul Abbott's. That portrait of Paul was so accurate, it was terrifying. It captured all his mania and compulsion and repetition. I thought, if I saw myself through that director's eyes, I'd never be able to deny that it's true. Never see yourself.

FROM: RUSSELL T DAVIES TO: BENJAMIN COOK, TUESDAY 23 OCTOBER 2007 00:45:50 GMT

RE: MORE WORK, LESS MAYBE

In TV land, things are moving fast. Steven's agent came in today to talk to Jane and Julie about *Doctor Who*, and then Jane and Julie interviewed Julie's replacement. In a year or so, Julie will step down. She'll exec next year's Specials, but there will be a new exec for Series Five. Julie wants to either move to the US and work there or… well, all sorts of top-secret plans are being discussed. But the interview turned out to be quite emotional for her. It suddenly struck her that she's leaving. Her replacement – if he accepts – is going to be Piers Wenger. He only got into TV because he saw *Queer as Folk*, so naturally I like him. Very exciting. Very good news for the show. I hope he accepts. But no Julie! Imagine!

FROM: BENJAMIN COOK TO: RUSSELL T DAVIES, TUESDAY 23 OCTOBER 2007 13:48:55 GMT

RE: MORE WORK, LESS MAYBE

I've met Piers before. He's lovely, wonderful and clever, although quite unlike Steven, I think, who's just as lovely, wonderful and clever, but in a different sort of way. Piers is softer and calmer. That contrast is exactly what the show would need, isn't it? What a team! (This is all horribly luvvie. I'm making myself retch. Shall I lie and say that they're both complete bastards and *Doctor Who* is doomed?) Who will complete the Holy Trinity? Who's going be the new Phil Collinson? What about Susie Liggat?

FROM: RUSSELL T DAVIES TO: BENJAMIN COOK, TUESDAY 23 OCTOBER 2007 18:03:49 GMT

RE: MORE WORK, LESS MAYBE

As for the actual producer, no one is sure yet. I don't think Susie would want it. I think she likes to move on every so often. But I'm glad that you like Piers. On a personal level, he's a proper old-fashioned gentleman. I wouldn't feel that the show was getting an exec who'd say, 'Davies was rubbish! That era is gone! Sweep it away!' Mind you, maybe that's what the newcomer *should* say. I just want to be gently enshrined. In gold leaf. Is that too much to ask?

Oh, but 4.11 is due in on Monday! MONDAY!!! Think back to all those leisurely months when I was musing over that episode. Well, now it's here. I've less than a week. Although, a little bit of me is quite excited…

FROM: BENJAMIN COOK TO: RUSSELL T DAVIES, TUESDAY 23 OCTOBER 2007 22:28:53 GMT

RE: MORE WORK, LESS MAYBE
How much has 4.11 changed now that it's Donna not Penny?

FROM: RUSSELL T DAVIES TO: BENJAMIN COOK, WEDNESDAY 24 OCTOBER 2007 20:12:24 GMT

RE: MORE WORK, LESS MAYBE

Well, we haven't seen the pivotal 'turn' scene in 4.1 as I'd planned, because it doesn't fit Donna's new motive, but it's quite fun working out exactly when her life did turn left or right. I reckon – this has been Maybe-ing away for months now – that her vital moment was when she went for the job interview at HC Clements. (HC Clements is back! Who'd have thought?) But then the story locks down in pretty much the same way, so it's no worry. Well, it's a little continuity-fraught. More than I'd have liked. Now I've got to back reference as far as 3.X – in fact, to events before 3.X that we never saw – but I can handle that.

FROM: RUSSELL T DAVIES TO: BENJAMIN COOK, THURSDAY 25 OCTOBER 2007 20:18:38 GMT

RE: MORE WORK, LESS MAYBE

The rushes are in for the 4.1 wine bar scene. It's exactly what I wanted – bizarre, panicky, funny and weird. Nice stuff. But as for the ladies' toilets rushes – well, I'm a bit peeved.[1] At the Tone Meeting, I stressed how vital it is that Penny and Donna should *not* be in neighbouring cubicles, or they'd both be aware of one another. And what have they gone and done? They're right next to one another! I might as well talk to thin air. That's a really subtle, important point, lost. I texted James. He texted back, saying, 'I completely forgot!' Yes. Yes, you did. I think we'll be able to cut around it slightly, but still that's a scene operating at 90 per cent instead of the full 100. That's a shame.

That's not quite a wrap on 4.1, because we have to reshoot Howard's stuff on the hillside. From what I hear, Bernard Cribbins is definitely in.

---

1 Unbeknownst to each other, Penny and Donna are both hiding in the toilets at Adipose Industries, waiting for home time, in order to do some snooping.

PARALLEL WORLDS

This e-mail exchange between Steven Moffat and Russell explores the similarities between their respective scripts for 4.10 and 4.11...

FROM: STEVEN MOFFAT TO: RUSSELL T DAVIES, THURSDAY 25 OCTOBER 2007 09:22:35 GMT

STUFF

Right, so I'm on Episode 10 now. It's coming just before Episode 11 (no flies on me!), which is the one where Donna is in a parallel existence, yeah? Living the life she would've led? Now, we've already had this conversation, but just to be extra careful...

One element of my Episode 10 is Donna finding herself in Girl's World, wondering what the hell happened, but starting to fit in, maybe falling in love (time moves differently there), with the Doctor trying to pull her back out – I'm trying to avoid spoilers here – as he runs about the Library, battling shadows and certain death.[1] How close are we, given the proximity? There are different ways I can play this, lots of different ways, so what do I have to avoid? For instance, the Girl's World is currently modern-day Britain, but that could change without huge upheaval. What do you think?

FROM: RUSSELL T DAVIES TO: STEVEN MOFFAT, THURSDAY 25 OCTOBER 2007 16:43:50 GMT

RE: STUFF

I suppose it is a bit of a worry, except mine's supposed to be delivered on Monday, so I get in first, ha ha. (Note the 'supposed'.) Episode 11 is a big What If story. Namely, what if Donna never met the Doctor? A nasty Time Beetle on her back causes this to happen. It's called *Turn Left*, because she turned left in the car one day to go for her job interview at HC Clements.[2] If she'd turned right and gone for some other job, she'd never have met the Doctor. But time changes (thanks, Time Beetle!), she does turn right... and the Racnoss Webstar attacks, it's blown up, and the Doctor is pulled out of the wreckage, dead, because Donna wasn't there to tell him to stop. That's all seen from newsreaders' points of view – and by Donna, standing behind the crash barriers, just an ignorant bystander.

So then the world gets worse and worse, as alien events happen with no one to stop them. The hospital from *Smith and Jones* disappears and is taken to the moon; it's delivered back, with everyone dead, along with – it says on the news – one Sarah Jane Smith, who gave her life to stop the Judoon. Sob! A little while later, with the Noble family conveniently out of London for Christmas, a replica of the *Titanic* lands on Buckingham Palace (this happens off-stage – I've got the cheap episode!), southern England is destroyed, irradiated, and the Nobles have to live like refugees in the north, 20 to a house. Worldwide recession. Some time later, the Sontarans invade, as in

---

1 The 'modern-day boy' mentioned in the Series Four Breakdown as featuring in Moffat's Space Library episodes is now a little girl. She is custodian of an artificial world, referred to here as 'Girl's World', in which Donna finds herself trapped.
2 Donna was working at HC Clements as a temp in 3.X.

4.4/4.5, and have to be defeated. This time the Torchwood team is reported as having lost their lives. Meanwhile, Donna is working in a field, planting crops. Life is crap and the world is going to hell in a handcart. Diseases are breaking out. Rioting. Looting. But what can one ordinary ex-temp-now-wheat-sower called Donna do to change the world? Except, she keeps bumping into this mysterious woman called Rose…

Basically, Rose is working with UNIT, who have salvaged the TARDIS. They can use it to send Donna back in time to stop herself turning right instead of left. Except Donna fails, and everyone dies. No, I made up that last line! (Well, I'm making all of it up. We both are.) Still, 4.11 is pretty joyless – Christ, it's grim – so for God's sake, Steven, put some jokes in 4.10. But it doesn't sound too like Girl's World, does it? I suppose we both have Donna in an unreal world, but I can compensate for that by making it sound like a pattern. Does that help? Maybe I can combine both our plots by making it sound like dark forces are conspiring to separate her from the Doctor – first of all, Girl's World, now the Time Beetle, because Great Events are coming. Sort of saying, mystically, that the universe is trying to bind Donna to the Doctor, like they're meant to be together, because she has some Greater Purpose To Fulfil. I haven't quite worked out what that is yet, but I'll sort it out in 4.13. Er, somehow.

FROM: STEVEN MOFFAT TO: RUSSELL T DAVIES, THURSDAY 25 OCTOBER 2007 17:25:35 GMT

RE: STUFF

So these mighty powerful influence-anything-they-want-to forces are of a broadly mystical nature? One of my plans is to make it heartbreakingly hard for Donna to leave her other life. Maybe the Doctor could muse, in the final scenes, that the efforts made to keep Donna in Girl's World seemed over the top, almost like something else was at work…

FROM: RUSSELL T DAVIES TO: STEVEN MOFFAT, THURSDAY 25 OCTOBER 2007 18:10:25 GMT

RE: STUFF

I haven't worked out if it's heartbreaking for Donna to leave my parallel world. In theory, she should have a husband and kids so that changing reality means she has to lose them, as the ultimate sacrifice… hmm, but we're both heading in the same direction there, aren't we? Shall I leave that alone? Do you want that?

FROM: STEVEN MOFFAT TO: RUSSELL T DAVIES, THURSDAY 25 OCTOBER 2007 18:53:20 GMT

RE: STUFF

Exactly where I was going. Oops! Okay, you're going first anyway, and I'm on *Tintin* for the next week, so you could see if it works for you. Very broadly, in mine, Donna would have kids, but she'd realise that they're not real. Just as she's about to leave Girl's World, one of her children is clinging to her, because he's got a suspicion that he stops existing every time that his mummy isn't looking – oh, the heartbreak!

FROM: RUSSELL T DAVIES TO: STEVEN MOFFAT, THURSDAY 25 OCTOBER 2007 19:13:43 GMT

RE: STUFF

Ooh, no, that's brilliant. You have the kids. (You've got kids! You do better kids!) I've been struggling with my other-world husband and kids, because the world is going to hell, so their life isn't up to much, and I've got London destroyed, Donna picking hops (do you pick hops?), Rose and a gutted TARDIS... yeah, I've got enough to be going on with.

Instead of making it How Can I Leave All This For A Different World In Which You Don't Exist?, I've got How Can One Ordinary Woman Change The Whole World?' Kids are yours!

Reproduced with kind permission

FROM: RUSSELL T DAVIES TO: BENJAMIN COOK, FRIDAY 26 OCTOBER 2007 20:44:09 GMT

STEVEN MOFFAT'S THIGHS

... are now mighty and impressive, because – mark the day – pending money and all that, the deal is done. As of today, Series Five is Steven's!

FROM: BENJAMIN COOK TO: RUSSELL T DAVIES, FRIDAY 26 OCTOBER 2007 21:04:32 GMT

RE: STEVEN MOFFAT'S THIGHS

Awesome news! I'm as delighted as you are... but are we *really* going to keep this subject line? I think I preferred 'Charlie Hunnam's Arse'.

FROM: RUSSELL T DAVIES TO: BENJAMIN COOK, SATURDAY 27 OCTOBER 2007 17:58:48 GMT

RE: STEVEN MOFFAT'S THIGHS

I started 4.11 today. Well, it made sense, what with prep starting on Monday! I'm going to overrun on this script now and miss the National Television Awards in the Albert Hall on Wednesday. I love that ceremony. I actually get to talk to *Hollyoaks* boys. This is a big event in my life. Damn.

Still, 4.11 is... interesting. A lot harder to rip through quickly, because it needs so much construction. The opening scenes in the Fortune Teller's den on the planet Shan Shen (where the Time Beetle jumps on Donna's back, and we flashback to Donna's life on Earth before she met the Doctor) are so complicated, with so much to be established, that they could have gone on for 20 pages. Even now, I don't get to the pre-titles cliffhanger until Page 7. I don't think it's ever been that late. After the titles, we're straight into the parallel world where Donna turned right instead of left, but I'm having a lot of trouble, because Steven has a sort of parallel-world Donna in 4.10, too. I'm having to write around his plans. But I can't wait to see what he's come up with.

In other news, we offered the part of Sky Silvestry in 4.8 to Lesley Sharp – and she's said yes! Brilliant! She needed some talking into it, because of the sheer amount of line-learning. I phoned her up and said we'd cast Jane Horrocks instead. She was hooting. I love Lesley.

FROM: BENJAMIN COOK TO: RUSSELL T DAVIES, SATURDAY 27 OCTOBER 2007 19:27:46 GMT

RE: STEVEN MOFFAT'S THIGHS

So you don't know what's coming in 4.10 until you read Steven's first draft? Doesn't he tell you? Do you really fight the spoilers?

FROM: RUSSELL T DAVIES TO: BENJAMIN COOK, SATURDAY 27 OCTOBER 2007 19:44:02 GMT

RE: STEVEN MOFFAT'S THIGHS

It's funny, isn't it? I ask him not to spoiler me. He's written 4.9 already, so I've read that. It's called *Silence in the Library*, and it has a character in it who I'm just sure is the Doctor's wife (!!!), but I don't like to ask. I want to find out in the second episode, like a viewer. It's the closest that I get to experiencing brand new *Doctor Who*. Not for long, though…

FROM: BENJAMIN COOK TO: RUSSELL T DAVIES, SATURDAY 27 OCTOBER 2007 19:56:11 GMT

RE: STEVEN MOFFAT'S THIGHS

In the Huw Wheldon Lecture that Nicola Shindler gave in 2002 (what can I say? I'm a swot!), she says:

> *There are a lot of ways to tell a story and, in my opinion, a lot of ways that shouldn't be used. I've got my pet hates, which drive the writers I work with mad. But they have to do a lot to persuade me to change my mind. I can't bear voiceovers and flashbacks. Interestingly, when you just lift them out of a script, it's amazing how well the story works without them, with no rewrites. I think they're often just a crutch for the writer and sometimes show lazy storytelling. I feel the same about voiceover. It's lazy. This is a visual medium, so don't have someone tell me what to think or what to watch; show me!*

Bearing in mind, Russell, that you've just started writing an episode that hinges on flashbacks, I wonder whether you agree with Nicola. You also used flashbacks and flashforwards aplenty in *Casanova*, and even *The Runaway Bride* employed flashbacks to fill in Donna's backstory (and let's not get started on *Love & Monsters*), while there were voiceovers in *Bob & Rose* (I'm thinking of the scene where Bob is in a nightclub, surveying the talent), for example, so where do you stand on this? What are the dos and don'ts of flashbacks and voiceovers? Plus, from a technical point of view, how do you write them into a script?

FROM: RUSSELL T DAVIES TO: BENJAMIN COOK, SATURDAY 27 OCTOBER 2007 21:22:33 GMT

RE: STEVEN MOFFAT'S THIGHS

I'm with Nicola – I think you should beware. The techniques are too often being used to disguise the truth, the real story, the heart of the script. It's all pyrotechnics and glitter, fuelled by insecurity. That 'Where do you start a story?' question can become so overwhelming that the writer goes mad, firing out shots all over the place. 'I'll start here! And now! And backwards!' Oh, why not just get on with it and write the story? Nic's dissatisfaction comes, I think, from having read so many scripts where the techniques are masking the skill. If I'm reading something new, especially by someone new, I want to know that they can write, I want to know how their characters talk, how the pace skips along, how the story hooks me, how passionate the writer is, how much I feel the whole thing. I'm not interested in admiring the artifice and thinking, oh, that's clever.

Of course, those devices *can* work. I remember being very careful with the use of Old Casanova as narrator in *Casanova*. The presence of an old and very much alive man was in danger of robbing Young Casanova's experiences of any vitality or danger. I'll admit, I wrestled with that, but I was experienced enough to be aware of the dangers and subvert them. The sequence that I'm most proud of is Young Casanova's duel, where obviously he's going to survive (Old Casanova says afterwards, 'Well, you didn't think I was going to die, did you?'), but it worked because it forced me to look at the duel from a different angle – a more important angle – namely, *why* is it taking place? What is the Duke of Grimani (who Casanova is duelling) actually thinking? Which leads to devastating insights into Grimani's life. The duel is actually irrelevant.

Even with Peter O'Toole in the role, Old Casanova's appearances are limited, especially as the story goes on. There are huge chunks where he doesn't appear. Even then, the role of narrator is potentially flat and dull, so it was vital – oh, crucial – that Old Casanova had a plot of his own. He had his relationship with fellow servant Edith and, more vitally, his hope that his one true love, Henriette, was still alive. Without that, if he'd just been a dying old man, it would have been passive and uninteresting. Peter knew that. When he was first offered the part, he wasn't so interested, because he knew how dull a narrator is – and that Young Casanova could upstage the whole thing! It was only when Peter read it, when he saw that Old Casanova had a story, that he accepted.

Even with voiceovers, take care. The greatest TV example these days is *Desperate Housewives*, but you have to consider the bigger framework at play. Firstly, *Desperate Housewives* isn't one particular character's story: it's Life On Wisteria Lane. That overarching structure, that authorial stance, allows the voiceover. It's part of the whole show. It's part of the show's ethos. I could listen to that actress, Brenda Strong, for ever. That voice is seriously, beautifully cast. But more's the point, that character, Mary Alice, is dead. Added thrill! In a show about secrets, the omnipresent narrator allows us to see into people's hidden lives. It's at its best at the end of an episode, when Mary Alice's voiceover calmly leads us to an otherwise silent image – the New Handsome Neighbour has a gun in his kitchen! – so it's actually a clever, witty way of framing a cliffhanger. Imagine how dull that Handsome New Neighbour scene would be if you just cut to his house, he's all on his own, he gets out a gun. Boring! The voiceover gives it a size and majesty; it leads you into the revelation and then quickly gets out, leaving you dangling. In a show that's seen as camp, pretty and funny, it's easy to miss how incredibly skilful that is.

That authorial/narrator's voice demands a certain wisdom in summing up events, because often it says stuff along the lines of 'That's the thing about love…' That's hard to write. You can end up with the Hallmark Cards voiceover. 'That's the thing about love: it hurts and wounds, and yet, when it's pure, you'll never feel so safe.' Yuck! The voiceover is a honey trap for bad writing. It has to exist for more reasons than 'here's a sweet way to end the episode'. That's why Nic is warning against it.

As with all this stuff, you're never sure if you've got it right, even after transmission. The first draft of *Mine All Mine* started at the end – or almost at the end – of the story, with the Vivaldi family on stage in the middle of a public concert in Swansea, the Vote Vivaldi climax from Episode 5. You were thinking, who are they? Why's everyone cheering? They *what?!* They own the town?! 'Tell us how this all started,' the MC said to Max Vivaldi – and then, on Max, we flashbacked to the beginning of the story. Now, Nicola cut that, because she thought, never mind framing devices, don't distract me, just tell the story properly. In other words: get on with it! And I agreed with her. I lost that opening. But still, sometimes, in the dark hours, I wonder… if that had opened the episode, you'd have seen what's at stake for that ordinary family, right from the start. You'd have taken hold of an essentially ephemeral and even silly notion – 'I own Swansea!' – and made it concrete, powerful and alive. Without that, the starting point of the story was: man gets off train and gets into taxi. Hardly thrilling. The flashforward opening would have given you scale, crowds, cheering and fireworks. Hmm. Difficult to say. I'll always wonder.

From a technical point of view, writing them into a TV script, usually a flashback demands a scene break, because it's a different place or a different time. I'd write:

```
1. INT. BEN'S KITCHEN - DAY

BEN is back from Rome. He unpacks his stuff, then leans
against the fridge, remembering…

                                               CUT TO:


2. INT. ROME, RESTAURANT - NIGHT

A RAT runs across the restaurant! PHIL screams!

                                               CUT TO:


3. INT. BEN'S KITCHEN - DAY

BEN laughs at the memory.
```

That doesn't use the word flashback at all. Although, in fairness, we've been talking about flashbacks, so you're expecting one. If this were a brand new script, I might read that and think, eh? What just happened? What rat? It might be better to write:

```
2. FLASHBACK - INT. ROME, RESTAURANT - NIGHT
```

Or even:

```
2. INT. ROME, RESTAURANT - NIGHT

FLASHBACK. Two nights ago. A RAT runs across the restaurant!
PHIL screams!
```

The most important thing is that it's nice and clear, and doesn't piss off the reader. Don't say:

```
1. INT. BEN'S KITCHEN - DAY

BEN is back from Rome. He unpacks his stuff, then leans
against the fridge and his mind goes back, back, back, to two
nights ago, when he was so happy. On a CU of his noble and yet
careworn features…

MIX TO: white frames, which pulsate and bleach, filling the
frame, then slowly bleed into fleeting defocused images, as we
gently flashback to the sounds of Roma herself, the pasta, the
people, and the rat, yes, the rat…
```

Blah, blah, blah, get on with it!

And voiceovers are simple:

```
1. INT. BEN'S KITCHEN - DAY

Ben is back from Rome. He unpacks his stuff, then leans
against the fridge, remembering…

                    BEN V.O.
    I remember that wonderful night in the restaurant in
Rome…
```

More often, I write 'V/O' instead of 'V.O.', just because I always have. Some people would write 'O.S.', which stands for 'Out of Sight'. However, in my multi-camera directing days, 'O.S.' meant 'Over Shoulder', so it makes me flinch. And don't write 'BEN OOV', because that's 'Out Of Vision', which literally means offstage but nonetheless present – i.e. there would be a second Ben calling through from the kitchen. (Maybe there is…? I know nothing about Chiswick.)

FROM: BENJAMIN COOK TO: RUSSELL T DAVIES, SATURDAY 27 OCTOBER 2007 21:46:56 GMT

RE: STEVEN MOFFAT'S THIGHS

Like Nicola Shindler, in her Huw Wheldon Memorial Lecture, you must have pet hates that drive the writers you work with mad. The other month, you cited the list of three adjectives (and I was curious, fascinated and amused), but any others…?

FROM: RUSSELL T DAVIES TO: BENJAMIN COOK, SATURDAY 27 OCTOBER 2007 22:28:30 GMT

RE: STEVEN MOFFAT'S THIGHS

I'm hesitant to list any particular devices like Nicola does, because, as she'd admit herself, all her dislikes *can* work. (She produced *Casanova*, remember.) A writer should never cut him- or herself off from something that might be useful one day. I'd be mad to say, 'I'll never do flashbacks!' Then again…

Dream sequences. I hate dream sequences. I hate them in novels, too. If I come to a dream sequence, I turn the pages until it's over. Nothing ever happens in a dream. It's all symbolic. Pathetically symbolic. Why get symbolic when you can show me what's *really* happening? Also, have you ever read or seen a dream sequence that actually feels like a dream? Really? I think it's impossible. Dreams are so odd and dislocated. I've never seen one captured properly. Matt Jones fell foul of this on *The Impossible Planet*. The cliffhanger ended with Rose being possessed by the Devil – her eyes went black and she said, 'I am the Beast Incarnate!' or something. It was wonderful – but then the next episode opened on the Tylers' estate. Back home with Jackie and Mickey, but a strangely different Jackie and Mickey, doing mysterious things, speaking with the wrong voices, being generally spooky, because, well, it was a dream. Inside Rose's head. I simply couldn't bear it. I was convinced – I'm still convinced – that nothing of any dramatic merit can happen in a dream sequence. So out it went.

Mind you, isn't Steven planning a dream sequence for 4.10, with Donna trapped in a fake reality? But he'll write it so well, it'll prove me wrong. I think the point there is that the Doctor is trying to get Donna *out*, so that injects drama into the whole set-up.

Another pet hate – and you'll see this three times a night on British TV – is scenes that end with one character storming off, and the other character just saying their name, plaintively or crossly. Angie storms out, and Tom just says, 'Angie!' Whenever that happens on TV, I sit there and say, 'Have you lost the use of your legs?' (I'm always talking at the TV. I love it.) Watch a week's output and count how many times a scene ends with the departing person's name being called out. It's not good enough! I could argue that people storm out of rooms very rarely. How often in your life have you actually stormed out? It happens 27 times a night on the TV. There has to be a better way. (The other night, on *Casualty*, a character storming out did at least have the good grace to say, 'Don't follow me!' That's some sort of solution, I suppose.) I don't think the writer even notices. They think it's acceptable. They've seen it happen 5,000 times, so they think it's natural. They're not really writing at all; they're just transcribing a weakened version of their overall television experience.

I can't even bear phone conversations that don't end in 'Bye'. *Everyone* says goodbye at the end of a phone call. Only a Wall Street banker or Joan Collins could conceivably just hang up. The laziness comes from having seen this on screen so many times that the writer thinks it's acceptable. Bad habits. This is my other favourite:

```
Angie goes to leave the room.

                    ANGIE
    Well then, I'll see you later.

At the door, she stops, looks back.

                    ANGIE (CONT'D)
    Oh, and Tom?

Pause. Tom looks at her.

                    ANGIE (CONT'D)
    Thanks.

And she walks out.
```

NO ONE HAS EVER DONE THAT! Pure TV artifice. It drives me bonkers.

I can't bear dialogue that's forced into unnatural shapes because of production circumstances. For example, it's almost impossible to include 'Let's go to the cinema' dialogue anywhere in TV drama, in any form, because it's hard to know what's going to be on at the cinema when you transmit. I remember one, just once, many years ago on *EastEnders* – Ricky Butcher said that he wanted to go and see *The Adventures of Baron Munchausen*, which was actually showing in cinemas at the time! That sentence was so odd, but brilliant, by being so rare. I've never forgotten it. Otherwise, you should find ways to write around it, not have dialogue that goes: 'D'you fancy seeing that new film tonight?' 'Yeah, great, I'll come with you.' That's never been said in real life, ever. (What film? Which cinema?) It gets worse: 'I'll meet you at eight.' 'Okay, see you then.' (Meet you where? Your house? My house? Outside the cinema? Where at eight? *Where?!*) It really is the curse of the soap opera. They find it acceptable to say, 'Fancy trying that new restaurant in town?' 'Yeah, let's go tonight!' (What restaurant? Where in town? Is that it?!) *STOP IT!* Writing like that is pure laziness.

I, of course, make no mistakes ever.

Er...

FROM: RUSSELL T DAVIES TO: BENJAMIN COOK, SUNDAY 28 OCTOBER 2007 23:45:35 GMT

RE: STEVEN MOFFAT'S THIGHS

I've had a terrible day. I'd half-forgotten that I had to give a talk at the Dylan Thomas

Centre in Swansea this afternoon. I've been so busy that I hadn't paid it much attention. (All I've wanted to think about is Donna and Rose.) I opened the brochure last night, about 3am, just to check details – oh Christ, it's a full-blown posh lunch with Dylan Thomas' daughter and the Mayor and 200 guests all paying £25 to see me! And I hadn't prepared a thing! I had close to a panic attack this morning, running around, frantic, in a flop sweat. My head was exploding. My dad in the audience and everything! Needless to say, it went marvellously. I'm a bastard with a microphone. I'm genuinely, properly arrogant with a microphone. I can understand Hitler with a microphone.

I haven't had time to write more script, but I'm going to give it a go now, see how far I get. Hey, I don't know London geography. If Donna is in Chiswick and the Racnoss Webstar is heading for central London, what direction is that? At the moment, Donna says west, because they always say they're going 'up west' on *EastEnders*. But that's not correct from Chiswick, is it?

FROM: BENJAMIN COOK TO: RUSSELL T DAVIES, MONDAY 29 OCTOBER 2007 01:38:03 GMT

RE: STEVEN MOFFAT'S THIGHS
No, it's flying east. Chiswick is in West London. They say 'up west' on *EastEnders* because… well, that's in East London. And on that bombshell…

FROM: RUSSELL T DAVIES TO: BENJAMIN COOK, TUESDAY 30 OCTOBER 2007 02:05:44 GMT

RE: STEVEN MOFFAT'S THIGHS
Is 4.11 too adult? I've already taken out lines about the mass graves in the south of England. But I do like that creating-a-whole-different-world thing. It's hard to do, but an enjoyable sort of hard. One minute, Donna and her family are normal people. The next, they're impoverished and homeless, all in a few short scenes. I sort of believe it, that it could happen to any of us, all of us, in the blink of an eye. One day, I want to write a huge-scale adult series with that happening. It's good for Donna, too. I love writing her. There's an indestructible core to her, like she's always determinedly at a right-angle to events. I'd love to be like Donna.

FROM: RUSSELL T DAVIES TO: BENJAMIN COOK, TUESDAY 30 OCTOBER 2007 18:44:40 GMT

RE: STEVEN MOFFAT'S THIGHS
I'd been hoping that I'd finish 4.11 by tomorrow afternoon, so I could hotfoot it to the Albert Hall for the National Television Awards, but that's buggered. I'm getting nowhere today. I'm always planning dramatic arrivals that never actually happen. Maybe everyone does.

FROM: BENJAMIN COOK TO: RUSSELL T DAVIES, WEDNESDAY 31 OCTOBER 2007 20:28:46 GMT

RE: STEVEN MOFFAT'S THIGHS
I'm e-mailing you in the dark. If I switch off the lights, the trick-or-treaters won't know

that I'm in. The National Television Awards start in half an hour. Are you there? (If you are, pointless question.)

FROM: RUSSELL T DAVIES TO: BENJAMIN COOK, WEDNESDAY 31 OCTOBER 2007 22:19:19 GMT

RE: STEVEN MOFFAT'S THIGHS
Happy Halloween! I'm stuck at home working, but I might as well have gone – I'm getting 50 texts a minute from the Albert Hall. Hey, *Doctor Who* won Most Popular Drama! And David is Most Popular Actor! He dedicated his award to his mum. I did that when I won Comedy Writer of the Year, but then had 107 people coming up to me afterwards, saying, 'Your mother must be delighted.' I spent the evening saying, 'No, she's dead.' That put the dampeners on it.

FROM: RUSSELL T DAVIES TO: BENJAMIN COOK, WEDNESDAY 31 OCTOBER 2007 23:46:09 GMT

RE: STEVEN MOFFAT'S THIGHS
Sad news. Howard Attfield died this morning. We've just heard. Coincidentally, we're watching the first edit of 4.1 tomorrow, which has the Geoff stuff edited into it, just so that we can get the feel of that sequence in the overall shape of the episode. That's going to be weird. Poor old Howard. It feels double-weird reading back the stuff in 4.11 where Sylvia and Donna mention Geoff.

Writing 4.11 is hard enough at the moment. Rose has to explain the whole situation to Donna. The problem is, the audience sort of knows what's going on, but you can't skip Donna's reactions, and there's so much to react to, so I have to keep it interesting, somehow new and slightly unexpected, while working out where to place what information and when. I'd hoped to finish tonight. Ah, sod it. That's enough for now. I've smoked too much.

FROM: RUSSELL T DAVIES TO: BENJAMIN COOK, THURSDAY 1 NOVEMBER 2007 11:55:03 GMT

RE: STEVEN MOFFAT'S THIGHS
I'm hotfooting it from the 4.1 Edit. First reaction: I am delighted. Mad, funny, weird, mental, it's oddly unpredictable, sort of unclassifiable. The genre keeps switching like crazy. There's a long way to go – I've three solid pages of notes, and Phil and Julie have tons more – but I know we'll get it to where we want it. Actually, I think the loveliest moment is when the taxi driver pulls up and says, 'Stacy Campbell?' It's a small part for an actor, but he says it perfectly. And Donna looks so lost. The night and the street and the sudden calm are just perfect. It feels real, in that moment. A little, insignificant moment just crystallises into everything that I wanted.

FROM: BENJAMIN COOK TO: RUSSELL T DAVIES, THURSDAY 1 NOVEMBER 2007 14:23:44 GMT

RE: STEVEN MOFFAT'S THIGHS
Have you ever been disappointed at an Edit? Like, *really* disappointed? Crushingly

disappointed? What do you do? Is it too late by then?

FROM: RUSSELL T DAVIES TO: BENJAMIN COOK, THURSDAY 1 NOVEMBER 2007 16:11:04 GMT

RE: STEVEN MOFFAT'S THIGHS

I live in a state of constant disappointment, but that's what makes you work harder, to act on that disappointment and eliminate it. The Edit tends to get skipped in all discussions of modern *Doctor Who*, like all we do is delete a few lines. But the Edit is tough, vigorous and merciless, because that's when you really shape all those words and pictures into the drama. It's like starting again. It's like production begins from scratch. No one ever takes the script into the Edit, because it's irrelevant by then. You're dealing with what you've got, not what you should have got. That's why we go through five, six, seven edits, with millions of notes from all of us, every time.

I'm making this sound very executive-driven, like Julie, Phil and I do all the work. Of course, the director and the editor do a hell of a lot before we even step in there. Having said that, *Doctor Who* has limited post-production time, so often we get to see the show at a stage when, really, the director and editor should spend another fortnight in there alone. But that's disingenuous, because we love going in there while it's still a bit raw. We know how to hammer something into shape. I'm always reading about interfering executives sitting in Edits, demanding that you shave a few frames off a shot, as a Great Evil Of Modern TV... but that's exactly what we do, and I think it's right. I suppose if your executive is a bonehead, you're in trouble. But then the US system is to lose the director from the Edit, so the producers take over completely.

A lot of what we do is eliminating the disappointment. Any moment that's only 90 per cent, we work at – try this, try that, cut it faster, lose that line, add music, play it off David, emphasise Catherine during that bit of dialogue – to make it 100 per cent. Any moment that's only fifty per cent, we'll move heaven and earth to cut. You sharpen and concentrate it, until you like it. The more you watch something, the more you like it, the more you forgive it, the more inclined you are to accept its faults, and that's why you have to remember the impact of that very first viewing, always. The most awful viewing was the first Edit for *The Runaway Bride*, because the director, Euros Lyn, and his editor hadn't had time – in a tricky episode, with that motorway chase and everything – to put on any music. (We always watch with temporary guide tracks, like movie scores and things.) It was the flattest hour of *Doctor Who* ever, particularly when it's supposed to be a big, blousy Christmas episode. The music is so vital to this version show. God, that was dispiriting! I was gutted. It was like watching an episode where David has a bag over his head.

I'm just describing a writer's life, really – and a producer's, a director's, an editor's. Everything is a work in progress. Potential is never reached. Do you remember how worried I was, on *Voyage of the Damned*, that the passengers and crew of the *Titanic* would appear to be human? That it looks like they're from Earth instead of just visiting? We played about with giving them bindis and stuff, although we abandoned that idea.

Well, just last night, it occurred to me that I should have simply had the people on the *Titanic* referring to 'the humans' a lot more. Like, a couple of dozen times, in the dialogue. It's so obvious! I can't believe it didn't occur to me earlier. Too late now, of course. Instead, we faffed about with sodding bindis. In 20 years' time, that'll still niggle me. It'll always be a work in progress.

FROM: RUSSELL T DAVIES TO: BENJAMIN COOK, FRIDAY 2 NOVEMBER 2007 03:12:03 GMT

RE: STEVEN MOFFAT'S THIGHS

Finito 4.11! I'm not sure it makes sense. Sod it, I'm posting it to the office now. They need prep. Ooh, I can sleep tomorrow.

The best news is – I looked at my watch, thinking of telling you this, and it was 9.15 tonight – I finally worked out how to write out Donna at the end of the series! This has been driving me mad. Quietly, desperately insane. There isn't time to tell you all the stuff going on in my head, but sometimes I leave out the most awful fears, because I don't even like admitting them to myself. It's been churning in my head – *how, how, how?* All day long, every day – *how?* She loves the Doctor, she loves travelling with him, she chose to be with him and went to extraordinary lengths to find him again, and she has precious little to go back to, so how could she leave? She gets injured? Dies? Sylvia dies? Donna gets lost in time, and I pick her up for one of the Specials (we find her years later, on an alien world, citizen of the universe, older and wiser, no longer needing the Doctor)? None of those ideas worked. They're all crap. They're all dull, actually. But then, tonight, I solved it. At 9.15pm. It's like it just went *wham!* Right now, I can't wait to write it. Huge stuff.

And I'm not going to tell you what it is! HA HA HA! It needs to sink into my head for a bit. But I don't think you should know. I think you should find out.

FROM: BENJAMIN COOK TO: RUSSELL T DAVIES, FRIDAY 2 NOVEMBER 2007 08:21:29 GMT

RE: STEVEN MOFFAT'S THIGHS

NOOOOOOOOOO!!!

Fine. I'll wait. Hmpf.

FROM: RUSSELL T DAVIES TO: BENJAMIN COOK, THURSDAY 8 NOVEMBER 2007 23:47:14 GMT

RE: STEVEN MOFFAT'S THIGHS

Episode 8 is shaping up nicely. We've cast Sam Kelly as Professor Hobbes, Lindsey Coulson as Val Cane, Daniel Ryan as Biff Cane (he was Rose's first boyfriend, Andy, in *Bob & Rose* – it's a Lesley/Daniel reunion!), and Rakie Ayola as the Hostess. That's an amazing cast. I'm so excited. Also, we've auditioned a very handsome Goth-type Jethro. Those eyes! His name is Colin Morgan. Oh, and did I tell you that we've cast Georgia Moffett as the Doctor's daughter in 4.6? Peter Davison's real-life daughter! She *really is* the Doctor's daughter! We didn't cast her for the publicity, honest. She's genuinely fantastic. She's going to have one hell of a career.

But I hit the roof the other day, because Episode 8 of *Sarah Jane* hasn't shaped up so nicely: it went out on the CBBC Channel with bloody atrocious credits. 'CASTING BY ANDY PRYGOR', that sort of thing! How amateur. I banged off an e-mail accusing Julie, Phil, Matthew Bouch and me of not looking after that show in post-production enough. We were all there for filming and the Edits, but then other work has overtaken us and we've neglected it. That was all a bit sour.

Also, I saw David and Catherine tonight, to explain the end of 4.13 to them. That went down a treat. Bloody lovely. They were enraptured. David kept on saying, 'That's *exactly* where it should end!' But I'm not going to tell you what that means.

FROM: RUSSELL T DAVIES TO: BENJAMIN COOK, WEDNESDAY 14 NOVEMBER 2007 00:14:58 GMT

SILENCE IN THE DISCO

I've been on the phone to Julie since 9.30pm. Sometimes the BBC is the maddest, stupidest place in the whole world. An example: it was proposed that the Christmas Special press launch – it's on 18 December – has a disco. Well, okay, fine. The place is booked until midnight. But the council says that the music has to stop by 11pm, so what happens between 11pm and midnight? Mrs Event Organiser says, 'I thought we could have a silent disco. It worked well when I was at MTV.' A silent disco – though you're 25 and probably know this – is when everyone puts on their iPods and dances in silence. At a *Doctor Who* press launch! To quote Julie, 'We're not launching bloody *Skins*!'

FROM: BENJAMIN COOK TO: RUSSELL T DAVIES, WEDNESDAY 14 NOVEMBER 2007 00:32:25 GMT

RE: SILENCE IN THE DISCO

Silent discos are fun. There was one at Glastonbury this year. Then again, there were Portaloos, pear cider, Lily Allen, and people swimming in their own excrement at Glastonbury, but none of that would go down very well at a *Doctor Who* press launch. You were right to scoff.

FROM: RUSSELL T DAVIES TO: BENJAMIN COOK, TUESDAY 20 NOVEMBER 2007 21:10:20 GMT

RE: SILENCE IN THE DISCO

This morning, we found out that lovely Sam Kelly, who was to be Professor Hobbes in 4.8, has been involved in a car crash and broken his leg. So he's out. We'll have to recast. Oh God…

I got a car back to Cardiff from Manchester last night, and it occurred to me, out of the blue, as we drove along… I should do a Davros origin story in 4.12/4.13! Like I did with the Master in *The Sound of Drums*. It sort of demands it, doesn't it? How did Davros become how he is? How did he get scarred? Well, he was Josef Mengele, wasn't he? The war, the wounded, the experiments. Blimey, that's good. (Interesting use of the word 'good', but you know what I mean.) Trouble is, in costing these episodes, I haven't allowed for that at all – digital mattes of Skaro, hospitals full of wounded – but it's worth pushing for, don't you think?[2]

FROM: RUSSELL T DAVIES TO: BENJAMIN COOK, THURSDAY 22 NOVEMBER 2007 13:23:02 GMT

RE: SILENCE IN THE DISCO

I received an e-mail from Janet Fielding this morning. She used to run the Women in Film and Television organisation, and I'm due to go to the WFTV Awards on 7 December, to give a Lifetime Achievement award to Verity Lambert. David is going, too, if he can be released from the schedule. But the e-mail is devastating. Verity's cancer has returned. She's been taken into palliative care. Janet, bless her, is apologising, because now they want the award to be collected by a friend of Verity's. As if I'd mind! I don't like to intrude and ask how bad it really is, but…

> **Text message from: Russell**
> Sent: 22-Nov-2007 23:22
> Verity Lambert died today. We've just heard. I'm ridiculously sad.

> **Text message from: Ben**
> Sent: 22-Nov-2007 23:32
> I'm speechless. Tomorrow is *Doctor Who*'s 44th anniversary. None of us would be doing what we're doing if it weren't for her.

> **Text message from: Russell**
> Sent: 22-Nov-2007 23:36
> I know. We're putting a dedication at the end of the Xmas Special.

> **Text message from: Ben**
> Sent: 22-Nov-2007 23:37
> I was going to suggest it, but then realised that of course you'd be doing that. Quite right.

> **Text message from: Russell**
> Sent: 22-Nov-2007 23:57
> Julie just said, 'Knowing our luck with graphics, it'll be spelt "Varsity Lamboot"!' I've been laughing so much, like you do when you're sad.

> **Text message from: Ben**
> Sent: 23-Nov-2007 00:02
> I'm just glad she lived to see *Doctor Who* become, once again, as brilliant and imaginative and important and loved as it was when she produced it.

2 A digital matte painting (DMP), added during post-production, is used to create virtual sets and backdrops.

> **Text message from: Russell**
> Sent: 23-Nov-2007 00:07
>
> Yes! And she really did watch it. When I met her last year, she said, 'All those Daleks flying into Canary Wharf! I wish we could have done that.' Oh, but you did, Verity. You made it all.

FROM: RUSSELL T DAVIES TO: BENJAMIN COOK, SATURDAY 24 NOVEMBER 2007 13:01:49 GMT

RE: SILENCE IN THE DISCO

Yesterday's read-through of 4.8 was a bit disconcerting. (Everyone else was happy, but sod them.) It just sounded slight and unimportant and weak. Maybe whacking great CUs of fearful faces will sell it. Lesley synced so well with everyone – it was an astonishing performance – so it sounded interesting rather than scary. It even started to sound natural. I do worry that a thin conceit has become a whole episode. I know that I've taken a big risk. I'm a bit worried.

The read-through of 4.11, on the other hand, was magnificent. Rarely have I been so pleased in a read-through. Catherine blazed her way through it. She did something I've never seen anyone do before: she said a line, made it hugely funny, everyone roared with laughter, then she looked up, looked around, and she laughed too! It was a look of absolute pure delight. Great moment. Catherine's capacity to perform anything really frees me up, to go anywhere, to say anything. There's a great bit in that script, when Donna is being sacked, and there's a *whumph!* as the Royal Hope Hospital is returned to Earth, offstage, but she's so full of her own problems, she turns to the office and says, 'Well, isn't that wizard?!' There's something about that line that proves everything I've been trying to say about dialogue, how free you can be, because I've never heard anyone say, 'Isn't that wizard?!' You'd never expect someone like Donna to say 'wizard'. It wouldn't seem to be in her vocabulary. I'm not even sure myself why she chooses it. But it works. Somehow, for reasons I can't even articulate, 'wizard' is exactly right for that moment. Moments like that, I like my writing.

> **Text message from: Russell**
> Sent: 25-Nov-2007 18:19
>
> Guess who we've cast as the Professor in 4.8? David Troughton!

> **Text message from: Ben**
> Sent: 25-Nov-2007 22:10
>
> Here's a marvellous thing: David Troughton appeared in the 50th *Doctor Who* serial, *The War Games*, back in 1969... and now you've cast him in the 50th episode of the revived series. FANBOY OVERLOAD!

FROM: RUSSELL T DAVIES TO: BENJAMIN COOK, THURSDAY 29 NOVEMBER 2007 23:45:19 GMT

RE: SILENCE IN THE DISCO

Everything is firing on all cylinders at the moment. We've two episodes filming at once, so it's only to be expected. Catherine and Bernard are brilliant together in 4.11, as are Catherine and Billie. Although, watching the 4.8 rushes is an odd experience, because it's all being shot in sequence. I'm seeing the story unfold, literally, day by day. The cast is starting to go stir-crazy on that *Crusader 50* set. They did the monster-knocking-on-the-outside-of-the-bus scene today. Both David and Lesley texted to say, 'We're scared to death!' More importantly, Colin Morgan is beautiful. You meet him in real life and think, yeah, nice, sweet. But he's one of those lucky bastards that the camera absolutely loves. All cheekbones and black hair and *mmm!* He's a seriously excellent actor, too. Every line, he makes a really interesting choice.

I would describe to you the fear and bile that's rising up with the approach of writing the series finale, but I can't bear to. Oh, that cold clutch of fear. Steven wrote to me today, saying, 'Don't you feel like sticking your head out of the window and yelling, "I DON'T KNOW WHAT I'M DOING!!!"' Yes, absolutely. Solidarity. Fear is always the same. Different worries with different scripts, but the same baseline fear.

FROM: BENJAMIN COOK TO: RUSSELL T DAVIES, FRIDAY 30 NOVEMBER 2007 00:02:56 GMT

RE: SILENCE IN THE DISCO

It can't all be fear and bile, can it? Aren't there bits of 4.12/4.13 that you're really looking forward to writing?

FROM: RUSSELL T DAVIES TO: BENJAMIN COOK, FRIDAY 30 NOVEMBER 2007 00:24:48 GMT

RE: SILENCE IN THE DISCO

It's not all fear and bile, no. Like, I've worked out the end to 4.13 – well, not the very end, that's Donna, but the climax to the plot and all the Dalek stuff. I went into a frenzy, playing Murray's Series Three soundtrack CD full-blast. I actually stood up and walked around the room. For ages, just striding. And hitting things. I was sort of banging work surfaces and stuff. Sometimes that happens. After about 20 minutes of frenzy, I was actually crying. In a good way. With relief. With happiness, actually. Because it works. I really think it works and will be magnificent. Right now, I believe in it with all my heart. So that's good. That's not fear and bile.

Of course, it's only one of a thousand problems solved – I don't know how I get everyone to the right positions yet, that's the tricky thing, the geography – but the sheer joy of that resolution is fantastic. It's so *Doctor Who*. It's so Doctor. It's so Donna. Sod off, Davros, you've no chance!

FROM: RUSSELL T DAVIES TO: BENJAMIN COOK, SATURDAY 1 DECEMBER 2007 14:35:44 GMT

RE: SILENCE IN THE DISCO

In the early hours of this morning, Steven Moffat delivered 4.10! At last! It's brilliant, of course. Such an imagination, it's staggering. I'm not sure I understand it yet, but then I read it at about 3am. We're trying to get Kate Winslet for River Song, who's sort of the Doctor's wife, and Michael Gambon or Ian McKellen for Dr Moon.[3] Fat chance!

I've just returned from Shan Shen, the fabled Chino planet. I have voyaged to the stars! In an alley behind Cardiff's Royal Infirmary. It's an amazing set. Smoke, lanterns, chickens, peppers, alien fruit... and it's only for two short scenes! It's starting to piss down now, but that's probably made it more *Blade Runner*-y. It's unsettling, though, going on set, because I feel such a stranger. Almost a fraud. All I do is type the words 'Shan Shen', that's easy, and then all those people have to slave away on a Saturday, in the rain, to create the bloody thing. I actually feel guilty. Julie and I laugh about what the crew must think of us when we turn up on set, because inevitably you're met with 'Nice of you to join us', like we've left our catamites and Leisure Palaces to walk amongst the workers. People talk as though you've never been on a set before, almost saying, 'This is the camera. This is the director. You'll have to be quiet because we're going for a take,' forgetting that we've spent 20 years on different sets in every sort of circumstance. You see yourself becoming that oft-joked-about, never-on-set producer. Like all that experience was for nothing. Hey ho.

> **Text message from: Russell**
> Sent: 03-Dec-2007 22:14
> We've just played the Christmas episode to Kylie, in London. She clapped and laughed and cried and even sang a bit. What a weird night!

> **Text message from: Ben**
> Sent: 03-Dec-2007 22:19
> Send her my love. Actually, she's probably forgotten who I am.

> **Text message from: Russell**
> Sent: 03-Dec-2007 22:21
> Oh, she's disappeared off into the night now. She's probably forgotten me already. She is not of this mortal Earth.

---

3 In the little girl's artificial world, Dr Moon is treating her.

Text message from: **Ben**
Sent: 03-Dec-2007 22:22
Yes. She's stardust.

FROM: RUSSELL T DAVIES TO: BENJAMIN COOK, THURSDAY 6 DECEMBER 2007 14:05:57 GMT

CRUSADER 52?

Time for an update. Phil wasn't part of the discussions about Donna's parallel worlds in both 4.10 and 4.11. Coming to it clean – this is why it's good to have someone coming to it clean – he's thrown his hands up in horror and said that we can't run both episodes consecutively. Yikes! He's right, of course. He wondered whether we should ask Steven to write out Donna's parallel life completely, but it's way too integral. And I've known about it all along, so it's my fault. As a result, we're shifting the transmission order. Steven's two-parter becomes Episodes 8 and 9, *Midnight* becomes Episode 10, and then Episode 11 remains the same, so there's a one-episode buffer in between Donna's two parallel worlds.

Tragically, that means that *Midnight* is no longer our fiftieth episode. My fanboy heart is broken. It might as well be the *Crusader 52* now. What a shame. (And we've lost your marvellous David Troughton/fiftieth episode fact!) Hand on heart, though, I think the new order is good. All the experimental stuff gets shifted further back in the series. I worry that running *Midnight* and *Turn Left* consecutively means two lower-budget episodes in a row – but actually that was the same as *Love & Monsters* and *Fear Her*, and the ratings went up, week on week, so I'm worrying for nothing. That doesn't stop me worrying, though.

Elsewhere, in Maybe land, it's a pit of despair! I even hesitated over that exclamation mark, because that's making it sound like fun. I know I had that moment of joy the other day, but it hasn't lasted. There's a greater fear, of course, and that's Christmas 2008. That's doing my head in, above and beyond 4.12/4.13. I haven't a clue – and it has to be written in February! I keep thinking of ways to escape. I could tell them that there just won't be a Christmas 2008 episode. 'Tough!' What would happen? The world wouldn't end. But Julie would die. I couldn't bear to let her down that much.

I'm not sure about Cybermen in the snow, in Victorian times. Would it be a retread of *The Unquiet Dead*? I spent a day wondering if the court of Henry VIII would be better, but that's not Christmassy enough. You'd have a banquet, but no turkey. It'd be flagstones, knights, swords and funny trousers, none of which feels Christmas Day enough. Plus, translating Victorian into Tudor is hardly a solution; it's just a disguise. How about something completely new? After the *Torchwood* press launch in London on Monday, I spent the night in a large, faceless Paddington hotel. I couldn't sleep, so I went for some ice at 2am. All the big, wide corridors were empty. Not a noise. The machine on Floor 2 wasn't working, so I went up to Floor 3. Still empty. The lift shafts were sort of humming, almost roaring. It was eerie. And I imagined, what if I was a dad and I'd left my family in the room, and when I got back... they were gone? Just gone. That's the start of a *Doctor Who* story! The whole hotel is empty, at Christmas, like it's been taken out of time or something, and creatures are beginning to stir, and the only other person in existence is this man called the Doctor. That sort of thing. Nice. But random. In need of an awful lot of thought – and I have to write this in February, so there's not enough time to develop it. I'm stuck with random, mad thoughts, desperately trying to plug a gap, but none of them quite working. It feels lousy. Sometimes I think, if I just died, all of this would go away. That begins to feel like a good option. It wouldn't be letting anyone down. I'd be blameless and free and martyred. Ridiculous, I know.

FROM: BENJAMIN COOK TO: RUSSELL T DAVIES, THURSDAY 6 DECEMBER 2007 15:18:15 GMT

RE: CRUSADER 52?

It's lucky that you're an atheist, then. Bugger all on the other side, and you know it. You'd *hate* that.

Besides, if you died, I'd never find out what's in store for Donna Noble. Reason enough to keep going, Russell.

> Text message from: **Russell**
> Sent: 07-Dec-2007 15:22
> Are you on set today? I hope the *Crusader 52* is fun.

> Text message from: **Ben**
> Sent: 07-Dec-2007 15:26
> I am on set, and it'll always be the *Crusader 50* to me. I helped name this bus! What am I supposed to do with my David Troughton/50th episode fact now, eh? The horror.

> Text message from: **Ben**
> Sent: 07-Dec-2007 16:16
> Hold the presses! I've just realised, *Midnight* IS still the 50th episode of new *Doctor Who*... to be shot! Filming on *Turn Left* started one day earlier, didn't it? So this is still (sort of) the 50th something after all. My fanboy mind is delighted.

> Text message from: **Russell**
> Sent: 07-Dec-2007 16:18
> Ha ha ha, oh, your fanboyness! I love it. Yes, *Turn Left* started a day earlier, so it definitely came first. That's cheered me up. I'll sleep easier in my bed tonight.

CHAPTER TEN

HOLDING
THE LINE

In which working on *Doctor Who* is likened to al-Qaeda,
Russell loses his trousers in Soho, and Catherine Tate
sparks a major diplomatic incident

FROM: RUSSELL T DAVIES TO: BENJAMIN COOK, FRIDAY 7 DECEMBER 2007 21:09:20 GMT

RE: CRUSADER 52?

Huge movements on Series Five. Piers Wenger has said yes to Julie's job – to the whole job, Head of Drama at BBC Wales, everything. However, with the usual *Doctor Who* madness, *The Guardian* has got hold of it, so a press release has had to go out, announcing Julie's departure… in 18 months' time! This is the only job where that gets reported so far in advance! Even Tony Blair kept us guessing for longer.

It's our production manager Tracie Simpson's farewell party on Monday. First Tracie, then it'll be Phil, and now Julie is off. It's the end, slowly. Piers and Steven had a train journey back from Cardiff together on Tuesday, so you could say that work on Series Five has already begun. That's weird. Actually, it doesn't feel weird – I'm not sure I feel anything at all about it. But as a fanboy – how exciting! That's a brilliant team.

FROM: RUSSELL T DAVIES TO: BENJAMIN COOK, MONDAY 10 DECEMBER 2007 03:21:07 GMT

RE: CRUSADER 52?

I spent today considering one tangible thing: whether to destroy New York in 4.12. That would be fun, wouldn't it? The idea came from the fact that all the Doctor's companions are found in England. I've a chance to expand on that, create a bigger world. Maybe Martha is in New York? She'd have to be saved, maybe by trying some experimental UNIT teleport that zaps her out of the building before Dalek lasers

267

hit. The only survivor! It suits Martha, that lone warrior feel, and brings her back to England with an easy zap. But destroying New York has its problems: it leaves heavy repercussions for the rest of *Doctor Who* history, because there's no reset button. I worry about that. Series Five is bound to have episodes set on modern-day Earth – and that might be hard to establish, because it'd be a very wounded world. It even deflates the end of 4.13, with the Doctor flying planet Earth back home, all happy and hooray... except for that smouldering crater with millions dead! These e-mails do influence things, definitely, because now I'm thinking, no, destroying New York is a bad choice. Typing it out in this e-mail made me realise that, but it's good to spend a day considering the option. This is the only job in the world where you can do that. Unless you work for al-Qaeda, I suppose. I might not destroy New York at all, but the thought is a good indication that I need to work harder to establish a worldwide feel.

I'm definitely doing Bernard Cribbins and the paint gun, though. Did I tell you this? He phoned me up a while back – I love getting phone calls off Bernard – and said, 'Is it true we're meeting the Daleks in the last episodes?' 'Yes, Bernard.' 'I've fought them before, you know!'[1] 'I know, Bernard, it was 41 years ago.' 'I've always had this great idea,' he said. 'You know those paint gun things? You could take out a Dalek with a paint gun, cos it's only got one eye. Bit of paint on the eye, it'd be blinded!' I was

1 Bernard Cribbins played police constable Tom Campbell in the 1966 movie *Daleks – Invasion Earth 2150 A.D.*, based on the 1964 *Doctor Who* television serial *The Dalek Invasion of Earth*.

hooting. I said, 'I'll see what I can do.' It could be brilliant – if only because Bernard Cribbins requested it. I'd better not tell the rest of the cast that I'm taking requests!

FROM: BENJAMIN COOK TO: RUSSELL T DAVIES, MONDAY 10 DECEMBER 2007 03:28:47 GMT

RE: CRUSADER 52?

Look, 3:21am that last e-mail was sent! Do you never sleep? Once again, we're both still up at ridiculous o'clock. Why don't we just work in offices, Russell? Wouldn't that be easier? Don't you think? Go on, tell me why you don't work nine-to-five in an office. Why isn't that the life for you?

FROM: RUSSELL T DAVIES TO: BENJAMIN COOK, MONDAY 10 DECEMBER 2007 04:05:01 GMT

RE: CRUSADER 52?

It's funny you should ask, because I *did* work in offices, in TV, for years and years, but I never fitted those hours. When I was storylining the soap *Revelations*, I was locked in an office with a brilliant man called Paul Marquess, who went on to create *Footballers' Wives*. We had such a laugh. One of the best times of my working life. I refused to start work at 9am. I physically couldn't. We'd be in the office at 9am every day, but we'd just hoot and gossip. We fancied a man down the corridor, called Tony Gregory, and invented excuses to walk past his door 15 times a day. We'd sit with Pritt Stick and Tipp-Ex and the photocopier, and invent *Revelations* paperback covers. We had a trainee called Jim who we'd torment all day, because he was the token straight in a sea of gays. But then, around about 4pm, we'd start work – and we'd be there till gone midnight, because then we'd work hard and properly. I loved storylining. Those ideas were watertight and insane. Looking back, I probably drove Paul mad. Every so often, he'd say, plaintively, 'Can we do some work now?' But I'd be busy cutting out cast photos and giving them moving mouths like Captain Pugwash, so I could act out the shows in puppet form! I was making a nine-to-five office job fit me. But that was the mid '90s, when I was already set on leaving to become a writer. I knew what I wanted. I was only storylining *Revelations* so that I'd get to write the best episodes. But before that…

I read those interviews with people who say 'I knew that I wanted to become a writer when I was six years old' with such envy. I didn't know. For a long time. Partly because being a writer didn't even seem like an option. It was like wishing to be a pop star or a mountaineer or a pianist. In my head, I was writing all the time, in the sense of making up stories, but I thought that was just *thinking*. Like, that's how people think. I thought everyone did it. Daydreaming. Doodling. Literally doodling – I'd draw all the time. All that energy went into cartooning. Just as a hobby, but a compulsive hobby. Everything I drew, I'd expand into stories. When I was 15, 16, I'd imagine being a Marvel artist. (A careers teacher said, 'You're colour blind. You'll never work in the graphics industry if you're colour blind,' and crushed that dream dead.) Even at Oxford University, I poured all that energy into drawing. I had a cartoon strip in the student newspaper. I'd illustrate the Student Handbook. Far more important to me than lectures. After Oxford, I went to Cardiff to do a postgraduate course in Theatre Studies, because I couldn't think what else to do with my life, but even then I was drawing all the time. I covered my bedroom wall with my own artwork. I became a poster designer for Cardiff's Sherman Theatre. Drew some of my best stuff ever. One of my first TV jobs was illustrating a *Jackanory*-type show for BBC Wales.

When I landed my first producing job, on *Why Don't You...?*, a magazine show with a gang of kids showing you things to do in the school holidays, my real passion was the Fact Pack, a free photocopy that we'd send out to viewers, packed with games, recipes, puzzles and stuff. I started to expand the illustrations into cartoon adventures. I was meant to be illustrating recipes, which was boring, so I thought it'd be fun if I brought a Potato to life. Then he needed someone to talk to, so I added an Egg and a Plastic Cup. They started to grow personalities, way beyond the gags. Potato was bullish and verbose, Egg was simple and sweet, Plastic Cup was sarky, sly and undoubtedly gay. Their simple lives started to develop into stories. I drew one where the Stationery Cupboard went to war with the Kitchen, which is still one of the best things I've ever done. Eventually, whole pages of the Fact Packs were given over to them, and their adventures became more and more epic. I was obsessive about it. At one point, I started sort of seeing a very nice hairdresser called Mark, but I had a Fact Pack to complete and gave it more time than I did him. Eventually, he said, 'This is never going to work. That drawing's more important to you than I am.' He was right. Obsession sounds like a bad thing, but it was more like love. I loved those cartoons. I still do.

During all this, I had the day job on *Why Don't You...?* proper. That was the office job. Organising schedules, material, rehearsals and stuff. Edits. Dubs. Lunch in the canteen. The nine-to-five job. But I glided through that. The real stuff, the creativity, for me, was drawing Potato fighting Paperclips, at night, at home, in the cartoons – and then the same thing started to happen to my *Why Don't You...?* scripts. I started to dramatise them. I couldn't help it. Scenes would link together. Gags would become running jokes. The kid presenters grew screen personalities – one daft, one cheeky, one mad – so that they could interact better. They started to have adventures. One week, they went off to explore Loch Ness, to find the Loch Ness Monster. That episode was the first time that I realised what I'd done. I remember, clearly, going home and thinking, take out the recipes and I've just written a drama! I only realised it after I'd written it. Not everyone liked it, of course. The Head of Children's Television, Anna Home, did comment, 'It's not supposed to be a drama. You're failing the magazine content.' That was true. I guess that was an official slap-down. But I ignored it. Like you do. You're cheeky when you're young.

In my final year on *Why Don't You...?*, for my very last episode, I really went for it: recipes and puzzles and makes were chucked out of the window, and the *Why Don't You...?* gang found themselves trapped in their cellar with an insane supercomputer,

MOFFAT'S NUMBER 5

December 2007, and work on Series Five is well under way...

FROM: STEVEN MOFFAT TO: RUSSELL T DAVIES, MONDAY 10 DECEMBER 2007 15:20:22 GMT

THE FUTURE

Russell! When you've some time, can we have a chat? I've a few practical points that I'd like to talk over with you. And since I'm starting to think about this for real (blimey!), I'm realising that I probably shouldn't hide myself away from spoilers like the whimpering fanboy that I am. Is it okay if I read your finale scripts when they're done, just in case there are any crossovers with all the nonsense currently in my head? If I wait to see the episodes, I'll be deep in new stuff, courses will be set, and it wouldn't be the first time that we've both blundered into the same idea.

One other thing, which I've been meaning to say. You're always so kind and positive, you'd never let it show, but I realise it can't be easy to hand over a show like this one – so please understand, I appreciate that and I'm hugely grateful for the chance that I'm getting. I'll try not to be some irritating little Scottish bastard measuring up your house for curtains. And boy do I need some more macho metaphors.

FROM: RUSSELL T DAVIES TO: STEVEN MOFFAT, MONDAY 10 DECEMBER 2007 20:35:22 GMT

RE: THE FUTURE

D'you know what? It *is* easy to hand over this show, now that I know it's to you. No kidding. No niceties. If it were going to some *Holby* committee, or some idiot, or some stranger, I'd be terrified, in a good old-fashioned fanboy way. But it's you. It's simply you. I think that's glorious. And I've genuinely had enough, while still loving it with all my heart. That feels good, getting out while still loving it. (Imagine going off *Doctor Who*!!!) So I'm really, really happy. You're not just measuring for curtains, you nonce. You're knocking down that wall, building an extension – hell, abandoning the whole thing, declaring it unsafe, and building a brand new house in its place. Like there's any stopping you!

When are we having this famous chat, then? I'm in London for the launch on 18 December. What if I came early? Are you free? Or how about the day after? Stories are beginning to prey on my mind, too. I'll park the Doctor wherever you need him. You decide! If you decide on more of an overlap, then the Specials can contain Series Five elements that'd be absolutely yours. I know, I'm so noble! But it's all for the good of the show. That's all that matters. If I'm taking time to think of the three Specials, and you've started formulating a whole series – oh, go on, you've started already, haven't you? – then we'll just swap roles, so you go first, you tell me what you're planning (not in too much detail, thank you – think of my fanboy heart), and I'll make sure that the Specials lead seamlessly into Series Five. That should work.

FROM: STEVEN MOFFAT TO: RUSSELL T DAVIES, TUESDAY 11 DECEMBER 2007 11:47:26 GMT

RE: THE FUTURE

I'm so glad that you still love it. I've asked you every year, but I was too nervous to this time. That's honestly a relief to hear.

FROM: STEVEN MOFFAT TO: RUSSELL T DAVIES, WEDNESDAY 12 DECEMBER 2007 09:37:50 GMT

RE: THE FUTURE

Actually, never mind all that, I'm wittering like a girl. I've worked out my opening episode! It's good, honest!

FROM: RUSSELL T DAVIES TO: STEVEN MOFFAT, WEDNESDAY 12 DECEMBER 2007 10:30:45 GMT

RE: THE FUTURE

I *knew* it! Exciting, isn't it?! Oh, I bet you're having fun.

>>I'm so glad you still love it<<

No kidding. Every second. Bloody love it.

which they defeated with an electric, lemon-powered skateboard. We *tripled* the ratings! Turning it into a drama sent that show from 0.9 million to 2.9. We were carried around Television Centre in a ticker-tape parade (not really, but almost). After I left, the show went back to its magazine format... and ratings fell to 0.9 million again. Ha! Seriously, that was me realising how powerful drama can be, how it can draw you in and build an audience. But I only did it because I like stories. Storytelling just bleeds out. Of course, much of it was disguised as drawing. I can still see cartooning in my work (cue internet insults), in the speed and the fast cuts, the visual gags, the pacing of the dialogue, but now my hobby is my life. That's why I never think of it as work, really, no matter how much hard graft I actually do. Even if no one ever saw this stuff, I'd be doing it anyway.

Nowadays, by the way, I run screaming from the notion of nine-to-five office life. Four years on *Doctor Who*, and I've never had an office. Never even had a desk. It'd be handy sometimes, to have somewhere to escape to or sit and think on my own when trapped in BBC Wales, but it wouldn't work. I'd end up drawing on the walls.

FROM: BENJAMIN COOK TO: RUSSELL T DAVIES, MONDAY 10 DECEMBER 2007 10:07:36 GMT

RE: CRUSADER 52?

>>I never think of it as work, really, no matter how much hard graft I actually do. Even if no one ever saw this stuff, I'd be doing it anyway.<<

I believe that. I'm going to quote it back at you next time it all gets too much. I'm going to make you write it out and stick it above your computer!

FROM: RUSSELL T DAVIES TO: BENJAMIN COOK, MONDAY 10 DECEMBER 2007 23:39:02 GMT

RE: CRUSADER 52?

I've just got back from Tracie Simpson's surprise farewell party. It was a genuine surprise, I think. She looked shell-shocked, instead of acting all fake-surprised. I think we really got her! Wonderful party. You can just tell that it's going to escalate all night. They're going to be off their heads. I've come home, genuinely sad. Deeply sad, actually. It's starting to sink in: this is the beginning of the end. Phil gave a beautiful speech. He described our very first block of filming, back in 2004, when, after one week, we were three weeks behind. Oh, those dark, dark days. With all our massive experience, we still had no idea how to make a show like *Doctor Who*. No one did. Tonight, Phil said, 'We had the BBC's new flagship in tatters, just one week in.' They were filming on the Tyler's estate, and Phil just couldn't take it any more. He burst into tears. He phoned Julie. Julie calmed him down, and then she said those fateful words: 'I'm sending you someone.' That someone was Tracie. From the next day onwards, the whole show ran better. We got it made thanks to Tracie. And in the history of *Doctor Who*, she's going to look like a footnoted crewmember. Amazing woman. Every single person in that room tonight loves her.

Anyway, gobsmacking 4.11 rushes today. No kidding, one of the finest pieces of acting I have ever seen – when Catherine realises that she's going to die. She's crying with horror. Absolutely perfect. I texted her to say thanks. She's a very private person, I'm never 100 per cent sure what she thinks about things, but she texted back: 'I'm so lucky to be doing all this. It's wonderful to be part of it.' That made me happy. Very happy. For many hours. But then I had a terrible conversation with Julie…

I'd e-mailed her asking about delivery dates. She e-mailed back saying that 4.12/4.13 is due by 7 January, and the 2008 Christmas Special (officially designated 4.14) is due by – gulp – 18 February. Ten minutes later, she phones up:

> JULIE
> I know why you're asking. This is impossible, isn't it?

> RUSSELL
> Well, I'll try.

> JULIE
> No, but this is really impossible, isn't it?

> RUSSELL
> Well… it's bad.

> JULIE
> Do you think you can do it?

> RUSSELL
> Episodes 12 and 13, fine, I'll have that done. Maybe not
> all by the 7th, but certainly 12, and enough of 13 to be
> going on with, and a good synopsis of the ending for you

to work from.

                        JULIE

But then you'll have to work on that, rewriting it and
getting the FX to budget. That's another two weeks at
least. That leaves you three weeks for Christmas 2008.
Can you do it?

                      RUSSELL

Um…

                        JULIE

I have a plan of attack. First option is the worst case
scenario: we just don't do a Special for Christmas 2008.

                      RUSSELL

Oh.

Long, long pause. Telephone wires humming. Then JULIE says,
quietly:

                        JULIE

That 'oh' is the happiest I've heard you sound in four
or five years.

                      RUSSELL

I just said 'oh'!

                        JULIE

No, that was a very big 'oh'.

                      RUSSELL

I meant 'oh', that's all, just 'oh'.

                        JULIE

That 'oh' was like, oh the relief. It was joyous.

                      RUSSELL

But what would the channel say?

                        JULIE

They'd be devastated.

                      RUSSELL

Then we can't do it.

                        JULIE

We have to, if you can't write it.

                      RUSSELL

But in times like this, when we're scared of the
schedule and feel like running away or stopping, you
always say, hold the line. We hold the line. You always
say that.

                    JULIE
    Right. Then that's what we'll do.

                    RUSSELL
    We hold the line?

                    JULIE
    We hold the line.

So we're blundering on. Into the darkness. That conversation has scared me. Julie is going to try to find money to give us an extra week so that we can stand down for seven days before filming 4.14. That would give me an extra week to write, so the deadline would be 25 February. Julie never, ever gives up. She fights. Also, she leads you into conversations like the one above. You find yourself speaking your darkest fears. They become tangible so that you can deal with them. You're not alone.

I think I would back down and give up if BBC One didn't have a new Controller, Jay Hunt, whose appointment was announced last week. We need her on our side, we need her to be waving the flag for *Doctor Who*, more than ever, so that we're not slipping back to become an also-ran. It's absolutely the wrong time for *Doctor Who* to fall out of the schedules. So. We hold the line. I keep going.

Which means I'm going to start 4.12, right...

... now.

FROM: BENJAMIN COOK TO: RUSSELL T DAVIES, TUESDAY 11 DECEMBER 2007 00:04:56 GMT

RE: CRUSADER 52?

You've started! (But have you *really* started?)

One question (but answer it later – don't let me distract you from 4.12): filming Series One, back in 2004, how, after one week, is it possible to be three weeks behind schedule?

FROM: RUSSELL T DAVIES TO: BENJAMIN COOK, TUESDAY 11 DECEMBER 2007 02:20:47 GMT

4.12

Julie is so sad tonight. She's crying. It really has hit home. The slow end. Funnily enough, it's sort of helping me – makes me determined to write. All those brilliant people on the crew, I've got to write something excellent for them, something that's worth all their time and effort. Yeah, how noble. That'll evaporate by tomorrow.

>>filming Series One, back in 2004, how, after one week, is it possible to be three weeks behind schedule?<<

It's the amount that you plan to complete each day. For his speech at Tracie's party, Phil had dug out our very first callsheets, and we couldn't believe them. Like, we'd planned four pages on the Tyler's estate in the morning – that was just the morning! – then a move across London and another four pages, with monsters and FX and closing off Whitehall. That number of pages – or more – is quite normal for most dramas, but we discovered that *Doctor Who* is more like four to five pages a day. That's why, after that first week, we had a backlog of three weeks' material still to shoot. (I can't believe that it was actually three – I think that's become a good legend – but the point still stands.) It was terrifying. And guess what Julie said? 'Hold the line!' I was offering to rewrite, to cut, to scale down, to seriously change the vision of what the show should be, to make it achievable, but no – 'Hold the line!' And we did, and we learnt, and we got more realistic, and faster, and better.

Anyway, 4.12 has begun. As an opening seven pages, it could hardly be more exciting. I'm stopping now, not because I'm tired but because I'm terrified. It's taken seven pages to get this far into the plot, which means that this episode might be 5,000 pages long! I'm going to have to get it moving.

FROM: BENJAMIN COOK TO: RUSSELL T DAVIES, TUESDAY 11 DECEMBER 2007 15:53:26 GMT

RE: 4.12

The Hub! Sarah Jane's attic! Chiswick! Only another 4,993 pages to go, Russell. Hurry up!

FROM: RUSSELL T DAVIES TO: BENJAMIN COOK, TUESDAY 11 DECEMBER 2007 17:55:06 GMT

RE: 4.12

I haven't even opened 4.12 today. I'm flinching slightly. It's like I wrote that in a blur. I can feel the million problems ahead. No, the zillion.

But I was asked on holiday today. By a 71-year-old woman in Cardiff Bay! I bumped into Gary Russell while I was having my daily coffee in the Bay – at Coffee Mania, and the fact that the man serving there was voted seventh in Wales' Most Eligible Bachelors has *nothing* to do with it – and we had a chat. Me and Gary, not me and Mr Eligible. Then Gary plodded on his way, to the dentist, and that's when the 71-year-old approached me. She said, 'I'm going to Malta in January, and I think the perfect travelling companion would be an older gay man.' Older?! Let alone the gay bit! I was just sitting there having a coffee. I wasn't exactly wearing a dress.

FROM: BENJAMIN COOK TO: RUSSELL T DAVIES, TUESDAY 11 DECEMBER 2007 18:22:33 GMT

RE: 4.12

Gary Russell got you a holiday to Malta? In January? Maybe he should go with her. Now, there's a drama. I'd have said yes like a shot. You've missed out, Russell.

Now that you're into 4.12/4.13, with its not inconsiderable cast list, I'm interested in how your approaches to writing, say, Rose, Martha and Donna differ? Is it *what* different characters say or *how* they say it that defines them, makes them 'come alive', makes them distinguishable?

FROM: RUSSELL T DAVIES TO: BENJAMIN COOK, TUESDAY 11 DECEMBER 2007 18:51:14 GMT

RE: 4.12

That's tricky. I don't type 'DONNA' and then think, now, how would she say this…? The fact that I've typed 'DONNA' means that she already has something to say. You can worry too much about speech patterns, about imposing different styles on the words, one for Rose, one for Donna, one for Martha, one for Sarah Jane. They're all women, on the side of good, in a sci-fi world, so their speeches aren't going to be radically different. It's not so much what they say, as why they say it and when.

But I suppose there's a basic characteristic that I bear in mind. An essence. Rose is open, honest, heartfelt, to the point of being selfish, wonderfully selfish. Martha is clever, calm, but rarely says what she's really thinking. Donna is blunt, precise, unfiltered, but with a big heart beneath all the banter. But we come back to what I was saying ages ago about turning characters. If Rose can be selfish, then her finest moments will come when she's selfless. If Martha keeps quiet, then her moments of revelation – like her goodbye to the Doctor in *Last of the Time Lords*, or stuck with Milo and Cheen in *Gridlock* – make her fly. Donna is magnificently self-centred – not selfish, but she pivots everything around herself, as we all do – so when she opens up and hears the Ood song, or begs for Caecilius' family to be saved, then she's wonderful.

FROM: RUSSELL T DAVIES TO: BENJAMIN COOK, WEDNESDAY 12 DECEMBER 2007 03:14:05 GMT

RE: 4.12

The line is holding! So far. Here's some more. I'm stopping now. I need to think ahead. There are three or four interesting options for what happens next, and I need to find the right one.

It's an odd script, isn't it? The concept is so huge that the dialogue is quite perfunctory and plot-based. I'm fighting to get any character in there. The Doctor and Donna have to talk about plot, plot, plot – it would sound mad if they didn't – and the others are talking in that sort of brusque signature dialogue. Like Martha's 'I'm not a soldier, I'm a medic'. Signature dialogue is saying 'This is who I am'. It's very obvious, but the size of the cast demands those simple distinctions. Also, I'm strangely aware of people watching this for the first time, even though it's an unashamed continuity-fest, so all the characters are stating their presence, as if for newcomers. And Ianto is quietly stealing the show. This is deliberate, so that Gareth David-Lloyd will love me. I'm only half-joking. Somewhere in the subconscious, I think you cast handsome men so that you can impress them. Yeah, and it really works. Well, maybe one day. Oh, just once.

I'm still fighting to keep the cost down. I wrote the last few scenes with loads of FX – Dalek space station, Dalek saucers, hurtling towards Earth – but I need the money later on. It was spectacular, but expensive, so I deleted all the FX and made the whole thing work with cheap radar graphics. I think it's better, actually. Captain Jack, Sarah Jane and Martha can't see what's happening, not until the Dalek ships (cont p281)

DEATH OF A PM

This sequence, written on 13 December 2007 and featuring UK Prime Minister Aubrey Fairchild, was cut from Russell's original draft of *The Stolen Earth*...

31. INT. NOBLES' HOUSE - NIGHT

WILF & SYLVIA watching the events of sc.35-40 on TV.

                                                        CUT TO:

32. INT. UNIT HQ, NEW YORK CITY - NIGHT

MARTHA & UNIT watching sc.35-40 on the big screen. (Don't see the screen here; ADR Trinity Wells will describe an American equivalent of events, a saucer approaching the White House, landing - but OOV!).[1]

                                                        CUT TO:

33. INT. SARAH JANE SMITH'S ATTIC - NIGHT

SARAH JANE & LUKE, watching sc.35-40 on MR SMITH.[2]

                                                        CUT TO:

34. INT. THE TORCHWOOD HUB - NIGHT

GWEN & IANTO watching the events of sc.35-40 on a computer, CAPTAIN JACK in b/g, on his mobile, desperate:

                          CAPTAIN JACK
    This is Captain Jack Harkness, I'm calling from
    Torchwood - I don't care, just tell the Prime Minster to
    get out of there!!

So sc.31-34 are layered in with:

                                                        CUT TO:

35. INT. NEWSREADER STUDIO - NIGHT

NEWSREADER TO CAMERA:

                          NEWSREADER
    - reports are confused, but... It's being said, one of the
    saucers is descending towards Westminster...

                                                        CUT TO:

----

1 Trinity Wells (played by Lachele Carl) is an American newsreader who first appeared in *Doctor Who* 1.4, and has since featured in several episodes of *Doctor Who* Series One to Four, *The Sarah Jane Adventures* and *Torchwood*..
2 Mr Smith is the supercomputer in Sarah Jane's attic.

(NB, sc.36-40 now entirely experienced as grainy TV FOOTAGE.)

HANDHELD CAMERA capturing SAUCER, as it descends on
WESTMINSTER.

CUT TO:

37. EXT. CITY STREET - NIGHT

GRABBED HANDHELD SHOTS of PEOPLE, running, looking back, and
up, in terror, fleeing from the saucer.

CUT TO:

38. EXT. CIVIC BUILDINGS - NIGHT

HANDHELD CAMERA, from a DISTANCE, capturing PRIME MINISTER
AUBREY FAIRCHILD, TWO AIDES and a BRITISH ARMY COLONEL walking
up to a scaffolding platform, like someone has quickly
arranged a public meeting.

(NB, no need for real Whitehall, just civic-type buildings in
darkness b/g, all shot close, grabbed, shaky).

NEWSREADER OOV
...we're getting pictures live from Westminster, we're
seeing Prime Minister Aubrey Fairchild... It seems he's
coming forward. To greet the visitors.

FX: WHIP PAN from Aubrey to a HANDHELD SHOT of a SAUCER,
lowering down...

CUT TO HANDHELD Aubrey & staff, buffeted by wind, but
remaining resolute, holding their ground...

CUT TO:

39. EXT. CITY STREET - NIGHT

GRABBED HANDHELD SHOTS - PEOPLE still running, but some have
stopped. Looking up in awe. Terror. One man joyous.

CUT TO:

40. EXT. CIVIC BUILDINGS - NIGHT
HANDHELD CAMERA jerkily ZOOMS INTO CU AUBREY FAIRCHILD, as he
goes to a microphone-stand. A brave man.

AUBREY FAIRCHILD
Visitors to Earth. We welcome you. We ask you for help,
in this strange wilderness. But most of all, I seek to
reassure you... The Human Race comes in peace.

FX: HANDHELD WHIP-PAN over to the SAUCER, as a huge BRONZE

DOOR begins to lower…

CUT TO AUBREY & STAFF, HANDHELD, their fear, their hope…

(Still INTERCUT WITH SC.31-34, Wilf & Sylvia staring, Sarah Jane holding Luke, terrified, saying quietly 'No, no, don't, no…', Captain Jack now back at the screen with Gwen & Ianto, muttering, 'Get out of there, just get out…')

FX: HANDHELD, the DOOR completing its descent, to become a RAMP. Beyond, the interior of the ship: PITCH BLACK.

And then…

Just a voice.

                    DALEK
    Exterminate!

FX: HANDHELD, ENERGY BOLT shoots out of the pitch-black –

FX: HANDHELD, AUBREY struck, skeleton, he screams & dies!

FX: HANDHELD: a SWARM OF DALEKS flies out!

                                        CUT TO:

41. INT. CRUCIBLE COMMAND DECK – NIGHT

THE CRUCIBLE is the Dalek ship at the heart of the web. Huge, dark space, with 1.13-type designs. Start close, shot tight, DALEK 1 gliding into position –

                    DALEK 1
    Dalek fleet in battle formation!

– tracking across DALEK 2, then 3, then 4, gliding in –

                    DALEK 2
    All systems locked and primed!

                    DALEK 3
    Crucible at 90% efficiency!

                    DALEK 4
    The Human Harvest will commence!

really arrive on Earth, which makes them more helpless. Good rewrite. Even if we could afford the FX, I think I'd keep it like that now.

FROM: BENJAMIN COOK TO: RUSSELL T DAVIES, WEDNESDAY 12 DECEMBER 2007 03:36:30 GMT

RE: 4.12

The Shadow Proclamation![2] Ooh, this is good! (Invisible Ben is on holiday in Cornwall. With Maria and her dad.)[3] Hey, the professor on the *Newsnight*-type show in Scene 14 should so be Richard Dawkins.[4] I bet he'd do it.

You say that you're considering three or four interesting options now. What are they?

FROM: RUSSELL T DAVIES TO: BENJAMIN COOK, WEDNESDAY 12 DECEMBER 2007 14:27:34 GMT

RE: 4.12

Richard Dawkins! Brilliant! I'm going to try that. Leave Invisible Ben in Cornwall. Visible Ben is full of good ideas. Mind you, if I was invisible and in Cornwall with Maria's dad, I know what I'd be doing…

The options… hmm, I haven't woken up with much clarity. I had a bad night's sleep,

---

2 First referenced in *Doctor Who* 1.1, the Shadow Proclamation turns out to be the 'futuristic space station complex where lots of alien races are gathered for a conference', mentioned in the Series Four Breakdown.
3 The *Sarah Jane Adventures* characters Maria Jackson (played by Yasmin Paige) and her father Alan (Joseph Millson) are, apparently, in Cornwall during *Doctor Who* 4.12/4.13, and Clyde Langer (Daniel Anthony) is 'with his mum', although Sarah Jane and her son, Luke (Tommy Knight), do feature.
4 In this draft, an 'elderly professor' (Professor Richard Dawkins in subsequent drafts and the transmitted episode) appears on a *Newsnight*-type TV show to discuss the 17 planets that have appeared in Earth's orbit.

and woke up in a sort of panic attack at about 5am, with vivid, weird images of Daleks and Martha and stuff. That, for the record, has never happened before. Maybe 'options' is the wrong word. It's more that I'm struggling with two contradictory directions. I want two things to happen: I want all the companions to link up, via their computers and phones, to combine their technology to send a signal that'll tell the Doctor where they are; at the same time, I want all these companions to hit the streets in the middle of the Dalek invasion, like freedom fighters in the night. I want both of these things to happen. I know all the scenes of both sequences, and now I'm trying to mesh them, to get the best of both worlds. Also, I'm trying to find the right moments for the Doctor and Donna's story to advance. The correct order. With a hundred choices. I always believe there's a correct order, a sequence that makes everything sing. I've just got to find it.

FROM: RUSSELL T DAVIES TO: BENJAMIN COOK, WEDNESDAY 12 DECEMBER 2007 15:49:36 GMT

RE: 4.12

Rather than do some real work, I've changed ELDERLY PROFESSOR to RICHARD DAWKINS. Nice one.

FROM: RUSSELL T DAVIES TO: BENJAMIN COOK, THURSDAY 13 DECEMBER 2007 02:21:32 GMT

RE: 4.12

Here's some more. Scary page numbers. I thought I'd be on Page 12 by now, but these events have taken me up to Page 20 already. I've thought about this for so long that I've become used to it, so it seemed smaller, more compact, in my head. I'm thinking ahead now and cutting huge chunks of future story as I go. New York has now becoming a pain in the arse, because it traps Martha there and her escape – 'Project Indigo' – is many pages long. It might have to be sacrificed.

FROM: RUSSELL T DAVIES TO: BENJAMIN COOK, THURSDAY 13 DECEMBER 2007 23:32:18 GMT

RE: 4.12

The Doctor is about to arrive at the Shadow Proclamation, but warning bells are ringing. He's meant to stride in with Donna, into some great hall, and, in a The Mill/Neill Gorton extravaganza, walk past every creature we've ever had. Krillitanes swooping. Judoon stomping. Slitheen farting. Maybe even an Isolus fluttering past. I've even thought of a way to include Margaret Slitheen, fleetingly.[5] But now I'm dreading it. It's going to eat up money. Money that is clearly better spent on the Dalek invasion of Earth. So I'm stalling. I hate writing something that might never be made. I haven't the time to waste! Trouble is, Will Cohen is *dying* to animate this sequence. He's been looking forward to it for months. So I'm writing to you instead of getting on with it. But I think typing that was therapy.

---

5 Blon Fel-Fotch Pasameer-Day Slitheen (played by Annette Badland) appeared in *Doctor Who* 1.4/1.5 and 1.11, having appropriated the identity and skin of human MI5 official Margaret Blaine. Following an encounter with the Doctor, Blon was regressed to an egg and returned to the hatchery on Raxacoricofallapatorius.

FROM: RUSSELL T DAVIES TO: BENJAMIN COOK, FRIDAY 14 DECEMBER 2007 02:05:49 GMT

RE: 4.12

I'm giving up for tonight. Just not connecting. I set myself the target of reducing 20 pages to 18. I failed, but lost a page and a half, so that's not too bad. It all helps.

I have to go to Manchester this weekend, because it's my boyfriend's birthday, and then Swansea, because it's my dad's birthday too – same day! – so work on this is royally buggered. I hate interrupting a script. It's hard to get the momentum back.

FROM: RUSSELL T DAVIES TO: BENJAMIN COOK, FRIDAY 14 DECEMBER 2007 19:35:54 GMT

RE: 4.12

The Judoon are back! Bo! Klo! Fo! To! Mo!

45. INT. TARDIS - DAY[6]

In flight, THE DOCTOR running round the console -

                    THE DOCTOR
     I'm trying to announce our arrival. No good just turning
     up! But that's weird… All frequencies jammed. They're on
     some sort of Red Alert…

He looks up.

DONNA is just standing against the rail. She's been crying,
doesn't like to show it. He goes to her, kind.

                    THE DOCTOR (CONT'D)
     I'll find them, Donna. I'll travel this whole wide universe
     to find them, I swear. It's not just your home. That daft
     little planet is the closest thing I've got.

                    DONNA
     Yeah. Sure.

ALARMS! The Doctor runs back to the console -

                    THE DOCTOR
     We're here! The Shadow Proclamation!

                                                        CUT TO:

46. FX SHOT

THE SHADOW PROCLAMATION. DMP only; a huge installation, metal
sc-fi towers ranged across a series of linked asteroids,
hanging in space, like a Roger Dean painting.

Over that, the sound of the Tardis engines…

---

6 Scenes 45–48, written on 14 December 2007, didn't make it to the shooting script.

CUT TO:

47. INT. SHADOW PROCLAMATION LOBBY - NIGHT

CLOSE ON THE DOCTOR & DONNA - who's recovering, brave face on
- both stepping out -

                    THE DOCTOR
     - right, the first thing we've got to do is -

Stops dead, as a PLATOON OF JUDOON march past, big, heavy
boots stomping, left to right - the Doctor & Donna nipping
through a gap in the formation, pushing forward -

                    THE DOCTOR (CONT'D)
     - whoops, 'scuse me, sorry -

FX: THREE KRILLITANES swoop down, the Doctor & Donna brushing
them off, still pushing forward -

                    DONNA
     Oy! Get off!

                    THE DOCTOR
     Keep your wings in, you lot!

- then stopped by TWO VESPIFORMS, buzzing right to left -

                    THE DOCTOR (CONT'D)
     - oh, mind those stings, thank you -

The Doctor & Donna then stopping to look properly. Gulp.

FX: WIDE SHOT. Big, white, open smart-sci-fi-building. Filled
with CROWD MULTIPLICATION JUDOON, CROWD MULTIPLICATION
SLITHEEN, a few HATH, two HELMETED SYCORAX, and CROWD
MULTIPLICATION SPACE-EXTRAS - some in big opera cloaks,
SISTERS OF THE WICKER PLACE MAT from 1.2, plus a lot of MONKS
& NUNS. Also, SHADOW POLICE - like Judoon, but Human, in big
stompy black uniforms. Flying through the air, KRILLITANES,
VESPIFORMS, GELTH. And in one corner, a huge 15ft ADIPOSE,
mewling. All busy, chaotic, emergency!

CUT BACK TO the Doctor & Donna.

                    DONNA
     Is it always this busy? What is the Shadow Proclamation
     anyway?

                    THE DOCTOR
     Police. Outer space police.

                    DONNA
     Name like that, I was expecting all druids and cloaks
     and incense.

> THE DOCTOR
> You should meet the Brotherhood of Darkened Time. That's
> the accountants.

TWO SLITHEEN & BABY SLITHEEN walk past, fast -

> DONNA
> Cor, what a stink!

> THE DOCTOR
> That's the Slitheen -

The Slitheen turn round, furious -

> SLITHEEN
> We are not Slitheen! Slitheen are criminals! We are
> Jingatheen!

> THE DOCTOR
> Sorry. Easy mistake. Tell me, what's everyone doing
> here?

> SLITHEEN
> The whole universe is on red alert! Planets have
> disappeared! Dozens of them! We have lost Clom!

> THE DOCTOR
> Clom's gone?!

> SLITHEEN
> Clom's gone!

> DONNA
> What's Clom?

> SLITHEEN
> Our twin planet! Without it, Raxacoricofallapatorius
> will fall out of the sky!
> > (turns to go)
> We must phone home -
> > (to Baby Slitheen)
> - this way, Margaret.

Baby Slitheen talks with the VOICE OF MARGARET BLAINE:

> BABY SLITHEEN
> Take me home, Daddy, I don't like the nasty policemen!

> THE DOCTOR
> …Margaret…?

> DONNA
> Come on, you!

And she shoves him forward, out of frame -

CUT TO A RECEPTION DESK, manned by Judoon, one unmasked with
RHINO HEAD. (All monks & nuns & opera-types crowding b/g, no
FX.)

A GRASKE is standing on the desk, furious.

> GRASKE
> Planet gone! Not good! Very bad!

THE DOCTOR & DONNA walking up, the Doctor just scooping the
Graske off the desk and putting him down out of frame -

> THE DOCTOR
> 'Scuse me, big fella -
> > (to the Judoon)
> I'd like to report a missing planet. Another one. It's
> called Earth -

> JUDOON
> Sco! Bo! Tro! No! Flo! Jo! Ko! Fo! To!

> THE DOCTOR
> Lo! Kro! To! Sho! Maho?

> JUDOON
> Sco! Sco! Blo! Do! Mo!

> DONNA
> Hold on, I thought the Tardis translated alien
> languages?

> THE DOCTOR
> Judoon are too thick.

> DONNA
> > (to the Judoon)
> Listen, you big Rhino. Earth. Missing. Six billion people!

Judoon holds out its translator, at her face.

> DONNA (CONT'D)
> Oy, what's it doing, what's that for, what are you
> doing, zoo boy?

The Judoon clips the translator into its chest-port. We hear
Donna's words back, fast, '*Oywhatsitdoingwhatsthatf…*'

> JUDOON
> Language assimilated. Designation: Earth English.

> DONNA
> Right, good, that's better, thanks - we need to report a
> missing planet, Galactic Location five delta omega -

                        JUDOON
    Take number. Stand in line.

                        DONNA
    But this is important!

                        JUDOON
    Take a number. Stand in line.

The Doctor takes a number from a supermarket-style dispenser -

                    THE DOCTOR
    Number one-six-two-five-eight-nine-

Looks up. DISPLAY: number 003.

                    THE DOCTOR (CONT'D)
    You're only on number three!
                    (psychic paper)
    I have been sent by the Judoon High Council, top
    priority, Ambassador Number One -

                        JUDOON
    Stand in line.

                    THE DOCTOR
                        (to Donna)
    I said so, thick!!
                    (to Judoon, angry)
    My name is the Doctor, I need to see the Chief
    Constable, right now, I can help you -

The Judoon raises its gun -

                        JUDOON
    Stand in line!

The Doctor steps back - other MONKS & NUNS pile in, taking
their place. The Doctor & Donna just figures in the crowd.

He puts his arm round her.

                                                CUT TO:

48. INT. SHADOW PROCLAMATION LOBBY - NIGHT

A LINE OF JUDOON stomping past…

Clearing to reveal DONNA, sitting alone. Haunted. MONKS, NUNS,
SYCORAX, etc, all around her. She glances across.

At a distance, THE DOCTOR, at the RECEPTION DESK, surrounded
by CROWD. He's filling in paperwork, arguing with Judoon.

Donna looks front. Lost in thought.

And as she stares into space...

Real sound fades away...

As she hears...

A heartbeat.

SLOW ZOOM IN on Donna staring to the distance, lost...

As it calls to her...

Then...

The moment breaks, as a FIGURE steps in foreground. Donna snaps out of it, looks up:

An ELDERLY NUN. Grave. Staring at her.

                    DONNA
Sorry, I was just...

                  ELDERLY NUN
There was something on your back.

                    DONNA
How d'you know that?

                  ELDERLY NUN
You have been marked, child.

                    DONNA
                  (chilled)
What does that mean?

                  ELDERLY NUN
You are something new. Something terrible and new.
                (touches her cheek)
Oh, but destiny is cruel. I'm so sorry for your loss.

                    DONNA
...my whole planet's gone.

                  ELDERLY NUN
I mean the loss that is yet to come. God save you.

And the Nun turns and goes.

Donna shaken, disturbed.

CUT TO THE DOCTOR, at the desk. Head down, scribbling through piles of Judoon paperwork, angry.

```
A SHADOW SOLDIER (i.e., Human) steps into extreme foreground.

                    SHADOW SOLDIER
    Can I help you with that, sir?


                     THE DOCTOR
    Triplicate! You've got 24 planets missing, and you need
    forms in triplicate! I'm the one and only person who
    could help, but no one's listening to me!


                    SHADOW SOLDIER
    I can listen. I did last time. And you saved my life,
    Doctor.

The Doctor looks up -

And the Shadow Soldier is MIDSHIPMAN FRAME!
```

I leave you with 4.12 cliffhanging on the best possible words! It may not be possible, but we'll see. I enjoyed typing it.

And I wrote the expensive stuff. It's actually the touch of a keystroke to delete it all. The same effect can be achieved with Judoon and a couple of Slitheen. Nice to try, though. I expressed my fears to Will, and he said, 'Oh, go on, do it!' So I did.

FROM: RUSSELL T DAVIES TO: BENJAMIN COOK, SATURDAY 15 DECEMBER 2007 14:09:44 GMT

ARSE, ARSE, ARSE!

I was hoping for a quiet weekend. No such luck. Catherine has just said on Jonathan Ross's radio show that this is David's last series! Poor Catherine. My heart sank. You could almost hear her swallowing the words as she said them. In fairness, it's so hard on *Doctor Who* to remember what's true and what isn't, what's possible and what's just speculation. But now it has all gone mad! Press on the phone! BBC News 24 is going to run it as a banner! It's like they threaten us. The biggest fight now, in your post-Hutton BBC, is to stop our Press Office from making a statement. Most people weren't listening to Jonathan Ross's show, for Christ sake! Just let it lie as rumour and gossip. 'No,' they say, 'we must have a "line".' So what's The Line?

FROM: BENJAMIN COOK, TO: RUSSELL T DAVIES, SATURDAY 15 DECEMBER 2007 14:22:15 GMT

RE: ARSE, ARSE, ARSE!

Why does the BBC have to confirm or deny anything? Shouldn't the BBC just shut up? Wouldn't that be less damaging?

FROM: RUSSELL T DAVIES TO: BENJAMIN COOK, SATURDAY 15 DECEMBER 2007 14:37:48 GMT

RE: ARSE, ARSE, ARSE!

Exactly! But it's a hard argument to maintain. Once this juggernaut starts rolling, it's difficult to stop – and it threatens to undermine Series Four. We all – Julie, Jane, David and me – have to work out an official response. That's David's call, really, though it's our job to help and protect him. And, of course, we've lost Jane Fletcher, who used to handle this magnificently. She's sorely missed.

We've just spoken to David. He's asked us to confirm, 'No decision has been made.' Poor bastard. He's the one who has to face the press on Tuesday night.

FROM: BENJAMIN COOK TO: RUSSELL T DAVIES, SATURDAY 15 DECEMBER 2007 17:39:31 GMT

RE: ARSE, ARSE, ARSE!

BBC News is reporting that David is leaving *Doctor Who*. Russell, how has your day gone since Catherine's gaffe? What goes through your mind when something like this happens? Honestly?

FROM: RUSSELL T DAVIES TO: BENJAMIN COOK, SATURDAY 15 DECEMBER 2007 21:12:29 GMT

RE: ARSE, ARSE, ARSE!

I get frustrated, really, because there's a barrage of confusing information about the show. If you're listening to all the news reports over the past few months – not as a hardcore fan, but as a more casual viewer – you'd have this bizarre whirlwind impression of the Doctor with three companions, and then the show is going off air because David regenerates, except he doesn't, and then Rose goes with him, and then James Nesbitt takes over or has he started already…? We sound *confused*. Publicity and public image depends on a strict, simple picture. A man and his police box. But now we sound like a mess. I really, really worry that we sound like old news, or bad news, or boring news. I worry profoundly about that. On Tuesday, at the press launch, all the journalists will want to know about this, putting David under terrible pressure and obscuring the point of the evening.

Meanwhile, this afternoon, the second wave started. I've given so many interviews over the years, a lot of journalists have my mobile number. I always give an interview on the condition that they don't use the number again. But of course they do. I'm thick. They phone up from BBC Stoke, BBC Cornwall, BBC Humberside, Galaxy FM, every bloody Radio Backyard. Though the BBC itself is by far the worst. When they talk about BBC cutbacks, they can start with those hopeless stringers sitting in Nowhere Land, imagining that they can break a big story by digging through their contact list. I suppose it's their job, and maybe sometimes it works, but imagine if I gave an exclusive to BBC Strathclyde!

The third wave is not just asking for a quote, but asking me to go on this chat show, that chat show, *Newsbeat*, you name it. The BBC has something called The Grid, a depository of phone numbers, which any BBC journalist can consult. I've asked a thousand times for my number to be taken off The Grid. It never is. People even deny its existence! So more and more calls come in, from complete strangers. I sort of hit my stride by late afternoon, telling them to sod off. If they persisted, I took their name and told them that I'm making a formal complaint within the BBC. That usually works. Eventually, I just stopped answering my phone. By tonight, it calmed down. But now it's out there, uncontrollable, on BBC News, everywhere, reported as fact. It can't be unsaid, ever. It's *Doctor Who*, for Christ's sake! You'd think we'd assassinated the Prime Minister. What the hell is it like on *real* news?

FROM: BENJAMIN COOK TO: RUSSELL T DAVIES, SUNDAY 16 DECEMBER 2007 00:48:39 GMT

RE: ARSE, ARSE, ARSE!

Amid all of this, what's Catherine saying on the matter? She must realise the storm that she's created. Poor Catherine.

FROM: RUSSELL T DAVIES TO: BENJAMIN COOK, SUNDAY 16 DECEMBER 2007 01:30:43 GMT

RE: ARSE, ARSE, ARSE!

That's the one thing I haven't asked. I don't like to. Like you, I wonder what she's said to David. Probably nothing. It was just a mistake, must have been, and they both adore each other, big time, so it'll just blow over, I presume. That's the last thing we need, actor wars. But they're both too intelligent for that.

Hey, I had the bloody *Mail* today describing me as having 'a large, soft, expressive face'. How bloody sexy do I feel? Soft!!!

FROM: BENJAMIN COOK TO: RUSSELL T DAVIES, MONDAY 17 DECEMBER 2007 15:42:36 GMT

RE: ARSE, ARSE, ARSE!

Is that the *Mail*'s article claiming that more than one companion in Series Four will 'confuse things', that it isn't 'very feminist that *Doctor Who* has gone from one assistant to a virtual harem', and describing Captain Jack's 'flamboyant sexuality' as a 'disruptive axis'? Is the jury still out on whether interviews with the *Daily Mail* are a good idea, Russell? Didn't your boyfriend tell you that he'd rather you didn't grant them interviews? I think I agree with him on this one…

FROM: RUSSELL T DAVIES TO: BENJAMIN COOK, MONDAY 17 DECEMBER 2007 16:08:47 GMT

RE: ARSE, ARSE, ARSE!

Far worse was the article's description of Martha as 'always going to be second best to Rose', followed immediately by a quote from me, making it sound as if *I'd* said second best! I'm still waiting to find out if Freema has seen that. I had a feeling that journalist was going to be dodgy, but I went ahead with it anyway. Why? Well, in the end, it's two pages in the *Daily Mail*. A great big photo of David and Kylie, a reminder that it's transmitted on Christmas Day (they printed the wrong time, of course – twice), and that's what matters. Harsh, but true. It's publicity. Moreover, that's two pages on me and my success, as a gay man, in a paper that vilifies homosexuality. Visibility is a good way of changing things, and that'll do me. As long as you don't get paid by them. I'd never accept that.

But it hasn't been a great weekend. On top of everything, Andy Pryor has discovered that Russell Tovey is in a play, *The Sea*, at the Theatre Royal Haymarket, from January to April, so that's our recording block buggered. (I really should have checked first.) Midshipman Frame was going to be vital. I had a lot of that planned out. And now… hmph. He would have been a junior soldier in the Shadow Proclamation. (After the *Titanic*, I imagined that he'd sort of followed the Doctor's example and set out to do good.) He could have helped the Doctor cut through the red tape at the Proclamation, but – and this is the best bit – when the Doctor goes on the run from the authorities, I wanted Frame to go with him. He'd become a companion! The Doctor, Donna Noble and Alonso Frame, on board the TARDIS, searching for the Earth. What a great team! But not for long. When they arrive on the Dalek ship in 4.13, then *zap!* Frame is killed! I wanted that to hurt. I wanted to show how cold the Daleks are, how vicious Davros is, how much danger they're in, so Alonso would have had to go. Except now he won't be in it at all. That's stalled a plot. What do I do instead?

> **Text message from: Ben**
> Sent: 17-Dec-2007 22:16
> How are you feeling about tomorrow's press launch, Russell? Also, will there be nibbles?

> **Text message from: Russell**
> Sent: 17-Dec-2007 23:28
> I'm dreading it. But there will be nibbles.

FROM: BENJAMIN COOK TO: RUSSELL T DAVIES, WEDNESDAY 19 DECEMBER 2007 11:20:01 GMT

RE: ARSE, ARSE, ARSE!

As press launches go, that wasn't too bad… was it? Well, the Science Museum was a fun choice of venue, at least.

FROM: RUSSELL T DAVIES TO: BENJAMIN COOK, WEDNESDAY 19 DECEMBER 2007 23:01:36 GMT

RE: ARSE, ARSE, ARSE!

I'm home now. I've been here for hours. I've been meaning to answer your e-mail about last night's launch, but I couldn't face it. I hated it. *Hated* it. I still feel sour.

It started badly. Me and Julie were running late. We had to rush for the train to London. We're always rushing. London is even more of a rush, because of the traffic, so Julie had to get changed in my hotel. She's running around in her bra and knickers – actually, it was a camisole. I had to ask, 'What's that called?' Like we're an old married couple. 'Why d'you have to moisturise your legs?' 'I shaved them yesterday.' 'Who's gonna know?' 'Oh, thank you!' (I'll leave you to guess who's who there.) Then we rushed to meet David and Jane for a drink. We had to work out The Line. Catherine claimed that David is leaving, so what's The Line on that? A one-line response, to be elaborated on at will, but one essential response from all of us, coordinated. I used to laugh at this, but it's needed if you're facing journalists. And what if the new BBC One Controller demands a 2009 series? What if someone asks about David's mother? Have we confirmed how long Catherine is staying for? What are we saying about Billie? What's The Line, The Line, The Bloody Line?! Except people are late, and gossiping, and pleased to see each other, so half The Lines don't even get discussed. Too late, we're behind schedule, go, go, go, into the cars, hurry up –

Actually, I'm making this sound funny. It wasn't funny. It was awful. At the first venue, where we met for a drink beforehand, I pretended that I didn't have any cigarettes, just so that I could walk out of the bar and away down the street for 15 minutes on my own. Head buzzing with Lines. Freezing cold. Christmas decorations. Best time I had all night.

When we arrived at the Science Museum – well, that's when it hits you, the sheer size of it. That launch was *massive*. A proper BBC event. We'd been chosen. It's good that we're chosen, it's important for the show, but I didn't enjoy it. It feels wrong somehow. It feels like it doesn't fit our show. We make the programme big, blousy and ballsy, but I think it's still sort of intimate, a daft little show, no matter how many spaceships are on display. It's certainly not corporate. That press launch was corporate. And there was no time to see anyone. Quick hello to my agent, I'm trying to see if Camille Coduri has turned up, I'm trying to see if you're there, but no time for that, there are people whose job it is to herd you in front of the journalists…

Next second, it's that parade of cameras, *GMTV*, *BBC Breakfast*, BBC News, *Newsround*, and you find yourself spouting The Lines, like a puppet. Worse, you slip into showbiz speak. I find myself saying things like 'There are lots of great surprises coming up.' Who talks like that?! Real people don't talk like that! In the middle of the line-up, I say hello to Russell Tovey. He's in front of *GMTV*. I'm with *Newsround*. We both look embarrassed. You can't say hello properly with lights and cameras in your face. Then you get shoved in front of the radio journalists, which is worse, because they're all in one gaggle, so ten different shows want ten different quotes, all at once. You have to be funny and sarky for *Newsbeat*, factual for Radio 2, factual-but-edgy for Radio 5, bland for Galaxy, all at the same time. That's probably where I go wrong. I should be myself. But everyone has a lot of different selves. I think that's why an evening like this is so dispiriting: I'm left wondering, who am I? And the funny thing is, while I hate it, I'm very aware that if, say, David is following me down the line, then no one actually wants to talk to me anyway. I'm left feeling like nothing again, but in a different way. The vanity!

Then it's the screening. We're hustled to our seats. 'That's Russell Tovey's boyfriend,' someone points out – and a whole fantasy night dies in my mind. We sit at the front, but The Lines are still buzzing in my mind, and everyone is doing a post-mortem on what just happened with the journalists. 'What did they ask? What did they say? Were they friendly? Did they ask about Catherine?' A hundred times over, in whispers – while Bernard Cribbins is saying hello, so that switchback personality is still flickering to and fro. 'Hello, Bernard!' (The journalists were fine) 'How are you?' (What did David say?) 'Nice to see you.' (Who's giving the first speech?) 'Wait till you see it!' (Where's my radio mic?)

Lights down, it begins… and I feel totally disconnected from it. I don't laugh. I don't cry. It's the size again – *Doctor Who* on a giant screen with 500 people watching. Not that a *Doctor Who* movie couldn't work, but *Voyage of the Damned* isn't a movie, it's for TV, so it looks wrong, sounds wrong. I sat there thinking about the differences between film and TV. I can see it in action. TV cuts faster, spends much more time in CU, so it looks awful on a big screen, too choppy, too close, too amateur. It's a clumsy and jittery piece of work, blown up. The lovely sound mix, on a sound system this big, is distorted, everything divided into clean, separate tracks – music from over there, booms from over there, all unrelated – instead of the proper mix you get on a telly. It's like a grotesque version of itself. It's a cheap tart. I just stare, feeling nothing. I love *Voyage of the Damned*, and this is making me hate it. Julie keeps saying, 'There's too much bass. Should we alter the bass?' until I snap, 'Leave it, just shut up.' And then I feel bad all night for snapping at her. She never complains. She's used to me doing that. I always snap at the one who'll take it. Is *that* who I am?

After the screening, we get speeches praising me. I would rather die, I swear. I just wish they'd stop it. I don't recognise that person at all. That's not modesty – I think I'm brilliant! – but I'm not the person in those speeches. It just gets so awkward. Do you clap when everyone claps you? I do, but then I feel stupid. I'm imagining someone saying, 'Look at that tosser clapping himself!' It's very hard to stop a clap once you've started. Then it's the Q&A. I hate the Q&A. I hate any Q&A. I'm 44 and balding and putting on weight, in a cheap suit because nothing else was clean and my alarm didn't go off; the last thing I want to do is sit in front of 500 people. I feel so self-conscious. But no one's asking Russell Tovey, Gray O'Brien or Clive Rowe any questions, and I feel responsible for them. Also, I'm trying to stop myself being 'funny', because I can put on 'funny' in front of a crowd, as a mechanism, but that default usually means swearing or being filthy, and there are kids in the audience, so I'm all constrained. At the same time, I'm scanning the audience for that journalist with a killer question – like the man from *The Times* at the *Rise of the Cybermen* press screening, who implied that the *Doctor Who* crew had been paid off by Motorola because a mobile phone logo was visible! He actually, literally, accused that brilliant crew of being corrupt, of accepting back-handers. And it escalated. The day after that, *The Times* phoned Motorola and other mobile companies asking if they had illegal deals with the *Doctor Who* crew, while we had to send the episode back to The Mill for all accidentally seen logos to be digitally removed, at quite some cost. That's how serious some dumb-arse little question can get. So I'm waiting, waiting, waiting, all the time, for some snake question like that.

Then it's the party afterwards. But I can't relax. It's all work. In three hours, I have half an apple juice and half a Coke. I have to speak to everyone. That's my job. Signing autographs for kids, which is nice, but then the MPs, the bloody MPs, then a man from the Youth Hostelling organisation ('Have you ever Youth Hostelled?'), then BBC bosses (so I have to be nice and ask for more programme money), then more MPs – they never, ever say which party they represent. For all I know, I could be thanking a Tory. Oh, but there's Annette Badland, except I haven't time to say hello. Actors and friends fly past. The people that you want to see get snatched away. I pop out for a cigarette, but there's Mark Thompson, the BBC Director-General, so suddenly I sound like this professional robot. And then he makes it clear that he knows that Steven is taking over, so suddenly I feel like yesterday's robot. And then more MPs, and they're getting red-wine mouths. Everyone is trying to grab a bit of you. 'I run this website. Will you join and endorse it?' 'Can we do dinner?' 'Can we, can we, can we?'

The one time I do get five minutes to myself, one of the sci-fi-magazine men is drunk and won't leave me alone, while I'm fending off his sly, smiling insults ('That was a fun episode, wasn't it? Just fun!'), and then I find myself with two gay boys who work as researchers in Parliament, and they're gorgeous, but it turns out that they're with the Shadow Secretary of Something. I'm thinking, would I sleep with a Tory? But then they're telling me that they were 13 when *Queer as Folk* was on, and I realise that I'm as old as George Bernard Shaw to them. They keep talking about how they watched *Queer as Folk* in secret on portable TVs in their bedrooms, so essentially we're talking about wanking, which is weird. Then it turns out that one of them knows the exact date of my mother's death, which is completely out of leftfield and the last thing that I want to think about. I've spent six years trying not to think too much about that, so I move on. But then someone else appears and he's all 'Why don't I ever see you? Why won't you have a cigarette with me? You have a cigarette with everyone else. Why not me?' I'm thinking, oh shut *up!* And then more bloody MPs, and there's the nice man from *The Guardian*, all smiles and hellos, the same man who wrote a *Guardian* blog last week describing *Doctor Who* as the Most Overrated TV Show of the Year, but I'm smiling back, because they can write what they like. And it goes on and on and on. When I say I hate it, I'm really so unhappy – and smiling like an idiot. A hundred versions of me, and every single one sounds like a fool.

Then it ends. Back to the hotel. So wound up. I don't get to sleep for hours. I just sit there, watching skiing and late-night poker on TV. Starving. I have a Coke and a Bounty from the mini bar. I worry about the price. On my wage, I worry about the price of a Bounty! And I sit there replaying everything I said to everyone, and all the people I missed, and all the stupid jokes I made, and I hate it. I hate myself. I just don't like myself very much. Well, who ever does? But when that self has been such a public self, all night, I feel prostituted, exaggerated, indistinct and stupid.

Still, the next morning is funny. I wake up, still sour. The 4.11 Edit is in Soho at 10am, so I wear my jeans and stuff, carry my suit on a hanger, go into Soho, have a coffee, buy the papers, have another coffee. After half an hour, I realise that my hanger is feeling rather light. I look. The trousers have slid off. I've lost my trousers. In Soho. I have to retrace my route through the cafes and newsagents, asking, 'Have you seen my trousers?' I never find them. Some tramp is looking smart for Christmas! But when I get to the Edit, I tell Phil, Julie, Graeme and Susie this story – and they laugh so hard, for so long, that I realise: *this* is why I love this job. These people. And whoever I am, if these people are my mates, then I can't be doing too bad.

FROM: BENJAMIN COOK TO: RUSSELL T DAVIES, THURSDAY 20 DECEMBER 2007 11:11:38 GMT

RE: ARSE, ARSE, ARSE!

I'm still laughing at your missing trousers! But I'm surprised that you're so worried about how you came across at the launch. I can understand you not enjoying it, and thank you for such honesty, Russell, but you're fantastic at dealing with the press, at putting on that public face. At least, you looked as though you knew what you were doing – how far to push it, and when, and with whom. You were asked who, living or dead, you'd like to see play the Doctor, and you answered 'Hitler' – *and got away with it!* Confident. Funny. Impassioned. It's sort of a shame that you don't think so.

FROM: RUSSELL T DAVIES TO: BENJAMIN COOK, THURSDAY 20 DECEMBER 2007 12:13:44 GMT

RE: ARSE, ARSE, ARSE!

Thank you. That cheered me up. I suppose what I'm saying is summed up in your phrase 'putting on that public face', because that's not a natural thing to do. I do know I'm good at it, but then that becomes a pressure in itself. People are expecting me to be good. You can sort of see why famous people go mad. I get one zillionth of that fame lark. Imagine being really famous, and famous for your face, your looks, your voice, famous for just being you. That's why the likes of Britney Spears and Amy Winehouse go berserk. I think it's one long cry of 'Who am I?'

FROM: BENJAMIN COOK TO: RUSSELL T DAVIES, THURSDAY 20 DECEMBER 15:35:34 GMT

RE: ARSE, ARSE, ARSE!

I meant to ask, did you finally meet up with Steven Moffat yesterday, in London, for that coffee? (Nice coffee, was it? Milk? Sugar?)

FROM: RUSSELL T DAVIES TO: BENJAMIN COOK, THURSDAY 20 DECEMBER 16:44:19 GMT

RE: ARSE, ARSE, ARSE!

It was a latte. Freezing, because I wanted to sit outside and smoke. Poor Steven. A kid called Karim recognised us and asked for a photo, and Steven said, 'You'll never know how historic this moment is!' But it was lovely. No great emotions. Well, I had a good time and we had a good chat, but I don't usually get emotional about stuff like that. Except in a good way. I *like* change. I love it when people move and leave and swap around. It felt good, healthy and natural.

I went for our coffee, full of things to tell Steven. I was bristling with them. But as soon as we sat down, I thought very clearly: I don't need to tell him any of this stuff. He knows scripts, he knows writers, he knows what's what. And he knows what he wants to do. He'll invent his own way of doing things. Experience – it's useless! Mostly we talked about the rewriting process, though it's a hard thing to discuss. As I talked, I thought I sounded power-mad. Genuinely. So I clammed up about it after a while. I didn't like the sound of myself. If anything, I felt a good old fanboy thrill down my spine, because Steven talked about the future in terms of … well, to the extent that I said, 'Don't tell me any more!' I want to find out as a viewer. I was even surprised, because I was half-expecting there to be a No Old Monsters rule under The Moff. But no. So that felt good.

I love this show, completely, and yet I will leave it without blinking. I've always been like that. I suppose I care about myself more than I care about any TV show. What I mean is… a funny thing happened that day. As Steven and I left Soho, we bumped into an ex of mine, Gareth. Lovely man, so we had a nice chat. As I wandered off with Steven, I explained that Gareth was my ex, and then I found myself saying, 'Actually, he's my *only* ex. I've only ever had two boyfriends, and he was one of them.' I'd never consciously thought that before, never mind said it out loud. I'm 44, and I've only had two proper relationships. Is that weird? I mean, I knew that to be the case, obviously, and yet I'd never really looked at the facts before so simply and easily. Two boyfriends! Just two! Steven must have thought I was really odd – not for only having two boyfriends, but for the way that I said it, because I was spelling it out, in words, carefully and slowly, for my own benefit. So really, for me, that – and losing my trousers – was what the last couple of days was all about. Not *Doctor Who*.

CHAPTER ELEVEN

DAY OLD BLUES

In which Russell hits rock bottom,
the Daleks learn German,
and Young Davros has a scream on Skaro

FROM: RUSSELL T DAVIES TO: BENJAMIN COOK, FRIDAY 21 DECEMBER 2007 02:02:51 GMT

THE ABOMINATION IS INSANE

Look, more script! Not enough, though. But also too much, because I'm on Page 32
when I should be on Page 23 or something. I'm not going to fit it all in. Still, I went
back and revised the end of Scene 47 and wrote a brand new Scene 48, cutting the
stuff with Donna and the Elderly Nun ('There was something on your back'), which
I'm keeping for a bit later.

Hey, guess what else? We've cast Alex Kingston as River Song in Steven's two-parter!
ALEX KINGSTON! I bloody love her. Alex Kingston is the Doctor's wife! And Dr
Moon is Colin Salmon. Classy cast.

FROM: RUSSELL T DAVIES TO: BENJAMIN COOK, SATURDAY 22 DECEMBER 2007 03:04:00 GMT

RE: THE ABOMINATION IS INSANE

I got rid of that whole Dalek descent on Westminster (Scenes 31–40). It's the Daleks
– why are they so diplomatic? When I read that back to myself on Thursday night,
having been away from the script for three days, I found my eyes skipping over those
scenes, and I woke up this morning and thought, get rid of them. I needed to lose
some pages anyway. You have to go down those blind alleys sometimes.

I'm not very fond of the Shadow Proclamation. The Chief Constable is the most thankless part ever.[1] She has to say terrible sci-fi lines like 'Perhaps if we scan for Zygma Energy' and 'The Tandocca Scale...' Some poor actor! Giving her detail, flesh and interest would just rack up the page count, so she's terribly stripped down. I keep wondering if I should cut the Shadow Proclamation completely, but without it... well, the Doctor would sit in the TARDIS, scanning things, until, yes, he finds the Earth. It would be strangely domestic. No struggle, no journey, no obstacles. He has to have a journey. Should the Shadow Proclamation be replaced with something more mystic, like a trip to a barren world to consult some psychic hermit? But that's equally bollocks. I hate that sort of spooky crap.

Also, I can feel the start of a cold. I *cannot* have a cold. I just can't. I won't.

FROM: RUSSELL T DAVIES TO: BENJAMIN COOK, SUNDAY 23 DECEMBER 2007 02:40:20 GMT

RE: THE ABOMINATION IS INSANE

I went back and fixed the Chief Constable. Her main problem was being a Chief Constable, so I decided – and it's funny how that e-mail to you yesterday clarified my worries – that since she has to say lame sci-fi lines, she can only work if she's a sci-fi creature. I've renamed her the Shadow Architect, made her albino and weird (hair scraped into a black snood, red eyes, solemn, swathed in black robes), and given her a slight mysticism – not hermit-in-a-cave mysticism, just an albino freakiness – so that she's sort of interesting now. Not fascinating, just interesting.

FROM: BENJAMIN COOK TO: RUSSELL T DAVIES, SUNDAY 23 DECEMBER 2007 07:30:09 GMT

RE: THE ABOMINATION IS INSANE

'Have you got a webcam?'

'She wouldn't let me. She says they're naughty.'

Ha ha ha ha ha! And three cheers for Bernard's paint gun. But surely, before repairing itself, the Dalek should say, 'MY VISION IS IMPAIRED! I CANNOT SEE!'...? Isn't that kind of obligatory?

Has Penelope Wilton signed up already?[2] Or do negotiations start now?

FROM: RUSSELL T DAVIES TO: BENJAMIN COOK, SUNDAY 23 DECEMBER 2007 10:32:01 GMT

RE: THE ABOMINATION IS INSANE

I'm glad you like the webcam joke. I love putting gags in the middle of The End Of The World, although that gag works because Wilf isn't being funny; he really means it. At the launch on Tuesday, as he was leaving, Bernard said, 'Are we doing that paint gun thing?' I said yes, and he was astonished. He was like, 'Really?!' What a lovely man. So no matter how many pages I'm over, I'm not cutting that. I know what you

---

1 The tough, efficient 'Chief Constable' (renamed the Shadow Architect in subsequent drafts) is the head of the Shadow Proclamation.
2 In *Doctor Who* 1.4/1.5, Penelope Wilton played Harriet Jones MP, who returned in 2.X as the UK's Prime Minister, before the Doctor deposed her.

mean about 'My vision is impaired' – it's a proper Dalek catchphrase, isn't it? – but, while he's saying that, Wilf and Sylvia would run away. It's already slightly dodgy that they just stand there.

God knows about Penelope Wilton. Julie and Phil have been nagging me to pay off Harriet's ending in *The Christmas Invasion* since… well, since *The Christmas Invasion*. (What a great episode title that was!) She's very hard to book, because she's so in demand. We only got her on *Bob & Rose* by the skin of our teeth. Imagine if we hadn't! That's why she's limited in this script to one location, one day's work. Easier to book. Julie has been expecting it, but I doubt she's laid any groundwork, because she can't until a script is in. We can't do anything until after Christmas now, but oh, fingers crossed. If not, I'm afraid it'll have to be Mr Copper from *Voyage of the Damned*. That would work. But I hope it's Harriet.

FROM: RUSSELL T DAVIES TO: BENJAMIN COOK, SUNDAY 23 DECEMBER 2007 11:40:13 GMT

RE: THE ABOMINATION IS INSANE

Ah! Got it! The Dalek says 'My vision is *not* impaired!' Good joke. Fanboy joke.

FROM: RUSSELL T DAVIES TO: BENJAMIN COOK, MONDAY 24 DECEMBER 2007 03:24:43 GMT

RE: THE ABOMINATION IS INSANE

I didn't finish. Damn and crap and bollocks! I don't think I've got time tomorrow. I haven't bought a single card or present yet, and I have to go to Swansea tomorrow night. Christmas with my blind dad. I sit and describe to him what's happening on TV. 'The Host have hooked arms with the Doctor, and they're flying him up, up, up through the ship…' I have a laugh doing that. I make things up. 'They're on fire!' There's no budget when you're blind.

I won't be back online until Friday now. Days off! Maybe a break will do me good. Although, I'll just be thinking about the script. It's Christmas Eve, and I'm dying to get back to work already.

> Text message from: **Russell**
> Sent: 25-Dec-2007 12:28
> Merry Xmas, Benjamino! Shame there's nothing good on TV tonight…

> Text message from: **Ben**
> Sent: 25-Dec-2007 15:34
> Oh, I don't know, I'm counting down the minutes till *To the Manor Born*! Ha!
> Merry Xmas to you and yours. I'm stuffed already. I'll have put on a stone
> by the time *Voyage of the Damned* is on.

Text message from: **Ben**

Sent: 25-Dec-2007 20:10

Watching *Doctor Who* with the family is so stressful. But it went down well.

Text message from: **Russell**

Sent: 25-Dec-2007 20:13

Various members of my family are now bleeding and wounded because they TALKED!!! For the love of Clom! The punishments will continue all night. Still, I might be biased, but I loved that Special. It worked well with the kids here too – just as it should.

Text message from: **Ben**

Sent: 26-Dec-2007 09:56

So what do you make of the viewing figures? An overnight estimate of 12.2 MILLION! OH MY GOD! Many congrats.

Text message from: **Russell**

Sent: 26-Dec-2007 10:08

F*****G HELL!!! I'm phoning Phil, Julie's phoning me, we're all going mental!

Text message from: **Russell**

Sent: 26-Dec-2007 11:31

Twelve point two!!! I just thought I'd spell it out in words to see how good it looks. I'm still laughing. I can't get over those figures. I am reeling. Everyone is so happy.

Text message from: **Ben**

Sent: 26-Dec-2007 11:38

And to think, just a week ago, you were walking around Soho with no trousers. That's some comeback, Russell.

Text message from: **Russell**

Sent: 26-Dec-2007 11:45

I hope my lucky trousers played some part in our ratings victory.

Text message from: **Ben**

Sent: 26-Dec-2007 11:51

The final, consolidated figure will be closer to 13 million, surely? That's incredible. It must make all the stressing worthwhile?

> **Text message from: Russell**
> Sent: 26-Dec-2007 12:42
> Oh yes, it does. Mind you, it's swiftly followed by the terrifying thought:
> NEXT YEAR! But sod that for now. You've got to take time to enjoy it.

FROM: RUSSELL T DAVIES TO: BENJAMIN COOK, THURSDAY 27 DECEMBER 2007 23:44:10 GMT

12.2 MILLION!!!

I'm back in Cardiff. I wasn't supposed to be back until tomorrow, but there's too much work to do, so I made my farewells. All is quiet and still in Cardiff Bay. Lovely.

I can't face opening 4.12. It feels like something that I wrote aeons ago. I've cancelled going to Billie's wedding next week. That's the last thing I need right now. Shame, but it had to be done. The script is more important. And that much-threatened cold is now descending over me fast. I'm snivelling away and starting to cough. Nooooo to the cough! The cough took me out for five weeks last year.

FROM: RUSSELL T DAVIES TO: BENJAMIN COOK, SUNDAY 30 DECEMBER 2007 02:28:05 GMT

RE: 12.2 MILLION!!!

Here's more… but it's absolute bollocks. I wanted to finish tonight, but I haven't. I failed. This cold is getting worse. My eyes are streaming and I can't see the sodding keyboard. Plus, this is now way, way, *way* too long. Seriously, I need another ten pages. I'm writing stuff that I know I'm going to cut. There are a couple of pages of lovely dialogue where finally the Doctor and Donna link up, over the scanner, with Jack, Martha and Sarah Jane, and Donna meets them all… but it's all going to be cut, I can tell. That's pissed me off. Dialogue that I've been dying to write, and now I've written it with a faint heart, because it's cuttable. What a waste of time and energy.

Tonight, this feels like a space-opera runaround. I don't like it much. It's too big, it's daft, the Doctor arrives too late and does nothing all episode. It's lame shit. It feels like we're going to spend millions of licence-fee-payers' money on silly rubbish. That's not the right mood to write in. And now tomorrow is buggered, because my boyfriend is coming to Cardiff for the New Year, but I must keep writing. I promised him that I wouldn't work over the next few days. Even though he has the patience of a saint, he's going to kill me. It's all going to get tense, and that's no mood to write in either.

FROM: RUSSELL T DAVIES TO: BENJAMIN COOK, SUNDAY 30 DECEMBER 2007 20:06:21 GMT

RE: 12.2 MILLION!!!

Sorry about last night's outpouring. I lost control of it. I woke up this morning, telling myself the thing that I have to tell myself a million times: I'm in control of it, it's not in control of me. I'm in a better mood now. I should finish tonight, but this cold is streeeeeaming…

FROM: RUSSELL T DAVIES TO: BENJAMIN COOK, MONDAY 31 DECEMBER 2007 04:35:22 GMT

RE: 12.2 MILLION!!!

FINISHED! I finished at about 1am, but it was 63 pages long, so I've been sitting here since then, whittling it down to 58. But it's still too long; it should be around 54. It's hard to tell with action scripts. When the FX budget is over – way over! – that'll help me prune back even more.

What a cliffhanger![3] And now I'm going to go and have a cold. Properly.

FROM: BENJAMIN COOK TO: RUSSELL T DAVIES, MONDAY 31 DECEMBER 2007 13:07:59 GMT

RE: 12.2 MILLION!!!

For once, just for once, could 4.12 *not* finish with a 'Next Time' trailer? Put a 'TO BE CONTINUED' graphic or something – anything! – but it'd spoil that amazing cliffhanger if we see the Doctor up and about in the trailer. Is the plan to convince people that this is David's swansong as the Doctor?

This is all very exciting. How are you feeling about it?

FROM: RUSSELL T DAVIES TO: BENJAMIN COOK, MONDAY 31 DECEMBER 2007 13:57:38 GMT

RE: 12.2 MILLION!!!

You're right, actually. A black, silent 'TO BE CONTINUED' card would be amazing. There are bound to be TV trailers that week, but you could just show lots of Daleks and a repeat of 'I'm regenerating…' We never send out preview discs of the last episode, so we might just get away with it. What a laugh! I feel happy now. Very. I think the script has lived up to the concept's promise.

Julie got back from New York this morning, sat down in the Virgin lounge to read it, but then Phil arrived to pick her up. She texted me: 'He's on time! He's never on time! I'm only on Page 30!' She's left in high suspense, but now she's got Billie's wedding all day and won't be able to read it till tonight. But I never send scripts to Phil at the same time as Julie. Maybe I should, but the whole thing is a headache to him – it's a terrifying budget sheet – so I leave him in peace. For now.

Of course, stopping has meant that this cold is sweeping over me. My hands are swollen. That's not good. What does that mean? Hey, what are you doing tonight? Dancing in fountains? I'm so sick and bleeargghhh, I'm just going to sit in front of the TV with my old fella and herald in the New Year from my armchair.

FROM: BENJAMIN COOK TO: RUSSELL T DAVIES, MONDAY 31 DECEMBER 2007 14:09:05 GMT

RE: 12.2 MILLION!!!

I'm out in Covent Garden tonight, and then on to Trafalgar Square – or maybe the Victoria Embankment to watch the fireworks.

---

3 The Doctor is shot by a Dalek, and carried to the TARDIS by Donna, Rose and Captain Jack, where he starts to regenerate...

Well, a rest should do you good. It'll give you a chance to shake off the cold. At least it won't take you five-and-half hours to get home tonight! Pity me.

Happy New Year, Russell.

FROM: RUSSELL T DAVIES TO: BENJAMIN COOK, MONDAY 31 DECEMBER 2007 14:16:27 GMT

RE: 12.2 MILLION!!!

Happy New Year to you, Benjamino! Seriously, my favourite thing about this year? This correspondence. I have loved it. It's been something new. New is good. I'm so glad that you thought of doing this. Thank you.

Get home safe. Subwave Network closing down.[4] Good night.

FROM: RUSSELL T DAVIES TO: BENJAMIN COOK, SATURDAY 5 JANUARY 2008 18:25:27 GMT

HAPPY NEW YEAR?

I'm starting to feel human again. I've spent half of the last week in bed. It's only a cold, but being a smoker makes it vicious. Yes, it's all my own fault. And I'm dying for a cigarette now!

The prep date for 4.12/4.13 is Monday, but they'll only have 4.12. There's plenty of work in that to be getting on with. Actually, I still haven't officially submitted 4.12; only you and Julie have read it so far. I keep meaning to go over it again, to reduce the page count, but then I sit here and cough, and want a cigarette, and fail to do anything. I'll give it the weekend. And I'll start 4.13. Any day now. Late already. Oh God.

New Year? They sold us a pup. It's the Old Year, with a bit of nail varnish.

FROM: RUSSELL T DAVIES TO: BENJAMIN COOK, SATURDAY 5 JANUARY 2008 19:29:50 GMT

RE: HAPPY NEW YEAR?

I've just realised, you sent me that first e-mail on 18 February… and that's now my exact deadline for 4.14. It's a year! Blimey. A year of sitting in this bloody chair. I'm depressed now.

FROM: BENJAMIN COOK TO: RUSSELL T DAVIES, SATURDAY 5 JANUARY 2008 20:38:30 GMT

RE: HAPPY NEW YEAR?

That's just the cold talking. Trust me, you've loved every minute of it! Ha ha.

>>I never think of it as work, really, no matter how much hard graft I actually do. Even if no one ever saw this stuff, I'd be doing it anyway.<<

Is now a good time to quote the above back at you?

---

4 The Subwave Network – created by the Mr Copper Foundation, and further developed by Harriet Jones – is a piece of sentient software, in *Doctor Who* 4.12, programmed to seek out anyone and everyone who can help to contact the Doctor.

FROM: RUSSELL T DAVIES TO: BENJAMIN COOK, SATURDAY 5 JANUARY 2008 20:45:23 GMT

RE: HAPPY NEW YEAR?

Ha ha ha.

No.

FROM: RUSSELL T DAVIES TO: BENJAMIN COOK, WEDNESDAY 9 JANUARY 2008 22:51:15 GMT

RE: HAPPY NEW YEAR?

I bumped into Freema in the Bay today. Big hug, hello, then I walked back to my flat, thinking about Martha in 4.13. I closed the door, and then I actually, really, said out loud to myself, all alone, 'You cannot let her down.' I really did that. Sometimes I say scary motivational things to myself out loud. Like it helps! It doesn't.

The good news is, Harriet Jones is back! Penelope Wilton says yes! Apparently, she said yes straight away, no doubt, no hesitation, bang, done. *Brilliant!* I wasn't expecting it to be that easy. So that's a thrill. She'll face the Daleks!

FROM: BENJAMIN COOK TO: RUSSELL T DAVIES, WEDNESDAY 9 JANUARY 2008 23:04:17 GMT

RE: HAPPY NEW YEAR?

>>'You cannot let her down.'<<

But why do you never talk about letting *yourself* down? Doesn't that worry you as much?

FROM: RUSSELL T DAVIES TO: BENJAMIN COOK, THURSDAY 10 JANUARY 2008 16:46:53 GMT

RE: HAPPY NEW YEAR?

I've been thinking about your question a lot. It struck a chord. It's partly because letting down Freema or Catherine or David or the production team *does* mean letting myself down. If we end up with a rubbish series finale, I'll be gutted. My God, I'll be suicidal. 'They' and 'me' exist simultaneously in that equation. They work for me, with me, because of me.

At the same time, the question went deep, because… well, this is kind of hard to say, but I never have, in my work, let myself down. Not ever. Not really. Not profoundly. Is that an outrageous thing to say? But that's why I'm successful. I'm good at what I do. I work exceptionally hard. That doesn't mean everything that I've done has been brilliant or that every script that I've written has been good, but actually every piece of work has been done with good intent, to the best of my abilities, within the limits of my own talent and stamina. Every Single Thing. Even some bloody awful Granada sitcoms that I was coerced into, where I ended up using a pen-name. Rotten scripts, rotten to the core… but I couldn't have made them better, at the time. I gave them everything. For all their awfulness, I still have a strange pride in them. I put everything into work. Everything. It's not always enough, and hindsight shows me a thousand different ways that I should have done things, but that's natural; I don't beat myself up over that. Or maybe I'm blind to the proper disasters. Maybe you have to be, to keep working. The problem is, there's no consolation in the above. I've only really thought about this when you posed the question.

But it's more than that… this is where it becomes a difficult question, in that it starts to define me, because I let myself down in a million other areas. I let myself down in my relationship with my father, in not phoning my sisters from one year to the next, in not giving my boyfriend enough time. When I do give him time, I mess that up too. I let myself down personally by smoking badly, eating badly, living badly. Do you see? *That's* where I let myself down. The real stuff. All the time. Is that because I work so hard? Or do I work so hard to absolve myself from blame? This is where work and life are simply indivisible. Ah, but that's what writing is. Looking at yourself all day, every day. Whether I'm thinking about monsters, gay men, religion, comedy… it's all me, in the end. With no answers and no clarity. Just more questions.

> **Text message from: Russell**
> Sent: 11-Jan-2008 13:57
> Final viewing figures for *Voyage of the Damned*: 13.3 million!!!

> **Text message from: Ben**
> Sent: 11-Jan-2008 14:04
> That's immense! Well done all. Hey, I'm texting you from a tunnel in Barry Island, on location for *The Doctor's Daughter*. I'm huddled in a corner, drinking soup. David texted me yesterday: 'It's not cold, actually – we're underground. It does smell like a wino's breath, though.'

> **Text message from: Russell**
> Sent: 11-Jan-2008 18:28
> I'm sat here doing no work. I'm scared now. Proper scared.

FROM: RUSSELL T DAVIES TO: BENJAMIN COOK, SATURDAY 12 JANUARY 2008 03:14:22 GMT

RE: HAPPY NEW YEAR?

It's only two pages. Don't get excited. An easy two pages. I always knew how to get out of those cliffhangers. I only did this tonight so that I don't wake up tomorrow in blind misery without even a file that says '4.13'…

FROM: RUSSELL T DAVIES TO: BENJAMIN COOK, SUNDAY 13 JANUARY 2008 01:43:22 GMT

RE: HAPPY NEW YEAR?

Steven Moffat e-mailed me earlier and said, almost in passing…

> *Another thing: I've started. I've written the first few pages of my first episode. Couldn't stop myself. It was like incontinence. Well, hopefully not completely like incontinence. But anyway.*

He's started! Oh my God, I'm old news.

FROM: RUSSELL T DAVIES TO: BENJAMIN COOK, SUNDAY 13 JANUARY 2008 19:52:22 GMT

RE: HAPPY NEW YEAR?

Yesterday was bad. Rock bottom, really. I went a bit mad. I ended up walking around the Bay at 3.30 this morning. But I think it forced some good thoughts out. I want to work tonight, but I feel so tired. Oh, moan, moan, moan. We'll get there.

FROM: BENJAMIN COOK TO: RUSSELL T DAVIES, SUNDAY 13 JANUARY 2008 20:15:19 GMT

RE: HAPPY NEW YEAR?

What good thoughts? It can't all have been doom and gloom...

FROM: RUSSELL T DAVIES TO: BENJAMIN COOK, SUNDAY 13 JANUARY 2008 21:18:31 GMT

RE: HAPPY NEW YEAR?

Mainly, it's the pattern of this episode. The chessboard. Who ends up where. I don't know how to get them there. The Doctor needs to be taken prisoner by Davros so that Davros can taunt him and, more handily, explain the plot. (This is where the Supreme Dalek is messing me up, because he's an additional element in an already busy cast. Life would be much better if the Dalek Crucible had just one badass in charge. But I simply can't bear it when Davros is in charge of the Daleks. They wouldn't let him; it reduces them to soldiers.) So, the Doctor with Davros, yes... but which companion in that room with them? I'd always imagined that it'd be Donna. I've a brilliant Donna-showing-compassion-for-Davros scene in mind. Plus, this is Donna's series; putting the Doctor with Rose weights the whole drama too heavily in her favour. And in some ways – which become important later on – Donna should have been in this room for a while. Simultaneously, the plot is demanding that Donna is in the TARDIS, touching the hand-in-a-jar, so she becomes the biological catalyst for Doctor #2 to be grown out of the original Doctor's hand. That's why Doctor #2 is half-human, because he's part-Donna, which gives him one heart. This means that when he goes to live in the parallel universe, with Rose, at the end, he's going to age at a normal rate, so they'll be a proper couple. None of that 'You'll wither and die while I stay the same' lark. It's the final solution to their biggest problem as a couple. Donna has to be in the TARDIS as Doctor #2 appears. So she spends most of the episode with him, right?

But hold on – look at your other options – because if Rose is going to spend the rest of her life with Doctor #2, shouldn't *she* be with him in the TARDIS as he springs into existence – and they spend the rest of the episode together, riffing off each other, both liking each other. And Doctor #2 is half-human, remember, so he can be more overtly sexualised than the original. Do you see how neat that is? If I don't take that option, she'll have to meet Doctor #2 in the last ten minutes. Pretty quick to fall in love. So, right, take that option – but that requires Donna to bond with the hand-in-a-jar, then think no more of it, waltz out of the TARDIS, with the original Doctor, to become Davros' prisoner, leaving the Doctor #2 birth to happen as if she'd had nothing to do with it. That's wrong. That's very wrong.

Also, it's a major piece of work simply to get the original Doctor out of the TARDIS with one companion, plus Jack, and to leave the other companion inside. Why would one stay behind? Why would Rose stay behind? Why would Donna stay behind? The other option: Rose *and* Donna stay in the TARDIS. Donna creates Doctor #2, while Rose is instantly attracted to him, and all three spend the episode together. Feels wrong, doesn't it? These scenes demand that the companion is alone, not two women together. The loneliness of it. And then the triumph! Remember way back, when I had to rewrite 4.5 very quickly, I told you that I'd stolen some of 4.12/4.13's plot to make 4.4/4.5 work? Well, here it is, coming back to haunt me. I stole the Donna-alone-in-the-TARDIS thread, where she finds herself alone on the Sontaran ship, and now I've got Donna alone in the TARDIS again in 4.13. It feels so similar. I've robbed myself. So maybe Rose should be in the TARDIS alone...?

FROM: RUSSELL T DAVIES TO: BENJAMIN COOK, SUNDAY 13 JANUARY 2008 21:34:36 GMT

RE: HAPPY NEW YEAR?

Oh, you asked me what good thoughts I'd had. I answered with the problems I've got! You only hear what you want to hear. Or maybe good thoughts and problems are the same thing.

FROM: RUSSELL T DAVIES TO: BENJAMIN COOK, MONDAY 14 JANUARY 2008 15:21:50 GMT

RE: HAPPY NEW YEAR?

I did no work last night. I went to bed. Set the alarm on my mobile, as usual. Placed my mobile far away from the bed, as usual. But then got a sheet of A4 and wrote on it in big, black Magic Marker: 'WORK, YOU STUPID ****!' That did the trick. I've been working since 11am...

FROM: BENJAMIN COOK TO: RUSSELL T DAVIES, MONDAY 14 JANUARY 2008 18:05:36 GMT

RE: HAPPY NEW YEAR?

GERMAN DALEKS!!![5] They've always been German, really, haven't they?

FROM: RUSSELL T DAVIES TO: BENJAMIN COOK, MONDAY 14 JANUARY 2008 18:53:18 GMT

RE: HAPPY NEW YEAR?

I've gone one better now: I Babel Fish-ed some dialogue for them, so now they're saying:[6]

              DALEKS
     Halt! Oder Sie werden geabschaffen! Sie sind ein
     Gefangener des Daleks!

5 Martha teleports to Germany, 50 miles outside Bremmen, where she encounters Daleks speaking German ('Exterminaten!').
6 Babel Fish is a web-based application that translates text from one of several languages into another.

Even then, I had a proper little conversation with myself about how Daleks would communicate in foreign countries – and how we, as the audience, would hear it. This tapped into another ponder, namely how much of the TARDIS translation facility Martha would have kept with her once she stops being a proper companion. Not much, I decided, or there would be all these polylingual ex-companions all over the place. That ability has to fade. Martha would hear German, so we should hear German. Daleks don't talk in standard English anyway, and would adapt to each country or planet. And yes, German, how apt for a bunch of Nazis.

FROM: RUSSELL T DAVIES TO: BENJAMIN COOK, TUESDAY 15 JANUARY 2008 03:11:59 GMT

RE: HAPPY NEW YEAR?

I'm terrified that there's no room for Jackie. I think we've asked Camille Coduri to keep the whole filming block of four weeks free, but now she's only going to be needed for one day at the end, when we return to Bad Wolf Bay. That's been worrying me all night. I e-mailed Julie about an hour ago, to ask where we stand with Camille and her agent. Not that Camille would complain, of course, but we're talking a living wage here. It's not fair. I did wonder, in my Julie e-mail, if Jackie could team up with Mickey and Sarah Jane (poor Julie hasn't even read 4.13 and won't know what I'm on about), but I regarded that as a desperate, last-minute option. Funny thing is, as the thought settles in, I realise that it could be rather good. It spoils the clean dynamic of the two Smiths together, but Jackie always comes up with good dialogue, and the thought of her and Sarah Jane is a bit tempting.

But would Jackie's early arrival bump up the length of the script? Also, I *really* worry that since Jackie has given birth and has little Tony at home (Tony Tyler!), she'd never enter a bloody battle zone. She'd stay at home. So I don't know what's best for the story, and I don't know what's good manners professionally.

FROM: BENJAMIN COOK TO: RUSSELL T DAVIES, TUESDAY 15 JANUARY 2008 13:16:44 GMT

RE: HAPPY NEW YEAR?

>>I e-mailed Julie about an hour ago, to ask where we stand with Camille and her agent.<<

And what has Julie said? What will decide: the story or the desire to give Camille a fair crack of the whip?

>>I *really* worry that since Jackie's given birth and has little Tony at home (Tony Tyler!), she'd never enter a bloody battle zone.<<

You could say the same of Sarah Jane, though. She has Luke waiting for her back home. If the world is about to end, I suppose you do whatever necessary to save that world and the people in it that you care about most.

FROM: RUSSELL T DAVIES TO: BENJAMIN COOK, TUESDAY 15 JANUARY 2008 13:40:41 GMT

RE: HAPPY NEW YEAR?

Julie has more or less told me to do what I want. Although, unusually for Julie, who always says 'write what you want', she did add, 'A bit more for Jackie would be great, though,' so I think that's a hint. I'm tempted to see what a Sarah/Mickey/Jackie combo would be like, so I might try it out this afternoon. I do love Jackie. But in the end: story wins. In the past, we've booked actors and then paid them off in order to get rid of them. A producer – a bad producer – will always say, 'But we've contracted them! We're paying them!' And I always reply, 'Yes, but we're paying them anyway, so it doesn't matter if they're in it or not.' Plus, you do spend less on them if you don't use them, on overnights and per diems. So there.

I don't think I need to worry about a reason for Mickey needing Jackie. That *would* start to get convoluted. I'm already having to shoehorn in lines about Dimension Jumps needing another half-hour to recharge and awful caveats like that, to stop the cast teleporting all over the place. Instead, I think it's very Jackie to just turn up. Like a nag. 'I'm not staying behind! Where's my daughter?!' There, motivation in one line, accurate character work and a bit of a laugh.

FROM: RUSSELL T DAVIES TO: BENJAMIN COOK, TUESDAY 15 JANUARY 2008 14:53:03 GMT

RE: HAPPY NEW YEAR?

I was on Page 19 and set myself a target: if I could add Jackie and make trims here and there so that the end result is *still* 19 pages, then she could stay. And I have. So she is. Hooray!

FROM: RUSSELL T DAVIES TO: BENJAMIN COOK, THURSDAY 17 JANUARY 2008 02:41:51 GMT

RE: HAPPY NEW YEAR?

The Doctor meeting Davros! Davros is hard to write. It's so easy to find yourself starting every line with 'So, Doctor…' and all that crap.

FROM: BENJAMIN COOK TO: RUSSELL T DAVIES, THURSDAY 17 JANUARY 2008 20:52:24 GMT

RE: HAPPY NEW YEAR?

I've just watched the first episode of Series Two of *Skins*. *Radio Times* biked it over to me. I'm interviewing Bryan Elsley for them next week. Oh, Russell… it's much better than Series One. I'm ridiculously happy about that. I can't wait for you to see this second series when it airs on E4 next month. Also, it seems that the blond gay one, Maxxie (played by Mitch Hewer), is the lead for the first half of the series, so you've *got* to watch. You're Number One Gay!

FROM: RUSSELL T DAVIES TO: BENJAMIN COOK, THURSDAY 17 JANUARY 2008 21:04:03 GMT

RE: HAPPY NEW YEAR?

Good for *Skins*! I mean that. I will watch, because I feel quite attached to that show, if only because we talked about Series One so much. (And did I mention Tony in his pants?) Isn't Tony all crippled and sick in Series Two? That's one way to reinvent a character. You can tell that Beautiful Maxxie is the new lead by the way that he dances half-naked through the trailer. And into my arms. Oh, they know their trailers, those *Skins* boys.

I fell asleep this afternoon. Bad move. I only woke up 20 minutes ago. Still a bit dazed. I spent today rearranging things (I've got Jackie and Mickey arriving at the same time now, in the same FX shot – of course, duh, how stupid was I?) and seeding information in the right place. I realised that Rose spent time in 4.11 telling Donna that she was super-important for reasons *beyond* 4.11's plot, but now she forgets to mention it to her, so I fixed things like that. Also, I realised that the Doctor is happily pointing to his hand-in-a-jar at the beginning, with Rose just standing there. Rose should be like, 'What?! Your hand *what?!*'

FROM: RUSSELL T DAVIES TO: BENJAMIN COOK, THURSDAY 17 JANUARY 2008 23:50:31 GMT

RE: HAPPY NEW YEAR?

I am writing. Jackie Tyler is about to die. I love Jackie about to die!

FROM: BENJAMIN COOK TO: RUSSELL T DAVIES, FRIDAY 18 JANUARY 2008 00:10:09 GMT

RE: HAPPY NEW YEAR?

You can't kill Jackie Tyler! She has a son now!

Kill him instead.

FROM: RUSSELL T DAVIES TO: BENJAMIN COOK, FRIDAY 18 JANUARY 2008 02:59:55 GMT

RE: HAPPY NEW YEAR?

I've started to write rubbish now. Always a sign. A sign saying: 'STOP'. I really wanted to write more, which means that I won't finish tomorrow after all, and then I have to go to Hull this weekend.

You wouldn't believe the stuff that I'm cutting as I go along. Stuff that I'd planned in my head, but then, no, too expensive or too long or just rubbish, so I never write a word of it. Even though it was alive and possible until... ooh, yesterday. Like, Doctor #2 and Donna were going to go back to the Shadow Proclamation and enlist a fleet of Judoon ships! And attack the Medusa Cascade! Blimey! Madness, I know. It would have been good, though. Roughly ten FX shots of Judoon ships flying and attacking Dalek saucers, etc.

FROM: RUSSELL T DAVIES TO: BENJAMIN COOK, SATURDAY 19 JANUARY 2008 03:24:20 GMT

RE: HAPPY NEW YEAR?

<u>60. INT. CRUCIBLE VAULTS - NIGHT</u>

THE DOCTOR & ROSE still in SPOTLIGHTS; looking up, hearing the sound of MASSIVE HYDRAULICS. DAVROS calmer, now:

> DAVROS
> It begins! Finally, we will achieve all that I have ever
> wanted. Peace. Everlasting peace.

> THE DOCTOR
> They'll kill you, Davros. Once it's done. Cos the
> Daleks despise you, for being flesh. Ohh, you will be
> exterminated.

> DAVROS
> As I said, Doctor. Peace.

Silence, as Davros glides away from them. Hold.

Only the noise of huge hydraulics from above. The Doctor
looking up, trapped, helpless.
But Rose is looking at Davros. She's quiet, sad:

> ROSE
> What happened to you? I mean your face. Your eyes. What
> happened?

> DAVROS
> Are you showing me pity, Miss Tyler?

> ROSE
> Someone must have. Once upon a time.

> DAVROS
> (quiet)
> Not for so many years. But I was like you, back then.
> Walking tall, so young and so proud. On a world called
> Skaro. A world at war.

> ROSE
> With who…?

> DAVROS
> With each other. My race, the Kaleds, in perpetual
> battle against the Thals. My very first memory; hiding
> underground, with the screams of battle above. I saw the
> surface of the planet, only once…

On CU Davros…

                                                    MIX TO:

61. EXT. SKARO - DAY

FX: CU DAVROS, the MAN. Gaunt, strong, in a dirty-white
medic's coat. FX for the BOILING RED SKY behind him…

FX: REVERSE. DAVROS a small figure on a VAST PLAIN. DMP of a
RUINED WORLD. A shattered domed city; weird, warped cliffs in
the distance. NUCLEAR CLOUDS in the sky.

                                                    CUT TO:

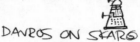

DAVROS ON SKARO

62. INT. CRUCIBLE VAULTS - NIGHT

                    DAVROS
  And I swore, then. To end it. I pledged my life, to help
  my people, to ensure their survival.

                                                    CUT TO:

63. INT. HOSPITAL WARD - DAY

These images are now cranked up, wild & jittery, only
glimpsed. It's like a WORLD WAR I WARD. But WINDOWLESS,
underground. INJURED SOLDIERS, bandaged, WOMEN in simple
nurses' uniforms, running, panicking.

JUMP CUTS of DAVROS the MAN, going from bed to bed. Studying
one SOLDIER, opening his eyelid, shining a torch; preparing
a syringe; injecting the soldier. The soldier thrashing in
agony; Davros & Nurse holding him down.

                    DAVROS OOV
  I studied the soldiers. Their frailty. Their pain. I
  sought to find a way, to free them from the agonies of
  the flesh. And then...

PRAC FX: EXPLOSION, Davros silhouetted against FIRE -

Glimpsed, jagged images - nurses - screaming - running -

CU Davros, his head now BALD, red, peeling; holding both hands
over his face, so he can't be seen. He's screaming.

                                                    CUT TO:

64. INT. CRUCIBLE VAULTS - NIGHT

                           DAVROS
    ...I became victim myself. Perhaps it was necessary. To
    inspire me.

                         THE DOCTOR
    ...except you weren't helping those soldiers. You were
    experimenting on them. You even experimented on your own
    family. Twisting the evolution of the Kaled Race, until
    they became the Daleks.

                         DALEK CAAN
                         (giggling)
    We were born! Out of blood!

                           DAVROS
                      (still at Rose)
    Can you imagine? I had one idea! An idea that has never
    stopped. Rolling out across the centuries. I have slept,
    and woken, and died, and every time I open my eyes,
    there they are. My Daleks. Outlasting eternity. And all
    from one man!

                         THE DOCTOR
    Oh, but every time you open your eyes, Davros... There's me.

> **Text message from: Russell**
> Sent: 19-Jan-2008 19:32
> Jane Tranter has just agreed to make 4.13 a 60-minute Special!

> **Text message from: Ben**
> Sent: 19-Feb-2008 20:15
> No need to worry so much about page count. Good news.

FROM: RUSSELL T DAVIES TO: BENJAMIN COOK, MONDAY 21 JANUARY 2008 01:47:02 GMT

RE: HAPPY NEW YEAR?

Just so you know exactly what happened on Saturday… I got *really* worried about page count. I can cut down anything, but this was getting absurd. The clincher for me was cutting two very simple, seemingly unimportant lines at the top of Scene 43 in the most recent draft. After Davros has activated the Holding Cell, he said, 'Excellent. Even when powerless, a Time Lord is best contained.' And then the Doctor said, 'Good to know you're still scared of me.' Cuttable, yes… except they're *not*, because those are two introduction lines to a big scene, they're a pause, a settling, a statement of intent. Signature dialogue. A signature that's saying, 'These two are going to talk now.' I thought, if I'm having to cut *that*, I'm in serious trouble. Let alone other stuff, like the fact that I was now writing in such shorthand that Davros didn't have time to recognise Sarah Jane, that I didn't have time in the TARDIS for the Doctor to tell

Captain Jack and Rose to put down their guns…

So I forwarded the script to Julie, saying what trouble we were in, to the extent of wondering: does something massive need to be cut? Like Sarah Jane? Or Torchwood? Something intrinsic, not just line-trims. Julie read it, loved it, phoned Jane and got instant authorisation for a 60-minute Special! It's not that simple, of course – Julie now needs to find funding, and contract Graeme[7] and all departments and the actors for another week – but if anyone can do it, she can. What support, though. Amazing.

FROM: RUSSELL T DAVIES TO: BENJAMIN COOK, MONDAY 21 JANUARY 2008 02:46:36 GMT

RE: HAPPY NEW YEAR?

I'm only tootling through that script tonight, slipping back lines that I wish I hadn't cut, such as this exchange between the Doctor and Rose in the Crucible Vaults, just after Davros has said that he wants 'Everlasting peace'…

```
Silence, as Davros glides away from them. Hold.

Only the noise of huge hydraulics from above. The Doctor
looking up, trapped, helpless.

Then, quiet, intimate, across the distance:

                    ROSE
    You never did finish that sentence.

                THE DOCTOR
    What sentence…?

                    ROSE
                  (smiles)
    Like you don't know. Last time I saw you. On Bad Wolf
    Bay. You said, 'Rose Tyler…'

                THE DOCTOR
    …isn't it cold?

                    ROSE
    Come on. Properly.

                THE DOCTOR
    Does it need saying?

                    ROSE
    Yeah.

  Pause; sad smile between them.

  Then, just as quiet:
```

---

7 Graeme Harper directed 4.12/4.13.

```
                        DAVROS
    Such intimacy. So different from the Doctor I once knew.
```

That's the sort of thing I mean, the sort of stuff that I was having to leave out by compressing into shorthand. It's at the heart of the whole thing. It'll pay off beautifully at the end. Of course, this script has to be ready for the Tone Meeting on Wednesday (it's going to be an endless meeting – we haven't even got the right amount of practical Daleks, let alone all the ones that I'm blowing up!), and I've just upped the page count, which gives me even more pages to write. Ah, something always bites me on the arse. That's a lot of work.

CHAPTER TWELVE

TIME FOR HEROES

In which *Skins* is the best thing on TV,
Russell gets chicken pox, and Rose Tyler
is a terrible racist... possibly

FROM: RUSSELL T DAVIES TO: BENJAMIN COOK, TUESDAY 22 JANUARY 2008 02:37:55 GMT

RE: HAPPY NEW YEAR?

I've almost finished... but I'm still a way off. I'm wondering whether to stay up and finish it. Technically, I *have* to, because this is supposed to be distributed to everyone tomorrow morning, but I don't know, I've had a weird day. I feel a bit strange, a bit dizzy and sick, just not myself. I've been typing away, without music, in silence. Normally, I love writing series finales. I get a real buzz. I'm not getting a buzz this time. It's laughable to think that I ever imagined fitting all this into 45 minutes. That's not helping. I feel stupid. I'm not sure I should continue, feeling like this, with big and lovely scenes to come. I feel like I might spoil them.

FROM: BENJAMIN COOK TO: RUSSELL T DAVIES, TUESDAY 22 JANUARY 2008 02:51:08 GMT

RE: HAPPY NEW YEAR?

>>It's laughable to think that I ever imagined fitting all this into 45 minutes. That's not helping. I feel stupid.<<

Yeah, but with the best will in the world, Russell, plenty of writers don't have enough story in their heads to fill 30 or 45 minutes of drama, let alone an hour. So think yourself lucky. Or gifted. But not stupid.

FROM: RUSSELL T DAVIES TO: BENJAMIN COOK, TUESDAY 22 JANUARY 2008 02:58:51 GMT

RE: HAPPY NEW YEAR?

You're too wise. That's actually worked on me. Right, I'll continue. Might as well forge on. More soon.

FROM: RUSSELL T DAVIES TO: BENJAMIN COOK, TUESDAY 22 JANUARY 2008 05:06:50 GMT

RE: HAPPY NEW YEAR?

In 40 minutes, Tesco opens for more cigarettes.

FROM: RUSSELL T DAVIES TO: BENJAMIN COOK, TUESDAY 22 JANUARY 2008 06:23:04 GMT

RE: HAPPY NEW YEAR?

Bloody hell. I must be five pages from the end. Just five. This is a long haul. Next, I have to write out Donna, but I can't bear it. I LOVE HER! Right, off to Tesco now, then I'll finish.

FROM: BENJAMIN COOK TO: RUSSELL T DAVIES, TUESDAY 22 JANUARY 2008 06:27:02 GMT

RE: HAPPY NEW YEAR?

STAY! WHERE! YOU! ARE!

Oh, all right, go to Tesco. But don't get run over by a bus on your way back. That would be *very* annoying.

FROM: RUSSELL T DAVIES TO: BENJAMIN COOK, TUESDAY 22 JANUARY 2008 06:27:58 GMT

RE: HAPPY NEW YEAR?

I just thought that. If I fell into the Bay, no one would know what happens to Donna!

I won't fall into the Bay.

FROM: RUSSELL T DAVIES TO: BENJAMIN COOK, TUESDAY 22 JANUARY 2008 06:46:00 GMT

RE: HAPPY NEW YEAR?

I didn't fall into the Bay. Mmm, croissant. Still warm. I love a little shop.

FROM: BENJAMIN COOK TO: RUSSELL T DAVIES, TUESDAY 22 JANUARY 2008 06:49:16 GMT

RE: HAPPY NEW YEAR?

Did you get hit by a bus, though?

FROM: RUSSELL T DAVIES TO: BENJAMIN COOK, TUESDAY 22 JANUARY 2008 06:54:39 GMT

RE: HAPPY NEW YEAR?

Yes, I'm typing from the ambulance. They say I'll never dance again. In fairness, I've had my day.

FROM: RUSSELL T DAVIES TO: BENJAMIN COOK, TUESDAY 22 JANUARY 2008 07:37:28 GMT

RE: HAPPY NEW YEAR?

This is too sad for words! I can't type because I'm crying!

FROM: BENJAMIN COOK TO: RUSSELL T DAVIES, TUESDAY 22 JANUARY 2008 07:41:49 GMT

RE: HAPPY NEW YEAR?

It's 7.40am. You've been writing through the night. You're allowed to cry. (What are you going to be like at the Final Mix? We'll bring tissues.)

FROM: RUSSELL T DAVIES TO: BENJAMIN COOK, TUESDAY 22 JANUARY 2008 07:49:29 GMT

RE: HAPPY NEW YEAR?

I can imagine Julie at the Final Mix. She'll die! I haven't even written Wilf's last speech yet. That's going to kill me. Dawn over the Bay is very beautiful. How's Chiswick?!

FROM: BENJAMIN COOK TO: RUSSELL T DAVIES, TUESDAY 22 JANUARY 2008 07:56:43 GMT

RE: HAPPY NEW YEAR?

Chiswick is fearing for the welfare of Donna Noble.

FROM: RUSSELL T DAVIES TO: BENJAMIN COOK, TUESDAY 22 JANUARY 2008 09:54:58 GMT

RE: HAPPY NEW YEAR?

It all ends in Chiswick.[1] That's so funny.

Oh, enough! Have it.

Phew.

Blub.

FROM: RUSSELL T DAVIES TO: BENJAMIN COOK, TUESDAY 22 JANUARY 2008 10:03:01 GMT

RE: HAPPY NEW YEAR?

And now, ten minutes after pressing send, I'm remembering all the lines and moments that I meant to put in. Always the way.

FROM: BENJAMIN COOK TO: RUSSELL T DAVIES, TUESDAY 22 JANUARY 2008 10:23:19 GMT

RE: HAPPY NEW YEAR?

Poor, poor Donna. That's worse than death, isn't it?[2] I think *I* might cry! At least Wilf remembers.

Donna was much better than Penny Carter would have been.

---

1 Donna Noble hails from Chiswick, in West London.
2 The 'biological metacrisis' that creates Doctor #2, when Donna touches the Doctor's hand-in-a-jar (following 4.13's cliffhanger resolution, in which the Doctor uses his severed hand as a store for unused energy from his aborted regeneration), proves to be a two-way transference; Donna becomes half-human, half-Time Lord. However, as her body is still human, she is unable to live with a Time Lord mind – and the Doctor has to wipe Donna's memories of her time with him so that she doesn't 'burn up' before he can return her home to Chiswick.

RISE OF THE CYBERMEN

These are the closing scenes of *Journey's End*, as written on 22 January 2008...

143. EXT. NOBLES' HOUSE - NIGHT

The Tardis noise now fading away. And all alone in the doorway, in the rain…

WILF salutes.

WIDE SHOT. The Tardis has gone. Only the rain. And Wilfred Mott gently closes the door.

                                              CUT TO:

144. INT. TARDIS - NIGHT

WIDE SHOT. In flight.

THE DOCTOR, all alone. He's a bit bedraggled, from the rain. Looks up at the Time Rotor.

Lost in thought.

Deep breath. Move on. He starts wandering round. Flicking switches. Recovering himself.

Nice and slow, taking his time. All the time in the world.

Then, eventually, there's a small bleep from the scanner. He wanders over. Only half interested. Studies it.

Then more curious…

                    THE DOCTOR
     What…?
                         (looks closer)
     What?
                           (closer)
     Whaaaat????!

And he's bending over, fascinated, unable to see -

TWO CYBERMEN rearing up behind him!!!

                              END OF EPISODE 13

FROM: RUSSELL T DAVIES TO: BENJAMIN COOK, TUESDAY 22 JANUARY 2008 10:30:07 GMT

RE: HAPPY NEW YEAR?

I know, imagine forgetting the Doctor! Catherine is *begging* to make an appearance in *The Sarah Jane Adventures*, because it's her daughter's favourite show, but I'm sitting here going, 'But *how?!*'

FROM: RUSSELL T DAVIES TO: BENJAMIN COOK, TUESDAY 22 JANUARY 2008 23:03:08 GMT

RE: HAPPY NEW YEAR?

I slept all afternoon. Fresh as the proverbial. People seem happy with the script, though Phil was seen to be weeping. Not at the sad ending; at the budget!

FROM: BENJAMIN COOK TO: RUSSELL T DAVIES, TUESDAY 22 JANUARY 2008 23:29:31 GMT

RE: HAPPY NEW YEAR?

You cried when writing Donna's goodbye, even though you knew what was coming, and now Phil is in tears… aren't you worried that it might be *too* sad for some viewers, especially the younger ones?

Also, if this isn't an odd question, why have you written that final scene with the Cybermen? What exactly do you think it adds to the plot? Isn't it a bit… superfluous?

FROM: RUSSELL T DAVIES TO: BENJAMIN COOK, WEDNESDAY 23 JANUARY 2008 00:04:57 GMT

RE: HAPPY NEW YEAR?

The final scene? Well, same reason as ever, really. Like the runaway bride appearing in the TARDIS at the end of *Doomsday*, like the *Titanic* crashing into the TARDIS at the end of *Last of the Time Lords*, to end on an upbeat note. To say that the story isn't over, don't stop watching *Doctor Who*, ever. The Doctor's life never stops, no matter how sad things get. Dry your tears, move on. New adventures to come. Otherwise, you might remember *Doctor Who* as a sad and bleak thing, which is maybe not so good if you're eight years old.

But am I worried that some viewers might find Donna's departure *too* sad? Not remotely. Not for a single second. I believe, hugely, massively, that TV isn't there to make you smile. Drama certainly isn't. That ending is devastating. I hope it's never forgotten. I hope people cry for years. In 70 years' time, kids watching it now will be in old folks' homes, saying, 'Oh, why couldn't Donna Noble have remembered just one thing?!' There's this great misconception that the Slitheen are for kids, and episodes like *Human Nature* and *The Family of Blood* are for adults. In fact, adults can enjoy daft green monsters, and kids can appreciate emotional, grown-up drama. Pixar understands that perfectly. JK Rowling does. If kids are upset, then they're feeling something, and kids feel things vividly. The death of a goldfish is like the end of the world. It's keen, real and powerful for them. But that doesn't make it something to be avoided. If they can reach that state through fiction, well, they're actually experiencing something wonderful. And important.

Of course, very young kids might not get it, because forgetting has no analogy with their lives. They understand grief and loss, that's easy, because they've all lost that goldfish, grandparent, mother, favourite pen, or been lost in a crowd, so they get it when they see the Doctor lose Rose to a parallel world, or Nemo's dad lose his son in *Finding Nemo*, or Harry Potter sees his dead mum and dad in the Mirror of Erised. It has an echo within them, whereas simply *forgetting* someone doesn't. What happens to Donna is actually, beneath its simplicity, a fairly sophisticated sci-fi idea, so I think a lot of younger kids might be puzzled. Or bored. That's why Wilf, with his lonely salute, is so important, because you can register his loss. For adults, too, he really sells the moment. But I can't think of a way in which a kid could think, even unconsciously, that's happened to me.

Then again, you can never predict how kids will react. They're bloody clever. All that instinct. The writer Pete Bowker tells the best *Doctor Who*-viewing story ever. His son, Eric, watched *Doomsday*, and didn't particularly react to Rose's departure, but then the bride, Donna, appeared in the TARDIS at the cliffhanger, and Eric turned to his dad and said, 'It's all right now, cos the good fairy has appeared to make the man better.' And that's not just cute: Pete said that to see such engagement with a story, so emotionally and pictorially, for the first time ever, was actually a family triumph.

FROM: BENJAMIN COOK TO: RUSSELL T DAVIES, WEDNESDAY 23 JANUARY 21:39:11 GMT
RE: HAPPY NEW YEAR?
How was today's Tone Meeting? Did you make it through? (Or are you still there? Have they locked the doors?)

FROM: RUSSELL T DAVIES TO: BENJAMIN COOK, THURSDAY 24 JANUARY 2008 00:22:08 GMT
SKINS WINS!
I just got a text from the Broadcast Awards – *Skins* Series One has beaten *Doctor Who* Series Three! You've been e-mailing the wrong person, Benjamino. You should be doing – no, wait for it –The Life Of Bryan. Ha ha ha.

The Tone Meeting wasn't as endless as I thought. I'm not about to say that 4.13 is easy, no way, but actually there's a lot of sleight of hand. The end of the universe actually takes place in six or seven separate rooms, three of which are standing sets, with a lot of spectacle purely CGI. I think it's achievable. (Remember me saying this. Next week the bills come in and I will bleed!) And that team is so excellent now. Piers was there to observe, and at times I thought, to him, we must be talking in shorthand. 'Scene 43, Shot 2, is a mid-shot green screen, no reverse, like in *Doomsday*, yeah?' There was a great moment when I was despairing of finding a location for the Crucible Test Area. I said, 'Let's face it, we're not going to find a big enough space that fits Dalek design. I might have to cut this sequence.'

And Ed Thomas said, 'Oy! I thought you were made of better stuff. Four years on this job and you've never wimped out before.' I loved him for saying that.

It was Phil's last Tone Meeting. We had a strange round of applause. Strange, because it was sad.

> **Text message from: Russell**
> Sent: 24-Jan-2008 19:44
> On set today, Alex Kingston walked up to me and shouted through her spacesuit helmet, 'Can you write me a part as a lipstick lesbian?!' I love moments like that.

> **Text message from: Ben**
> Sent: 24-Jan-2008 20:18
> It's great going on set at the moment, isn't it? Everyone is just gutted by what's in store for Donna in 4.13!

> **Text message from: Russell**
> Sent: 25-Jan-2008 11:16
> Bernard Cribbins just phoned me up: 'I have read Episode 13. I have been crying for two days.'

FROM: BENJAMIN COOK TO: RUSSELL T DAVIES, SATURDAY 26 JANUARY 2008 00:22:08 GMT

RE: SKINS WINS!

Where do you stand with the Christmas Special right now? How's life in the Christmas Maybe?

FROM: RUSSELL T DAVIES TO: BENJAMIN COOK, SUNDAY 27 JANUARY 2008 09:00:23 GMT

RE: SKINS WINS!

Lordy God. Panic. I've been having a lot of thoughts – nothing coherent, not yet – for ages, but the rush of scripts has been so great that I haven't had time to tell you. Cybermen, Victoriana, a swordfight on the roof with Cybershades (Cyberman heads in flowing black robes, like wraiths, sort of creepy half-Cybermen), workhouse kids as slaves… That's all the normal plot stuff. The real heart of it is the beginning: the Doctor arrives, hears a damsel in distress, the Doctor steps forward to save her… when this *other* man swings in, dashing, brilliant, amazing, clever, witty, saves the day. The Doctor says, 'Who are you?' The man says, 'I'm the Doctor!' Good scene. The Doctor becomes *his* companion. I like that. Sweet. There will be a beautiful woman too, of course, but really it's the Doctor paired with a new Doctor. That's a lovely story and it's got great potential. It would be wonderful if I had a month or two to let it stew. But it's due in three weeks! I can hardly bear to look at it. The furnace!

Quite apart from the time in which I have to write it, it's like relaxing-after-the-thirteenth-episode-is-delivered is hardwired into me. I can feel bits of my brain and body closing down. It's Herculean to keep going. And I'm not Hercules. I'm really, properly, feeling old. I used to have the stamina to steamroller through this sort of schedule, but it's lacking now. The last time I had my eyes tested, the optician asked my age and said, 'You'll need bifocals soon. Your lenses won't be able to cope with reading for much longer.' Lo and behold, a few months later, it's like someone's thrown a switch. Suddenly, overnight, my glasses are on and off, on and off. Proper, undeniable ageing. You sort of think it'll never happen, but your body has other ideas.

Nah, it's worse than that. It's not just Grumpy Old Men stuff. Far worse is the snaky little thought: if you had some coke, you'd have twice the energy and stay awake for longer. I haven't thought that seriously for years. This is the first time, in ten years or so, of thinking, I *need* it. I know it's bollocks, I know, I know. I think I needed to type it out to see how stupid it looks.

FROM: RUSSELL T DAVIES TO: BENJAMIN COOK, THURSDAY 31 JANUARY 2008 01:11:06 GMT

RE: SKINS WINS!

Well, 4.13 is 170 FX days over! I've found about 88 to cut, and Phil has found 120, but they're a bit severe, so I'm fighting them off. Never mind, we'll get there, I'm sure of that. It's just that the actual getting there is such a slog.

I know what's *really* preying on my mind, though, and stopping me moving onto the Christmas Special. Julie said, 'That scene on Bad Wolf Bay isn't working, is it?'[3] And she's absolutely right. I love a good note, because it's like someone has articulated the voice at the back of your head. That scene doesn't work. I have always known that, from the moment I typed it out, but I don't know how to fix it. Rose has to be stupid to fall in love with Doctor #2. No matter what I do, that's not her Doctor. I can Elastoplast over it by saying that Doctor #2 needs Rose, but that's slight. You don't *feel* that. Why doesn't Rose hop into the TARDIS and go with the real Doctor? The walls of the universe are open enough for her to pop to and fro. She's always wanted to get him back, so why does she stay on Bad Wolf Bay? The hardest thing of all in that scene – and Billie might yet have problems with it – is getting Rose to walk away from the TARDIS in the first place. That, indeed, is the problem with the whole scene, that Rose has to act out of character to stay on Bad Wolf Bay. She's utterly, marvellously selfish, and would push past anyone to get to her Doctor.

I have to work out whose scene it is, too. In many ways, it's the Doctor's, the real Doctor's. David thinks it's a tragic scene, because it's all about the original, but that's exactly what has reduced Rose's intelligence; she's doing what the plot demands, not what *she'd* demand. That's always wrong. But follow Rose's impulse and we're off into…

---

3 The Doctor drops Doctor #2, Rose and Jackie 'home', on Bad Wolf Bay, on the parallel Earth.

well, plots that we can't shoot, pages of arguing, the Doctor denying her a life with him for no good reason other than my need to tie up the loose ends. Oh, it's driving me mad. In *Doomsday*, Bad Wolf Bay was the best scene ever, and now I've made it the location of the most unconvincing scene ever – and I don't know how to fix it. All sorts of false notes are chiming. I think I hate the kiss between Rose and Doctor #2. That's when Rose's intelligence is zero. It makes me feel nothing, when I should be feeling everything.

When I get this stuck, I start lying to myself. I tell myself that the Bad Wolf Bay scene mustn't be that sad, because the really sad scene is Donna's departure. You can't have tragedy after tragedy. Well, there's a certain amount of sense in that, but it's still a lie. I'm telling myself that to soothe myself for not getting the scene right in the first place. I'm supposed to be thinking about 4.14, but this Bad Wolf Bay scene has become a logjam in my head. It's all I can think about. Julie first made her comment about five days ago, and I've been thinking about it ever since. One thing I do know: this isn't a couple-of-lines rewrite. It's more fundamental. Julie keeps e-mailing with suggestions, like Rose saying to the original, 'But he's not you', which only makes me say, 'So why stay with him?!' This isn't a dialogue problem. There's no sentence that will paper over the cracks. It's a plot rewrite. I've got the story wrong. And that's massive, potentially. In an episode that's already over-length (it's been timed at 67 minutes, damn it – this is getting ridiculous) and over-budget, how do I think of a new story?!

FROM: BENJAMIN COOK TO: RUSSELL T DAVIES, THURSDAY 31 JANUARY 2008 01:41:18 GMT

RE: SKINS WINS!

Yes, I suppose the original Bad Wolf Bay scene, in *Doomsday*, worked because the Doctor and Rose *had* to be separated. This scene isn't working because they choose to be. The imperative has gone. Ouch!

FROM: RUSSELL T DAVIES TO: BENJAMIN COOK, THURSDAY 31 JANUARY 2008 01:51:04 GMT

RE: SKINS WINS!

Well, exactly. And that raises another problem: if I work out a version in which they *have* to be separated, aren't I repeating the first bloody version? Argh! Do you see?

FROM: RUSSELL T DAVIES TO: BENJAMIN COOK, MONDAY 4 FEBRUARY 2008 10:45:39 GMT

RE: SKINS WINS!

I've made further FX cuts. Not just for FX, but also for page count. Firstly, the Shadow Proclamation Lobby has gone. Completely. Slitheen, space extras, monks and nuns. Poor Louise Page – I hope she hasn't spent money on this already. (As we have with Margaret Slitheen's voice. Annette Badland has already recorded her line!) Hey ho, something substantial had to go. The TARDIS now lands directly in the Shadow Architect's office. We'll still need the Judoon – they'll be there with some 'Bo! Klo! Fo!'

dialogue – but we only have four of them now.

All the stuff on Skaro with the Young Davros has been cut, too. The FX, plus the ward and the nurses and the soldiers, everything. It's heartbreaking, but what can you do? Will Cohen is devastated.

However, I have asked for two extra FX shots – that's all we need – around Rose. Brand new ones. Similar to the Voidstuff shots with the 3D glasses in *Doomsday*. This should fix the problems with her plot. The Voidstuff surrounds anyone who crosses from one universe to another, so I can say that it's now contaminated or something, as though – because of the Daleks' dimension-rupturing – it's become lethal if you're in the wrong universe. Rose has to stay in the parallel world – or she'll die. She has no choice.

> **Text message from: Russell**
> Sent: 04-Feb-2008 22:04
>
> I feel... blurgh! I get dizzy every time I turn my head. My eyes are all puffed up. Oh well, it'll pass. I have to get on with work tomorrow. It can't wait any longer.

FROM: RUSSELL T DAVIES TO: BENJAMIN COOK, TUESDAY 5 FEBRUARY 2008 14:15:12 GMT

RE: SKINS WINS!

Chicken pox! I've got bloody chicken pox!!! I woke up today like a *Doctor Who* monster. More lumps and bumps than... well, my normal lumps and bumps. I feel like crap. I'm going back to bed now. Must not scratch.

FROM: BENJAMIN COOK TO: RUSSELL T DAVIES, WEDNESDAY 6 FEBRUARY 2008 01:08:38 GMT

RE: SKINS WINS!

Chicken pox?! Didn't you get it out of the way when you were a kid? It's supposed to be less of a bastard when you're young. (Sorry, not helping.) My mum used to make me go round to play at the houses of kids with chicken pox, hoping that I'd catch it!

> **Text message from: Ben**
> Sent: 06-Feb-2008 19:45
>
> Feeling any better? Today was fun. I was on set for *Silence in the Library*. Swansea in the sunshine! Gorgeous set. AMAZING lunch.

> **Text message from: Russell**
> Sent: 06-Feb-2008 19:51
>
> Amazing lunch? In Swansea?! I'm worse today, because I was allergic to the pills, so my mouth blew up till I was having trouble breathing. I had to go to casualty. On a Wednesday morning. Not glamorous. Now my lips are so big, I look like a cartoon duck.

Text message from: Ben
Sent: 06-Feb-2008 20:18

Casualty?! Russell, I hope you aren't working tonight. That shouldn't be your priority. For once, let other people sort out the shit.

Text message from: Russell
Sent: 06-Feb-2008 20:22

I know, you're right, I'll stop soon. But no one else can rewrite this bastard script. I'll work till Friday, then I can stop and have a whole weekend off in lovely Manchester.

Text message from: Russell
Sent: 07-Feb-2008 12:16

I'm hobbling today. It's on the soles of my feet. There ain't no dignity.

FROM: RUSSELL T DAVIES TO: BENJAMIN COOK, SATURDAY 9 FEBRUARY 2008 18:18:09 GMT

RE: SKINS WINS!

Manchester, hooray! My boyfriend, my clothes, my CDs, my… everything. Even my full-sized Dalek in the hall. (I've got to get rid of that. It's too much like work now.) With a bit of luck, I can stay here for ten days or so, but I'm itchy, scratchy and tired, and I still have to rewrite 4.13. And I just realised, my plan to make the Bad Wolf Bay scene work – the one involving Voidstuff – won't work, because I'd forgotten that Mickey has to be free to stay in our universe. Bollocks. Julie's upset. She's saying, 'Leave Mickey in the parallel universe,' and I'm saying, 'Too late! We promised Noel that we'd bring him back in *Torchwood* Series Three.'

FROM: BENJAMIN COOK TO: RUSSELL T DAVIES, SATURDAY 9 FEBRUARY 2008 19:01:46 GMT

RE: SKINS WINS!

Why not have Rose admit that she's a terrible racist and she wants to stay in the parallel world to rid herself of Mickey? Yes, that'll do. Rose Tyler: Terrible Racist. That's not just an idea, it's a spin-off.

FROM: RUSSELL T DAVIES TO: BENJAMIN COOK, SATURDAY 9 FEBRUARY 2008 19:24:12 GMT

RE: SKINS WINS!

That's brilliant! Or maybe Freddie Ljungberg, Russell Tovey and Charlie Hunnam could run past in speedos, and Rose thinks, hmm, okay, I'll stay here, thank you very much. That would work.

FROM: RUSSELL T DAVIES TO: BENJAMIN COOK, MONDAY 11 FEBRUARY 2008 23:55:16 GMT

RE: SKINS WINS!

I watched the new *Skins* tonight, finally. But, but, but… that first episode is EXCELLENT! What a change. What a show! Moments of absolute beauty – like Tony with Maxxie's mum, when she has to help him piss, and then they started laughing, that was perfect. The tiny little fact that Maxxie's mum used to clean for Tony's mum. I loved it.

FROM: BENJAMIN COOK TO: RUSSELL T DAVIES, TUESDAY 12 FEBRUARY 2008 01:57:01 GMT

RE: SKINS WINS!

I'm glad you're watching. It's much better, isn't it? It's extraordinary and fascinating that they had to destroy Tony in order to let the show breathe. I hear rumours that Series Three will have an almost entirely new cast, to keep the show about 17- and 18-year-olds. I think that's an incredible idea. Brave, aren't they?

How are you feeling today?

FROM: RUSSELL T DAVIES TO: BENJAMIN COOK, TUESDAY 12 FEBRUARY 2008 13:15:36 GMT

RE: SKINS WINS!

Sick as a dog. The moment I stopped work, everything leapt on me. Today, it's bronchitis! And I still haven't rewritten 4.13.

FROM: RUSSELL T DAVIES TO: BENJAMIN COOK, MONDAY 18 FEBRUARY 2008 02:14:07 GMT

RE: SKINS WINS!

I've whittled down 4.13 from 78 pages to 71. That's a miracle. I can't believe I'm delivering the final draft on the day that they start filming! That's horrific.

The Bad Wolf Bay scene still isn't working, but do you know what? No one's giving me good notes on it, when they should, so sod it. It's slightly better now, and I've cut the kiss between Rose and Doctor #2, but it still sucks.

I know exactly what's wrong with it: it's too complicated. Emotionally, I mean. It has no echo, no resonance, it's empty sci-fi. When the Doctor and Rose were separated into parallel universes in *Doomsday*, that felt like every love you've ever lost – even if it's only the ones that you've lost in your head, like teenage virgins pining over love songs in their bedroom. But when you've been separated into different universes, but now have a double of the man that you loved, who's not quite the same, but who's better because he's mortal, but worse because he's not the original… well, you're going beyond human experience. There's no parallel with real life. No equation. Therefore, no feeling.

FROM: BENJAMIN COOK TO: RUSSELL T DAVIES, MONDAY 18 FEBRUARY 2008 02:22:06 GMT

RE: SKINS WINS!

I agree with some of what you said about the Bad Wolf Bay scene (you're right, it's still not *quite* working), except for the bit about Rose's departure, as written, having no resonance. We've all loved someone and it hasn't worked out, for whatever reason, so we've found someone else. We've moved on. Even the teenage virgins find someone real, someone who exists beyond the posters on their bedroom walls. And yet we know – we always know – that the next love is *not* the same, they're *not* as good, we're settling for second best. We're all just making do. Like Judith in *The Second Coming*, we're all hoping that someone better will come along, someone as incredible as our First Love or as perfect as the girl or boy in the posters on our bedroom wall. Or is that just me? Oh God…

FROM: RUSSELL T DAVIES TO: BENJAMIN COOK, TUESDAY 19 FEBRUARY 2008 14:18:55 GMT

RE: SKINS WINS!

I take your point about accepting second best, making do with Doctor #2, and how we can all recognise that, because we've all done it (we lie to kids, we tell them that those bedroom posters are fantasies – bollocks, they're the *best!* Everything else is a pale imitation), but the problem is, none of us does it THAT QUICKLY. Not in three pages. Accepting second best is a quiet, passive condition – universal, yes, but you have to slide that into a drama. It's what Rose has done with Andy in *Bob & Rose*, it's what Vince does when he goes out with Cameron in *Queer as Folk*… they're making do with compromises and imagining themselves happy, wishing themselves happy, even if it isn't true. But no one does that in a crisis. It's gradual.

I'll think on. I'm sure that I'm going to rewrite that scene again before it's shot.

FROM: BENJAMIN COOK TO: RUSSELL T DAVIES, TUESDAY 19 FEBRUARY 2008 22:05:31 GMT

RE: SKINS WINS!

I wonder whether Rose's decision works *because* it's quick. If she had time to think about it, of course she wouldn't stay on Bad Wolf Bay. As I read it, Rose accepts second best, Doctor #2, because her Doctor, the original Doctor, manipulates her into doing so. That's why it happens so suddenly. The whole 'He's too dangerous to be left on his own' speech – 'He needs you. That's very me.' The original Doctor knows how to hit a nerve, doesn't he? He's pushing Rose away, making a magnificent sacrifice, because he loves her. That's why you describe him in the script as 'Heartbroken'. You're hung up on the idea that Rose must be dumb to choose to stay on Bad Wolf Bay, but she doesn't choose, does she? Not really. He does.

FROM: RUSSELL T DAVIES TO: BENJAMIN COOK, FRIDAY 22 FEBRUARY 2008 18:08:59 GMT

PANIC!!!

Sorry I haven't written for a few days. On Monday, I've just two weeks to write the Christmas script… and I haven't a clue. There have been no Maybe thoughts while I've been ill, and now I'm worried because I'm still feeling ill. I've got this cough that

I can't shake off, I'm losing sleep because I'm coughing so much, and naturally I think it's cancer because, well, that's what smokers think. I'm cocking things up like buggery here. I'm going back to Cardiff on Monday. I need to be there, to lock myself away, to panic some more and bang my head against the wall.

FROM: BENJAMIN COOK TO: RUSSELL T DAVIES, FRIDAY 22 FEBRUARY 2008 19:16:03 GMT

RE: PANIC!!!
>>I never think of it as work, really, no matter how much hard graft I actually do. Even if no one ever saw this stuff, I'd be doing it anyway.<<
    Ahem.

FROM: RUSSELL T DAVIES TO: BENJAMIN COOK, FRIDAY 22 FEBRUARY 2008 19:18:16 GMT

RE: PANIC!!!
SOD OFF!
    You're right, though.

> **Text message from: Ben**
> Sent: 25-Feb-2008 23:12
> Please don't tell me you missed tonight's *Skins*...?! How shocking was Sid's dad's death? That long, lonely day in Sid's house, that was just wonderful. Bryan Elsley, all is forgiven!

> **Text message from: Russell**
> Sent: 26-Feb-2008 00:32
> That episode was brilliant. BRILLIANT! Isn't it weird? *Skins* has got so much better by bringing the parents right into the centre and by sidelining the shagging and clubbing somewhat. In some ways, it's the opposite of what it was. Bloody marvellous, though.

FROM: RUSSELL T DAVIES TO: BENJAMIN COOK, SATURDAY 1 MARCH 2008 16:28:17 GMT

RE: PANIC!!!
I've rewritten Bad Wolf Bay again. Finally, I've got it right!
    Basically, I've given more of the decision to Rose, put her in control, and used that control to push away the original Doctor. And the kiss is back in! Then the scene finishes as before: Rose saying, 'No – !', as the TARDIS fades away, Doctor #2 taking her hand, and a wide shot of the now-empty beach. Julie is happy, David is happy, phew, good. Series Four, final rewrite, done.

FROM: BENJAMIN COOK TO: RUSSELL T DAVIES, SATURDAY 1 MARCH 2008 16:47:51 GMT

RE: PANIC!!!

Ahh, that's the one! That Bad Wolf Bay scene is better now, isn't it? Never mind Julie and David... are *you* happy with it, Russell?

FROM: RUSSELL T DAVIES TO: BENJAMIN COOK, SATURDAY 1 MARCH 2008 17:13:56 GMT

RE: PANIC!!!

I am delighted. That is such a weight off my mind. Knowing that it wasn't working was driving me mad. It hung over me, during Chicken Pox Fortnight. Literally, all the time. I tell you what helped: I watched the footage of the 4.12/4.13 read-through. They filmed it for *Doctor Who Confidential*, then edited it together fast so that I could see it – and they had to read the first draft of 4.13, because that's all that I'd written. It was so slow! (I'd been worried that cutting all that history-of-Davros stuff had gutted the script and left it a bit vacuous, but then I realised that it's the best cut I could have made, because the read-through drags terribly around about those scenes.) I could see what worked and what didn't, and I realised how good the kiss was, but equally that the kiss had no consequence. That's why it wasn't earning its place. But it's obvious, in the end, isn't it? The scene is about Rose choosing between two Doctors. So, on the last draft, finally, I've written clearly, obviously, Rose making that choice. Rose is in control.

The rushes have helped, too. When Rose is in the TARDIS with Doctor #2, Billie is looking at him with sheer *lust*. As only Billie can do! That, too, puts the power into Rose's hands. The mechanics start to work...

FROM: RUSSELL T DAVIES TO: BENJAMIN COOK, MONDAY 3 MARCH 2008 23:50:38 GMT

RE: PANIC!!!

Hey, did you see *Skins* tonight? Blimey! It's not afraid to take risks, is it? It's a different show each week. A lot like *Doctor Who*, actually. But every episode has such a strong, wonderful, unique voice. I don't know whether that comes from Bryan Elsley or from his team of young writers. But *Skins* makes me feel so out of touch with domestic drama. I kind of dread going back to writing that stuff, like it's something I've forgotten. No, not forgotten, something that I've moved too far away from. And a world which is working perfectly well without me. Damn them!

Sometimes I think of giving up writing, and that thought seems utterly wonderful. Like bliss. Like a release. Freedom. Imagine having no deadlines ever again. Sometimes I think very strongly that I really could stop for ever. That shouldn't feel so brilliant, should it? I don't know. Maybe it's the pox talking. No, it's just the middle-aged businessman talking, that's all. But I do get so tired of Scene 1, Scene 2, Scene 3, on and on and on. Maybe I should try to write a book...?

FROM: BENJAMIN COOK TO: RUSSELL T DAVIES, TUESDAY 4 MARCH 2008 00:07:55 GMT

RE: PANIC!!!

You couldn't stop writing, Russell. You wouldn't last six months.

How does a writer know when they've found their voice, do you think? *Can* you know? Or is it for others to tell you? Must your voice be unique? Aren't writers – like musicians – imitators by trade? Does finding your voice begin with imitating other, more accomplished writers, do you think?

FROM: RUSSELL T DAVIES TO: BENJAMIN COOK, TUESDAY 4 MARCH 2008 02:18:21 GMT

CYBERMAN ARSE

Ha ha, you're right, I couldn't stop writing for ever. Not even for six months. What would I do? I'm a slave to this job. Oh dear…

Look, I finally started 4.14. Christ, I hate starting. It just says: such a long way to go. Funny to think, the last Christmas script, that was the very first script that I ever sent you, and now we're onto next Christmas already. This one hasn't exactly got Kylie and the *Titanic*, but it's got a different sort of hook…

```
1. INT. TARDIS - NIGHT

REPEAT the end of 4.13; THE DOCTOR alone. He walks around the
console. A bleep from the scanner, he studies it…

                    THE DOCTOR
    What?
                        (looks closer)
    What??
                        (even closer)
    Whaaaat???

And he's bending forward, staring, not noticing… the TWO
CYBERMEN rearing up behind him!!

NEW MATERIAL. The Doctor spins round - !

                    THE DOCTOR (CONT'D)
    What?!

FX: THE TWO CYBERMEN… fade away…

The Doctor looks round, hearing a whoosh…

FX: THE TWO CYBERMEN reappear, fading up at the top of the
ramp. Both flailing, slowly, as if falling…

The Doctor takes a step towards them, boggling!

FX: and the two CYBERMEN fade again. A second later, one fades
back into existence, right by the wooden door; it's as though
```

they're phasing through the Tardis.

FX: CU that Cyberman fades, gone.

The Doctor runs to the console, throwing levers –

                  THE DOCTOR (CONT'D)
  Falling through the Vortex! But heading for where…?

The Tardis lurches, CAMERA SHAKE! The Doctor running around
the console, feverish, levers, buttons, switches, then –

Bump! Landed! The Doctor runs to the door, heading out –

                                  CUT TO:

2. EXT. VICTORIAN STREET – DAY

THE DOCTOR steps out of the Tardis.

Snow! In a STREET MARKET. It's a working-class area of London,
all busy and bustling…

Vendors, cocky lads, working girls, crones, braziers, beggars
in doorways, hot chestnuts, smoke, steam, the works.

The Doctor walking through. Gradually relaxing into a smile.
Soaking it in. He's loving it, the sheer colour and bustle and
noise; this is what he travels for.

Throughout all this, a CAROL can be heard; a new Murray Gold
Christmas Carol. Jolly & sinister, like the best hymns. The
Doctor passes the CAROLLERS, stops for a listen.
Then he wanders on, calls out to an URCHIN:

                  THE DOCTOR
  You there, boy, what day is this?

                    URCHIN
  Christmas Eve, sir!

                  THE DOCTOR
  In what year?

                    URCHIN
  You thick or something?

                  THE DOCTOR
  Oy! Answer the question!

                    URCHIN
  Year of our Lord 1851, sir.

                  THE DOCTOR
  Good, right, fine, and I don't suppose you've seen any

```
men, sort of tall, sort of metal, men made of metal,
with ears, like handles, big handle things, metal, no…?

Suddenly, a woman's voice, a distance away, yelling -

                    ROSITA OOV
Doctor!

                    THE DOCTOR
… who, me?

                    ROSITA OOV
Doctor!!!

Big grin!  And he's running - !

TRACK with him, racing through the snow, exhilarated -
he's actually glad to hear someone calling his name -
```

The best title for this episode would be *The Two Doctors*… but maybe not. *The New Doctor*, perhaps? Or *The Next Doctor*? I quite like *The Next Doctor*. I'm glad to have started, though worried by what's to come. I had a fair bit of Cybermen-in-Victoriana worked out, but this two Doctors story, the *real* story, is so strong that it's sort of knocking out everything else. That's good. It shows that it's a strong concept. But it's kind of left me clutching broken bits of story. Then again, a lot of that Cybermen stuff was dark – graveyards and things – whereas this new stuff is fun and lively, it's even going to get knockabout, and that's good for Christmas Day.

You ask how a writer finds their voice. Now, *that's* a question! Everyone has a voice, in life and in print, but finding it in print takes time. There's no technique for finding it, I don't think, and it's never 100 per cent individual. Yes, imitate like hell. Everyone does. But I'm not sure that it happens on purpose; it's a natural process. We all do it in speech, maybe even with thought. I can hear conversational riffs in my speech patterns that are torn from my friends, dozens of people, and writing is the same. Gaining a voice, whatever that is, comes with experience and practice – and the writing, again, is indivisible from the person. Your voice tends to be something that other people talk about, about you. It's not something that you think about much yourself, and certainly not whilst writing. I never – *never* – sit here thinking, what's my voice? You might as well ponder, who am I? It is, in fact, exactly the same thing. You can wonder your whole life and you'll never get an answer to that.

After all these years of wondering, I've never realised those last four sentences quite so clearly! This Great Correspondence does me good.

So the voice exists simply because you exist. You find your voice by writing, by experience. It doesn't matter what exactly you're writing, just that you *are* writing. Then one day someone will say, 'You've really found your voice with that piece', and you'll think, eh? Really? Everyone said it to me on *Queer as Folk*. It was kind of obvious, an easy remark, since that series was so close to home – so close that it still staggers me to watch it from afar, now. I did, in some ways, find my voice, but I wasn't aware of it. All this analysis exists outside the script. I just got on with it and wrote the next piece.

You can see voices in scripts, can't you? The difference between Steven's and mine? And it's always such a reflection of the person. I mean, look at Steven: he's all tough and Scottish, full of lethal gags (both in life and in script), and quite a lustful man, I think, a writer clearly driven by sex. More significantly, under that gruff exterior, a wonderful and romantic man, who hates to give that away – except in his writing. Again, again, again, scripts don't just live in Script World; they exist alongside everything else that you love and hate in your whole, wide, mad, lovely life. You copy from – or rather, are influenced by – everything.

I'm sure a lot of this e-mail correspondence amounts to Handy Tips, and that's fine, but everyone should find their own way to write. You must. Thing is, copying isn't just copying; it's selecting. It's not a dumb process. You can be aware of the fact that, yes, you've taken that phrasing or spacing off me, or Moffat, or Bryan Elsley or whoever, but what you're not so consciously aware of is the stuff that you're choosing *not* to use. If, say, you happen to like my one-line-pause technique, you'll know that you lifted it off me. At the same time, you'll have discarded techniques from my scripts that you don't like. That's not merely copying, but selecting, editing and adapting. It's a good, intelligent process of choosing, not imitating. So grab it all. From anyone. Read scripts, lots of them. Not just *Doctor Who* scripts. Go into the TV department of your nearest bookshop, grab any and every script book and bury yourself in them.

If you're thinking of writing your first script (oh, go on!)… well, I know what it's like. It's so easy to put off. Maybe you just don't write until you're ready, but I worry that's too easy an excuse, because then you could spend your whole life being not-quite-ready. You've got to start. The kids writing *Skins* are in their teens and early twenties! There is no time to waste! The whole world is full of unwritten scripts. There's a marvellous bit in *Peer Gynt* where he's surrounded by Songs, and they sing, 'We are songs, / you should have sung us. / A thousand times / You have curbed and suppressed us. / In the depths of your heart / we have lain and waited… / We were never called forth – / now we poison your voice.' That must feel terrible – and obviously feels true of everyone, even if you've written as many books as Stephen King or Agatha Christie. Don't be stifled and strangled.

It's so important to start writing, because then the process never, ever ends. Finding your voice isn't the last stage, just another stage along the way. You reach the top of that mountain, only to see a whole bloody, endless range of mountains waiting beyond. You've a million more things to reach for, a million more variations on your voice to articulate. Because your writing always lacks something. Mine does, Moffat's does, even Paul Abbott's does, everyone's does, and that's why we spend the rest of our lives, still typing away in the dark, trying to get better. Until we die.

There's a note to end on!

BOOK TWO

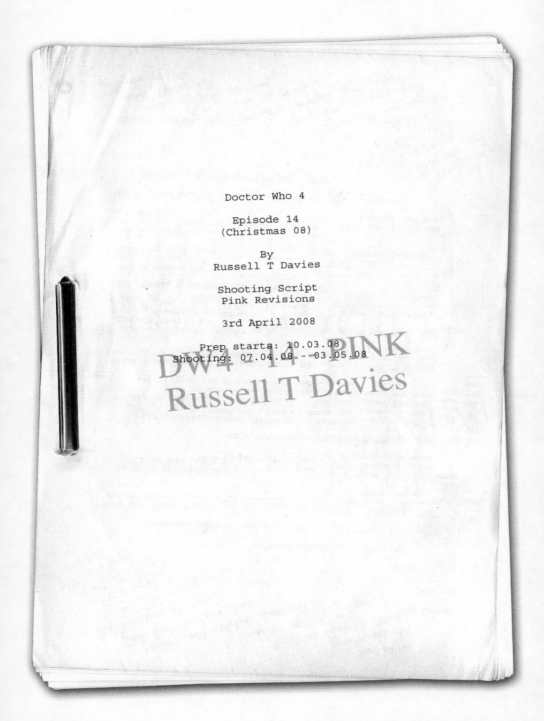

Doctor Who 4

Episode 14
(Christmas 08)

By
Russell T Davies

Shooting Script
Pink Revisions

3rd April 2008

Prep starts: 10.03.08
Shooting: 07.04.08 - 03.05.08

DW4 14 PINK

Russell T Davies

CHAPTER THIRTEEN

WHAT HAPPENED NEXT

In which the CyberKing rises,
Russell contemplates kissing Davros,
and Ianto's fate is sealed

FROM: BENJAMIN COOK TO: RUSSELL T DAVIES, TUESDAY 4 MARCH 2008 22:01:34 GMT

BOOK COVER

Russell, take a look at the attached jpeg. It's Ebury's mock-up cover for *The Writer's Tale*.[1] We're a book! A proper book! With a cover and everything! The 'Foreword by Philip Pullman' line is a placeholder. We'll never get him. Worth asking, though. Always worth asking.

Thoughts?

FROM: RUSSELL T DAVIES TO: BENJAMIN COOK, THURSDAY 6 MARCH 2008 00:46:41 GMT

RE: BOOK COVER

Hello Benjamino,

Sorry I didn't reply yesterday. I sort of went into shock. It never really occurred to me that a book co-written by me, about me, would have me on the cover. Duh! Obvious. But oh, it's horrifying. I'm sorry, I really am quite horrified. It looks like vanity publishing. Stood there on the TARDIS set, it looks like I *am* the bloody Doctor. I'm not arguing, really, because I can see that it makes sense. But ouch! I mean, be honest, imagine seeing yourself as a book cover. Christ almighty. It's a lovely

---

1 BBC Books is an imprint of Ebury Publishing, a Random House Group company, and publisher of *The Writer's Tale* and *The Writer's Tale: The Final Chapter*.

design. I'm not knocking the design. But, but, but... before we commit, is there any other option? Like a scrapbook sort of cover? I.e. a cover that isn't me? Don't mistake this for modesty. Genuinely, I wonder how much a photo of my face would actually help sell a book...? Not at all, I'd think.

As you said, worth asking.

P.S. Love a foreword. Philip Pullman is a great idea. Nice one. But how the hell do we get in touch with Philip Pullman?

FROM: BENJAMIN COOK TO: RUSSELL T DAVIES, THURSDAY 6 MARCH 2008 01:16:39 GMT

RE: BOOK COVER

Listen, if you're uncomfortable with that cover, I'll argue that we should go for something else. You have to feel comfortable with this book. All of it. There are always other options. But... look, I'd give it a few days. See how you feel after the weekend. Personally? I love that cover. (But would it work better in colour, do you think?) And it is only a first draft. Ebury are saying that we can do another, newer photo shoot for the cover proper...

FROM: RUSSELL T DAVIES TO: BENJAMIN COOK, THURSDAY 6 MARCH 2008 02:33:58 GMT

RE: BOOK COVER

Sorry, it's just... oh, the shock. I'll think on it. I promise.

In the meantime, I'm sending you more 4.14 script. It includes a stunt sequence that's so complicated I can't see how the hell we shoot it.[2]

FROM: BENJAMIN COOK TO: RUSSELL T DAVIES, THURSDAY 6 MARCH 2008 15:14:18 GMT

RE: BOOK COVER

'The CyberKing will rise, indeed. How like a man.' Ha!

FROM: RUSSELL T DAVIES TO: BENJAMIN COOK, THURSDAY 6 MARCH 2008 18:00:02 GMT

RE: BOOK COVER

Yes, bit dodgy, that line.

FROM: BENJAMIN COOK TO: RUSSELL T DAVIES, THURSDAY 6 MARCH 2008 18:06:09 GMT

RE: BOOK COVER

I love that line.

FROM: RUSSELL T DAVIES TO: BENJAMIN COOK, THURSDAY 6 MARCH 2008 18:10:15 GMT

RE: BOOK COVER

Okay, I'm keeping it! I'm just hoping no boring bastard questions it.

---

2 The Doctor and the 'next Doctor' lasso a Cybershade, which drags them up the wall of a nearby building, through the top-storey window and along the floor, heading for another window. Rosita, companion to the 'next Doctor', arrives in the nick of time and cuts the rope with an axe.

FROM: RUSSELL T DAVIES TO: BENJAMIN COOK, MONDAY 10 MARCH 2008 03:09:42 GMT

THE NEXT DOCTOR

I wrote loads today. Having the who-is-this-other-Doctor mystery is a helpful guide rope. It pulls me through the story… which doesn't mean the story is good. It could still fall to shit in my hands. Is it obvious who the 'next Doctor' is? Well, not obvious, but how much is it fooling anyone? It's hard to tell. Is it even interesting? It's unusual for a Christmas Day episode to have this much plot. I'm not sure it fits. It's more of a night for spectacle, though I suppose the soaps do well at Christmas, so people do follow a twisting plot. But it still feels like more of a Boxing Day story.

As of today, these first 34 pages of script have been distributed to the production team. Some of them saw the first ten pages last week, but since then I've made changes right from the start. I've changed the look of the Cyberleader, for instance. He has that visible-brain-in-a-head now, like the Cyber Controller in *The Age of Steel*. But only if we can afford it.

FROM: BENJAMIN COOK TO: RUSSELL T DAVIES, MONDAY 10 MARCH 2008 22:23:07 GMT

RE: THE NEXT DOCTOR

Fantastic day! It was Julian Bleach's last. His final shot was exposing Davros' decaying torso. Time was running short, but Graeme Harper was just about holding it all together. Peter Bennett told him, 'You'd bloody better finish – or we'll leave you here on your own with a camera!' Poor Graeme.

I interviewed Julian afterwards. Lots of concise and straight-to-the-point answers, but a thoughtful and courteous man. I like him. 'Davros was very probably inspired by Hitler,' he said, 'and I found that to be quite a useful reference point, particularly in some of his more dogmatic speeches.' (He added, 'I am actually creating a whole new race at the moment, but to say any more would spoil the surprise!' Ha ha.)

FROM: RUSSELL T DAVIES TO: BENJAMIN COOK, TUESDAY 11 MARCH 2008 22:33:34 GMT

RE: THE NEXT DOCTOR

I've just seen the Dalek Crucible rushes. Davros' torso!!! That shot is marvellous, and alarming. Oh, you can see panic in the air, the way there are so many single takes. But it's fantastic. There's Sarah Jane, and Rose, and Jackie, and two Doctors watching Catherine Tate save the universe! I think those drugs went deeper into my head than I ever realised. The best bits are the explosions, when all the women scream like girls – and Jack too, probably! (Hey, was everyone getting on, or was there companion rivalry?)

I'm excited by Davros. Very excited. A much cleverer mind than the Master, I think – look what he's achieved, compared to the Master. Empires! The Master never achieved so much. While I wrote the Master as a genius in Series Three, he's fatally flawed by his jealousy/hatred/love of the Doctor; that's what allows the Doctor to defeat him, in the end, because it's so personal. Much less of that with Davros. In their big confrontation, Davros' key tactic is to stop the Doctor from speaking. Because that's how the Doctor works. He talks himself out of things. All that wit and banter and intelligence. Deprive him of that, and the stakes get higher. Of course, you can't make that an absolute rule, because you're dying for *some* of those Doctor-villain exchanges. But as a keynote, it's interesting. And isn't Julian Bleach brilliant? He's rather fit under that mask, but I really can't start fancying Davros. Sod it – yes, I can! Imagine kissing Davros.

FROM: BENJAMIN COOK TO: RUSSELL T DAVIES, TUESDAY 11 MARCH 2008 23:04:20 GMT

RE: THE NEXT DOCTOR

>>was everyone getting on, or was there companion rivalry?<<

They were getting on better than I'd have ever thought possible.

FROM: RUSSELL T DAVIES TO: BENJAMIN COOK, TUESDAY 11 MARCH 2008 23:08:18 GMT

RE: THE NEXT DOCTOR

Phew. I would have been so sad if there were tension. I hope John Barrowman's kept his trousers zipped. We can't have Lis Sladen suffering that indignity.

> **Text message from: Ben**
> Sent: 12-Mar-2008 16:32
> I'm back in London, on set with ITV's *Demons*. I've just interviewed Mackenzie Crook. Quite shy, but so enthusiastic about *Doctor Who*. How come you've never cast him?

> **Text message from: Russell**
> Sent: 12-Mar-2008 16:50
> We've asked Mackenzie Crook a million times, but the dates have always clashed. In fact, he was almost cast as Clive in Episode 1 – the very first Episode 1 – before we got lovely Mark Benton instead.

FROM: RUSSELL T DAVIES TO: BENJAMIN COOK, THURSDAY 13 MARCH 2008 02:49:30 GMT

RE: THE NEXT DOCTOR

More script. The mystery revealed.[3] I suppose it's not much of a surprise, but I'm not sure I want it to be. I like it when it creeps up on you, ahead of the action – or maybe that's my excuse for not hiding it better. I'm writing a mystery – unusual for me, I don't often do that – so maybe I should learn to hide things, like Steven hides things…? Oh, I don't know.

I got ridiculously hung up on how the Cybermen could know a lot about the Doctor

---

3 The 'next Doctor' is revealed to be Jackson Lake, a Victorian gentleman who believes that he's the Doctor – a fugue state brought on by the murder of Lake's wife and kidnap of his son by the Cybermen.

– Time Lord, TARDIS, his history. The Cybermen at Canary Wharf in *Doomsday* – this lot are survivors of the battle at Canary Wharf – knew nothing about all that Time Lord stuff. They only kept the Doctor alive because he knew all about the Daleks. (I had to go back and look it up. They registered his 'increased adrenalin'. Didn't notice two hearts, did they? Dumbos!) So, I've got this ridiculous line – 'stolen from the Daleks inside the Void, I'd say' – about how the Cybermen got the information, which the Doctor tells Jackson Lake and Rosita for *no reason at all*. He might as well turn to camera and tell us! Damn.

FROM: BENJAMIN COOK TO: RUSSELL T DAVIES, THURSDAY 13 MARCH 2008 08:55:16 GMT

RE: THE NEXT DOCTOR
You've said that you aren't comfortable with writing scenes out of order, so what do you do when you're working on a scene like that, with a line like your 'stolen from the Daleks', that you're really not happy with? Do you say to yourself, 'I'll go back and change that later,' even if you never do? Or have you resigned yourself already to the fact that this scene will never be as good as you want it to be?

FROM: RUSSELL T DAVIES TO: BENJAMIN COOK, THURSDAY 13 MARCH 2008 14:48:25 GMT

RE: THE NEXT DOCTOR
If I'm really stuck on a line, I'll write something like a placeholder, and move on. But not often. That's rare. I'll usually hammer away at it, on the spot, until it's right. That isn't to say that it won't change later, or the next morning, when I look back at it. The line that I um-ed and er-ed over so much last night wasn't even a 'real' line. It has no character, it's info-dump, it breaks the fourth wall, and it talks to the audience. It has no heart. Maybe that's why I struggled.

More often, I get stuck on why does this scene exist, how do I solve this plot, and, crucially, where is this heading? But every time I cut that 'stolen from the Daleks' line, I fretted and put it back. I keep thinking of all those eight-year-olds who love this stuff and follow it, and would be asking that question.

Text message from: **Ben**
Sent: 13-Mar-2008 22:32
Night shoot. DALEKS! ACTUAL DALEKS! ON THE STREETS! (Why is it so exciting to see Daleks on real streets? It just is.) It's like *Blade Runner,* in Cardiff! With Daleks!

Text message from: **Russell**
Sent: 13-Mar-2008 22:40
Argh, I can't wait to see the rushes. Graeme is doing such a good job. Mind you, you won't be so happy at 5.30am.

> **Text message from: Ben**
> Sent: 14-Mar-2008 00:20
>
> It's so cold, my hands have dropped off. My career as a journalist is over. I'm useless to everyone.

> **Text message from: Russell**
> Sent: 14-Mar-2008 00:26
>
> You can always teach. Ho ho. I'm writing the Doctor finally meeting Miss Hartigan.[4] 'Yet another man come to assert himself against me in the night!'

> **Text message from: Ben**
> Sent: 14-Mar-2008 00:37
>
> Not camp at all, then! It's raining now.

> **Text message from: Ben**
> Sent: 14-Mar-2008 02:48
>
> We're huddled in the camera truck, reminiscing about the Brandon Estate.[5] Phil: 'Thank God we don't have to film there any more.' Billie: 'Never say never.' Can't you bring her back for the Specials?

> **Text message from: Russell**
> Sent: 14-Mar-2008 02:50
>
> There's a thought.

FROM: RUSSELL T DAVIES TO: BENJAMIN COOK, FRIDAY 14 MARCH 2008 03:16:02 GMT

RE: THE NEXT DOCTOR

Here you go. More script. If you're not too frozen. (Stay in the camera truck.) It's so stupid, this writing lark. I spent all day stuck, not writing, because I couldn't work out a way for the Doctor to meet Miss Hartigan. You've got to have the Doctor meeting the villain, but I was in danger of everyone heading underground to the Cybermen's stronghold, and the Doctor and Miss Hartigan having no sort of encounter at all. I couldn't work out how to do it, where to do it, when. All day, gone. Pissed off. Then I sat down to write, with no solution, and... thought of it! Immediately. Obvious. Simple. If I'd started sooner... ah, the only way to write is to write. For all my banging on about what to do if you're really stuck on something, there's nothing dumber than sitting there writing nothing at all. Stupid bastard job.

---

4 Miss Mercy Hartigan (played by Dervla Kirwan) is the Cybermen's human ally in *Doctor Who* 4.14.
5 The Brandon Estate, in South London, served as the location for the fictional Powell Estate, where Rose and Jackie Tyler live in *Doctor Who* Series One and Two.

FROM: BENJAMIN COOK TO: RUSSELL T DAVIES, FRIDAY 14 MARCH 2008 06:05:51 GMT

RE: THE NEXT DOCTOR

I'm actually frozen! Dead from the waist down. (Or is it the waist up?) That was one hell of a shoot. Nerves on edge. Tempers fraying by the end. The first day on this block that was genuinely tense. The footage looks incredible, though. David and Billie shot their slow-mo sprint towards each other, from 4.12. (David: 'Should I dance as I run?') It's epic and perfect. Long way to go, I know, but it's bound to be one hell of an episode. And then Graeme asked David not to wince so much as the lone Dalek exterminated him. David: 'But that was my best acting of the night!' Billie: 'This is no time for acting.'

I interviewed Billie. She talked about watching Freema as her replacement in Series Three. 'I think it bothered me for about a day – and then I just got over it. I thought I'd be a lot more jealous of Freema than I was.' Interesting. One of Billie's reasons for coming back for these episodes is, she says, the chance to work with Freema and Catherine. See, they really do love each other. Sickening, isn't it?

But the quote of the night? As Billie cradled a dying David in her arms, Johnny B informed her that she has a moustache! To which she replied, 'It's low times for Rose Tyler. She hasn't used a waxing strip since she last saw the Earth. Razors are in short supply on her parallel world!'

Right, I need sleep. I haven't slept for 23 hours. I'll read the 4.14 script when I wake. I'm cold and exhausted, and that's no condition to enjoy Cybermen.

FROM: RUSSELL T DAVIES TO: BENJAMIN COOK, SATURDAY 15 MARCH 2008 02:54:15 GMT

RE: THE NEXT DOCTOR

Oh, that's enough. I sat down to write five hours ago, but I've hardly written anything. Two scenes, that's all… and the first one is dull. But I'm sitting here thinking, really. Building up to the grand finale. It had better be grand. This is all quite tame so far. Hmph.

When you're working late on a Friday or Saturday, do you get mates texting, off their heads in clubs? Yeah, yeah, have a nice time. There were tons tonight. Shaddup, the lot of you.

FROM: RUSSELL T DAVIES TO: BENJAMIN COOK, SUNDAY 16 MARCH 2008 04:01:28 GMT

RE: THE NEXT DOCTOR

Here's more nonsense. I'm worried that it's sort of descended into a runaround. That's why I've made Miss Hartigan even more powerful towards the end, when she becomes the CyberKing. I wasn't planning that. I invented it tonight, on the spot, but it's galvanised me. That character is really taking off.

I hope I finish it soon.

FROM: BENJAMIN COOK TO: RUSSELL T DAVIES, SUNDAY 16 MARCH 2008 11:21:48 GMT

RE: THE NEXT DOCTOR

Any further thoughts on titles? *Court of the CyberKing*, perhaps?

FROM: RUSSELL T DAVIES TO: BENJAMIN COOK, SUNDAY 16 MARCH 2008 11:39:13 GMT

RE: THE NEXT DOCTOR

It was *Court of the CyberKing* (how did you guess?), but I'm so attracted by the thought of 4.13 ending with that traditional credit, now saying, '*Doctor Who* will return at Christmas in… *THE NEXT DOCTOR*'. The speculation! There would be a genuine buzz. It's what this would be called if it didn't have Special status. The Cybermen are window-dressing; it's all about Jackson Lake, really. I'll run it past Julie, see her reaction.

The whole script is due in tomorrow. We've the bloody Tone Meeting on Wednesday. Do you know what? I might get there. With a CyberKing about to rise, and a hot-air balloon waiting in the wings, it's not hard to see what's going to happen…

FROM: RUSSELL T DAVIES TO: BENJAMIN COOK, MONDAY 17 MARCH 2008 00:45:18 GMT

RE: THE NEXT DOCTOR

A nightmare on set tonight. They're in the big police traffic-control centre, doubling for UNIT HQ in New York – because it looks good, it's got lots of screens and things – but we secured the location on the condition that they'd have to commandeer it back if there was anything like, say, a major road traffic accident. Two hours into filming: major road traffic accident! Far more important than a *Doctor Who* schedule, I know, but… do they stop? Don't they? Everyone on a knife-edge, whilst completely – and genuinely – sympathetic. But they're carrying on. For the moment. Knowing the plug could be pulled any minute if some Chief Constable walks in and says, quite rightly, 'What the hell are these people doing here?!'

Anyway, I'm so close to finishing *The Next Doctor*. So tired! But while I said I don't get sentimental over work, that doesn't stop me getting celebratory. It's like there's a big party building up in my head… but I've got to crush it, because I haven't quite got there yet. Onwards! You still up?

FROM: BENJAMIN COOK TO: RUSSELL T DAVIES, MONDAY 17 MARCH 2008 01:00:11 GMT

RE: THE NEXT DOCTOR

Yeah, still working. Done myself a chicken stir-fry. It sounds like hell on set.

FROM: RUSSELL T DAVIES TO: BENJAMIN COOK, MONDAY 17 MARCH 2008 04:47:26 GMT

RE: THE NEXT DOCTOR

The Next Doctor is done! I'm very pleased with it, I think. I'll go to bed now. I probably won't get up until about 11am.

FROM: BENJAMIN COOK TO: RUSSELL T DAVIES, MONDAY 17 MARCH 2008 04:52:58 GMT

RE: THE NEXT DOCTOR

You've finished? Are you ridiculously happy? You must be. I suppose it's not quite over, though. You've got to afford it. All those weeks of FX and design wrangling... but the toughest bit is done. Celebrate good times, come on!

FROM: RUSSELL T DAVIES TO: BENJAMIN COOK, MONDAY 17 MARCH 2008 04:58:40 GMT

RE: THE NEXT DOCTOR

Yeah, and *Torchwood* Series Three storylining starts next Tuesday. Christ alive! But right now I feel brilliant. Well, no, too knackered to feel brilliant. Sex is brilliant. Cassoulet is brilliant. My friend Tracy is brilliant. I just feel tired, and smoky, and bleary. But I've a quiet day tomorrow. I might feel brilliant then.

> Text message from: **Russell**
> Sent: 18-Mar-2008 16:27
> Are you on set? How's the former Prime Minister?

Text message from: **Ben**
Sent: 18-Mar-2008 16:34
No, I'm on my way there. They're filming in a cottage in Dinas Powys, a village known affectionately as 'Dinky Pooh'. Is this befitting a former PM?

> Text message from: **Russell**
> Sent: 18-Mar-2008 16:35
> You just want to see her die in Dalek death rays, don't you?

Text message from: **Ben**
Sent: 18-Mar-2008 16:39
Yes. Well, that and the free dinner.

> Text message from: **Russell**
> Sent: 18-Mar-2008 16:41
> I would hope it's all tablecloths and candelabra with Dame Wilton on set. We must have standards.

Text message from: **Ben**
Sent: 18-Mar-2008 16:42
It'll be chicken wings and chips as per usual. She's a FORMER Prime Minister.

Text message from: **Russell**
Sent: 18-Mar-2008 16:43
Mmm... chicken wings.

Text message from: **Ben**
Sent: 18-Mar-2008 21:48
I've just interviewed Penelope. 'I would do anything for Russell T
Davies,' she said. 'I think he's an incredible writer, and he's created
a wonderfully witty person in Harriet Jones.' Bet you wish you hadn't
exterminated her now.

Text message from: **Russell**
Sent: 18-Mar-2008 22:03
You're right. I'll bring her back.

Text message from: **Ben**
Sent: 18-Mar-2008 22:10
After each take, Phil's screaming, 'NO, SHE ESCAPES!' Poor deluded
Phil.

Text message from: **Russell**
Sent: 19-Mar-2008 14:55
I'm stuck in Upper Boat. It's the 4.14 Tone Meeting. I still haven't seen
last night's rushes, but Phil has acted out Penelope's death scene for
us. At length.

Text message from: **Russell**
Sent: 19-Mar-2008 21:03
Dear God. Tone over. Survivors ate the dead.

Text message from: **Ben**
Sent: 19-Mar-2008 21:39
How much do you have to cut?

Text message from: **Russell**
Sent: 19-Mar-2008 21:41
Oh, not much. No CGI Cybershades, only practical ones... but that's it,
the rest is intact. So far. They're the best team in the world.

FROM: BENJAMIN COOK TO: RUSSELL T DAVIES, SUNDAY 23 MARCH 2008 02:04:12 GMT

HELLO AGAIN!

I've been thinking. I know, I know, I really should stop doing that. It only leads to trouble. But there's something I've been meaning to say. Something that's been bothering me. It's about 4.13. Bear with me...

It's a nine-out-of-ten script. One thing is standing between that nine and a ten... and it's the final scene. Back in January, I remember asking you why exactly that scene was there at all. 'To end on an upbeat note,' you said. To remind us that there are 'new adventures to come'. But I can't help thinking... doesn't that defeat the object of that ending? It's *supposed* to be sad. It's meant to be tragic. The Doctor and Rose are parted again (for ever this time?), and Donna is right back where she started, with no recollection of how amazing a person she can be. That's tear-jerking. Maybe a little bit bleak. But also it's brilliant, deeply affecting and, above all, an incredibly brave ending. It's noble! And then the bloody Cybermen pop up in the TARDIS and... well, that spoils it a bit. It's too easy. It's not even shocking. It's a bit rubbish, really. It's a watered-down version of the endings to Series Two and Three, even down to the 'What? What?? Whaaaat???' gag. Ending on Wilf, standing there in the rain, saluting the Doctor, or on the Doctor alone in the TARDIS... isn't that a hundred times better? What does that scene with the Cybermen add to the plot? Nothing at all. So what if you leave us in floods of tears? That's *great* television.

Besides, you don't really need a scene at the end that throws forward to the Christmas Special: for the first time in four years, you'll have filmed the Special by the time that Episode 13 airs, so you can include a trailer after the end credits. Moreover, what's the one thing in *The Next Doctor* script that doesn't really work either? The opening scene! (Well, isn't it? You know it is.) The Doctor pushes some buttons on the TARDIS console and – oh, look – the Cybermen disappear. If you cut the final scene of 4.13, you can cut the opening scene of 4.14, the cliffhanger resolution, and improve both episodes immeasurably. C'mon, you know it makes sense.

Invisible Ben is dead. Long live Visible Ben. Etc. Ha ha. Tell me to sod off if you want.

FROM: RUSSELL T DAVIES TO: BENJAMIN COOK, SUNDAY 23 MARCH 2008 02:35:31 GMT

RE: HELLO AGAIN!

Damn it, Benjamino, I'll do anything for a ten-out-of-ten script. But... but... yes, it's a sad ending, yes, it's tragic, but that's not the keynote of *Doctor Who*, is it? Well, maybe it's becoming so. But this is a show about danger, and monsters, and a mad man in a blue box. The Doctor versus the monsters, that's what you get from the Cybermen ending. The tragedy of poor Donna – it's like a death – I don't think that's the right note to end on. The finality of it. You could almost turn your telly off and say, 'Right, that's the end,' and it's my job to make sure that people never, ever do that. The story goes on, the Doctor survives. The final scene does add to the plot, because it's a *new* plot. Yes, I've done that 'What? What?? Whaaaat???' twice before, but that's the point. It's a running gag. I'd like to think that it's almost expected now. Imagine it without that ending. People would be saying, 'What, no "Whaaaat???"…?'

Hmm. I'm saying all that, but… well, you have tapped into something there, maybe, because there was a problem with that scene. They had to phone me from set. The problem being: how wet is David? He's just stepped out of the rain, then he's got to run straight from that TARDIS scene and directly into the Christmas Special, chasing Cybermen. But he can't spend the whole of 4.14 soaking wet. Over the phone, we reached a compromise: David is a bit tussled, he's dried off his jacket, so it's a few minutes later when he meets the Cybermen. That's what they shot. But it's one of those on-the-spot decisions that's put my teeth on edge. (My fault.) You should feel that the Doctor has just left Wilf, that he's still thinking of Donna. By putting in an offstage break, it's kind of interrupted the sadness. Plus, they didn't shoot the-Doctor-walking-around-the-console-sadly for long enough. You can imagine the music swelling, the tragedy of it all… but not for only ten seconds! We need longer, so we've already set that aside for a reshoot. Gaps are opening up in that scene.

But I do like it. Honestly. You should see it. When the Cybermen stand into shot, it's like… wow! Cybermen! Great ending!

FROM: RUSSELL T DAVIES TO: BENJAMIN COOK, TUESDAY 25 MARCH 2008 22:30:02 GMT

RE: HELLO AGAIN!

Do you know what? It takes time. For notes to sink in, sometimes. And I've kept thinking about what you said, about the Cybermen. It's kept niggling. Partly because you've spent most of these e-mails being Invisible Ben, so for you to pipe up, you must feel it strongly…

Oh God. What I'm saying is: you're right. I *think* you're right. Hand on heart, when you get a good note, it chimes with something that you're already thinking. Right at the back of my mind, I think I'd always thought, right from the moment I typed that last scene, that the runaway bride was brilliant, the *Titanic* was brilliant, and the Cybermen… aren't. They're kind of a poor cousin to those first two cliffhanger surprises. Catherine Tate and the world's most famous ship were just gobsmacking. Cybermen, not so much. I knew that. It just took me a long time to hear it.

And I'd completely forgotten that we'll have shot the material to run a proper Christmas Special trail. Good point! Everything I'm saying about 'new adventures to come', we can achieve that after the credits.

Also, we're way over on the 4.14 FX list, and Scene 1 has a good 15 days of FX, as the Cybermen vanish and tumble through the Time Vortex, heading for Victorian England. If I cut those 15 days, we'd be back on track. Plus, plus, plus… yeah, the thought of the Doctor landing in Scene 1 of 4.14, just arriving, fresh and happy and unbound by continuity to 4.13, is rather lovely. New episode, new start, Christmas Day, off we go. And another thing

This page: Scenes from the 2008 Christmas Special *The Next Doctor*.

Top: The Doctor (David Tennant) does battle with the Cybermen in Victorian London.

Left: Dervla Kirwan as the deliciously devilish Miss Hartigan.

Above right: Grabbed by the Cybershades!

Above: David Morrissey (Jackson Lake) and David Tennant on location for *The Next Doctor*.

Left: Operation Cobra is GO-GO-GO!!! David Tennant announces he is to leave *Doctor Who* – live on ITV1.

Below: The Brigadier (Nicholas Courtney) and Mrs Wormwood (Samantha Bond) return to the world of *Doctor Who* in *The Sarah Jane Adventures* Series Two.

Above: The deserts of Dubai make a stunning backdrop for the first of 2009's Specials, *Planet of the Dead*.

Left: David Tennant is joined in Dubai by Michelle Ryan as Lady Christina De Souza – along with a very badly dented London bus.

Top: The cast and crew in sandy Dubai.

Above: Michelle and David enjoy the heat...

Right: ... while the Doctor and Christina generate some heat of their own.

Below: Russell and Benjamin embark on their book tour to promote *The Writer's Tale*.

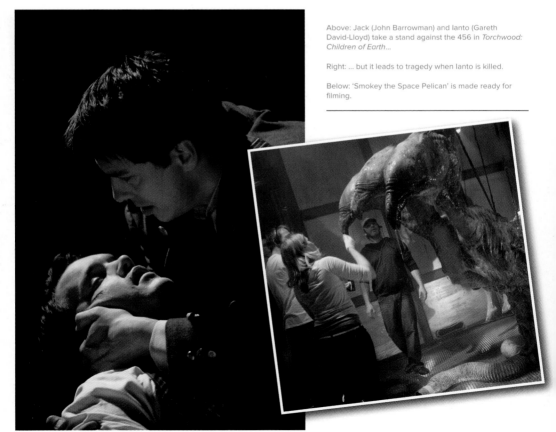

Above: Jack (John Barrowman) and Ianto (Gareth David-Lloyd) take a stand against the 456 in *Torchwood: Children of Earth...*

Right: ... but it leads to tragedy when Ianto is killed.

Below: 'Smokey the Space Pelican' is made ready for filming.

This spread: The beginning of the end for the Tenth Doctor in *The Waters of Mars*.

Above: Trouble for the Doctor on the red planet.

Right: Lindsay Duncan as Adelaide Brooke.

Below: Terrifying Water Monsters run amok on Bowie Base One.

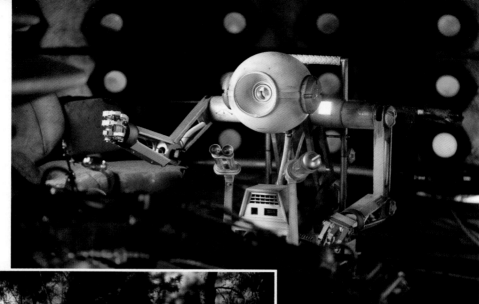

Above: Gadget gets to grips with the Doctor's TARDIS.

Left: A pair of Water Monsters dry out between takes.

Below: An emotionally charged final confrontation for the Doctor and Adelaide.

Overleaf: We glimpse a darker Doctor at the end of *The Waters of Mars*.

– I've been thinking about this a lot! – confronting the bride and the *Titanic* was fun, but starting 4.14 with Cybermen phasing in and out of reality is such a sci-fi opening. In a bad way. It's kind of off-putting. Besides, if we're reshooting the end of 4.13 anyway, the Doctor can now be wet and bedraggled and sad, so that problem is solved too.

Oh, all right, you win! Well, hold on, I'll talk to Julie tomorrow. She does love her 'What? What?? Whaaaat???'

> **Text message from: Russell**
> Sent: 26-Mar-2008 14:06
> Benjamino! I just talked Julie through changing the end of 4.13 – no cliffhanger, no Cybermen, run a trail instead – and she likes it! I told her it was my own idea, so ha! I hope that script gets a 10/10 from you now...

> **Text message from: Ben**
> Sent: 26-Mar-2008 17:25
> Much better! Yes, it's a 10/10 episode now.

> **Text message from: Russell**
> Sent: 26-Mar-2008 18:25
> You and this correspondence have changed the script! The whole ending to the series! Now the world is going to spin off its axis. Beware the power, Ben. Power corrupts! No, but seriously. Thank you. See you later.

FROM: RUSSELL T DAVIES TO: BENJAMIN COOK, SATURDAY 29 MARCH 2008 10:10:45 GMT

THAT'S A WRAP

We wrapped at 9.45am today! That's Series Four finished. My last Episode 13. My last season. Blimey.

FROM: BENJAMIN COOK TO: RUSSELL T DAVIES, SATURDAY 29 MARCH 2008 10:28:14 GMT

RE: THAT'S A WRAP

Wrap? At 9.45am?! Unheard of! Were you on set? It's the end of an era.

FROM: RUSSELL T DAVIES TO: BENJAMIN COOK, SATURDAY 29 MARCH 2008 10:31:45 GMT

RE: THAT'S A WRAP

It's the end of an *error*. I was going to go on set, but they wrapped before I could brush my teeth.

FROM: BENJAMIN COOK TO: RUSSELL T DAVIES, SATURDAY 29 MARCH 2008 10:34:02 GMT

RE: THAT'S A WRAP

Make them do it again. Get them all back in, and make them wrap with you there.

FROM: RUSSELL T DAVIES TO: BENJAMIN COOK, SATURDAY 29 MARCH 2008 10:40:57 GMT

RE: THAT'S A WRAP

Good idea. I'm sending pink pages right now, in which Quintus falls through a time storm, naked, and lands on Midshipman Frame.

FROM: BENJAMIN COOK TO: RUSSELL T DAVIES, SATURDAY 29 MARCH 2008 10:43:19 GMT

RE: THAT'S A WRAP

I can see where this is going.

FROM: RUSSELL T DAVIES TO: BENJAMIN COOK, SATURDAY 29 MARCH 2008 10:47:36 GMT

RE: THAT'S A WRAP

It's too early to fantasise like this. This is why I shouldn't drink gin.

FROM: RUSSELL T DAVIES TO: BENJAMIN COOK, SATURDAY 29 MARCH 2008 23:53:27 GMT

RE: THAT'S A WRAP

I can't delay looking at the 4.14 FX cuts any longer. I'm so tired tonight. I actually think that those two gins have had a knock-on effect. Drink exhausts me now. I think I'm still knackered after 4.14, but I haven't had time to *be* knackered. I'll have the odd quiet day, but then *Sarah Jane* and Edits and Dubs come along. Even this morning was spent with Julie, sorting out the trail to run at the end of the Series Four press launch tape. I haven't had time to slump yet.

It's a stupid life sometimes. It's a Saturday night, and I'm sitting here all alone, staring at FX sheets, at midnight. (And we're about to lose an hour at 2am!) It's a weird sort of quiet, passive, sexless life. Half-lived. On Saturdays, you can't help thinking of everyone else getting laid... but I'm just sitting here. Like so many Saturdays. It's like my obituary could say, 'He sat and typed.' I should spend my money. I should close down this computer, and go to New York. Right now. I could work on the FX cuts in a Manhattan diner. I could just fly off and do it.

But I never do.

FROM: BENJAMIN COOK TO: RUSSELL T DAVIES, SUNDAY 30 MARCH 2008 00:03:32 GMT

RE: THAT'S A WRAP

So, why don't you? What stops you getting up and leaving? Why don't you do more with your money? Fly off to New York!

FROM: RUSSELL T DAVIES TO: BENJAMIN COOK, SUNDAY 30 MARCH 2008 00:15:00 GMT

RE: THAT'S A WRAP

I've a nasty suspicion that, fundamentally, I think I don't deserve it. Hmm. There now, all this late-night introspection is making me *glad* to turn to FX lists. Thank you, Benjamino!

FROM: RUSSELL T DAVIES TO: BENJAMIN COOK, SUNDAY 30 MARCH 2008 03:37:00 GMT

RE: THAT'S A WRAP

I've lost 229 FX days, and an hour of my life. These bastard clocks.

FROM: RUSSELL T DAVIES TO: BENJAMIN COOK, SUNDAY 30 MARCH 2008 11:14:44 GMT

RE: THAT'S A WRAP

Off to buy the papers. It's preview time! What will they make of *Partners in Crime*? Apparently, the *Sunday Times* refers to Donna's age, twice, and her lack of athleticism. Here it comes: the hate of a strong woman. God, 13 weeks of this!

In other news, Steven's second Series Four episode is now called *Forest of the Dead*.[6] (So the new *Radio Times* will be wrong.) He changed it yesterday. We had a laugh with possible titles. He thought up *A River's Song Ends*, but I thought *Forest Under CAL's Kingdom* was better.[7] Or *CAL's Untimely Node Transition*.

FROM: BENJAMIN COOK TO: RUSSELL T DAVIES, SUNDAY 30 MARCH 2008 12:12:41 GMT

RE: THAT'S A WRAP

Don't worry, they're good previews. Only the *Sunday Times* is sniffy. The *Mail* says (of David and Catherine): 'It works!' *The Observer* says that Catherine is 'a joy to behold', and that *Partners in Crime* is the 'best series opener to date'.

FROM: RUSSELL T DAVIES TO: BENJAMIN COOK, SUNDAY 30 MARCH 2008 13:40:04 GMT

RE: THAT'S A WRAP

You're right, they're glowing. Lots of TV covers and photos. Plus, with *The Observer*, a free bar of chocolate. Nice.

FROM: RUSSELL T DAVIES TO: BENJAMIN COOK, MONDAY 31 MARCH 2008 00:31:42 GMT

RE: THAT'S A WRAP

The hand of Visible Ben has reached out… and done good! This is the rewrite of 4.13 – Christ, that's gonna make people cry – and a brand new opening to 4.14. With your fingerprints! I'm channelling Visible Ben. Good rewrites. Not just your bit! The whole episode is six pages shorter, minus 220 FX days, and I swear you won't notice a thing has gone. Good. I'm happy with that.

FROM: RUSSELL T DAVIES TO: BENJAMIN COOK, MONDAY 31 MARCH 2008 02:42:00 GMT

RE: THAT'S A WRAP

I just recounted my FX shots. I haven't lost 220. I've lost 190. Bollocks, arse, mathematics, shit.

----

6 Up until now, *Doctor Who* 4.10 had been called *River's Run*.
7 The little-girl custodian of 'Girl's World' is known by the acronym CAL (her real name being Charlotte Abigail Lux) and appears in The Library as a Node, a robot-like drone with Charlotte's human face.

FROM: BENJAMIN COOK TO: RUSSELL T DAVIES, MONDAY 31 MARCH 2008 02:56:23 GMT

RE: THAT'S A WRAP

Now might be a good time to break open that free bar of chocolate…?

FROM: RUSSELL T DAVIES TO: BENJAMIN COOK, WEDNESDAY 2 APRIL 2008 22:31:38 GMT

RE: THAT'S A WRAP

Blimey oh blimey, Episode 13. The TARDIS flies the entire Earth back home! Then Bad Wolf Bay! Then the tragedy of Donna Noble! Even watching a rough assembly (it wasn't a proper Edit; we were just there to lock FX), Julie and I were crying. It's gobsmacking. Hell of an Edit to go – it's a sprawling beast – but we've done that before. We'll make it magnificent.

But then I went and spoilt it all by having a proper strop, and chucking my toys out of the pram. I'll have to apologise to everyone now. That takes longer than losing your temper. I just snapped. I've been up since 7am, for *BBC Breakfast*, and then a Tone Meeting for 4.14, then the 4.14 read-through, then all the way back to Cardiff for the FX meeting… and now I've got to do the rewrites after the notes on 4.14 – not big, but that's fiddly work, and it's my last chance to get the script right, by tomorrow – and I missed *The Apprentice*. I know it's on iPlayer, but a strop's a strop. A full-blown temper. I won't describe it. I'm too embarrassed. A lot of swearing and… oh, bollocks. I've come home knackered, and ashamed, and sick to the heart of this never-ending workload. While I'm typing this, Julie is e-mailing with apologies – like it's her fault! – and solutions, and practical ways of solving things, and that makes me feel like even more of a bastard.

Tomorrow at 9am, I've got a big two-day meeting about *Torchwood*, in which I've got to reinvent the whole bloody thing for five episodes on BBC One next year. I've got to be impressive – I've *got* to be – but I haven't had a second to think about it. Pete Bennett (who's producing this series of *Torchwood*) is going to be there, for whom I want to make it marvellous, and Euros (who's directing) will be there, for whom I want it to be the best thing ever, and John Fay is coming, a writer I *hugely* admire and who's only stepped out of a fantastic ITV career because he wants to work with me. I'm going to sit there like a dumbass, clearly improvising and bluffing, and actually I'm ashamed of how little work I've put into this. Two days of everyone *looking* at me. Oh God. I am dreading it. I feel out of my depth.

Still, yesterday's Series Four press launch was fun, wasn't it? That *Voyage of the Damned* launch last year really was bloated. This one felt normal again, and manageable. Jane Tranter said she'd written a speech that was quite elegiac, because she was so aware that it was our last full series – me, Julie, Phil, David. Half an hour before, she chucked that page away. Wrong time, wrong mood, we're here to launch this, now, right now, and that's all. Positioning! And I loved the episodes. Loved them! To be honest, everyone's going, 'Pompeii, Pompeii, Pompeii,' as they should, because it's loud, extravagant, and heartbreaking. But it's got its problems. It's a funny mix of linear and convoluted. Mind you, the end made me cry. I was sitting there thinking, DON'T CRY! Because I knew I had the Q&A minutes after.

Best of all, the mime sequence in *Partners in Crime*, the Doctor and Donna meeting through the windows – that got such big laughs! Proper, big laughs. In all the right places. Building to that reveal of Miss Foster watching. Bloody lovely. That was my favourite part of the night, to feel a big comedy sequence click into gear in just the right way. (Of course, it did occur to me what a communal laugh that was, that it could be so unfunny watched sitting on your own. Ah, sod it.) When I first pitched *Doctor Who*, I used the example of all those gangs of mates and families sitting around the telly together for the *Pop Idol* final. Event TV. That's still what I'm writing. I'm writing for group viewing. Maybe that's good, maybe that's bad, but it worked in that cinema. That moment was the best feeling I've ever had at a screening.

I suppose it was a shame that there weren't drinks afterwards, because it would have been nice to see people. Except, that's not true. You always end up avoiding the same old drunk idiots who can't handle their alcohol. So bollocks to that.

FROM: BENJAMIN COOK TO: RUSSELL T DAVIES, THURSDAY 3 APRIL 2008 12:45:18 GMT

RE: THAT'S A WRAP

A strop about what? (Missing *The Apprentice*?! No!!!) You don't have to tell me, if you'd prefer not to. But it can't be that bad, can it?

Wasn't the Series Four press launch magnificent, though? The madness of those Adipose! Only in *Doctor Who*. The cradle sequence is so exciting on a big screen. But no Rose Tyler cameo, ha ha! That'll be a shock, when she pops up on transmission.

I guess you're in *Torchwood* Meeting Hell now. Here's hoping that your brain hasn't turned to liquid.

FROM: RUSSELL T DAVIES TO: BENJAMIN COOK, FRIDAY 4 APRIL 2008 14:59:20 GMT

RE: THAT'S A WRAP

The *Torchwood* meeting was good. Poor Ianto, he dies from an alien virus in the corridors of Thames House. In Jack's arms. I did try to convince them that it was a clothes-shredding virus, or it should happen in a sauna, but no one's on my wavelength.

>>A strop about what? (Missing *The Apprentice*?! No!!!)<<

I wish my strop *was* about *The Apprentice* (I've caught up on iPlayer now – God, I love that thing). It was about... oh, everything. I was stupid. About my workload. Script after script after script. For Christ's sake, I'm a packhorse. This year was meant to be lighter; now it's a blur of work. We've been so busy that we've avoided looking at the terrible truth. I should have seen it earlier. I brought it all on myself. I'd already suspected that I might have to give away one Special to another writer – but only one, the Easter Special, because I'm not missing Christmas, and certainly not the regeneration – but I've still got to storyline all five *Torchwood*s, and write at least one of them...

There's only one option left: I give up the Easter *and* Christmas Specials, and go straight on to writing the regeneration this summer. That works. Back on schedule. But damn! We talked about which other writers to use for the Specials. We thought Gareth Roberts for Easter, because that's a space-opera episode. (I really must update you on all that thinking.) I've always wanted to see him write something like that. And Phil Ford for Christmas, because he really is the most reliable writer of all, across *Torchwood* and *Sarah Jane*. He deserves the reward. He's saved our lives on the other shows, and deserves a crack at the Big Show before we all depart. One possible problem: he's never been rewritten by me, which might be a sticking point. But he's a very nice man, so I'm sure he'd be okay. And he's bloody good at nailing formats. I'd probably have less rewriting to do than with any other writer.

Damn, damn, damn. I'd have loved those Specials. Especially with a bit of time to think and recharge the batteries. But what the hell. I'm so tired. Funny week. Everything kicking me off. I think that's Launch Week. I get jittery. Or maybe it's simply that I'm properly knackered, and now with the added pressure of 4.14, every tiny thing seems bigger. It's just me being temperamental. I don't think our e-mails have properly gone into my temperamental side... well, obviously, since I want to make myself sound good. I try to make the e-mails as honest as possible, but everyone filters themselves.

Sorry, that was a bit of a rant. I might just sleep all weekend. Hey, new *Doctor Who* tomorrow! The Rose scene!

FROM: BENJAMIN COOK TO: RUSSELL T DAVIES, FRIDAY 4 APRIL 2008 20:47:43 GMT

RE: THAT'S A WRAP

You've just decommissioned yourself out of two scripts! Well, you've admitted that your mind keeps skipping over Easter and Christmas and ahead to the regeneration episode, so now you can skip ahead officially, right? Since you'll be rewriting the first two Specials anyway, why don't you decide now, before you approach Gareth and Phil, that you'll take a co-writer's credit? It's no use complaining after the event (which you will, won't you?), when you feel that you're not getting the credit that you deserve.

FROM: RUSSELL T DAVIES TO: BENJAMIN COOK, SATURDAY 5 APRIL 2008 00:59:06 GMT

RE: THAT'S A WRAP

I know what you mean about the co-credit. Talking of skipping ahead to David's regeneration, Euros has agreed to direct it! Isn't that brilliant? We're so happy. David just loves him, so we're all excited. You've got to be on set that day. Book a seat now. That'll be in about a year's time. I still won't have left this chair.

FROM: BENJAMIN COOK TO: RUSSELL T DAVIES, SATURDAY 5 APRIL 2008 02:22:08 GMT

RE: THAT'S A WRAP

They can wheel you in, yeah? With dolly-bird nurses on either side. Like Young Mr Grace.[8] 'You've all done very well.'

Hey, *Partners of Crime* is on today.

> **Text message from: Ben**
> Sent: 5-Apr-2008 18:26
> It's on now! The Adipose are coming!

> **Text message from: Russell**
> Sent: 5-Apr-2008 18:27
> Ssh! He he.

> **Text message from: Russell**
> Sent: 5-Apr-2008 19:24
> I love that ending with Wilf looking up at the TARDIS. I think I got that idea from your text this time last year, about children looking up at the moon. Now they can look for a blue box. Now I spend the rest of the night worrying about what the viewing figures will be.

> **Text message from: Ben**
> Sent: 5-Apr-2008 19:48
> My mum says she enjoyed tonight's episode. That's all that matters.

> **Text message from: Russell**
> Sent: 5-Apr-2008 19:53
> My work is done. Good woman. I peeked onto the forums online, got burnt alive – COMEDY!!! ARGH!!! – and ran away.

> **Text message from: Russell**
> Sent: 6-Apr-2008 10:04
> Hooray, hooray, 8.4 million. By the time that's consolidated, that should be higher than last year's Episode 1. Ha ha ha.

> **Text message from: Ben**
> Sent: 6-Apr-2008 10:28
> Amazing. Especially considering the earlier start time.

8 The co-owner (with his brother, Old Mr Grace) of the fictional Grace Brothers department store, in British sitcom *Are You Being Served?*

FROM: RUSSELL T DAVIES TO: BENJAMIN COOK, MONDAY 7 APRIL 2008 23:08:23 GMT

RE: THAT'S A WRAP

I was mobbed tonight! MOBBED! I went to Johnny B's concert at the Millennium Centre. (He sang 'You're So Vain'!) The fangirls were out for Johnny B… and settled for me instead. They had to get security to come and save me. God knows what David's life is like. He has it all rehearsed: enters the auditorium after lights have gone down, runs for backstage as the lights go up again, Jennie Fava at his side like the perfect bodyguard – it's amazing to see them in action. But what a life.

It was brilliant, of course. Fair dos to John, he is a one-off. He had 2,000 people in the palm of his hand. It was weird, though, sitting there watching him do his Captain Jack shtick. Julie and I were talking about it afterwards. There's David, soon to be Hamlet, Johnny B the unstoppable, Catherine with her stellar career, Billie who's just… well, Billie, and they're all doing *Doctor Who*. It's the biggest, most spectacular cast in the whole of the UK!

I'm going to make time tomorrow to update you on the Maybe. It's been lying fallow for a while. But vague ideas are storing up. You've seen how they can change, so it's a good time to make notes. (*The Writer's Tale 2*! Ha ha! How about it, Ben?) Problem is, my mind keeps skipping ahead to the regeneration, because I want it to be so magnificent, and I keep avoiding the two bloody adventures in between.

FROM: BENJAMIN COOK TO: RUSSELL T DAVIES, MONDAY 7 APRIL 2008 23:29:21 GMT

RE: THAT'S A WRAP

The Writer's Tale 2? I thought you'd never ask.

You had me at hello.

BBC Wales

"Doctor Who"
Amended Shooting Schedule
(Issued: 07/04/08)
Episode 14 Shoot Dates:
Monday 7 April – Saturday 3 May

Producer: Susie Liggat
Director: Andy Goddard
Line Producer: Catrin Defis
Co-Ordinator: Jess van Niekerk
Designer: Edward Thomas
Chief Art Dir: Stephen Nicholas
DOP: Ernie Vincze
Gaffer: Mark Hutchings
Sound: Julian Howarth
Costume: Louise page
Make-Up: Barbara Southcott
Loc Manager: Gareth Skelding
First AD: Richard Harris
Second AD: Jennie Fava

This schedule is a guide only. For up-to-date information please see the daily call sheet
and advance schedules contained therein. All artiste calls will be given by the 2nd AD.

CHAPTER FOURTEEN

THE GREAT WOBBLE

In which the Doctor boards the Starship *Enterprise*,
Russell spends £230 on a cake,
and Michael Grade waves a gun about

FROM: RUSSELL T DAVIES TO: BENJAMIN COOK, WEDNESDAY 9 APRIL 2008 20:49:26 GMT

RE: THAT'S A WRAP

I'm so tired. I was doing ADR until 3am, and then had to get in a taxi at 8am for meetings, meetings, meetings, and a *Sarah Jane* read-through. The day ended with having to look at *Sarah Jane* costumes ('Yes, that waistcoat's lovely'), by which time my brain was crawling out of my ears. At one point, I was so rude to Gareth with *Sarah Jane* script notes (I sort of lose my filter when I'm knackered), I was saying, 'This scene's shit, you're writing shit, I'm reading shit.' Julie had to say, 'Russell, you're too tired. I think you should stop now.'

I'm supposed to have written a treatment for Episode 1 of *Torchwood* by Friday. The plan is to have me writing Episode 1, John Fay writing Episode 2, and James Moran writing Episode 3, all simultaneously, with a continuing plot, so we've got to know what each other's episodes contain. My mind is in revolt. TREATMENTS?!!! I don't write treatments. I'm fighting myself. This is going to be an interesting day.

FROM: RUSSELL T DAVIES TO: BENJAMIN COOK, THURSDAY 10 APRIL 2008 18:55:46 GMT

RE: THAT'S A WRAP

Everyone else has just this second delivered their *Torchwood* summaries. I haven't written a word. I'm e-mailing you instead.

FROM: BENJAMIN COOK TO: RUSSELL T DAVIES, THURSDAY 10 APRIL 2008 19:06:28 GMT

RE: THAT'S A WRAP

You've got your priorities all wrong.

No. Hang on. *Right*! Priorities all *right*.

FROM: RUSSELL T DAVIES TO: BENJAMIN COOK, THURSDAY 10 APRIL 2008 23:43:15 GMT

RE: THAT'S A WRAP

I've given up on *Torchwood*. I'm having a mini strike. I'm watching *Supernatural* on ITV2 instead. Those *Supernatural* boys turn me into a teenage girl. They're literally sooo handsome. OMG!!! The other *Torchwood* treatments are a mess. We've got so much to do. I can't bear it. So much work. I can see ways to fix it all, but sometimes I feel like I'm this dumb story machine. It's not that I'm running out of stories; it's more like I've got too many of them, and too many solutions, and they won't stop pouring out. I'm sick of it. So, I'm not going to do anything. I'll walk into the meeting tomorrow and busk. Well, it's in London, so that gives me a train journey to work things out.

Did you know, they're not making an Adipose toy because – get this – they think they won't sell?! I can't believe –

Oh! WAIT! Sod the Adipose. I knew I had something to tell you. According to Julie, Steven Moffat has given David the weekend to decide whether he wants to do Series Five or not. The thing is, David is thinking about it!

FROM: BENJAMIN COOK TO: RUSSELL T DAVIES, FRIDAY 11 APRIL 2008 00:58:04 GMT

RE: THAT'S A WRAP

Really? I thought it was a done deal. I thought David had decided.

FROM: RUSSELL T DAVIES TO: BENJAMIN COOK, FRIDAY 11 APRIL 2008 21:45:44 GMT

THE WOBBLE

Manchester! I've forgotten how to type on this keyboa5**(rd.

Everything is still in flux. I think David is just having a wobble. End of filming in sight, only the Specials, the size of *Hamlet* staring him in the face, then out of the blue an e-mail from Steven saying, 'Let's have a chat about the future.' That sort of wobble. That doesn't make it insignificant, the wobble could go either way, but we'll remember this as the Great Wobble. Or not.

I was on set with David this morning – he was about to battle the CyberKing from a hot-air balloon, like you do – but we didn't talk about it much. I'll just back him, personally and professionally, and help him no matter what he decides. Although… I can't help thinking, would I have done a fourth year if I'd known that I'd be handing the Tenth Doctor over to someone else anyway? I wonder. I could be long since gone. I could be far away, doing something else. But it's down to me to swallow that. Doesn't really matter.

Maybe I should have been more opinionated today? I spend so much time being nice to people, sometimes I think I'm a mug. Someone said the other day, someone who hadn't seen me for ages, 'You haven't changed a bit. None of this success has changed you.' I thought then, I'm a mug. People *should* change in life. Isn't that the point? I struggle so hard to be liked that I retard my own development. Oh, I suppose that's my wobble. The Great Wobble spreads. I'm allowed one or two. But anyway – Steven has said that he's starting to write *Doctor Who* next week, so that's David's deadline. That's so exciting, isn't it?

In other news, the *Torchwood* meeting was good. I think and hope that John Fay is a genius. He's truly exciting to be with. It was invigorating to be with a man who pushed me, and said no to me a lot, and was really inspiring. Further reports to follow. I'll stay in touch from the frozen north. It's cold up here.

FROM: BENJAMIN COOK TO: RUSSELL T DAVIES, FRIDAY 11 APRIL 2008 22:21:11 GMT

RE: THE WOBBLE

You can see why Tom Baker ended up staying for seven years. This show is supposed to be a rolling review, but you can't help becoming attached.

FROM: RUSSELL T DAVIES TO: BENJAMIN COOK, SATURDAY 12 APRIL 2008 17:15:55 GMT

RE: THE WOBBLE

Look what I just discovered on my Manchester computer. (Yes, it's the sort of afternoon where I'm going through old files.) From July 2004, this is my very first drawing of a Toclafane![1] Back in Series One, when we thought we'd lost the Daleks and I had to think of something for Rob Shearman to replace them with, I came up with this.[2]

1 The cyborg Toclafane, human heads integrated into spherical, mechanical shells, appeared in *Doctor Who* 3.12/3.13.
2 The estate of Dalek creator Terry Nation, which holds the rights to the Daleks, temporarily blocked their use in *Doctor Who* Series One due to a disagreement over licensing. The changed story for Shearman's 1.6 featured an alien akin to a child who kills for pleasure, an idea that eventually evolved into the Toclafane in 3.12/3.13. Ultimately, the BBC was able to secure the rights for the Daleks from the Nation estate, and 1.6 became Dalek once again.

They weren't called Toclafane back then, they were just Future Humans. And those are the sort of boots that I imagined Chris wearing. I love a big boot. No, don't reply. Just don't.

FROM: RUSSELL T DAVIES TO: BENJAMIN COOK, MONDAY 14 APRIL 2008 11:33:46 GMT

RE: THE WOBBLE

Not much to report. Apparently, Steven is going to Cardiff on Wednesday to meet David. I might dress up as a waiter and eavesdrop. Yes! I shall become an industrial spy, much like Donna Noble. Or like Rose and Pete sneaking into the Cyberfactory: give yourself away and… well, you'll be taken to the Cyberleader, and given plenty of time to destroy him![3] Never got that quite right, did we?

I don't think there will be any more news today. Far more importantly, I'm trying to get my lift back to Cardiff brought forward so that I'll get home in time for the *Skins* series finale.

FROM: RUSSELL T DAVIES TO: BENJAMIN COOK, MONDAY 14 APRIL 2008 23:19:47 GMT

MORE WOBBLING

Oh, *Skins*! We'll hate Series Three now. We'll be *Skins* ming-mongs, insisting that it's not as good as the old days of Series Two. But I thought they were properly 18 years old tonight. You can't often achieve that with teenagers, because their lives and dialogue have to be so thought out, in a drama. But tonight they were full of hopes, and dreams, and daftness, and spunk, and wisdom, and jokes, and tears, and everything. Wonderful. Beautiful dialogue just skimming past you. And Tony and Sid… oh, that was perfect. So skilled. I want to track down Bryan Elsley. I want to tell him that he's brilliant. I'm not sure I would've stuck with *Skins* if it wasn't for you, Benjamino. Good call.

And now I've got 67 e-mails waiting for me. But sod that. On Thursday, I've lunch with MICHAEL GRADE at THE IVY! I'm being headhunted. Wa-hey!

FROM: BENJAMIN COOK TO: RUSSELL T DAVIES, MONDAY 14 APRIL 2008 23:37:40 GMT

RE: MORE WOBBLING

Here I am adding to your 67 e-mails, but I have to hand it to Bryan Elsley: that *Skins* finale was faultless. We've had to wait two bloody series, but every line, every scene, every single bloody moment was perfect. How often can you say that about a piece of telly? The car chase! With the coffin! Anwar's chat with Sketch, on the sofa, about friends moving on. ('They just take longer to reply.') Jal's eulogy at Chris's funeral. That was magnificent. The fireworks! Tony just nods and there are fireworks! Maxxie's line about no one wearing pants in London. Sid leaving Tony at the airport, then coming back through the revolving doors. (Predictable, but so what?) And Tony telling Sid, 'You were

---

3 In *Doctor Who* 2.6, Rose and her dad, Pete, infiltrate the Cyberman Headquarters.

always my favourite.' That closing moment, with Effie, reminding us of what's to come in Series Three. Oh, and the scene with Tony and Michelle in the car, where they break up without either one of them using the words 'breaking up'. Such *brilliant* writing.

The whole episode was about knowing when to stop, really. Knowing when to let go. They stopped short of depicting Cassie and Sid's reunion. They stopped short of showing us Jal's abortion. They didn't hammer anything home, but let it be. Russell, can you believe this is the same show that did a *Carry On Russia* episode in Series One? This finale was perfection. That is a fact. Yes, you should e-mail Bryan Elsley, and tell him.

FROM: RUSSELL T DAVIES TO: BENJAMIN COOK, MONDAY 14 APRIL 2008 23:48:36 GMT

RE: MORE WOBBLING

You're so right. I loved that episode because it made me *think*. About when I was 18. Getting those A level results – which was barmy, because my parents were away, so we'd been having a two-week party in my house (I was that *Skins* boy!), and everyone was drinking wine for breakfast, and we all staggered off to school, got the results, then staggered back to the wine. Cheap, bad wine. I didn't drink wine for years after that summer. Oh, all those mates of mine! A lovely boy called Julian – blond, a dancer, he was like Maxxie. He died a few years later – so young. Christ, the '80s were strange. It made me think of all that, for the first time in years. Quite apart from being a beautiful piece of telly, that alone made watching the whole two series worthwhile. And they really did capture it – all the hope, the ambition, the fear, and the still-working-out-who-you-are.

Funny thing is, after all these years, I'm not sure I can remember what my A level results were. Three As and one B? Two As and two Bs? Something like that. I'm in a job where I've never, ever been asked my qualifications. God, if I could have told myself that at the time!

> Text message from: **Russell**
> Sent: 15-Apr-2008 10:52
> I'm doing the shoot for our book cover today, on the TARDIS set (I'm dreading it), but I can't get *Skins* out of my head. How brilliant.

> Text message from: **Ben**
> Sent: 15-Apr-2008 10:52
> Good luck. Don't let the photographer bully you.

> Text message from: **Russell**
> Sent: 15-Apr-2008 17:11
> The photographer was rather good, actually. I looked vaguely human and not 10,000 years old. We have a cover!

LETTER TO BRYAN

This is the e-mail that Russell wrote to *Skins* co-creator Bryan Elsley a few days after transmission of its Series Two finale, along with Bryan's reply...

FROM: RUSSELL T DAVIES TO: BRYAN ELSLEY, SUNDAY 20 APRIL 12:35:56 GMT

HELLO

Dear Bryan,

I hope you don't mind me writing out of the blue. I cadged your e-mail address off a mutual friend of ours, Charles Martin.

But anyway, hello. I'm a writer too. I'm the *Doctor Who* man. I've always wanted to meet you. I think you're brilliant, but now I've been driven to cadging e-mail addresses, because I had to write and say that *Skins* is just PHENOMENAL. I bloody love it. I enjoyed the first series, but the second series just flew. It became something so rare, and beautiful, and wise, and funny, and brave, and mental and new. Ending with a final episode that was just about perfect. Nothing's ever perfect! But that was!

And I've got to say, the penultimate episode, when you took that dazzling, huge, brilliant leap to New York, was one of the most amazing things that I've ever seen. I've never seen a story take such a jump. I can't imagine how you even thought of that. But it was lucid, and true, and heartbreaking, and I will never forget it.

I'm going to sound like a stalker soon, so I'll stop in a minute, but also I think everything you've done with that young writers' team is wonderful and shames the rest of us. I read an interview with you, years ago, in the *Sunday Times*, I think, where you spoke about new forms of narrative, how our TV-watching generation is becoming outdated and the next generation will have new ways of storytelling. I just nodded, sadly. But then you went out and did something about it! You're an inspiration.

So thank you for *Skins*. Good luck with the next series. And good luck with the BAFTAs tonight. If you don't win, it's a scandal!

All the best,

Russell

FROM: BRYAN ELSLEY TO: RUSSELL T DAVIES, MONDAY 28 APRIL 16:45:18 GMT

RE: HELLO

Dear Russell,

I'm sorry that it's taken so long to reply to your lovely e-mail. I've just acquired a baby and it's 20 years since I had my last one, so I've had to be sent away for re-education.

Anyway, I'm finally back in my office and just want to say thank you for being so encouraging. It means a lot to me, because you're the writer who, a few years ago, reassured me that it was still possible to do something meaningful, funny and entertaining in TV drama, and that these things can coexist, just at the point when I was about to give up trying. It's hard to relate just what *Queer as Folk* meant to me, but I'm sure lots of people say that to you. I just hope that isn't boring or frustrating, given all the other fantastic work that you've done. It happens to be true, that's all.

Next year on *Skins*, on Series Three, we're kind of pushing it out. All the writers except me are under 23, and four of them under the age of 20. All the characters are gone, to be completely replaced with a set born from the imaginations of the young creative team. The possibilities of going on our arses are too numerous to think about. We'll be hanging on for dear life again. If you ever fancied coming by our writers' meeting on a Wednesday afternoon and spending half an hour telling a bunch of kids how you go about things, we would be so happy. In the meantime and failing that, it would be nice to finally meet up at some point.

We didn't get the BAFTA, of course. Quite a long evening when your award comes and goes in the first 45 seconds...

Best regards,

Bryan

FROM: RUSSELL T DAVIES TO: BENJAMIN COOK, TUESDAY 15 APRIL 2008 18:37:29 GMT

RE: MORE WOBBLING

I'm only writing to make a promise, so that I see the promise through later. Tonight, you're going to see the return of the Maybe. It's been ages. I've got to whack these Specials thoughts down before they develop too far, or die.

FROM: BENJAMIN COOK TO: RUSSELL T DAVIES, TUESDAY 15 APRIL 2008 23:19:23 GMT

RE: MORE WOBBLING

I eagerly await the Maybe!

Hey, are you going to David's birthday bash on Friday? I've got an invite, so I'll try to make it down. And have you seen *The Sun* today? Apparently, Jennie Fava is dating David Tennant! Where do they get this stuff?

FROM: RUSSELL T DAVIES TO: BENJAMIN COOK, TUESDAY 15 APRIL 2008 23:27:48 GMT

RE: MORE WOBBLING

Jennie said, 'It says that I was at the John Barrowman concert! Now everyone's going to know! And they'll think I actually *am* dating David!' Ha ha. Mind you, it's slightly serious. Julie had to warn her to tell her family and everything, because reporters may well turn up at her parents' house, track down old school friends, all that shit.

Yes, I'm going to David's party. Julie and I have bought the cake. For 200 people. It's cost us £230! It had better be TARDIS-shaped.

I'm about to tackle the Maybe. I might not stop typing till 3am.

FROM: BENJAMIN COOK TO: RUSSELL T DAVIES, TUESDAY 15 APRIL 2008 23:32:07 GMT

RE: MORE WOBBLING

>>Julie and I have bought the cake.<<

Is Phil Collinson jumping out of it? Or is that for when David leaves?

FROM: RUSSELL T DAVIES TO: BENJAMIN COOK, TUESDAY 15 APRIL 2008 23:35:11 GMT

RE: MORE WOBBLING

Phil is so jumping out of a cake at David's leaving party.

FROM: RUSSELL T DAVIES TO: BENJAMIN COOK, WEDNESDAY 16 APRIL 2008 01:18:45 GMT

RE: MORE WOBBLING

Right. So. The Maybe.

Bear in mind, thinking of that five-episode *Torchwood* storyline took an awful lot of thinking, and stunted some of my *Doctor Who* time. That's my excuse. Can you believe that I've got to deliver a *Torchwood* script in three weeks' time? Bloody hell! I haven't had a second to think about it. I've had to bloody cancel Kylie in Paris in May. That would have been such a laugh. But my mind is screaming. Anyway –

We've three Specials: Easter, Christmas, and the 2010 regeneration. Unless David accepts Steven's offer later today, and the 2010 Regeneration gets knocked out, in which case we only make two Specials. Blub. But let's ignore that for now. Easter is very empty. This will probably be given over to Gareth. Julie is insisting that I accept a joint credit. She says it's necessary. It attracts guest stars. They expect to see my name on the front of the script. But I'm still queasy. It'll look, in hindsight, like I *didn't* write any of *The Fires of Pompeii*, or *The Satan Pit*, or… well, most of them.

Since Easter is the only proper, standalone episode next year, I fancy something outer-spacey, wild and whizzy, spaceships and lasers. Lots of *POW!* Also, one proviso: the time between shooting and transmission will be incredibly tight, so the script has to have CG-only elements, with no live-action inserts, so that The Mill can prep and finish some FX while we're still shooting. In other words: spaceships. It was meant to be. I've always wanted to see *Star Wars*-type dogfights, two sorts of zippy spaceships racing against each other, battling, zooming, cartwheeling… and the TARDIS materialises right in the middle, and really gets involved. Like the wing of a spaceship whacks it! The TARDIS tumbles through space, the Doctor inside getting jolted about, really funny, he's going 'Oy!', hits another ship, tumbles again. Taking a dogfight and making it funny. Lovely *Doctor Who* subversion. Then an X-wing fighter screeches to a halt in front of the TARDIS – literally, with a screech of brakes, that makes me laugh – and talks to the Doctor over the scanner. Female pilot (this episode's companion) being all tough: 'This is a restricted area!' With the Doctor being all Doctor-ish: 'Well, how should I know?!'

They're all without a regular companion, these three Specials, so we get Companion Of The Week. That was always the plan. Then I wobbled big time over that, having written *The Next Doctor*, because it's so hard to write with no companion. Jackson is so lost in his own story that he can't fill the companion's role very well. The Doctor does mutter to himself a lot. So, I spent that chicken-pox fortnight thinking that we need one companion for all three Specials. Then I realised that's bollocks. Jackson's circumstances are unique. We won't have an amnesiac again. The plan is back on.

So, the Doctor and the female pilot... The Doctor lands at the Military Space Base – all boiler suits and alarms. It's a dirty, gritty, grimy war. People really are dying in these dogfights. Two opposing armies. Fighting over what? I've no idea. That's as far as it goes. Big gap there. But if you've got starfighters, then at some point the Doctor has to get into the cockpit (small set, easy) and enter the fray... except I'd love him to join the battle with some sort of weapon-stopping device on board, so everywhere he flies – zipping in and out of zooming starfighters – he jams engines and guns. Literally, spreading peace. All the ships end up hanging there like hunks of junk. Nice image.

As a final image, I'd love him to enter the TARDIS, laughing. I know that sounds odd and small, but we've done a million sad departures. Imagine him at Easter, sailing off, hooting at something, with the pilot left behind (voluntarily), hooting too.

I've been toying with one other idea, a variant on this, although I don't think it works. I would so love to see the Doctor on board the Starship *Enterprise*, puncturing all that Starfleet pomposity with his sheer Doctor-ness.[4] When we began in 2004, *Star Trek: Enterprise* was still on air, and I told Julie, in all seriousness, that I wanted to do a *Doctor Who/Star Trek* crossover. It was on our list of plans, until *Star Trek: Enterprise* was axed. (The crossover would have been so brilliant, though. In an official crossover, the Doctor would have had to learn that Starfleet is wonderful, but that's a small price to pay.) But I've wondered ever since whether to do it anyway: invent a ship called the *Endeavour*, give it a bridge, a captain, a science officer, a funny-foreheaded lieutenant, all of that... then let the Doctor loose. Enormous fun.

But too much fun? If it's not the real *Enterprise*, it starts to become a pastiche. If these are my last stories, why waste one on *Star Trek*? Oh, but I could so write it! So could Gareth. It is tempting me. I wonder. Hey, are you Invisible Ben again now as we enter new territory? Or are you going to become visible? I like Visible Ben. But it's your call. (Hmm, does that mean I'm waiting for you to tell me that the *Endeavour* idea is rubbish? Am I just begging that reply?)

I've spent a long time wondering if we link from the Easter Special into the Christmas Special with a 'What? What?? Whaaaat???' exit. (Yes, Ben, it's back!) It's unusual, this

---

4 The USS *Enterprise* is the name of several starships in the *Star Trek* science fiction franchise. Starfleet is the fictional peacekeeping armada of the United Federation of Planets.

Easter episode, because I think there are going to be a lot of kids devastated that the show isn't on again next week. Does a 'What? What?? Whaaaat???' ending help, or make it worse? I think a one-off, self-contained episode would be best, but I'm here to tell you the Maybe, so I'd better flag the other options. You could end with a knock on the TARDIS door – yes, a plain old knock – and the Doctor says, 'What?' He walks to the door. It knocks again. 'What??' And he opens the door... and there's HELEN MIRREN!

'Whaaaat???'

And we're into the credits. Because the Christmas episode, right now, is still that Empty Hotel idea that I came up with last December, inspired by my night in the faceless hotel in Paddington, do you remember? And I think we could maybe get Helen Mirren if we planned this far in advance. She's turned us down in the past, but always nicely, because she's been too busy, so we could try to lure her with this much notice. Or Judi Dench. Jane Tranter says that there's definite interest from Judi Dench. I'd love the Doctor with an older companion. Difficult to do too much running and chasing, but...

So, the Hotel. Big, noisy, middle-class family, heading off to a posh hotel for Christmas, a proper, huge, city-centre Dorchester-type place. Noise, noise, noise, all the way. Mum, dad, kids, their granny, all yammering away in the car, and as the porters take the luggage, then all the way up in the lift, spilt drinks, tears, nagging, get to the hotel room (two or three rooms, connecting doors)... by then, Gran has had enough. Really fed up. Says something like, 'I wish you'd all disappear!' Storms out. Goes to the ice machine. Corridors empty. Spooky. Creepy. A sudden wind blows through the halls. Gran gets the ice, goes back to the room. Empty. All disturbed and messy, but no people. She goes downstairs. Foyer, empty. No one. Goes outside. Streets, empty. (At night.) No traffic. London, deserted. Nice CG shot of Nelson's Column, Christmas tree, no people. So, Gran walks along, her phone's not working, but she sees a police box, knocks on the door... ah ha!

Now it gets expensive. And this is really what's blocking me. Vastly expensive. We've got the Doctor and Gran in an empty world, and he's as lost as she is, but they're not investigating for long before creatures start to appear. Weird, spindly, eight-legged creatures with human torsos, like centaurs. Except, in my mind, they're the wrong size. They're small and creepy. They're singsong, strange and delicate. These creatures are the forerunners, the sentinels, of the aliens. They've frozen Earth for one second in time, to make it, for one night, their carnival. Creatures parading through the streets. This bizarre carnival procession, on a vast scale. (And this is just the first 15 minutes! Christ alive! The Doctor and Gran are the only ones who are human. Everything else is CG, or at least prosthetics. I try not to worry about money, but that really is seriously blocking me.) Huge, weird, bug-like creatures, with crowns, sceptres, slaves, robes. The Doctor and Gran in hiding. It's all a bit magical. A sinister fairytale. Creatures who have come through a gap in reality. Not literally supernatural, but feeling like it.

There's an echo of that old JK Rowling plot in here.

But how did Gran avoid the time-slip? And how do you sustain the Doctor and Gran in hiding for an hour? The threat has to escalate. The aliens are only here to live out one night in this magical suspended second, but if, say, the Doctor and Gran are seen, then Earth is surrendered and becomes the aliens' home. That doesn't make any sense at all. Rather, it depends on witchcrafty ideas and language. The supernatural thread is really very strong. Also, it needs to bring the family back into the action, somehow. Gran has to be fighting for them, not just the world. Kids in danger. Brilliant. And Mum and Dad. Do the aliens unlock them out of time once they know that Gran is a danger? To tempt her out? Something to do with a Christmas present? Like, whoever opens that box is destined to... oh, that sort of thing. I just can't see it yet.

The size of this! We have to make these Specials slightly cheaper, because they haven't got a supporting series to amortise the costs. Julie is raising a good bit of money, as she always does, but it's hardly the right time to go mad with scale. Still, however that story ends, we definitely link into David's last story. Regeneration is on the way. He stands there in the final Christmas scene, in the snow, by the TARDIS, saying goodbye to Gran, having saved the world... then he sees, far off, through the snow, but staring at him... an Ood. And then it's gone. But he knows. The Doctor knows. He's being summoned. He must return to the planet of the Ood, because the end is near. His song must end soon. The Ood have seen it. He's going to die. (He doesn't say that, but it's in the air.) Sad farewell to Gran. His final journey. Off he goes.

The Ood, by the way, are living in vast ice palaces now that they're free – huge, carved landscapes – with an Ood Consciousness that is seeing through time. They're filling in for the Time Lords, in terms of being a higher race with massive knowledge and authority, to direct and summon the Doctor. Good old Ood! Who'd have thought? The Ood have blossomed into the species that they were always meant to be, infinitely wise and calm.

I've got to read *Sarah Jane* scripts now. I'm not sure I'll be able to return to the Maybe tonight, because I've got an interview with the *New York Times* tomorrow morning, so I can't do an all-nighter. Ben, you're going to kill me!

FROM: BENJAMIN COOK TO: RUSSELL T DAVIES, WEDNESDAY 16 APRIL 2008 01:55:03 GMT

RE: MORE WOBBLING

The Doctor on board the *Enterprise*, puncturing Starfleet pomposity with his sheer Doctor-ness. This is my favourite idea. (So long as it's not a simple *Star Trek* parody. That would be too easy.) If you give it a good story, and make the captain, the science officer and everyone *real* after the initial cheap shots (you need a few cheap shots!), and make us care for them, then we'll get the joke *and* get involved. And you could give the starship an Easter-y sort of name. In fact, the Easter Special is the 200th *Doctor Who* serial. (Yeah, I counted!) So, you can call the ship *Voyager 200* or *Endeavour 200* or something. Or maybe call one of the crew Ash Wednesday. No? Please yourself.

But I'm not quite sure how you'd make the 'What? What?? Whaaaat???' cliffhanger work. A knock on the TARDIS door. The Doctor opens it. It's Helen Mirren. That wouldn't be much of a surprise to him, would it? Not really. Unless Helen Mirren was playing herself! (She wouldn't be playing herself, would she?) So, you'd have to have a line or two explaining that everyone's vanished – but that's exposition, when the cliffhanger should be all about images. The newly regenerated Doctor! The bride in the control room! The *Titanic* smashing through the TARDIS wall!

FROM: RUSSELL T DAVIES TO: BENJAMIN COOK, WEDNESDAY 16 APRIL 2008 02:30:43 GMT

RE: MORE WOBBLING

The *Enterprise* is your favourite idea? I didn't see that coming. It is fun, isn't it? But I fear that the parody would be all-pervading. Even if I wrote it well (or if Gareth did, of course), it would still look like a sketch. And yet...

You're right about Helen Mirren, too. 'Look, it's Helen Mirren!' No matter what she's wearing, she would, by then, have filmed 4.16, so we'd have announced her casting. She wouldn't be a surprise like the runaway bride. Damn.

One other idea: what if David has aged between his penultimate and final episodes? It could pay off beautifully if the Ood summon the Doctor at the end of the Christmas episode, and then he steps out of the TARDIS in the 2010 episode... looking older! A little bit of grey. A little bit tired. Like he did *anything* to evade that summons. He went everywhere, did everything, to avoid discovering his destiny from the Ood. He ran away. Travelled to the furthest stars. Got married. Broke his heart. Did unspeakable things. All to avoid this. He will do anything to avoid dying. That fits in with the whole final episode. (How like a Time Lord, to live a whole lifetime in one week.) But the Ood have waited, with infinite patience. He couldn't put it off any longer.

FROM: BENJAMIN COOK TO: RUSSELL T DAVIES, WEDNESDAY 16 APRIL 2008 02:45:19 GMT

RE: MORE WOBBLING

But if an Ood appears at the end of 4.16 to tell the Doctor that his song is ending soon, isn't it sort of cheating to have him run, run, run for a lifetime? It's like that line that you like in *Tooth and Claw*, when Queen Victoria says that whoever owns the Koh-I-Noor diamond must surely die, and the Doctor replies, 'Well, that's true of anything, if you wait long enough.'

FROM: RUSSELL T DAVIES TO: BENJAMIN COOK, WEDNESDAY 16 APRIL 2008 03:09:57 GMT

RE: MORE WOBBLING

You can go around philosophising with 'Everything has its time', and 'Everything must die', and all that shtick, but when an Ood says, 'It's your turn now,' you'd be like, 'RUUUUUUNNNNNNNNNNN!!!!!' (I certainly intend to.) But I like that. It makes the Doctor so much more real. I should actually *say* that. Old King Ood should say, 'Everything has its time,' and the Doctor says, 'Yeah, but not me.' The Doctor's arrogance and determination to outwit death should become part of his last story, like it really is time that he dies before he becomes too powerful. That's interesting.

But I'm definitely off to bed now. Night.

FROM: RUSSELL T DAVIES TO: BENJAMIN COOK, WEDNESDAY 16 APRIL 2008 23:05:47 GMT

RE: MORE WOBBLING

David met with Steven and Piers today at 5pm. They outlined Series Five to him. David said to Julie afterwards, 'It's genius, seriously, absolute genius… but I want to watch it, not be in it.' In other words, he's letting go. The Wobble is steadying.

But other options are still being bandied about. It's like we've all had a Wobble, and that Wobble has sort of cleared more space, made us look at what we're doing in a new light and ask new questions, because now we're wondering: do we make more Specials? Why just three? How about a mini-series with David in early 2010, with Steven's Series Five and new Doctor shifted to the autumn? Julie and I are seeing Jane tomorrow night in London – Michael Grade first! – so we'll try to make sense of it all then. But overall I think it's done. David has made his mind up, and so has Steven. The plan stands. The plan is good.

You know what? Steven is so lucky. A whole new Doctor ahead of him. Brilliant!

FROM: BENJAMIN COOK TO: RUSSELL T DAVIES, WEDNESDAY 16 APRIL 2008 23:12:37 GMT

RE: MORE WOBBLING

When will it be announced that Steven is taking over? If him and Piers are going to start looking for a new Doctor, word will spread like mad, very soon. Have you and Julie got a plan for that? You always have a plan.

FROM: RUSSELL T DAVIES TO: BENJAMIN COOK, WEDNESDAY 16 APRIL 2008 23:32:04 GMT

RE: MORE WOBBLING

Well, there's half a plan. Rumour is that he's won the Best Writer BAFTA for *Blink*, and that's announced in a fortnight or so. Well, I keep saying that we should announce it the day after. But I don't think anyone is really listening.

> **Text message from: Ben**
> Sent: 17-Apr-2008 15:43
> How was your meeting with Michael Grade?

> **Text message from: Russell**
> Sent: 17-Apr-2008 16:06
> First thing he said: 'Were you one of those people who wrote to me when I axed *Doctor Who* in 1985?' I said, 'No, you were right, it was shit,' and he hooted! He was lovely. What a raconteur! A proper showman. Loved him.

FROM: RUSSELL T DAVIES TO: BENJAMIN COOK, MONDAY 21 APRIL 2008 20:32:03 GMT

RE: MORE WOBBLING

Long e-mail. Beware. A lot to catch up on.

First of all, Michael Grade said some fascinating stuff at that lunch the other day. He said, 'Do you know the difference between drama and melodrama? Melodrama is: I've got a gun, I'm pointing it at you, I hate you, I want to kill you, my finger is squeezing the trigger... and the gun jams. Drama is: I've got a gun, I'm pointing it at you, I hate you, my finger is squeezing the trigger... and I can't do it.' I think that's brilliant. And he mimed all that, pointing his hand at me. In the Ivy!

Funny thing is, it cropped up the very next day. Because the same difference applies to drama and science fiction. Gareth has written a *Sarah Jane* script where she meets her parents in 1951, but she knows that she's got to get away.[5] So, she drives out of the village, but the roads keep twisting back, space folding in on itself. She's caught in a loop. Every path she takes brings her back to where she started. She can't escape. But the drama version is: Sarah Jane knows that she's got to get away, and she tries to drive out of the village.... but she can't. She knows that it's wrong, but she turns the car around, to go and meet her destiny. Thank you, Mr Grade! Quite apart from anything, it's nice to sit in meetings and quote Michael Grade.

Anyway. When we Maybe'd last, the Doctor had caught a glimpse of an Ood in the Christmas snow and headed off to face his destiny. Now, since the Great Wobble of 2008, Jane has suggested making the regeneration story a two-parter. David is fine with this, apparently. Quite when the second part is aired, I don't know. No one knows. Jane was wondering if the whole two-parter could run at the top of Series Five, so it's a 15-week season. Two weeks of David, 13 weeks of the new guy (or girl)... but Steven has been talking about how good the gap between early 2010 and Easter will be – a few months waiting for an Easter resurrection – and he's absolutely right, I think. On Friday, Julie and I told Jane our fears – which felt a bit off, because I felt like I was talking on Steven's behalf. But it turned out that Jane had been suggesting 15 weeks as an extreme solution, to open up our thinking so that we could imagine that anything is possible. She wasn't clinging to the 15-week idea at all. She more or less handed it back to us, saying that she'd trusted us this far, and our gut instincts had always been right, so she was happy with whatever we wanted to do – we could play a regeneration two-parter in January if we wanted. I DON'T KNOW! One episode or two?! Julie wants two. I'm not sure. Maybe writing this e-mail will help.

This is the one-part version. (Or one of the options, at least.) The Doctor – older, tired, having lived that life in a week – arrives back on the planet of the Ood, and they tell him that his next journey will be his last. He's calm with the Ood, and understanding, but still... who the hell wants to die? And it's not fair. He's saved

---

5 *The Sarah Jane Adventures* 2.9/2.10.

empires and universes; why is there no one to save him? That's not overt, not at first, but it's there. I love that dark side to David's Doctor. It's subtle and, because of that, so powerful. Gareth said in an interview the other month that he loves David leaning on the Radiation Room door, talking to Jack, in *Utopia*; that it's like there's something dark stirring underneath. Yes! I love that idea. And there's that bit in *The Doctor's Daughter* where he's telling Jenny about the Time War, and he actually sneers at her for a second. It's magnificent. Terrifying! Something kept inside. After all, this is a man who has lost so much, and seen so many terrible things.

With all that ticking away, off he goes… and this is where it really becomes a one-parter. He lands in some poxy, battered little ship, creaking away in the middle of nowhere. It's nothing. It's not a Time War, or the Master's revenge, or the realm of Davros. It's tiny. Four people on board. A family. I'd love them to be a prosthetic family. I could call them the Prosthetix. (Not really!) All with blue alien faces. Mum, dad, son (handsome if blue) and daughter. They're stranded in the middle of nowhere. All they've got is a leaky engine. This stupid, simple, daft bloody leaky engine is going to irradiate the Doctor, and kill him.

This family isn't important. They're no one. The kids won't grow up to become Leaders of the Universe. And that's the point: they're as important as anyone. But it's a great way of bringing out the Doctor's growing resentment. 'You're nothing! You're no one! I give my life for you?!' He's bordering on 'Do you know who I am?!' He should actually say that. It's the twenty-first-century marker for vanity. All this emerging arrogance, all his rage and fear, all his loneliness. To dispel that, he's got to go into the Engine Room. I'm sure he'll have to replace someone in the Engine Room. Ordinary dad is in there, willing to give his life for his kids – but the Doctor has no one, so he's the one who steps in there instead. Because he's got to. There could be some sort of twist. In venting the engines, the energy becomes the Sun, our Sun, and so the Doctor's sacrifice creates the Solar System. Nice bit of grace at the end, a bit *Terminus*, and I never expected to be channelling that story![6] But also it's the only option left, after the *Terminus* ship created the universe and the Racnoss caused the Earth to form. I'm running out of things for the Doctor to create –

Oh, what if it were Gallifrey? He created Gallifrey! I just thought of that now, typing to you. Nah, not as effective, is it? He created Space Men In Big Hats. Who cares? But something like that. And then he's irradiated. Dying, gently. But there's one last thing that he has to do…

And I'll come to that after describing the two-part version, because the actual ending will be the same no matter which version I go with. The problem with this one-part version is that it's so small. That's deliberate, but you can't help feel the anticlimax. David's last story, *Radio Times* cover, all the press coverage… and he's saving the bloody

---

6 Four-part 1983 *Doctor Who* serial *Terminus* postulates that the Big Bang was the result of a jettison of unstable fuel from a spaceship.

Prosthetix family! You're expecting The Ultimate Battle For The Universe, and what you get is a creaky old cargo ship, filmed in oh-so-familiar South Wales factories. I'm fighting the disappointment. My own disappointment.

So, then there's the two-parter... for which I'd have to bring back John Simm as the Master. I said that to Julie and Jane, and they sat bolt upright! That was lovely, but worried me, because the Prosthetix family would never get a sitting-up response. Julie and Jane went, 'Ooh!' I like an 'Ooh!' The audience should be going 'Ooh!' I've always known what I'd do, to bring back the Master. I loved him so much, I couldn't help but work it out, in idle moments, just daydreaming...

You'd still have the Ood prologue, the Doctor leaving them, knowing that this trip will be his last. But then you'd cut to Lucy Saxon, in a women's prison.[7] Cowed, silent, beaten. She's quiet and withdrawn. She's had a nervous breakdown. She never talks to anyone. Maybe all the other prisoners hate her, because she's posh. (She was the Prime Minister's wife)! So, she's led through the corridors, to the visitor's room, where there's a journalist waiting to interview her. The mystery of What Happened To Harold Saxon is still unexplained, to the public. (Also, this works as a handy update for viewers.) The journalist is a middle-aged woman. With red fingernails, and an evil agenda. As she says goodbye, she slips something into Lucy's palm, with a cunning glance at the bulldyke prison guards, her conspirators. It's the Master's ring![8] 'Take care of this.' Lucy is an innocent in this. She has got no idea what's going on. (Maybe the journalist leaves the cell, and Chief Bull Dyke says, 'Now, have her killed.' There are wheels within wheels. Nah, maybe not.)

Night-time. Prison. Lights out. In secret, the guards come for Lucy. This regiment of bulldykes. They take her down to the basement, where there are chalk circles and symbols drawn on the floor. It's as close to a Satanic ritual as we can get on the BBC. Lucy is made to kneel while they chant. This is the Sect of Saxon! His devoted followers, determined to bring him back. If I could, they'd cut Lucy, they'd use her blood and pour it on the ring, like she's part of him, genetically, if only because she had sex with a Time Lord. (Not sure how to phrase that. 'You have known him' or something.) Ritual. Power building. Huge FX extravaganza. Lights dipping, wind blowing, floor cracks open, smoke and fire, whole country shaking, and out of the firestorm steps Himself, reborn. (After that, I need the Master on his own. He's got to get rid of these disciples. Maybe he drains their bodies, in order to become corporeal. And he kills Lucy. Poor Lucy.) Far across the universe, in his TARDIS, the Doctor looks up, spider senses tingling. LOVELY! Now I'm sitting up.

But then... ah, but then... a big bloody blank. I have no idea. Well, obviously,

7 In *Doctor Who* 3.12/3.13, Lucy Saxon (played by Alexandra Moen) is the wife of Harold Saxon, aka the Master, during his tenures as Defence Minister and Prime Minister of the UK. Later, she shoots the Master, apparently killing him.
8 Having been shot by Lucy Saxon in *Doctor Who* 3.13, the Master dies, refusing to regenerate, unwilling to be the Doctor's prisoner. The Doctor cremates him on a pyre. However, soon after, a female hand with bright red fingernails picks up the Master's ring from the pyre's remains.

huge battle with the Doctor, but what's the actual plot? He can't *just* be battling the Doctor. That's the worst kind of Doctor/Master story. (Well, no, the worst kind of Doctor/Master story is when the Master has miniaturised himself by mistake, and needs someone to lift him out of his box... Dear God!)[9] The Master needs some huge plan. Probably Earth-based. This feels Earth-based. I don't have to write it for a good few months. I could probably wait till August. That's four months away. But that doesn't feel like long enough to cook up a super-duper two-part epic. Or am I being a wimp? Maybe I'm tired. Then again, ever since our Great Correspondence began, I knew what would happen in *The Stolen Earth*. Actually, I'd kept that story up my sleeve since the first year. It was always going to be my last series finale... and now I've been asked to cook up finale number two, and quite quickly, and it's like my heart is dying.

I can't tell you how much I'm worrying about myself, and how much I'm worrying about the story. It's not a healthy start, is it? It's not a healthy start for a two-parter. There's no story that I'm burning to write, yet. Plus, once I face the inevitable and get it down to the Doctor/Master head-to-head, surely I've played every variation on that? What could I do with the two of them that's new? That Series Three climax really did push every button. The Master, this time, would probably have to die and give his life-energy to save the Doctor. But that's awful! That's the opposite of what he'd do. But it's the only variation left. Unless he could somehow do that unwillingly...? But how does that work? Then again, how could you ever run out of material with two such brilliant characters?

But both the one- and two-parter would have the same ending. And this I love! I could write this now. The Doctor is dying, but with only a gentle radiation shimmer and regeneration glow on his hand – so he goes on his last, private odyssey. He goes to say goodbye to those that the Tenth Doctor has loved...

Captain Jack is walking across the Bay. He sees, a huge distance away, the TARDIS. The Doctor, standing there. The Doctor salutes him. Jack is gutted, because he knows, he just knows, what this means. He salutes back. A farewell. Oh, this is going to make me cry.

Cut to Martha Jones. She's with UNIT troops in some sort of abandoned factory, fighting a lone Sontaran. A Sontaran sniper. He's in a window, aiming his gun, got Martha right in his crosshair. He's squeezing the trigger, like Michael Grade... then *BAM*! The Doctor is behind him with a mallet, having hit the Probic Vent on the back of the sniper's neck. The Sontaran falls to the ground. Martha is unaware of this. All she hears is the sound of the TARDIS fading away.

In Ealing, Luke Smith is running along, running into the road. A car is coming. The screech of brakes! A hand reaches out, pulls him out of the way. It's the Doctor. Luke runs off to fetch Sarah Jane. She comes rushing out of 13 Bannerman Road... but the

---

9 This is the plot of 1984 *Doctor Who* serial *Planet of Fire*.

TARDIS is a long, long way away, and the Doctor is stepping inside. He gives her a final wave. And she knows. She just knows. This is really making me cry.

The next one is so indulgent, but if ever I'm to indulge myself...

In Waterstone's. A book signing. A queue of people. At a table, the author, with her book, *A Journal of Impossible Things*.[10] It's Jessica Hynes![11] She barely looks up as the next man asks for an autograph. 'To John, please.' He asks her if the book is really true. She says yes, she found her grandmother's diaries, from 1913, and she really did fall in love with a man from the stars. The man asks what he looked like. She says, 'He was tall and thin, with big wide eyes...' As she looks up, there's the Doctor. And she knows. He asks her if Joan was happy in the end. She says, 'Yes. Yes, she was.'

Then, a church. There's confetti and laughter, and there's Donna the bride again, pregnant, laughing away, her old self. She doesn't spot the Doctor watching from afar. But Wilf and Sylvia see him, and go to him, and say that the husband is a good man, he'll look after her, with some hint that Sylvia is now a lot nicer to Donna. The Doctor gives Wilf and Sylvia an envelope. It's a wedding present for Donna. Back outside the church, Wilf gives Donna the envelope. She opens it. A lottery ticket. And the Doctor walks away... back to the TARDIS, so tired, to regenerate all on his own.

As he regenerates, intercut with Jack, Martha, Sarah Jane, even Donna, just pausing to look at the sky. So sad. As though they can feel it. And then, maybe, only then, cut to the Doctor #2 and Rose, in the parallel universe, as they look at the sky, holding hands, because they both know what's happening.

And the Tenth Doctor dies.

Bloody hell, I really am crying. Ridiculous! If it makes me feel that much, then it's got to be good. I had to pause for an hour there. That upset me. I'm such a bloody girl. Oh, but reading back this e-mail, maybe I just answered myself. I should write the story that I *feel* the most. Which is the one-parter.

Or is there a way of getting both? Can I invent a two-parter that has the size of the Master story (not necessarily with the Master), but with the focus of the one-parter? Maybe that Prosthetix spaceship isn't in the middle of nowhere; maybe it's in the middle of a great big nasty war, and you fill the two episodes with that, while still reaching the realisation that it's all about this one little, unimportant family. Epic and intimate at the same time. I don't know. I seem to be stretching stories out of their natural shape. By combining them, I seem to be losing them – or maybe that's judging them too soon. I should let that thought simmer.

Argh, one or two parts? What do you think, Ben?

ENOUGH TYPING! Christ alive, sorry about that.

---

10 John Smith, the Doctor's human identity in *Doctor Who* 3.8/3.9, kept *A Journal of Impossible Things*, in which he recorded his strange and vivid dreams – actually memories of his life as the Doctor.
11 Jessica Hynes (née Stevenson) played Nurse Joan Redfern, John Smith's sweetheart in 1913, in *Doctor Who* 3.8/3.9.

FROM: BENJAMIN COOK TO: RUSSELL T DAVIES, TUESDAY 22 APRIL 2008 04:44:39 GMT

RE: MORE WOBBLING

Thank you so much for that e-mail. I don't know why you're apologising! I *want* to be updated, however long, complicated, and candid it may be. It's all good. And there, right at the end, you ask what I think, which is asking for trouble…

>>you're expecting The Ultimate Battle For The Universe, and what you get is a creaky old cargo ship, filmed in oh-so-familiar South Wales factories. I'm fighting the disappointment. My own disappointment.<<

I think you've answered your own question there. You say that the story you *feel* the most is the one-parter, but imagine pitching it to David. Describing the Prosthetix story to David. Telling him it out loud. I know you'd make it work, but it's too small for a swansong. I think – for what it's worth – the Master story is better. Much more exciting.

Couldn't you feature the Prosthetix family as a subplot in the two-part story? The Doctor battles to save everything, The Ultimate Battle For The Universe, and all the while we're thinking that's how he's going to die… but he doesn't. He survives. He lives. He's not supposed to live! But then, in the aftermath, he does something tiny, something personal, like saving the Prosthetix family from a leaky engine, or stopping Luke from running out in front of a car – and *that's* what kills him. He's saved the universe, but he keeps going, keeps fighting, because he wants to save *everyone*. He dies saving the little people. That's very him. A hint of arrogance, and a bloody great dollop of compassion.

Or have the Doctor hit by a bus or a truck. Yeah! Like Tony in *Skins*. Then he can go visit Captain Jack, and Martha, and Sarah Jane, and Little Miss Redfern, all covered in blood, and on crutches, and with one of his eyeballs hanging from its socket. What do you mean 'no'? Hey, come back! HEY!!!

>>once I face the inevitable and get it down to the Doctor/Master head-to-head, surely I've played every variation on that? What could I do with the two of them that's new?<<

Last time, the Master was Prime Minister. He was all-powerful. He was king of the bloody world. This time, can't you make him the underdog, pathetic, desperate, scrambling… and therefore more dangerous than ever? Like Lord Voldemort in the *Harry Potter* novels. Reborn, but vulnerable. He-Who-Must-Not-Be-Named was always scariest as that mutant-baby creature in *The Goblet of Fire*, compelling others to kill on his behalf, or strapped to the back of his victim's head in *The Philosopher's Stone*. (How nuts was that? Only JK could get away with it!) What if the Master didn't want to take over the universe, but was just trying to survive – or is that not what the Master is about, really? (He refused to regenerate at the end of *Last of the Time Lords*. He *wanted* to die.)

>>I can't tell you how much I'm worrying about myself, and how much I'm worrying

about the story.<<

Where do you think this insecurity is coming from?

FROM: RUSSELL T DAVIES TO: BENJAMIN COOK, TUESDAY 22 APRIL 2008 09:03:00 GMT

RE: MORE WOBBLING

I've got to go to London now, to appear in John Barrowman's documentary about being gay.[12] STOP LAUGHING!!! Christ alive, my poor career. But I couldn't refuse him.

Thank you for your 04:44 e-mail. I think you've just talked me into doing a two-parter! That's not Visible Ben; that's Boss Ben. You bastard.

Must run. I'll write more tonight.

FROM: RUSSELL T DAVIES TO: BENJAMIN COOK, TUESDAY 22 APRIL 2008 23:14:06 GMT

RE: MORE WOBBLING

That was a day and a half. I turned up, and Johnny B had no idea I was even coming! I suspect that we'll come across as revoltingly Out Media Gays. (OMG!) He even high-fived me at one point. On camera. Oh, we're going to look gross. Plus, as a gay man, who wants to be seen sitting next to him? I forgot to wear a sack on my head – though people may think that I am.

>>Where do you think this insecurity is coming from?<<

Right at the start, we agreed that you'd be signing up to every neurosis, you poor, *poor* bastard. So, here goes. Maybe the fact that I've got no full series to charge into next is making everything feel different. I'm lacking that engine. Maybe it all feels faintly off-colour because it's ending. Except, I don't think so. It's not the series. It's me. I keep wondering – I can't help it – whether this Great Correspondence, whether *The Writer's Tale*, has changed the scripts, or my reaction to them. (Don't worry, I'm not backing out!) Does opening up the scripts to you weaken them somehow? Did sharing them make me lose the loneliness of the job? The isolation? For want of a better word, the *suffering*? I told you at length, in those early e-mails, how this job drives me mad. Although I've had some bad times this year, none feels quite as bad as Series Three. *Last of the Time Lords* drove me demented. If I could measure it, then Series One, Two and Three were a ten on the Loony Scale. But this year, Series Four, feels like a seven. Was it writing to you? Did that take the pressure off? Did it stop being such a lonely job, and become a bit more fun?

Are the scripts less focused as a result? Or are they as good as they always were, and all I'm missing are the by-products, the angst, the secrecy of writing, the privacy, the proud and testosterone-fuelled feeling of 'I did this all on my own'? Maybe writing to you acts as a safety valve, takes away some of the pressure, and makes me feel better.

....
12 *The Making of Me: John Barrowman.*

I've been hesitant about saying this, because I don't want you to think that you've interfered or anything. I still love all this stuff. At heart, it might be the simple fact that I *need* something to worry about. Since the book is new, that's become my new worry. Also, if the job has driven me slightly less mad, isn't that good? It's healthier. Everything is a work in progress, so maybe I'm more aware of that process now. By keeping the doubt, maybe I'll keep questioning, and get better at writing. That's all I want to do, get better. I don't feel as burnt by the writing this year, so I think what I'm lacking is the sense of victory, the having-survived-it-all. Which is the process, not the script.

Or maybe I just worry too much. Talking of which…

>>it's too small for a swansong<<

I haven't quite abandoned the one-parter, but I can feel it weakening. It's still All Options Open, though. You say, 'Imagine pitching it to David,' but I'm only writing to you in depressive Great Correspondence mode. If I had to pitch that story as a beauty, then I could. 'Deep space… one, tiny, helpless spaceship drifts along. Inside, the most ordinary family in the universe… so ordinary that the Doctor's entire fate will hinge around them.' All said in that movie-trailer voice!

Interesting thoughts today, staring at a blank canvas with the Master: I thought, I like him homeless. Just for a bit. Great image. He'd have to hide, since everyone on Earth would know his face. I woke up this morning thinking that the best possible end to Part One would be planet Earth EXPLODING INTO PIECES!!! That's very Master, and a great thing to wake up thinking.

It did strike me, standing on Paddington Station today, that of all the blank canvases to have, this one's a beauty. So, no panic. Yet.

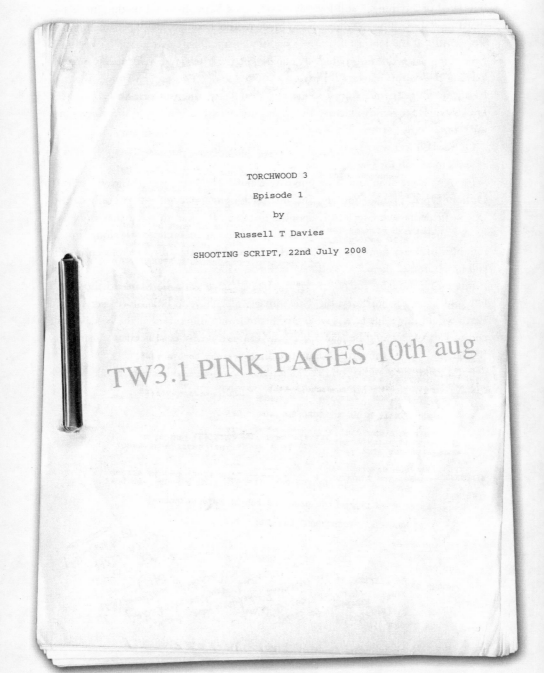

TORCHWOOD 3

Episode 1

by

Russell T Davies

SHOOTING SCRIPT, 22nd July 2008

TW3.1 PINK PAGES 10th aug

CHAPTER FIFTEEN

THE GOOD, THE BAD, AND THE QUEEN

In which *Beauty and the Beast* is praised to the skies,
The Matrix causes controversy,
and Russell receives a letter from Her Majesty

FROM: RUSSELL T DAVIES TO: BENJAMIN COOK, THURSDAY 24 APRIL 2008 23:14:06 GMT

HELLO

Sorry, I've been quiet for a day or two. Filming of *The Next Doctor* has been mental. Last night, they had about a thousand onlookers turn up in Gloucester! It's a nightmare for David, though he handles it so well. But I'm knackered. Julie too. I wondered to her whether we're getting slower. She said, 'No, we're just exhausted.' We've been doing this for five years now. Sometimes I forget.

FROM: BENJAMIN COOK TO: RUSSELL T DAVIES, FRIDAY 25 APRIL 2008 13:24:51 GMT

RE: HELLO

Russell! I just got off the phone to Catherine Tate. Lovely interview. She says that *Doctor Who* is now the job that she will measure all future jobs by. How nice is that? She admitted that, had you all been doing another series, she wouldn't have hesitated in signing up for it.

FROM: RUSSELL T DAVIES TO: BENJAMIN COOK, FRIDAY 25 APRIL 2008 13:40:17 GMT

RE: HELLO

I am *amazed* that Catherine said that about a second series – and gutted, because imagine how incredible a second series with Catherine and David would have been. But I'm hugely, properly, genuinely honoured. Thanks for telling me that.

RE: HELLO

Hey, happy birthday. Six Welsh BAFTAs for *Doctor Who*, and one for *Torchwood* – not a bad birthday present.

RE: HELLO

You've outed me. I'm 31 today.

Yes, I'm just back from the Welsh BAFTAs. Good night. Steven was there, on fine form. I gave an award to Glyn Houston ('I'm earning a fortune from that *Hand of Fear* DVD!').[1] I made merry with Gethin Jones. I told him that I loved him. On stage. Out loud. Got a big laugh. I'll do anything for a big laugh. But thank God I didn't tell anyone it was my birthday, or it would have been unbearable.

RE: HELLO

Here are some chapters of *The Writer's Tale* to read through – see attached document. I want to make sure that you're okay with all this being published. It's mostly harmless, but you've got to be happy.

RE: HELLO

Exciting! I've got to go do podcasts and commentaries with David now – the poor man, they're packing his days full of every bloody thing, because he's leaving Cardiff properly at the weekend – but I'll be back later. Can't wait.

RE: HELLO

Good stuff! Publish and be damned. It's weird, though, reading back our e-mails from last year. When I read what I wrote about being so excited about the end of 4.13, walking around the kitchen, banging things, ending up so happy that I sort of cry... it's kind of horrific, but also fascinating. Sitting here now, quite calm, I have a hard time recognising myself. It's as though I'm talking about a completely different person. I'd never have written stuff like that if I'd been doing a series of stone-cold-sober Essays On Writing. I'm so glad we did this.

THE MASTER'S BACK!

Hot news, right this very second: JOHN SIMM SAYS YES!!! You're the fourth person

---

1 Glyn Houston played Professor Owen Watson in 1976 *Doctor Who* serial *The Hand of Fear*.

to hear. (Andy Pryor, then Julie, then me, if you're counting.) John is filming in South Africa, but his agent phoned him to sound him out, tentatively, for returning for David's farewell episodes. It was an immediate yes. He'll move anything, clear everything, to do it. I'm so pleased, if only because when people say, 'Oh, I loved doing *Doctor Who*,' I can't help wondering if they *really* did. But obviously it's true.

I had a vague Master thought this morning. Standing by the tills in Tesco's, at 10.45am, I meshed the Doctor Will Do Anything Not To Die story with the Master Returns story. I thought, what if he really will do anything? What if the Doctor and the Master team up? What if the Doctor is so tempted by an offer of life – or survival – from the Master that he begins to compromise himself? I'm not sure where that's going, but it's interesting.

Also, I saw a great edition of *The Real Hustle* on BBC Three the other day (it was a repeat, I think), where they warn you how thieves and fraudsters operate… and it was perfect for the Master! Like, if you're dining in an open-air café, the thief waits until your glasses and plates are empty, then slings a towel over his arm, approaches the table like he's a waiter, clears your stuff, asks for your credit card, and then scarpers! It's amazing how people just handed their cards over. Imagine the Master doing that. He's the ultimate modern identity fraudster. You get this fast montage of him, literally, building up a new, fake life – first a credit card, then he buys a suit, then he steals a laptop, through the laptop he taps into someone's bank account, next thing you know he's smart and rich, and he's catching a flight to Geneva. Yeah, Geneva. Geneva is lurking in my head for some reason. I'm not sure why. It feels like the Master needs to leave the country. He'd know that the Doctor is looking for him, and it'd be good for this showdown, whatever it is, to go beyond England.

In other news, Samantha Bond has said yes to returning to *The Sarah Jane Adventures*. Andy Pryor's e-mail says, 'Mrs Wormwood lives!' Not camp at all.

FROM: BENJAMIN COOK TO: RUSSELL T DAVIES, THURSDAY 1 MAY 2008 12:12:01 GMT

RE: THE MASTER'S BACK

THE MASTER… REBORN! Phenomenal news. I'm on set at the minute, on the BBC's wireless connection. David has been soaked for the re-shoot of the climax to 4.13 – much better! – and now him and David Morrissey are heading towards a green screen, with wild looks in their eyes. More later…

FROM: RUSSELL T DAVIES TO: BENJAMIN COOK, TUESDAY 6 MAY 2008 00:58:38 GMT

RE: THE MASTER'S BACK!

David, Julie and Phil are off to Paris tomorrow, to see Kylie in concert… with an empty seat for me. They're staying at the George V, which is the poshest hotel in the city. Bloody *Torchwood* deadline! Look, I've failed to even start the script before midnight, and therefore I won't write anything tonight. Bollocks.

Oh, but I'm interviewed in the new issue of *Arena* magazine. It's rather nice. It doesn't feminise me, for once. Mind you, I'm called a 'celebrity writer', which I can't deny, but that's pretty horrific, isn't it?!

> **Text message from: Russell**
> Sent: 6-May-2008 20:15
> I'm getting texted photos from Kylie's concert. This just isn't fair!

> **Text message from: Ben**
> Sent: 6-May-2008 20:26
> Text them back one of you sat at your desk. Sobbing.

> **Text message from: Russell**
> Sent: 6-May-2008 20:33
> John Fay and James Moran have delivered Episodes 2 and 3. This makes me feel like a cheat and a fraudster.

> **Text message from: Ben**
> Sent: 6-May-2008 20:35
> Are the scripts any good?

> **Text message from: Russell**
> Sent: 6-May-2008 20:36
> For first drafts, they're marvellous.

FROM: RUSSELL T DAVIES TO: BENJAMIN COOK, WEDNESDAY 7 MAY 2008 17:29:22 GMT

RE: THE MASTER'S BACK!

I still haven't started my *Torchwood* script… but this morning, walking through the Bay, I said to myself, 'Stop beating yourself up about it.' So, I have! I feel much happier today. It's *The Apprentice* tonight. I'm just going to sit and watch it without worrying about what I should be doing.

FROM: BENJAMIN COOK TO: RUSSELL T DAVIES, WEDNESDAY 7 MAY 2008 20:26:47 GMT

RE: THE MASTER'S BACK

Cue the sound of something far off going very wrong somewhere…

FROM: RUSSELL T DAVIES TO: BENJAMIN COOK, THURSDAY 8 MAY 2008 20:11:31 GMT

RE: THE MASTER'S BACK!

We had a great big summit today — me, Julie, Piers, phoning Steven, David and Jane — about when to announce David's departure. Of course, stuff will leak and rumours will spread, but should we Hold The Line and say nothing? David wants to hold out until after Christmas, but we're all hoping to wait even longer, really. Top of the agenda was that Steven is keen to be announced as the new showrunner as soon as possible, and this will create a lot of David speculation. But we'll all just keep our heads down. It's worth it.

Also, watching 4.13 today (oh, it's good), we discussed how to end 4.12's mock-regeneration. Full trail? After the titles? Close-ups of the other characters? I announced, solemnly, 'I think it should end with no trail, only the words "TO BE CONTINUED".' That's *your* idea! Claimed as my own! Ha ha ha… oh, wait, now Julie is going to read this. Damn.

> **Text message from: Russell**
> Sent: 9-May-2008 18:27
> Julie has sent me home, because she says I look too tired. That makes a man feel good. Sent home! Still, today's *Torchwood* meetings were exciting. (Alien: 'We want ten per cent.' Civil Servant: 'Of what?' Alien: 'Your children!')

FROM: RUSSELL T DAVIES TO: BENJAMIN COOK, SUNDAY 11 MAY 2008 15:26:00 GMT

RE: THE MASTER'S BACK!

There's nothing better than going for a walk in the Cardiff sunshine, and bumping into Gareth David-Lloyd. He looks good. Yet again, that's one of those odd meetings where I want to say, 'We're going to kill you!' I suppose only writers and hitmen ever think that. But I can't tell him. It's not professional, until everything is signed and sealed and we know that the scripts work.

Talking of which, I'm so bloody dumb. You know that sequence I was envisaging of the Master acting out *The Real Hustle*, pretending to be a waiter, etc? Well, he's Harold Saxon! Everyone knows his face! That hit me like a thunderbolt today. I can't believe I forgot that. D'oh! Oh well. I'm an idiot.

FROM: BENJAMIN COOK TO: RUSSELL T DAVIES, FRIDAY 16 MAY 2008 19:16:22 GMT

BIG ANNOUNCEMENT?

Right, I'm hearing whispers that the Steven Announcement is likely to be next week. What's The Line, then? 'RUSSELL T DAVIES QUITS DR WHO'? 'STEVEN MOFFAT TAKES UP THE REINS'? Or is the Beeb going to try both?

FROM: RUSSELL T DAVIES TO: BENJAMIN COOK, FRIDAY 16 MAY 2008 21:43:59 GMT

RE: BIG ANNOUNCEMENT?

No, it's all very positive. To celebrate! The future! I am but a footnote. Apparently, it's going into *Broadcast* magazine this Wednesday.

FROM: BENJAMIN COOK TO: RUSSELL T DAVIES, SATURDAY 17 MAY 2008 23:51:59 GMT

RE: BIG ANNOUNCEMENT?

Russell! How's *Torchwood* coming along?

FROM: RUSSELL T DAVIES TO: BENJAMIN COOK, SUNDAY 18 MAY 2008 00:50:35 GMT

RE: BIG ANNOUNCEMENT?

Slowly. Oh, so slowly. We've had this brilliant idea of blowing up the Hub at the end of Episode 1, but sort of forgot to work out *why*. Small detail. I'll get there. At least I've started.

But I won't send you this script. I'll spare you the grief.

FROM: RUSSELL T DAVIES TO: BENJAMIN COOK, SUNDAY 18 MAY 2008 20:45:06 GMT

RE: BIG ANNOUNCEMENT?

Oh. My. God. I'm just going through my Manchester mail –

I have been offered an OBE.

HA HA HA HA HA HA HA HA HA HA HA HA HA HA HA HA HA HA HA HA HA HA!!!

FROM: BENJAMIN COOK TO: RUSSELL T DAVIES, SUNDAY 18 MAY 2008 22:33:06 GMT

RE: BIG ANNOUNCEMENT?

CONGRATULATIONS!!! That'll be for saving Buckingham Palace last Christmas. Turning the Royal Family into werewolves in *Tooth and Claw*? Not so much.

FROM: BENJAMIN COOK TO: RUSSELL T DAVIES, SUNDAY 18 MAY 2008 22:37:33 GMT

RE: BIG ANNOUNCEMENT?

Um… will you accept it? You will, won't you?

FROM: RUSSELL T DAVIES TO: BENJAMIN COOK, SUNDAY 18 MAY 2008 22:45:15 GMT

RE: BIG ANNOUNCEMENT?

I really don't know. I am torn. TORN! The 'British Empire', for God's sake! But it would make my father happy. He's 83 and blind. All the right reasons make sense – my father and my sisters, and this going to a gay man, and a writer – but I really think it's nonsense, and I'm not sure if I think it's *wrong*. I've never had to think about that before. I never thought I'd have to.

FROM: BENJAMIN COOK TO: RUSSELL T DAVIES, SUNDAY 18 MAY 2008 22:50:10 GMT

RE: BIG ANNOUNCEMENT?

If it's good enough for Verity Lambert…

FROM: RUSSELL T DAVIES TO: BENJAMIN COOK, SUNDAY 18 MAY 2008 23:09:35 GMT

RE: BIG ANNOUNCEMENT?

I might ask Paul Abbott what he thinks. I can't help thinking that he must have turned down an OBE or two over the years.

Maybe I've been offered it because my parents once helped to abduct a spy.

FROM: BENJAMIN COOK TO: RUSSELL T DAVIES, MONDAY 19 MAY 2008 00:01:46 GMT

RE: BIG ANNOUNCEMENT?

Look. Russell. You know what my next question is going to be. You just know.

FROM: RUSSELL T DAVIES TO: BENJAMIN COOK, MONDAY 19 MAY 2008 00:19:58 GMT

RE: BIG ANNOUNCEMENT?

It was back in the '50s. My mum and dad were very big in Swansea Rugby Club, it was their whole life (see how I've followed them?), and there was a visiting team from... er, here I get vague. Romania? Somewhere like that. My mum and dad could both speak French, which was the only language they all had in common, so they were enlisted as translators. But then some men from the Foreign Office came to our house. They said that one of the rugby team wanted to defect, and it was 'in our interest' that he did so. (Okay, I'm making up the 'spy' bit, but it's close!) So, they arranged the whole thing. One night, there was a big do for the visiting team at some posh hotel in the Gower. At a certain time, my mum had to keep the blokes in charge talking, while my father was instructed to take The Man out into the gardens for a walk and a chat, which he did, and then men leapt from the bushes, bundled The Man away, and that was that. Disappeared into the night.

Ever since then, to this day, my parents have received Christmas cards off the Foreign Office. I only found this out because, when I was 13 or 14, I saw one of the cards and said, 'What's this for?' I'm from a family of spies!

FROM: BENJAMIN COOK TO: RUSSELL T DAVIES, MONDAY 19 MAY 2008 00:20:19 GMT

RE: BIG ANNOUNCEMENT?

You're in the wrong job, clearly. Writer? Pah! Spy? Oh, unless you combine the two. You are Jessica Fletcher, and I claim my five pounds.[2]

FROM: RUSSELL T DAVIES TO: BENJAMIN COOK, MONDAY 19 MAY 2008 00:29:07 GMT

RE: BIG ANNOUNCEMENT?

If I were Jessica Fletcher, you'd be dead by now. Everyone close to her cops it. You'd think the police would notice.

I once walked past Angela Lansbury at the BAFTAs. She was astonishingly beautiful.

---

2 Mystery writer and amateur detective Jessica Fletcher is a fictional character (portrayed by Angela Lansbury) in long-running American TV show *Murder, She Wrote*.

FROM: BENJAMIN COOK TO: RUSSELL T DAVIES, MONDAY 19 MAY 2008 00:35:11 GMT

RE: BIG ANNOUNCEMENT?

She was the voice of the teapot in *Beauty and the Beast*, wasn't she? 'Off to the cupboard with you now, Chip. It's past your bedtime.' Amazing.

FROM: RUSSELL T DAVIES TO: BENJAMIN COOK, MONDAY 19 MAY 2008 01:06:23 GMT

RE: BIG ANNOUNCEMENT?

Beauty and the Beast was my best experience in a cinema ever. (No, stop!) I went along to a Manchester cinema on a Tuesday afternoon, ages after it was released, and I was the only person in the auditorium. That's how films should be seen. It's so liberating. I laughed, I cried, I cheered when all the furniture decides to fight. Plus, it's easily the best Disney film. I've seen it dozens of times. I love it. It's sacrilege to say so, but that golden period of the late '80s to the '90s produced the *best* Disney cartoons of the lot.

And what about *The Little Mermaid*? It's beautiful. Really, truly beautiful. I've even got an Ursula mug somewhere (with the words 'I'm a very busy woman')![3] Best thing about that film? You cannot see where the happy ending is coming from. They all look doomed, the world is ending, all those ships are stirred up from the ocean floor… and then about six seconds before it happens (honestly, I timed this on the video once), you see the sharp prow of a ship turning round and heading for Ursula. Completely out of the blue… and yet it's the shipwreck in which they were playing in the very first scene. Oh, that's clever.

FROM: BENJAMIN COOK TO: RUSSELL T DAVIES, MONDAY 19 MAY 2008 01:10:04 GMT

RE: BIG ANNOUNCEMENT?

Yeah, *The Little Mermaid* is inspired. That scene where the Little Mermaid's father, Triton, is all alone, having lost his daughter, and he says in that deep, echoing voice, 'What have I done…?' God, I love that film. So few people like this stuff. No, that's not true. So few people *admit* to liking this stuff. Even Disney executives, I think.

FROM: RUSSELL T DAVIES TO: BENJAMIN COOK, MONDAY 19 MAY 2008 01:13:50 GMT

RE: BIG ANNOUNCEMENT?

It's the songs, stupid! A few years ago, they decided to make their cartoons with less songs… resulting in song-less, joyless, jokeless, singalong-less films, nowhere near as loved as those classics.

> **Text message from: Ben**
> Sent: 20-May-2008 18:06
> The Steven Announcement was today?! I've just read it! How's it gone for you? History in the making and all that. Or has it all been a bit anticlimactic?

---

3 Ursula the sea witch is *The Little Mermaid*'s chief antagonist.

> **Text message from: Russell**
> Sent: 20-May-2008 18:30
> I'll update you by e-mail later tonight. (By tomorrow, everyone will have forgotten who I am.)

> **Text message from: Ben**
> Sent: 20-May-2008 18:44
> Perhaps it's time to wear a name badge. It'll help them identify you when you sign on.

FROM: RUSSELL T DAVIES TO: BENJAMIN COOK, WEDNESDAY 21 MAY 2008 00:49:51 GMT

RE: BIG ANNOUNCEMENT?

So, blimey. Today. It was all a bit rushed at first, because the press release was meant to go out on Thursday, but *The Guardian* got a whiff of what was going on, and started chasing Steven, so we rush-released it. And then... well, nothing. Honestly! I bet Steven is being bombarded, but I've carried on as normal. I've had all of two e-mails and three texts. Two of those texts were from you! Oh, and my father thinking I'm unemployed. And it was on the eight o'clock BBC One news summary. That's very mad. Producers on the news! Phil Collinson phoned up, because he was in the gym with headphones on, and saw my face flash up on BBC News, and he thought I was dead. I told him, in that event, all channels will go to black.

But I don't really feel anything. In my heart, right down deep in my heart... nothing. I wish it felt like more, really. But it doesn't. Just a slight dismay that a lot of reports are calling it 'DAVIES LEAVES' instead of 'MOFFAT STARTS', but what can you do? Oh, and five seconds of fury, because a blog on *Media Guardian* says that I made the show 'too childish, too camp, and too gay'. TOO GAY? What the hell does 'too gay' mean? Seriously? You'd expect that from the *Mail*, but this is *The Guardian*. Still, that's the nature of blogging. No Standards Required.

I have, however, been singing *Beauty and the Beast* songs to myself all day. The villagers sing, 'We don't like / What we don't understand / In fact, it scares us...' Major psychology in two lines of a song. Ahh, Disney.

FROM: RUSSELL T DAVIES TO: BENJAMIN COOK, THURSDAY 22 MAY 2008 19:26:47 GMT

RE: FW: DOCTOR WHO

Oh dear. We've hit a sudden, screeching halt on *Torchwood*, because Freema might not be available after all. *Law & Order: UK* (loving that colon) wants to cast her in a lead role. That's a brilliant headhunting swoop from Richard Stokes and Chris Chibnall. They've moved straight from *Torchwood* to *Law & Order*, and they've pounced on Freema. Good move. Clever move. Can't blame them. Bless Freema. It's 13 episodes! On ITV! *(cont p396)*

MISS JONES

This sequence from Russell's first draft of *Torchwood: Children of Earth*, Episode 1, features Martha Jones. Actress Freema Agyeman had, at one stage, been pencilled in for the full series, but proved unavailable, so this cameo – ultimately unused – was written instead.

So, it's a Monday morning. At 8.40am, every child in the world just stopped – stopped in their tracks – for one minute, before continuing as though nothing had happened...

```
33. INT. MARTHA'S FLAT - DAY

MARTHA JONES - just dressed for work, going round picking up
keys & papers, busy, while on the mobile -

                    MARTHA
    - there's a UNIT Captain in Washington, Steve Davy,
    he's got a son and a daughter, he took them in for
    testing. Blood tests, sugar levels, that sort of thing,
    they even checked for radiation -

                                                    CUT TO:


34. INT. TORCHWOOD HUB, JACK'S OFFICE - DAY

INTERCUT with Martha, sc.33.

CAPTAIN JACK on his phone.

                    CAPTAIN JACK
    He let them experiment on his kids? Nice man. I like
    him.

                    MARTHA
    They're not experiments, they're tests. And they found
    nothing. No traces of anything.

                    CAPTAIN JACK
    Can you send me the results?

                    MARTHA
    No need. There's nothing to show.

                    CAPTAIN JACK
    ...Martha Jones, are you pulling rank on me?

                    MARTHA
    If I have to.
                        (beat)
    Look, this is worldwide. That puts UNIT in charge. It's
    not one of yours, Jack, Torchwood's more...
```

                         CAPTAIN JACK
    You calling me provincial?

                         MARTHA
    Well it's Cardiff, isn't it?

                         CAPTAIN JACK
    I keep telling you. Hand in that badge! Come and work
    with us.

MARTHA going to the window, pulling back the blinds…

FX: MARTHA set against DMP of NEW YORK, at sunrise.

                         MARTHA
    Yeah, like I'm really gonna move to South Wales, right
    now.

                         CAPTAIN JACK
    How's Tom?[1]

                         MARTHA
    He's good, yeah. You'd better come across for the
    wedding.

                         CAPTAIN JACK
    Oh, I don't want to start a fight. He is so jealous of
    me.

IANTO pops into the office.

                         IANTO
    You were right! He's back!

                         CAPTAIN JACK
    Ianto Jones just walked into my office, naked.

                         IANTO
    Martha, he's such a liar!

                         MARTHA
    Tell him hello from me!

                         CAPTAIN JACK
    Speak to you later — and keep me informed, yeah?

                         MARTHA
    Will do, see ya —

Jack hanging up, crossing to Ianto, both heading out —

                         CAPTAIN JACK
    What's he doing?

1 Thomas Milligan appeared in *Doctor Who* 3.13. In Series Four, it was revealed that he has become Martha's fiancé.

```
                            IANTO
        Waiting. Exactly like you said.


                                            CUT TO:


    35. INT. TORCHWOOD HUB - CONTINUOUS

    JACK & IANTO heading for a terminal, GWEN at her computer.

                            IANTO
        He's been there for 20 minutes.

                            GWEN
        Who has..?

    Gwen crossing to join them -

    ON SCREEN: CCTV FOOTAGE, HIGH ANGLE of Roald Dahl Plass. And
    standing there... RUPESH.²
```

2 Rupesh Patanjali (played by Rik Makarem) is a doctor from Cardiff's fictional St Helen's Hospital. Captain Jack considers hiring him as Torchwood's new medical officer.

A huge transatlantic crossover! But, but, but… unless that's solved tomorrow, which is unlikely, that leaves our *Torchwood* scripts in disarray. Ah, the show that lurches from emergency to emergency. (We're hoping that Freema will still be free for a few days on *The Sarah Jane Adventures*. Have I told you that? Martha and Sarah Jane battling Mrs Wormwood and a Sontaran in the series finale!)

In other news, Steven and I were both in Broadcasting House today. The Two Who Rule. It's lovely, actually. If there's a problem or a decision or a press release, I can turn to him and say, 'Up to you.' The relief!

FROM: RUSSELL T DAVIES TO: BENJAMIN COOK, WEDNESDAY 11 JUNE 2008 20:45:43 GMT

SORRY!

I can't stand it. I simply CAN'T STAND IT.

I can't *not* send you a script! It's been driving me mad. I've spent a ridiculous amount of time thinking about the not-sending. I'm not kidding. I've been closing down the script every night and feeling like there's something *missing*! So, it just makes life easier for me if I send you this bloody *Torchwood* script. I am sorry. I told you that writers were creatures of habit and superstition, and now you're hardwired in. God help you. You don't even have to read it. Honestly. Even if you do read it, you don't have to like it.

I really am sorry. I hate to lumber you. It won't be for life. (Or if it is, have me killed.)

FROM: BENJAMIN COOK TO: RUSSELL T DAVIES, WEDNESDAY 11 JUNE 2008 20:52:19 GMT

RE: SORRY!

Never worry about sending me scripts! Of course I love reading them. How could I not?

Even now, while cooking steak (yes, Wednesdays are all about steak and *The Apprentice*), I couldn't resist peeking at the first few pages. The Hub blows up![4] I know you said that you were going to destroy the Hub – but right at the top of the series? And we see it from the outside? That's going to be expensive. But what an incredible opening.

FROM: RUSSELL T DAVIES TO: BENJAMIN COOK, WEDNESDAY 11 JUNE 2008 23:09:01 GMT

RE: SORRY!

Steak. Damn. I just had a tuna sandwich.

Hey, thank you. For accepting the script. I do like that central idea of aliens broadcasting through children. That's creepy.

Someone rang me during *The Apprentice*. Can you believe that? I was so cross, I decided to answer the phone instead of ignoring it, just to tell them to sod off. But I'm glad Lee won.[5] Good old Lee. Rugged Lee.

FROM: RUSSELL T DAVIES TO: BENJAMIN COOK, THURSDAY 12 JUNE 2008 14:42:44 GMT

RE: SORRY!

This morning was the Dub for Episode 12. It is the most magnificent, bollocking mental, bloody wonderful extravaganza ever seen on screen. That is a fact. It's like having chocolate, and whisky, and steak, and cigarettes, while making love to a porn star on a luxury yacht in outer space. Dear God, it's brilliant. And you know what? The best bit is your idea to end with no trail, only 'TO BE CONTINUED'. The three words slam in, one at a time, in big gold lettering, TO! BE! CONTINUED! We rose up from our seats and applauded. We really did. What a great idea.

FROM: BENJAMIN COOK TO: RUSSELL T DAVIES, THURSDAY 12 JUNE 2008 15:36:20 GMT

RE: SORRY!

>>The best bit is your idea<<

Yes, it's all me. My work here is done.

FROM: BENJAMIN COOK TO: RUSSELL T DAVIES, FRIDAY 13 JUNE 2008 15:54:05 GMT

RE: SORRY!

You're an OBE! It's been announced! It's in the papers, so it must be true. It had better go to your head – I want an opportunity to turn to you and say, 'Oh Russell, you've changed.'

FROM: RUSSELL T DAVIES TO: BENJAMIN COOK, FRIDAY 13 JUNE 2008 16:10:59 GMT

RE: SORRY!

Yes, it's the OBE news. My phone is ringing, and ringing, and ringing. Of course, in

---

4 In Russell's original draft, the final scene of the episode – in which Gwen bursts out of the Torchwood Hub, running for her life, as Roald Dahl Plass explodes – was placed at the beginning of the episode, before cutting to the titles, then picking up the story from 24 hours earlier.
5 Lee McQueen, an IT recruitment sales manager from Princes Risborough, who won Series Four of *The Apprentice*.

amongst the ringing phone calls, there are my sisters. I'd forgotten to tell them. I really am terrible at this family lark. No, I haven't changed at all.

FROM: RUSSELL T DAVIES TO: BENJAMIN COOK, SATURDAY 14 JUNE 2008 11:07:23 GMT

RE: SORRY!

I'm only writing because at about 9.20am, I had a Very Good Idea… but I have to go to London now, so this e-mail is just a marker. I'll tell you when I get back. I've been puzzling for weeks now, what does that Master actually *do* when he returns? What's the most gobsmacking plan? He conquered the Earth for a whole year in Series Three, so how the hell do I top that? It's been driving me mad. I've been surly with Jane and Julie – and you! – for wanting him back, because I can't think of a scheme grandiose enough. And then, today, I did. It's a rare 'where do you get your ideas from?' notion that just popped into my head, and made me very happy. I'm so excited.

FROM: BENJAMIN COOK TO: RUSSELL T DAVIES, FRIDAY 13 JUNE 2008 15:54:05 GMT

RE: SORRY!

Another cliffhanger! You always do this. You were born to be a dramatist. I bet there is no London trip. You're goading me. (It's working.) I await your return from 'London'. I am gnawing my own arm off in anticipation. By tomorrow morning, all I shall have left is a stump.

FROM: RUSSELL T DAVIES TO: BENJAMIN COOK, SATURDAY 14 JUNE 2008 11:07:23 GMT

RE: SORRY!

So, right, anyway: what the hell does the Master do? For ages, I thought, blow up the Earth in the cliffhanger. Modern-day Earth, gone! But, hmm, no. It's always going to be re-created, isn't it? You don't really *believe* that. (Maybe you do, if you're eight years old. I haven't completely discounted that yet. It could happen somewhere.) Then I spent a long time thinking about body-swapping – so the Master becomes the Doctor and vice versa, which would give us Evil David Tennant. That would be fantastic, especially in his swansong. But again, it's predictable. And they'd only end up swapping back. Also, in David's swansong (why is it called a swansong?), I want to see the Doctor, not an evil version. I want him in all his wonderfulness, centre-stage. Plus, I've done body swaps in *New Earth*. So, what, what, what?! What brilliant, new, amazing plan could the Master come up with? Yesterday, bolt out of the blue, I thought –

Well, I thought of the end bit first, and then added what must vaguely happen beforehand, so… we're on Earth. There's some sort of science project researching human genomes. I don't know what for. Immortality, maybe. That always sounds good. Yeah, *The Immortality Gate*, that's a good title. It would have to be more advanced than human technology, so maybe there are aliens at work behind the scenes, maybe harmless aliens using the place as research or something, adding to the technology – and the Master is infiltrating the place, the Doctor hot on his heels – and then somehow this technology, whatever it is, needs to be transmittable. Or *made* transmittable by the flick of a switch, by the Master. This is the point. He puts *himself* into the machine. He transmits *himself*. Every single person on Earth falls to their knees. Their faces judder, fast, like that Jacob's Ladder effect, all blurred and violent as they change...

When they look up, EVERY SINGLE PERSON IS THE MASTER!!! He transmits himself into the human race. Everyone looks like him. Everyone *is* him. Men, women, kids – all the Master. The human race *becomes* the Master. All six billion of us. FX shots of hundreds of John Simms, all in the clothes they fell down in. Women, too! John Simm in drag! But the kids would still be little. They would be small John Simms. Teenagers as John Simm. A baby in a pram?! The Doctor runs into the street, and everyone is the Master – with the Master's consciousness, I suppose. (Or would they? What if they remain themselves, mentally? That's tempting. But difficult. They'd just go bonkers. It needs to be a world full of Masters, not a world full of people freaking out.) The Doctor's beloved race becomes his arch enemy. The faces! All those faces! Soldiers marching, all John Simm. Families together, all John Simm. Streets full of John Simm. It's the most striking image. It's nightmarish.

It's very *Being John Malkovich*, of course. But I only thought of that comparison afterwards. I was thinking along the lines of: the Master enslaves the human race, he projects himself into them, mind control to the nth degree, so they all become his slaves, all mentally controlled by him... no, boring, but... hold on, he projects himself *into* them... and those words sort of triggered the image of the faces. Of course, it's an FX nightmare. Any scene with a human in, after that, becomes a multi-green-screen extravaganza. (Imagine how many days John will have to spend on green screen!) That's where those harmless aliens become handy, because we might need to get off-world pronto. Anyway, all those problems to come – and I suppose it still has the inbuilt problem that of course it'll be switched back at the end. But so what? It's worth it, to see that nightmare image. It's worth it to see the Doctor's face, never mind the Master's.

Right. *Torchwood*. Prep starts in 15 hours!

FROM: BENJAMIN COOK TO: RUSSELL T DAVIES, SUNDAY 15 JUNE 2008 18:57:17 GMT

RE: SORRY!

I don't know which bit of your e-mail to reply to first! But I think I'll go with:

>>John Simm in drag!<

No, no, I won't. Really, I won't. I think I'll go with:

>>why is it called a swansong?<<

It refers to a dying swan that's mute until the moment of its death, when it sings a heavenly song – a bit like the Ood's song, I imagine. And then it dies. Hence, swansong. But I only know that because Tennyson wrote a poem about it.

>>The faces! All those faces! Soldiers marching, all John Simm.<<

Terrifying, yes! Nightmarish! It brings to mind *The Matrix* – the second one, I think, *The Matrix Reloaded*. I gave up after that. (Wachowski Brothers, what were you thinking?!) It's just like the Hugo Weaving character (is it Agent Smith?), in a black suit and tie, multiplied over and over and over. Brrr!

So, what's the next step? I mean, before you can develop this idea further, do you have to run it past The Mill? Maybe if you completely 3D-model John's head, you can transpose a lot of those faces without John having to replicate every single position…?

FROM: RUSSELL T DAVIES TO: BENJAMIN COOK, SUNDAY 15 JUNE 2008 19:44:44 GMT

RE: SORRY!
THE MATRIX!!!!!!

Bollocks.

I hate you.

Damn, damn, damn, that didn't even occur to me. I literally hadn't thought of that. But it's exactly the same! A multiple person, like a million Hugo Weavings! (And what the hell were those films about in the end? No wonder I'd blanked them.) That is such a pisser. If you'd seen my face when I got your e-mail…! But I've had 20 minutes and a *Coronation Street* to think about it, and I think I'll go ahead, partly because of the lack of other ideas, partly because a good idea is a good idea, and partly because I know that I didn't think, 'Oh, I'll do a *Matrix*.' Besides, it'll be so different. Completely different. Bloody hell, though. *The* bloody *Matrix*.

P.S. Swansong. That's beautiful. I like that.

FROM: RUSSELL T DAVIES TO: BENJAMIN COOK, MONDAY 16 JUNE 2008 01:49:08 GMT

RE: SORRY!
The Matrix! I am still staggered.

Here's a bit more *Torchwood* script, mostly rewriting. Today, we heard that Freema is completely booked up – no wonder, with 13 episodes of *Law & Order* to film – so she can't appear in the *Sarah Jane Adventures* finale either. Scripts all written, filming in three weeks' time. Nightmare! Etc. These things happen from time to time. Agents cock up dates. I've had to write her out of *Torchwood* completely. Not even a cameo. Poor Martha Jones.

> **Text message from: Russell**
> Sent: 16-Jun-2008 12:17
> Today's big idea: to replace Martha in *Sarah Jane* with the Brigadier![6]

6 UNIT's Brigadier Alistair Gordon Lethbridge-Stewart (played by Nicholas Courtney) first appeared in *Doctor Who* in 1968, and returned regularly from 1970 to 1974. His final appearance was in 1989 serial *Battlefield*.

> **Text message from: Ben**
> Sent: 16-Jun-2008 12:28
> OH YES! HOW BRILLIANT! Just don't get confused, and put the Brigadier in *Torchwood* snogging Ianto.

FROM: RUSSELL T DAVIES TO: BENJAMIN COOK, TUESDAY 17 JUNE 2008 02:30:17 GMT

RE: SORRY!

Here's more *Torchwood* script. It's getting quite interesting now. I had such a good time this afternoon, writing scenes of people chatting in kitchens. Gay people in kitchens. Ordinary stuff. It's been so long since I could do that. Four years? Five? I think that's why this script has taken so long; I've been gearing up to finding that style again. (Or did I find it too easy? Ah, never happy.) But how nice to write *Torchwood* characters as real people, with families, feuds, aches, and pains. That's the direction I always wanted to take it in for Series Three. Back to home and hearth. Chris Chibnall wrote such beautiful stuff at the end of Series Two by writing a prequel story for every character in *Fragments*, and a magnificent Gwen-based story in *Adrift*. He really paved the way. He showed me where to go. Come home, he said. Come home.

Meanwhile, some sort of phone call is on its way to John Barrowman. He has a couple of naked scenes this series. Although he's got a fantastic body (we've all seen most if it!), no actor is ever too happy about naked scenes. It's one of Andy Pryor's terrible jobs. He phones the agent, the agent phones John, and John can then talk to Andy or me direct, if he wants.

FROM: BENJAMIN COOK TO: RUSSELL T DAVIES, TUESDAY 17 JUNE 2008 02:40:27 GMT

RE: SORRY!

If one actor will strip off without hesitation, it's John… isn't it? Surely it's John?

FROM: RUSSELL T DAVIES TO: BENJAMIN COOK, TUESDAY 17 JUNE 2008 03:02:53 GMT

RE: SORRY!

You'd be surprised. I'm really quite interested to see what his reaction will be to this. But Captain Jack is blown to smithereens with a bomb in his stomach, then all his cells sort of draw back together, so there's no way he can wake up fully clothed.

The things I do to see arse.

FROM: RUSSELL T DAVIES TO: BENJAMIN COOK, WEDNESDAY 18 JUNE 2008 14:07:40 GMT

RE: SORRY!

I am within a spit and a cough of finishing this *Torchwood* script. I've been sitting here typing for ten days solid. Please. Help. Me.

I went downstairs earlier, and found Lis Sladen sitting on the floor in the lobby. Sarah Jane Smith! Just sitting there! 'I don't know what time my pick-up is.' So, I sat with her.

On the floor. For 20 minutes. I love that woman. You look into her eyes and think, 'Christ, she still looks 21.' How does she do that?

FROM: BENJAMIN COOK TO: RUSSELL T DAVIES, WEDNESDAY 18 JUNE 2008 14:09:10 GMT

RE: SORRY!

Portrait in her attic, I reckon.

FROM: RUSSELL T DAVIES TO: BENJAMIN COOK, TUESDAY 24 JUNE 2008 00:56:36 GMT

RE: SORRY!

I've got a stinking cold, so I didn't go to the *Sarah Jane* read-through today in case I gave the Brigadier pneumonia. Yes, THE BRIGADIER! Nicholas Courtney himself! Julie texted to say that he was fantastic, and she's not one to be all loved-up with the old series.

> **Text message from: Russell**
> Sent: 4-Jul-2008 20:54
> I'm stressing about *Journey's End*. We've promised so much with last week's cliffhanger to *The Stolen Earth*, and the frankly astonishing level of news coverage over the past week has surprised us all. I'm worried that people will switch off in disgust after the first scene tomorrow evening.[7] Foolish people.

> **Text message from: Ben**
> Sent: 4-Jul-2008 21:00
> Everyone will love every moment of Episode 13... until the end, when they'll feel let down by the lack of a 'What? What?? Whaaaat???' cliffhanger featuring the Cybermen.

> **Text message from: Russell**
> Sent: 4-Jul-2008 21:06
> He he. You killed *Doctor Who*.

FROM: BENJAMIN COOK TO: RUSSELL T DAVIES, SUNDAY 6 JULY 2008 10:30:12 GMT

JOURNEY'S END

My God! Have you seen the overnight viewing figures for *Journey's End*?!

FROM: RUSSELL T DAVIES TO: BENJAMIN COOK, SUNDAY 6 JULY 2008 10:40:20 GMT

RE: JOURNEY'S END

I know! 9.4 MILLION!!!!!!! This writing lark, eh? It's not bad, is it? The most watched

7 The cliffhanger to *Doctor Who* 4.12, broadcast on 28 June 2008, sees the Doctor start to regenerate.

programme of the week! Ha ha ha! It's *Doctor Who*'s first time in the Number One position in its whole 45-year history. It's gobsmacking. Someone should write a book about how we did it…!

FROM: RUSSELL T DAVIES TO: BENJAMIN COOK, MONDAY 7 JULY 2008 15:36:09 GMT

RE: JOURNEY'S END

Remember all that wrangling earlier this year over the two-Doctors-and-Rose scene on Bad Wolf Bay, because it didn't feel anything like human experience? Well, I've received an e-mail from lovely Pete Bowker…

> *In having one Doctor grieve for his lost love, while the other Doctor went off with that same lost love, you have written of that moment we all have when we make a choice. It is the grieving for the love we never had (and the sex we never had) because of the choices we made.*

It did work! I love that e-mail.

FROM: BENJAMIN COOK TO: RUSSELL T DAVIES, MONDAY 7 JULY 2008 16:22:51 GMT

RE: JOURNEY'S END

Camden ahoy! I'm moving my stuff into my new place on Wednesday. All this packing is sending me insane. So much stuff! Although, wasn't Camden bombed by the Daleks in *The Stolen Earth*? Epic location fail.

FROM: RUSSELL T DAVIES TO: BENJAMIN COOK, TUESDAY 8 JULY 2008 17:21:57 GMT

RE: JOURNEY'S END

Moving house, along with BT Internet, is the worst evil known to man. God help you.

I had a Very Good Idea today. Well, it was on Sunday, but I e-mailed this to Julie today, to see what she thinks:

> *Last Special. The Doctor up against the Master. Who better to have as a faithful companion, in the TARDIS, then Wilfred Mott?! I could make it work! It means Catherine cameoing in the background a little more than we'd planned, but just an extra day's filming on top of that wedding scene I'd mentioned. She wouldn't get her memory back. It would be a hoot. People love Bernard Cribbins. And it's such a shame that he never got to go on board the TARDIS and have a proper adventure. David would love it, too.*

Julie has just replied with the words 'GOLD DUST'! That's a deal, then. Both Bernard and Wilf have been ticking away in my head ever since I watched those final scenes of *Journey's End*, with him saluting the TARDIS in farewell. That's why you should watch stuff on transmission – it's inspiring! I thought, isn't it a shame that he never got to look inside the TARDIS? Remember when we first booked Bernard, and he thought he was going to travel in the TARDIS? He never did. Today, those thoughts coalesced.

All of a sudden, clear as day, I thought: I cannot let him go. I cannot let it end like that. I can't, I can't, I can't. I *must* write more stuff for him. Wilfred unleashed! We wanted different sort of companions for these Specials, so what could be better than Gramps?

As I said to Julie, bringing back Wilf will mean including a bit more Donna (hooray!), but she's not getting her memory back. No way. That's fixed. That really would spoil past stories. You'd have to glimpse her throughout this new story, just in the background, the Doctor having to avoid her, Wilf filling in the Doctor on what's happened to her life, with so much sadness. Like in *Journey's End*, when he says to the Doctor: 'But she was better with you!' I love that line. I'm not spoiling that.

Oh Christ, Donna is getting married! I have to include that for the ending. But that could act in my favour: she's all busy and distracted, the wedding-mad Donna of *The Runway Bride*, so Wilf is free to get out of the house and have an adventure of his own. I can see that scene quite clearly... the Doctor and Wilf sitting in a café, Donna pulls up opposite, she's come to pick up Wilf, she's beeping the horn, the Doctor looking at her through the café window (scenes through glass are always nicely shot – directors love them), while Wilf says, plaintively, that her life just isn't as good. Why doesn't she get out of the car to pick up Wilf? Won't she see the Doctor? I know she met him as John Smith at the end of 4.13, but this should feel, now, like he shouldn't ever be seen by her. Anyway, details, I can fix that.

What's more, Wilf has reminded me of that story that I described to you in the very first chapter of *The Writer's Tale*: the old codgers with their Alien Watch gang. Do you remember? I realised that I was imagining Wilf and the Doctor in that café with other people around them, a few old codgers, funny and wheezing away, plus a nice old lady that Wilf's taken a shine to. Enid, maybe? Nice name, Enid. My godmother was called Enid. Sweet, lovely characters. And I was thinking about this quite happily, until I realised that it's that Alien Watch group from Chapter 1 of our book! Those old codgers have sneaked back in. *The Writer's Tale* is intruding into the script, but in a good way. I believe the Alien Watch, that's the crucial thing. I believe that Wilf, having known the Doctor, would be watching the skies for aliens and fighting the good fight. Since Donna can't.

I know what I'm thinking of, too, with this greasy-spoon café: there was a brilliant scene in Paul Abbott's *Reckless: The Sequel*, where Robson Green's character, Owen, sits in a café with, er, someone – can't remember who – and pours out his problems. As the scene goes on, all the old men and women who sit about in greasy spoons all day begin to chip in to the dialogue, giving him advice. Lovely, slightly surreal scene. I've never forgotten it. Where do you get your ideas from? Paul Abbott! Best answer yet.

FROM: BENJAMIN COOK TO: RUSSELL T DAVIES, TUESDAY 8 JULY 2008 19:08:19 GMT

RE: JOURNEY'S END

I knew it! I knew you'd use that Alien Watch idea somewhere, eventually. It's too good and too funny to waste. Imagine them tracking down the Doctor!

FROM: RUSSELL T DAVIES TO: BENJAMIN COOK, TUESDAY 8 JULY 2008 19:33:26 GMT

RE: JOURNEY'S END

Also, today, I thought, let's make the Master part-skeleton! What do you think? He was as good as dead until the Sect of Saxon brought him back, so how about now, every so often, he shudders and transforms into a living skeleton? The Mill can do skeletons, although they're expensive and time-consuming (that's why we see so few Dalek exterminations), but this could be a proper skeleton, with real eyes. There's nothing creepier than eyes in a skeleton. In my experience! You only get flashes of it. The Master starts to shiver, and shake, and... he's a living skeleton! Scary.

FROM: RUSSELL T DAVIES TO: BENJAMIN COOK, THURSDAY 10 JULY 2008 21:28:09 GMT

RE: JOURNEY'S END

You on set with *Sarah Jane* tomorrow? I was going to come down, but now I've got to do phone interviews with Australia all morning. For three hours! I'll try to come along in the afternoon. What they don't know on set is that we haven't quite secured the rights to use the Brigadier yet! Oops. We're soldiering on (ho ho) in the hope that we can fix it, but there's always a brand new piece of madness to take us by surprise.[8]

Then, this afternoon, *Torchwood* turned out to need so much work that I had to cancel my trip to San Diego. Julie and I were supposed to be going at the end of the month. It's the huge Comic-Con convention, with about 100,000 guests (the room for the *Doctor Who* session has 4,000 seats!) and I'm supposed to go to promote *Doctor Who*... but no, I'll be in Cardiff Bay. Julie has people lining up for dinner, like the *Lost* people and an invite to the Skywalker ranch, so I'm even more pissed off that I'm not going.[9] I would have loved all that. A bit of sci-fi schmoozing. Still, she'll be wonderful. It turns out that Steven is going, and he's the Big Boss now, so that might actually be better for the show. All the same, today's been a real pisser.

Never mind that. Hooray for your new home. And our book goes to print tomorrow, in Germany. *Exterminieren*! So, good times, really. Hope you're really happy in Camden, Ben. With many adventures.

8 Shortly afterwards, Henry Lincoln and Mervyn Haisman, the writers who created Brigadier Lethbridge-Stewart back in the 1960s, granted the BBC permission to use the character in the *Sarah Jane Adventures* Series Two finale.
9 Skywalker Ranch, in secluded cut open country near Nicasio, California, is the workplace of George Lucas.

118   CONTINUED: 118

                              YOUNG CLEM
                    What's in there? What is it?

                              CAPTAIN JACK
                    Just go. Into the light.

                              YOUNG CLEM
                    It's safe, though. Isn't it?

                              CAPTAIN JACK
                    Yeah. It's safe.

                                                      CUT TO:

119   INT. WAREHOUSE - NIGHT 3   119

         CLEM scared, holding on to GWEN; she's fearing the worst,
         but trying to fight it. CAPTAIN JACK so still, so quiet.

                              GWEN
                    - no, but that's what he does, he
                    fights them, he fights aliens,
                    isn't that right, Jack?

                              CAPTAIN JACK
                    No.

                              GWEN
                    Then why were you there?

                              CAPTAIN JACK
                    I gave them the kids. It's all my
                    fault. 1965, I gave them 12
                    children.

                              GWEN
                    ...what for?

                              CAPTAIN JACK
                    As a gift.

         END OF EPISODE 3.3

CHAPTER SIXTEEN

EVERYTHING CHANGES

In which *Torchwood* climaxes with an anti-puberty drug,
Madonna moves in next door,
and the Eleventh Doctor arrives

FROM: RUSSELL T DAVIES TO: BENJAMIN COOK, THURSDAY 17 JULY 2008 17:06:09 GMT

THE BIG DINNER

Things are moving fast here, faster than I can say. *Torchwood* is in a desperate state. DESPERATE! The final episode climaxes with the classic line, 'Tell the professor we need that anti-puberty drug NOW!!!' I'm not kidding. And it's all my fault. I never paid the final episode enough attention. I am weeping. So –

First, a bit of context. Last night was a Big Dinner with Julie and Jane, discussing plans for the future, which boil down to: next May or June or July, whenever the Specials are more or less finished, I go to LA. To live! Seriously, that's what they're suggesting! With Jane arranging it all. (I'm like a baby in a pram.) I was bleating protestations like, 'I can't drive. Everyone drives in LA.' Jane says, 'Right, we'll get you an assistant. She can drive you.' I said, 'He.' She said, 'Yes, okay.' They were talking about where I'd like to live ('Hills or beach?'), and what I'd do (adapt *Bob & Rose* for the American market as a long-runner, or maybe *More Gay Men* set in LA, or maybe something brand new and unexpected), and it was just… mind-boggling. You wouldn't have recognised me at this meal, because I hardly said a word. I just sat there nodding and going 'uh-huh', but I was thinking… well I wasn't even thinking. My brain was spinning. In turmoil! Like… really?!

I got back to the hotel, and I just sat there for hours. I wish I'd had e-mail. I almost phoned you up, but then thought I'd sound too girly. But I was thinking… oh, a million things, like I'm too old for this, I should have gone when I was 30, not 45, it's too hot out there, I won't know anyone, I haven't told my boyfriend, I'm a bloody liability on my own in a city that's full of temptation.

I travelled back to Cardiff on the train this morning, read *Torchwood* Episodes 4 and 5, and then sat for six hours giving notes. I asked if we could delay production, and Julie said no, because it would cost us £250,000, and then, because there's no way out of it, I found myself volunteering to write Episode 5 – and maybe even Episode 4 – myself. That's two new scripts in the next fortnight, and it's going to kill me. And I sat there looking at this schedule, and the chaos, and the mess, the same old mess for the thousandth time, the mess that you get on every single sodding show anywhere ever, and suddenly I thought, clear as day, sod this, I'm going, I'm off to LA. I'm going to meet new people, and do new things, and learn new stuff. If I do end up in a meeting with scripts that need this much work – which I will, because it's the same the world over – then at least I will be doing so beside the pool, in the sun.

So, there we go. What strange days! It still feels far off and unreal, especially now that I'm back here in Cardiff, in the same old seat, like none of it ever happened. But look at this year: two more *Torchwood*s to write, two Specials to be co-written with Gareth Roberts and Phil Ford, plus the final two Specials all on my own... so it's like the rest of 2008, the whole bloody year, has vanished into a pit of work.

Right now, I think I'm going to sit and just watch bad TV. This will be my last chance to sit and do nothing for weeks.

FROM: BENJAMIN COOK TO: RUSSELL T DAVIES, FRIDAY 18 JULY 2008 01:47:58 GMT

RE: THE BIG DINNER
Tonight, I attended the UK DJ Championships Final, at Carling Academy Islington! Lots of scratching, spinning, beat-boxing and... actually, it was a lot of bloody noise. I spent the whole time texting my mate Alex, who'd gone to see *Mamma Mia! The Movie* (I think he's having 'a crisis'), trying to decide who's having the sillier night.

I got home to find an e-mail from another mate that says, 'You and Russell have sold out the National Theatre, almost! I could only get tickets in the circle!' Our Platform Event on 7 November, to promote the book, has 18 seats left out of 880! It only went on sale a week or so ago. Meanwhile, Roger Moore on 16 October has 283 unsold seats. Russell, you're officially more popular than James Bond! I think we should add another date, due to popular demand.

It sounds as though you've had an *incredible* couple of days. The Big Dinner! You're off to LA! Possibly! OH. MY. GOD!!! But the far-off and surreal will become very, very real ridiculously quickly. Was this offer from Jane really that unexpected? You must have known it was coming. It's the logical next step. You've all but conquered British TV – or will have, once you've overseen the definitive third series of *Torchwood* (I have faith) and David's *Doctor Who* finale – and maybe, dare I say it, you've outgrown it. If you don't make the move to LA, you'll always wonder, won't you? What could have been, etc. Besides, you've got to go, for the sake of *The Writer's Tale 2*! You're the main protagonist, and the main protagonist would head off into the sunset in the final chapter. But are you ready to be a small fish in a big pool, rather than British TV King?

Seriously, though – wow! Huge congratulations. Look, whether you stay here or go to LA, you'll do amazing things. I mean, what's left to say? If only I had some well-chosen words with which to end this e-mail... wait a minute, I know, Russell, listen...

Tell the professor, we need that anti-puberty drug! NOW!!!

FROM: RUSSELL T DAVIES TO: BENJAMIN COOK, FRIDAY 18 JULY 2008 02:26:02 GMT

RE: THE BIG DINNER

DJ Championships? Sadly, I'm with your mate Alex – I'm dying to see *Mamma Mia!* but can't find anyone who wants to see it with me. It would be too sad to sit there on my own. (My mate Peter was out in Greece when they were filming that, and Pierce Brosnan offered him a lift in his car! Pierce Brosnan!!!)

It's weird, this LA stuff. After I sent you that e-mail, I thought, I bet Ben is imagining that I've had all sorts of conversations about this over the last few months, and I just haven't bothered mentioning it, but... no, not really. It's sort of happened around me. It was mentioned, ages back, and I said, 'That'd be good,' and since then Julie has talked about it as definite, like 'When we're in America,' and I've just nodded. But that's it, really. That's all. I've sort of been swept along. Rather, I *let* myself be swept along. Maybe that's my version of cunning. But even at the dinner with Jane, she didn't exactly make an offer. It wasn't that formal. It was more of a nice chat, like, right, how are we going to do this? Very strange. I'm still trying not to think about it too much. But when you say that I'll be a small fish in a big pond, which is absolutely right, I instinctively think, oh good! I really do. That would be lovely. All that 'celebrity writer' stuff pisses me off. (That *Voyage of the Damned* press launch feeling has never really gone away.) I'm lucky, because I'd be small, but not poor – and not quite unknown, because the effect of the US *Queer as Folk* still rumbles on out there. Also, if the whole thing stinks, I could just come straight back here. Thank God, there aren't enough good writers in the UK for me to be out of work. That's horribly true.

I'm off to bed now. I've got the *Torchwood* Tone Meeting From Hell first thing tomorrow, sitting there saying, 'Ah yes, this scene won't actually happen. Nor this one. Nor this one. Nor...' Etc.

P.S. WE'VE SOLD OUT AT THE NATIONAL!!! Does that mean we have to sign 880 books afterwards? Ben, I think it does. Bloody hell. Equally, how fantastic!

FROM: RUSSELL T DAVIES TO: BENJAMIN COOK, SUNDAY 20 JULY 2008 02:25:32 GMT

RE: THE BIG DINNER

Friday's Tone Meeting lasted NINE HOURS! And that was only Episodes 1 to 3.

There's so much to do, and muggins here doesn't bloody know how the whole thing ends. (Well, I do – Jack has to kill his grandson, that's a given – but I don't know how and why we get there.) I think I was a bit cornered. When that happens, I'm rude to people. I've a feeling that I upset some people around that table. It kind of sums me up, that I can't actually tell if I have or not. I'm blind to myself. But the consequences were flying about this morning in e-mails and phone calls, and I... went to bed! I went to bed at 11am, and woke up at 6pm. I just closed down. That's one way to escape your problems. I recommend it. When I woke up, everything had calmed down and gone away. Well, until tomorrow.

Anyway, I want to update you on the *Doctor Who* Christmas Special. For ages, I've been thinking of doing that story about the family in the hotel on Christmas Eve, where Gran wishes they'd all disappear and they promptly vanish. As does everyone in the whole wide world! And then she meets the Doctor. Cue titles! Always loved that story – and always worried about it, because I can tell how hard it is to generate story out of an empty world. But now I've had another idea...

Christmas on Mars! A Mars base in the near future. It's not all wild and clever; it's much more real. Proper airlock doors that are difficult to open instead of just swooshing. We'd make that primitiveness part of the story. We could look at genuine NASA plans for a Mars colony, and extrapolate from that. Plus, added monster. I mentioned this Mars idea to Julie, and she liked it, but she said, 'Let's press ahead with the hotel idea for now.' We had a meeting with Phil Ford last Friday (11 July), in Pizza Express, and he loved the hotel idea. He came out with one brilliant, pivotal image, which really sold the story to me: imagine if the whole world is empty, and then you hear the lift ping! Something has arrived. That simple ping becomes the most terrifying sound in the world. Nice one. He's great to work with. He grabs ideas, and twists and turns them for all they're worth.

I'm still uneasy, though. It feels more Halloween-y than Christmas Day. Let's see.

FROM: RUSSELL T DAVIES TO: BENJAMIN COOK, MONDAY 21 JULY 2008 17:05:19 GMT

RE: THE BIG DINNER
I received Typo Of The Week this morning, a letter asking me to talk at the Oxford Student Union. 'Your work, including *Queer as Folk* and *The Second Coming*, confirms you as one of the television writers working in Britain today.' Do you think they meant to put an adjective in there? Sexiest? Tallest? Welsh-est?

FROM: BENJAMIN COOK TO: RUSSELL T DAVIES, TUESDAY 22 JULY 2008 03:01:29 GMT

RE: THE BIG DINNER
Oxford Uni ain't what it used to be.

FROM: RUSSELL T DAVIES TO: BENJAMIN COOK, TUESDAY 22 JULY 2008 10:15:03 GMT

RE: THE BIG DINNER

This *Torchwood* stuff is so bad, and so late, and so impossible to fix, that I went for a coffee in the Bay yesterday – and sat there for *four hours*. I just couldn't come home and face it. Four hours! I bought every newspaper and magazine under the sun (*New Scientist*!), just to delay coming back to this seat. What a disaster.

FROM: BENJAMIN COOK TO: RUSSELL T DAVIES, THURSDAY 24 JULY 2008 10:30:21 GMT

RE: THE BIG DINNER

Have you heard the latest from Ebury? *The Times* wants to buy the first serial rights for *The Writer's Tale*! How insane. They envisage publishing two extracts in the *Times 2* arts section. I think we should do TV adverts, too, in which you and I sit in leather wing-backed chairs, smoking pipes, promising a fascinating insight into art and culture and... shit.

FROM: RUSSELL T DAVIES TO: BENJAMIN COOK, THURSDAY 24 JULY 2008 13:07:18 GMT

RE: THE BIG DINNER

Serialised! In *The Times*! I'm still laughing. My first proper laugh in weeks. Since Friday, I've had two weeks to rewrite two episodes of *Torchwood*, and guess how much I've done? NOTHING. I am sitting here all day, every day, frozen in terror. Not writing a single word. I haven't got a clue how the whole thing ends. This is severe.

FROM: BENJAMIN COOK TO: RUSSELL T DAVIES, THURSDAY 24 JULY 2008 13:32:46 GMT

RE: THE BIG DINNER

When I've asked you whether you start writing a story with the ending in sight, or whether a leap into the dark is sometimes more thrilling, you've said that you always know the *emotional beats* of the ending. You know how it *feels*. You know which characters survive, and which don't. (Poor Ianto.) At this stage in the scripting process, I imagine you as playing, like, a giant game of Tetris, frantically manipulating a barrage of narrative elements (falling from the sky, in pretty-coloured blocks!) to form complete, workable storylines. Marvel at my metaphors, yeah! It must feel easier in hindsight, of course, but is this the first time that you've absolutely no idea how to fit together the pieces of story, to resolve the plot emotionally *and* structurally? Or has it ever been even more skin-of-your-teeth?

FROM: RUSSELL T DAVIES TO: BENJAMIN COOK, THURSDAY 24 JULY 2008 14:49:34 GMT

RE: THE BIG DINNER

The ending of *New Earth* was fairly skin-of-my-teeth, with those magical potions and things.[1] But the *real* ending, with Cassandra meeting her younger, human self, was always planned. This is why I, literally, cannot write scenes out of order. By not writing the Cassandra-and-Chip ending first, the climax gained in strength from everything that it had picked up along the way.[2] For example, in Rose and Cassandra's first encounter in *New Earth*, Cassandra calls Chip her 'favourite pattern'. But that line was a complete throwaway. It sounded camp and uncaring, I figured, for Cassandra to think of a clone as a swatch of fabric. However, once in place, I *used* that line. I thought, why is Chip her favourite pattern? Ah, because the Chip pattern was the last 'person' to tell her that she was beautiful. I knew that Future Cassandra (transplanted into Chip's body) would die in Human Cassandra's arms, but I hadn't planned on Future Cassandra calling her beautiful. That only occurred to me when I was writing Rose and Cassandra's encounter. When Cassandra said then that the last time she had been called beautiful was on that night long ago, I knew that it would form part of the ending. But of course it feels easier in hindsight.

Endings are at their most satisfying when the pieces of story slot together like… yeah, like Tetris! Great metaphor. Even on the soaps, I think you get the most satisfaction from those rare one-off episodes that impose a Beginning, Middle and End. Production mechanics – and the sheer volume – force different shapes on soaps. Most of the time, they're simply One Scene After Another. There's no intrinsic shape, but we're happy to watch that, because there's a different shape in our heads: our own knowledge of our working week, and the pattern that the soap will form across those five days. A string of lanterns across the week. *That's* the shape. So, planning a soap means that there are all sorts of technicalities to bear in mind – ones that don't relate to the actual story, but to the transmission itself. If, say, you always get your highest viewing figures on a Friday, then maybe you plan your Big Events for a Friday – or maybe, on the contrary, you plan Big Events for a Monday, so Monday's figures start to equal Friday's.

The tentative plan for *Torchwood* is that all five episodes will be show across one week, from Monday to Friday, on BBC One. The plotting is a whole science in itself, and fascinating. It's a story being written according to the transmission and cast workload. But then that's often the case on *Doctor Who*. Production rules.

FROM: RUSSELL T DAVIES TO: BENJAMIN COOK, MONDAY 28 JULY 2008 16:28:25 GMT

I ONLY WROTE TO SAY HELLO, BUT…

Last night, we went to see Kylie at the O2 Arena. She was brilliant. Truly amazing. I'm not really into those big arena shows, but this one was spectacular. Kylie's life must be so strange. I think she's even more magnificent now, for handling it so well. It's impossible, looking at her in that setting, to think that we got her to Upper Boat for

---

1 To save the infected, zombified humans in a hospital in New New York, the Doctor empties intravenous medical solutions into a disinfectant shower, and sprays the mixture on the diseased humans, who are instantly cured. The Doctor encourages them to spread the cure to the other sufferers through touch.
2 In *Doctor Who* 2.1, Cassandra has a devoted force-grown clone assistant called Chip.

three weeks! How the hell did that happen?

After the concert, we went backstage. Have you been backstage at one of these things, to see the life of a superstar?! You enter this cryptic world of whispers, and signals, and hints. It's like the Russian secret service. First of all, you go to a bar. But that's just a holding area. On the signal, you get taken to a smaller bar, which is really just an improvised dressing room, while people like Will Baker hint that Kylie *may* appear. 'Give it half an hour. See what happens.' Fair enough. She's just performed for two-and-a-half hours in the biggest show ever. I wouldn't blame her for telling everyone to piss off. But then comes the nod. We're all led down the corridor, to her dressing room… which is tiny, but decked out like a Hawaiian beach, complete with cocktail bar, and cocktail-bar woman who'll make you whatever you want… and there's the Pop Princess! Looking utterly beautiful in a dress that's beyond glittery!

Kylie is honestly so lovely. She greeted strangers like my old fella with a hug and a kiss, which made his day, and she was genuinely happy to see people like Louise Page. But all of this in some strange, fake Hawaii, in the echoing concrete jungle that's backstage at the Millennium Dome. The fact that Morvin, Foon and Midshipman Frame were there – and Russell Tovey's mother! – made it all the weirder. Russell's boyfriend was there, too. His beautiful, handsome, policeman boyfriend. Does his boyfriend know how lucky he is? Actually, I think he does. Bastard! Hmph.

Earlier in the day, we had the *Doctor Who* Prom at the Royal Albert Hall (have you read Caitlin's piece about it in *The Times*? It's so lovely, and so right), with the most awful *Torchwood* storms still raging. Me and Julie with fixed smiles, poor Euros unaware of quite how bad it is, and even my old fella, who I never talk to about work, asking, 'Has something gone wrong?' I'm wondering how long it'll take me to describe. I'll be quick…

John Fay has written some truly magnificent stuff for Episode 4, so I won't have to write that one after all – he's lovely, he can take the notes, and get it up to speed easily – but the gaping void of Episode 5 is staring at me, and we're seriously running out of time. When I said to you the other day that it's all my fault, I'm only just beginning to realise what has happened, in this new five-episode process. A long time back, we stared, all of us together, at the emptiness of Episode 5. We had no solution. Nothing. We had bits of plot, but no story, no essence, no real reason for the show to exist. So, I took a deep breath and… well, I gave away one of the best ideas I've ever had. The point being, it wasn't a *Torchwood* idea. It was a notion I've had in my head for about 20 years, and a series that I've always been dying to write, and something I'd talked about at length with Nicola Shindler, and Phil Collinson, and Julie, hoping that we could make it together one day. They loved it. They always said, 'Let's do it,' ahead of any other idea I've ever had.

It was, essentially, a family drama, in which the world goes to hell, ending with our nice, safe, comfy western society descending into anarchy or a military state. Those nightmare regimes that we see in Africa, or Bosnia, or in history – but right here, on our doorsteps, with ordinary people like you and me, and our mums and dads, and our brothers and sisters, not just watching it, but part of it. Brilliant idea. And now I find myself using it up on *Torchwood*. I love *Torchwood*, but this was a good six hours of drama, maybe 12 hours, maybe three years of drama, that I've been planning for decades, condensed onto the ending of a sci-fi spin-off thriller.

So, the raging that I mentioned, that raging has been me. I feel like I've cannibalised my own work, like my head is going into revolt. I've got a blank script, and I've got the material with which to fill those 70 pages, and yet… and yet my brain can't, won't, will not do it! While the clock is ticking. While everyone is waiting. While no other solution is appearing. Christ, I've been sour with people. I've been unbearable. Add to this the fact that I have to rewrite James Moran's Episode 3, and we're filming in three weeks! We're trying to book actors, but the classy ones – we're trying to get Peter Capaldi in as the civil servant (a distant descendant of Caecilius, I like to imagine, without his strapping son, sadly) – want to know the full story before they accept… and we haven't got one.

So, at the height of all this, I sort of walked out. I went to the cinema with my phone off. I saw *The Dark Knight* (very good, not brilliant), *WALL-E* (wonderful), and *Wanted* (great fun), just sitting in the dark all day long, with a flat mobile, wishing every bastard dead. I got back, eventually…. and I'm not sure anyone had even noticed I'd gone. What a walkout! I can't even do that properly.

It's still not resolved. We might have to split filming into two blocks, and get a new director in for Episodes 4 and 5, because they'll be so late – if they ever exist, because I can't think of a bloody ending – which takes us into September, October, all my 'spare time' gone, all impacting on the *Doctor Who* Specials. Oh, that's Christmas ruined. But that's par for the course, really.

FROM: BENJAMIN COOK TO: RUSSELL T DAVIES, MONDAY 28 JULY 2008 17:23:14 GMT

RE: I ONLY WROTE TO SAY HELLO, BUT...

Ouch. Ouch, ouch, ouch. You have to rewrite Episode 3 before you can tackle Episode 5, right? Isn't the read-through next Friday?! Do you think you're leaving it this late so that the sheer panic will provide the adrenalin?

FROM: RUSSELL T DAVIES TO: BENJAMIN COOK, MONDAY 28 JULY 2008 17:30:11 GMT

RE: I ONLY WROTE TO SAY HELLO, BUT...

Yeah, probably. What a stupid way to work. I'm finding it impossible to summon up the resources. Current progress on Episode 3 is zero pages. But it wasn't a completely wasted day. I had one good idea for Gareth's *Doctor Who* Special this afternoon –

To update you, we've moved on from spaceships, lasers and X-wing fighters, or even the Doctor on board the Starship *Enterprise*. There's a lot of promise in those ideas, but the conversations haven't taken off. Shame. Except, talking about dogfights and space bases, we wondered who or what the tough, female pilot (the Companion Of The Week) is fighting. I suggested the Chelonians. The Chelonians are man-sized tortoises from Gareth's '90s *Doctor Who* novel *The Highest Science*, so he owns the copyright. Neill Gorton would have a brilliant time creating spaceship-flying tortoises, with flying-helmet goggles on. I did float another idea: a classic double-decker bus in outer space. The image has been floating about in my head for ages. An ordinary bus, full of ordinary people, goes through a wormhole, ends up in the middle of a dogfight in outer space. ('Where does the bus get its oxygen from?' Oh, shut up!)

Gareth went away to write up a treatment. He e-mailed to say, 'If this is a war, with a space base and soldiers, it's going to be gritty, right?' 'Okay,' I say, 'follow the story. Make it gritty.' But when he phoned me to describe his story, he had the Doctor and the pilot reach the space base only to discover that it's… an outer-space hotel, with bellboys, and lifts, and mysteriously disappearing guests! (They were being taken down to the planet below, to be implanted with alien eggs, because eggs = Easter.) Gritty? A hotel?! That's not gritty. That's *Thoroughly Modern Millie*. Besides, I hated the hotel. A sci-fi hotel could make a good episode of *Doctor Who*, but it has to be the central premise. This story had the hotel, but still with the dogfights, and the war, and the pilot. That's a ramshackle shed-load of random ideas jammed together.

So, we went back to the bus idea, the red double-decker bus in space, and actually the boring question of 'How do they breathe?' was more important than it first seemed. You could magic up an oxygen field – maybe the Doctor is carrying it with him, just in case! – but it all seemed a bit lucky. Right, okay, forget outer space. What if this bus goes through a wormhole and lands on a planet? That's still a great, surreal image, maybe even better than space. But film where? A beach? A quarry? There are some amazing, empty beaches further along the coast, windswept and bleak –

Ah. Hold on. At this point, someone (I can't remember who) pointed out that we're filming in January. It's going to be freezing. Worse, we'll have very little sunlight. This alien vista doesn't feel like a night shoot somehow. It should be open, and wide, and amazing. So, I open my gob… and cannibalise myself! Again! Ages ago, I'd asked Julie whether we could have foreign filming for 4.17/4.18. It was way back, just after the transmission of *The Fires of Pompeii*. I'd thought, why aren't we aiming for those visuals again? I'd said, 'Let's find a desert. Let's have the last confrontation between the Doctor and the Master in a wide-open desert. Sky. Sun. Bleached bones. Epic.' And Julie had said yes, because she makes things happen. But now, but now… ohh, I had to say, heavy-hearted, 'Well, if we're going to a desert, what about using it for Gareth's story? A bus, in the desert, for real.' Julie said, 'What about the two-part Master story?' I said, 'Tough. I'll have to think of something else.' So, it was done. Gareth delighted, obviously.

At the same time, the flying idea lingered, because I knew that there was only one ending: to get out of the desert, back through the wormhole, the bus has to fly. Antigravity clamps or something. Maybe another alien ship has crash-landed, too. It's staffed by Friendly Outer-Space Flies (no longer Chelonians, because we can't ask an actor to wear a tortoise suit in the bloody desert – we'd kill him), and the Flies provide the clamps. The triumphant image at the end is the double-decker bus, driven by the Doctor, soaring back through the wormhole, and flying over London. Hooray! (Never mind that red double-deckers are no longer in service. They are in *Doctor Who* world.)

We'd lost a lot, though. No dogfights meant no pilot. No companion! The Companion Of The Week has to be someone on the bus instead. Okay, plucky young girl, we can do that. What if the double-decker is an open-top tourist bus, and she's the guide? Gareth worked that up: alien planet, CGI stingray-creatures about to use the wormhole to swarm to Earth (nice!), and a tour guide called Rebecca. Except, the tour guide isn't working. This is what Gareth e-mailed me this morning:

> *My idea is that she's our version of Tracy Turnblad from* Hairspray – *a big, happy, fat girl – and she's the guide on the tour bus. It's a job that's not going anywhere, and she's been wandering through life aimlessly, but apparently happily. But now she's getting older, and none of her big dreams ever worked out… until this day, when, thanks to the Doctor, the entire universe and all its possibilities unfold around her. She's the kind of person that can only come good when there's a crisis on. Over the episode, we see her get more confident, more capable, more serious. At the end, I'd like her to head off into space with the Chelonians as an ambassador between them and other races. Earth was just never big enough for her.*

But I'm not keen. Much as I love Tracy Turnblad, I can't quite see her in *Doctor Who*. However, we're running out of time. All our leisurely spare months of development are disappearing. Then, this afternoon, I had a sudden fit of ideas…

What if she's a jewel thief? A top-class, glamorous cat burglar? The Black Canary, that sort of thing.[3] Scene 1, she's flying down on wires to steal something valuable from a top-security vault. (Something that'll be handy in solving the plot at the end, as it happens. A jewel would be fantastic, but I've done that in *Tooth and Claw*. Some sort of software…?) Alarms go off, she's on the run, skedaddles out of the building. Hermione (I'm calling her Hermione) reaches the street, but sees her getaway driver surrounded by police. She runs off, and we're into a busy London street, crowds, people – she walks past a police box! – she's walking along fast, clutching her prize, but there are more policemen ahead of her, on walkie-talkies. So, she does the only thing she can do. She steps onto a bus. The nearest bus. The London double-decker. With the Doctor on board! This is all fast, only two pages. She's clutching her stolen goods, maybe a police car appears behind the bus, so she's getting tenser and tenser (the Doctor maybe noticing, maybe not, because he's got a gadget that's reading strange space-time shenanigans), maybe the police see her and start to give chase.

---

3 The Black Canary is a DC Comics superhero, noted for her martial arts skills. She was created by writer Robert Kanigher and artist Carmine Infantino, and first appeared in *Flash Comics* #86, in August 1947.

Next thing you know, the bus has gone into a tunnel, *whoosh*, wormhole, bright lights… and they drive onto an alien planet! The Doctor and Europe's greatest cat burglar (armed with wires, clamps and weapons in her little black bag), thrown together to survive. The middle of the story is still empty, but back home, at the end, Hermione thinks she's about to run off – maybe she thinks she could travel with the Doctor? – but she's arrested. Or maybe, even better, she's arrested, but then we see her escape, with a final smile at the Doctor, like 'Until we meet again!' Nice. Sexy. Fun. That's just a rough idea, but a good character, instantly sell-able to a guest actress, and a great partnership for the Doctor – a sexy, sassy, hard-but-lovely woman with the heart of a thief.

That is how to invent a story.

FROM: BENJAMIN COOK TO: RUSSELL T DAVIES, MONDAY 28 JULY 2008 17:48:30 GMT

RE: I ONLY WROTE TO SAY HELLO, BUT…

Too many writers tackle a) character and b) story as though they're separate things, but it's one big intermingled whole, isn't it? Who Hermione is *is* the story. (Even more so since she's the Companion Of The Week.) Not sure about the name Hermione, though. And can you really get a double-decker London bus into the desert on a BBC budget?

FROM: RUSSELL T DAVIES TO: BENJAMIN COOK, MONDAY 28 JULY 2008 17:53:27 GMT

RE: I ONLY WROTE TO SAY HELLO, BUT…

Ben, with this team, anything is possible. Julie and I took Ed Thomas to one side and said, 'Bus. Desert. Can we do it?' A pause of about one and a half seconds. 'Yes.' I absolutely love that man. Anyone else would run away. Or punch us. He just said, 'Yes.' And then he said, 'Morocco would be best. I'll do some sums.' That's all so far, although I think Tunisia is also a possibility (long history of sci-fi filming there, because of *Star Wars*, etc), but we'll see. We might yet end up in the Gower. In January.

FROM: RUSSELL T DAVIES TO: BENJAMIN COOK, TUESDAY 29 JULY 2008 22:11:38 GMT

RE: I ONLY WROTE TO SAY HELLO, BUT…

I discussed Hermione with Gareth today. It has, literally, galvanised him. He lit up. I could hear his mind whirring – or I would have, if it hadn't been over e-mail. That's got to be good, for a writer. We've scheduled a face-to-face meeting for Friday.

Meanwhile, Phil Ford's outline for the Christmas Special arrived today. It doesn't work. I knew it. He's worked so hard on it (and it's called *A Midwinter's Tale*, which is beautiful), but it's come out as sword and sorcery. I hate sword and sorcery. It's got an alien princess with a funny name, who's come to Earth to be married. The lift goes ping, the Doctor and Gran are terrified, they run to see who's there… and out steps the Queen of the Shi'ar, with two muscled bodyguards. Now, I love a muscled bodyguard, but only in real life. (I see them often.) The plot ends up with them chasing through secret corridors underneath Buckingham Palace. Normally, I'd work on any storyline to get it moving, but this feels like a dead end. Not Phil's fault. I feel guilty, because it's taken him ages to fill these pages, but I don't think we can proceed with this. I don't want to. I don't want to spend licence-fee-payer's money on it. I don't *believe* it.

So, Christmas on Mars! Poor Phil. But he's a grown-up. He won't mind.

FROM: RUSSELL T DAVIES TO: BENJAMIN COOK, FRIDAY 1 AUGUST 2008 01:52:28 GMT

RE: I ONLY WROTE TO SAY HELLO, BUT...
DISASTER!!! Noel Clarke has pulled out of *Torchwood*. He's got a part in a Michael Winterbottom film. Damn, damn, damn. I mean, that's brilliant for Noel – you watch it, he's a star, that man, just watch him rise – but yikes! We've lost Mickey! Those scripts are like splintered matchsticks. They're in pieces. Tiny pieces. It's so drastic, I'm actually laughing.

FROM: BENJAMIN COOK TO: RUSSELL T DAVIES, FRIDAY 1 AUGUST 2008 01:59:02 GMT

RE: I ONLY WROTE TO SAY HELLO, BUT...
I hadn't realised that Mickey was going to be in this series of *Torchwood*. He isn't in your Episode 1, and that's all I've read. Why hadn't you booked Noel for *Torchwood* already? The read-through is next Friday!

FROM: RUSSELL T DAVIES TO: BENJAMIN COOK, FRIDAY 1 AUGUST 2008 02:10:29 GMT

RE: I ONLY WROTE TO SAY HELLO, BUT...
To book actors, you need specific dates, which means that we need a schedule. The schedule can't be fixed until the scripts are ready. The *Torchwood* scripts are nowhere near fixed. (Noel would have appeared in Episodes 4 and 5.) In other words, it's probably my fault again. But this isn't unusual. The schedule/booking/script conundrum lies at the heart of every TV drama ever made, and it explains why the whole of the industry operates in a panic all the time, everywhere, because no one ever has the money to block-book guest actors for the whole filming period. That's partly why films cost so much, so they *can* book actors throughout.

Sometimes, if someone has two jobs, you can wrangle dates with the other production company, but apparently this Winterbottom film can't change its dates at all. Maybe we're being equally intransigent. Still, it's shocked me out of that not-writing-anything depression, like a jolt. No time to sit about moping. I'm typing like the wind! I managed 24 pages today.

In other news... oh, who am I kidding? There is no other news. My life is a *Torchwood* hurricane. If there's a Series Four, I'm running for the hills.

FROM: BENJAMIN COOK TO: RUSSELL T DAVIES, FRIDAY 1 AUGUST 2008 02:17:18 GMT

RE: I ONLY WROTE TO SAY HELLO, BUT...

Is this the worst situation you've ever found yourself in during the scripting of a TV show? If not, can you think of a worse example? Go on, it'll make you feel better! It'll put this into perspective. Yes, Russell, perspective.

FROM: RUSSELL T DAVIES TO: BENJAMIN COOK, FRIDAY 1 AUGUST 2008 02:20:55 GMT

RE: I ONLY WROTE TO SAY HELLO, BUT...

Is it the worst? I had to have a think. Truth be told, the production problems are never the worst, because they're exciting. I'm invigorated. Honestly, I am. I'm full of energy. When Julie phoned to tell me the Noel news, I thought of the answer on the spot. (We're not replacing him. That would be awful. We're just reorganising the entire story so that we never need him in the first place – which is more work, because it affects the movements of every other character, but it tightens the whole thing.) The really bad times are the actual writing, new writing, starting from scratch. That's when I end up walking around the Bay, doing my head in, because that's just emptiness. Nothing exists. Or too many options exist. This problem, at least, has 75 pages of Episode 3 yelling at me, waiting to be fixed –

Hey. You're right. That *has* made me feel better.

FROM: RUSSELL T DAVIES TO: BENJAMIN COOK, FRIDAY 1 AUGUST 2008 02:31:03 GMT

RE: I ONLY WROTE TO SAY HELLO, BUT...

Actually – I'm still thinking about it – the worst times are when you have to lie. I hate that. I hate lying. It catches up with you in the end. Always. Never lie!

FROM: BENJAMIN COOK TO: RUSSELL T DAVIES, FRIDAY 1 AUGUST 2008 02:35:00 GMT

RE: I ONLY WROTE TO SAY HELLO, BUT...

I want to know more about lying. (Yes!) Don't you have to lie all the time in this business? At every press launch, for a start? In every interview? Even at Tone Meetings? And auditions? And every time you're asked, 'How's the writing going?'...? Isn't writing one big fat lie? Or is that the one place where the truth can out?

How much have you lied over the course of this Great Correspondence?

Honestly?!

FROM: RUSSELL T DAVIES TO: BENJAMIN COOK, FRIDAY 1 AUGUST 2008 02:38:37 GMT

RE: I ONLY WROTE TO SAY HELLO, BUT...

I like your lying questions. I mean, I like your questions about lying. I must finish more *Torchwood* tonight... but I will give lying some thought (ha ha!), and get back to you. I promise.

FROM: RUSSELL T DAVIES TO: BENJAMIN COOK, SATURDAY 2 AUGUST 2008 22:17:12 GMT

RE: I ONLY WROTE TO SAY HELLO, BUT...

Great meetings with Gareth and Phil yesterday. In Starbucks! Phil was especially lovely. It was clear how much he'd suffered to make a story out of the Gran and the hotel. I'm kicking myself, because I should have stepped in sooner and saved us all time. So, yes, a Mars base, 2030 or 2050, not the far future, nice and reachable. We're still thinking of someone like Helen Mirren. She could be the wise, tough boss of the base. We all thought of her as Russian. The monster should be some sort of creeping possession, taking over crewmembers – something from the air? The soil? And the thing I love most about this, the thing that I keep stressing, is... messages from home. Those flickering videos of wives and kids, beaming from Earth on Christmas Eve, messages of love across outer space. Marvellous. There has to be some way to make that pivotal, not just texture. But we were all very happy. Big smiles. You can *feel* this filling up with character, and incident, and action, and fun.

Today, Phil asked whether we can call it *Red Christmas*. Hmm. Nice. But I prefer *Christmas on Mars*. Does exactly what it says on the tin. The *Red* is clever, but sounds a bit shlocky to me, like red = blood. You'd call a Hammer Horror Christmas film that. Still, we'll see.

FROM: RUSSELL T DAVIES TO: BENJAMIN COOK, MONDAY 4 AUGUST 2008 02:31:46 GMT

RE: I ONLY WROTE TO SAY HELLO, BUT...

Listen to this. Torchwood is spying on a government/alien meeting, with a mole on the inside called Lois Habiba, who's using the Magic Contact Lenses that Martha wore in *Torchwood* 2.6. Through them, Torchwood can view whatever Lois sees, as though the contact lenses are cameras. Torchwood can send Lois instructions, by typing out messages that appear as text in the lenses, in her POV, like, right in her eyes. But contact lenses can't convey sound, obviously. (The lenses did convey sound waves in *Torchwood* last year, but I've got rid of that because... well, that's silly magic!) So, if someone is talking, Lois has to look at them. The lenses have software that can lip read, and translate that into a computer voice, which plays out at Torchwood's end... but Lois still has to be looking right at whoever's talking. If she's not, or can't, she has to scribble it down on a piece of paper, and look at that instead, to transmit it back to Torchwood. Plus, the alien hasn't got a mouth and talks through speakers, so Lois has to write, and then look at all the alien's words, too. As if that wasn't complicated enough, she writes everything in shorthand –

AAAAAAAAARGH!!! It's doing my head in. It's so tricky to write. Literally, I have to write what's happening, then Lois's version of that, then Torchwood's end of that, then the written words, then the texts, then the computer voice... AAAAAAAAAARGHAHAHAHAH!!! Great scene, great ideas, really classy thriller stuff, all being jammed together at 2.30am, in a rush, with no time to explore the potential. Such a shame.

FROM: BENJAMIN COOK TO: RUSSELL T DAVIES, MONDAY 4 AUGUST 2008 02:38:00 GMT

RE: I ONLY WROTE TO SAY HELLO, BUT...

Better to be grappling with a great idea at 2.30am than ploughing on with a terrible one.

FROM: RUSSELL T DAVIES TO: BENJAMIN COOK, MONDAY 4 AUGUST 2008 02:41:39 GMT

RE: I ONLY WROTE TO SAY HELLO, BUT...

Hmm, that's actually worked. I'll keep going. For now.

FROM: RUSSELL T DAVIES TO: BENJAMIN COOK, TUESDAY 5 AUGUST 2008 00:07:18 GMT

RE: I ONLY WROTE TO SAY HELLO, BUT...

Finally, I finished that script at 6pm. I guess I underestimated how much there was to do. But then I sat down, and channel-hopped, and there was *Voyage of the Damned* on BBC Three. I'm now calling *The Writer's Tale* back from the printers, because I want to say, 'That episode is BLOODY BRILLIANT!' It was like seeing it as new. My God, it's good.

FROM: BENJAMIN COOK TO: RUSSELL T DAVIES, THURSDAY 7 AUGUST 2008 12:02:23 GMT

RE: I ONLY WROTE TO SAY HELLO, BUT...

Have you seen David's *Hamlet* reviews? They're sensational. And the ones that aren't are only because he's off the telly. It was on the front page of *The Times*! He really is such a big star now. It couldn't happen to a nicer man. And you can't often say that.

FROM: RUSSELL T DAVIES TO: BENJAMIN COOK, THURSDAY 7 AUGUST 2008 13:18:16 GMT

RE: I ONLY WROTE TO SAY HELLO, BUT...

I couldn't agree more. I've been reading the reviews, too. Wonderful! It feels like only yesterday that you were with him on his very first day on *Doctor Who*, him in his dressing gown, facing down Harriet Jones. You in your hoodie, scribbling away on a notepad.

FROM: BENJAMIN COOK TO: RUSSELL T DAVIES, THURSDAY 7 AUGUST 2008 13:37:35 GMT

RE: I ONLY WROTE TO SAY HELLO, BUT...

We were on that waste ground in Brentford, weren't we? Next to the old Beecham's Pharmaceuticals factory. You're right, it does feel like only yesterday. After his first take, David announced, 'You can send wee Jimmy Krankie home! She's not needed! You can't get rid of me now.' Ha ha. Do you remember him saying how exciting (and terrifying) he'd found that first day? He said it felt as though he'd overdosed on tartrazine! Ah, I loved that shoot. Filming for a week at Clearwell Caves, in Gloucestershire. The Sycorax spaceship! With the crew lugging all the equipment up and down those bloody caves! And David's swordfight on the wing of the spaceship, filmed in a quarry on Barry Island, by the sea, in the blazing sunshine.

I interviewed David on Barry, in his stripy pyjamas. He said – I've just looked it up – 'How many other dramas do you get to have fantastic speeches, full of brilliant one-liners, and then do a sword fight? It's like, "Thanks, Russell! I'll take that, cheers." It's pretty cool.' Oh, and he mooned the paparazzi out at sea. I'd forgotten that. There was a speedboat circling, so he just went, 'I'm going to show them my arse,' and pulled down his pyjama bottoms. One of the make-up girls was standing right behind him. He hadn't realised. 'It's okay,' she said, 'it's nothing I haven't seen before.'

FROM: RUSSELL T DAVIES TO: BENJAMIN COOK, THURSDAY 7 AUGUST 2008 13:43:01 GMT

RE: I ONLY WROTE TO SAY HELLO, BUT...

It was such a strange time, *The Christmas Invasion*. Strange and thrilling. And scary! It was the first time we were making a programme that we knew to be a success – people were watching! My God, the extra pressure. That feeling never went away. I've always maintained, ever since then, that success is a lot harder to deal with than failure. Nice problem to have, I know, but all the same... the return of *Doctor Who* had gone from being this potentially odd, cult, short-lived experiment to a primetime bonanza – now with a Christmas Day slot! I think that's when we really set our eyes on the horizon, and decided to go for it. All our ambition unfurled, properly – me, Phil Collinson, Julie, Ed, everyone. That's when the show became a long-term, life-absorbing, time-eating commitment. I think you can see it in that episode. We didn't have any extra money for it – well, apart from having an extra 15 minutes' worth, because it's an hour long – but there's a massive size and boldness to that story. *Aliens of London* had been trying to go that far, but I was still testing the boundaries. It's one thing to have a spaceship hit Big Ben, but once you've got the Prime Minister appearing on TV, begging for the Doctor's help, then you're entering a completely different fictional world – *Doctor Who* itself in a very new shape. And I loved that shape. Never looked back. Yeah, love that episode.

And that's without even mentioning David's arrival!

FROM: BENJAMIN COOK TO: RUSSELL T DAVIES, THURSDAY 7 AUGUST 2008 13:59:26 GMT

RE: I ONLY WROTE TO SAY HELLO, BUT...

Yeah! My favourite moment from *The Christmas Invasion* was filming David's arrival on location at the Brandon Estate. The Tenth Doctor emerging from the TARDIS for the very first time (David: 'I can't believe this! I'm inside the TARDIS!'), David doing his big speech – 'Here we are, then. London, Earth, the Solar System, I did it. Jackie! Mickey! Blimey!' – in the middle of which an old man in a dirty mac wandered right through the middle of shot! Everyone staring at him, open-mouthed... and as he shuffled past Noel, this old bloke went, 'Bloody BBC. Full of poofs and homosexuals.' Completely ruined the Doctor's big entrance! As David said afterwards, 'I like how he specified poofs *and* homosexuals. Heaven forbid.'

FROM: RUSSELL T DAVIES TO: BENJAMIN COOK, THURSDAY 7 AUGUST 2008 20:12:14 GMT

RE: I ONLY WROTE TO SAY HELLO, BUT...

Phil Ford has delivered his *Red Christmas* treatment. It works! Good! Mind you, it's a bit too sci-fi smart for me. The inhabitants keep flying in a shuttle from one base to another. There should just be one base. This place should feel brave, desolate, raw and exposed, not part of a complex. And Phil has them terraforming, which I don't like, because that's massive and hugely sci-fi. It means they're taking over the whole planet. This should be a lonely, valiant bunch of scientists, fighting against the odds, not powerful at all. Still, wonderful characters. It's a delight to work with Phil. A constant delight. I'd be lost without him.

One other thought, which I've passed on to Gary Russell, to talk about with Phil: what if this is a doomed colony, famous in (future) history for everyone having died, for reasons unknown? Only the Doctor realises. It gives the story an epic quality. The Doctor is fighting history as well! What if he breaks the Laws of Time, he saves everyone, and that's his final arrogance? When the Ood appears at the end, it's like this time the Doctor has gone too far. It's time to die. There's an inevitable sense of justice behind his final summons.

FROM: RUSSELL T DAVIES TO: BENJAMIN COOK, MONDAY 11 AUGUST 2008 09:41:27 GMT

RE: I ONLY WROTE TO SAY HELLO, BUT...

I'm in Manchester, but heading back to Cardiff tonight. Julie has worked her magic with the schedule, and given me a slight reprieve, so I have until the end of August to write a completely new *Torchwood* Episode 5. I think I've thought of a way to end it. We had the read-through of Episodes 1 to 3, which was half fun, half agonising. Fun because I could see how much potential there is in this format, but agonising because I'm not sure we're going to get there. I was surrounded by actors saying, 'What happens to my character in the end?' I simply didn't know!

Blah, blah, blah. It's the usual lurching from one crisis to another.

FROM: RUSSELL T DAVIES TO: BENJAMIN COOK, TUESDAY 12 AUGUST 2008 00:46:00 GMT

RE: I ONLY WROTE TO SAY HELLO, BUT...

Ooh, I knew I had something to tell you...

I've read Steven's first script! Series Five, Episode 1!

FROM: BENJAMIN COOK TO: RUSSELL T DAVIES, TUESDAY 12 AUGUST 2008 00:55:49 GMT

RE: I ONLY WROTE TO SAY HELLO, BUT...

DON'T JUST SAY THAT!!!

What's it like? Is it brilliant? I bet it's brilliant. Please say it's brilliant.

FROM: RUSSELL T DAVIES TO: BENJAMIN COOK, TUESDAY 12 AUGUST 2008 00:59:54 GMT

RE: I ONLY WROTE TO SAY HELLO, BUT...

It is BRILLIANT. Of course it is! I so want it to be a big success. I love *Doctor Who*, and I love reading Steven's stuff best of all. It's a great story about... oh, I'm not going to spoil it for you. Only a year or so to wait! You'll survive.

But it's scary.

FROM: BENJAMIN COOK TO: RUSSELL T DAVIES, TUESDAY 12 AUGUST 2008 01:02:37 GMT

RE: I ONLY WROTE TO SAY HELLO, BUT...

How scary?

FROM: RUSSELL T DAVIES TO: BENJAMIN COOK, TUESDAY 12 AUGUST 2008 01:03:10 GMT

RE: I ONLY WROTE TO SAY HELLO, BUT...

Very.

FROM: BENJAMIN COOK TO: RUSSELL T DAVIES, TUESDAY 12 AUGUST 2008 01:04:44 GMT

RE: I ONLY WROTE TO SAY HELLO, BUT...

How very?

FROM: RUSSELL T DAVIES TO: BENJAMIN COOK, TUESDAY 12 AUGUST 2008 01:21:14 GMT

RE: I ONLY WROTE TO SAY HELLO, BUT...

More news. I forgot! We had proper interviews and everything – because Human Resources made us – and Tracie Simpson is now producer of the *Doctor Who* Specials. HOORAY! Well, she's doing Easter 2009 and the final two-parter, and Nikki Smith – who's been in charge of Series Two of *The Sarah Jane Adventures*, and who's absolutely lovely – will produce the second 2009 Special, because a) Easter 2009 has to be finished so fast that Tracie will have to sit right on top of post-production while the next Special is still being filmed, and b) Nikki really deserves this. Good news. They'll both be wonderful.

FROM: BENJAMIN COOK TO: RUSSELL T DAVIES, TUESDAY 12 AUGUST 2008 01:25:41 GMT

RE: I ONLY WROTE TO SAY HELLO, BUT...

So, when does the search for the new Doctor begin? And how does that even work? Who makes the offer? Is it Piers? Or Steven? Or Jane Tranter? Do they hold auditions? Take prospective candidates out for lunch? How did you do it with Chris and David? Also, these days, how do you think playing the Doctor affects an actor's career? Any negatives?

FROM: RUSSELL T DAVIES TO: BENJAMIN COOK, TUESDAY 12 AUGUST 2008 01:48:52 GMT

RE: I ONLY WROTE TO SAY HELLO, BUT...

Depends who they choose. Normally, Jane would make an offer of this size, though actually that wasn't true of Chris or David. Jane was involved with the discussions, but Julie made the actual offers. The change partly reflects how much bigger the role of the Doctor has become since David took over. If the offer is huge, or if you've never worked with the actor before, it's normal to approach the agent first. Julie and I asked David before his agent got involved, and Julie asked Catherine to come back before approaching her agent, but that's because we had a working relationship with them already. Even then, some agents could get prickly. It's always supposed to be agents first, so our very next words, as soon as we'd spoken to David, were 'And we'll phone your agent first thing tomorrow.' That's not because agents are power-mad or anything. Imagine if David had hated us on *Casanova*, and thought what we'd done to *Doctor Who* was an embarrassment; it would have been very awkward for him to face us. An agent protects you from that. (It's like when someone asks me direct to write a script. I hate that. I always tell them to go to my agent.) But with David, as with Catherine, we were sure that we were on safe ground – with them as people, not just as actors – before starting the conversation.

There are all sorts of other factors. What if Piers and Steven want to approach an actor who has a movie profile? An actor who doesn't *need* the part so much? An actor who won't bite off the BBC's hand? Or an actor whose agent is very film- and theatre-based, who looks down on TV? It's surprising how many of them are like that. Also, this will all be so top-secret (so secret that I'm being told nothing at this stage), with the worry that a non-TV agent might not understand the sheer secrecy of *Doctor Who*, and will waft past the post boy and casually tell him, so it could be online by tomorrow. (Do we get a press release ready?!)

>>how do you think, these days, playing the Doctor affects an actor's career?<<

Put simply, it has the most enormous beneficial effects. Look at David! Remember him in 2005? Stood in his pyjamas in Brentford? Or flashing his bum at the paparazzi on Barry Island? He's just about the country's most famous man now – apart from David Beckham, and he's abroad. For 99.999 per cent of actors, *Doctor Who* is the best opportunity in the world.

> **Text message from: Russell**
> Sent: 12-Aug-2008 17:49
> I've got Madonna living next door! She's staying at the St David's Hotel for ten days while she rehearses her new tour at the Millennium Stadium. This afternoon, we had a helicopter buzzing the hotel!

> **Text message from: Ben**
> Sent: 12-Aug-2008 18:02
> But has she sold out at the National Theatre? I think not.

RED CHRISTMAS

These are Russell's notes on Phil Ford's *Red Christmas* treatment.

FROM: RUSSELL T DAVIES TO: JULIE GARDNER; GARY RUSSELL, THURSDAY 14 AUGUST 2008 00:38:37 GMT

PHIL FORD'S RED CHRISTMAS

This is great. Really good stuff.

The base needs to be more primitive, and more distinct. More noble. Prouder. More unique. It's the very first base on Mars ever. It's not terraforming; surely the first real Mars bases will just be there to examine, and do tests and things? (We need dates on that. When are they planned for, or just hoped for, in real life?) The science should be closer to ours. And the fact that Valentina is a Mars veteran spoils it somehow.[1] This should be the first, first, first. If they're expedition number 16, it sort of makes the whole thing less epic. Think in headlines. The First Base! The First Pioneers! The Brave! The Bold!

For that reason, I don't like flying off to – or even the existence of – the algae farm.[2] This isn't a complex; it's one base. It should be wonderful, and central, and amazing. Whether it's two domes or one, it should be simple and central. That's tough, I know, but all that claustrophobia and trapped-ness will be brilliant. Of course, it needs to expand, to give us visuals and movement. We need a set-piece chamber, like the Strut in *Voyage of the Damned*. An Oxygenation Chamber, full of CGI pistons, and levels, and spinning machines (okay, maybe a bit in advance of real science), in which the Doctor will perform daring deeds, and CGI stunts, and save lives, and be amazing. An FX-driven, stunt-driven, visual set-piece chamber.

Okay, thinking about it some more… maybe some sort of algae farm could work (not for terraforming, just for food and air), but the story begins to work if it's 200 yards away. If you can *see* it. If something has gone wrong, it closes down and seals itself off, and no one inside will reply or can reply. They have to walk to the base, but with tension and scares. Maybe walk across the surface of Mars, or maybe walk through the now-dark-and-undoubtedly-deadly tunnel that connects the two domes. Do you see what I mean? The smaller and tenser this gets, the better it is. Cut all the sprawling, sci-fi shuttle stuff. Make these people and their situation more physical, more real.

If we're seriously going to try for Helen Mirren, I'm not sure Valentina should be Russian. Helen Mirren was Russian in that *2010* film. She'd be unlikely to repeat herself. Besides, a bit of British pluck would be wonderful here. They're odd beasts, these Christmas ones. They're not subtle. We can let rip with the characterisation, a bit. We need to concentrate massively on Valentina, to put her at the centre. And the other characters barely register. They're all a bit Crewman A and Crewman B. These characters have to a) not fill up much space, and b) be very distinct. They have to be

---

1 In Phil Ford's original treatment, set on Christmas Eve 2079, Valentina Kerenski is the leader of the Mars base ('Camp Bowie'), having been on the first manned mission there in 2050 and several times since.
2 In the original treatment, the agricultural team on Mars, based some distance away from 'Camp Bowie', is cultivating plains of algae that are slowly releasing oxygen into the thin Martian atmosphere.

like Morvin, and Foon, and Mr Copper, distinctive, simple, archetypal, to make me care about them, but quickly. It sounds like a contradiction, but it isn't.

I get very little sense of what this creature is.[3] Or what it looks like. It kills some, but infects others. Surely the infection spreading is more interesting, more and more mutated crewmembers on the loose?

Big problem: the Doctor cannot summon the TARDIS by remote control. Ever. Bang go two-thirds of all stories, if he can! I know that's a bugger, and the Christmas tree is so effective, but… no.[4] God knows how to solve that, cos having the TARDIS outside with all the spacesuits ripped is brilliant, but… no!

Julie predicted that this would be lacking in Christmas, and she's right. That's not just detail to be filled in elsewhere. It's integral. This will always be lacking in Christmas unless we tackle it now. Those video messages from home must become part of the whole structure, the mood, the ethos of the thing. Bind them in, and then spin them, find the tragedy in those messages, the love, the hope, the joy, the vital information, the lies, the everything. They're not a detail. They're at the heart of it.

A stray thought that I discussed in passing with Gary the other day… what if the Doctor knows that Bowie Base (which sounds better than Camp Bowie!) is the Famous Lost Expedition. It's part of history. They all died. No one ever returned. By saving them all at the end, the Doctor is defying the Laws of Time. When the Ood appears at the end, there's a sense, without quite saying it, that he's gone too far. He has been too arrogant, and Time is calling him in for his final story, in which he'll pay the price. I know this is hard to reveal, because the Doctor is never going to turn around and say to the crew of Bowie Base, 'Oh, you're all going to die.' He'd be a bit bonkers to do that, even in the worst circumstances, so I can't quite work out how to swing that yet (without the Doctor looking at the TARDIS scanner and talking to himself, which doesn't work)… but just because something doesn't work immediately doesn't mean that it won't work ever. It's worth niggling at that idea. It makes things more epic, more heartfelt.

So, this is a really, really good start – and a thousand times better than my last duff idea. You can see Phil starting to fly with this one, and that's fantastic. But it's not quite there yet. Sci-fi off-world episodes are so hard to write. They really are the toughest of the lot. But once the base works, once it has a reality, a logic, a toughness, an integrity, then like the video messages, like the algae farm, like the Oxygen Chamber, like the creature, like Christmas, everything will tie together and become some sort of whole. This story is about the base. Work on the base, and the story will lock into place, I promise.

I think we should go for another treatment, but we'll get there soon. It's very exciting.

3 There is something in unrefined Martian water that the farmers have been drinking unwittingly, infecting them.
4 The unidentified creature has torn apart every spacesuit on the base – including the Doctor's – leaving him no way to reach the TARDIS outside on the surface. With various cables and adjustments, the Doctor uses the base's fake, metal Christmas tree as a transmitter to signal to the TARDIS, transporting it into 'Camp Bowie' by remote control.

FROM: RUSSELL T DAVIES TO: JULIE GARDNER; GARY RUSSELL, THURSDAY 14 AUGUST 2008 13:30:37 GMT

PHIL FORD'S RED CHRISTMAS

Also! I was thinking overnight…

Robots. A base robot. A clunky, very real sort of robot – all white metal with black joints, like real Japanese robots are these days. I'd think, like, a practical build. A real little thing, trundling around on caterpillar tracks, like Wall-E, with mechanical arms picking up soil outside, or offering crewmembers their turkey pill, or whatever.

But then, when it goes mad (and quite why it would go mad requires a lot of work), the arms can become CG, and whirr, and whizz, and spin, and cut, and be terrifying.

I love a robot!

FROM: RUSSELL T DAVIES TO: BENJAMIN COOK, THURSDAY 14 AUGUST 2008 21:16:18 GMT

RE: I ONLY WROTE TO SAY HELLO, BUT…

Phil Collinson sent me the most beautiful e-mail today. He was in Cardiff, so I went for a coffee with him, and told him about LA. I voiced all my fears. Am I too old? Is it too mad? Is it wrong to go to America and start again, while worrying that I can't go back to my same old Manchester life after all this? (It would just be too small.) Phil sympathised, like you do, but then we saw a handsome man and changed the subject, and then Phil had to go, so he got on the train. But then he sent me this e-mail:

> I can't stop thinking about what you'll do when IT'S over, as I chug interminably through the countryside. You're right to be worried. The time we've had is amazing. The way Doctor Who has been so demanding of every living minute of energy, brain power… the huge sacrifices made so easily… the sheer joy it gives back every day… just the whole SIZE of it… all means that when you wake up the day after they've dubbed your last episode, a huge hole is left behind. So, what I'm saying is, GO TO LA! It'll be the perfect distraction, and just so huge and exciting and frightening and wonderful. Not just the job of it, but the living in a strange country bit.
>
> And I'll have somewhere else to stay when I visit…

Bless Phil for that. 'A huge hole is left behind.' How honest. I think that e-mail has made up my mind. He's right. I'm going.

FROM: BENJAMIN COOK TO: RUSSELL T DAVIES, THURSDAY 14 AUGUST 2008 23:05:04 GMT

RE: I ONLY WROTE TO SAY HELLO, BUT…

You're going!

You'd better have e-mail in LA.

FROM: RUSSELL T DAVIES TO: BENJAMIN COOK, FRIDAY 15 AUGUST 2008 00:38:37 GMT

RE: I ONLY WROTE TO SAY HELLO, BUT…

I think LA will have e-mail. Call it a wild stab in the dark, but I think so.

I told my old fella about it at the weekend. There really should be a whole other book saying how marvellous he is. The absolute first thing he said was, 'You've got to go.' (Hey, is he having an affair? Wait a goddamn minute! Is he glad to be getting me out of the way?!) I'm lucky to have him. He really is a saint. I've spent five years beetling between Manchester and Cardiff – and beetling less and less, staying in Cardiff instead, because it's easier – but all the time saying, 'I'll be back home soon.' And then I sit down and say, 'I'm moving to another country.' He really is the most gracious, kind man. He'd never try to stop me going. He can't move out there – he's got a staff job, like a job for life, he can't give that up on a whim – but he'll save up his holidays, and come out for months at a time, and I'll be coming back lots. My old dad is 83. It's no time to disappear. Besides, I'm still convinced that I'll get there, decide it's too hot, and come back within a fortnight.

I'm trying not to think about it too much. Times like this, with huge decisions, I don't think or talk much. I sort of bob, like a cork – yes, Ben, like a cork – and see which direction I float in. And I'm floating west.

IN THE
MIDNIGHT HOUR

This interview with Russell, by Benjamin, was originally published in
Doctor Who Magazine 400, on 18 September 2008...

In his most candid interview ever, **Russell T Davies** *invites DWM readers into his
Manchester home to reveal the truth about the 2009 Specials, lying in interviews,
the darkest corners of fandom, and 'twisty-turny, timey-wimey'...*

'**E**very year, you wait for it to fail. Every year, you wait for the ratings
to die, because no good luck lasts forever, no matter how hard you
work at it.' That, says Russell T Davies, is why now is the right time
for him to quit *Doctor Who*, the show that he was responsible for
resurrecting in 2005, after a 16-year hiatus, and turning into a commercial and
critical success. 'It's achieved everything that I wanted it to, and more. I've pushed it
as far as I can. It's time for a completely new eye on it.'

After this year's Davies-penned Christmas Special, set in Victorian London and
involving the Cybermen, he'll oversee just four more Specials in 2009 (the first two
of which he's co-writing, and the final two he's scripting alone), before Steven Moffat
takes over as showrunner for Series Five in 2010. 'It feels like I've got other things
to do,' says Russell. 'Four years just feels good. It feels right, I think. I'm absolutely
always thinking that I must get out before I get bored of it. They did ask me to do a
fifth series,' he reveals. 'I think that's when I realised for sure that I just didn't want to
do it.'

It's 2pm, on 20 August 2008. Russell has been up since first light, in his house in
the Victoria Park area of Manchester, working on the script to Episode 5 of the third
series of *Torchwood*, which will run on BBC One next spring. In this house, he wrote
all of his *Doctor Who* scripts up to and including Series Three opener *Smith and Jones*.
He prefers writing here to his Cardiff residence, where work dictates that he spends
most of his year. Not for much longer, though.

Russell's Manchester home perfectly encompasses the two obsessions in his life: his writing, and cartooning. The hand-drawn theatre posters in the entrance hall are his own work, from the mid 1980s, when he designed the flyers for Cardiff's Sherman Theatre. For a long time, Russell wanted to be a graphic artist. As a kid, he loved Marvel comics and Charles M Schulz's *Peanuts* strips. On the wall in his front room is his prized possession: a framed *Peanuts* sketch autographed by Schulz himself.

'He was a *genius*,' says Russell of Schulz. 'The rhythms of his jokes, the repetition, the silent third frame of four, the way that the punchline is immediately followed in the same frame by a follow-up line, which becomes an extra punchline in itself... oh, I use *all* of it. It's so ingrained. The day he died I was so sad.'

Russell gives *DWM* a guided tour of the house. It's surprisingly *Who*-lite. Okay, so there's the life-sized 1980s-style Dalek in the entrance hall ('I should get rid of that,' he says), the dozen or so toy Daleks that take up a whole shelf in his kitchen, and the complete set of Target novels in his office upstairs, but you're reminded that *Doctor Who* represents just four years of a career in television that spans two decades. Russell landed his first proper writing and producing job, on children's magazine show *Why Don't You...?*, in 1988. He can't quite believe that it was that long ago.

His cluttered office is his personal sanctuary. 'It smells of cigarettes,' he apologises. The walls are lined with hundreds of files, books, videotapes and DVDs. Next to the computer, on his desk, is a signed photo of Andrew Hayden-Smith. It was acquired, insists Russell, long before the former CBBC presenter was cast in *Doctor Who* as Jake Simmonds. The office walls are adorned with photos commemorating Russell's earlier work – from short-lived, early-1990s ITV daytime soap *Families*, to 1999's *Queer as Folk*, the Channel Four series about gay men living in Manchester, which first put Russell on the map.

'I used to be a very florid writer,' he says, lighting a cigarette back downstairs in the living room. It's the first of several that he'll smoke during our three-hour conversation. 'My God, you should watch *The Grand*,' he says of the hotel-set period drama that he wrote in the 1990s. 'Talk about Baroque! But I'd had a soap training, in which it's every character's job to stand there and tell us everything that they're thinking, usually in lists of three adjectives. I knew that it wasn't working. I knew that I was in a stylistic dead-end. Literally, I taught myself how to write better. In Episode 16 of *The Grand*, I had Steven, the posh son, finishing his engagement with posh Christina. Such an empty character,' he adds, laughing. 'I called her Christina Wyndham-Price, because it rhymed with "plot device".'

'That scene was a massive breakthrough for me,' he continues. 'They started the scene happy; five pages later, the engagement was off, and not once did either of them use the word "engagement" or say "I love someone else" or "it's over". I pared back all those words and phrases, because they didn't need saying. Both characters just *knew* what was happening. They realised it during the scene. Honestly, that scene changed the path of my whole career. I wrote better from that point on.

'That led directly to *Queer as Folk*, which is the ultimate in not saying what's actually going on. Ten episodes of a love story, ten episodes of Vince in love with Stuart, and I *never* had Vince say, "I love you." Never. Writing is, equally, what you *don't* write. I think that's why *Queer as Folk* succeeded. The audience felt involved, because they had to work hard. They weren't being given everything on a plate. I remember shooting one of the opening scenes, where Hazel is running after Bernie, shouting, "It's only a t-shirt!" – which is never explained. Everyone – actors, crew, extras – was wondering what she was going on about. Pam Tait, the costume designer, said, "This script isn't just minimal, it's gnomic." I think that's one of my best compliments.'

Before we continue, your intrepid *DWM* reporter has something to declare. In February 2007, Russell and I entered into a correspondence, a pretty-much-daily exchange of e-mails, that continued for more than a year and has been collected together in a book, called *Doctor Who: The Writer's Tale*, which is published by Ebury this month. It's like a year-long interview with Russell T Davies. It's all there: courting Kylie Minogue, signing up Catherine Tate, turning down Series Five, the search for Russell's successor...

'I've been asked to write a book about writing a few times before,' explains Russell, 'but I'm wary of a lot of the books out there, the ones that simply teach technique without any passion. They're all theory... whereas I like your description of our book as the diary that answers back. Yes, with you as the diary! It's the perfect format. It's writing in action.'

For someone better known nowadays by his PR face, his 'Marvellous' side, the 'Hooray!'-studded rhetoric of countless *Doctor Who Confidentials* and breakfast TV interviews, the Russell T Davies of *The Writer's Tale* is surprisingly frank. It's full of angst and self-doubt. No more Mr Marvellous...? 'I think that's the only way to talk about writing. I knew I had to break myself open in order to be honest about scripts. It's fascinating to see Julie [Gardner, executive producer] and Phil [Collinson, producer] read it, because they know me very well, but even they had no idea of what I go through.

'I think I've realised, more concretely than ever before, that I'll never be happy. I think that's quite positive, that I'm always worried, that I always think the next script is going to kill me, that I always think I'll never get there. I take a slight comfort in that now, as I face a million more deadlines. It's like therapy. After Steven Moffat had read our book, he e-mailed me saying, "I thought you just sat there typing all day, laughing." I imagined *he* did that, too. In a way, all writers are the same. Well, *good* writers. It's a cry for solidarity. We're all tearing our hair out, living with a massive pressure. If I use my "publicity voice"... well, that's too easy now. It's a lie.'

Not that he's been lying in previous interviews, you understand... or has he? He grins. 'Lying can be good. That and being able to read upside-down. I've spent my career reading documents upside-down on people's desks and it's got me an awful long way, let me tell you. But if I'm honest about my writing... well, I've realised that I don't care what people say about my scripts, because I criticise them on levels that they'll never even touch. They might criticise my decisions, or the way that I lead my life, or the speed at which I write, which I bet will come in for some criticism, but you might as well wish that I were blonde, or shorter, or not Welsh.'

Knowing that he's leaving *Doctor Who* helped Russell put 'a bit more energy' into his Series Four scripts. 'It made them more muscular if anything. In some ways, it took the pressure off. It was bold, all the different directions that we went in this year. If *Midnight*, for example, had been the greatest disaster in the history of the world, I wouldn't have cared. If people had said, "That was terrible, all the kids were bored," it wouldn't have mattered. I'd still be happy with it... whereas if I'd been signed up for a fifth year, I'd really have been questioning my judgement.'

As it happens, the *Midnight* gamble paid off: a 45-minute slice of prime time family drama, featuring a small cast on a single, claustrophobic set, with minimal special effects, was watched by over eight million people, helping Series Four to achieve some of *Doctor Who*'s highest ratings this century. Of course, had the show averaged a weekly audience of three million ('I'd have died on my arse,' chips in Russell), no doubt he'd be sat here now reminding us that the BBC shouldn't be chasing ratings, that *Doctor Who* is a fine piece of public-service broadcasting, and that plenty of fantastic shows don't attract huge audiences...?

'Very true,' he says, with a chuckle, 'except *Doctor Who* is absolutely designed to be seen by everyone. Yes, I'd argue the opposite if we hadn't got the ratings... but the BBC wanted us slap bang at the heart of the schedule, when they thought that Saturday nights weren't working.' He's referring to the dark days of 2004, before *Doctor Who* had transformed the televisual landscape. 'Everything I've ever worked on, I've wanted ten million people watching. Well, I've finally got it. Every year, I've set myself these targets, which I've never talked about before in case we fail. Let's face it, one day the ratings will sink back down. But we're meant to be getting millions. We're meant to be beating ITV. We're not making a drama about Solidarity in Poland, or the Gulf War; it's just very powerful entertainment. I can't believe that some people still don't watch *Doctor Who*! I find that mad. They're idiots.'

DWM wonders where the current success of *Doctor Who* leaves Russell's successor. In taking over from Russell, is the challenge facing Steven greater to the one that Russell faced in bringing back the show in 2005? 'I'm absolutely confident that whatever Steven is planning will be brilliant,' rattles off Russell. But he's sidestepping the question. *DWM* tries again. Isn't Steven's dilemma that he'll want to make his mark on the show, and yet Russell has already hit upon a formula that patently works? 'Well... yes,' replies Russell, 'it's hard, isn't it? I think that's what people will say to him – that it's harder, because he's got to replicate success. I think that's what will be said, and I think he won't care. He's too clever to worry about that.

'When I was bringing it back, people told me, "It'll never work." Every single year, *The Guardian* has called it "the make-or-break series". They're always ready for it to fail, and there's a great joy in proving them wrong. I bet Steven is discovering that joy already. Besides, a lot of what I've done with the show is common sense, like having a season finale. It's not like I *invented* the season finale. I would bet my back teeth that Steven's seasons will build to some sort of twisty-turny, timey-wimey climax. You know how he loves laying clues and pulling tricks on the viewers. His writing is so complex, so structured, so clever, so thought-through...

'Plus, no matter what I did to the format, it's still a man in a police box, who turns up in a different place every week and has an adventure. Honestly, fundamentally, I didn't change a thing. I just fine-tuned the parts of the formula that interested me, like the role of the companion. Steven writes very different episodes to mine, but they fit beautifully into that format. So what's to worry about? Nothing, really.'

Last December, Russell and Steven met up in London for coffee and a chat. 'I remember going to this meeting bristling with things to say. I had a million things to tell him, about BBC Wales, BBC Drama, how to handle the publicity, all that sort of stuff... and I remember, vividly, the moment I sat down, I thought, I don't need to tell him any of this. He knows it already. He's produced shows before. We actually had very little to say. I've told him that he can phone me at any time, but I bet he won't.' Is Russell secretly hoping that he will? 'No, because I hate it when people phone up and ask for advice,' he smiles. 'Experience counts for nothing. I might give him bad advice, and then I'll look like an idiot.'

Get Russell talking about the state of television today, and he's quick to denounce what he describes as 'so-bad-it's-popular programming', citing such shows as *Rock Rivals* and *Hotel Babylon*. 'I find that sort of TV mystifying,' he says, 'and cynical, actually. I don't understand the cynical heart that makes those things.' He's more charitable towards the increasing number of aspirants to *Doctor Who*'s crown, such as *Primeval* ('a great show – it did very well for ITV') and the BBC's new Saturday teatime drama *Merlin* ('a really, really fine piece of work'). The producers of both shows have talked openly of their debt to *Doctor Who*, with *Merlin* even including a "Thanks to Russell T Davies" acknowledgment on the end credits.

'*Merlin* is the first proper rival to *Doctor Who* that I've seen,' says Russell, 'and that's my finest compliment. I think it does us good to have rivals snapping at our heels. It *is* a competition, frankly. It's honest-to-God rivalry, and I like that. It fuels everyone to keep going.' But the strongest motivator, he says, is his fear of letting down *Doctor Who*'s cast and crew…

'When you've got David [Tennant] there, and Catherine Tate has agreed to give up a whole year of her life, *that's* the greatest pressure of all. I couldn't look them in the eye if we're not doing them proud. That's been the benefit of changing our cast every year – which wasn't the plan, but I loved that in the end. Every year, if the show had failed, the press would have blamed the new cast member, and we must never, *never* allow that to happen. That's a fantastic pressure on everyone to keep up the standard. It wouldn't have mattered if they'd been given rubbish scripts, or had terrible sets, or bad directors; the press would have looked at the face on screen and said that it's the newcomer's fault. They'd have said that Catherine had destroyed *Doctor Who*, or Freema [Agyeman], or David.'

In his Foreword to *The Writer's Tale*, Philip Pullman describes Russell as 'pugnacious, and rightly so, when faced with narrow-minded prejudice', highlighting in particular 'the relentless and merciless idiocy of internet "criticism"'. How does Russell regard the adverse reaction, in some quarters, to Catherine Tate's casting in Series Four? 'I think it's a bit horrific,' he confesses. 'Of course people are free to say whatever they want, but it seems that they're even freer when the subject is a successful woman. Successful women are considered to be fair game, especially by female columnists. Women beware women. That's the truest phrase ever said.

'The problem is that a lot of journalists go online to find their material, quoting the internet forums and that area of fandom that reacts as if the world is ending, as though by casting Catherine we're destroying the show. That's embarrassing, quite frankly. To be absolutely blunt, it's the only moment in my entire four years that I was actually ashamed of fandom. I'm not talking about fandom full stop; I'm talking about those dark corners that react in that way. As if we didn't know what we were doing! After four years! All of us – Julie, Phil, David, all of us – were utterly confident of what a fine actress Catherine is and how brilliant she would be. The proof is there now, in 14 episodes. She's every bit as magnificent as I promised she would be.'

In the past, Russell has insisted that he never goes online to read what people are saying about him. But this isn't true, is it? 'Now and again, I have a look,' he admits. 'But I don't do it constantly. I wonder if Steven does? My boyfriend's a civil servant, so he sits at a computer all day, every day, and sometimes he goes online over lunch. I ask him, "What are they saying?" He says, "They're slagging you off again." But I refuse to take it personally. I'd die if I did.' What's the worst thing that he's read about himself online? 'That I'm lazy. That always gets me. Fair enough if you don't like what I do… but lazy?! It's a ridiculous view of television. It's an assumption that we're all swanning around in chauffeured limousines, drinking champagne. That annoys me. It's facile. But it doesn't annoy me for long. *I* know I'm not lazy.'

Is life behind the scenes on *Doctor Who* really as cosy and controversy-free as the people who work on it make out? 'I know that some people think that *Doctor Who Magazine* is sort of cheerleading when you report that everything's nice and happy,' he considers, 'and it's human nature to want to know great, dark secrets... but c'mon, look, we work hard to create a comfortable working atmosphere. I'm sorry if people don't like that, but you know what? Tough shit.'

DWM invites Russell to whet our appetites for the forthcoming 60-minute Specials. The Christmas one is shot already ('It has a *very* exciting title,' he says, 'which may or may not get people up in arms'), and next year's Specials will commence production in January. 'They're all very different. They're all very colourful. They hit the ground running.' When asked about settings, he says, 'There are at least two alien planets, maybe more.' What about returning aliens? Here he chooses his words carefully: 'I would say... how can I put this? Two new monsters... no, three! Yes, three.

'The Doctor is travelling alone. Each story will have a different companion, a woman or a man of the week to team up with, some great guest casting... and it won't always be a young girl.' In the Christmas Special, it's David Morrissey, playing 'a brilliant character'. And just to confirm – is David Tennant staying on for all five Specials? 'Yes, every single one. He is the Doctor.'

In each of his annual end-of-series interviews with *DWM*, Russell has spoken of the show's future with the same mix of bravado and enthusiasm that's marked every stage of his career. This time around, however, the question is how Russell's next project can possibly top *Doctor Who*? Will the next thing he writes simply not be as good? 'The next thing I write will just be different,' he reasons. 'It'll be like I learnt nothing from *Doctor Who*. You do just start again with every show.' He's rumoured to be planning a six-part drama known only – 'ridiculously,' he says – as *More Gay Men*. 'I don't know what it's about, just gay men. There's probably a 40-year-old gay man, and maybe a 20-year-old gay man, not an affair, just the different generations. I think they both work in the same office.'

Will Russell write for TV's *Doctor Who* again? 'No, I'm looking forward to watching it as a viewer, for the first time in 21 years. I can't wait.' What if one day there's an episode that he doesn't like? Has he forgotten what that feels like? Will he be on the internet within minutes, registering his complaint? 'Oh, but I've always loved *Doctor Who*, even during those periods when it was considered to be terrible... let's say *Time and the Rani*, which was the first episode I ever saw in Manchester, actually, on a black-and-white portable. It was probably better in black-and-white.' It was still shit, though, wasn't it? 'It was a low moment, but no way did I stop watching. No way did I ever give up on Sylvester McCoy. If *Time and the Rani* were repeated today, I'd still sit and watch it and have a good time. It has that very handsome man in it, Mark Greenstreet [Ikona]… dressed as a lizard, admittedly! But there's something good about every episode.'

Has he overseen any real clangers during his tenure? 'There probably have been weaker episodes in the past four years, but now, for me, it's hard to see which ones. It's probably my fault if an episode is weak. I mean, okay, we all talk about *Aliens of London* with a slightly regretful tone, because we were learning, we'd never worked with prosthetics before, and the schedule was impossible… well, do you know, I watched it on BBC Three the other night – and what a classic episode! The Doctor's in Downing Street. A spaceship flies into Big Ben. Penelope Wilton [Harriet Jones] is watching Slitheen murder people. Frankly, it's brilliant. If I'm absolutely honest, I think some fans don't yet realise how good these last four years have been. And it'll be just as fantastic once Steven has taken over…'

By which time, Russell will be riding off into the sunset. No tears, no regrets, just Allons-y, straight ahead and out, press the button, dematerialise, new planet – next stop, everywhere! Isn't he going to miss this show? 'No,' he says first off, but then he considers the question. 'Julie worries sometimes. The sheer size of this show… I suppose it's hard to imagine just going back to Manchester, and sitting there writing a six-parter… because the next thing I write will go out at nine o'clock, it'll be an adult drama, it'll get three million viewers, and there won't be half as much fuss about it. It won't get a *Radio Times* cover. I'll miss the size of the job, I think. I'll miss the energy that goes into it, actually. The creativity.

'Then again, I worry for my health. I mean, doing that book with you, seeing it written down, the day-to-day workings of this show… I do think, I'm 45 now, that number of late nights, with that amount of smoking, with that amount of coffee, seriously, that's not good.' He stubs out his cigarette as he says: 'I'd like to see 55. That'd be nice.

'But each new drama creates it's own new world, and it's own problems, and I know that'll fill my head,' he says. 'I'll be looking at the latest issues of *Doctor Who Magazine*, going, "Hey, didn't I used to work on that show, way back…?"'

Same time next year, then, Russell? For now, he says nothing. He just smiles. He knows what we're thinking. Yeah, maybe we won't see him for dust.

THIS EDITION OF

DOCTOR · WHO

THE

WRITER'S TALE

SIGNED BY THE AUTHOR,
IS LIMITED TO 1000 COPIES
OF WHICH THIS IS NUMBER

400/1000 !!!

CHAPTER SEVENTEEN

BEST-LAID
PLANS

In which *Torchwood: The Musical* is considered,
Chris Moyles turns out to be extraordinarily lovely,
and Russell and Benjamin go on tour

FROM: RUSSELL T DAVIES TO: BENJAMIN COOK, SATURDAY 23 AUGUST 2008 16:20:26 GMT

CANAL STREET

It's Manchester Pride this weekend. I'm avoiding it. I've too much work to do. Although, they've an AIDS vigil on Monday night – which is rather beautiful, all candlelit in the park in the middle of Canal Street – so I promised to go to that.

On Friday morning, I had to walk down Canal Street, because I was on my way to do an interview for one of the gay magazines. Canal Street was deserted. I hadn't set foot there in years. I haven't been clubbing there at night for, ooh, about four or five years, I think. Since *Doctor Who*, really. Lots of new bars. Old bars with new names. I thought, blimey, I used to own this place. Honestly, after *Queer as Folk*, it was like I knew everyone there. That place was my life. I wish I'd realised that at the time. Now, I am the past. It was a trip down memory lane. So many bars that I got pissed in. So many dark corners. All plain and ordinary in the daylight.

By the time I left the interview hours later, they were starting to erect the barriers for Pride, and the bars were filling up, and it was sunny, so lots of beautiful and not-so-beautiful boys were sitting outside, so I had another stroll up and down. Within ten minutes, I'd bumped into five or six people. The same five or six people I used to bump into in 2000! I thought, 'God, they're all still here.' Older, fatter, thinner on top, but the same old faces. It made me feel glad that I've moved on and done different things. It would have been so easy to stay there, and write gay scripts for the rest of my life.

Enough reminiscing! I just watched an assembly of the first week's filming on *Torchwood*, and it's marvellous. That was a nice surprise. Euros is so brilliant. That show has never looked better. It's nice to hear those characters saying my dialogue again. So, that's cheered me up. It's inspired me, actually. It's spurred me on to get Episode 5 right. Not that I've written a word yet, of course.

Meanwhile, Julie, Andy and I have been talking casting for the *Doctor Who* Easter Special. Tricky. Sexy cat burglar? There aren't many actors who can carry that off. But the fact that it's proving so hard to cast has made me wonder: a cat burglar and a bus? Isn't that a clash? Just as bad as a hotel and a dogfight? Cat burglars don't get on buses. Well, glamorous, posh ones don't. In fairness, Gareth has already wondered aloud about this. 'Make it work,' I said. But while he's working away on the script, it's kept ticking away in my head. I haven't told Gareth this, I'm letting him keep typing, but the thought has been growing and growing for weeks now. The clash of styles inherent in those decisions. The clash of genres. Good clash or bad clash? Two sides, fighting each other. How far have we wandered since our days of shop girls and ordinary lives connecting with the Doctor? How far have we wandered from our original brief, back in 2004? I had a nice chat with Jane Tranter the other day, and she was reminiscing about *World War Three*, and how much she loved Downing Street intercutting with the Tylers' council flat. It's her absolute favourite episode, the one that she keeps referring back to. It's the essence of *Doctor Who*, for Jane. But a jewel thief? A character who's never actually existed in the real world, ever? It gets those alarm bells ringing.

The other day, I thought, what if we make this Companion of the Week the sort of woman who *would* get on a bus? Never mind posh Hermione; what if she's plain Eileen? Played by someone like Kathy Burke! I love Kathy Burke. Or Brenda Blethyn. Or maybe Gwen Taylor. That sort of actor. Classy, heartfelt, down-to-earth. Instant connection with the audience. The most ordinary housewife in the world, teamed up with the Doctor. Scene 1, she's at home with her dull husband, Trevor. He's reading out the horoscopes. She says, 'Read mine.' He says, 'When's your birthday?' And she's almost in tears. She's lived with this man for ten years. He doesn't know when her birthday is. She's crying as she goes out of the door, going to the shops, and she gets on the bus (do you see? She fits the story!)… and there's the Doctor, and… how good would that be?!

FROM: RUSSELL T DAVIES TO: BENJAMIN COOK, MONDAY 1 SEPTEMBER 2008 00:34:40 GMT

RE: BACK IN CARDIFF...

I'm dying here. I'm on Page 8 of this *Torchwood* Episode 5 script. You know how fast I write – you know better than anyone – but this time it's taken me four days to reach Page 8! I had the worst night's sleep in years last night. It was nightmarish, with images of Jack, and Gwen, and Ianto (not in a good way), and Peter Capaldi, swimming about. Seriously, their faces looming in my head. Their disappointment! This cast is so huge that paying them all off in the final episode is the hardest job I've ever had, let alone defeating the bastard alien. The alien is making demands. For the third episode in a row. I hate aliens.

FROM: BENJAMIN COOK TO: RUSSELL T DAVIES, THURSDAY 4 SEPTEMBER 2008 02:15:08 GMT

RE: BACK IN CARDIFF...

How's *Torchwood* coming along? Any better?

FROM: RUSSELL T DAVIES TO: BENJAMIN COOK, THURSDAY 4 SEPTEMBER 2008 02:29:17 GMT

RE: BACK IN CARDIFF...

Not bad at the moment, dare I say. I read an interview with Alan Moore recently, in which he said – I'm paraphrasing – 'When you're young, you plan everything. As you get more experienced, you fly on instinct. That means putting things in scripts that you've go no idea why they're there, but as you work at it, as you write, they rise up, they assert themselves, they become more and more vital, like they were always meant to be there.' Less mystically, what he means is, you use ideas once you've created them, you work at them and bind them in. And tonight's one of those nights...

Back in Episode 3, I gave Ianto's sister a makeshift crèche, for no good reason – I just thought it livened up ordinary domestic scenes, made the house noisy and fun, gave her not-much-story-husband more to do ('Ten quid a kid!'), and helped spell out the whole *Children of Earth* theme. (That's what we're calling this series, *Torchwood: Children of Earth*.) Nice idea, that's all. But tonight, oh, tonight – like a bolt of lightning, the thought went 'OH!!!' in my head – the crèche has become spectacular, and vital, and epic, and potentially brilliant. Like I'd carefully seeded that in, way back in Episode 3. I hadn't, I was just having fun, but something in my head must have worked at it until it was staring me in the face.

That's why, I realise, *Torchwood* has been so painful, because that's how I work now, very much on instinct. This one story has been spread across three writers, demanding that it's planned in detail, in advance, so it's been split across three minds, and that sort of flourishing hasn't been possible. It's only now that I'm pulling it all together and making it my own again that the synapses are firing. Connections are being made. But mark the moment, because I don't often say it: right now, I'm happy.

FROM: BENJAMIN COOK TO: RUSSELL T DAVIES, THURSDAY 4 SEPTEMBER 2008 02:30:08 GMT

RE: BACK IN CARDIFF...

I'm documenting that for *The Writer's Tale 2*. ('This time, it's personal!') It's 2.30am, on 4 September, and Russell T Davies is writing... and he's happy! Ha ha ha. It won't last.

When's Episode 5 due in, then? Wasn't it the end of August?

FROM: RUSSELL T DAVIES TO: BENJAMIN COOK, THURSDAY 4 SEPTEMBER 2008 02:55:10 GMT

RE: BACK IN CARDIFF...

It was due on 30 June. No kidding. Christ, I've made this production a mess. Yet again.
There, now I'm unhappy again.

FROM: BENJAMIN COOK TO: RUSSELL T DAVIES, THURSDAY 4 SEPTEMBER 2008 02:58:21 GMT

RE: BACK IN CARDIFF...

I told you it wouldn't last.

FROM: RUSSELL T DAVIES TO: BENJAMIN COOK, THURSDAY 4 SEPTEMBER 2008 23:55:30 GMT

RE: BACK IN CARDIFF...

If we didn't have this photo shoot in London tomorrow, I'd stay up and finish this
Torchwood script.[1] Yes, finish. But I'm knackered. I'll have to go to bed soon, or you
and the Dalek will have your picture taken next to a living corpse. So, I'll have to
finish this over the weekend. But the end is in sight. And the rushes continue to be
marvellous. Wait till you see Captain Jack's daughter taking out a government assassin
with a breadboard in her back garden! I think this series might work.

FROM: RUSSELL T DAVIES TO: BENJAMIN COOK, MONDAY 8 SEPTEMBER 2008 01:28:15 GMT

RE: BACK IN CARDIFF...

One page to go. ONE!!! But then I've got to go back and fix a lot of stuff, and cut a
lot. It's too long and too expensive. Same old same old, in other words. But hey, yes,
the production team will wake up tomorrow to find Episode 5 in their inboxes. The
story is complete at last, after all these months. I think it hangs together. There's a
great climax, which has nine pages without a single word of dialogue, so I'm rather
pleased with that. But imagine the read-through! I'll have to read out all those stage
directions!

You up to anything exciting?

FROM: BENJAMIN COOK TO: RUSSELL T DAVIES, MONDAY 8 SEPTEMBER 2008 01:37:19 GMT

RE: BACK IN CARDIFF...

No. No, I'm not. I'm hanging out my washing to dry. You, on the other hand, are
killing Ianto. (You bastard. Etc.) How did Gareth David-Lloyd take the news?

FROM: RUSSELL T DAVIES TO: BENJAMIN COOK, MONDAY 8 SEPTEMBER 2008 02:39:55 GMT

RE: BACK IN CARDIFF...

Ianto doesn't even make it to Episode 5. He's dead at the end of Episode 4. Poor Ianto.
Julie and Pete told Gareth the news, in London. I was mid-rewrite, or I'd have been

---

1 On Friday 5 September, Russell and Benjamin were photographed in London, with a Dalek, for *The Times*.

there for something that important. Julie said it was okay. He was just fine. Simply that. It's an actor's life, isn't it? I had a word with him later, at the read-through, and he was fine, and happy, and smiling. He keeps himself to himself, but I'm sure he's all right. Funny to think of Ianto gone, though. The man who was so bright and chirpy in the very first episode of *Torchwood*, flirting instinctively with Jack before he even knew what that really meant, now cut down in his prime by an alien bastard. Hey, this stuff is real to me!

Look, it's almost 3am, and the e-mails are still coming in from Julie, who's out in LA at the moment. It's teatime out there.

FROM: BENJAMIN COOK TO: RUSSELL T DAVIES, MONDAY 8 SEPTEMBER 2008 02:41:19 GMT

RE: BACK IN CARDIFF...

That'll be you in nine months' time. It'll be 3am here in the UK, and you'll only just be settling down for an evening's work in LA. Oh my God, I'll have to e-mail you at 3am! That'll be a bit different! Imagine that! Um...

FROM: RUSSELL T DAVIES TO: BENJAMIN COOK, MONDAY 8 SEPTEMBER 2008 03:48:04 GMT

RE: BACK IN CARDIFF...

It's done! *Torchwood* sinks slowly into the west. I must stop typing now. My letter 'a' has broken. I have to reinsert the 'a' manually every time I want to use it. 'Manually' was a right hassle. Good night.

FROM: BENJAMIN COOK TO: RUSSELL T DAVIES, MONDAY 8 SEPTEMBER 2008 10:45:02 GMT

RE: BACK IN CARDIFF...

If you want to cut down on vowels, perhaps you could e-mail me in Welsh. Or you could just buy a new keyboard. Yeah, do that. Hey, did you ever do that interview about your desk with... was it the *Observer Magazine*? Did you find enough to talk about? Were they impressed with your Cassandra action figure and waning keyboard?

FROM: RUSSELL T DAVIES TO: BENJAMIN COOK, MONDAY 8 SEPTEMBER 2008 11:19:54 GMT

RE: BACK IN CARDIFF...

It ws odd, tht interview. They kept trying to put things on my desk tht hve never, ever been there. I kept sying, 'But tht's not wht it's like.' My desk just wsn't interesting enough! 'Hve you got something from *Queer s Folk*?' they wondered. 'No,' I sid. In the end, we hd to tlk bout the view. It might not be their most thrilling insight into a writer –

OOH, I'VE FIXED THE 'A'!!! LOOK!!! I hit it really hard, and it worked. Oh, that's brilliant. (That's the most exciting thing to happen all morning. I'm weeping.)

Anyway, the photographer from *The Observer* said, 'The editor of American *Vogue* was so excited that I'm meeting you. I've done George Clooney and Isabella Rosselini, but you're the first name that's impressed him!'

And then he handed me his script to read.

4.15

Gareth Roberts has delivered his first draft of the Easter Special… and it's bloody brilliant! He's really, really worked hard, and concentrated. Do you know what he said? He told me that after I rewrote *The Unicorn and the Wasp*, he sat down with both scripts – his last draft, and my rewrite – and laid them out together, page by page, to see what I'd changed, and why. I have to say, fair dos to him. I spend so much time moaning and griping about other writers, but I was… well, certainly impressed, but actually sort of honoured.

The surprise is, against all our expectations, he's made Christina work. (She's called Christina now, the cat burglar. Not Hermione.) A long way to go, but she's fun, and different, and larky. So, Eileen the housewife, or Christina? That's our dilemma. The ordinary or the posh? I'm really not sure.

RE: 4.15

Can't you cast a sexy Christina, and save an Eileen-type character for the following Special? It's set on the Mars base, right? Put Kathy Burke or Brenda Blethyn or Gwen Taylor into the middle of that, as a greasy mechanic wielding a spanner and… no, that doesn't really work, does it?

RE: 4.15

No.

RE: 4.15

Thought not.

RE: 4.15

We had a script meeting with Gareth for 4.15 in London today, on the Sixth Floor of TV Centre. I love the Sixth Floor. It's just what you expect TV to be like – all smart and swish, with classy, uncomfortable settees. But before I could see Gareth, Jane grabbed me, pulled me into a little glass office, and told me the news. (You're going to love this.) The plan is… for David to announce that he's leaving live at the National

Television Awards next month![2] Presuming he wins, of course. Turns out, it's actually David's idea. He's such a showman. I love it! He's worried that it's becoming more and more likely, what with potential Eleventh Doctors being approached, that word will leak that he's leaving, and he wants to be in control of the announcement. Jane asked me what I thought, but I was too busy laughing. That's a big audience! On ITV! Live! Oh, that's mental. We have to do it.

Best part was, I said that me and Julie and Jane could be sitting in the audience… and act all surprised! Angry even. Or burst into tears. We could pretend that we didn't know. Jane loved that. We practised our faces. We were very convincing.

FROM: RUSSELL T DAVIES TO: BENJAMIN COOK, SATURDAY 13 SEPTEMBER 2008 18:01:07 GMT

RE: 4.15

It's sunny today. I went to the Bay. The fans were out in force. I was swamped! This gang of four 14-year-olds on roller skates came up to me. 'Can my mate have a hug?' A hug? Seriously? 'Yeah, me too, give's a hug.' Really?! I thought they were winding me up, sticking a note on my back or something. But no. They hugged me. All four. Bony teenage arms. It's weird, hugging someone on roller skates. They move. Then off they went. Boys hug now?

You were right, though, I'm sort of happy these days. I was walking to Tesco's, and realised that I had this stupid smile on my face. *Torchwood* finished, Gareth and Phil writing without me, and I'm not about to start rewriting yet (I'm having thoughts about those scripts, for when I take them over, but nothing concrete), so I'm happy. This leads me to conclude that writing = unhappiness, therefore why do I work so hard? What is it, punishment? Why not stay happy? But I won't follow that thought. I might stop smiling.

FROM: BENJAMIN COOK TO: RUSSELL T DAVIES, SATURDAY 13 SEPTEMBER 2008 18:40:58 GMT

RE: 4.15

>>I'm having thoughts about those scripts, for when I take them over<<

Shouldn't you share your thoughts with Gareth and Phil? Or is that going to delay their writing? Or risk derailing them?

FROM: RUSSELL T DAVIES TO: BENJAMIN COOK, SATURDAY 13 SEPTEMBER 2008 18:49:00 GMT

RE: 4.15

I think it's easier – meaning an easier life for me – if I just leave Gareth and Phil alone for now. Although, one thing that keeps growing in my head for *Christmas on Mars* is that robot, the little drone, pottering about on the planet. I've been to see *Wall-E*, and I'm inspired. We could make this thing really cute, and mechanical, and important.

---

2 David Tennant was nominated for Outstanding Drama Performance at the National Television Awards 2008, for his role in *Doctor Who*. Catherine Tate was also a nominee in this category. The annual awards are broadcast live on ITV.

Who doesn't love a cute robot? (Cue the voice of the internet! Point proven, thank you.) I think we can do something brilliant with that. Our own K-9! I wonder how much it costs to actually build a real, moving, gizmo-armed little thing. I want to try.

FROM: RUSSELL T DAVIES TO: BENJAMIN COOK, MONDAY 15 SEPTEMBER 2008 16:16:37 GMT

RE: 4.15
I've told Gareth everything now. I came clean. I couldn't stop thinking about Eileen. Yes, Christina is brilliant, but if there's a housewife version possible, too, then it's so tempting. Fair dos to him, Gareth loved the housewife idea. One of the exciting things about these Specials is that we *can* deliberate like this. For all of a month or so, we can go into a holding pattern, instead of rushing into a decision. Both stories could work. It's kind of a win-win situation. Or maybe the opposite is true. Maybe we have too much spare time, so our decision-making is becoming vague, less immediate and instinctive. Adrenalin is good. Still, Andy Pryor has put on his thinking cap (it's a light mauve) for the housewife, to think of possible Eileens. This feels good, playing with alternative characters. It feels healthy. It feels experimental.

FROM: BENJAMIN COOK TO: RUSSELL T DAVIES, TUESDAY 16 SEPTEMBER 2008 08:12:15 GMT

THE TIMES
Day One of our serialisation! I'm pictured with a Dalek, in *The Times*, on the same page as a photo of JK Rowling! My mum will be pleased. A great picture of you on the cover, too. And they've made an additional news story out of your 'JK Rowling's imagination becomes real' and 'Russell Tovey would make a great Eleventh Doctor' e-mails. The *Telegraph* has picked up on this already: 'RUSSELL TOVEY TIPPED AS THE ELEVENTH DOCTOR WHO!' It looks like the Russell Tovey thing will provide the bulk of the press speculation, at least for today.

FROM: RUSSELL T DAVIES TO: BENJAMIN COOK, TUESDAY 16 SEPTEMBER 2008 11:33:07 GMT

RE: THE TIMES
I texted Russell Tovey to warn him. He thought it was all very funny, and sent his mum out to buy a copy of *The Times*, so he's fine with it all. He texted again a few minutes ago: 'Whoa!! It's everywhere!' Poor Russell Tovey.

I've only just bought *The Times* myself. It took me this long to pluck up the courage. It looks good (nice photos, too), but it's weird seeing that serialisation. I feel sort of... naked. (I'm not.) Like it's me sort of exposed. I never tell anyone anything about what I'm thinking, and now there it is in a national newspaper. A book seems more contained and controlled, but when you see it in newsprint... I read it for about ten seconds, then ran away, and ate, and smoked a lot. Yikes. Still. Scary is good.

Hey, we're live on *BBC Breakfast* tomorrow. No staying out late tonight! We've got to sparkle. Yes, Ben, sparkle.

> **Text message from: Ben**
> Sent: 18-Sep-2008 09:50
> My friends are questioning my choice of footwear. Since when are trainers a 'brave' choice for *BBC Breakfast*?

> **Text message from: Russell**
> Sent: 18-Sep-2008 09:54
> Nicola Shindler was watching, too. She's texted to say that I'm sexier than you. This proves that she is a True Friend.

FROM: BENJAMIN COOK TO: RUSSELL T DAVIES, THURSDAY 18 SEPTEMBER 2008 10:25:32 GMT

RE: THE TIMES

This morning, I got an e-mail from Geoff Hoon's son, Chris (we were at uni together), congratulating us on the *Times* stuff.[3] His dad found your 'bloody MPs' comment, apropos the *Voyage of the Damned* press launch ('Signing autographs for kids, which is nice, but then the MPs, the bloody MPs…'), very funny. Apparently, Geoff is a massive *Doctor Who* fan. He has his own sonic screwdriver! No, really.

FROM: RUSSELL T DAVIES TO: BENJAMIN COOK, TUESDAY 16 SEPTEMBER 2008 20:34:47 GMT

RE: THE TIMES

I stand by my previous statement. Bloody MPs.

For me, the most amazing thing was a text last night from my friend Tracy, my oldest and bestest friend since I was 11. She practically *is* Rose from *Bob & Rose*. I gave her a copy of the book last week, then out of the blue she sent this to me:

> *It's fantastic. But it made my cry, too. I was learning about you. How hard it's been. A separate life. You must have your own subtle knife to cut between worlds. Thank you for being my friend.*

In the whole 34 years I've known her, Tracy has never said anything like that. She doesn't even talk like that! It's lovely, but really threw me. When I say to you, 'I don't tell anyone this stuff,' I bet you think, 'Yeah, apart from your best mates and things.' But no. There's the proof.

FROM: BENJAMIN COOK TO: RUSSELL T DAVIES, THURSDAY 18 SEPTEMBER 2008 20:43:21 GMT

RE: THE TIMES

It's a funny old way to reach your best friends, by publishing a book about yourself. Proves what a media creature you are! What do your family think?

---

3 Former Secretary of State for Defence Geoff Hoon was, at this time, Chief Whip of the House of Commons. He became the Secretary of State for Transport in October 2008, a post he held until June 2009.

FROM: RUSSELL T DAVIES TO: BENJAMIN COOK, TUESDAY 16 SEPTEMBER 2008 20:56:59 GMT

RE: THE TIMES

My family? God knows. They don't even know about it yet. I never tell them a thing. I got a text off my sister this morning: 'Have you got a book coming out?' Whoops. I did mean to say something. Honest.

Oh, and today Andy Pryor came back with a list of who's free to play Eileen, and none of the names excited us all that much – all the lovely, clever actors of a certain age were booked up ages ago – so this means CHRISTINA LIVES! I'm really, really glad, actually. She's a great character.

FROM: RUSSELL T DAVIES TO: BENJAMIN COOK, FRIDAY 19 SEPTEMBER 2008 18:23:05 GMT

RE: THE TIMES

Tomorrow, I'm on Radio Berkshire. What went wrong?

FROM: BENJAMIN COOK TO: RUSSELL T DAVIES, FRIDAY 19 SEPTEMBER 2008 18:41:16 GMT

RE: THE TIMES

Don't worry. This morning, I was interviewed for *What's On Birmingham*, to promote our book signing there next month. My 15 minutes of fame are over. In another couple of days, we'll be sat in our respective homes, unshaven and penniless, watching VHS recordings of our *BBC Breakfast* interview over and over, and e-mailing each other about the 'good ol' days' when we used to be on the telly. We'll be like Cannon and Ball.[4] Rock on, Russell.

FROM: RUSSELL T DAVIES TO: BENJAMIN COOK, SUNDAY 21 SEPTEMBER 2008 19:47:51 GMT

RE: THE TIMES

Julie is back from LA! She landed five hours ago. The work rate has doubled already. She went looking at properties and things out there. She treated that holiday like a proper recce for when we move.

In other news, the National Television Awards plan is ruined. David is on stage that night. D'oh! It took Julie to point out The Bleedin' Obvious. The NTAs are on 29 October, when David is on stage, in *Hamlet,* in Stratford-upon-Avon. We all assumed that the NTAs were on a Sunday, like the BAFTAs. Oh, we're idiots. I'm gutted. I was so looking forward to it. Heaven knows how we're going to announce David's leaving now. I can't imagine anything else as public as the NTAs. Bollocks! That was going to be so much fun.

FROM: RUSSELL T DAVIES TO: BENJAMIN COOK, TUESDAY 23 SEPTEMBER 2008 15:07:34 GMT

RADIO TIMES

Benjamino! Thank you for that *Sarah Jane* article in the new *Radio Times*. You probably

---

4 Cannon and Ball are a comedy double act consisting of Tommy Cannon and Bobby Ball.

don't know how excited we get by coverage like that, especially on a show like *Sarah Jane*, which has to fight to be seen. Lots of texts and e-mails flying about this morning. Nikki saying, 'Have you seen today's RT?!' Julie demanding, in capitals, 'GET ME A COPY!' And ten minutes later: 'OH, IT'S BRILLIANT.' Everyone is thrilled. It's lovely. And you mentioned my mum.[5] Which made me cry. It was so sudden and unexpected, it just got to me.

By the way, we're not giving up on the NTA plan. Julie said, 'What if we ask the NTAs for help? A prerecord? They could play an insert of David announcing his departure?' But that's risky. A prerecorded tape is asking to be leaked. We've dealt with the NTA people before, and they're hugely trustworthy, but that information is dynamite. And that's *if* he wins, which they won't know until the night itself. We could have a prerecord that never gets used! (Great DVD extra.)

FROM: BENJAMIN COOK TO: RUSSELL T DAVIES, FRIDAY 19 SEPTEMBER 2008 17:23:10 GMT

RE: RADIO TIMES

Can't you do one of those live links to the theatre, timed to coincide with the interval? (Isn't Hamlet off stage for a good while?) Or is that too risky? So many ways for it to go wrong, I suppose.

FROM: RUSSELL T DAVIES TO: BENJAMIN COOK, FRIDAY 19 SEPTEMBER 2008 20:19:48 GMT

RE: RADIO TIMES

They *could* get a live link backstage at *Hamlet*, and time his award for the interval, but Julie is worried. 'Won't it take David's mind off *Hamlet*, and ruin the production?' Me: 'Shut up. It'd be brilliant.' Seriously, though, he's carrying that whole three-and-a-half-hour text in his head. We don't want to ruin that night's production. (I'll pay refunds.) We'd have to take the NTA people into our confidence, but maybe not fully, because they love a live link anyway.

FROM: RUSSELL T DAVIES TO: BENJAMIN COOK, THURSDAY 25 SEPTEMBER 2008 09:41:36 GMT

RE: RADIO TIMES

Do you listen to Chris Moyles? He's on the TARDIS set tomorrow, but no one has booked any stars to appear with him! John Barrowman is off filming. Catherine is on holiday. Billie is pregnant. David is in panto. (Er, *Hamlet*.) Moylsey has been making huge capital out of this all week. 'No one's there!' Except bloody me. Oh, I'm shamed.

I JUST REALISED, IT'S PUBLICATION DAY!!! WE'RE AUTHORS!!!

---

5 The *Radio Times* article promoting Series Two of *The Sarah Jane Adventures* mentions Sarah Jane's parents, Barbara and Eddie, who died in 1951: 'Russell T Davies chose the name Barbara because it was his late mother's name.' In 2.9/2.10, Sarah Jane goes back in time to see them.

THE REGENERATION

This e-mail exchange between Steven Moffat and Russell considers the Tenth Doctor's regeneration...

FROM: STEVEN MOFFAT TO: RUSSELL T DAVIES, WEDNESDAY 1 OCTOBER 2008 18:14:46 GMT

HELLO

Can we make sure David is wearing his tie when he regenerates? It's for a new bit in Episode 1.

You're going to tell me he defeats the baddies by blowing up his tie or something...?

FROM: RUSSELL T DAVIES TO: STEVEN MOFFAT, WEDNESDAY 1 OCTOBER 2008 23:55:38 GMT

RE: HELLO

Yes, he will be all tied up. (You know what I mean.) Do you want to see the new Doctor at the end of David's last episode? We've talked about this, but I have a head like a sieve. It'll end with INT. TARDIS, blaze of light, all the usual shenanigans... and then the New Man appears? Feels nice and traditional. But maybe you want to see him for the first time when he arrives in Series Five, Episode 1. Your call, boss!

FROM: STEVEN MOFFAT TO: RUSSELL T DAVIES, THURSDAY 2 OCTOBER 2008 08:29:19 GMT

RE: HELLO

It's definitely BOTH our calls. My thinking at the moment: if we get it right, and we will, we'll have built up this regeneration to a national event. If we DON'T see the new Doctor, it'll be a big fat let-down. If I were eight, I'd be spitting. Furious! It's so *Doctor Who* to flip it all with a big 'But never mind, eh?' Same with the runaway bride and the *Titanic*, in fact. Conscious echo?

Clincher: it's the only time we'll see the Eleventh Doctor (!!) in the old (!!) control room. And that's not just the fanboy completism that drives me every waking and sleeping moment of my life: it somehow matters. Everything is about saying it's the same man. I mean, it's tempting, holding him back, because it's a good entrance in Episode 1 – but you get that anyway.

But what do you think? To hell with whose call it is. Nothing is more important than getting this right. Except the other 900 things that nothing is more important than.

FROM: RUSSELL T DAVIES TO: STEVEN MOFFAT, THURSDAY 2 OCTOBER 2008 10:21:05 GMT

RE: HELLO

>>it's a good entrance in Episode 1<<

Hey, I'll be the judge of that! Me and my fanboy mates. I will be posting on the message boards.

Oh, I think we both agree. Partly because it feels like tradition, but also because I've sort of precluded ending on a regeneration cliffhanger with *The Stolen Earth*, because a lot of people would feel like they've seen it before. If we show Doctor Eleven, lots of kids will feel that natural dismay, they'll go 'I don't like him!' as soon as they see him, but in a way I *loved* feeling like that as a kid. It's part of the process. And it never stopped me watching. Because then you watch his first full episode, and fall in love with him. You're right, seeing the new guy reminds you that Life Goes On, instead of Oh, It's Finished.

Hooray. We agree. We are good bosses. And I think it would be really, really funny to slip into the end credits, 'Last line by Steven Moffat.' Seriously. What a handover!

Reproduced with kind permission

FROM: BENJAMIN COOK TO: RUSSELL T DAVIES, THURSDAY 25 SEPTEMBER 2008 10:50:20 GMT

RE: RADIO TIMES

This morning, Chris Moyles spent five minutes on the phone to Billie, live on air, asking her what you're like. 'He's enormous.' 'What, he's fat?' 'No, he's just enormous. And he wears glasses.' 'Has he got a beard?' 'No, why?' 'I imagine he looks like a junior Santa.' 'No, he's nice.' 'Yeah, but I've got him for three-and-a-half hours!'

You'll be fine.

FROM: RUSSELL T DAVIES TO: BENJAMIN COOK, FRIDAY 26 SEPTEMBER 2008 23:35:39 GMT

RE: RADIO TIMES

Well, Chris Moyles was a hoot. He really is extraordinarily lovely. You realise, like an idiot, how much of that radio persona is a performance. He hugs you! Big, proper, warm hugs! He looks you right in the eye when he interviews you, like he's encouraging you. And he introduced me to his brother, who's a breathless, over-excited fanboy. Great team. All of them, genuinely excited to be there. Then a big hug goodbye. Completely the opposite of what I was expecting. I had a brilliant time. Ah, showbiz.

Lunch with Julie today was surreal. (Pizza Express, Salad Nicoise, thank you.) She got out a map of LA. 'Now, I think you should live near me. These are the areas I recommend. Venice Beach is good. It's all cleaned up, but still bohemian. Lots of writers live there. Views of the sea. You might like it, because the temperature is lower than in town. Or there's Larchmont. More suburban, but close to BBC Worldwide. Or there's Sunset Strip. You like Sunset Strip, remember?' And there are these photos of *incredible* houses, just stunning. Blimey! I can't live somewhere like that. That's ridiculous. I can't believe that this is really happening. So, I stopped thinking about it. We talked about Phil Ford's robot instead.

Then, tonight, we went for dinner with John Simm at the St David's (well, I say dinner – bar food, peanuts and crisps). What a hoot! God, he can tell an anecdote. I've thought of him as the Master for so long, I'd forgotten what brilliant company he is. And he's the most incredible mimic. I never knew that. He was telling us stories that had pitch-perfect impersonations. (Amazing stories. I'll have to tell you one day.) He loved the Master-as-a-skeleton stuff. Loved the eyes. Also, he was raving about *The Dark Knight*, and he wants a bit of the Joker's insanity in the Master this time – which is fine, that's where I was heading. I wanted to make him madder. Brilliant!

FROM: RUSSELL T DAVIES TO: BENJAMIN COOK, SUNDAY 28 SEPTEMBER 2008 20:07:33 GMT

RE: RADIO TIMES

I got a text off Gareth David Lloyd last night: 'Thanks for your comments in the book. I'm flattered!' How embarrassing. All I do is say how sexy he is.

I went into town today to buy a copy, since I've given all mine away. I like to have one at my side. I wandered into Borders, and practically bumped into a *pillar* of them! Yes, a pillar. It was horrifying. I just thought, oh, please don't let this pillar still be untouched by 2012. There were big signs announcing our October book signing. 'RUSSELL T DAVIES & BENJAMIN COOK SIGNING'. Or maybe it said 'SINGING'. We could do that.

Anyway, I bought one, came home, read all the Gareth David Lloyd references, and blushed to my boots. It's complicated, having a book out.

FROM: RUSSELL T DAVIES TO: BENJAMIN COOK, FRIDAY 3 OCTOBER 2008 22:02:08 GMT

RE: RADIO TIMES

This bloody OBE. You're allowed to bring three people. I've got 1) my boyfriend, 2) my sister, 3) my other sister, and 4) my father. Now, my father had said that he didn't want to come, because he's blind, but last night I made the mistake of saying, out of duty, 'Are you sure?' Blow me, he changed his mind! So, who out of the other three do I get rid of? Everyone is digging their heels in. No one is volunteering to take the bullet. Bloody hell.

FROM: BENJAMIN COOK TO: RUSSELL T DAVIES, SATURDAY 4 OCTOBER 2008 01:47:23 GMT

RE: RADIO TIMES

We're in the middle of a credit crunch, with unemployment everywhere, and mounting debt, and your biggest problem is 'Who do I take to Buckingham Palace?'!!

Listen, something struck me today, as I was flicking through *The Writer's Tale* for the 53rd time. I was reading our exchange of texts last Christmas Day, and thinking… David's swansong is a two-parter, yes? So, when is it actually scheduled for? You've been saying some time in early 2010, possibly… but why not show both parts on Christmas Day? The Mars Special could be on Halloween instead (you'd have to take out the Christmassy bits), or in November, or the week before Christmas – anywhere but Christmas Day itself – then David's final adventure, both parts, could give us the Best Christmas Day Ever! Like the two Christmas Day episodes of *EastEnders* that we get each year. For once, *Doctor Who* could bookend *EastEnders*! (And it'd mean that we wouldn't have to wait so long for *Christmas on Mars*. Easter to Christmas is one hell of a stretch. Easter to November less so.)

Plus, it was meant to be, because David's first episode was *The Christmas Invasion*, broadcast on Christmas Day 2005. That's poetic, that is! He was born and died on Christmas Day. Like Jesus. If Jesus had died on Christmas Day. Oh, go on!

FROM: RUSSELL T DAVIES TO: BENJAMIN COOK, SATURDAY 4 OCTOBER 2008 02:20:18 GMT

RE: RADIO TIMES

Dare I say it, that's not as barmy an idea as you might think. A double-bill of Christmas Day Specials? That's almost irresistible. I wonder…

FROM: BENJAMIN COOK TO: RUSSELL T DAVIES, SATURDAY 4 OCTOBER 2008 02:25:22 GMT

RE: RADIO TIMES

Claim it as your idea! Yeah, then it might happen!

FROM: RUSSELL T DAVIES TO: BENJAMIN COOK, SATURDAY 4 OCTOBER 2008 02:27:11 GMT

RE: RADIO TIMES

I'm e-mailing Julie now. I won't mention you yet. But the idea will always be yours. The Great Correspondence cannot lie.

FROM: RUSSELL T DAVIES TO: BENJAMIN COOK, SUNDAY 5 OCTOBER 2008 00:37:31 GMT

RE: RADIO TIMES

I'm just back from Cardiff's Gay Film Awards, where I presented Best Short Film.[6] Actually, I was dreading it. I thought, 'I'm bound to end up bored and slinking home at midnight to catch up on *The X Factor*.' But do you know what? It was brilliant! I was honoured to be there, I really was. There were filmmakers there from across the world, and it was all *Queer as Folk* this, *Queer as Folk* that, *Torchwood*, gay, bisexual, blah, blah, blah, and an award-winner made an acceptance speech saying, 'Thank you to Russell T Davies, because he was my inspiration.' That made me feel as old as the hills, though. I'm like the gay Santa.

There were no taxis to be had on a Saturday night, so I've walked all the way home from town in the pissing rain. But here's an e-mail from Caitlin Moran:

> *I'm reading your book. Aside from fainting with joy at ME-ME-ME-ME-ME being mentioned, my main reaction is: I never realised how mental you are. You missed your calling. You could have been the greatest actor the world has ever known. Your public carapace is mighty and convincing. You always come across so… Aslan.[7] With a fag.*

---

6 The Iris Prize Festival, in Cardiff, celebrates gay and lesbian films from around the world.
7 Aslan the 'Great Lion', the guardian and saviour of the magical kingdom of Narnia, is the central character in the *Chronicles of Narnia* novels by CS Lewis.

It's odd to think that she even had a notion of me that needed reassessing in the first place. But that's good, I think. Feels healthy.

FROM: BENJAMIN COOK TO: RUSSELL T DAVIES, SUNDAY 5 OCTOBER 2008 00:53:42 GMT

RE: RADIO TIMES

Does that *Queer as Folk* association ever get tiresome? Don't you wish that people wouldn't bang on about it? You've said, when it comes to All Things Gay, it's important to stress visibility, and your Gay Writing has been the making of you, but don't you wish that you were recognised for Writing, for Drama, for Storytelling or whatever, irrespective of the Gay tag? Is it even constructive to label *Queer as Folk* as Gay Drama? Most of the people who watched *Queer as Folk* were straight. Well, statistically. (Unless Charlie Hunnam's Arse turned them all.)

FROM: RUSSELL T DAVIES TO: BENJAMIN COOK, SUNDAY 5 OCTOBER 2008 17:04:36 GMT

RE: RADIO TIMES

I know what you mean, but it doesn't bother me at all, the gay thing. A lot of writers would die for a label! I'm proud of it, I really am, which is lucky, because I reckon it's going to stick. The whole *Doctor Who* thing might die down after a while, especially as Steven takes over, and then someone after him, and someone after them, and I suspect I'll be left with the epitaph of *Queer as Folk*. The thing is, I think I *am* a Gay Writer, when I write anything. If I wrote a drama exclusively about a man and a woman who've been married for 40 years, I still think I'd be writing a gay version of that – or rather my insights, as a gay man, into that relationship.

I'm slightly in PR mode here, because I had to do 27 quick interviews after the Gay Film Awards. You have to be automatically positive – in the context of a gay film festival, you *must* be – but I don't have to fake that response. I really, really mean it.

Most crucially, I don't think it's ever affected my commissions. I'm not aware of anyone ever having said, 'He can't write that because he's gay.' Well, it might have been thought, subtly and insidiously. When people write off my scripts as 'lightweight', I think that's bound up with their perception of my sexuality, even if they aren't conscious of that. But there's always someone who's going to say they don't like my writing because of this, that or the other. Equally, they might say, 'Gay or straight, I think you're rubbish.' Fair enough. I think they're rubbish, too! Then again, the man who commissioned *Bob & Rose* and *The Second Coming* for ITV was Nick Elliott: older, straight, millionaire, all whisky and horseracing. But he loved me, frankly. He loved my work. The trendy, iconoclastic Channel 4 turned down *The Second Coming*, but the populist ITV gent understood it. Who'd have thought? In the end, you can't worry. That's the truth. I have never, ever worried about it. It's only when asked about it that I have to consider it.

Maybe I'm blind to a lot of what goes on, and is said, around me. But isn't that always the case?! Tonight, one young filmmaker told me that he'd been watching *Queer as Folk* when he was 13, and he watched Stuart and Nathan having sex, and then, more significantly, watched them rush off to the hospital, and that complicated scene between Stuart and Vince on the roof, where they hug – and he said that suddenly so many things made sense to him. He went into school the next day, and told all his mates – all girls – that he was gay, and they were all happy for him, and he was fine. Now, I'm sure that it was a bit more complicated than that, and the story was narrowed down to be said to my face, but that's probably the hundredth time I've been told something like that, and I will never, ever get tired of it.

FROM: RUSSELL T DAVIES TO: BENJAMIN COOK, SUNDAY 5 OCTOBER 2008 17:48:39 GMT

RE: RADIO TIMES

There was me, blathering on about the gays, and I forgot to tell you… Julie LIKES your Christmas plan! 'Fascinating,' she said. None of us had ever thought of it! I came clean to her in a phone call last night, and admitted that it was your idea – which she loved, because she thought it was brilliant to get an outsider's opinion on the whole thing. (An outsider? I think you're secretly running the whole shebang!) She's run it past Jane, and there's definite interest. Apparently, one of the most attractive things about your idea is hitting the Saturday *before* Christmas with the Mars episode. Julie said, 'It makes it a completely *Doctor Who* Christmas!' She said that we might have to run the first part of the finale on Christmas Day at 6pm, to make room for *EastEnders* and stuff, and do I have a problem with that? But I think it's fine.

She's only had a quick conversation with Jane, so they're going to talk about it more next week. Long way to go. And there are problems. If the Mars episode goes out the Saturday before Christmas, then does that hit the *X Factor* final? (Is the last *X Factor* the Saturday *before* the last Saturday so that they can get the Christmas Number One slot?) But there you go. The wheels are turning. You have turned them. Do you fancy running the LA office?

FROM: BENJAMIN COOK TO: RUSSELL T DAVIES, SUNDAY 5 OCTOBER 2008 18:18:26 GMT

RE: RADIO TIMES

Last year's *X Factor* final was the weekend *before* the weekend before Christmas. Ditto the year before. This year's will probably be 13 December, but it's hard to call whether the 2009 final will be on the 12th or 19th. I predict 12 December, to give them time to get a Christmas Number One.

>>Do you fancy running the LA office?<<

I am already. Who do you think rigs every Oscars night?

FROM: RUSSELL T DAVIES TO: BENJAMIN COOK, SUNDAY 5 OCTOBER 2008 19:28:39 GMT

RE: RADIO TIMES

I'm studying this year's *X Factor*! It looks to me like they'll have whittled down the contestants to three by 13 December this year, because there's always three in the final. This means that we have a chance! The Saturday before Christmas is *Factor*-less! I can't believe I've just sat here with a calendar working that out.

I have just typed out the Christmas 2009 calendar, complete with the *X Factor* dates, and sent it to Julie! I'm obsessed.

FROM: RUSSELL T DAVIES TO: BENJAMIN COOK, MONDAY 6 OCTOBER 2008 15:34:17 GMT

RE: RADIO TIMES

Julie has spoken to David about the NTAs. He's up for the live feed! It's tricky now, because we'll have to start talking to the NTA people without making it obvious what's going on. Then again, they must be thinking that David stands a good chance of winning, so they'd want a live backstage camera just in case, surely? (At the same time, male and female actors are put into the same category this year, so Catherine is up against David. That could split the vote. Christ, we've never needed David to win so much! Poor Catherine. I wanted her to stand up there with a trophy for Donna Noble.) The only option is to start talking to the NTA people now. I even think, a few days beforehand or maybe on the day, we should let them know the big picture about David's announcement, because that's only fair. Live TV is a nightmare, and they wouldn't thank us for giving them a big shock. They need to be able to handle it.

I was on set for *Torchwood* this afternoon, in Cardiff Bay. It's so happy! It's a joy to be there. They're buzzing. That's because of Euros, and Pete, and the fact that *Doctor Who* isn't filming, so they're the Number One Show. Psychologically, I think that's having a huge impact. And I really do think it's found a good, new shape. This five-hour thriller feels great. I'm absolutely sure it works. (That'll come back to haunt me.) I'm glad they're happy. They deserve it.

FROM: RUSSELL T DAVIES TO: BENJAMIN COOK, TUESDAY 7 OCTOBER 2008 22:19:34 GMT

RE: RADIO TIMES

I had a script meeting in London today, with Gareth. Beforehand, Jane grabbed Julie and me. Into the secret glass office. Not laughing so much today; serious face on. The NTA Plan is accelerating. But we need to take a second and concentrate. Should we do this? Is it wise? Jane has had to let the Heads of Publicity know, and it sounds as though they're worried. They think it'll be hard to control. (It's better than the control we usually have!) They think the press will be furious, for giving them no warning. (Isn't that what happens with news?!) And I think, quietly, they're worried that it's on ITV, not the BBC. (I love that! *Doctor Who* all over the rival channel, upstaging everyone!) I suspect that Jane was only scratching the surface, that there's a lot of opposition to this idea, but she keeps loving it, saying things like '*coup de théâtre*'.

Talking of which, we're off on our book-signing tour tomorrow! How mad. See you in the morning, Benjamino. Bright and early.

ON TOUR!

From Wednesday 8 to Friday 10 October 2008, Russell and Benjamin embarked on a series of signings in bookstores around the UK. Originally published in *Doctor Who Magazine* 402, this is Russell's account of their three days on tour...

I'm on tour! Yes, it's me and Benjamin Cook from this very magazine, going round bookshops, signing *The Writer's Tale*. (Later, we're told that a blogger says we look like Bannakaffalatta and a Slitheen. Worse than that, it's Margaret Slitheen! Hmph.) David Tennant sends a text: 'Have you got a tour bus?' Um. No. We've got a car. But it's a very nice car, driven by the man who drives Alan Titchmarsh, so there. We're on a three-day, whistle-stop tour – London, Birmingham, Manchester, Bristol, Cardiff. 'That's funny,' I say, 'every time we stay overnight, it's in a city where I've got a home.' 'Yes,' says Ed the Book Man wearily.[1] 'You'd almost think it was planned.' Oh, right, sorry, thanks.

We've got no idea what to expect. Ten people, 35 maybe? What if no one turns up? I once saw Richard and Judy sitting in a shop with nobody.[2] I ended up buying their book out of sympathy. But when we arrive in the first store, we're told the queue is snaking out of the door! It turns out, that's for Julie Walters, but never mind. I declare her our mortal enemy. In London, the staff say, 'You've got more than Jamie Oliver and Alan Carr,' and I'm happy for the rest of my life. And when the Manchester shop says, 'You've beaten Sir Bobby Charlton,' I decide to run for President.

It's a bit like being a gangster. The car pulls up in a deserted loading bay; big burly men march you through concrete corridors; you're taken to meet the boss in a subterranean office. Then she offers you apricot cake, and the analogy falls apart. But we're actually nervous and jittery, me clutching a Sharpie, Ben mainlining Red Bull, until we're led through to the table, and then, all of a sudden – it's brilliant! Absolutely brilliant. We end up having the time of our lives. Thing is, it's so *smiley*. Everyone's smiling! That's the wonderful thing about *Doctor Who*, in the end: it just makes you smile. A hovering journalist asks snidely, 'Are you sick of pretending to smile?' Hey, back off, hack! The smile's genuine. How could it not be?

People have been queuing for ages, so Ben and I are genuinely frantic to make it worth their while. If you've never been to a signing, this is what happens: you're given a Post-It in the queue, to stick on the flyleaf and write down the dedication you want, and more importantly how to spell the name, otherwise it would take forever. Especially that woman called Anniina ('It's from Finland'). Then it becomes a blur of names and smiles. Hello Angela, Michael, Freya, Jason, Rosalind, Minea, Team Lesbian, a man called Jesus (Ben writes 'God bless'), women dressed as Captain Jack, teddies dressed as Captain Jack, and, best of all, the kids. Little, round, giggling faces. I ask, 'What's your favourite

1 Ed Griffiths is Publicity Manager at Ebury Publishing.
2 Richard Madeley and Judy Finnigan are husband-and-wife TV presenters.

episode?' A lad called Alyn says *Rose*, which I've never heard anyone say before. He'll be the producer in 2028. But two little boys just stare solemnly. 'Favourite episode?' Silence, stare. 'Favourite companion?' Silence, stare. 'Favourite monster?' Silence, stare. 'I think you two are secret *Primeval* fans.' 'Oooh yeah!' they chime, huge grins. Mum says sorry and takes them home to be beaten soundly.

Then it's back to the autographs – and a signature under pressure becomes something very odd indeed. I find myself writing Result Davies. Peanut Davies. Runt Davros. One of them even looks like Pam Dance. Ben's is morphing into some weird alien pictogram [...]

Our favourite story comes from Birmingham. The woman in charge, Amanda – who should be in charge of the whole country, frankly – says that the manager of the Nationwide next door has asked for the queue to be removed. Why? 'It looks like there's a run on the bank!' So if the worldwide financial markets have since collapsed, and you're reading this in the firelight of your own furniture while fighting off wild dogs, now you know why. *Doctor Who* brought down civilisation. But what a way to go.

And as the queues go on and on – the girls who bring birthday cake, little Emily who can't stop laughing, Karen and her husband ('We got engaged at a convention, and our dog's named after Katy Manning'), *The Angels Have The Phone Box* t-shirts, the sheer goodwill of it all – I can't help thinking, *this* is fandom.[3] At its best. Cos I live in a very closed *Doctor Who* world, and the subject of fandom is usually brought up by provocative, negative journalists so that I often react in a provocative, negative way. As though the fans are a problem. But that's just restricting the discussion to the extremes, the couple of hundred angry, shrill voices who dominate the conversation. Now, these three days open my eyes. I'm an idiot! Because I can see so clearly, right in front of me, that the majority of fans are happy and fun and barmy, just like the show. And the most joyous thing of all is that every one of us – those in the queue, and us two signing away – have got a little blue box spinning somewhere in our heads. Spinning forever.

Then it's back to the Post-its and the faces, hello Aaron, Giovanni, handsome Stefan, Matt from Aardman, Mikee with two Es, Susan, Nige, Ben, meet Ben!, Erica, Harriet, Paula, Connor, Hayz, Ramsey, Owen, Joshua, Jonathan, Johnny, John, Jon, Jo...

MEANWHILE:

Far away from the scribbles and name-dropping, in a cold and forgotten corner of Cardiff...

A small red light blinks in the dark. Printers sit poised. Computers count away the seconds in a dusty, abandoned room. A sign on the door bears the legend: *Doctor Who* Production Office.

Soon, so soon, the waiting will be over. And preproduction on the Specials will begin.

Monday 24 November.

Tick tock, tick tock...

---

3 'The Angels have the phone box' is a much-quoted line from *Doctor Who* 3.10.

FROM: RUSSELL T DAVIES TO: BENJAMIN COOK, SATURDAY 11 OCTOBER 2008 01:25:33 GMT

RE: RADIO TIMES

Benjamino! Hope you survived the Dalek-strewn streets of Cardiff after our signing. My night turned to crap. I was just about to get an early night, when I got called out to the *Torchwood* set in Pontcanna. A huge location has just fallen through – the entire climax to Episode 5 was written around it – because there's asbestos in the roof. So, more rewrites. The rewrite pages will soon start hitting mysterious colours like goldenrod. You know you're in trouble when you've hit goldenrod.

And now I am engaged in a complex and ridiculous discussion with the *Doctor Who* Sound Department (they never sleep) about what a Cybershade sounds like. For Christ's sake, I don't know! Maybe sort of... *raaawr*.

What a week though. Just brilliant. I'm glad we didn't fall out and storm off, like bands do on tour.

FROM: RUSSELL T DAVIES TO: BENJAMIN COOK, MONDAY 13 OCTOBER 2008 00:59:46 GMT

CHELTENHAM

I have come back from the Cheltenham Literary Festival itching. Bites, Ben. Insect bites. Some sod has had their photo taken with me, and given me BLOODY FLEAS!!! Otherwise, I had a really good time. We missed you, though. Especially as I walked into the signing room, and everyone does that clapping thing, and I had to sit down and sort out my Sharpies with them all staring at me. That felt weird on my own.

Caitlin Moran interviewed me on stage. She sends her love. She completely hadn't thought about kids being in the audience. I saw one of the questions on her pad: 'You say writing is sexual. What does that mean?' I said, 'How am I going to describe that with kids sitting there?' 'Kids?' she said. 'KIDS?! *All* of my questions are about sex! There are kids?!' She dived into the dressing room for 20 minutes to rewrite everything. Then, we got shown into the auditorium for a sound test. It was *huge*. Like 2,500 seats! We both stood there staring, and suddenly it wasn't funny any more. I haven't been that nervous in ages. I went outside, and smoked for half an hour. As it began, we had to walk backstage and wait behind a curtain to be introduced. The noise of 2,000+ people! Terrifying! (I should have known this was going to happen, really, but I never pay any attention to the schedule.) But then on we went, and everyone was clapping, and of course it was lovely. Again, all that goodwill. *Doctor* bloody *Who*.

It was only 15 minutes of me on my own, then Johnny B came bounding on, and then it really was a hoot. OMG! LOL! I luv him! SQUEEEE! He's so relaxed, and slides from anecdote to anecdote – and then ever-so-serious, heartfelt speeches – with so much ease. He's the gay buccaneer one minute, the children's hero the next, and everyone just worshipped him. Three women in the front row were literally OMG-ing in their no-doubt-*Torchwood*-branded pants. Then it was the Q&A, and lots of kids asked questions, which is guaranteed to make everyone smile. Someone asked what our favourite episode is. I gave the stock answer – 'It's like asking you to choose your favourite child' – and Caitlin said, 'Oh, I can do that!' He he. And then there was more clapping, and it was over. Phew.

But nothing is without an agenda. Nothing, not ever. The man who always drives Anthony Hopkins when he's in Wales drove my car on the way to Cheltenham. I said casually – okay, not so casually – that I'd love the great man to be in *Doctor Who*. 'I'll have a word,' he said. Seriously, he's got to e-mail Sir Hopkins tomorrow, and said he'd mention it!

FROM: RUSSELL T DAVIES TO: BENJAMIN COOK, MONDAY 13 OCTOBER 2008 04:03:53 GMT

RE: CHELTENHAM

Julie sent an e-mail at 2am saying, 'The papers are reporting that you called Prince Charles "a miserable swine" at Cheltenham.' Did I?! On stage, we talked about him not appearing in *Voyage of the Damned*, so I must have said it then. Can't remember.

FROM: BENJAMIN COOK TO: RUSSELL T DAVIES, MONDAY 13 OCTOBER 2008 04:28:40 GMT

RE: CHELTENHAM

That'll make 28 November interesting. Isn't that the day you collect your OBE from his mother?

FROM: RUSSELL T DAVIES TO: BENJAMIN COOK, TUESDAY 14 OCTOBER 2008 16:30:12 GMT

RE: CHELTENHAM

Half an hour ago, I received an e-mail from Julie: 'We are a GO for backstage filming in the *Hamlet* interval.' The NTA Plan is on! For God's sake, go and vote, Ben! Vote David! Vote now! I've done it already. Felt weird and wrong, skipping over Catherine's name. It's for the greater good of *Doctor Who*, but all the same…

Meanwhile, here's something to make you hoot. This afternoon, Julie and I received an e-mail from Mark Cossey, a producer at the BBC. Lovely man, great supporter of ours, he oversees *Doctor Who Confidential*. Apparently, an entertainment company, with considerable experience in these things, has approached Mark to ask us what we think of *Torchwood: The Musical* as a concept! 'They have the two chaps from ABBA on board to write the music,' Mark explained. 'I wasn't quite sure what to say, but I did promise to pass it on.' Of course, after I'd finished laughing, I e-mailed straight back: 'But, what, do you mean Björn and Benny?[8] Really?!' Mark e-mailed back: 'Yep. Björn and Benny love *Torchwood*. Maybe you have the power to re-form ABBA.' Oh, that's funny. That is the best thing ever!

FROM: BENJAMIN COOK TO: RUSSELL T DAVIES, TUESDAY 14 OCTOBER 2008 16:43:37 GMT

RE: CHELTENHAM

HA, HA, HA, HA, HA, IT'D BE AMAZING! LITERALLY, AMAZING! I'm

8 Björn Ulvaeus and Benny Andersson from 1970s/80s Swedish pop group ABBA.

bristling with anticipation. In fact, I think Bjorn and Benny should write *Torchwood* Series Four...

(To the tune of ABBA's 'Voulez-Vous')

> *Weevils everywhere*[9]
> *A pterodactyl flying through the air*[10]
> *Eve is at the bar*
> *You cum so hard, you don't know where you are*
> *And here we go again, we know the start, we know the end*
> *John is in this scene*
> *Been on TV before, now it's the law, to see some more*
> *Of John on our TV screens*
>
> *Torchwood Four (ah-ha)*
> *Take it now or leave it*
> *Now is all we get (ah-ha)*
> *Nothing promised, no regrets...*

Etc.

FROM: RUSSELL T DAVIES TO: BENJAMIN COOK, TUESDAY 14 OCTOBER 2008 16:57:08 GMT

RE: CHELTENHAM

That is so brilliant! Look, this could be the end-of-Act-One ballad.

(To the tune of ABBA's 'Fernando')

> *Did you cum so hard, Fernando?*
> *I remember long ago another Torchwood Hub like this...*

Fernando is a Tiny Space Monkey who's fallen through the Rift and is trying to take over the world with his Evil Pop Music. It'd pass the time.

FROM: BENJAMIN COOK TO: RUSSELL T DAVIES, TUESDAY 14 OCTOBER 2008 17:14:27 GMT

RE: CHELTENHAM

Forgot to say, the NTA news is ridiculously exciting. Imagine being in the audience for that! How nervous will you all be? IT'S LIVE! ANYTHING COULD HAPPEN! What a plan! I love it so much.

Look, while I'm e-mailing you about the NTAs, ABBA, and other acronyms, we've received an e-mail from Ebury: 'Excellent news! Richard and Judy have selected *The*

---

9 The sewer-dwelling Weevils are the 'resident alien' of *Torchwood* Series One and Two.
10 The Torchwood team keeps a pterodactyl as a pet. The creature came through the space-time Rift.

Writer's Tale for their Christmas Books strand. It will be endorsed by R&J on their new TV programme as a perfect Christmas gift.' Bollocks, just as they sink to 50,000 viewers. But we're in the R&J Book Club!

FROM: RUSSELL T DAVIES TO: BENJAMIN COOK, TUESDAY 14 OCTOBER 2008 17:20:18 GMT

RE: CHELTENHAM

BLIMEY! FANTASTIC NEWS!

Let's say no.

Oh, all right then, yes.

FROM: RUSSELL T DAVIES TO: BENJAMIN COOK, WEDNESDAY 15 OCTOBER 2008 23:30:27 GMT

RE: CHELTENHAM

Anne Jowett from *Radio Times* e-mailed me today:

> *Christmas-wise, it looks as though we'll run the* Doctor Who *cover the week* before *the Christmas issue – at the moment, there are compelling reasons why we can't run it two weeks before – but the good news is that although I can't promise absolutely, we're gunning very hard for Christmas 2009.*

I forwarded that straight to Julie, adding:

> *PROOF!!! I'm telling you, it's meant to be. The* Doctor Who *Christmas!*

Julie e-mailed back saying, 'I am on it. I promise.' So, that's exciting. Your plan!

When things are set in motion with Julie, they often fall off my radar for a while, because she has meetings with... well, I don't know who she has meetings with, but she talks to Jane, and schedulers, and all sorts of bosses that I don't even know exist, and e-mails fly around that would make *The Writer's Tale* look like a pamphlet. I think I show off sometimes, and make myself sound like I'm on top of these things – I can catch the odd draught of me doing that in the book – whereas in fact Julie adds it to her mountain of work, and I sit back. Then, with e-mails like that one from Anne, I don't imagine that Julie has forgotten about Christmas, but I become a nag. Essentially, it's me saying, 'I WANT!' I'd deplore it, but it works. I dump the workload and responsibility on Julie, and flounce off. She is so marvellous.

In other news... poor *Sarah Jane* is suffering. Down from one million viewers last series to half a million this week, presumably because the programme is now shown half an hour earlier this year. That's got to be playing a part. Just when Series Three is looking at big budget cuts – at least one-fifth off the budget. We've worked out how to make the show for less, but it's worrying us. I'd hate that wonderful cast to be unhappy with what we're doing. So, an interesting choice cropped up today – and I don't know what to think, which is unusual for me. Jane Tranter didn't know about the budget cuts, because it's a Children's Department commission (only the pilot was part-funded by Drama), but when she found out, she was instantly brilliant. She offered to bump us up more or less to our original budget... but the show would have to go on hiatus for a year, because the money isn't available yet. It would then play at 5.30pm on a Sunday, with repeats on CBBC later that week. (There's a lot of speculation there. CBBC might not like that. The money and the slot can't be definite yet. Plus, Jane is leaving.) But what would we prefer? To carry on with Series Three now, or risk the hiatus? Christ. I don't know.

I know a 5.30pm slot sounds wonderful, but I was in the *Sarah Jane* Dub today – a beautiful, tender story written by Joe Lidster – and here's the thing: it's just not a 5.30pm-on-Sunday show. If I were inventing a Sunday *Doctor Who* spin-off, it would be very different. We've got these kids running around, and a supercomputer built into the wall, and lots of daylight, because kids can't work nights, and a lovely ethos that smacks of weekday teatime telly. (Which, yes, okay, kids aren't watching. Shaddup!) We'd have to reinvent it. Should we? Should we reinvent a spin-off? How far from its origin is it sliding then? I sat watching it today with 5.30pm-on-Sunday in mind, aware of the changes that we can make, and it felt wrong. Yet, if the extra money keeps it looking handsome and stylish… oh, I'm really stumped. So is Julie.

FROM: BENJAMIN COOK TO: RUSSELL T DAVIES, THURSDAY 16 OCTOBER 2008 01:44:18 GMT

RE: CHELTENHAM

Thanks for the update on, well, everything. Can I ask, how important is a *Radio Times* cover? Is it more about publicity or prestige?

Oh, but poor *The Sarah Jane Adventures*! That's a tough call. I'd say continue for a year with a lower budget, and then switch to Sundays for Series Four. Sorted.

>>We've worked out how to cheapen the show, but it's worrying us.<<

What have you worked out? How can you cheapen *The Sarah Jane Adventures*?

FROM: RUSSELL T DAVIES TO: BENJAMIN COOK, THURSDAY 16 OCTOBER 2008 02:37:54 GMT

RE: CHELTENHAM

A *Radio Times* cover *is* important. It's one of those things that fans consider to be important, but do then turn out to have real value. Not in terms of ratings, really, but in terms of prestige. It's symbolic, really. It sends out a signal to other press outlets. It gives you stature, and helps to drive the whole campaign. A Christmas cover is gobsmacking. That 2005 one, with the TARDIS in the snow, was amazing to all of us. Daft, really, isn't it? Sounds silly when you describe it like this. But it's real. You go into a Publicity meeting and say, 'We've got the *RT* cover for this episode,' and everyone sits up, so we do work hard on them. In fairness, the *RT* loves *Doctor Who*, and really supports us. (You might have noticed!) I can remember the days when I'd long for an *RT* cover. *Casanova* was the first one that I ever had. I was so excited. They brought it to the press launch. I got such a kick. Not just me – Nicola, Julie, everyone. And there on the cover was David Tennant! Nothing has changed.

>>What have you worked out? How can you cheapen *The Sarah Jane Adventures*?<<

We'd have to strip it back, and be lethal with the schedule. At the moment, each episode has six days filming. We'd have to make that five, but a strict five. It would allow five locations (or less, preferably) per episode, but you couldn't move location within any one day, because you'd need to complete up to eight pages a day. It all depends on the writer, to script a full and strict day's work per location. No half days. We could go further. We're debating whether to break the director's ownership of the material. I started that conversation, and it's kind of a runaway train. If, say, Episodes 3, 4, 7, 9 and 11 have scenes outside Sarah Jane's house, at the moment we'd go to the house exterior once for Episodes 3 and 4, then again, weeks later (and probably with a different director), for Episode 7, then again for Episode 9, then a fourth trip to complete Episode 11. That's a normal TV schedule. Under the new system, you'd film all those scenes outside the house in one day, across all the episodes, with one director (this means getting *all* your scripts in, in advance), so directors wouldn't own episodes as such; they'd own locations. On the downside, it could increase cast costs (you'd have to have cast Episode 11 while you're shooting Episode 3, which might mean paying an actor for a longer stretch), but also might affect the calibre of director that you can appoint. A lot of directors would refuse to work that way.

Director-ownership is one of the most expensive parts of drama budgets. They're paid for weeks of prep, weeks of filming, weeks of post-production. If we cut back the prep, make them shoot whatever is convenient to us, then shift them on to shoot new material, which removes them from post-production and leaves the Edit in the hands of the editors… it's actually closer to the American system, where directors get two or three days in post-production to give notes, then they're off, and the producers run the Edit. It's a bit radical. It's horrific for the director. All over the industry, the director is becoming the fall guy for these budget deficits. That's a real tragedy. It would affect our schedules as producers, too. More work for us. Great.

But I'm not sure the changes on *Sarah Jane* will be that big. I'm not sure they need to be, not yet, because we can make additional savings with the FX, and the grade, and the size of the guest cast. But it's good to have discussions like this, to open everything up to examination. That's what the job is going to become, more and more – cost-cutting. It's a good skill to have. Part of me actually enjoys flexing those muscles, if I'm honest – and I'm an amateur next to people like Julie. One day, they'll have honed an entire shoot down to a Polaroid and a passing dog. Though maybe we could cut the dog…?

Hey, the *Torchwood* team finished filming on the Hub tonight. The end! The very last scene before the place blows up. They had cakes and champagne. Even if there's a fourth series, I wouldn't bring back the Hub. We're done. Move on. I wonder what we'll do with that set. Turn it into matchwood, I suppose.

Right, I'm off. Script meetings at 10am tomorrow. Zzzzz…

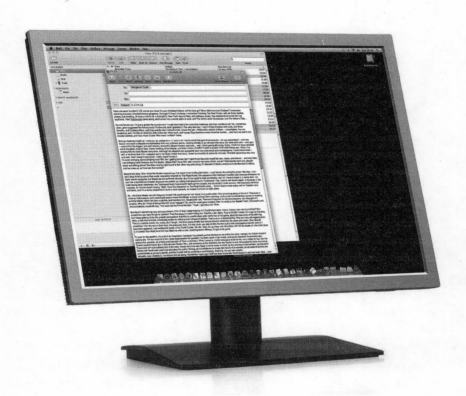

CHAPTER EIGHTEEN

THREE E-MAILS (AND AN EPIPHANY)

In which the Tenth Doctor's final words are revealed,
the Master slashes up a businessman in a toilet cubicle,
and thick, putty-coloured gloop drips down soft, sticky faces

FROM: RUSSELL T DAVIES TO: BENJAMIN COOK, FRIDAY 17 OCTOBER 2008 02:57:25 GMT

4.17/4.18

Have you seen the date?! (Of course you have! It's your birthday!) Where did the time go? When did it become October? I remember planning this year; it looked bloody gorgeous. I thought I'd have a holiday. I remember finishing *The Next Doctor*, with all those months ahead, and thinking, I'll have a *month* off. A fortnight in New York, trips to Paris, and ordinary, lovely, free weekends at home with my boyfriend. Then *Torchwood* came along, and turned into a whole stack of work, and *The Sarah Jane Adventures*, and *The Writer's Tale*...

No one forced me. I'm just a glutton for punishment. I could have had a few executive meetings, and then wandered off. No, I remember when Jane suggested the five-episode *Torchwood*, and I *grabbed* it. The very next day, I was in Pizza Express with Julie, and Brian Minchin, and Lindsey Alford, outlining exactly how it should work. I knew the plot – those alien-voiced children – immediately. No one twisted my arm. I'm like an alcoholic with a free bar. More work, and I jump! Days become weeks become months... and here we are in mid bloody October, and how much *Doctor Who* have I written? None.

Enough beating myself up. I owe you an update on 4.17 and 4.18. I had in mind that quiet final episode – do you remember? – with the Doctor on board a clapped-out-spaceship with very ordinary aliens, meeting his fate in an intimate little story. But

Jane and Julie – and you! – pushed for the bigger, two-part version, where the Master returns, and now… well, I think you're all wrong. Sorry. I think I've been tempted out of my good, original idea. I keep thinking of the Master, and then I think: I HAVEN'T GOT A STORY FOR HIM! Worse still, I think: I've already told the best Master story ever. Although my clapped-out-spaceship story sounded small and unimpressive, I had a lot of detail – well, a lot of the *feel* of it – mapped out in my head. I knew that story. I knew its mood for its entire 60 minutes. That little spaceship was nice and safe. And I swear it was good. I really regret losing it.

I'm even worrying about bringing back Wilf. Am I getting too fan-ish? I said these Specials would be new, clean, uncluttered… and now here I am bringing back Gramps and the Master. (Good title!) I love Wilf, and I want to see more of him, but isn't that exactly when you should leave something alone? But then I swing right round to the other way of thinking: it's Bernard Cribbins, everyone loves Bernard Cribbins, and he loves us, so how can that be bad?

Back to the story. Ever since the Master cropped up, I've known how to bring him back – Lucy Saxon, the women's prison, the ring – but I can't stop thinking about that waiter sequence inspired by *The Real Hustle*, the sequence that I realised I couldn't use because everyone on Earth would recognise the Master as the ex-Prime Minister. But it's too good to lose completely, isn't it? I have to keep it, in some form. He can't be a confidence trickster, because we ended up nicking that sequence for *Torchwood*. Yes, I had to rob myself again. In Episode 3, the Hub having been destroyed, the Torchwood team has to build itself up from scratch, but we couldn't work out how. We reached a bit of an impasse, so I found myself saying, 'Well, I saw this sequence on *The Real Hustle* once…' Damn! But it works really well for Captain Jack and Ianto, and it's a funny sequence in quite a dark episode, so maybe it's found its right place.

So, I think the Master should disguise himself. He could dye his hair blond. In a public toilet. He's scrubbing away at the sink. That puts in mind an Ortonesque, post-watershed scene where the Master is dying his hair like a rent boy, and a smart businessman comes in cruising, and the Master takes him into a cubicle, and murders him. Maybe after sex. That won't happen, for obvious reasons, but I thought of it anyway. Why do I think of things that will never happen? Oh, and he could grow a beard, then he really is the Master! Yeah, that could work. And somebody could still say, 'You look like the Prime Minister.' 'Yeah, I get that a lot.' Nice.

But there's something very obvious about 4.17/4.18 that I keep missing: it's David's last story. I know, I know, how obvious is that?! But sometimes you take things for granted. Past few days, it's been hitting me. David's. Last. Story. That is HUGE! I mean, it's huge for the fans, but I keep getting hit by the greater perspective, that this is a world-class actor at the top of his game, about to leave one of his defining roles, a role that is loved, absolutely loved, by millions and millions of people. That is such a responsibility. This isn't any old regeneration. This is a cultural event. No, really, don't laugh, it is! It's a piece of telly that people should remember for years and years. Kids should remember it for the rest of their lives. No pressure, then. It's only when you see all this *Hamlet* stuff in the newspapers that the size of it becomes apparent. I am writing the death of the Tenth Doctor. Oh. My. God. It's up there with Who Shot JR?[1] Or the death of Little Nell![2] (Sod it, it's better than that!) And this has filled me with a cold, clutching terror. Blimey, it's got to be good.

To look for the positive, it's a bit of an inspiration, because it's pointed out the obvious to me within the story: namely, the Doctor doesn't want to die. I'm too much of a fan, I take regeneration for granted; I've been stuck in fan-mode, seeing the eleventh incarnation as a production process, as a fairly ordinary part of Time Lord fiction. What I mean is, it's felt strangely small to me, very matter-of-fact, like the Doctor wouldn't care. But in this all-new *Doctor Who*, with emotions at the forefront, like the Doctor is *real*, this suddenly feels enormous. This event isn't just subtext; this is the story. Never mind the new body to come (bear in mind, by the time this is transmitted, the Eleventh Doctor will have been seen out and about in public, filming, so his existence is a very real fact for the viewers, on all sorts of levels); the current body is going to perish, and the Doctor will do anything to avoid dying. Anything. As any man would.

Actually, now I realise it, I've known this all along. Remember ages ago I told you that I knew the Tenth Doctor's very last line? Well… and this is a real birthday present, Ben… here's the line. Ready? It's simply:

```
                    THE DOCTOR
            I don't want to go.
```

Said all alone, standing by himself in the TARDIS, with the old, orange, regeneration glow beginning to burn. Nice, simple, and sad. 'I don't want to go.' So true of the Doctor, and of David, and of all of us watching. 'I don't want to go.' Oh, poor Doctor. It's like I've known how sad his reaction would be, but I just didn't realise what a strong story that little sentence contained. Because now, in my head, that story is rocketing! This is life and death! This feeds back into the Master. The Doctor and the Master are always so opposite, and yet so similar, and now this story is about the Master surviving, too – doing anything to escape death.

You know what? Sod that *Real Hustle* stuff. What a waste of time. That's way too easy. The Master is *dying*, and desperate to survive, and so is the Doctor. They're on a collision course. So, back in that women's prison, in the satanic rite with Lucy Saxon… oh, she's not dumb, she's been waiting for him. She knew about the ring. She's been waiting all this time for the cult to gather around her and show its hand. As the vortex

---

1 'Who Shot JR?' was an advertising slogan created in 1980 to promote Season Four of US soap opera *Dallas*. In the final scene of Season Three, the character JR Ewing was shot by an unknown assailant; viewers had to wait eight months to learn whether he would survive and which of his many enemies was responsible.
2 'Little' Nell Trent is the heroine of Charles Dickens' novel *The Old Curiosity Shop*.

of light appears and the Master is reborn, Lucy has a… I don't know, a weapon (what sort of weapon can she have hidden in prison?!), and she smashes the ring, just as he's manifesting, just *before* he's complete. Explosion! The entire prison destroyed! The Master consumed in fire! What happened? When the Doctor arrives on Earth from the Ood-Sphere, the TARDIS lands outside the smouldering remains of the prison… but it's a few days later. The few days later are crucial; a little slip in time that puts the Master ahead. There are stories that as the prison burned, a strange half-shadow creature scuttled out of the flames and ran away…

The Master is like Voldemort. The half-formed Voldemort. (Well, that's going to cost. We can't afford that many FX, to make him a CGI creature. Maybe he's just John Simm looking rough.) He can't steal wallets and clothes; he's a wretch, he's homeless, he's living in the hinterlands of the city like a wild, lost thing. Well, no, still with a bit of charm and wit. But he's dying (that fits in with my earlier half-skeleton idea – it was meant to be!), he's powerless, he's feeding off the life force of tramps and things. Sinister scenes set near the docks, with old tramps huddled around braziers, thinking that the Master is one of their kind ('You look a bit like that old Prime Minister…'), then he flashes into a skeleton – and pounces! Drains the life force! Bodies are being found, dead tramps reduced to husks. This is nice, because I've had Wilf's Alien Watch on my mind all this time, but I've been a little worried that I'm not sure what they're up to – what UFOs are they watching exactly? All they had was a funny little scene in a café. They were little more than set dressing. But now – oh, now – they're on the trail of this evil vampire who's killing the homeless at night. Without knowing it, they're hunting down the Master! That's how the Doctor meets them.

That's nice, but I'm skipping over the fact that all of these ideas fill about half of 4.17. I have no bloody idea what happens in 4.18. Empty. It is empty. HELP! Empty, empty, empty, the story is empty. No, bollocks, worse, I know what's haunting me, and this haunts every writer… I HAVE RUN OUT OF IDEAS. That's a permanent subtext to everything I ever do. I'm not sure I've admitted that before, or even looked it in the eye. (Oh Christ, this e-mail has taken a sudden, blind turn into darkness!) But it's a very big worry, all the time, maybe for everyone who's ever written anything, ever. The terror – and the profound belief in the possibility – of running out of ideas. Sometimes, a journalist asks it. 'Do you think you'll ever run out of ideas?' Said with a smile, the bastards. And I bet every writer gives a cheery little answer, hiding the clutch at their throat, because the unsayable has just been said. It does haunt you. Always. Literally, always. And it must be possible. It must be.

I can remember clearly when the opposite of that happened. There was a very definite moment when I first gained some confidence in my ability to generate stories, when I realised that I was genuinely full of ideas and stood a good chance of making it as a writer. (And I don't often dwell on the positive, you might have noticed, so let me try for once.) It must have been 1995 or 1996, and I was working on *The Grand*. That show was a nightmare. Writer after writer would get sacked, and I'd have to replace them. It was supposed to be written by a team, but I ended up writing the entire first series, and most of the second, and every member of the cast needed a story, every week. There was a regular cast of 12 or so, and you had to think of story after story for them. It was merciless. It was a story machine. One day, on Series Two, another script had fallen through at the last minute, and I had to fill the space in about ten days. I was walking away from Granada in a sweat, because my head was empty. I had no story of the week. Absolutely nothing. I was walking past the law courts – which isn't relevant, but it's vivid in my memory – and staring at the blank space in my head, when I simply thought, suddenly, out of the blue, with no planning: what if Esme Harkness had children?!

Esme Harkness (I love that surname) was a retired prostitute living in faded elegance in the hotel. She was played by Susan Hampshire, who was glorious and brilliant. Esme was everyone's favourite character. (In the very last episode, she inherited a fortune – and bought the hotel!) It struck me that a woman like that, in the 1920s, would have had children years ago – and abortions, too, but imagine if she carried two kids full-term, who had been given away, maybe brought up in good homes, never knowing about their real mother. Then, in this episode, cue a blackmailer who knows the whereabouts of Esme's now-grown-up kids, and can give her the information in return for money. Well, I wrote it. And it worked. It was a bit dark and internalised as stories go, and I got a bit symbolic by making the whole thing revolve around a game of cards (you tend to write symbolic when you're young, because you think it's deep), but Susan Hampshire made the whole thing thrilling, and the blackmailer was played by Ian Dury – I've worked with Ian Dury, isn't that brilliant? – so it was a nice piece of invention. Out of desperation.

The point is, back at those law courts, in one footstep, I went from an absolutely blank page in my head to a full 60-minute plot. Simple as that. The whole plot downloaded from nowhere in a single second, it really did. And I can remember the moment so clearly, so acutely, because in that very same second, I thought, I can do this job. I was young then, still wondering whether this was the right job for me, whether I'd end up starving in an attic, whether I would run out of ideas, and in that single second, that one moment, I proved my worth. To myself. I've never forgotten it. Trouble is, it's no consolation now. Well, it is during some dark hours, but that positive stuff just isn't as insistent and pervasive as the bad stuff. I love thinking about that moment, but it's precious and fleeting. What If I Run Out Of Ideas? lingers every bloody day. And here it is, flexing its muscles with 4.18.

This e-mail is so long that I'm beginning to get paranoid – if my PC freezes or something, it'll be lost (I should write this safely in a Word document, but e-mail feels more immediate and real) – so it's nowhere near finished, but this is a good point to send anyway.

Many happy returns, Benjamino. Hey, this is your present.

FROM: BENJAMIN COOK TO: RUSSELL T DAVIES, FRIDAY 17 OCTOBER 2008 03:30:51 GMT

RE: 4.17/4.18

>>I've already told the best Master story ever<<

You're wrong. You've told the second-best Master story ever. Since he was all-powerful in *The Sound of Drums* and *Last of the Time Lords*, smooth, smarmy and oh-so-New Labour, the way to go in 4.17/4.18 is to make the Master scrabbling and desperate. Hobo Master. Voldemort Master! I remember saying to you, months back, how much I love that idea. Vampire Master, yeah! I swear you're on the right track.

What do you mean you've run out of ideas? Nonsense. Listen, that scene in the public toilet, with the businessman, is brilliant. Okay, so you don't show it all. You can't. You show *some* of it, maybe. You don't show the Master slashing up a businessman, obviously. Or shagging him! But you show the businessman entering the toilets, the Master at the washbasins, an exchanged glance, that's all, the Master turns back to the mirror, the businessman enters a cubicle... and the very next shot is the Master walking away from the toilet block, in the businessman's clothes. Brrrrr!

It's the most exciting part of your entire e-mail – honestly – because there, in your description of that one, thrilling scene, is precisely what's new, and fresh, and so wonderfully unsettling about these episodes. That scene feels raw, and rough (good rough!), and different – and sordid, actually. No, not sordid. Avaricious! That's the word. (Is it? Do I even know what that means?) That's the Master this time around. He's avaricious (I'm sticking with it), and that's electrifying. You've nailed it already. I keep thinking of *The Dark Knight*. Heath Ledger in *The Dark Knight*. The Joker. Scenes in back alleys, gutters, and prison cells. Who needs Christmas cheer?! You'll blow *EastEnders* out of the water.

You're doing exactly what I said in my Introduction to *The Writer's Tale*: you're driven by expectation – by meeting it, by confounding it, by surpassing it. You've got the Master hanging out with tramps. The former Prime Minister! Living like a vagabond. Like a bum. Like a monster. How angry would that make him? And angry is good. Angry is scary. Desperate Master is much more frightening. Desperate and mad. Hypnotising tramps!

Also, if he's Hobo Master, Bum Master, a down-and-out, hanging with drunks, drug addicts and bums, then you could call the episode... wait for it... wait for it... are you ready? You could call the episode... *The Sound of Bums*! Me so funny. Oh, my sides. I should turn professional. But seriously – stop complaining that you haven't got enough story, because this sounds amazing. Really, honestly, I promise. I'm right. Because you know what? I'm hooked already.

And David's last line is pure class, for so many reasons. It's beautiful, and understated, and unexpected. See, there you go again, confounding expectations.

FROM: RUSSELL T DAVIES TO: BENJAMIN COOK, FRIDAY 17 OCTOBER 2008 19:03:48 GMT

RE: 4.17/4.18

I'm really surprised. I'm kind of gobsmacked. Do you really like it that much? (That's rhetorical. I'm not fishing for compliments.) Wow! That's made me so happy. I just went out to Tesco's – that long walk I walk every day, usually with sloping shoulders, and bowed head, and heavy heart, because all the problems weigh me down (I hate that walk!) – and I sort of strolled along thinking, yes, maybe I can do it. That felt wonderful. Is it really that good?! I should read those e-mails back to myself. I just sort of splurged it all out. And I've got more to say. But Christ, turning all these ideas into a script is a whole heap of hard work, about to start any day now.

The funny thing is, do you know what happened in that last e-mail? I've written you a treatment! That did me good last night. I had a powerful night's sleep. I woke up invigorated. (You may charge me a psychiatrist's fee.) There am I crowing that treatments are beneath me, but that's what I just did – and it worked.

Right. So. More. Onwards. Back to the plot. I keep wondering whether the Doctor should have an Ood Spirit Guide throughout the story, appearing behind his shoulder during quiet moments, or even frozen moments of action, talking cryptically, like spirit guides do. He's really there; he's not in the Doctor's imagination. He's projecting himself, mentally, into the Doctor's journey, not just to advise, but also to judge. Except, while I've had this image in my head for months now, it isn't suggesting any dialogue or great moments. It's a bit dreamlike, isn't it? I hate dream material. And now that I've shoved Wilf into the mix, there's no need for the Doctor to have a secret mentor. He can talk to Gramps. I keep picturing Wilf and the Doctor together – running, laughing, hunting the Master across urban wasteland – and gradually Ood Boy just fades.

Talking of Wilf, I keep coming back to that café scene. I could never work out how or why they were sitting opposite a Donna who doesn't barge into the actual scene. What, do they see her by coincidence? That's rubbish. Eliminate coincidence! Then, today, it occurred to me: it's Wilf's plan. He takes the Doctor to this café deliberately. The Doctor is wondering why. What's so special about this place? Turns out it's opposite where Donna works. No, opposite where her fiancé works! Wilf has brought the Doctor to spy on her. (Great chance to see Donna with her not knowing she's being watched, parking on double yellows, beeping the horn, arguing with the traffic warden, salty old pre-Doctor-Donna. I love that Donna.) The fiancé comes bumbling out – nice, big, harmless man – but Wilf is so sad. This man (Sam, Samuel, Sammy?) is a dreamer, a romantic, a bit like the Doctor, but with none of the Doctor's gumption. He has these wild and crazy schemes that end up losing money. God help the two of them. They're going to end up living in a tiny, rundown flat. Oh, and Donna steps out of the car… and she's hugely pregnant! It's all a bit wistful, setting up the final scenes of 4.18, where the Doctor appears at the church and gives Donna a wedding present. A lottery ticket. 'I'll keep that. You never know, I might get lucky for once!' Ahh, Donna Noble, millionaire. (Oh, she'd be married. She'd have a new surname. A new surname for Donna?! Lyons? Donna Lyons?)

Do you see what I mean about not needing Ood Sigma in there? Although, he'd serve a nice cuppa in the café. It's funny how much I love that café. It's absolutely central to me. Never mind the sci-fi, or the story, or the monsters; that café scene is where the heart of it is. Two people connecting over a cup of tea. Two ancient, wise men, keeping themselves warm, just before Christmas.

Elsewhere, that Geneva thing keeps lingering. A few months ago, remember I mentioned the Master flying out to Geneva, after his *Real Hustle* stings? Why Geneva? I feel like the Master, this identity-fraud Master, with his new persona, Mr Smart Businessman, needs to find something on Earth that will give him power, so he uses his new contacts – he can hack into UNIT or Torchwood databases, and all sorts – to find, well, I don't know, some sort of project, some sort of science project, that he can take control of and turn into a world-dominating machine. (What, though? Mind control? He's done that. He's done bloody everything!) Maybe some top-secret, James Bond-type lair in the Swiss Alps, one of those houses built into a mountainside, incredibly swish and sleek, where some multimillionaire is working on... well, I keep thinking of *The Lazarus Experiment*. Bloody Lazarus has beaten me to it! Because that's exactly what I need here. I need an old man pouring money into genetic research. When the Master turns up, he has all the knowledge to take over the experiment and turn it into what, what, what?! But that's a good shape for a story. I'd just have to work hard to un-Lazarus it. Then again, Harold Saxon funded the Lazarus research, so I could use that to make the similarities look deliberate. (That's a bit fan-ish, isn't it? I loved *The Lazarus Experiment*, but it's hardly the one that I expected to be referencing for the big finale!)

Mind you, it's all a bit dry – Switzerland, the sleek base, the experiments, the millionaire, it's dull for kids. This top-secret project needs aliens! It needs to be clever enough, scientifically, to have required alien involvement. They should be *secret* aliens. The millionaire shouldn't know that they're there. They're disguised as humans, only unmasking when they go behind-the-scenes for secret alien conversations, like aliens do. 'The plan is proceeding!' and all that. Although, actually, they don't feel evil. I don't know why, but they feel like they're there to *help*. The Master is there to be evil. He's centre stage.

I was walking past Techniquest this morning, and I realised that I'm channelling *The Faceless Ones*![3] Because this alien race needs to be sick, or dying, and they need help. They need some sort of genetic thing that will cure their race, so they're using the millionaire's top-secret scientific project for their own ends. Not nastily, though.

3 *The Faceless Ones* is a 1967 *Doctor Who* serial concerning the Chameleons, an alien race that has been damaged by an explosion on their home world and is reliant on a scientific process of identity theft to sustain and extend their lives.

No one's going to be hurt. They'll just take the end result, whatever it is, and go home to cure their people. The Master would suss that they're there immediately. So would the Doctor, though he's got to be one step behind for this part of the story. Maybe the Master could befriend the aliens, pretend to help them, then turn the tables on everyone, like he does.

I like these aliens. I was thinking today, could we have faces that are runny? There needs to be something wrong with them, genetically, like they're melting. Imagine if they had soft, sticky faces, all drooping jowls and hangdog expressions – because they could be quite funny, this lot – and I wonder if Neill Gorton could build something where, maybe, they have concealed holes at the top of the prosthetic mask through which a runnier version of their skin is pumped, constantly. Not water, something thicker and gloopier. Throughout every scene, they've thick, putty-coloured gloop dripping slowly down over their eyebrows and mouths. They're constantly wet and runny. Ewww! Nice, though. Good for kids. The Runny People! (The Bashboli. Is that a good name? Hmm, maybe.) They'll be the last alien race I create.

Talking of monsters… I phoned up Will Cohen the other day, to ask about my plan for every human on Earth to become the Master. Expensive, obviously. He promised to get back to me, but hasn't had time yet. However, there's a certain amount of doable FX that we can take for granted – multiple passes against green-screen, maybe even modelling a full CGI John Simm-head, getting people to wear green masks, then imposing John's face on them for huge crowds. But I worry about how much FX it's going to take up. If there are three people in a scene, that's three Masters. The multiple passes are going to break the budget. I've got to get the Doctor off the planet quite early in 4.18, I think, so I was thinking about the Runny People and… well, they'd have a spaceship off-Earth, wouldn't they? In orbit. With a handy transmat. The Doctor transmatting away from the Master's evil plan is a lot like Martha at the end of *The Sound of Drums*, but hey ho. Now, I hadn't seen this coming, honestly, this isn't deliberate, but if the Doctor escapes to the spaceship… and the Runny People, they're humble, they're ordinary, they're even a bit amateur, so… look, it's that ordinary alien spaceship! It's back! The original idea for the one-part finale, bleeding though! Weird how things like that happen. Actually, maybe it's not weird at all. It's a natural process of using what I've got.

But is it right that an epic two-parter ends with a showdown on a crumbling little ship? Actually, put like that, it sounds attractive. Maybe if I work hard on the ship itself, if I make it like *The Little Engine That Could*, then it might pay off in the end. It had better pay off, because this bloody spaceship is determined to appear, no matter what. I can't stop it.

Anyway. Look, I've never articulated this, but it's time I told you about the Two Doors. Yes, the Two Doors! I'm not a hundred per cent sure what the Two Doors are yet, but they've been in my head for such a long time now. I've never even told you about them, because it's easier to talk about the Master, and Wilf, and Runny People. Actually, they've become so embedded, I haven't told you about them, because it's like mentioning that the sky is blue. But I'm beginning to worry about them. Big time. You see, *Army of Ghosts* and *Doomsday* were written around Two Levers. Everything that happened pivoted around the fact that Two Levers opened the dimensional breach between our universe and the parallel one in which Rose would become trapped, and ultimately the Doctor would hold on to one lever, and Rose would fall from the second. Literally, the whole architecture of that story is built around those levers. And now I've got Two Doors. Except, the Two Doors are more complicated than the Two Levers. I keep thinking about them, and I can't work out how they operate, and that's going to be vital. The closer these scripts get, the more it's bugging me. This is what I mean...

The millionaire's top-secret project has some sort of power plant within the main chamber. Two Doors. Two separate booths, maybe. Two small, glass rooms. It's like – I don't know, I'm guessing, I can't *see* it, it's maddening – it's like some sort of pressure system, a radiation room, whereby an operator has to be in one of the rooms at any one time. This whole chamber is massively radioactive, all being siphoned through these two rooms, somehow, and the safety devices demand that one operator is present at all times. No, the operator has to be actually *inside* the booth. Only by closing the first door can the second door open to let the occupant out. You have to go through the first door, close it behind you – the closing is vital – and then press the door control inside that booth so that the second booth will open and the operator inside can go on his tea break. Is this making sense? It's a bit blurry. These Two Doors need to be strongly established. We need to see them operate in 4.17, really clearly, even boringly, we should see them operate two or three times, and repeat in 4.18. And here's why...

This is how the Doctor will die. He's going to have to step inside Booth #1 to free someone in Booth #2, and that's going to irradiate him. Because – oh, I've never told you this, it's obvious – it's *not* the Master who causes the Doctor to regenerate. No way. Oh no. You should spend the whole story thinking that's going to happen... and then the story ends, the Master has been destroyed (maybe he should be reduced to dust this time; we can't have another dead body for the Doctor to grieve over), and the Doctor is standing there, shattered, amazed, 'I'm alive!' Not even grieving for the Master – well, maybe a line or two – but actually thinking he's changed events to prevent his regeneration. And then – this is the point – he realises, behind him, there's some dumb bloody technician stuck in Booth #2, which is going to flood with radiation. Someone has to open Booth #1 to let him out. In stepping into Booth #1, and triggering Booth #2's door, the Doctor opens up the radiation – the whole glass booth floods with red light, agony, and he's dying. It's a slow death. His hand gives a warning glow, but he can fight it for a little bit; that's when he says goodbye to Wilf ('I'll see you at the wedding'), and sets off on his last trip, to visit Sarah Jane, and Martha, and Jack, and everyone.

The key is the technician. The dumb sod who got trapped in Booth #2. This man should have had only two or three lines throughout. He should have been *no one*. Just a bloke. (I wondered if he should be a Runny Person, but no, he should be completely ordinary.) He's unimportant. He's insignificant. He's useless. The Doctor gives his life for a no one. (Because there's no such thing as a no one.) And the Doctor shouldn't do it easily. He knows what's going to happen. Oh, the drama in it! The sheer drama! He should rant and rave at this man through the glass before opening the door. 'Who are you? Who the hell are you?! Who the hell are you to do this to me?!' Railing against death. But then of course, with dignity, the Doctor opens the door. He steps inside. He saves the nobody's life. Because he's the Doctor. He has no choice. The Tenth Doctor's ending should be so small and intimate, after all the sturm and drang. He's saved the world already; now he saves one man called Keith. And in doing so, dies.

But I'm still faking those Two Doors. Explaining it here has made it feel a little better. Even if I don't manage to build the Two Doors into the script, the sacrifice will be the same; giving your life for a stranger. How Doctor is that? At the same time, I'm thinking, if you're eight years old, have you waited all this time for a bloody glass door to open? A man called Keith vanquishes your childhood hero! Shouldn't the Doctor be suspended over a precipice – or, better, holding a dying Wilf in his arms, and giving his life force or something to save the old man? Hmm. But maybe I can play with those expectations. Maybe you'll be expecting the Wilf sacrifice. I can even foreshadow that with red-herring lines like Wilf saying, 'Don't worry about me. I'm not important!' You're convinced that Wilf is going to die somehow, and then Keith takes you completely by surprise and –

Hold on.

Oh God.

OH MY GOD!

What if it's Wilf in Booth #2? Tapping on the glass? With the radiation count rising, about to flood? Poor Bernard's sad face. The Doctor realising that he has to open Booth #1 to save the old man. He survived the Master, but it's bloody Wilf who brings him down! The marvellous thing is, Wilf would *know* what's at stake. Wilf would be saying, 'Leave me here. Don't do it. I'm old. I've had my time. Don't kill yourself. You're more important than me.' I've been living with Keith the stranger for all these months – I love him, I love the randomness of it – but now, oh, just think of the *acting*! Bernard and David! Through glass! Christ, I'm tearful just typing this. I'm not kidding, I really am. It's making me cry. Oh wow. Bernard bloody Cribbins! Like it was always meant to be, that strange destiny binding together the Doctor and the Noble-Motts all this time. Ever since he bumped into that funny little man in a deserted London on Christmas Eve, with Kylie Minogue, it's been destined for Wilfred Mott to end his life. Ohhh yeah!

Ben, Ben, Ben, this Great Correspondence is MAGNIFICENT! I thought of that idea right here and now. 'Where do you get your ideas from?' HERE!!! I'm typing so fast that this is full of typos, and I'll have to go back and correct it once I've calmed down. The Tenth Doctor gives his life for Wilfred Mott. OH MY GOD. Or even OMG! That's a real OMG! Oh, I'm thrilled. Those sad eyes of Bernard's. David staring at him. 'Doctor. Let me die.' CHRIST! I did love Keith. I loved the Doctor's fleeting rage at Keith, although he could still do that with Wilf. 'Why did you step inside there?!' That's exciting. I'd never thought of that, yet it's been staring me in the face.

Brilliant, brilliant, brilliant. I love that. Brilliant. I do laugh at the thought of saying to you, 'I've run out of ideas,' when these e-mails are bloody endless, and they've made me feel a little better...

But then, hold on, wait a minute, I look at 4.18, and the vast hollows of empty space. Look at me saying, 'The Master is reduced to dust,' when I've got no bloody idea how. Oh, bollocks, there goes the excitement. That didn't last long, did it? That constant panic at the back of my head feels like a dull scream. Actually, it's not even that exciting. It's more like a moan, or a clock ticking or something. From the moment I wake up. Following me everywhere.

Where were we? *The Immortality Gate.* There's a title for 4.17. It's the millionaire's project. *The Lazarus Experiment* was about growing younger (yes, please!), but this project is about becoming immortal, a self-renewing cell structure that would last for all eternity. Who wouldn't want that? (Me!) It involves some big gate, some sort of arch in which you stand and get zapped and immortalised. This is where the Master stands, having replaced the controls with, er, some sort of, um, human-slash-Time-Lord-genetic-broadcast system, transplanting himself into every human on Earth. But I like that name, the Immortality Gate. That's good. More importantly, it's what the whole story is about. (Listen to me, using a theme!) The Doctor wants to live, the Master wants to live, and this millionaire's top-secret project is about living for ever. Neat. Nice. That could sing.

A couple of days ago, we were talking about casting with Andy Pryor. I said that I'd love to cast Julie Andrews in something. She'd be perfect for the millionaire. She'd be seeking immortality for her children. Yeah, I'd believe that. That would give this millionaire more character. But I've been stuck with this Julie Andrews character being located in Switzerland, because her plot fitted the old identity-fraud Master, but now that the Master is a seething, dying wreck, eating tramps on wastelands, how the hell does he get to Geneva? How do those two plots tie together? Then, today, it sort of clicked. I've always wanted a sequence where the Doctor, Wilf and the Alien Watch hunt down the Master at night, running over derelict buildings, hounding the beast – and they corner him, and the Doctor is so wary, because he knows he's going to die, and the Master is skeleton-ing on and off, wanting the Doctor's life force... when a blazing light slams down! Troops abseil in! There's a helicopter right above them! These private security troops grab the Master, and haul him up into the air. They're taking him to Switzerland! Those in the know, like Julie Andrews, have been following events in London, they know that an insane alien genius is on the loose (the Lucy Saxon/ burning prison link would interest a lot of people), and they've been hunting him down, too, because Julie Andrews needs a genius to complete the Immortality Gate.

That all clicked into place because *Silence of the Lambs* was on ITV2 tonight. You know that scene where Hannibal Lecter is transferred to another city, and they hold him prisoner overnight in this huge room, surrounded by guards and squads of police, because everyone knows he's so dangerous. That's what the Master would be in Switzerland. Julie Andrews (it's very funny, typing 'Julie Andrews') would be so cautious of this madman, while still needing his knowledge. The image of a psychotic, brilliant man in that film is so powerful, I'm inspired. Especially when Hannibal escapes. Of course, the Master won't escape in the same way as Hannibal. He won't cut off people's faces and wear them as a mask. (Maybe not!) You never know, though. The Master's powers of hypnotism could give me an equivalent of that. I've never used those. Well, I did, I made it worldwide with the Archangel Network – but a bit of old-fashioned 'Look into my eyes' wouldn't go amiss now, especially if those eyes are in a skeleton head.[4]

Thinking about the Master and the Immortality Gate… those Runny People are kind of pesky. Why would any alien race need to come to Earth to do their research? They've got to be cleverer than us. But hold on! What if they're there to *stop* the millionaire's project? Because immortality is banned. That still makes the Runny People quite benign; they're just there to throw in a bit of sabotage, and then sod off. *That's* why Julie Andrews' experiment isn't working. That's why she needs the Master. The Runny Men become victims of the Master's coup, too. I still can't work out how the Master switches the project from 'immortality' to 'every human looks like me', but I suspect I'll have to use my greatest technobabble flimflam yet. Or maybe just 'he's switched the circuits'! Yes, that'll do. Yes.

Christ oh mighty, I'm taking a break now. More to come. Yes, more! I haven't even got to Donna yet. (Me to Julie this afternoon, about halfway through writing this e-mail: 'What if Catherine was in this Special *properly*, not just in the background. Like, Donna Noble is back!' Julie: 'Oh, well, good! God, yes.' We'll see. I'm still not sure. That's a separate chain of thoughts to describe.) However… while I've been typing to you, all hell has been breaking loose. BBC News has contacted us saying that they're considering running a story that would basically say that the *Doctor Who* team have been seriously considering and talking to various actors about taking over from David, and so it's looking likely that David may soon announce when he's leaving. The cheeky bastards. We're being undercut by our own bloody news service! E-mails are flying like crazy. It's mental.

---

4 In *Doctor Who* 3.12/3.13, the Archangel Network was the main phone network on Earth, broadcasting a signal of four beats, designed by the Master for the purposes of mind control.

We think we've shut them down for now, but this'll make you laugh – it's from Piers – 'I'd suggest sticking to Operation Cobra, unless people start coming forward with tangible evidence that David is leaving.' Operation Cobra! The plan for David to announce his departure live on air at the NTAs, should he win, is officially called Cobra! We use that in *Torchwood*. It's the government's crisis name for Cabinet Office Briefing Room A. And now we're using it for David! That's made me hoot. But if BBC News ruins our NTA plan, I'll... I'll... oh, I don't know. Bollocks.

CHAPTER NINETEEN

THE COBRA'S TALE

In which Richard and Judy are compromised,
David Tennant's face is carved into a pumpkin, and Operation
Cobra is launched, then aborted, then launched again

FROM: BENJAMIN COOK TO: RUSSELL T DAVIES, FRIDAY 17 OCTOBER 2008 21:04:35 GMT

RE: 4.17/4.18

And... and... AND?! What about Donna? What happens next? Damn you and your cliffhangers.

Hey, am I part of Operation Cobra now that you've, um, told me about Operation Cobra? Was that information classified? Will you have to kill me? Isn't the first rule of Operation Cobra: never talk about Operation Cobra?

FROM: RUSSELL T DAVIES TO: BENJAMIN COOK, SATURDAY 18 OCTOBER 2008 19:03:48 GMT

RE: 4.17/4.18

I'm off on my travels: Swansea tonight, and London tomorrow to present one of the Teaching Awards (the New Teacher of the Year works at the school where my mum, dad and granddad taught), and then Manchester on Monday.[1] Phew! Bad timing, though, because I want to tell you more about Donna. Still, that can stew for a few days. My ideas might improve with age.

Besides, I'm dying to know how it all ends. Got any ideas?!

---

1 Natalie Richards, a drama teacher at Bishop Gore School in Sketty, Swansea, was named the SSAT Outstanding New Teacher of the Year at the annual Teaching Awards ceremony at the London Palladium, on 19 October 2008.

FROM: RUSSELL T DAVIES TO: BENJAMIN COOK, THURSDAY 23 OCTOBER 2008 14:22:47 GMT

OPERATION X-MAS

Ah well. We got so close with your Christmas transmission plan. Yet, not all is lost…

Julie just phoned. This has been batted to and fro between the schedulers and us for over a week now. In the end, they thought that two episodes of *Doctor Who* on Christmas Day would be too much. They've a double *EastEnders* and a double *Cranford* to schedule, both of which, in fairness, have ratings to match ours. But the key point was range. The BBC has to show its range on Christmas Day, as a showpiece. This means *Doctor Who*, *EastEnders*, *Cranford*, the news, and probably a sitcom.

But! Jane still loves the idea of scheduling 4.16 a little earlier in the year. So, how about 4.16 on Saturday 19 December, 4.17 on Christmas Day, then 4.18 on New Year's Day? Bear in mind, New Year's Day is traditionally the highest-rating day of the lot. That's a magnificent slot. It makes sense. You can *picture* it. That's been my worry, inconstant scheduling, with 4.18 in some sort of two-days-after-New-Year, neither-here-not-there slot… but New Year's Day is big. It's branded. Julie asked me whether I liked it, and it is very attractive. The human race transformed into the Master on Christmas Day, cue credits, come back next week! Lovely.

It forces a strange dogleg into the story, because 4.17 would be set on Christmas Day or Christmas Eve, then the action would carry on, continuously, into 4.18… but a Christmas Day setting would look odd on New Year's Day, wouldn't it? But I can write around that. Everyone still has their decorations up on New Year's Day, so the setting would make sense. I'd just avoid any specific references in 4.18 to the actual day. When the Doctor goes off on his sojourn to visit all his ex-companions, at the end of 4.18, *then* it's New Year's Day. Donna's wedding is on New Year's Day. That's sweet. All those church bells ringing, people celebrating, out with the old and in with the new… oh, that fits a dying Doctor. I could write that beautifully. New beginnings. We'd see the new Doctor on the first day of 2010. Better still, the Tenth Doctor's epitaph would read '2005–2010'. Julie said, 'They always wanted us to do five years, and now we have.' (Well, six, technically, but I know what she means.) It feels good, and right, and proper, and celebratory. I know we don't get the symmetry of a Doctor born and dying on Christmas Day, but it's only one week extra.

Of course, plans change, and Jane will move on, so Julie is on a mission to demand that this is set in stone. I'm going to start writing it any day now (er, maybe), and I need to seed in all this Christmas and New Year stuff. The last thing I need is a scheduler changing his mind next November. Fingers crossed. For now, though, I'm happy. In a big and busy BBC, it's not half bad.

FROM: BENJAMIN COOK TO: RUSSELL T DAVIES, THURSDAY 23 OCTOBER 2008 18:35:07 GMT

RE: OPERATION X-MAS

The more I think about it, the more I like it. David regenerating on New Year's Day,

I mean. Not *Cranford*. Boo to *Cranford*. All those bonnets make me edgy. Besides, the Christmas Day cliffhanger is irresistible…

FROM: RUSSELL T DAVIES TO: BENJAMIN COOK, THURSDAY 23 OCTOBER 2008 23:50:18 GMT

RE: OPERATION X-MAS

I did wobble on the thought of a Christmas Day cliffhanger, but I think I've wobbled back. It's odd, and different, and new, but we've sort of survived anything – transmitting before 7pm, changing companions every year… all the things that shouldn't work have worked, so the sheer newness of the Christmas Day cliffhanger seems exciting to me. (The Master should turn to camera and say, 'Merry Christmas… no, Merry Mastermas!' Or is that crap?) It's definitely the best scheduling we're going to get (and I love *Cranford* – don't knock the ladies in bonnets), so it's time I turned it to our advantage. It's better than our old pattern of 4.16 on Christmas Day, then the remaining two episodes thrown away God knows when. I hated the vagueness of that – it was driving me mad – so I'm really, properly glad that you kick-started this discussion. We've ended up in a much better place as a result. I know the story is about death, but actually the bigger story, the whole *Doctor Who* story, is about the new guy. That's what the marvellously named Operation Cobra is all about. New, new, new. Once the Eleventh Doctor appears at the end of 4.18, that's what everyone's going to be talking about. 'Did you see him? What did he say? What's he going to wear?' Kids will go crazy until the start of Series Five, and that's absolutely right.

FROM: BENJAMIN COOK TO: RUSSELL T DAVIES, FRIDAY 24 OCTOBER 2008 01:51:19 GMT

RE: OPERATION X-MAS

Well, I'm convinced. But not by the 'Merry Mastermas' line. You're right, that's crap, leave it.

FROM: RUSSELL T DAVIES TO: BENJAMIN COOK, FRIDAY 24 OCTOBER 2008 12:18:33 GMT

OPERATION COBRA

The Cobra team – Cobra!!! – is secretly arranging an interview with David on Tuesday, to be filmed by *Confidential*, confidentially, and released to all media outlets on Wednesday night as soon as he's made his announcement, should he win the award. They need someone to interview him, and your name is on the list! Don't get excited, because it's been nixed since, with the thinking that it needs to be an official BBC person. But how funny! My name was on the list, too, along with the note: 'Perhaps a little too cosy for this release?' *Cosy*?! That's worse than 'jolly'.

Everything is changing with Cobra every half-hour. It's all so jittery and tense, partly because it's the first combination of both production teams: Piers and Steven are included in this, too. In fact, it's more their announcement than it is ours.

FROM: BENJAMIN COOK TO: RUSSELL T DAVIES, FRIDAY 24 OCTOBER 2008 18:19:21 GMT

RE: OPERATION COBRA

What with all this Operation Cobra jazz, maybe we should have a code name for this e-mail correspondence.

FROM: RUSSELL T DAVIES TO: BENJAMIN COOK, FRIDAY 24 OCTOBER 2008 18:39:25 GMT

RE: OPERATION COBRA

We should be Operation Asp. I don't know why, but Asp is a very funny name for a snake. Cleopatra should have tried some other means. I always used to laugh in school.

FROM: BENJAMIN COOK TO: RUSSELL T DAVIES, FRIDAY 24 OCTOBER 2008 18:19:21 GMT

RE: OPERATION COBRA

That'll do.

FROM: RUSSELL T DAVIES TO: BENJAMIN COOK, SATURDAY 25 OCTOBER 2008 01:06:05 GMT

RE: OPERATION COBRA

I've spent a lot of the past two days trawling through *The Next Doctor*. Almost all the FX work is done, and it's looking fantastic (oh, the CyberKing!), but there are still bits that don't work. An FX shot of the Cybershade jumping onto the wall. Bad green screen. Bad wire work. Odd jump cuts, from CUs to wide shots, which I didn't like at the time but just sort of accepted. My fault, really. I should have flagged it up earlier, but I was knackered. Yesterday, I decided that I couldn't watch those mistakes go out on Christmas Day, so I waded in. Back to the Edit. We trawled through the original rushes, finding alternative shots, and new orders to sequences, and the repairs are looking much better. We might need to reshoot a Cybershade, but I'll be glad we did it, come 25 December.

I've failed to conclude last week's Maybe update. I will, I will, soon, I promise. It's by choice, though. This Donna stuff is clashing in my head, big time, and I'm letting the thoughts settle. E-mailing you might interrupt the process. But maybe not, because that bit in last week's e-mail when I thought of trapping Wilf in the booth, while actually writing to you, was very exciting. I can't work out what's best: do I a) stick to the original plan and keep Donna in the background, or b) she's Donna, it's Catherine Tate, she's loved, she's a brilliant actress, it's Christmas Day, so why not use her? I can think of several brilliant Donna and Master scenes that would make it worthwhile. Plus, the Master turns the human race into copies of himself, but I've got no one to *observe* it, apart from the Doctor and Wilf. I need someone to see it, to be terrified, and I reckon Donna's altered brain structure, following *Journey's End*, could make her immune to the takeover, so she'd be watching as Sylvia transforms in front of her...

Donna runs into the street, freaked out. Neighbours opening doors – John Simm,

John Simm, John Simm, they're all John Simm! Maybe they stare at her and howl. They howl when they see someone who's not like them. They chase her. All these John Simms chase her, like a witch-hunt. Anyone unchanged is hunted down. This isn't awakening Donna's memory, but there's a danger that it could, at any minute. Until it does, she's the old Donna, scared and horrified, not knowing what to do. The Doctor, who's in Geneva, would know this and would need to save her, which gives him something *personal* to fight for. 'I've got to save the world' isn't half as powerful as 'I've got to save Donna!' Especially if he adds, 'Without awakening her memory!' She's cornered in an alley, surrounded by a circle of Simms, and it should feel like they're going to rip her apart. They're snarling! As the Simms advance (how many FX shots is this going to need?), CU on Donna, because she's *starting to remember*! Wild images of Ood, and Davros, maybe even a Giant Wasp, flickering in front of her eyes – and she hasn't a clue what's happening – then as a Simm reaches out, she shouts, 'NO!!!' FX circle of energy blasts from her head, knocking out the Simms! She's left surrounded by unconscious bodies. What the hell did she do? (We'll discover later that the DoctorDonna part of her mind is turning itself into a weapon. Or something.)

Or maybe a great big spaceship descends and saves her, beaming her up – because the Doctor and Wilf, by now, have escaped to the Runny People's ship in orbit.

Or both! She blasts the circle of Simms, and then a great big spaceship descends –

Look, I was going to type all that on Monday, but I couldn't stop. Still, it's noticeable that out of those options, a) is one line, and b) is a big paragraph. Is that telling me something? Or am I so short of plot for 4.18 that I'm just inventing incident? I don't know.

FROM: BENJAMIN COOK TO: RUSSELL T DAVIES, SATURDAY 25 OCTOBER 2008 01:39:08 GMT

RE: OPERATION COBRA

>am I so short of plot for 4.18 that I'm just inventing incident?<<

Um. Isn't that your job?

FROM: RUSSELL T DAVIES TO: BENJAMIN COOK, SATURDAY 25 OCTOBER 2008 01:47:01 GMT

RE: OPERATION COBRA

I walked into that one. Thing is, you're right. The worry is, the more I use Donna, the closer I creep to using what's inside her head. I certainly can't have her saving the day at the climax of 4.18, because she did that in *Journey's End*. Then again, the chance to have a witch-hunt through the streets, with all those John Simms, that's the *point* of the Master taking over the human race. That's the pay-off. The sheer nightmare of it all. Who better than Donna to go through that?

The other day, I described the Master-in-disguise idea – living on the streets, feeding off the life force of tramps – to John Simm, and he loved it. He really loved the blond hair. Actually, he suggested *white* hair. It'd be good if it were all rough and punky. Also, he suggested, every time the Master kills a tramp, he leaves the letter 'M' scrawled onto a nearby oil barrel or something. A calling card. I love the 'M' idea, like he's luring the Doctor with it. What's that old film, an old black-and-white film, where Peter Lorre plays a murderer – I think he's a child-murderer – but someone sees him and chalks 'M' on his back, so all the homeless and street urchins track him down? Great film. (Is it called *M*? Yes, it is.) Peter Lorre whistles all the way though it, this creepy little tune. It's really sinister.

Of course, I looked at my diary tonight, and realised that I ran out of time to start writing the script, ooh, about four weeks ago. Ring any bells, Ben? Have we been here before?

FROM: RUSSELL T DAVIES TO: BENJAMIN COOK, MONDAY 27 OCTOBER 2008 12:17:21 GMT

RE: OPERATION COBRA

Cobra week is getting exciting. I keep saying that since the NTAs have agreed to send a live camera to David on Wednesday, surely he's won…? 'No,' says Julie. 'These NTAs are scrupulous.' They're very nice people, and we can charm them all we like, but they won't budge an inch and tell us how the voting's going. Damn them. They have to check and double check and all that.

People always think that award ceremonies are a lie, and that you're told in advance, but you're not – honest! Imagine if winners had to clearly lie on camera. It would be obvious. ITV would be taken off air for fraud. So we're powerless – which we're not used to! We love a bit of power, Julie and me! But we've just got to sit back and cling on for the ride. The only reason we'll know a bit in advance – like, an hour or so, after the voting has closed and it's all been counted – is because of the live feed, and the RSC, and the sheer complexity of getting David to the right place at the right time. They have to provide for every option. In effect, it's no different to all those awards ceremonies where the winner can't be there and there's a pre-recorded speech… but this is *Doctor Who*, and therefore has to be more complicated, more secret, and more insane.

FROM: BENJAMIN COOK TO: RUSSELL T DAVIES, MONDAY 27 OCTOBER 2008 12:19:44 GMT

RE: OPERATION COBRA

I did wonder. I didn't think voting closed until Wednesday afternoon.

FROM: RUSSELL T DAVIES TO: BENJAMIN COOK, MONDAY 27 OCTOBER 2008 12:25:19 GMT

RE: OPERATION COBRA

The phone lines close at 6pm on Wednesday, so Julie thinks we might be told by 6.30pm, if at all. But I've just realised, you and me are going on *Richard & Judy* that afternoon… but it's not being shown until Friday.[2] It'll be old news by then! It'll look

---

2 Topical chat show *Richard & Judy's New Position*, made by Cactus TV and shown on UKTV digital channel Watch, was recorded 'as live', but not transmitted until two to four days later.

weird that we're not discussing David's departure. But I can't alert anyone. Operation Cobra bans me from telling Ebury or Cactus TV or anyone. Yikes.

FROM: BENJAMIN COOK TO: RUSSELL T DAVIES, MONDAY 27 OCTOBER 2008 12:30:18 GMT

RE: OPERATION COBRA

Perhaps I could look pale and exhausted, then faint and cause a commotion if David's name crops up during the show. This is a Very Good Idea. Nothing can possibly go wrong.

FROM: RUSSELL T DAVIES TO: BENJAMIN COOK, MONDAY 27 OCTOBER 2008 16:39:11 GMT

RE: OPERATION COBRA

Look, it's *real*! Here's the press release that our PR people have prepared for Wednesday evening (attached to this e-mail). 'David Tennant has announced that he will leave the award-winning BBC drama *Doctor Who* when he has completed filming of four special episodes, which will be screened in 2009 and early in 2010…' Boo! Even by forwarding this to you, I've set off alarms in Cobra HQ.

FROM: BENJAMIN COOK TO: RUSSELL T DAVIES, MONDAY 27 OCTOBER 2008 16:47:26 GMT

RE: OPERATION COBRA

On David's regeneration, you're quoted in the press release as saying: 'I might drop an anvil on his head. Or maybe a piano. A radioactive piano.' Um, you're not taking this seriously, are you?

FROM: RUSSELL T DAVIES TO: BENJAMIN COOK, MONDAY 27 OCTOBER 2008 16:52:06 GMT

RE: OPERATION COBRA

The PR people e-mailed me about that quote: 'You've got a day in which to change your mind.' Everyone's a critic.

FROM: BENJAMIN COOK TO: RUSSELL T DAVIES, TUESDAY 28 OCTOBER 2008 23:57:26 GMT

RE: OPERATION COBRA

It's very almost Cobra Day! Happy Cobra Day, Russell! I keep thinking about our interview with Richard and Judy – isn't it going to be virtually unusable? Chances are, David's resignation will be all over the papers come Thursday morning, and they're transmitting Friday night. (That'll teach them not to transmit live.) What do we do if we're asked about, like, how long David is planning to stay for? Seriously? I can't *really* pass out.

FROM: RUSSELL T DAVIES TO: BENJAMIN COOK, WEDNESDAY 29 OCTOBER 2008 00:27:07 GMT

RE: OPERATION COBRA

Happy Asp Day! I'm quietly in a sweat about tomorrow's *Richard & Judy* interview.

I should have seen this conflict of dates way off. I was seduced by a Book Club! It just didn't occur to me. I'm really worried that it's unprofessional of me. It cocks up their show. I know the producer well enough to have a quiet word, but the way that word could spread is horrific. Those TV galleries are staffed by *Doctor Who* fans. Also, it's been decided that the BBC will issue the press release about David's decision at 7pm – when everyone is safely inside the Albert Hall, with just enough time to alert the NTA staff and, more importantly, to give the papers time to prepare stuff (providing he's won, of course). That means a scant few hours between *Richard & Judy* in the afternoon, and the press release at 7pm... but I can't risk it. I CAN'T!

FROM: BENJAMIN COOK TO: RUSSELL T DAVIES, WEDNESDAY 29 OCTOBER 2008 00:41:23 GMT

RE: OPERATION COBRA

What if you had a quiet word with Richard and/or Judy before the interview? They can be trusted, can't they? Ask them not to pose any specific questions about David. (They'd guess why, but so what?) Or is even that too risky?

FROM: RUSSELL T DAVIES TO: BENJAMIN COOK, WEDNESDAY 29 OCTOBER 2008 01:00:52 GMT

RE: OPERATION COBRA

I could just say, 'Lay off the David stuff.' I've wondered that. I do know R&J well enough to give them a quiet hint, which might be better than the woman-in-charge, because once she's given even the smallest hint, it's her duty to protect *her* show, not mine. Fair enough. Except Richard is fantastically barmy, and literally says anything that pops into his head. There's no guarantee that I'd get to see them beforehand anyway. Usually, you just meet them when you go on set, with all the mics on. If I *asked* to see them, that might set alarms ringing, because that would be so odd... Christ, what a tightrope! It's doing my head in. It's only now that we're actually here, on the day, that I realise how bad this timing is.

FROM: BENJAMIN COOK TO: RUSSELL T DAVIES, WEDNESDAY 29 OCTOBER 2008 01:03:21 GMT

RE: OPERATION COBRA

I've always imagined Richard to be more professional than he comes across on screen. Isn't it all a bit of an act? Or is he really that unpredictable?

FROM: RUSSELL T DAVIES TO: BENJAMIN COOK, WEDNESDAY 29 OCTOBER 2008 01:07:50 GMT

RE: OPERATION COBRA

No, Richard is mad. Brilliantly mad! When I was on their show to promote *The Second Coming*, he said, 'This is so fascinating, because if ever we have a guest on, and I really want to get to know them, I ask what their religion is, because that opens up the conversation and leads to fascinating stuff.' And I thought, no, you don't! You just made that up! He's never done that, ever. I've been watching. I'm that faithful viewer.

But in that moment, I swear, he really believed it. I can't help it, I love the man.

Get fainting, Ben. Make a swoon noise.

FROM: RUSSELL T DAVIES TO: BENJAMIN COOK, WEDNESDAY 29 OCTOBER 2008 10:27:24 GMT

RE: OPERATION COBRA

I'm jittery. Ridiculously so. God knows what it's like in Cobra Command. We just don't know what's going to happen today. Plus, I left my black shoes in Manchester. These things are important. Not as funny as losing my trousers in Soho, I know.

FROM: BENJAMIN COOK TO: RUSSELL T DAVIES, WEDNESDAY 29 OCTOBER 2008 10:38:23 GMT

RE: OPERATION COBRA

>>Not as funny as losing my trousers in Soho, I know.<<

The day isn't over yet. See you on *Richard & Judy*. (The show. Not the couple.)

> Text message from: **Ben**
> Sent: 29-Oct-2008 11:47
> News just in... the BBC has suspended both Russell Brand and Jonathan Ross.[3] This is bound to steal column inches from Operation Cobra. NOOOOOOOO!!!

> Text message from: **Russell**
> Sent: 29-Oct-2008 11:50
> WHAT?!!! OH NO! The Cobra just became an Adder. I might insult Julie Walters on *R&J* to gain some ground.

> Text message from: **Ben**
> Sent: 29-Oct-2008 11:47
> And I'll leave some vulgar messages on Jimmy Krankie's answering machine.

[*That afternoon, Russell and Benjamin record an appearance on the Halloween edition of* Richard & Judy's New Position, *at TV studios in Lambeth, South London. By 4.15pm, they're heading home (Benjamin) and to the National Television Awards (Russell), in separate cars. But the texting continues...*]

3 In a pre-recorded edition of his Radio 2 programme *The Russell Brand Show*, broadcast on 18 October 2008, Brand and fellow Radio 2 DJ Jonathan Ross left a series of 'lewd' messages on 78-year-old actor Andrew Sachs' answering machine, discussing the actor's granddaughter, Georgina Baillie. After little attention, the incident was reported in tabloid newspaper *The Mail on Sunday* on 26 October, prompting a record number of complains (38,000 by 2 November) about *The Russell Brand Show*, its presenters, and the BBC's editorial decisions. On 29 October, Brand resigned from the BBC. The Controller of Radio 2, Lesley Douglas, followed suit on 30 October, and Ross was suspended for 12 weeks without pay, pending investigations by the BBC Trust and broadcast regulator Ofcom.

Text message from: **Russell**
Sent: 29-Oct-2008 16:15
Julie is nervous. She's thinking that David hasn't won. ABORT! ABORT!

Text message from: **Ben**
Sent: 29-Oct-2008 16:20
Stop panicking. Unless... oh, what if Catherine's won instead?! Is she in on Cobra?

Text message from: **Russell**
Sent: 29-Oct-2008 16:21
She's half in on it. Lis, Noel and Camille are not in, until 6pm, at which point they'll be inducted. I'm loving this!

Text message from: **Ben**
Sent: 29-Oct-2008 18:10
Oh. Russell Brand has just RESIGNED.

Text message from: **Russell**
Sent: 29-Oct-2008 18:12
If he keeps upstaging us...!

Text message from: **Ben**
Sent: 29-Oct-2008 18:15
No prizes for guessing the headlines in tomorrow's papers. 'BBC LOSES TWO STARS IN ONE NIGHT!' See if you can force Babs Windsor to resign – for the hat trick.

Text message from: **Russell**
Sent: 29-Oct-2008 18:17
I will kill her.

Text message from: **Russell**
Sent: 29-Oct-2008 18:52
We've heard from the NTA people! Operation Cobra is GO-GO-GO!!!

Text message from: **Ben**
Sent: 29-Oct-2008 18:55
Good old Cobra! I never doubted it. (Ahem!) Isn't the press release issued in five minutes?

> **Text message from: Russell**
> Sent: 29-Oct-2008 19:05
> The NTAs aren't allowing our press release any more, so it's literally LIVE!!!

> **Text message from: Ben**
> Sent: 29-Oct-2008 19:26
> When do the NTAs kick off? 8pm? I'm sat at home in my tux, in front of the TV, waiting...

> **Text message from: Russell**
> Sent: 29-Oct-2008 19:54
> FIVE MINUTES TO GO!!!

> **Text message from: Ben**
> Sent: 29-Oct-2008 19:55
> WHAT ARE YOU DOING TEXTING ME, THEN?!

> **Text message from: Russell**
> Sent: 29-Oct-2008 20:44
> We've got no idea what order these awards are in. It's a nightmare.

> **Text message from: Ben**
> Sent: 29-Oct-2008 20:45
> When's the *Hamlet* interval? Can't you work it out from that?

> **Text message from: Russell**
> Sent: 29-Oct-2008 20:52
> No, because the NTAs are running behind schedule. Whenever that interval is, we're in trouble...

[*A few minutes later, at the Royal Albert Hall, David Tennant is announced as the winner of the National Television Award for Outstanding Drama Performance. 'Hello, London!' he says, via satellite from Stratford-upon-Avon's Courtyard Theatre. 'This is really, really very exciting. Thank you to everyone who works on* Doctor Who. *It is the best bunch of people in the world – Russell and Julie and Phil, our producers; Catherine Tate, who should win won of these...*

'I'm very excited,' he continues, 'because, in January, I go back to Cardiff to make four new Specials, which will see Doctor Who *all the way through 2009. But,' he says, pausing*

dramatically, 'when Doctor Who *returns in 2010, it won't be with me.' There are gasps and boos from the Albert Hall audience. 'We love you David!' shouts one woman. 'Now, don't make me cry,' he replies. 'I love this part, and I love this show so much, that if I don't take a deep breath and move on now, I never will – and you'll be wheeling me out of the TARDIS in my bath chair. I think it's better I don't overstay my welcome. So it's been the most brilliant, mad, life-changing time over the last three-and-a-half years… but it's not over yet. I've got a whole other year to go. I'm not quitting. There's a whole 2009 to go before I leave.'*]

> **Text message from: Ben**
> Sent: 29-Oct-2008 21:25
> YOU DID IT!!! Operation Cobra – top marks! History! Well, slightly.

> **Text message from: Russell**
> Sent: 29-Oct-2008 23:57
> Back at the hotel. Exhausted. But we actually did it! The tabloids are furious that we beat them. That's going to be a very happy memory. Full report once I'm back in Cardiff tomorrow.

FROM: RUSSELL T DAVIES TO: BENJAMIN COOK, THURSDAY 30 OCTOBER 2008 23:50:10 GMT

RE: OPERATION COBRA

What. A. Bloody. Night. I don't mean yesterday's NTAs (I'll update you on that soon, I promise); I mean tonight…

I'd promised to re-open the Cardiff Bay *Doctor Who* Exhibition. Nice refit, much bigger, and with a Supreme Dalek rising out of the ground that I could have watched forever. I was only expecting about 20 people to turn up. (It's in a Cardiff shopping centre, on a Thursday night.) When will I learn? This show! A good 300+ people turned up. Still, all very nice, and my speech was funny, and two Cybermen burst through a polystyrene door. Great fun. Then it all went wrong. I was shown through the exhibition, barely realising that all 300 people were following me. All well and good, until I reached the end. There was this little boxed area where we just sort of paused, photographers were snapping away, and I was told to wait, because they wanted me with the Cybermen, so I waited… and then 300 people appeared. Not all of them, obviously. Not at first. First of all, it was just three nice boys – autograph, photo, thanks – and then two nice girls – autograph, photo, thanks – then a lesbian couple who wanted me to sign a bowling skittle (honestly!), then a dozen people, then two dozen, then three…

Imagine one of our book signings, but with no control, no order, no queue, no table, no system, no one in charge, no Post-Its, no pens, no space, just people, people, people. It was a nightmare. It just wouldn't stop. As it started to get worse, people from BBC Branding and Worldwide tried to stop it and turn people away, except there was no away for them to be turned to. 'Anyway,' I said, 'you can't,' because there were wide-eyed kids all jamming forward, holding out annuals, storybooks, and bloody napkins to be signed, and parents with those cameras, those bastard cameras that never bloody work. I'm trying to sign things with nothing to rest on. It's so impossible to sign something flimsy in mid-air. Especially when the pen won't write. And the Post-It, Ben! The Post-It is a thing of genius. Take away the Post-It, and you find yourself shouting at some goggling kid, above the noise, 'What's your name?' 'Meep.' 'What's your *name?*' 'Meep.' 'WHAT'S YOUR NAME?!' 'Meep.' 'What, Jack? Jason? John? Joe? What. Is. Your. NAME?!!!' And that's just the first stage. Next, it's 'How do you spell that?' One girl's name was Jessamond. Lovely kid, but 'J, E, double S –' What, sorry, pardon? WHAT?!

But I can cope with that. I thought, if I have to stay here for three bloody hours, I can do it. Except then – and it's dark in this exhibition, and the space is tight, and no one knows what the hell is going on – I have a genuine, proper, rare panic attack. You'll never have seen me like that. It hardly ever happens to me these days. It happens to me in crowds, in tight spaces, if the situation is unexpected. Certain situations trigger it, and it's horrible, because everything goes hyper. It's like I can see and hear everything faster – and like I think faster, way too fast. It's all scrolling in my head. The physical signs are: I start to shake a bit, and I sweat. It pours off me. It really pours. There are, literally, drops of sweat falling off my head, not just once or twice, but all the time. *All the bloody time.* Kids are actually going, 'Ewww,' because they're getting hit by my sweat. Can you imagine?

Oh God, I'm shamed. I've had those attacks before, but never, *never*, in all my life, with everyone taking photos. It's going mental in my head, and all the time I'm grabbing pieces of paper – 'What's your NAME?!' – and stooping down to two-foot-four to have my photo taken with some bloody toddler who doesn't even watch *Doctor Who*, and the camera doesn't bloody work. By now, I'm actually losing control. I'm swearing in front of these kids. Well, not at them. I was hissing at the BBC people, 'Bloody stop them!' One of the Branding Team had twigged that something was wrong, except I'm too bloody embarrassed to say anything properly, and my hands are full of Sharpies and annuals, and then he starts shouting, 'Everyone get back!' But I'm going, 'Stop bloody shouting!'

I should have just stopped and walked away, but I'm beyond anything sensible by that stage. I'm shivering. I'm dropping the pens and napkins, scrabbling for them on the floor, and kids can't even say their own names, and people *keep taking photos*. I've all these little trip-words and conditions in my head that I can repeat to calm myself down… but like I said, I've never been in that situation before, with everyone talking at me, looking at me, and photographing me, so nothing was working. Eventually – and this goes on for a solid ten minutes, an endless ten minutes – I realise that I'm trapped into signing anything that's offered, so the solution is to stop people even seeing me, which means cutting off the procession at the corner. I'm hissing, 'Stop them! That corner! STOP THEM COMING ROUND THE F*****G CORNER!!!' Some teenage girl said, 'You shouldn't swear,' and she's lucky I didn't f*****g punch her.

The Branding and Worldwide people wade in, and stop the whole exhibition. And I get out. I walk out of the shopping centre – still being chased by kids and families – and I'm ice cold with sweat by now, feeling ridiculous, still shaking. Oh God. Stood in the cold. I smoked five cigarettes in a row. Calmed down. Even then, I'm ashamed, because the Branding and Worldwide people won't leave me alone. They're still dancing attendance, so I have to explain myself – 'I have a problem with crowds' – knowing that will be all around the office in the morning, like I'm some bloody nutjob. I'd never tell them that normally. Oh, Christ knows what they'll say about me tomorrow. Sod 'em.

Anyway. There we go. But then it got funny. I still had a job to do. I had to do press interviews. The first one was with a 10-year-old girl, a reporter for *First News* or something, 'The world's only primary-school newspaper'! Her name was Talia. She was from Hampstead. Being 10, she wrote out all my answers in longhand. 'When… David… de…cided… to… leave…' Christ almighty.

Phew. So, that was a night and a half.

FROM: BENJAMIN COOK TO: RUSSELL T DAVIES, FRIDAY 31 OCTOBER 2008 10:53:06 GMT

RE: OPERATION COBRA

Yesterday sounds horrible. I'm really sorry that happened. Especially after the euphoria of Wednesday night. I never knew that about you and crowds. I can't imagine it, to be honest. I don't mean I don't believe you; it's just that… well, you're so confident, and loud, and bright in public, it's hard to imagine you panicking like that. All those people swamping you – and once you've signed an autograph for one kid, you can't turn anyone down, can you? – sounds dreadful for anyone, under any circumstances. Let alone… hmm.

If you want to write about something happier, tell me about Wednesday.

FROM: RUSSELL T DAVIES TO: BENJAMIN COOK, FRIDAY 31 OCTOBER 2008 16:34:13 GMT

RE: OPERATION COBRA

It's ironic, because I suspect that I'm good with crowds. It's only an *unexpected* crowd that throws me. It's a weird little glitch in my head. Most days, it doesn't bother me. If it's a speech, or the NTAs, or even a Tone Meeting, I'm ready. It's not like I spend the day before meditating or anything, but I know that it's coming, and there's a little tic at the back of my head preparing me. But when it comes out of the blue, then bloody hell. Sometimes, I think, the older you get, the more your defences crumble. After all these years, for me to have a night like that again makes me think, oh, here it comes, it's not gone, it only waited.

The stupid thing is, it's *my* fault, but the repercussions are reaching Brandgate proportions (well, not quite), because BBC Worldwide is mortified by it all, like it was their fault, and they're sending e-mails today that say:

> We would like to apologise deeply. We feel there are some significant learnings and points for review in terms of the event and press management. I just wanted to let you know that I am on the case and will be feeding back thoughts to you more fully once I've had the chance to consult with a few people this end.

It's an investigation! Bloody BBC. I'm trying to say, 'No, it was a mistake, it's me, not you! Argh, just leave it alone!' It's so bonkers.

You're right, an NTA e-mail will cheer me up. I will write that. It'll be fun. But thank you for that last e-mail. Noel and I had a lovely chat about you at the NTAs – he really does love you, that big, tough fella. He said the loveliest things. I said you were a bastard, of course.

P.S. Talking of bonkers, *Torchwood* was out in the wilds of the Brecon Beacons on Wednesday night, and it *snowed* on them! In October! Huge nightmare.

FROM: BENJAMIN COOK TO: RUSSELL T DAVIES, FRIDAY 31 OCTOBER 2008 16:46:14 GMT

RE: OPERATION COBRA

We're on *Richard & Judy* tonight, but I can't watch it. I don't get Watch. I want to hear what you said, because I couldn't make out a word from where I was, imprisoned in the 'Star Bar' bit of the studio. Christ, that was weird. (Still, free drinks – can't complain.) Everything about that day was odd.

FROM: RUSSELL T DAVIES TO: BENJAMIN COOK, FRIDAY 31 OCTOBER 2008 19:08:20 GMT

RE: OPERATION COBRA

I can't get Watch either. I've only got a plain Freeview here in Cardiff. Damn. I wanted to see Rufus Hound calling you 'an attractive man' during your interview. I was hooting! Oh God, it'll probably cut to me hooting. Never hoot in public. And then he showed you his tattoos![4] Rufus was lovely, actually, wasn't he? It was weird, though. I was sat there with Matt Dawson, discussing a pumpkin with David Tennant's face carved into it. Bizarre. Maybe Freeview's limitations are a good thing.

Anyhow. The NTAs. It's funny looking back, because I can see, with hindsight, how much the hype had hyped *us* up. Of course David was going to win, and of course it would go without a hitch. But we'd all made the day so potent – so sort of symbolic. We've known for ages that David is leaving, we knew that it'd be announced some day, we knew that they're already looking for an Eleventh Doctor, and yet the whole thing seemed so massive. So important. Maybe it was more about us. Then again, it was

---

4 The show's 'comedian in residence' Rufus Hound interviewed Benjamin in the 'Star Bar' – then, off camera, flashed him the tattoo, on his left upper-arm, of monkeys fighting robots, including a Dalek. Meanwhile, Russell and his fellow guests (retired rugby player Matt Dawson, and actor and impressionist Kevin Bishop) had to pass comment on a *Doctor Who*-themed pumpkin-sculpting challenge. It was that kind of day.

certainly important for *Doctor Who*. Perhaps we're so tuned in to protecting the show that there's precious little difference between it and us these days. Still, I love waking up on days like Wednesday, when you're awake immediately and your first thought is, oh my God, big day! Julie is the same. We're adrenalin junkies. The worst thing is, I woke up really feeling bad about Richard and Judy, like I was seriously compromising them. Professionally, it felt so wrong – and personally, too, because I've been on their show lots of times, and they're always so nice to me. I did feel bad about it. I still do. I've written to the producers since to explain.

On the train to London, Operation Cobra was going mental. Julie phoned up to say that they'd got David's video interview ready to upload onto the website, and they'd added the Christmas Special trail at the end. I said, 'Which trail? The *Journey's End* trail? Because that's the right one, just ten seconds long. Not the Comic-Con trail?' (The one that was shown at Comic-Con in San Diego is 50 seconds long, way too much material, shots that we're holding back for December.) 'No,' said Julie, 'they won't have put on the wrong trail. I'll go and check.' She phones back: 'They've put on the wrong trail.' Bollocks. 'What do you want me to do?' she asks. 'Can you change it?' I say. 'The tapes have been sent out,' she tells me. 'We'll have to call them back.' 'Then call them back! Now!' Then I get to London, get in the cab, calm down, phone her back: 'Hold on, the Comic-Con trail is great. Let's release it.' 'I've called all the tapes back now.' 'Send them out again.' Do you see, just jitters, jitters, jitters? We were going loony.

By the time you arrived at the Cactus studios, Ben, I was outside in their smoking bit, 'The Garden' (it's an alley, with tables), on the phone to Julie, both of us trying to work out a *Richard & Judy* line. In the end, we worked out an escape clause: if Richard or Judy started to say, 'What about David?' or 'How long is he –' then I'd leap in with 'I think *you'd* make a good Doctor, Richard!' – in the hope that it would send him off on an Ali G-type riff, and the starting point would be forgotten.[5] I had three or four trigger sentences like that, all stored in my head. All useless, probably. You rarely get to use those planned sentences. Anyway, when you were in make-up, I left quite quickly because I went to tell Ed from Ebury the full story. He blanched: 'Oh my God!' I was going, 'You can't tell anyone!' (Why did I tell him, then? I'm still not sure. I think I was just so wound up that I needed to say it out loud. And I trust him completely. I thought he should be part of it, in case any trouble blew up afterwards, so he'd be ready.)

Like I said, it was all hype and jitter about nothing, because while you were missing it all in the 'Star Bar' – that mad, mad bar area of the studio – Richard and Judy were being lovely and kind. They skirted close when Richard said something about Judy fancying David – 'How many women do you know who, like my wife, carry

---

5 Famously, Richard Madeley once dressed up as comedian Sacha Baron Cohen's alter ego Ali G on ITV breakfast show *This Morning*, which Madeley presented with Judy Finnigan from 1998 to 2001.

a torch for David Tennant?' – and my mind was whizzing at a thousand miles an hour, thinking, do I use my Richard/Doctor clause or will that *make* them ask when he's leaving? I wittered. And then we judged a man who'd carved David's face into a pumpkin. And one of the fanboys from the 'Star Bar' asked me how the timeline of Harriet Jones's three terms in power could have been altered. My mind was swinging all over the place! It's no wonder I went a bit mental on Thursday night. And then I emerged into the corridor to find Rufus Hound showing you his tattoos of famous robots fighting famous monkeys. I can't leave you alone for a second! That was the funniest and strangest thing I'd seen in ages. (Has he turned up at your house yet? I bet he doesn't show those tattoos to everyone.)

Before I knew it, I was at the hotel. Same old crap, same old panic, there's never enough time. I'm ironing a shirt, and texting Julie, and you, and Phil, and the taxi is due, and I'm late. I'd be on time if I were just going to the awards, but no, of course, there's the pre-drinks, the sodding pre-drinks, the bane of my life, the bloody pre-drinks with everyone. I'm going to have that carved on my gravestone: 'Killed by pre-drinks.' Why can't we just turn up? And I'm really, seriously believing that David hasn't won, because there's been no word. I was really sour for a good 20 minutes. All those plans! All that excitement! What a waste of time. Now we'll have to tell everyone he's leaving in some flat, poxy press release. And I'm feeling clumsy, and old, and stupid, getting into my clothes, having come all this way for nothing. And I forgot to bring my black shoes, so I'm wearing Doc Martens, which look ridiculous with all that posh nonsense… and then Julie rings… and WE'VE WON, and I LOVE this night, and my DMs look BRILLIANT, and I AM ONE SEXY BASTARD!!! Even the pre-drinks turned out to be okay. Steven was there, too. I said to him that the night felt like a real, proper handover, from me to him. That was part of the Cobra plan. Everything we said and did had to move on from David, onto Series Five, onto new, new, new. Exactly right. Protect the programme.

But then it descended into chaos, like it always does. Catherine wanted me to walk in with her, so she wouldn't be on her own on the red carpet, but she was late, and then her car got lost and couldn't find the carpet – and Julie was on the phone to *Torchwood*, who were stuck with children in the Brecon Beacons, and it was snowing, so they were having to cancel the whole shoot, with no way of rescheduling it. You should see Julie at times like that, standing on the red carpet, photographers all around, with fanboys in the crowds shouting 'Julie! Julie!' at her, while she's on her mobile sorting out *Torchwood*, with my mobile in her other ear, literally, at the same time as she's guiding Catherine in. But really, by this stage, it's a laugh. It's a complete bloody big laugh, as we're all signing autographs, and Dannii Minogue sweeps past, and Simon Cowell arrives – the cheers, my God! – and *GMTV* asks if Catherine is coming back, to which I say, 'No, I'm done with her. She's old news!' See, with crowds like this, I'm fine. Well, I'd known for weeks that this would happen, and I'd been there before. Easy.

Throughout it all, we're counting down. Julie is Head of Cobra. She's getting messages and muttering, 'The camera's in place at Stratford. The link's working.' Even then, it had to be complicated: what if the live link breaks down? David has pre-recorded his stage-door speech, just in case. (I wonder what happened to that tape. Nice DVD extra.) Oh, but what if *Hamlet* starts late? Julie is grim and powerless. If an entire coach-load of the audience has been delayed, the RSC will delay the start of the play, because that's more important to them than our camera. Very true, but... yikes! Even then, new Cobra briefings are being passed down from on high. The Head of BBC Publicity has said that under no circumstances must we suggest Russell Brand as the next Doctor. No. Way. Well, that tempts me. I'm dying to say it now. But Julie is deadly serious: 'Do not say anything that connects *Doctor Who* to that unholy mess.' She's right. Not funny.

The Albert Hall is packed with everyone that you've ever seen on telly ever. Times like that, I realise that I'm a thousand years old, and have been in TV for too long, because I know so many people. The real-life Bob who inspired *Bob & Rose* is there, and his wife. And Annabelle Apsion, who's the mum in *Shameless*, begs me for a part in *Doctor Who*. 'It's the reason I became an actor!' And while I'm by the *Shameless* seats, Sean Gilder says hello. Ahh, lovely man. The Sycorax Leader! Killed by a satsuma! They're bizarre, those events, because everyone starts talking to everyone. It's sort of communal. I had a lovely chat with Arlene Phillips, who can't have known who the hell I was. But there are far too many A Gays there, all coiffed and groomed – Jason Gardiner from *Dancing on Ice*, that man from *EastEnders*, Craig Revel Horwood – and I'm thinking, they're all so smart and I'm wearing bloody Doc Martens. How embarrassing.

Anyway, the ceremony starts. We're live on ITV! Even then, the work doesn't stop. Julie is five seats away from me, so she's texting: 'Should all the cast go up on stage if we win Most Popular Drama?' I text back: 'No, the NTAs asked for only me and Catherine.' Julie: 'I know, but it would be so nice.' Me: 'That's true. Let's do it.' So, whispers go along the line to Camille, Noel, and Lis – change of plan, pay attention! Also, Cobra Briefing #15 from the PR people was: if *Doctor Who* wins Most Popular Drama, and you go backstage after collecting the award, don't get in the lift, because that takes you to the Press Area on the second floor, where they take photos and ask questions, and you haven't got time for that. Come straight back to your seat, to be ready for David. Got that? Do. Not. Get. In. The. Lift. Okay? So, we win – and I kiss the Duchess of York, ha ha.[6] And then we're taken backstage. I'm thinking, Do Not Get In The Lift. But we're being led towards the lift. I'm thinking, I'm sure we're not meant to go in here...? But people with earpieces and clipboards are herding us, and they seem to know what they're doing, so we become dumbos, like sheep. Catherine, Lis, Noel and Camille are all chattering away, and they don't object to the lift. Surely

---

6 Sarah Ferguson, the Duchess of York, presented the 2008 National Television Award for Most Popular Drama.

they had Briefing #15? Am I wrong?! I end up thinking, they said, 'Do Not Get In The Lift,' but is this the lift they meant? Maybe this is the First Lift. We won't get in the Second Lift. If there's another lift after this, I definitely won't get in it.

So, we get in the lift. The NTA woman presses the button for the second floor. 'That's the Press Area,' I say. 'I thought we weren't meant to be getting in a lift.' But I say it quietly, so no one actually hears me. We arrive on the second floor, and the lift doors open… and standing there is the Head of BBC Publicity, and the *Doctor Who* PR team, looking at us like we're idiot children. They have arms outstretched, trying to stop the tide. 'Didn't we say, "Do Not Get In The Lift"?' 'Oh,' I say, '*this* lift?' 'What lift did you think we meant?' 'There might have been another lift.' 'No, it's this lift.' 'Oh. We shouldn't have got in, should we?' 'No.' We press the button and go back down. We're hooting. Lis says, 'I enjoyed my trip in the lift.' When we get back out at the bottom, the people with clipboards and earpieces are staring at us. 'Why've you come back down?' they say. 'No idea,' I reply. 'It's mad up there.'

And then, finally, we get to the whole point of the evening: David Tennant wins Outstanding Drama Performance! But this was the most surprising thing of all, because I looked up at this huge screen looming over the Albert Hall, and THERE'S DAVID! It really hit me. I was so *delighted* to see him. I can't explain how powerful that moment was. It wasn't the announcement to come; it was just *seeing* him, because I realised, in that second, that I hadn't seen him for ages and ages, and we spend so much time thinking about him, and talking about him, and about the Tenth Doctor, and the sight of him on that screen, even though it had been planned for months, was astonishing. I was really gobsmacked. There was something about his face, too, because he looked kind of raw, and open, and emotional. Or maybe I'm projecting that onto him. Maybe that's how I felt. It was bizarre being so close to him, yet so far away, all of us sharing the same thoughts, but not really knowing what each other is thinking. It was so strange, but the strongest feeling. Maybe all my predictions about how unemotional I'm going to be when I leave this show are wrong. Maybe I'm going to be a sobbing mess. Then again, maybe there will never be a moment as focused as that – certainly not one as public. Maybe that was it! Gaping at a big screen. Very appropriate.

So, David said his stuff – and I've watched it back since, and it seems perfectly normal, but at the time it was like his pauses were endless. Time in slow-motion. Agonising! We all thought it – me, Jane, Julie, Phil, we all said afterwards, 'I thought he wasn't going to say it!' But the best bits were the moans and groans of dismay that went around the Albert Hall. I'd been worried that the audience wouldn't really listen. It's noisy at the NTAs, full of people screaming and yelling. A lot of that is filtered out by microphones on TV, but on the spot it's a box of noise. I actually thought that David's words could be missed. But no. The dismay! That felt wonderful. That's when we all started looking at each other, with the biggest grins. Perfect! It worked.

But then work took over, and it was off to the second floor. (I got in the lift.)

The press asked questions – 'Are you shocked by David's announcement?' – and it all dissolved into nonsense. And then the party afterwards, where the man who plays Niall in *Hollyoaks* was gorgeous and failed to ask me out, and I met Paul O'Grady, and Lee McQueen, and that nice man from *The Bill* who was once a Cyberman.[7] But I couldn't be bothered. I just wanted to leave. So I did. Back to the hotel. It was the same hotel I was in on the night that we announced Chris Eccleston's casting as the Doctor, when I stayed up late to watch it break on the news channels – and here I was again, watching BBC News 24 talking about David's departure. Funny little coincidence.

It took me ages and ages to unwind. I pottered about till about 4am. But it did me good. That announcement unlocked some stuff in my head. At one point, I was lying on the bed, fully clothed, and the whole Rose thing suddenly made sense. I've been massively worried about how to include her at the end of 4.18, when the Doctor revisits all his old companions. How can you see her, when she's stuck in a parallel universe? I'd thought of cutting to her and Doctor #2, the blue-suit Doctor, in their parallel world, sort of realising that the original Doctor is dying, feeling it somehow… but what are they doing? Building another TARDIS? Living with Jackie and Pete? Travelling the wilds? Should Rose have a baby? Whichever way you look at it, that's an odd scene, and distracting. But on Wednesday night, I realised how to do it… and I'm not telling you, ha ha ha! I really don't want to write it down. I need to save it.

On the train back to Cardiff on Thursday morning, I described the scene to Julie. She sat back in her seat. She was silent. I thought, she doesn't like it. Then I realised… she was crying. She actually burst into tears. I'll take that as a good sign. When I got back here, I sat at the computer and all sorts of 4.18 scenes poured into my head. That brave little spaceship proves to be the key. I haven't told you about the head of panic building up about 4.18 – well, to some extent, I don't want to repeat myself. If I'm building up to a script, then I'm terrified, take it as read. Thursday afternoon, though, I had a rare moment of looking at the whole of 4.18, and thinking: I can do this. It's going to be good. Yes, I can write it. Very rare. Like a powerful rush of warmth towards the episode. I don't think I've ever felt that in all of this Great Correspondence. I really do think Wednesday night released all of that – partly because of the relief, and partly the fear of living up to people's expectations.

Operation Cobra might have been mental, but I think it did me good.

---

7   Niall Rafferty, played by Barry Sloane, is a character in Channel 4 soap *Hollyoaks*. Graham Cole, best known as PC Tony Stamp in ITV police drama *The Bill*, appeared in various episodes of *Doctor Who* in the early 1980s, often uncredited, including as a Cyberman.

                         THE DOCTOR
          He says the drive system stalled.
          Ten miles up, they fell out of the
          sky. But what caused that?

                         SORVIN
          <Chirrip chup.>

                         CHRISTINA
          Which means, no idea.

                         THE DOCTOR
          Yup. But wait a minute... that's
          a Crystal Nucleus down there, yes?

                         SORVIN
          <Chip!>

                         THE DOCTOR
          And it looks like it survived the
          crash. If the Crystal's intact...
          Oh yes, that's better than diesel!

                         CHRISTINA
          What, you can use the Crystal to
          move the bus?

                         THE DOCTOR
          I think so. The spaceship's a
          write-off, but the 200's small
          enough.

                         CHRISTINA
          How does a Crystal drive a bus?

                         THE DOCTOR
          In a super-clever outer-spacey
          way, just trust me! Look -

Runs to a broken, tilted WALL MONITOR, clicks it on -

ON SCREEN: THE CRYSTAL CHAMBER (as in sc.66, to come). A
small room at the bottom of the shaft. Burnt metal.
Centre; the CRYSTAL - a fist-size YELLOW DIAMOND, held in
place by FOUR METAL CLAMPS, all held on a metal bed, like
a PLATE (NB, Crystal, clamps & plate are actually quite
small, portable; the surrounding technology gives it size.)

                         THE DOCTOR (CONT'D)
          That's the Crystal. Have you got
          access shafts?

                         SORVIN
          <Chirp chip chirrip chup.>

                                        (CONTINUED)

CHAPTER TWENTY

SMOKEY THE SPACE PELICAN

In which Gallifrey is resurrected,
Russell remembers his childhood,
and the 456 has a gas at Upper Boat

FROM: BENJAMIN COOK TO: RUSSELL T DAVIES, WEDNESDAY 5 NOVEMBER 2008 08:16:22 GMT

THE STAR-SPANGLED BANNER

BARACK OBAMA WINS!!! U – S – A!!! U – S – A!!! I think I might move there too now. It looks great. A Brave New World. A lot like the old world, but with one less idiot in power. I woke up to the news. I was going to stay up to follow the results, but I was too shattered. Wasn't Obama's first speech as President-Elect fantastic?

FROM: RUSSELL T DAVIES TO: BENJAMIN COOK, WEDNESDAY 5 NOVEMBER 2008 11:55:20 GMT

RE: THE STAR-SPANGLED BANNER

O – BA – MA!!!

OMG! ETC.

You have, literally, woken up to a Brave New World. Oh, it's exciting. History! This is so wonderful. Also, on the news, they're saying that they can clone mammoths. It's the future they promised us, with jetpacks and monorails. My silver jumpsuit is looking good. Mind you, just to be pessimistic (it's hardwired into me), this will send out a wave of change that will sweep across this country and let in the bloody Tories. Bollocks. I know, I'll move to America! Ha ha. Yes, it's all about me.

Anyway, yes, what a speech. Mind you, John McCain's concession speech was gracious and dignified. Okay, that's enough, sympathy over. It was actually a bit boring, staying up to watch the coverage, because Obama had obviously won, but the networks didn't dare say so until bloody 4am. But then, oh, the cheering in Chicago. Amazing. Apparently, exactly 40 years ago, JFK said that in 40 years' time there could be a black man in the White House.

In other news, I've had a very good couple of days. Gareth's latest draft is excellent. He's a good lad. I'm so happy. I wanted a great big, funny, mad old romp, just before it all turns dark for Christmas – and that's exactly what we've got. A jewel thief, a double-decker bus, giant flies, swarms, a psychic old woman, and UNIT! Gareth has never written a script that's so joined-up before. It's a real whole. Less work for me, too. (Just as I finally get a co-credit! That's making me laugh.)

Oh God. I've read it. I've started. I'm back on *Doctor Who*.

FROM: RUSSELL T DAVIES TO: BENJAMIN COOK, WEDNESDAY 5 NOVEMBER 2008 23:50:42 GMT

RE: THE STAR-SPANGLED BANNER

I'm off to London tomorrow. I've agreed to appear on *Charlie Brooker's Screenwipe*, because he's doing a Special about writers. Apparently, it's inspired by – wait for it – our book! Yes, really. He couldn't put it down, I'm told. Unless they're saying that to lure me. Every single writer asked is turning up. I think everyone's too scared to say no to Charlie Brooker.

And then, on Friday, it's the Great Correspondence On Stage! At the National! Oh, and are you coming to Cardiff for this Children in Need thing at the weekend? It's the Upper Boat Open Day. Have I told you about that? Guided tours of Upper Boat – winners via a competition phone line, to raise money for charity – with your tour guides being Julie, me, Johnny B and Eve Myles! It's barmy. I've no idea what it entails. I haven't had a script, or a timetable, or anything.

FROM: RUSSELL T DAVIES TO: BENJAMIN COOK, MONDAY 10 NOVEMBER 2008 17:48:19 GMT

COUP DE THEATRE

I'm in Manchester. It's probably the last time I'll get back here until Christmas. I love this office of mine. I'm having a lazy day today, and then I'll panic for the rest of the week. (Can you believe we were on stage at the National on Friday? That's so mad. I loved it, though. I thought it was really good.)

The Children in Need thing was mad, but lovely. You could just tell that BBC bean-counters were lurking, calculating how much money they would make if they opened up a tour full-time. A fortune, I reckon. But why not? People were genuinely delighted to be standing on the real TARDIS, where David Tennant has stood. Best part was, the punters got taken onto a huge, new *Torchwood* set, the government chamber where the alien 456 ambassador – the aliens are called 'the 456' – is revealed in a tank full of gas, and some kid says, 'It's a pelican!!!' In fairness to Neill Gorton, it wasn't anywhere near complete. They're not actually filming it until Thursday. They've got a good few days to wire up the animatronics, and then cover it with blood and gunk and stuff, to make it better. But I love that. A pelican! Torchwood versus the Space Pelican!

FROM: RUSSELL T DAVIES TO: BENJAMIN COOK, THURSDAY 13 NOVEMBER 2008 16:11:56 GMT

RE: COUP DE THEATRE

We're hitting money problems. It was always going to be hard to raise the cash for the *Doctor Who* Specials, on the simple basis of fewer sales, lower returns – plus, there's no 13-episode pot of money to amortise the costs – but now, of course, along comes the worldwide recession. International sales for the show are down, which is usual after a big expansion, but people are buying less, naturally. Canada bailed out before Series Four, and now we've lost Japan, too. This means that BBC Worldwide has less money to give us. DVD sales are down too, across the board, for everyone. Interestingly, when Worldwide's money is low, usually they go to 2Entertain (who publish the DVDs) for more cash, and 2Entertain go to Woolworths... but they've been sending out very big signals recently saying that Woolworths might be going bust! Can you believe it? Woolworths! (Sell those shares!) It's haemorrhaging all over the place. This is truly the recession in action.

Do you remember what I said about how Julie has to balance all this? Yesterday, she and I had a very tough conversation about our options. We've got to be prepared to concede, and compromise, and shift strategies, for the good of the show. Two things might happen: firstly, we might have to reduce the final two-parter to two standard-length 45-minute episodes; alternatively, we might have to drop an episode altogether, which we both agreed would be Phil Ford's pre-Christmas story. (Poor Graeme Harper. He's directing that episode. Poor Phil, too.) This is still worst-case scenario. It might not happen. But neither is it nonsense. It really *might* happen. At the same time, I'm sending out warning flares, saying that 4.17/4.18 is expensive. Julie and Jane are both saying that we'll find the money. 'Keep going, and stay ambitious!' That's why I can never complain about any budget issues, because we really are so supported by the BBC, and always have been.

FROM: BENJAMIN COOK TO: RUSSELL T DAVIES, THURSDAY 13 NOVEMBER 2008 16:51:07 GMT

RE: COUP DE THEATRE

>>we might have to drop an episode altogether<<

Surely BBC Worldwide want *more* output, not less?

FROM: RUSSELL T DAVIES TO: BENJAMIN COOK, THURSDAY 13 NOVEMBER 2008 17:01:24 GMT

RE: COUP DE THEATRE

Yes, but for some reason – which, frankly, I don't understand (you're having this relayed to you by a financial idiot) – Worldwide's input would remain constant, even if we did three episodes instead of four, thereby making three more affordable.

FROM: BENJAMIN COOK TO: RUSSELL T DAVIES, THURSDAY 13 NOVEMBER 2008 17:05:21 GMT

RE: COUP DE THEATRE

I don't really understand that logic.

How's life in the Maybe?

FROM: RUSSELL T DAVIES TO: BENJAMIN COOK, THURSDAY 13 NOVEMBER 2008 17:30:31 GMT

RE: COUP DE THEATRE

>>I don't really understand that logic.<<

No, me neither, but I've had to put a clock on it, because 4.17/4.18 plans are advancing in my head. If they're to be whittled down to 45 minutes, I need to know now. Julie has promised a decision by next week – which might not be possible, but soon, anyway. She's so magnificent at forcing through money (on *Sarah Jane* Series Three, for example, the problems have almost disappeared), so we're proceeding as normal, for now. Imagine, though, what Julie goes through every single day, juggling all these sums – and doing so without ever getting bored, without ever losing her passion for these shows. She's amazing. I've never worked with better. Never.

Back in the Maybe (isn't it so much warmer and more fun than the real world?)... To leap straight in, the biggest dilemma is still Donna. It's Catherine. The temptation to use her, to make her a big part of that Master story and not just a cameo. I can't get that out of my head. I've spoken about it to Julie, and we've both had the same reaction: ooh, the temptation! But tempered with the same caution: she can't get her memory back. So, how do I do that? I got far down a long line of plot, which was rather good... the Doctor has taken refuge in that battered old spaceship, with the Runny People and Wilf, and he flies down and rescues Donna. But once rescued, she's frantic – spaceships! Runny People! Memories! – so lovely old Wilf has to anesthetise her or something, just knock her out, while the Doctor is frantically trying to think of a way to bring all this to an end, in case it kills her. All of which still has to dovetail with Donna getting her happy ending with the wedding, somehow. But on and on and on it went, in my head...

Until yesterday. I was brushing my teeth, and I thought very clearly: no. One word, like that. A sign went up in my head: wrong way. Initially, I'd thought of having Donna only in the background, so... trust your instincts. That's how it should stay. This plot is about the Doctor and the Master. Donna is a bystander. Maybe she'll turn into the Master, along with every other human. Wilf can even be on the phone to her at the time. That's nice and scary. And that's that.

Good. Phew. That's been weeks and weeks of thought. It hasn't helped seeing Catherine at the NTAs and stuff, because I so want to write more for her, but that's the wrong instinct. I have decided. It really was like a big, sudden, unbidden 'NO' in my head. I've never had that before. I rather liked it. It makes life easier.

I'll sign off for a bit now – more to report soon – because my landline stopped working this afternoon, and BT needs me to test every bloody socket and handset, blah, blah, blah. I hate BT.

FROM: RUSSELL T DAVIES TO: BENJAMIN COOK, FRIDAY 14 NOVEMBER 2008 00:03:24 GMT

RE: COUP DE THEATRE

Back to 4.17/4.18... The millionaire character is expanding nicely. Anthony Hopkins. Or Julie Andrews. I can fill that character with vigour. Some characters just feel alive, and he or she is one of them. I can sort of feel him/her bristling across the screen, earning his place in the story, because he/she's a plot machine. In a good way! I keep veering between options – does he want this Immortality Gate for himself, or for his children? Or even grandchildren, if he's old enough? There's something marvellously selfless about a man who's doing it for his children. But thinking about the millionaire – who should be a billionaire, really – I keep coming back to... Switzerland? Geneva?! Why do I imagine that he lives abroad? How weird to have a pivotal *Doctor Who* story set in the Alps. I invented that when I had the *Real Hustle* Master stealing a passport and leaving the country, just because that looked so smart and clever, but now the Master is a shuddering cadaver, so I don't need that old plot any more.

Yes, *Doctor Who* is at its best in England. It should be a stately home, with a huge sci-fi lab built right into the heart of it – all those consoles and computers set against big French windows, sweeping curtains, busts on plinths, oil paintings and things. Nice contrast. Ed would do that brilliantly. The Christmas scheduling decision is informing this, too. A millionaire. The millionaire's kids. Grandchildren. Christmas. Stately home. Big tree. Feels good. It's time to bring the story back home. Sod the Alps! Why the hell did I wander off there?

Then, after my last e-mail, I had a brainwave. A BLOODY GREAT BRAINWAVE! All along, I've been persecuted by the problem, what does the Master *want*? He transplants himself into every human, but that's just the first episode. He can't spend the entire second episode hunting for the Doctor. He has to have a plan, a universal scheme, like in *Last of the Time Lords*, but not too much like *Last of the Time Lords*. I've done power, war, spaceships, etc. But then, this evening, I was sitting here at the computer and I thought... GALLIFREY! He wants to restore Gallifrey!!! That's nice, because it tempts the Doctor, too. The Master won't succeed, of course, but we'll get a few fleeting seconds of it, glimpses of the planet. Oh, the temptation. (Oh, the budget.)

I know where it came from. Nothing comes out of thin air. Ages ago – well, a good few weeks ago – Julie sat down opposite me and said, out of the blue, with real longing in her voice, 'D'you know what I want in the finale? Gallifrey. Can we go to Gallifrey?' Which completely took me by surprise. That's the last thing I was expecting her to say. But she'd just been to the Edit of the *Doctor Who* Prom footage, and that had a Gallifrey sequence, with Murray's score, and those images from *The Sound of Drums* where we glimpse the Doctor's home world in a flashback, and she said, 'It's so powerful. It *means* so much. It's the Doctor, and his home, and his longing, and his whole mythology.' And I said no. Immediately. Partly because that's often my first instinct – it's selfish, like saying, 'Get off my turf!' – and partly because I thought that Gallifrey would be just too expensive, all hallways, and arches, and cardinals, and echoes, and chambers. 'Every single shot would be an FX shot,' I said. 'We couldn't do it.' 'Oh,' she said sadly, and that was that. But I was listening. The fanboy part of my mind was saying, 'No, no, no,' because it's burdened with too much continuity, etc. However, Julie isn't full of *Doctor Who* lore. She wasn't being fan-ish. What she actually wanted was that myth, that temptation, that call of home.

Today I thought, what if the Master can pull Gallifrey out of the Time War (with a handy bit of un-timelocking) by replacing it with Earth? A planet-swap. Earth gets thrown into the last seconds of the Time War, to die a horrible death, and Gallifrey replaces it in the solar system. The Time Lords live! Except, the Master has this Master-body-projection thing now, so all the Time Lords can become him. Why would he be happy becoming just the human race? He'd want to be every Time Lord! Of course, the Doctor would arrive in time to stop him throwing the switch. No, in fact, he'd arrive just after the switch had been thrown. Out of those windows – those French windows – an old, familiar breeze blows in. That scent. Snow in the air. The Doctor and the Master look out, and the fields beyond the house, the fields of Earth, are fading away, the orange mountains are appearing, those mountains of High Endeavour or whatever I called them in *The Sound of Drums*, with the Time Lord Capitol gleaming on the horizon. Gallifrey restored! The Doctor in awe! And then the Doctor blows up the whole shebang. Everything reverts back to Earth. Hooray. But that simple moment of him standing with the Master and seeing Gallifrey, breathing it in, tempted, so tempted to allow it to survive… that's worth a million quid. That scene sells it to me. That's what Julie meant. Not the planet, but the legend.

Julie phoned tonight, about something or other, and I was so excited, I said, 'I've found a way to do it! You're getting Gallifrey!' She was ridiculously excited, too. But then I thought, for all I know, that's what Steven is planning to do in Series Five. I fired off an e-mail, and he replied almost straight away. 'No, fine, have it.' He said he loves it. He thinks it's a brilliant way to end David's tenure.

FROM: BENJAMIN COOK TO: RUSSELL T DAVIES, FRIDAY 14 NOVEMBER 2008 00:35:46 GMT

RE: COUP DE THEATRE

Gallifrey *is* exciting! Julie is right. She was responding as someone who loves the Doctor, the man, his life, and his history, not as a raging fangirl. But can we see some more Time Lords, please? Can we, can we, can we? Thanks. (Seriously, can we?) It's not fan-ish any more, Gallifrey, is it? It's all wrapped up in the Doctor, and his loneliness, and the Time War – and like ten million people know the ins and outs of that. TEN MILLION! (Probably more, let's face it.) We're all fans now.

FROM: RUSSELL T DAVIES TO: BENJAMIN COOK, FRIDAY 14 NOVEMBER 2008 02:03:24 GMT

RE: COUP DE THEATRE

You like that story? Oh, good. The moment I read your e-mail, I went downstairs to make a cup of tea, and all sorts of Gallifrey stuff came into my head. It became real! I hadn't thought about seeing Time Lords, or hearing them, but now… hmm, maybe. (Fleetingly!) Oh, that's good. Phew. Right. Gallifrey it is. (Maybe not the Time Tots. I won't mention them. Though I might give them to CBeebies as an animated series!)

FROM: RUSSELL T DAVIES TO: BENJAMIN COOK, FRIDAY 14 NOVEMBER 2008 21:23:34 GMT

RE: COUP DE THEATRE

I woke up this morning and thought: the Gallifrey idea is shit. I really did. My heart was in my boots. Gallifrey seems so backward-looking. Restoring it almost seems like fan fiction. (Then again, so does the Daleks meeting the Cybermen, and I made that work.) Also, I'm thinking, how?! How does the Master planet-swap? The Master turns himself into every human being, and then what? He finds a convenient, long-buried Gallifrey Restoration switch? Buried at Stonehenge or something? That's handy! He's stuck on Earth, and he rules the planet, but how the hell does he shift into an almighty planet-swapper? I'm haunted, again, by the ghost of *Last of the Time Lords*, in which I played every beat of a Master story possible. In that story, he had the TARDIS. It would be wonderful if he had the TARDIS again here, because I could believe that it could be converted into an almighty planet-swapping device. But I've *done* it. Also, to get really ming-mongy, if the Master can find a way to restore Gallifrey, why didn't he do that last time? He ruled the Earth for an entire year, but faffed about with Toclafane. Why wasn't he aiming at Gallifrey then? Why?!

This is weird, because I was flushed with excitement about it last night. Maybe I'm having some sort of adrenalin comedown today. Gallifrey gives me something that really links the Master and the Doctor – unites them even, beautifully so, just for that one scene. That's rich, that's powerful, that's good… except I've woken up not liking it. Mind you, Steven sent another e-mail today, just to say how much he *really* likes it. He's never done that before, so I should listen to him. (Unless he's out to sabotage me. Yes, that will be it. He's setting up Series Five as the cure for all ills, the bastard.) I'll just have to keep on thinking about it. To Gallifrey or not to Gallifrey? I suppose it does tie up the last four years quite nicely, in which the Time War, and the Doctor's loss and loneliness, have been so central – stuff that Steven is, naturally, going to want to move on from, I suspect, because it's about time we did, so it's the last chance to play that story.

On a much more trivial level, I keep wondering what to call the final episode. I've used up so many classic apocalyptic titles – *The End of the World*, *Doomsday*, *Journey's End*… what's left? *The Final Reckoning*? Maybe *The Final Battle*. That's okay. Hang on, no, it isn't. 'Battle' is a shit word. *Death of the Doctor*? Hmm. No.

Oh, but I'm so terrifyingly late already. I should have started on Gareth's rewrite ages ago. Hell, I should have finished Gareth's rewrite by now. I should be onto Phil's. But I'm building myself up. Psyching myself. But there's an extra element this time, a funny sort of reluctance nagging at me now, because actually, for the first time ever on this job, the end is in sight. In a couple of months' time, I will have finished *Doctor Who*. That feels like a very significant stage in my life. But it's having a detrimental effect, because there's a big part of me that doesn't *want* to finish. Not just for sentimental reasons, though they are strong – I love this job, and the people – but also because the future beyond *Doctor Who* is an empty void. I imagine myself sat in some stark Hollywood flat, bored to tears in American meetings... and coming home. In fact, I went to Tesco's on Tuesday night, and walking there I absolutely convinced myself that I shouldn't go to America – that I should stay in Manchester, lock myself away in my office, and write, just like the old days. I was so convinced that I had this apologetic e-mail to Jane and Julie all written out in my head. Word for word. It was a fact. I felt good. I had changed my mind. I was staying here. But then I came home, and forgot all about it. Like you do.

I spent a lot of the day pottering about here in this house, running through the stuff that needs fixing, in my head, in 4.15 and 4.16. It's comparatively little with 4.15. For example, I'm not sure the information about Christina's life is seeded correctly throughout the episode. I'm not sure that she and the Doctor reveal themselves to each other in quite the right order yet – or with enough style and fun. This is more than fixing dialogue. It's kind of the spine of the whole thing. So, I'm working on that, if only in random thoughts. With 4.16, we're waiting to see if The Mill can realise Water People as CGI, with complete 3D models – because that will affect the episode substantially, if it's beyond the software. It's looking possible, right now. Will Cohen has sent me some water-software adverts that were beautiful, but he needs to go and do tests. That will take him a fortnight or so.

But while I sit here, regretting not-writing, one little detail can bring me to a grinding halt. Right at the start of 4.15, there's a problem that I can't get around: Christina the jewel thief is robbing that vault, she lowers herself down from the roof towards that precious goblet thing, and it's surrounded by laser beams, which she lowers herself through... but that's where I halt. She lowers herself through the beams? Well, they're rubbish beams, then, aren't they? That doesn't work. She has to find a better way around the lasers, and yet this is just a pre-titles sequence. It's meant to whizz by. Maximum speed. There's no time for too much intricacy. So, what does she do? I swear, that single thing is stopping me. You know I have to work on things in order, and that's Page 1! I've various fixes that I could drop into later scenes, no problem, but I simply cannot do it till Page 1 is working. Every day that passes, I'm losing time.

One other thing happened today: I've been asked to write the Foreword for the 30th anniversary publication of *The Hitchhiker's Guide to the Galaxy*. I am *so* honoured. That

This page: Preparing for *The End of Time* itself!

Top: Wilf (Bernard Cribbins) meets the mysterious Woman (Claire Bloom) in church.

Above: Lucy Saxon (Alexandra Moen) isn't as helpless as she seems.

Left: Director Euros Lyn discusses a scene with the Elder Ood.

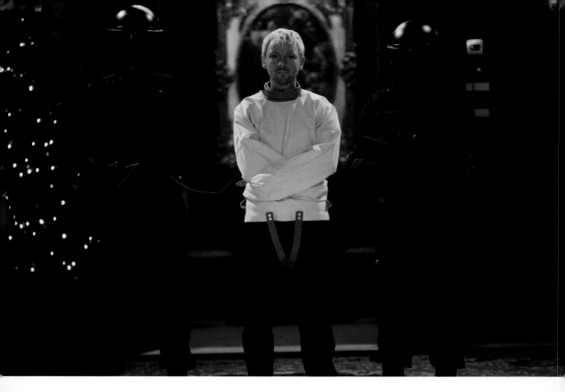

This spread: The many faces of the Master (John Simm).

Above: A prisoner of Naismith.

Left: Markers on John Simm's face help with his CGI transformation into the skeletal Master.

Below: The Master becomes a Chinese army officer, newsreader Trinity Wells and a UNIT General.

Facing page: The Master is captured by Naismith's troops.

Above: The Time Lords make their triumphant return.

Left: Timothy Dalton as Rassilon, Lord President of Gallifrey.

Below: Green-screen filming for the massed ranks of Time Lords seen in *The End of Time*.

Above: These innocuous-looking booths in Naismith's mansion will cost the Doctor dearly...

Right: Addams (Sinead Keenan) in her Vinvocci form.

Below: Abigail (Tracy Ifeachor) and Joshua Naismith (David Harewood) toast their success.

Facing page left: The Doctor faces a final, terrible choice...

This page: The Doctor finally gets his reward.

Above: Verity Newman (Jessica Hynes) meets the man who broke her great grandmother's heart.

Above right: The Doctor does a spot of match-making between Captain Jack (John Barrowman) and Alonso Frame (Russell Tovey).

Right centre: Newlyweds Martha Jones (Freema Agyeman) and Mickey Smith (Noel Clarke) hear a familiar sound for the last time.

Right: It's second time lucky for Donna Noble (Catherine Tate).

Below: A final – and first – meeting for the Doctor and Rose (Billie Piper).

Above: The dying moments of David Tennant's Tenth Doctor...

Right: ... and the first moments of Matt Smith's Eleventh Doctor.

Below: The two Doctors!

book, of all books. When I was 16, that book was as cool as punk rock, and drugs, and sex, it really was. Everyone carried it around with them at school. In a plain old Swansea comprehensive. And now I'm writing the Foreword! I can't believe they've asked me.

FROM: RUSSELL T DAVIES TO: BENJAMIN COOK, MONDAY 17 NOVEMBER 2008 02:55:37 GMT
CARDIFF
I'm back in Cardiff, starting to root through 4.15. The script attached to this e-mail is Gareth's, but I'm writing inside it, so the asterisked sections are my changes. But he's written his best script so far, so I'm mostly just tidying up and clarifying.

FROM: BENJAMIN COOK TO: RUSSELL T DAVIES, MONDAY 17 NOVEMBER 2008 03:01:29 GMT
RE: CARDIFF
You're still up? Of *course* you are. Thanks for the script. It's a really mad old romp.

FROM: RUSSELL T DAVIES TO: BENJAMIN COOK, TUESDAY 18 NOVEMBER 2008 02:36:50 GMT
RE: CARDIFF
Here's some more 4.15 script.

Meanwhile, in Upper Boat, they're filming Torchwood versus Smokey the Space Pelican. We focus on that creature for three whole episodes, and it's so obscured by smoke that we're all wondering if it's going to work – a very uncertain feeling, creeping through the production team, while Peter Capaldi has to act with glass and smoke. (Which he's doing brilliantly. The man is amazing.) I've been wondering if we can enhance the alien with extra swirly CGI or something. I had a long conversation with Julie about that this afternoon. All I can suggest is ripping some of the CG out of, say, *Doctor Who* 4.16, and spending that on *Torchwood*. Not that cash is that easily transferable, but… it is when Julie is in charge. Hey ho. Sci-fi fun.

FROM: RUSSELL T DAVIES TO: BENJAMIN COOK, WEDNESDAY 19 NOVEMBER 2008 02:08:01 GMT
RE: CARDIFF
More script. I'm really getting into the swing of it today. It feels good and proper – and fun! – to be sitting here writing *Doctor Who*. And today we saw an edit of Smokey the Space Pelican, which ain't too bad after all. The smoke really makes you stare. So! Good all round.

FROM: RUSSELL T DAVIES TO: BENJAMIN COOK, THURSDAY 20 NOVEMBER 2008 01:25:47 GMT
SWANSEA AND BACK
I'm too tired to write tonight. Strange old day. I was in Swansea for the funeral of one of my mum and dad's old friends. Lovely Myra Blyth. One of the best. She was 86, sat down in a chair, went to sleep, never woke up. Nice way to go. I have to go to one or

two of these funerals a year. They're dropping like flies. My mum and dad had a real gang of mates. All their adult lives, a proper gang, 20 or 30 of them, 40 maybe, I've never counted, with each of those people expanding over the years into family trees of sons, daughters, grandkids, who all became part of the gang, too. They used to traipse in and out of our house, usually pissed, and I mean very pissed. Great drinkers, all of them. The backdoor would open, any time of day, and one of them would stride in, usually with some outrageous story (often filthy), told with the skills of a true storyteller, with punch lines, riffs, and crescendos. Loud, wild, barmy characters, all ferociously Welsh. This entire community was based around Swansea Rugby Club. Their entire lives satellited around that place, all day, every day. It was their world. It still is. These funeral wakes are always held in the Rugby Club. Sometimes I think that's where mine will be. It'll just be automatic.

What a ferocious social life it was. Way beyond anything else I've seen in my life. The men were all just out of War. They all went off to fight at 16, just kids. The Rugby Club still lists all the names of the boys who were blasted to bits. Billy Williams, who died at 16, swimming in burning oil. Never forgotten. My father had to hose down boats of refugees to stop them entering the harbour, because no one wanted them. But those Swansea men fought, they drank, they had sex… and then they returned home, still kids, and had to go back to living with their mothers. No wonder they escaped to the Rugby Club. They're way beyond sports fans; they lived for that place, and for each other. Truly, the most ferocious and loyal friendships. My dad was there, always. The only time you could guarantee him being in the house was Christmas Day, when he'd sit there burning in a silent hangover, then he'd go to bed at five in the afternoon. On Boxing Day, the rugby started again, and off he went. And they weren't just spectators: so many of the men went on to play for Wales, while the women became rugby wives, the powers behind the thrones. Kingsley Amis was a lecturer in Swansea, and wrote a book about that crowd, *The Old Devils*, which won the Booker Prize. BBC Two dramatised it a few years ago, and people would phone me up saying, 'That's your mum and dad! They've dramatised your mum and dad!' This was a drama with hairy old men pissing in gardens at midnight, while the women drank so much gin and tonic that they'd fall over and sleep in their clothes.

I loved that crowd. Every Friday and Saturday night, they'd all pile in from the Rugby Club, at two in the morning – plenty of booze in our house – all off their heads, yelling, and bawling, and hooting, and singing, singing like you'd think the Welsh didn't, really. I used to lie in bed and listen, and think it was marvellous. When I was very young, I didn't even know if these people were uncles and aunts or whatever; they were literally like an extended family. Even now, at that wake today, I'm not actually sure who's whose son or cousin or wife. They're just one great big gang.

But Christ, old age. Old age is savage. It's brutal. If you'd taken a snapshot of them just ten years ago, they'd all be wrinkled, smiling, hearty and pissed. But then they were hacked down, one by one. With no dignity. These vivid, grand people end up felled, and it simply doesn't stop – cancer, strokes, Alzheimer's. My mother had an aggressive blood cancer for two years, and never told anyone, not a living soul. She hid it ferociously and brilliantly, until the week before she died, because she didn't want to be one of these walking wounded. Some of the women used to go for lunch together, every Wednesday, every single Wednesday, for decades, a regular gang of 15… and now there's five of them left. Just five. But those five are still smiling, still hooting, still drinking gin and tonic, now telling stories of their broken hips, dead husbands, and children living on the other side of the world. Such an extraordinary gang, woven into each other's lives, and now each other's deaths. They all turn up at the funerals, still bristling with news, and gossip, and anecdotes. Faithful to the last.

Good old Myra. Went in her sleep. One of the few who got it right. And we all sat in church, and listened to the vicar telling us, with all his heart, that she's with her husband now, and 'whosoever shall believe in me shall have eternal life', and you just think, no wonder we make this stuff up. It's so needed. It must be wonderful, to be a Christian.

And I said I didn't want to write! I just wanted to write something else for once.

FROM: BENJAMIN COOK TO: RUSSELL T DAVIES, THURSDAY 20 NOVEMBER 2008 01:45:34 GMT

RE: SWANSEA AND BACK

I can see why richly defined characters – and bright, sharp dialogue – are such anchors of your scripts. The sorts of people who populate your writing were there, in your front room, as you lay in bed and listened to them singing downstairs.

Can I ask – if you don't *mind* me asking (I don't wanna be intrusive) – what was your mother like? I've never really asked you about her before. You talk about your dad sometimes, because he's still alive, you visit him and that… but your mum, not so much. What kind of mum was she? Which aspects of her do you see in yourself?

FROM: RUSSELL T DAVIES TO: BENJAMIN COOK, THURSDAY 20 NOVEMBER 2008 02:31:01 GMT

RE: SWANSEA AND BACK

Ah, never mind the 'intrusive'… Although it is hard to give an answer – what is a person like? They're an infinite number of things. There's that marvellous Stephen King quote, where he says that the most layered, complex, fascinating fictional character is nothing but a bag of bones compared to a real person. My mum is hard to describe without making her sound like Mother Of A Gay Man. Shame on me for even worrying about that. But she was immensely strong and clever. Like so many women, the glue that holds a family together. (I remember standing in the hospital, an hour after she died, and my sister saying, 'How are we all going to stay in touch with each other now?') But I loved her. I loved seeing her. I really miss seeing her.

We weren't close in the ways that you'd expect us to be close. We wouldn't have long, intimate conversations, but I never felt that we needed to, because I'm like her in many ways, sort of private and self-contained. We could both talk, and talk, and talk all day, without giving too much away. She was quite private, I think, and liked being private. She had lots of friends – those great Rugby Club friends, those powerful, exotic, larger-than-life figures – but for all that, at the same time, I think there was a whole secret life, going on in her head. I like that. I don't spend any time wondering what she was doing, what she was thinking, or wishing that I'd known more. I'm just glad she was like that, because I'm like that. When I describe her as strong, I don't mean that she was domineering or loud; she wasn't at all. But her presence was strong. I think that's what I mean when I say how much I liked simply seeing her. She was like a still centre. She didn't need to shout, or nag, or intervene. She'd just potter about in the kitchen – all day, every day in the kitchen – while the whole family revolved around her, without her needing to even try.

She was an only child. Maybe that helps you to live in your head, I don't know. When she was very young, they were as poor as anything, living out on the Gower in a tiny cottage. It'd be worth a fortune now. That's where the rich people live. My grandmother would clean houses and pubs, and even make tea in the garden for passers-by, to make money – while my grandad was a bit of a mystery. He'd disappear abroad. He joined the American army, took cargo boats to Jamaica, and all sorts of strange, wanderlust things. When he was home, he'd take my mum to the edge of the cliffs, and dangle her over the edge by her legs so that she could collect plover's eggs from the nests, because they could be sold for good money. My nan used to scream at him, 'You've been dangling that child again!' Then, when my mum was – I don't know – seven or eight, she spilt a pan of hot chip-fat down herself, had terrible burns, so the whole family had to move into town so that she could be closer to the hospital for years of grafts. That's when we became a Swansea family instead of country folk. No wonder she was strong. No wonder she was so self-contained. What a thing to go through.

It was all summed up by the way she died, really, when she had cancer and lived with it for two years without telling anyone. The strength of that! No one in my family has ever felt hurt or betrayed by that, by her silence – which is remarkable because, when a parent dies, you go through all those wild and contradictory reactions. But we never regretted her decision, none of us, or blamed her, because we all knew what she was like. She kept herself to herself, even when surrounded by family and friends.

Well, hmm, there's one time when I wish she'd said a bit more, or that *I'd* said a bit more. Towards the end, I'd worked out that she was ill (long story, I'd type for ever), and I went to see her, to ask her. She admitted it, though didn't say how ill she really was. (It was a blood cancer, so it was very invisible). We'd talked – really calmly, really ordinary stuff, while watching TV and flicking through newspapers, because real life is so un-dramatic, most of the time, no tears, no angst and stuff – and then she drove me to the station, but we stopped off in Tesco's on the way, and pottered about in the aisles, just chatting away, buying stuff for my sister… when this really polite, kind, elderly man walked up and said, out of the blue, 'Excuse me, I hope you don't mind my saying this, but you're bleeding.' And her arm was covered in blood. There was blood trailing across the supermarket floor! But she was mystified. There was no cut, there was nothing wrong with her. Really bizarre. Where's all that blood from?! She ran to the toilets, to clean herself up, and I got the staff to clean the floor. And when she came back, there it was – the tiniest pinprick on her thumb. The sort of cut you get in picking up, I don't know, some bit of shopping, like the smallest of paper cuts. Literally, a pinprick. As small as that. But because she was on some sort of blood-thinning drugs, that tiny little incision bled, and bled, and bled. And then we just carried on, she kept on chatting and shopping, but she was mortified. Everything she'd been keeping secret was suddenly visible, bright red, in public.

So, she took me to the train station. We had one of those daft little family traditions – the traditions that you don't even think about, you just do – where whenever one of us gets on a train, the other stands on the platform and waves it off. Even if you have to wait ten minutes before the bloody thing moves, stuck there in a dumb show. It's just a Davies thing. I got on that train, and she was on the platform, and I must have spent 20 seconds turning away, putting my luggage on the rack or whatever, and when I turned back… she was gone. Impossible! Honestly, impossible. We just don't do that. I went to the window, looked up and down, and there was no sign of her. She must have actually had to run to get out of sight in time. And that's when I really knew how ill she was. She must have thought that would be the last time she'd ever see me. And she was right. I saw her in hospital, when she was dying, just a couple of weeks later, but she was insensible by then. Bloody hell, I hate that image, an old woman running down a station platform – so she didn't have to look at me, or I didn't have to look at her.

Ah, you see, you ask about my mum, and I talk about her death. Because it's still incredible to me. They always say that you get over these things, and only remember the happy times. Well, maybe not. It's eight years ago now, and I can't exactly say that I smile whenever I think about her. I still think: she's dead. I still think it's wrong. Out of thousands of years of great literature, novels, poetry, essays, diatribes and philosophy, the Death Of Your Mother seems to be quite a small theme. It should be massive. I can't work out if it's too huge, or too ordinary.

That's cheered me up. You bastard! Ha ha. No, it hasn't made me miserable. Not really. I'm glad you asked, even though I don't think I've really answered. I just told a good story instead. Because that's what I do.

FROM: BENJAMIN COOK TO: RUSSELL T DAVIES, THURSDAY 20 NOVEMBER 2008 02:40:56 GMT

RE: SWANSEA AND BACK
Have you ever written her, do you think? Because your scripts are full of strong women, clever women, you write mums so well – Hazel in *Queer as Folk*, Monica in *Bob &*

Rose, Jackie in *Doctor Who* – and your mum sounds very like them in some respects, but quite unlike them in others. And what did your mum make of your chosen career? Did she approve? Oh, but she must have! She must have been so incredibly proud.

FROM: RUSSELL T DAVIES TO: BENJAMIN COOK, THURSDAY 20 NOVEMBER 2008 03:04:19 GMT

RE: SWANSEA AND BACK

I'm sure she was proud of me. It's a shame that she never saw this big, popular success that's *Doctor Who*. All she saw was the *Queer as Folk* controversy, which can't have been easy for her. Mostly, she worried about my job, because 'writer', to my parents, sort of equals 'bohemian' or 'unemployed'. It was only right at the end – that last time I saw her properly – I told her how much I earned. She was staggered. Maybe that's why she ran away – she was going to the bank!

I don't think I've ever written my mum, though. I don't think I've ever written anyone directly. At the same time, I'm always writing everyone I know. I suppose there are echoes of her in Val Vivaldi, the mum in *Mine All Mine* – always in the kitchen, married to a difficult man, living a secret life – but that still wasn't anywhere near her, really. I write strong mothers, but I write strong women full stop. Rose Tyler. Rose Cooper. I sometimes wonder if I write women well because I'm not hampered by fancying them. But perhaps that's bollocks.

FROM: BENJAMIN COOK TO: RUSSELL T DAVIES, THURSDAY 20 NOVEMBER 2008 03:20:06 GMT

RE: SWANSEA AND BACK

Or maybe you just write everyone well, because you're a good writer. Just a thought.

Since we're talking about your family and childhood, can I ask you something that you've been asked a hundred times before, I suspect… not by me, though… when did you come out as gay? In fact, when did you realise you were gay? Were your parents okay with it? What did the local community make of it? In Swansea. In the '70s. I've never asked you that before.

FROM: RUSSELL T DAVIES TO: BENJAMIN COOK, THURSDAY 20 NOVEMBER 2008 03:53:14 GMT

RE: SWANSEA AND BACK

>>Were your parents okay with it?<<

They still don't know. I've never told them. Ho ho.

When did I realise I was gay? I've never reached a satisfactory answer to that question – I look back and I can't think of any one specific moment – because I suppose I've always known, even before I had the right words for it. There was no choice. It was always men. My first crushes were on boys. (Is anything in your adult life as strong as those very first crushes? The burning madness of them! Does everything get duller as you get older?) I've no sense of ever going off girls, because I was never 'on' them. Even at nine or ten, when I probably didn't know what sex was or how it worked, there was always a fevered attraction towards boys, so I really can't remember when I first applied the word 'gay' to myself. It never felt wrong, I never hated it, but I knew that I should keep quiet about it… not in a tortured way; it was just automatic. That was what I did, naturally. I envy those 15-year-old boys and girls nowadays who can come out of the closet. Like life is so much better now…? But I wonder. They have more choice than I ever thought I had, but maybe that causes more angst. To announce myself simply didn't exist as an option for me, or for any gay boy or girl of my age, and I'm not saying that's good – theoretically, morally, it's absolutely wrong – but to live that life, not saying anything…? Yeah, I could do that. And I did. It just felt like waiting.

I'm sure I'm scratching the surface here – looking back into that young head is like staring into a furnace – but really, in the end, it felt all right. I'm making it sound very calm, but I suppose I was helped because I found a safe space to live in: the youth theatre company that I belonged to, which was wonderful. That, not school, was my real life. Naturally so. It was a collection of brilliant, funny, clever people, in which even the straightest of lads could camp it up. Very few were overtly gay, though some older boys were. It was brilliant, I realise now, to see out gay men just a few years ahead of myself, and to know that there was a life to be led. Great place, great fun, great friendship. The most magnificent training ground, not just for theatre, but also for life. So much of my character was formed in that youth theatre. I don't think the staff who ran it will ever really know how marvellous they were, and how important.

I only told my parents that I was gay once I'd already left home. Even then, they must have guessed. My dad – with the only observant thing he's ever said in his entire life – just said, 'You've always drawn men.' He was right. I used to draw constantly back then, all the time, like a compulsion, sketching and doodling all day long, and it was always handsome cartoon-y men, with strong jaws and big quiffs of hair. So, yeah, mum and dad were fine – not delighted, let's be honest, but they both loved me way beyond any issue. But with a big, loud, fey, arty son, let's face it, it must have been screaming at them. I know that my mum worried, because she associated 'gay' with drugs and promiscuity. I went on to write *Queer as Folk*, which didn't help! But we didn't talk about this stuff much. It's weird, isn't it, because you're essentially talking about sex – well, it's far more than that, but that's the baseline – and most parents don't talk to their kids about that, whether gay or straight.

I know what you mean about Swansea in the '70s, but I think there's a lie told about small communities – whether that's rural places, small towns, or closed groups – that they claim that they 'don't know any homosexuals'. Look a little deeper, and they do, and always have, for generations. There's always been funny old Uncle Douglas, who never got married; those two stern women who live together in that old house; someone's camp little son who doesn't like football. It's there, and it's accepted, quietly, tacitly. The moment that it becomes too overt, too sexual, too challenging, then the headlines flare, the blood pumps, and the extreme reactions get trotted out – maybe because people are scared, because they simply haven't thought about it, or because they love to strike an official stance, or because they're embarrassed by sex in any shape or form. But when all that dies down, Uncle Douglas, and the two women, and Walter the Softy, they're still there, and not driven out.

It's a funny subject, this one, because 'coming out' sounds so simple. As though it happens once. But I think I still come out in some shape or form, somehow, somewhere, to someone, almost every day. I'm always aware of it, a lurking 'does he know?' Yes, even me. A friend of mine, who's my age and has had roughly the same experiences as me, astonished me only a few years ago when he said, 'I think I need a year off. I think I need to move house, or maybe just go away, so that I can come to terms with it.' With what? 'Being gay.' That staggered me, because it sounds so true. I'm really not sure what that means, and I'm certainly sure there's no magic answer to it all, but something is ringing a bell there. It's never over... is it?

FROM: RUSSELL T DAVIES TO: BENJAMIN COOK, THURSDAY 20 NOVEMBER 2008 19:52:06 GMT

MORE 4.15

Great 4.15 Tone Meeting today! It's so good to be back. There's an energy about *Doctor Who* that lifts everyone. I thought today, Steven and Piers are so lucky to be inheriting this workforce. It solves half their problems before they've even started. The best part of all was a big round of applause to welcome Tracie Simpson. The crew loves that woman. Brilliant idea, promoting her. And she was fantastic. I'd wondered last night whether she might seem nervous or daunted. Not a bit of it. She was as strong, and as brilliant, and as fun as ever. In a short orange dress, and long leather boots. Since we're filming in a desert, Tracie and Ed arrived wearing sheikhs' headgear! How funny. Plus, we've a new accountant who's very handsome, and very tall, and possibly gay. Unfortunately, he didn't laugh at any of my jokes. Ah, you can never laugh a man into bed. Out of bed, yes...

Oh, and we're going to Dubai! That's our desert! The double-decker bus sets off in December, because it will take five weeks to get there.

And then I came home, and watched the death of Ianto Jones on the rushes. Killed by Smokey the Space Pelican. I cried! Like an idiot! I created that man. It's a bit of a sentimental scene, but we can trim it down in the Edit. A good death, well told. I'm really proud of that.

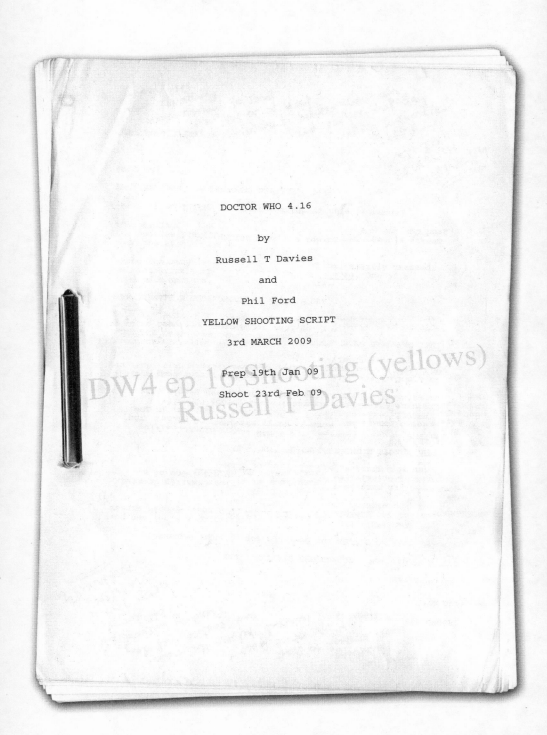

DOCTOR WHO 4.16

by

Russell T Davies

and

Phil Ford

YELLOW SHOOTING SCRIPT

3rd MARCH 2009

Prep 19th Jan 09

Shoot 23rd Feb 09

DW4 ep 16 Shooting (yellows)
Russell T Davies

CHAPTER TWENTY-ONE

MR SMITH AND THE RUNAWAY TRAIN

In which Prince Charles apologises, octopus tattoos are
envisioned, and Matt Smith's name isn't mentioned once

FROM: RUSSELL T DAVIES TO: BENJAMIN COOK, SUNDAY 23 NOVEMBER 2008 01:38:23 GMT

RE: MORE 4.15

Ah, I'm too tired. I was going to stay up all night, but… zzzzz. And I have to write with
that balcony door open, or this place gets smoked like a kipper, so now I'm a block of
ice. It's freezing. But I've *got* to finish 4.15 tomorrow, or the whole week is wrecked. I
love Gareth's stuff, but it's turning into a bigger rewrite than I thought.

FROM: BENJAMIN COOK TO: RUSSELL T DAVIES, SUNDAY 23 NOVEMBER 2008 02:19:52 GMT

RE: MORE 4.15

I wonder if you're changing stuff just because you can. Do you ever worry about
that?

FROM: RUSSELL T DAVIES TO: BENJAMIN COOK, SUNDAY 23 NOVEMBER 2008 10:10:48 GMT

RE: MORE 4.15

That's probably true. No, it's very true. Then again, I read back my stuff and think it
works, so… God, they must call me a bastard. Imagine those writers sitting in the pub,
calling me everything under the sun. Oh well.

FROM: RUSSELL T DAVIES TO: BENJAMIN COOK, MONDAY 24 NOVEMBER 2008 18:02:53 GMT

RE: MORE 4.15

Ta-daaa! Pom-pom! I've finished 4.15! One script down. Three to go. (Or even two.

We haven't decided whether to cut 4.16. Julie says that she's still lacking £300,000 from the budget.) I thought I'd finish yesterday, but it turns out that one episode of *Torchwood* is running under by five minutes, and they finish filming this week, so I had to cook up five extra minutes of stuff.

But now I can shut the balcony door for a bit. Thank God.

FROM: RUSSELL T DAVIES TO: BENJAMIN COOK, TUESDAY 25 NOVEMBER 2008 20:36:48 GMT

RE: MORE 4.15

I'm watching *Torchwood* rushes – AND THERE'S NICK BRIGGS!!! The voice of the Daleks! On screen at last! He plays Rick Yates, the Deputy Prime Minister and Foreign Secretary. He is really, properly wonderful on screen. Huge presence. Utterly believable. Wonderful eyes. That man has really, really got it. I'm so pleased. And the scenes that he's in are riveting. It's the government deciding how to cull ten per cent of Britain's children. Oh, it's good. I'm really excited. Good old Nick.

In Specials Land, we've now got until the end of the week to decide whether to cut 4.16, because of course Julie has to talk to David about it and see how he feels. Though, there's still no sign of the missing £300,000. I'm wondering if there's a version of 4.16 that's very, very cheap, to save money that way.

Still, the rest of my week is turning to shit. On Thursday, I'm in London to talk to the BBC Drama Writers Academy at Elstree. On Friday, I collect my OBE. (Oh Lordy.) Saturday, the BAFTA Children's *Doctor Who* Day (I don't know what this is, but it involves Any Effects, which means something will explode).[1] Then, on Sunday, the actual Children's BAFTAs, where I'm presenting a lifetime achievement award to the Chuckle Brothers.[2] Mental week. But annoying, because I should be working. Just think, if 4.16 is cut, I'll have to start writing the finale IMMEDIATELY!

FROM: RUSSELL T DAVIES TO: BENJAMIN COOK, THURSDAY 27 NOVEMBER 2008 01:14:17 GMT

RE: MORE 4.15

Julie said the funniest thing today. Someone from Branding told her that in order to gain admission to the BAFTA Children's Event on Saturday, she'd have to take a child with her. No adults are allowed in without a child. Not even her. Julie: 'Where am I going to get a child from? Do they think I've got one in my cellar?' That's been making me laugh all day.

No, I still don't know what the BAFTA Children's Event is.

But we spoke for an hour on the phone today, about this 4.16 wrangle. I think I'm writing to you because – well, I do anyway – but I want to lay it out, because I simply don't know what I think. I always have an opinion. Always! But this time… I just don't

---

1 Any Effects provide physical effects for *Doctor Who*, *Torchwood* and *The Sarah Jane Adventures*.
2 The Chuckle Brothers are a comedy double act consisting of Barry and Paul Elliot, best known for their work on BBC children's show ChuckleVision, for which Russell wrote three episodes in the early 1990s.

know! Money is getting tighter. Goodbye Woolworths. Julie says that the financial bite is terrifying. *Doctor Who* has more resources than most, but this is getting tough. It would still be easier for us to spread the money that we've got over three episodes instead of four, but we haven't worked out all those costs yet. We don't know how much we'd lose by paying off Graeme, David, Nikki, all those people. Of course, there are ways of absorbing those costs. For example, David is dying to appear in an episode of *The Sarah Jane Adventures* next year, so maybe *Doctor Who* money could cover that? Etc. Anyway, no matter how much money you have to pay out for a cancellation, nothing is as expensive as actually making an episode.

In a funny way, this is all your fault. Yes, you, ha ha. Because 4.16 is suddenly in a vulnerable position. Now that we've come up with the idea (your idea!) of the Christmas regeneration (all right, spread into New Year's Day, but the point still stands), then, to be blunt, we don't *need* the Saturday-before-Christmas Special. The 19th is kind of irrelevant now. The two-part finale will be huge, and will soak up all the publicity and viewers we need, so 4.16 is the last vestige of a plan that changed a while ago. So, you did it. You knackered it. Ha ha ha.

Julie spoke to David today. She didn't quite stress the financial angle, because it's not fair to worry him about that. (Also, there is no one higher up at the BBC demanding that we make this cut. It's entirely generated by Julie and me.) David's reaction was as clever and canny as you'd expect. He was 'disappointed' at the thought of doing three Specials, not four, but wise enough to know that the big finale is the thing to be protected. He didn't throw his hands up in horror and say that we're doomed. Instead, he wondered if we'd throw away 4.16 on 19 December, and where else would it fit? Halloween? But that would put us up against *The X Factor*.

Then, David had the stunning idea of *Children in Need* night – which we talked about for ages, because it's tempting. Except, in the end, that's a charity night – which does very well, with ratings exceeding *Doctor Who*'s in places – and editorially we couldn't justify interrupting a major fundraiser. Children in Need might love it, but we're both still doubtful. They want singing newsreaders. Imagine the pressure to include Pudsey, or a plot in which children are in danger.[3] Let alone the on-screen telephone numbers. Or splitting the Special into ten-minute chunks. Or... oh God, you see? Hostage to fortune. Potentially damaging. Anyway, it's wrong. We'd be parasites. I doubt that Jay Hunt would sanction it. Possibly even asking her to sanction it would make *Doctor Who* a pain in the arse. Never let anyone on the Sixth Floor think of *Doctor Who* as a problem, in any context, ever. Rule Number One

So, what do we do? Julie is going to Jane, because she's more of a final arbiter and has a better grandstand perspective. She can help us see the wood for the trees, and other metaphors. But we've got to decide soon, because I should start writing 4.16 – or 4.17

---

3 *Children in Need*'s mascot, Pudsey, is a yellow teddy bear with a bandage over one eye.

– on Monday. (It won't be Monday. Did you guess?) Right now, the word that attracts me like a magnet is 'disappointed'. Bless David, he would be disappointed. Hardly the strongest word in the world, but a heartfelt one. I never want to do anything that disappoints David. (Rule Number Two! My personal rule.) So, that word alone is enough to push me into action and go for four episodes. Add to that, how do we announce that we're cutting an episode without it saying 'BBC IN FINANCIAL CRISIS'. Or is that good, to make public the fact that we're acting on a genuine shortfall? Once upon a time, only the fans would have noticed or cared, but *Doctor Who* attracts automatic headlines now, with the press gunning for the BBC in any way possible.

Hmpf. Typing it out didn't help. Well, maybe it'll sink into my head a bit, and I'll wake up tomorrow with a clearer idea – just like Charlie Brown's sister puts a French book under her pillow in the hope that it'll sink in while she sleeps.[4] (Doesn't work.)

> **Text message from: Ben**
> Sent: 27-Nov-2008 22:58
> Good luck for tomorrow. Don't let them forget that the Doctor saved Buckingham Palace last Christmas.

> **Text message from: Russell**
> Sent: 27-Nov-2008 23:02
> Thank you! Oh, and Julie has raised all the money – all four Specials are on!

> **Text message from: Ben**
> Sent: 27-Nov-2008 23:06
> Has Julie considered helping out Woolworths? She'd get them back on their feet in no time.

> **Text message from: Russell**
> Sent: 27-Nov-2008 23:07
> She's manning the pick 'n' mix as we speak.

> **Text message from: Ben**
> Sent: 28-Nov-2008 13:17
> I've just seen you on the news! At the Palace! Very smart. You were chatting to Prince Charles for ages.

---

4 Charlie Brown is the main protagonist in Charles M Schulz's *Peanuts* comic strip.

> **Text message from: Russell**
> Sent: 28-Nov-2008 13:26
> On the news?! Oh no! He was talking about David as Hamlet, and that
> he was sorry he couldn't appear in *Doctor Who* last Christmas. How
> bloody mad. It was ridiculous and hilarious. Full report to come.

FROM: BENJAMIN COOK TO: RUSSELL T DAVIES, SATURDAY 29 NOVEMBER 2008 22:45:36 GMT

PRINCE CHARLES' ARSE

How was the Mysterious BAFTA Children's Event? Did Julie get in? Did she find a
kid in the end? Where from?! My neighbour has several going spare, I think. I should
have mentioned this earlier.

FROM: RUSSELL T DAVIES TO: BENJAMIN COOK, SATURDAY 29 NOVEMBER 2008 23:17:59 GMT

RE: PRINCE CHARLES' ARSE

I'm back in Cardiff for a few scant hours. This morning was mental! The Mysterious
BAFTA Children's Event. I still don't know what it was for or why we did it, but it was
good fun. We had to get in at 7am to rehearse, and the show was at 10.30am, so we
barely knew what was happening. I thought I'd be on stage for ten minutes. I was on
for an hour-and-a-half! But it was brilliant, and Kirsten O'Brien was a hoot, and 1,000
kids screamed at the Cybermen and Daleks, so there we go. This show is truly mad at
times. I was on stage at the Barbican! First the National, now the Barbican!

I'll give you a full Palace update when I'm back properly (off to London again
tomorrow for the Children's BAFTAs), but even just a day later, it all seems very
strange and far away.

FROM: RUSSELL T DAVIES TO: BENJAMIN COOK, WEDNESDAY 3 DECEMBER 2008 15:05:03 GMT

MY ANKLES' ARSE

Yeah, my ankles. My ankles hurt. Ankles! I'm like a Jane Austen lady with weak ankles.
It's been like this for ten days. It's like I've got little coins of pain – like a hot 10p piece
– in the side of both ankles. I feel like I'm about to fall over all the time. Since it's
both ankles simultaneously, that probably means it's arthritis or something. Oh God!
Ankles?!

Anyway! Proper update! When I last wrote in detail, 4.16 was teetering on the brink.
Funnily enough, that e-mail *did* do me some good. It unlocked the problems, and I lay
awake afterwards buzzing with ideas. I couldn't get to sleep, because suddenly it was as
clear as day: we were all talking about 4.16 as expendable, so the answer is… make it
unmissable! Make it vital! Make it earn that Saturday-before-Christmas slot. It's hard
to do that with just a monster and a Mars Base, but there's a lovely little subplot ticking
away in Phil's script: the Doctor knows that the Mars Base of 2050 is mysteriously
destroyed, and that it's (conveniently) one of those fixed-point-in-time things, so he

should leave well alone and let them die. But he doesn't. Nice, okay. But that night, it just clicked: that's not a subplot, it's the WHOLE PLOT!

There's a tiny key lurking in 4.15, where the Doctor says – for the first time in twenty-first-century *Doctor Who* – that he stole the TARDIS. To new viewers, he must seem best of mates with the Time Lords, all that rebel stuff has been put to one side – and quite rightly, since I imagine that became irrelevant once the Time War broke out. He was hardly going to carry on a personal grudge once the whole of creation was at stake. No, he went back home and joined up, albeit in a maverick-y, Doctor-y way, I'm sure. (Maybe I should write that Time War novel one day? I've got so much of it worked out in my head.) By bringing back that element, the rebel, suddenly he becomes fascinating in a whole new way. All that stuff in *The Fires of Pompeii* about not breaking the Laws of Time – suddenly in 4.16, for the first time, he realises: who says so? Why not?! The rebel, reborn! He's the only Time Lord left. He *is* the Laws of Time! He can do what he wants! It's like the grief is over, and he realises who he is now. It's not just a nice emotional, brave decision to save the Mars colonists; it's arrogance, it's the Doctor extending his powers… until the Ood calls him to his death at the end. Pride, then a fall.

This feeds into this new format, the companionless Doctor. I've always believed what Donna says at the end of *The Runaway Bride*, that the Doctor is dangerous on his own, that he needs a human with him. I'd been vaguely worried that none of the Specials was proving this, but here's my chance. (Always listen to those worries!) Also, it's what I wanted from that first notion of David's last episode, before it became a two-parter – the story set on board the clapped-out spaceship, which was probably the Tenth Doctor battling with his id, his dark side, his monstrous power. Now, we get the chance to play that on Mars!

Oh, that was a good night. It was brilliant to feel everything click. For the first time, I *needed* 4.16, to complete the Tenth Doctor's story. The next day, I got in the car with Julie, going to Elstree, and described all this, and we were very excited. 'It's become a trilogy,' she said. We were buzzing. So, then we went to Elstree, talked to the Writers Academy, all very nice, then Julie had to head off early… 15 minutes later, she phoned from the car. All the money problems solved! The cash is in! Thank God we went through that process with 4.16, because it's strengthened it hugely. Maybe that's always a good test for an episode: threaten to axe it, and then see how it adapts under pressure.

Everything else is going well. The recce in Dubai was wonderful, apparently. They've even taken plate shots, so you could say that shooting has begun. Sort of. The double-decker bus is being kitted out with made-up adverts. I thought it would be nice to tie it in with the finale somehow, and mention the millionaire's name, so the mobile phones on the bus adverts are made by 'Naismith'. Nice name. Yes, the millionaire is now called Naismith. That was the name of one of the villains in *Century Falls*. I've always liked it.

Oh, and then the Palace. It was just weird. I woke up that morning in a stinking temper. Really foul. I couldn't work out where it came from. Then I realised – that's how much I hate not being in control. Being thrown into someone else's schedule, and someone else's protocols, for someone else's reasons, with a regime, and discipline… oh God, I hated it. (My sister got told to put away her camera in the Palace, and I wanted to punch the footman. We pay for that place!) But that's scary, realising how much I like to be in charge. America will do me good. Cut that bastard down to size! (Just don't hurt my ankles.) Poor Andrew had been in charge of the arrangements, and I was bloody unbearable.[5] 'Where do we go? Where do we get the taxi to?' 'It just says the Palace.' 'But which bit of the Palace? Have you *seen* Buckingham Palace? It's got hundreds of doors. It's got gates to the left, and gates to the right, and a gate in the middle. Which gate do we go to?!' Turns out, it was the gate everyone else was going through. Oh, I was wound up. But then we got inside, and it was all rather matey, everyone else feeling out of their depth, too. And then a footman fanboy'd me in the cloakroom, so that made me laugh. He said, 'I'll get sacked for doing this, but can I have your autograph?!'

All the OBEs got shoved in one room, MBEs in another, Dames and Sirs somewhere else (I bet their room was posher). Anna Wintour was standing across the room, looking truly, impossibly glamorous. There were soldiers, mayors, and posh people. I ended up with the dwarf. There was a dwarf called John, from Motherwell, in a wheelchair, and I thought, I'll go and talk to him. Plus, I'm 6'6", so I thought it would look funny. And he was lovely. Dead tough Scotsman. He does charity work, and works for the government and for disabled rights, and helps out with kids in amateur football, and I'm thinking, I just write TV. I felt a fraud. But that's nothing new.

Then, we all head in – John abandoned his wheelchair, because he was determined to walk – and actually it's quite a laugh, because it's so relaxed. They do so many of these functions, it's the most well-oiled machine imaginable. With really friendly staff. Fair dos to them, they were lovely. God help me, I'm becoming a royalist. You can see the audience as you queue up, and my sisters look so funny in their hats! I was just laughing. The Band of the Coldstream Guards plays music throughout the whole thing. When I went in, it was *Greensleeves*. So, you stand there, and bow – I thought I'd hate the bow, but what the hell, when in Rome – and Prince Charles was actually quite smiley and twinkly. Before you approach him, a Very Handsome Soldier whispers in his ear, telling him who you are. Imagine him saying, 'Writes *Doctor Who*, sir.' Ha ha! So, he said how marvellous David Tennant was in *Hamlet*. (David texted later saying that Prince Charles had actually sent him a long letter saying how marvellous he was.). Then he said that he understood we'd asked him to appear in *Doctor Who*, that he'd only heard about it

---

5 Andrew Smith, Russell's boyfriend.

recently – oh God, I wonder if he heard the 'miserable bastard' bit – and that while he'd love to, he just gets too many requests like that. And I said, 'Never mind that, are those ears real?' Yes, I really did.

And suddenly it's all over, it's photos outside, and it turns out the photographer's assistant's daughter was in school with Lis Sladen's daughter. Only *Doctor Who*! It will be there, somehow, for ever.

I was really knackered after that weekend. I've done barely anything all week, just rested my ankles. I'll have to panic and gibber from this weekend onwards, but that's the deal –

Oh no, wait, I did have some grand thoughts this morning. It was actually making me laugh, by the end. Since Gallifrey is returning, I let myself get completely carried away, imagining a fanboy version of 4.17/4.18. I imagined *starting* there – Scene 1, Gallifrey! Christmas Day, Gallifrey! The President hurrying through an ancient temple. Subtitle: 'The last days of the Time War'. Time Lords gathering in cloisters, scared, exhausted, under siege – explosions offstage, Daleks on their way, no one knows where the Doctor is – and they convene to form some Grand Plan. (It turns out, in the end, that they have anticipated – via some creepy Time Lady Seer-type-figure – that the Master will try this planet-swap one day, and they must take action to safeguard the future by planning against him…) All that shit. Then I slapped a great big label saying 'FANBOY' over the whole thing, and ditched it. Fun, though. Even typing it out now, I still wonder… no, don't. No. Funny how you shift, though. Five years ago, even imagining that would have been impossible. Now, it's actually transmittable, and horribly seductive. Fanboy levels rising! Definitely time to go.

FROM: BENJAMIN COOK TO: RUSSELL T DAVIES, WEDNESDAY 3 DECEMBER 2008 17:04:00 GMT
RE: MY ANKLES' ARSE
Gallifrey – oh, you know you want to! Imagine that narrative jump between the opening scene on Gallifrey, all cloisters, temples, and Time Lord grandeur… and five minutes later, the Master in a grubby public toilet, on Earth, all sordid and filthy. Besides, after all these years, do you really imagine that that brilliant crew couldn't pull off Gallifrey? Of course they could. In fact, you *owe* it to them. (Oh, that's not fair. I'm joking. No, really, I am.) You owe them Gallifrey. (I'm still joking. Honest.) But go on. Please. It'd be amazing. Imagine being seven years old and watching Scene 1, Gallifrey. You'd wet yourself.

Imagine it.

Go on.

They'll wet themselves, Russell! WET THEMSELVES!

FROM: RUSSELL T DAVIES TO: BENJAMIN COOK, FRIDAY 5 DECEMBER 2008 01:05:06 GMT
RE: MY ANKLES' ARSE
They've done a timing on 4.15, and it's only 54 minutes. Bollocks. I'll have to invent

some more. That's annoying. After all this time, you still can't tell how long a script is going to be.

And weirdly, tonight, Steven's Series Five, Episode 4 arrived in my inbox. Completely unexpected, unasked for. They seem to be thinking, you're showing us the Specials, so we'll show you our scripts, too. How could I not read it? It's just spectacular. And terrifying! And funny. And everything. Amazing stuff.

FROM: BENJAMIN COOK TO: RUSSELL T DAVIES, FRIDAY 5 DECEMBER 2008 02:36:10 GMT

RE: MY ANKLES' ARSE

Stop showing off. (Sob!)

FROM: RUSSELL T DAVIES TO: BENJAMIN COOK, FRIDAY 5 DECEMBER 2008 18:45:02 GMT

RE: MY ANKLES' ARSE

I ran my latest Gallifrey idea past Julie today. She loved it. You bastards. You win!

BUT! I've shifted it to the top of the last episode. Honestly, trust me, opening on Christmas Day, with Gallifrey at the top of 4.17, is wrong. But at the top of 4.18? Yes, please! (Julie still hates those headdresses, though. I said that the guards in the background could wear them, while the speaking Time Lords – the President! – could just have skullcaps and robes.) God knows how we'll afford it, though. I'm not having them waffling on in a Welsh castle.

FROM: RUSSELL T DAVIES TO: BENJAMIN COOK, WEDNESDAY 10 DECEMBER 2008 15:10:15 GMT

DAVID TENNANT'S BACK

Bad news. David is going into hospital! They're operating on his back! Yikes. It's a prolapsed disc. Ow ow ow ouch.

Oh, the poor man. He must be devastated. That's terrible. Ouch. He has to drop out of the West End run of *Hamlet*. He thinks he might make some of the run, maybe after Christmas, but they're saying six weeks off.

FROM: BENJAMIN COOK TO: RUSSELL T DAVIES, WEDNESDAY 10 DECEMBER 2008 15:16:15 GMT

RE: DAVID TENNANT'S BACK

Holy crap! Poor David. SIX WEEKS?! Knowing his work ethic, he must be devastated. At least he'll be back for filming, fingers crossed. (He'll miss *The Next Doctor* press launch, though, won't he?)

FROM: RUSSELL T DAVIES TO: BENJAMIN COOK, WEDNESDAY 10 DECEMBER 2008 15:10:15 GMT

RE: DAVID TENNANT'S BACK

Yes, the press launch is knackered. We're wondering whether to cancel, more as a gesture of support. I'm not sure that makes sense, but... oh God!

FROM: BENJAMIN COOK TO: RUSSELL T DAVIES, WEDNESDAY 10 DECEMBER 2008 15:34:17 GMT

RE: DAVID TENNANT'S BACK

It does make sense. At this stage, and without David, what's the point of a press launch? Most media outlets have everything they need by now, surely? Short of actually watching the thing, and spoiling the plot twist. That's the only story left to tell. Why not keep it a surprise? And that's coming from someone who loves a good launch (mmm, nibbles!) and is gagging to see the finished episode.

FROM: RUSSELL T DAVIES TO: BENJAMIN COOK, WEDNESDAY 10 DECEMBER 2008 23:22:55 GMT

RE: DAVID TENNANT'S BACK

Mark this day in your diary. Today, Steven told us whom he and Piers have cast as the Eleventh Doctor.

YES!!! REALLY!!!

Oh, it's exciting! I think it's BRILLIANT! Genius, in fact. I never saw that coming. Oh my God, there's a new Doctor. He exists! And you're going to hate me. Really, really hate me. But – I can't tell you who it is. Ha ha ha. This is Controller-of-BBC-One-level secret. If I told you, I'd actually have to kill you. I'm serious. And who would I e-mail then?

FROM: BENJAMIN COOK TO: RUSSELL T DAVIES, WEDNESDAY 10 DECEMBER 2008 23:25:24 GMT

RE: DAVID TENNANT'S BACK

WHAT?!!! Oh, Russell! Suddenly this subject line seems a bit inappropriate. COME ON, WHO IS IT?! Okay, okay, you can't tell me, I understand (you bastard!), but… one question… please… is it wee Jimmy Krankie? Finally?!

FROM: RUSSELL T DAVIES TO: BENJAMIN COOK, WEDNESDAY 10 DECEMBER 2008 23:27:40 GMT

RE: DAVID TENNANT'S BACK

It isn't wee Jimmy Krankie.

FROM: BENJAMIN COOK TO: RUSSELL T DAVIES, WEDNESDAY 10 DECEMBER 2008 23:28:09 GMT

RE: DAVID TENNANT'S BACK

Fine. Is it Rufus Hound? He has the tattoos for it.

FROM: RUSSELL T DAVIES TO: BENJAMIN COOK, WEDNESDAY 10 DECEMBER 2008 23:32:29 GMT

RE: DAVID TENNANT'S BACK

No.

FROM: BENJAMIN COOK TO: RUSSELL T DAVIES, WEDNESDAY 10 DECEMBER 2008 23:29:21 GMT

RE: DAVID TENNANT'S BACK

How about Richard Madeley? With Judy as his companion.

FROM: RUSSELL T DAVIES TO: BENJAMIN COOK, WEDNESDAY 10 DECEMBER 2008 23:32:29 GMT

RE: DAVID TENNANT'S BACK

Enough with the guessing! (He he, I'm loving this.) David texted me from hospital today, in bed, watching *The Next Doctor* on DVD. 'I feel much better already,' he said. Bless him. His operation is at 8am.

FROM: RUSSELL T DAVIES TO: BENJAMIN COOK, THURSDAY 11 DECEMBER 2008 16:08:30 GMT

THE RUNAWAY TRAIN

We've got another runaway train at work. Whenever things escalate, Julie and I phone each other up and yell, 'Runaway train!' And then hoot. And then climb on board. But Piers was wondering how to announce the new Doctor, and was musing that it would be best on TV... when I piped up and said, 'Why not do an interview, and broadcast it after *The Next Doctor* repeat on New Year's Day? Complete surprise!' So off they go, steaming ahead... with Julie and me left behind on the platform, shouting, 'Wait!!! Have you guaranteed secrecy? Are you using the *Confidential* crew? Has anyone told David?!' It's a runaway train, and I started it!

FROM: BENJAMIN COOK TO: RUSSELL T DAVIES, THURSDAY 11 DECEMBER 2008 16:24:05 GMT

RE: THE RUNAWAY TRAIN

But how's that going to work? How are they going to find an extra five minutes in the TV schedules to announce Richard Madeley as the Eleventh Doctor?

FROM: RUSSELL T DAVIES TO: BENJAMIN COOK, THURSDAY 11 DECEMBER 2008 16:28:10 GMT

RE: THE RUNAWAY TRAIN

That's part of the Runaway Train. That's the schedulers, screaming from First Class, with Julie wading in, saying, 'For God's sake, it's the AFTERNOON, just SHIFT things!' Meanwhile, in the driver's seat, Jay Hunt is saying, 'This is so good, we should *announce* it in the schedules!' With all of us screaming, 'No!!!' Because then there will be so much attention that some tabloid will go to ferocious lengths to spoil it. That's like asking for trouble. Once these trains run away, they really run away.

P.S. Of course it isn't Richard Madeley. (He'll be in 4.18 as Rassilon, obviously.)[6]

FROM: BENJAMIN COOK TO: RUSSELL T DAVIES, THURSDAY 11 DECEMBER 2008 16:34:43 GMT

RE: THE RUNAWAY TRAIN

I can see Jay Hunt's point. Imagine the viewing figures! Then again, who gives a toss about viewing figures when you could announce the new Doctor live on air *as a surprise*? Then again, if you kept it a secret, wouldn't lots of people miss it, because they'd be too busy watching ITV?

---

6 Rassilon is the founder of Time Lord society on the planet Gallifrey.

FROM: RUSSELL T DAVIES TO: BENJAMIN COOK, THURSDAY 11 DECEMBER 2008 16:50:46 GMT

RE: THE RUNAWAY TRAIN

Yes, Jay has a point… except Julie is wary that we're crossing a line, and becoming pretentious with too much hoo-hah, and putting too much on the new man's shoulders. (Or the new woman's shoulders. Yes, Ben. Woman.) The current thinking is to *drive* people to it, with a promise on the official website of news on BBC One later in the day. Mind you, how many people are watching websites on New Year's Day instead of just going, 'Bleurgh!'? Oh, I don't know. I'm too busy shovelling coal. Get off the tracks!

FROM: RUSSELL T DAVIES TO: BENJAMIN COOK, FRIDAY 12 DECEMBER 2008 01:30:08 GMT

RE: THE RUNAWAY TRAIN

Good day today. We saw *Torchwood* 3.1, which was mighty fine. Normally, you edit one episode at a time, so there are a few weeks between each one, more or less, but this has got three editors working on five episodes at once, with Euros running between editing suites. Madness. I think it's something to do with completing it before the financial year is out, even though it's not being shown until next summer. But that's what leaves Euros free to direct 4.17/4.18 (he can write them, too, at this rate), so it's all worthwhile.

FROM: RUSSELL T DAVIES TO: BENJAMIN COOK, FRIDAY 12 DECEMBER 2008 20:37:13 GMT

RE: THE RUNAWAY TRAIN

The Eleventh Doctor plans changed again today. Jane Tranter thought that the New Year's Day announcement was slightly thrown away, so they've commissioned a half-hour documentary to go out on Saturday 3 January, on BBC One, covering the history of all the Doctors, all the way up to the new man, hopefully keeping him as a surprise at the end! The *Confidential* team has just a few days to knock all that together.

Meanwhile, *The Next Doctor* press screening is back on. (Don't! I know! Don't even start me!) I might die of blood pressure if I tell you all the Publicity/screening shenanigans. No, they're not shenanigans, shenanigans are fun. This is far from fun. But I'll tell you one bit. They said that if we cancelled the screening, a journalist might use the Freedom of Information Act to find out how much cancelling the room – which we'd have to pay for now, at this late stage – would cost. For Christ's sake! The dull bastards. This is what it's like now at the BBC.

FROM: BENJAMIN COOK TO: RUSSELL T DAVIES, SUNDAY 14 DECEMBER 2008 23:53:49 GMT

RE: THE RUNAWAY TRAIN

I just Googled 'Richard Madeley Doctor Who', and got nothing. It seems that He Who Cannot Be Named is still, er, unnamed. Whoever it is, I hope it holds.

How's your weekend been?

FROM: RUSSELL T DAVIES TO: BENJAMIN COOK, MONDAY 15 DECEMBER 2008 00:05:27 GMT

RE: THE RUNAWAY TRAIN

A bloody lame weekend (surprise, surprise), pacing about this bloody flat on my own, doing sod all, just panicking in my head. Last night, I even slept on the settee, because somehow... well, I think I imagined that put me nearer the computer. Like that would help. What a bloody idiot. Instead, I just slept badly, and felt like shit all day. I just can't get 4.16 to work. I read Phil's last draft last week, and it's a brilliant piece of work, both Gary Russell and Julie have said that it's marvellous, but it still needs work. Jamming in the stuff that I want to write is impossible, so I've stalled. There's this logjam in my head. The bastard thing is, this is going to ruin Christmas now. I'm so pissed off. Ah, the usual. You've heard it all before. It doesn't get better, though.

London tomorrow, to sort out my US deal with the BBC, and then it's Jane Tranter's leaving do. Might be a laugh, but not in this mood.

FROM: BENJAMIN COOK TO: RUSSELL T DAVIES, WEDNESDAY 17 DECEMBER 2008 06:45:22 GMT

RE: THE RUNAWAY TRAIN
How did it go? Spill the beans!

FROM: RUSSELL T DAVIES TO: BENJAMIN COOK, WEDNESDAY 17 DECEMBER 2008 19:49:23 GMT

RE: THE RUNAWAY TRAIN

I've been all over the place. Three cities in one day, yesterday. Jane's party was a hoot, but too full and busy. Mainly, I ended up talking to Freema, who was on sparkling form. (I asked her to come back for one day in 4.18. She said, 'Oooh yes!') Nice chance to catch up with Chris Chibnall as well. I realised how much I'd missed him. I love old Chibs. My friend Annie Harrison-Baxter – who produced *Bob & Rose*, *The Second Coming* and *Mine All Mine* – was there too, and said, 'You're so successful now, you've got no idea how much people out there hate you.' Ha ha. She's right, too. People say, 'You're so successful,' as though that makes my life all stardust and happiness. If you know the slightest thing about human nature, you'll know that the opposite is true. It just makes me a target. I get so cocooned in Cardiff, I forget how vicious and mean it is in this industry. It's a high-end business, and I'm at the highest end of it, so that leaves me open to attack. People keep asking why I'm not bothered by moaning fans, forgetting that the whole industry is that nasty. Frankly, I don't really care, and I've always given as good as I get. So, that was a bit salutary, I suppose. But I walked away laughing, and sort of vindicated by that. If that sort of thing loses me a friend or two, then they were useless friends in the first place.

Anyway, it's been chaos, because we were meant to be using the Specials to shift, finally, on to high definition. Until yesterday, when the HD money was pulled out. Some department turned around and told us that it was too expensive. Like we hadn't been telling them that for four years! But no, they decide now, when we've done camera tests, and booked equipment, and taken HD plate shots in Dubai. They said, 'You didn't keep us fully informed about costs.' Julie replied, 'Does that include the day I personally phoned you from the camera hire shop in Dubai? Was that not enough information?' She's brilliant in a scrap. But this could wreck the budget, because we were using the HD money to amortise costs elsewhere. All of a sudden, I have to lose 90 FX days out of 4.15. (The Special is called *Planet of the Dead*. A nice, traditional sort of *Who*-ish title for the 200th story.) I'm good at cutting costs, but that was impossible. My poor boyfriend, I only went north for his birthday, but I sat there with a spreadsheet instead.

But then, today, they buckled. HD is back on. But with less money. So, 4.15 has to steal FX money off 4.16, which I'm having to make monstrously cheap. We had a lovely ending with monstrous CG Water People on the loose… which will now be three men in wet spacesuits. And funny eyes, maybe.

And now David Morrissey has had to pull out of tomorrow morning's press screening, so the whole thing is useless, but no, we're still going ahead. But with no Q&A! What's the point?! It's mental right now.

> **Text message from: Ben**
> Sent: 18-Dec-2008 14:04
> Have you seen today's *London Evening Standard*? The headline is: 'FEARS GROW FOR DR WHO'. The paper is claiming that David's back injury might jeopardise filming of the Specials.

> **Text message from: Russell**
> Sent: 27-Nov-2008 23:02
> The stupid bastards. That is literally the opposite of what I said today in interviews at the press screening. I said, 'No contingency plans, no delay, no rewrites.' THE OPPOSITE!

FROM: RUSSELL T DAVIES TO: BENJAMIN COOK, THURSDAY 18 DECEMBER 2008 19:27:52 GMT

RE: THE RUNAWAY TRAIN

I am home. Lovely to see you at today's screening, briefly. What did you think of it? People seemed happy, although they're hardly going to say anything else to my face. Bless Jane Tranter, though, on the edge of tears during her speech – she's been like that all week. She's *Doctor Who*'s greatest supporter, with the power and money to back that up. Piers and Steven will miss her more than anything.

FROM: BENJAMIN COOK TO: RUSSELL T DAVIES, THURSDAY 18 DECEMBER 2008 22:36:27 GMT

RE: THE RUNAWAY TRAIN

The press screening? Nice nibbles. Even the speeches weren't shit. (Press launch speeches are always shit. But not this time.) Jane Tranter loves *Doctor Who*, doesn't she? Really, properly loves it. I don't think I'd realised quite how much until today. And she called Nick Briggs 'one of the best actors in the UK'! I'm never letting him forget that. 'Get him! One of the best actors in the UK!' At Pizza Express afterwards (yeah, we're well classy – you do The Ivy, me and Nick do Pizza Express), every time he opened his mouth to speak, I'd jump in with, 'Pray silence for one of the best actors in the UK!' It got old. But he was touched by what Jane said.

In other news… how's David? What's the latest? Are you going to have to rewrite 4.16 at all? Is there even a hint of truth in the *Evening Standard*'s story?

FROM: RUSSELL T DAVIES TO: BENJAMIN COOK, THURSDAY 18 DECEMBER 2008 23:26:30 GMT
RE: THE RUNAWAY TRAIN
Seriously, there will never again be a Controller of Fiction who knows the name of the actor who does the Cyberman voices. She is extraordinary. She's so eloquent and passionate about *Doctor Who*. It's not just other people saying it's her pinnacle; it's her too. She spoke at lunch about the moment that she realised she could get the show back on air, and it was so beautiful. Have a look at the BAFTA website: there's a video in which she's interviewed, and talks about *Doctor Who*, about the courage she needed to bring it back in 2005. It's really wonderful and inspirational.

The best part of that screening was the secret interviews after. Yes, secret interviews! For this top-secret Eleventh Doctor *Confidential*. They wanted me talking about the new guy (or gal), and Jane and Julie, too, so they booked a room in that hotel where we had the screening, then whisked us up in the lift as soon as we left the cinema so that we could wax lyrical about the genius of He Who Cannot Be Named. Hilarious! With all those journalists downstairs, missing the scoop. Honestly, even saying his (or her) name out loud on camera felt odd, like it was breaking some sort of law. They filmed me next to a plaster leopard. I'm worried that it'll look like they filmed me at home, where I have plaster leopards.

Oh, and David T is fine. It's all going really well. He's up and about. It seems to be a properly successful operation. So, no delays, contrary to what the *Evening Standard* might say. That hoarding was brilliant, wasn't it? 'FEARS GROW FOR DR WHO'. I practically ran into the newsagents when I saw that, which proves that it sells papers.

Right, back to *Planet of the Dead* – which is still three minutes short, so I'm inventing nonsense for Malcolm, UNIT's scientific adviser. Nice nonsense, though. Plus, we've cast Michelle Ryan as Christina. Great casting. I'm so tired, though. I got all insomniac last night, and ended up with two hours sleep. Two hours! I'm surprised I wasn't falling asleep at the press screening.

FROM: BENJAMIN COOK TO: RUSSELL T DAVIES, FRIDAY 19 DECEMBER 2008 00:49:21 GMT
RE: THE RUNAWAY TRAIN
I meant to tell you, the Christmas issue of *NME* chooses *Doctor Who* as the TV highlight

of the festive season. The magazine calls it the 'Best show on TV by miles'. The *NME*! Finally, *Doctor Who* is cool. The preview also says: 'Sadly this heralds the beginning of the end for David Tennant's reign. While we're on the subject of the new Doctor, please let it be Liam Gallagher: "Daleks, they're just dicks in bins."'

FROM: RUSSELL T DAVIES TO: BENJAMIN COOK, FRIDAY 19 DECEMBER 2008 01:02:35 GMT

RE: THE RUNAWAY TRAIN

The *NME*? That is cool! Blimey. Ah, that's nice. It's really hard to tell what the ratings will be this year, what with it being on an hour earlier than last year, and without Kylie. Obviously, they won't be stratospheric, but we should do fine, I think.

FROM: RUSSELL T DAVIES TO: BENJAMIN COOK, FRIDAY 19 DECEMBER 2008 03:28:44 GMT

RE: THE RUNAWAY TRAIN

Here's my *Planet of the Dead* rewrite. That might well be the shooting script. (Boring, fiddly changes, though Malcolm's new stuff is rather funny.) Do you know, whenever I read other people's Doctor dialogue, I'm always telling them off for making him sound trite and glib. It drives me mad. Then I go to rewrite the dialogue... and I make the Doctor's even funnier and dafter! Thing is, I reckon my dialogue is funny, and no one else's is. I am a monster.

It's 19 December already. It's Christmas soon. So soon! Haven't bought or done a thing. Bollocks. Whatever will today bring...?

FROM: BENJAMIN COOK TO: RUSSELL T DAVIES, FRIDAY 19 DECEMBER 2008 21:22:09 GMT

RE: THE RUNAWAY TRAIN

I spent this afternoon with Piers at TV Centre. I love that Sixth Floor. He bought me a coffee. We nattered about *Doctor Who*. I like Piers. He seemed stressed. (I wonder why!) These are tense times. I mentioned Richard Madeley, but Piers didn't blink, so maybe I'm on the wrong track. (Unless it's Richard Whiteley? That would be a coup.) Nice coffee, though.

But I'm all *Who*-ed out now. What a day! I'm off for drinks with my mate George. With any luck, he won't ask me about *Doctor Who* once.

FROM: RUSSELL T DAVIES TO: BENJAMIN COOK, FRIDAY 19 DECEMBER 2008 23:10:03 GMT

RE: THE RUNAWAY TRAIN

Who-ed out? Tell me about it! I've started 4.16 (exactly 365 days before it's actually transmitted, probably, which is kind of funny), but on the Friday before Christmas, when everyone else is out getting pissed and pulling boys. I'm sat at home, typing. I'd love to be out drinking with mates. (Hope you're behaving!) Instead, I'm typing 'EXT. MARS'. That dark and perverse power works on many shows.

Still, I'm glad that your chat with Piers went well.

FROM: RUSSELL T DAVIES TO: BENJAMIN COOK, SUNDAY 21 DECEMBER 2008 03:04:18 GMT

MORE 4.16

Lordy, 17 pages in one day! It's all quite straightforward, until we hit Page 13 or so, when suddenly there's a brand new way of telling the story from the Doctor's point of view – he realises that this Mars base is doomed – and that's got to be good.

FROM: RUSSELL T DAVIES TO: BENJAMIN COOK, TUESDAY 23 DECEMBER 2008 01:33:26 GMT

RE: MORE 4.16

Here's some more. Better day today. (The last couple of days have been rubbish. Five or six more pages, that's all.) The monsters have arrived! Once the monsters arrive, and the action starts, it all begins to motor. Action might be a bastard to write, but at the same time, if you follow it, it solves a lot of problems. Plainly and suddenly, there are things that *must* happen. Keep control of them, and you've a rope to pull you through. I think.

No way will I finish before Christmas, though.

FROM: RUSSELL T DAVIES TO: BENJAMIN COOK, WEDNESDAY 24 DECEMBER 2008 02:12:57 GMT

RE: MORE 4.16

More script. I'd hoped to get further. There's a lot of set-up in this episode, and I can feel in my bones that it's about to get massively action-packed and non-stop in about ten pages' time – which is great, but the thought of it defeats me for now. I haven't got the energy for action scenes. This whole Christmas lark drains it away. You can feel the world stopping around you. Funny thing is, I keep picking up *The Writer's Tale*, and wondering where I was this time last year. It's more or less the same! I was halfway through 4.12 on Christmas Eve, kicking myself for not finishing. See a pattern there? Mind you, last year, I had one-and-a-half episodes to go. This year, I've two-and-a-half episodes. But I'm sure the filming of 4.17/4.18 is later than 3.12/3.13 was... surely? Must be? I don't like to check in case I'm wrong. (Hey, I'm using the book as a guide! Everyone should write a book.) I just have to keep going. I might write that on a Post-It – 'KEEP GOING!' – and stick it above the computer. Or get it tattooed on my forehead. Yes, I'll do that. Are there any tattooists open in Cardiff on Christmas Eve?

In other news, Julie wants me to pitch a New Gay Show to Showtime in the US (they made the American *Queer as Folk*), which is exciting – though I'm not sure, because I've got two or three other ideas jostling for space. I'm not sure which one is going to come to the front of my mind first. Still, clear evidence that my mind is moving on from *Doctor Who*.

Anyway, I never ask how you are. Actually, that's terrible. I'm all me, me, me. How is your new life in Camden? Is it good or bad? I don't even know if you're in love with anyone, man or woman or beast, or even just enjoying yourself or... well, as long as you're happy. Where are you spending Christmas?

FROM: BENJAMIN COOK TO: RUSSELL T DAVIES, WEDNESDAY 24 DECEMBER 2008 03:03:26 GMT

RE: MORE 4.16

Christmas? Yes! With my parents, in Brighton. Are you heading back to Swansea? Is there *any* chance you'll finish 4.16 today? Or will it be hanging over you all Christmas? 'Keep going' is good advice. The tattoo on your forehead, less so.

My friend George is getting an octopus tattoo on his arm next year. An octopus! And some other seafaring stuff, like an anchor and a ship's wheel. He isn't a sailor; he just likes the sea. His tattooist on Frith Street, Soho, has an eight-month waiting list! It will take 14 visits over several months to complete George's tattoo, which will cover half his torso and cost the best part of his student loan. I wish I'd spent my student loan on a tattoo. Apparently, it'll be so painful, he might have to have his arm in a sling afterwards. And that's everything I know about tattoos. Before this evening, I didn't even know that.

FROM: RUSSELL T DAVIES TO: BENJAMIN COOK, WEDNESDAY 24 DECEMBER 2008 09:43:01 GMT

RE: MORE 4.16

Christmas Eve. A fine old fog across the Bay. Beautiful! Your friend George sounds marvellous. How brave! I'd never have the nerve. But Christ almighty, his arm in a sling?! I didn't know it *could* hurt that much. On reflection, I don't think I'll bother getting the 'KEEP GOING' tattoo. I'll stick the Post-It on my forehead instead. Yeah.

FROM: RUSSELL T DAVIES TO: BENJAMIN COOK, WEDNESDAY 24 DECEMBER 2008 13:18:20 GMT

RE: MORE 4.16

Right, I'm off to Swansea. I've been thinking about it, and I might come back with an octopus tattoo. But I might not.

Have a lovely time in Brighton. The CyberKing will rise! (Etc.)

FROM: BENJAMIN COOK TO: RUSSELL T DAVIES, WEDNESDAY 24 DECEMBER 2008 13:20:57 GMT

RE: MORE 4.16

Good luck with the octopus tattoo. It might suit you. (It won't.)

> Text message from: **Russell**
> Sent: 25-Dec-2008 12:40
> Swansea calling Brighton! Merry Christmas! Shame there's nothing on TV tonight. (It's the annual joke.)

Text message from: **Ben**
Sent: 25-Dec-2008 19:24
Merry Christmas from Brighton! I enjoyed *The Next Doctor*. A great big Cyberman marched over London – what's not to love? And later it's *Wallace & Gromit*.[7]

Text message from: **Ben**
Sent: 25-Dec-2008 20:58
Gromit has just saved the day in a hot air balloon! Where do they get their ideas from?

Text message from: **Russell**
Sent: 25-Dec-2008 20:59
I'm watching! Thank God we were on first.

Text message from: **Ben**
Sent: 25-Dec-2008 21:00
And now the plucky young female (dog!) is saving the day on a forklift truck. You should sue.

Text message from: **Russell**
Sent: 26-Dec-2008 09:52
11.7 million!!! And over 50% audience share! That's such a relief. Honestly, I thought we'd fall to eight or nine.

Text message from: **Ben**
Sent: 26-Dec-2008 09:54
Only 0.5 million less than last year, despite being on an hour earlier. Good work.

Text message from: **Russell**
Sent: 26-Dec-2008 10:16
We came second, after *Wallace & Gromit*. I hate *Wallace & Gromit*.

Text message from: **Ben**
Sent: 26-Dec-2008 09:54
Plasticine doesn't count. You're still the top-rated TV show of the day to feature real human beings.

7 Half-hour animated TV short *A Matter of Loaf and Death*, created by Nick Park and featuring man-and-his-dog double act Wallace and Gromit, was first broadcast on BBC One on Christmas Day 2008.

FROM: RUSSELL T DAVIES TO: BENJAMIN COOK, SUNDAY 28 DECEMBER 2008 15:04:36 GMT

SANTA'S ARSE

I'm back in the Bay. Back on e-mail! Christmas was fantastic. Yes, really. I had a marvellous time. I think it's the first Christmas in years that I haven't had a cold or a bad back. Even though I've got those scripts hanging over me, they hardly bothered me at all. I cut off completely, and my sisters weren't too mad, and my dad didn't cause any trouble, so that's a rare old time. And we got 11.7 million! When you think that we were ecstatic with *The Christmas Invasion* and *The Runaway Bride* getting nine-or-so million on the overnights... what the hell is happening with this show?! It's a mystery. But I love it.

Tomorrow, I'm getting a rough cut of that *Confidential* documentary for 3 January. The Eleventh Doctor! Talking! About the role! I'm so excited. Oh, and I'll tell you what's bugging me: those BBC One Christmas idents, with Wallace and Gromit in the bloody snow. Yes, lovely, etc. But why isn't that *Doctor Who*? Why isn't it David and a TARDIS, spinning about? I want that next year. I want the ident! I'm going to start a campaign.

That's all the news. Julie is off to New York today. I'll go back to Manchester on Tuesday. And I'm deliberately not thinking about the nightmare January and February that I've got ahead of me. Hope all's well with you.

CONTAINER TERMINAL - 1
JEBEL ALI PORT
DUBAI - U.A.E

DP WORLD

Box Line Agent: _UASC - DAS_
cc : MT Yard: _____
Reefer Yard: _____
Vessel File: ✓

CONTAINER CONDITION/DAMAGE REPORT

DATE: _04-01-09_

MV: _IBN AL ROOMI_ VOY NO: _M001_ ROT NO: _638277_

CONTAINER NUMBER: _UACU4264307_

CONTAINER DESCRIPTION:
☐ 20' ☑ 40' F/R ☐ REEFER
☐ TANK ☐ EMPTY ☑ LADEN
☐ ALUMINIUM ☐ STEEL ☐ FIBERGLASS

DAMAGE CODES: B (BRUISE) C (CUT) H (HOLE) BR (BROKEN)
M (MISSING) R (RUST) S (DISTORTED)

1. CORNER FILLING
2. FRONT TOP RAIL
3. BOTTOM END RAIL
4. TUNNEL
5. CROSS MEMBERS
6. LEFT SIDE
7. FRONT SIDE
8. TOP SIDE RAIL
9. TARP TIEDOWN RINGS
10. CORNER POST
11. SIDE POST
12. FORK POCKETS
13. HINGS

14. DOOR GASKET
15. LOCKING BAR
16. LOCKING BAR RETAINER
17. REAR BOTTOM RAIL
18. SIDE RAIL
19. DOOR HOLD BACK
20. LOCKING BAR HANDLE
21. CORNER POST
22. RIGHT SIDE
23. OPEN TOP TARPAULING
24. LOCKING BAR KEEPER

REMARKS: _DURING YARD DAS DAMAGED._
CONTATS OF CARGO
BADLY DAMAGED.

SUPERINTENDENT SIGNATURE: _____ INCIDENT DATE & TIME: _05-01-09 0500 HRS._

SUPERVISOR: _____

TALLY CLERK NAME: _____ ID NO: _____

REVISION : 03

JUNE, 07

DPW-CAR-CON-003-F03

544

CHAPTER TWENTY-TWO

GUNS DON'T KILL PEOPLE, TIME LORDS DO

In which a double-decker bus is crushed, a space captain
shoots herself, and Matt Smith sings the *Doctor Who*
theme down the phone from Starbucks

FROM: RUSSELL T DAVIES TO: BENJAMIN COOK, MONDAY 29 DECEMBER 2008 20:21:13 GMT

RE: SANTA'S ARSE

It's Bernard Cribbins' 80th today! I phoned him up. He said, 'Get off the line! Wrong
number! There's only a 24-year-old in this house!' Good old Bernard.

Then, I watched the *Confidential* documentary. It's called *The Ten Doctors*. Or *The
Eleven Doctors*. The new Doctor looks so handsome, and interesting, and deep. David
looks noble. Jane and Julie look glamorous. I look tired.

FROM: BENJAMIN COOK TO: RUSSELL T DAVIES, MONDAY 29 DECEMBER 2008 21:08:33 GMT

RE: SANTA'S ARSE

>>The new Doctor looks so handsome, and interesting, and deep.<<

It's definitely not Richard Madeley, then. Damn.

FROM: RUSSELL T DAVIES TO: BENJAMIN COOK, WEDNESDAY 31 DECEMBER 2008 14:25:47 GMT

HAPPY NEW YEAR'S ARSE

I'm back in Manchester, and I'm going to have a nice time tonight. My mates Tracy
and Bobby are up from Swansea. Phil C is coming round. The house is stocked with
booze, food, cheese and everything, and we're going to play cards all night. Yes, cards.
We love playing cards. It's cards night. I'm really looking forward to it. (Consults *The
Writer's Tale* – yes, much better than last year, when I was missing Billie's wedding with

a bad cold in the Bay.)

But what a year! Let's never forget how amazing it's been. Hope you have a good time tonight. Good luck!

FROM: BENJAMIN COOK TO: RUSSELL T DAVIES, WEDNESDAY 31 DECEMBER 2008 21:08:33 GMT

RE: HAPPY NEW YEAR'S ARSE
Yes, what a year. I'm ending it as I began it: in central London, watching fireworks. At least this year, it shouldn't take me four hours to get home.

P.S. HAPPY NEW YEARRRRRRR!!!

FROM: RUSSELL T DAVIES TO: BENJAMIN COOK, THURSDAY 1 JANUARY 2009 16:08:18 GMT

RE: HAPPY NEW YEAR'S ARSE
HAPPY NEW YEARRRRRRR to you, too! I didn't actually drink last night. I was too busy being host. (And there was so much alcohol in the house, I thought I could wake up on a dredger to Montenegro.) But Phil was on great form. Singing away! It was brilliant to see him so relaxed, and having such a laugh. Even the cards descended into chaos. By two in the morning, they'd all discovered fennel vodka in my cupboard. I didn't know that fennel vodka even existed. But there it was. By three in the morning, my Swansea women had decided they fancied Phil and wanted to kiss him, and chased him around the house until he fled in a taxi. So, the Swansea contingent is only now waking up. These are my last hours of holiday – I've got to start writing again tomorrow – but they're all still over the limit, so they're staying another night. Hey ho.

But all in all, a great New Year.

Text message from: Ben
Sent: 2-Jan-2009 16:22
The producer of *BBC Breakfast* just phoned. They want me to go on Monday morning's show to discuss the new Doctor. Is that okay? Thought I'd best check. (And is it okay if I go on dressed as Bannakaffalatta? I want to create an impression.)

Text message from: Russell
Sent: 2-Jan-2009 16:25
You're their *Doctor Who* expert! Of course it's fine. (Not Bannakaffalatta, though. Go dressed as a Cybershade.) I think the news that the announcement is tomorrow is about to go live on the BBC website. Madness ensues...

FROM: BENJAMIN COOK TO: RUSSELL T DAVIES, FRIDAY 2 JANUARY 2009 19:36:14 GMT

RE: HAPPY NEW YEAR'S ARSE

When was David told the Eleventh Doctor's identity? What was his reaction?

FROM: RUSSELL T DAVIES TO: BENJAMIN COOK, FRIDAY 2 JANUARY 2009 22:33:59 GMT

RE: HAPPY NEW YEAR'S ARSE

He's been first-to-be-informed at every stage, I think. He was kept up to date on the auditions throughout the whole process. That's both a courtesy (it would be awful if he found out major news through a leak!), but also because his advice is genuinely sound.

I don't know how he actually feels, although I did get a great text off him after *The Next Doctor*, saying, 'Can't we just keep the Christmas ones?!' I bet he feels fine, though, or he wouldn't be leaving the show.

FROM: RUSSELL T DAVIES TO: BENJAMIN COOK, SATURDAY 3 JANUARY 2009 14:06:55 GMT

RE: HAPPY NEW YEAR'S ARSE

It's on the news! The BBC News! Not the announcement, but the announcement about the announcement! Insane. I've got friends texting me asking who it is. (I am remaining stern and professional.)

FROM: BENJAMIN COOK TO: RUSSELL T DAVIES, SATURDAY 3 JANUARY 2009 14:47:11 GMT

RE: HAPPY NEW YEAR'S ARSE

Tell me about it! I've had so many texts. Never been so popular. Why do they presume I even know who it is? I'm tempted to tell them that the Eleventh Doctor is 'now safely tucked away in the Celebrity Big Brother House… whoever he or she may be!' Oh God, I hope we make it through to 5.30pm! That's when *The Eleven Doctors* is transmitted, right? I can't bear the suspense. Oh, that BBC press release, which quotes Piers: 'I just can't wait to tell everyone who it is – it has been a nail-biting Christmas trying to keep this under wraps!' Well, quite.

FROM: RUSSELL T DAVIES TO: BENJAMIN COOK, SATURDAY 3 JANUARY 2009 15:26:58 GMT

RE: HAPPY NEW YEAR'S ARSE

It's so exciting, though. It's amazing to see the size of this speculation. This show has become something truly mental. I'm getting texted by people it's really hard to say no to, people like Freema, so I've just stopped replying. I'll leave it till tomorrow. But Piers e-mailed about five minutes ago, and he's really happy with how it's going. It's still going to be a massive surprise to most people – like it was with Tom Baker back in the '70s, I suppose. I just want to stay in all night and read the internet. Proof, if proof were needed, that I really should be leaving this job. Oh, but I bet it'll go bonkers out there.

And David might be going back on stage tonight! Well, he needs the work now. Ha ha! Julie just phoned him, and he's loving all the Eleventh Doctor frenzy. Wait till you see Lis Sladen in tonight's documentary. She's backstage at her *Peter Pan* panto, in full costume as Mrs Darling, so it looks like she dresses like that at home! (Which might even be true.)

RE: HAPPY NEW YEAR'S ARSE

MATT SMITH IS THE DOCTOR!!!

How many people will be saying, 'Who?!' I did know him, actually. No, I did! He's the one who was so superb in those BBC adaptations of Philip Pullman's Sally Lockhart novels, and wasn't Billie Piper. He has the right look, doesn't he? I hope he keeps the hair –

No, wait a minute. He's 26. Oh my God. *I'm* 26! He was born 11 days after me. I've just checked this on the internet. Doctor Who is younger than I am! Sob! I'm old.

RE: HAPPY NEW YEAR'S ARSE

Yes, younger than you. Younger is the way to go. (A motto that's seen me through life.) Piers loves him, Steven loves him, Jane loves him. Jane says that they had dinner at Steven's last month, with Matt, and it was lovely. This is going to be brilliant. Seriously, I think this is genius. I'd been sitting here for months, quietly thinking about who I'd cast as the new Doctor if I had a choice – and I'd been blank. I'm too close to David, I suppose. But with this bit of casting, it's like it swept into my head and cleared away the cobwebs. I can see Matt as the Doctor. I thought he was amazing in *Party Animals*, did you see that? I only watched it because I once had a very strange phone call with a member of the cast's mother – long story – but then I stayed to watch because of this amazing Smith bloke. It's sort of what I was reaching for way back, maybe, when I was imagining someone like Russell Tovey in the lead – all sort of unexpected and unpredictable. Exactly what *Doctor Who* needs. The shock of the new. I think that's such a clever decision.

RE: HAPPY NEW YEAR'S ARSE

I'm finding it difficult to get into 4.16 at the moment… mainly because I'd rather be on 4.17/4.18. I'm kind of looking forward to their problems. I should have three weeks each for those last two, which is tight, but not as tight as it has been, and I'm hoping a blast of energy as I spot the finishing line will get me through the last episode. The end! The very end! (I must not get a cold. The last thing I need now is a bloody cold.) I'm really going to try to work diligently this time. I'm sick of my own system of leaving stuff, and leaving stuff, and leaving stuff, then flying by on adrenalin and panic. I'm determined to start on 4.17, and give myself a comparatively calm schedule of four or five pages a day. That's how I used to write, in the first two series, before the workload became so mental. I'm going to try to get that rhythm back, maybe not working all night, maybe keeping those four or five pages to daylight hours so that I'm not so knackered. That's the plan. Don't laugh.

FROM: BENJAMIN COOK TO: RUSSELL T DAVIES, MONDAY 5 JANUARY 2009 13:00:55 GMT

RE: HAPPY NEW YEAR'S ARSE

How does 4.17/4.18 feel at the moment? Still loose and empty? Or bursting with ideas?

I'm heading back to TV Centre in a bit, to do two hours of down-the-line regional radio interviews about Matt Smith. He gets cast, I do the interviews – how did that happen? I should have said no. It's going to be gruelling.

FROM: RUSSELL T DAVIES TO: BENJAMIN COOK, MONDAY 5 JANUARY 2009 13:22:24 GMT

RE: HAPPY NEW YEAR'S ARSE

My main worry at the moment is the Christmas Day episode – to make it really fit Christmas Day. The Doctor is on a dark, personal quest to meet his own death, and the Master is a gibbering cadaver, and there's a loneliness haunting the whole thing... but I have to remember that it's 6pm or 7pm, on 25 December, with everyone watching. Somehow, for Christ's sake, keep the fun! More pressingly, the episode has to have an identity in itself, not just as the first part of a two-parter. It's never going to feel standalone, but it needs to, I don't know, have a sort of completion about it so that it's a good watch in itself, not relying solely on the New Year's Day episode.

Gallifrey keeps swinging to and fro in my head. Yes, there's the solemnity and pomposity of those old men in big collars, which is thrilling, but are they the villains, in the end? Did the Doctor have to destroy them, because an eternity of war with the Daleks had turned them into vile (gibbering, Master-like?) monsters? No, not monsters, but bastards. Men who will *want* the Earth destroyed, if it brings Gallifrey back. Does the Doctor end up fighting the whole lot of them?

Having just typed 'Does the Doctor end up fighting the whole lot of them?', I've realised that the only answer to that is 'yes'. Blimey. Bad Time Lords! But hold on – aren't I bringing them back because I was inspired by Julie's desire to see their beauty, and awe, and majesty? Why am I undercutting them now? Although, I can sort of feel that it's possible to have both – to have the majesty in 4.18, Scene 1, Gallifrey, the cloaks, the solemnity... ready for a final reveal that they're bastards. Maybe.

Have a good time on the radio. Tell them all that I'm the best and Series Five will be rubbish. Yeah, do that.

FROM: BENJAMIN COOK TO: RUSSELL T DAVIES, MONDAY 5 JANUARY 2009 13:27:05 GMT

RE: HAPPY NEW YEAR'S ARSE

I'm literally on my way out the door, but...

>>aren't I bringing them back because I was inspired by Julie's desire to see their beauty, and awe, and majesty? Why am I undercutting them now? Although, I can sort of feel that it's possible to have both<<

Of course it's possible to have both. BRING ON GALLIFREY! The most beautiful men are the biggest bastards. Think of it like that. Except that's not true. That's only true of women.

>>Tell them all that I'm the best and Series Five will be rubbish.<<

Will do.

FROM: RUSSELL T DAVIES TO: BENJAMIN COOK, MONDAY 5 JANUARY 2009 13:32:54 GMT

RE: HAPPY NEW YEAR'S ARSE

>>Except that's not true. That's only true of women.<<

You'll have to be my expert on that. I will pay you a consultancy fee.

> **Text message from: Ben**
> Sent: 5-Jan-2009 15:37
> I'm bleeding from the forehead here — 17 eight-minute interviews! I'm down to BBC Essex, and running out of new ways to say that Matt Smith will be amazing.

> **Text message from: Russell**
> Sent: 5-Jan-2009 16:15
> You media whore! Just snap and storm off.

> **Text message from: Ben**
> Sent: 5-Jan-2009 16:21
> I'm so bored that I'm making things up. 'I think Britney Spears should be the new companion. She could mime the lines, badly.'

> **Text message from: Russell**
> Sent: 5-Jan-2009 16:36
> Keep going! Fly the flag!

FROM: RUSSELL T DAVIES TO: BENJAMIN COOK, TUESDAY 6 JANUARY 2009 02:44:31 GMT

RE: HAPPY NEW YEAR'S ARSE

Here's more 4.16. Mainly, I've been through the first 40 pages altering where we meet people and introduce different rooms. It's quite an art. Really tricky to get right. Like, do you see the sickbay only when it's needed, or do you seed it in advance, to give the place more size and complexity? Usually, I'd say just see it when it's part of the plot. However, when a story is as internal and claustrophobic as this one, you need to flex your muscles,

CASTING COMPANIONS

This e-mail exchange between Russell, Julie Gardner, Tracie Simpson, Peter Bennett (first assistant director on 4.17/4.18) and Andy Pryor charts the production team's attempt to book all of the Tenth Doctor's companions for one-off appearances at the end of 4.18...

FROM: JULIE GARDNER TO: RUSSELL T DAVIES; TRACIE SIMPSON, MONDAY 5 JANUARY 2009 16:25:05 GMT

CASTING – TWO-PARTER

Can I confirm which regular cast you want to return for this? Is it as follows: Catherine Tate – three days? To be shot in scenes with Jacqueline King and Bernard Cribbins? One location? Their house? Bernard Cribbins – to book through the block. Jacqueline King – three days or less? Billie Piper – one day. John Barrowman – one day. Freema Agyeman – one day. Jessica Hynes – one day. Do you need Noel Clarke? Is there anyone I'm missing?

FROM: RUSSELL T DAVIES TO: JULIE GARDNER; TRACIE SIMPSON, MONDAY 5 JANUARY 2009 16:58:12 GMT

RE: CASTING – TWO-PARTER

Yes, and Noel Clarke – one day. Noel's day will be with Freema, the same scene. And Lis Sladen and Tommy Knight, together – one day. This might also need (want?) Daniel and Anjli as well, but is the budget going through the roof?[1]

Catherine and Jacqui are tricky. Three days, certainly – but maybe more. I'd need Catherine at 1) the Nobles' house, 2) the road outside a café, 3) ext. church. All daytime – or day-for-night int. house. But I might need Jacqui for 1) Nobles' house, 2) ext. church, 3) city shopping streets, but that last one would be at night. And I can't guarantee that this won't expand a bit (though not hugely). Equally, tell me what I can and can't have now, and I won't write it!

All these appearances would be daytime, except for Billie – she'd be a night shoot. Don't panic, Tracie, but that could be a night shoot on the Tylers' estate. With a snow machine. Lordy. On the same night, we'd need Camille.

Blimey, does this make sense? Incidentally, I have mentioned this to Freema, and she said yes, so that's a good start...

FROM: JULIE GARDNER TO: RUSSELL T DAVIES; TRACIE SIMPSON, MONDAY 5 JANUARY 2009 17:10:21 GMT

RE: CASTING – TWO-PARTER

BRILLIANT. Thank you.

Tracie – let's coordinate how we call everyone, because they may all talk, so we should put in calls together at the same time before Andy contacts the agents officially. I could find call time on Wednesday afternoon, if that's any good?

---

1 Daniel Anthony and Anjli Mohindra play Clyde Langer and Rani Chandra respectively in *The Sarah Jane Adventures*.

FROM: ANDY PRYOR TO: TRACIE SIMPSON; JULIE GARDNER; PETER BENNETT, WEDNESDAY 7 JANUARY 2009 15:18:18 GMT

RE: CASTING – TWO-PARTER

Okay, folks, I've done some sums on all of this, and it will depend on several factors – whether the dates are spread out for Catherine and Jacqueline, whether we can get agents to accept the same rates as last time, and whether we can negotiate a favoured nations, one-off fee for those people coming back for one day. I've attached a document detailing all the costs depending on what scenario we go for.

Let me know your thoughts and we can decide how to approach this.

FROM: JULIE GARDNER TO: ANDY PRYOR; TRACIE SIMPSON; PETER BENNETT; RUSSELL T DAVIES, WEDNESDAY 7 JANUARY 2009 16:27:59 GMT

RE: CASTING – TWO-PARTER

I think we must push for favoured nations on the one-days. I feel we have to do this in the current climate. We really need to be sensible. The budget is going to be well and truly spent across these episodes. Russell – do you agree, as you'll be facing a possible rewrite if we fail on this?

FROM: RUSSELL T DAVIES TO: JULIE GARDNER; ANDY PRYOR; TRACIE SIMPSON; PETER BENNETT, WEDNESDAY 7 JANUARY 2009 16:48:25 GMT

RE: CASTING – TWO-PARTER

Oh, of course. Anyone falling out would have a knock-on effect, though, I've got to say. If, for example, any one companion said no, then the omission would look weird. It's inviting a tabloid story saying that we snubbed them, or that they snubbed us. More importantly, for kids, it would just look odd – from the Doctor's point of view, he'd never leave one of them out! If that happened, we'd have to drop *everyone*, except Billie and Camille (because that's going to be a nice coda to the whole of our time on the series), and Donna (because Donna, via Wilf, is more woven into the story). But let's see, as we go along. If we did lose one of them, then we could try something very clever and have the Doctor looking on from afar with previous footage. Oh, I'm cunning! Easier said than done, mind you.

Having said that, if there's a problem with Jessica Hynes, then that scene is a bit of a luxury and is independently droppable.

and explore the location a bit more. Also, it's hard trying to iron out the bits that are too reminiscent of *The Satan Pit* or *42*. (Did they worry about this in the '60s? When *The Moonbase* was the same as *The Ice Warriors*?[1] No, they did not.) These outer-space-crewmember stories are the hardest to write. Everyone is trapped in functional jobs. Actually, back in the '60s, you can see why stories like *The Moonbase* had that ahead-of-its-time multiracial casting. They had to, or everyone's the bloody same!

---

1 *The Moonbase* and *The Ice Warriors* are both 1967 *Doctor Who* serials.

FROM: RUSSELL T DAVIES TO: BENJAMIN COOK, WEDNESDAY 7 JANUARY 2009 03:16:11 GMT

RE: HAPPY NEW YEAR'S ARSE

I'm very happy with the latest few scenes of 4.16. So happy, in fact, that I thought of the opening line of 4.17, and went ahead and wrote it. It has begun! The beginning of the end. That feels good, to have a file named '4.17', even though it's just one line. But I've been trying to think of that line for ages. Something mythic and huge. Then I was standing in the kitchen, boiling the kettle, and thought of it.

```
1. FX SHOT - PLANET EARTH

FX: THE EARTH, suspended in space, in all its beauty.

Over this, the NARRATOR. A stranger; an old, wise man.

                    NARRATOR
      It is said that in the final days of Planet Earth,
      everyone had bad dreams.
```

FROM: RUSSELL T DAVIES TO: BENJAMIN COOK, THURSDAY 8 JANUARY 2009 08:57:58 GMT

FW: BUS DAMAGED

Oh my Lord.

Oh shit.

The bus arrived in Dubai.

Someone dropped a cargo container on it.

Oh my God. Off to Cardiff. More later!

FROM: BENJAMIN COOK TO: RUSSELL T DAVIES, THURSDAY 8 JANUARY 2009 19:49:36 GMT

RE: FW: BUS DAMAGED

But, but… OH. MY. GOD!!! How did that happen?! How can you crush a bus?! It can be written around, can't it? Oh God! A journey through a wormhole is bound to cause damage to such a primitive piece of technology as a London bus. Failing that…

WE'RE ALL DOOMED!!!

FROM: RUSSELL T DAVIES TO: BENJAMIN COOK, THURSDAY 8 JANUARY 2009 19:22:29 GMT

RE: FW: BUS DAMAGED

Someone at the port in Dubai dropped a cargo container on it! What are the chances?!

So, we convened in Cardiff. I was in charge, because Julie was trapped in London. It was very exciting! The options are… film with the damaged bus, because that's what wormholes do to buses. (Yes, good call, Ben. I thought of that, too, within 30 seconds of seeing the photo.) Problem with that is, we don't know how much work the damaged bus needs to make it safe, and to transport it into the desert. We don't even know if it can stand up, or whether it's leaning on something and will fall apart as soon as someone whispers at it. It's impossible to tell from that single photo. We've people itching to fly out and inspect it for health and safety, but the port is closed for the weekend, so we can't get to look at the bus until Sunday night.

But! If we go for the second option – to ship our second, clean bus out there (the made-to-look identical bus that we've got in Cardiff, to shoot all the Earth scenes) – then it needs to leave in 11 hours' time! Yikes! Plus, if we do ship out our clean bus, we have the problem of buying a *third* bus to shoot the Earth scenes. Money isn't a problem for any of this, because we should be covered by insurance. (Although, when I got to the office, it turned out that we'd only checked the marine insurance so far, which is useless, because the bus was on dry land when they dropped a bloody great container on it. But looking at that bus, it's hard to imagine an insurance company protesting.) Amazingly, buying a third bus has turned out to be the biggest headache of the day. They're not easy to find. Especially since we'd found a bus that fitted the specifics of the story – hydraulic doors, no middle door, an open drivers' cab, etc. It's hard to match the two that we've got already. Finding a third bus could take three to four weeks – yes, *weeks*! – and that's just the start of the workload, as then the bus has to be declared part of the BBC fleet (!), and insured, and covered with our own non-copyright adverts and logos. Plus, the bus sent to Dubai had to have its wiring removed so that we could control it, and the hydraulics taken out of the door for safety during transport, and the hydraulics then reinstalled, etc, etc, etc. (I had no idea how hard these departments work.) So, if we're buying a Bus #3, and sending out our clean Bus #2, we have to decide TODAY, because Bus #2 has to leave NOW.

Or do we film on a beach in the Gower?

If, however, we go with Bus #1 in its damaged state – well, The Mill has started to model the clean bus (for the CG shots of it flying) and will have to completely rework the model to make it damaged. Can they do that in time? It turns out, yes, but they'll need detailed photos of the damage, to reproduce it – which doesn't allow for the fact that the damage might change and shift the moment that the smashed bus moves. Oh, and the damaged bus can't drive to the desert now, and will have to be put on a low loader all the way. Shit.

And then, no, hold on – even if we use the wrecked Bus #1, we'll still need to buy a Bus #3 to film on in Cardiff, because we're using the interior of Bus #2 in studio, to be shot before Dubai, and the downstairs interior of Bus #1 in Dubai is so wrecked that we have to replicate that somehow on our bus in Cardiff – and because of the schedule, locked into vital road closures, we'll need Bus #2 intact *after* we've shot the interior scenes in studio. In other words, Bus #2 cannot be wrecked for our studio shooting at all.

Oh, that's like one-tenth of today's conversations. In the end, we decided that the only concrete fact was that a duplicate Bus #3 would be impossible to find and sanction for use in time, so we have to go with Bus #1, in Dubai, in its wrecked state. With the Dubai shoot at the end of the run, that gives Ed Thomas' team four weeks to fly out there and make the bus safe. We went all the way back to our very first solution! Also, it's the solution that got Ed's eyes fired up with excitement, and that's the most powerful weapon we've got. Once that man is determined to do something, then he makes it happen. He is marvellous. As you said straight away, the bus will arrive through the wormhole, trashed. I think that's going to look magnificent. It's better! The Doctor has to fly this creaking, hissing, clapped-out wreck back through the wormhole and over London!

Bloody hell. But as ever – what a brilliant team. Everyone focused, determined, laughing, inventive, honest, and absolutely committed to making it work. They are all geniuses. I love them. I truly love them.

And now I have to read 12 *Sarah Jane* scripts by tomorrow morning. I am dying.

FROM: RUSSELL T DAVIES TO: BENJAMIN COOK, SATURDAY 10 JANUARY 2009 00:26:40 GMT

RE: FW: BUS DAMAGED

Joe Lidster is a genius. This is a fact. If he works hard, gets his head down, and realises what he's capable of, then in ten years' time, he could be… me. Sorry, no other way to end that sentence! Me! He could have his own studio, turning out his own shows, and be king of all that he surveys. He has just handed in a new *Sarah Jane* story; it was an emergency commission when another script fell through; it's the cheap episode.[2] He wrote treatment after treatment, in a rush, and they were all lacking, until I actually

---

2 *The Sarah Jane Adventures* 3.3/3.4.

lost my temper just before Christmas, told him to stop bothering me and just write something… and then he handed in a first draft that's poetic, and beautiful, and clever, and made me burst into tears at the end. But the best bit was the meeting with him today, because he clearly has no idea how he does it, or why. He flies on instinct and imagination, so much so that he can barely explain what he's written. This isn't just being bad in meetings, which a lot of writers are. Joe really *doesn't know*, yet every instinctive choice is fascinating. And right.

Thing is, if he doesn't start believing in himself, he could get torn apart in this career. Script meetings are all 'Why does this character do this? Why does she do that?' And that's where the script process starts to fall apart, if the writer isn't robust. When the writer can't answer clearly, then everyone leaps in – trying to help, genuinely – saying, 'What if he did this? What if she did that?' If you're not careful, that creative process becomes invasive. Most writers sitting in pubs saying 'They've destroyed my work' caused the problem themselves, because they weren't vigorous enough, because their script invited changes. Producers are trying to build something tangible out of something that's simply an act of the imagination, and very often a flawed act. Of course idiots can do damage, but most of them are trying to help. Everyone's happy if a script works. Everyone's life is easier.

It's such a fine line. Writers have to be strong, if only because there are so many forces battering them. We're a marvellous team, and we understand Joe, or we try to understand, so I hope we're getting the best out of him. But if you're Production Company A dealing with New Writer B, and you're faced with his vagueness and uncertainty, then… well, Joe will become the writer complaining in the pub. What do you do, though? What do you say to make a person strong? Well, you say all this. But you're working on someone's character, and I haven't got the magic words to make that change, no matter how much I blather on. But I do think, after all these years, and all those meetings, and all those writers clutching their scripts, I can tell who is, or who is *going to be*, a good writer. Not just on the page, but because of who they are. What they think. How they make their way through the world.

I feel really moved by today's meeting. I can't get it out of my head. I had to write that down. It really affected me, how precious and precarious this whole thing is. Although, in the end, I think talent will out. There aren't enough good writers for genius to be thrown away. Joe will get better, and he'll get stronger. I worried about this. I was quite harsh with him. I worried that I went too far. But then I went outside for a cigarette, and looked up at those blue metal walls of Upper Boat, and thought, seriously, in ten years' time, this could be Joe's, with the Thirteenth Doctor running about inside.

In other news… you'd never have dreamt that a bus was trashed in Dubai yesterday. Everything is carrying on as normal. Nothing can't be solved. It was Ed's 40th birthday, so we had drinks and balloons in the Meeting Room. Meanwhile, Julie has moved into Upper Boat, because Piers is moving into her office now, and they're already calling her the mad woman in the attic! She was in at six this morning. But during all this, as she cheers the troops along and solves 57 problems with her left hand, her mum has been diagnosed with bone cancer. Julie is sitting there wondering whether the treatments will work, and how long they will take, because it's so hard to face. It's exactly – literally, stage by stage – the same as my mum. This is how it ends. Slowly. You can be surrounded by doctors, and goodwill, and charts, and drugs, and hope, making it so hard to see. Poor, lovely Julie.

Anyway, no more script tonight. I'm too tired. Those *Sarah Jane* script meetings lasted eight hours, and I've a long, savage weekend ahead. I have to finish 4.16 by Monday, for the start of prep. Then, on Wednesday, there's a read-through of *Planet of the Dead*. David Tennant, back in the room! I can't wait.

FROM: RUSSELL T DAVIES TO: BENJAMIN COOK, MONDAY 12 JANUARY 2009 01:30:19 GMT

LIFE ON MARS

I'm ten pages from the end. Do I keep going all night? Or finish it off tomorrow? I've got an empty day tomorrow, so I could write all day, and deliver by late afternoon. But prep starts tomorrow. There's nothing better than them arriving at their desks in the morning, to find the script waiting for them. Psychologically, that's a good start. But I'm knackered. This is all one, long action sequence – the last 30 pages are one big fight. I've had a whole weekend, fighting on Mars. Like you do.

FROM: BENJAMIN COOK TO: RUSSELL T DAVIES, MONDAY 12 JANUARY 2009 01:42:44 GMT

RE: LIFE ON MARS

Get some sleep! Even if the script arrives at their desks in the morning, they won't read it until 2pm. Adelaide Brooke and the crew of Bowie Base One – or those that are still alive, at least – can wait until morning.[3]

FROM: RUSSELL T DAVIES TO: BENJAMIN COOK, MONDAY 12 JANUARY 2009 02:19:39 GMT

RE: LIFE ON MARS

You're right. Too much to do. Not finished. But almost! Tired. Zzzz.

FROM: RUSSELL T DAVIES TO: BENJAMIN COOK, MONDAY 12 JANUARY 2009 18:24:25 GMT

RE: LIFE ON MARS

Done! Finito!

```
136. EXT. LONDON STREET - NIGHT⁴

     FX: THE TARDIS materialises.
```

....

3 Adelaide Brooke, the captain of Mars' Bowie Base One, was called 'Valentina Kerenski' in Phil Ford's original script.
4 This is Russell T Davies and Phil Ford's original ending to *The Waters of Mars*, in which the Doctor bids Adelaide farewell back on Earth, outside her London house, having changed history and saved her life, along with the lives of Mia Bennett (a geologist on Bowie Base One) and Yuri Kerenski (the base's nurse).

THE DOCTOR strides out - ADELAIDE following, then MIA, running out, scared, away from the Tardis - YURI last -

> THE DOCTOR
> The 19th of December, 2059. Five more shopping days to go, merry Christmas! Yuri, help that Gadget-thing out of the Tardis.[5] Much as I love a funny robot…

(NB, cutting away, around the moment of Gadget's actual exit from the Tardis!)

> ADELAIDE
> …that's my daughter's house. It's London. I'm home.

> THE DOCTOR
> And it's snowing!

> YURI
> No, that's the Carbon Wash, cleaning up the atmosphere, we get this at eight o'clock every night.

> THE DOCTOR
> I'm calling it snow.

> MIA
> …but what is that thing??! It's… bigger, I mean it's bigger *inside*, who the hell are you?? What is he??

And she's so freaked out, she runs away -

Yuri looks to Adelaide for permission -

> ADELAIDE
> Go after her.

> YURI
> Yes ma'am.
> > (to the Doctor)
> Thank you.

Then he turns, runs. Following Mia, off into the night.

Gadget trundles after them. A little wave of its hand.

> GADGET
> Gadget-gadget!

Leaving Adelaide and the Doctor alone, in the snow.

---

5 Gadget is a three-foot-tall Wall-E-type robot probe on tracks. It has big camera-lens eyes. The script says: 'Despite being in advance of anything today, it looks low-tech, dented and abused. Gadget has two arms, complete with skeletal hands. From its body hangs a full selection of tools – a tool for every job.'

And she's just as scared of him; though equal to him. The Doctor now with a strange new arrogance.

> ADELAIDE
> They're a couple.

> THE DOCTOR
> We'll see. Early days.

> ADELAIDE
> No, but if they stay together… say, there's a child, a child born into the world, who was never meant to exist. Let alone me.

> THE DOCTOR
> Time will compensate. I can feel it, even now. Captain Adelaide inspires her granddaughter face-to-face, isn't that better? Just get Susie Fontana Brooke on board that light-speed ship in 30 years' time, everything's back on track.

> ADELAIDE
> But you can't *know* that.

> THE DOCTOR
> If I say so, then it happens.

> ADELAIDE
> No one should have that much power.

> THE DOCTOR
> Tough.

Silence. She steps away, unnerved by him.

> THE DOCTOR
> Adelaide. I've done it before. In small ways. Saved some little people. But never someone as important as you. Oh, I'm good!

> ADELAIDE
> 'Little people'? Who decides they're so unimportant, you?

> THE DOCTOR
> There was a war. A long time ago. And ever since then, I thought I was just a survivor. But I'm not. I'm the winner. That's who I am. The Time Lord Victorious.

> ADELAIDE
> And there's no one to stop you?

                                    THE DOCTOR
        No.

And then, but then, he hears…

A song.

An old, familiar, haunting song.

He looks up…

Behind Adelaide, a good distance away…

An OOD. Ood Sigma. Surrounded by snow and Ood-song.

Staring at him.

The Doctor stares back. Defeated.

Hold on him: blinking, upset, all this sudden arrogance draining
away. Like he's collapsing inside. Then:

                                    THE DOCTOR
        …I've gone too far.

                                ADELAIDE
        What is it, what's wrong?

She looks round.

The Ood has gone. No one there.

The Doctor recovering, quiet.

                                    THE DOCTOR
        I think I've been summoned.

                                ADELAIDE
        What for?

                                    THE DOCTOR
        My death.
                                (pause, then:)
        Go home, Adelaide Brooke. Go to your daughter, and her
        daughter. Hold them tight.

And she's so scared.

Runs towards the house.

The Doctor walking towards the Tardis, heavy-hearted…

But she stops. Looks back. Upset. Calls out:

> ADELAIDE
> Will I ever see you again?

> THE DOCTOR
> No. Never.

He goes inside the Tardis.

Adelaide stays watching.

FX: the grind of ancient engines, in a flurry of snow; the Tardis fades way…

And Adelaide is crying. For him.

CUT TO:

137. INT. TARDIS - NIGHT

THE DOCTOR at the controls. Manning the console, grave.

Slowly, closer and closer on him. He's breathing hard. Summoning up the energy, the nerve, the fight.

And then he decides:

> THE DOCTOR
> No.

CUT TO:

138. FX SHOT: TIME VORTEX

The TARDIS hurtles away, down the Red Vortex.

The final journey.

END OF EPISODE 4.16

FROM: RUSSELL T DAVIES TO: BENJAMIN COOK, TUESDAY 13 JANUARY 2009 13:29:35 GMT

RE: LIFE ON MARS

I'm in the middle of a 4.16 rewrite, because I woke up realising something horrible about that script, and I'm not sure what to do. The only way to find out if I'm right is to write it. Here's the e-mail that I just sent to Julie:

> *I thought of this while I was writing yesterday, and rejected it. Then, I woke up this morning, knowing that I'm right. Adelaide Brooke has to die. And to do so, she has to take her own life. Yikes! Keep reading! I can make this discreet. The whole*

thing is about the Doctor fighting the Laws of Time, and growing in arrogance, and power, until he's brought down at the end. Nothing can show him the unstoppability of time, and the foolishness of his actions, more than Adelaide's death. He's launched into his final story by this tragedy – and his need for a human companion. Look what's happening to him! A man seeking redemption. It's so tough, this, because it's seriously the only ending that this story should have. (That's why I want Easter to be such a lark – see where we're heading!) But you don't kill heroes easily. Maybe this has to be done.

And while I was typing to you, Julie just phoned – she hadn't read that e-mail, but had read the script, and was phoning to say that she had a problem: Adelaide must die! Ha ha ha. Oh, she's good.

FROM: BENJAMIN COOK TO: RUSSELL T DAVIES, TUESDAY 13 JANUARY 2009 15:02:01 GMT

RE: LIFE ON MARS

Adelaide kills herself! On BBC One! At teatime! And it's the Doctor's fault! Now, that's dark. But it's the right ending to that story, isn't it? Good move.

P.S. Piers just e-mailed. It looks like I've secured Matt Smith's first magazine interview about his casting as the Eleventh Doctor! It's this Thursday.

FROM RUSSELL T DAVIES TO: BENJAMIN COOK, TUESDAY 13 JANUARY 2009 16:13:15 GMT

RE: LIFE ON MARS

OH MY GOD about the Matt Smith exclusive! World first! That's so brilliant. Get in there with the new boy!

Here's the new ending to Scene 136...

ADELAIDE

The whole of history could change. The future of the human race. Doctor. No one should have that much power.

THE DOCTOR

Tough.

She steps away, scared of him.

ADELAIDE

But I believed you. Right from the very first second, how did I believe you?[6] Unless it was *right*. That I knew, even then, I knew my place in time. That I should die.

THE DOCTOR

Adelaide. I've done it before. In small ways. Saved some little people. But never someone as important as you. Oh, I'm good!

---

6 When the Doctor and Adelaide meet on board Bowie Base One, he gives her his word that she can trust him: 'And 40 million miles away from home, my word is all you've got.' She looks at him, and somehow she does trust him...

CHAPTER TWENTY-TWO: GUNS DON'T KILL PEOPLE, TIME LORDS DO

> ADELAIDE
> 'Little people'? What, like Mia and Yuri? Who decides
> they're so unimportant, you?

> THE DOCTOR
> For a long time now, I thought I was just a survivor. But
> I'm not. I'm the winner. That's who I am. The Time Lord
> Victorious.

> ADELAIDE
> And there's no one to stop you?

> THE DOCTOR
> No.

> ADELAIDE
> This is wrong, Doctor. I don't care who you are. The Time
> Lord Victorious is wrong.

> THE DOCTOR
> That's for me to decide. Now, you'd better go home.
> (of the house)
> All locked up, you've been away. Still, that's easy.

He points the sonic screwdriver at the house, whirrs.

The clunk of locks; one upstairs light comes on.

> THE DOCTOR
> All yours.

> ADELAIDE
> Is there nothing you can't do?

> THE DOCTOR
> Not any more.

And she turns away from him -

Runs to her house.

Stops by her door.

And as she turns to look back at him.

SLOW MOTION.

THE DOCTOR, still watching her, in the snow, standing tall, so
confident, so proud. Unstoppable.

And in slow motion, she turns to her door.

As she steps inside, just a glimpse of…

She's taking her gun out of her pocket.

The door closes.

CUT TO the Doctor. Still in slow motion, he turns away from the house, to walk back to the Tardis. In the snow, and the night, in perfect command.

And then REAL TIME SLAMS BACK IN, as -

Bang!

From the house. A flare of gunfire in a darkened window.

Then silence.

On the Doctor - CU, slam into FLASHBACKS, as in sc.12 -[7]

FLASHBACK: the photo of Adelaide, unchanged. Slam into the date of death, unchanged: 2059.

Intercut with CU Doctor, his horror -

FLASHBACK: headlines, *Mystery of Location… Alien Intervention?* Then -

Daughter pledges to continue her work. Then -

A photo of a proud, strong woman, looking skyward. *Susie Fontana Brooke. First Lightspeed Ship. Proud heritage.*

Time slamming back into place.

The Doctor, defeated.

Hold on him: shattered, all this sudden arrogance draining away. He's collapsing inside. Sinks to his knees.

CU on him. His grief.

Music, filling this moment. Haunting, soaring. But then, gradually, realise…

The Doctor can *hear* this.

It's a song.

----

7 In Scene 12, the Doctor sees flashbacks depicting newspaper reports of the deaths of Adelaide and her crew. (Headline: 'Mars Disaster.' Smaller headline: 'Bowie Base One Destroyed. World in Mourning.')

An old, familiar song.

He looks up…

A good distance away…

An OOD. Ood Sigma. Surrounded by snow and Ood-song.

Staring at him.

> THE DOCTOR (CONT'D)
> …I've gone too far.

Ood Sigma just stares at him.

The Doctor stands. Calls out:

> THE DOCTOR (CONT'D)
> Is this it? My death? Is it time?

A flurry of snow, and…

The Ood has gone. No one there.

The Doctor recovering.

Looks back at the house. So sorry.

Then walks to the Tardis, head bowed.

Steps inside.

FX: the grind of ancient engines, and the Tardis melts away, into the snow and the dark…

FROM: RUSSELL T DAVIES TO: BENJAMIN COOK, TUESDAY 13 JANUARY 2009 23:43:14 GMT

RE: LIFE ON MARS

The new ending is loved. I'm chuffed to bits with it. That's as dark as we'll ever go! But I love the worry. Drama should make you anxious, and push things to the limit. There's a worry that we'll have to get this past BBC Editorial Policy – and every word that anyone says anywhere is now the source of twitching at the BBC – but that's a fight that I'm ready to face. In fairness, Editorial Policy has always been massively supportive of us, right from the very first day.

Actually, I did think of that ending yesterday, in the afternoon, mid-rewrite, but I pushed it out of the way, because I could only see it literally – the gun, at Adelaide's head, bang, blood, splat, on the Doctor, yikes. I thought, what, cut to a wide shot so that it's not too grisly? What happens to the body? Outside her daughter's house – does the daughter come running out? Impossible. But then I woke up this morning, knowing that it wasn't just a good idea; it was, in fact, the *only* way that a story like this can end. It's naturally tragic. Fight time, and it fights back. It's what we all do. And we all fail. But it wasn't until I thought of the house – the dark, abandoned, spooky house – that I knew how to make it work. The death becomes an image, a flash, a gunshot. It's almost symbolic. Because it's all about the Doctor, not the corpse. That would be a great way to play it even if this were a 9pm drama.

So, I'm happy. And the *Planet of the Dead* read-through is tomorrow. Michelle Ryan phoned me up tonight. She's lovely. And there's a chance, just a chance, that we might get Lee Evans to play Malcolm, UNIT's scientific adviser! But now I've got to do Pink Pages to allow for the wrecked bus. I suppose this will be the first and last time that I have to rewrite for a damaged double-decker.

FROM: BENJAMIN COOK TO: RUSSELL T DAVIES, THURSDAY 15 JANUARY 2009 16:20:19 GMT

MATT SMITH

I think I am in love.

That is all.

FROM: RUSSELL T DAVIES TO: BENJAMIN COOK, THURSDAY 15 JANUARY 2009 16:31:43 GMT

RE: MATT SMITH

You're fickle! David is weeping. But you can't leave me on that cliffhanger!

Oh, you have.

FROM: BENJAMIN COOK TO: RUSSELL T DAVIES, THURSDAY 15 JANUARY 2009 21:07:25 GMT

RE: MATT SMITH

I'm heading out in a bit, but thought I'd update you on Matt Smith first, because he really was awesome. Chatty, charming, bursting with enthusiasm… the crew will love him. He was full of praise for David, too. He knows that he's got big shoes to fill. ('Well, it's lucky I've got big feet,' he said.) He's quite a talker. He kept going for 45 minutes. Sentences ran away with him – adjective after adjective to describe how excited he is at being cast. 'I'm going to try to make my Doctor as varied, and brilliant, and dark, and unpredictable, and happy, and sad, and funny as I can – every facet of me, really – and explore it with bravery and courage,' he said. (Phew!) 'I'm going to do it my way.' I thought he was about to break into song. And then he did! He sang the *Doctor Who* theme at me down the phone! I told him, 'A few weeks ago, you can't have imagined that you'd be sat in Soho, in Starbucks, singing the *Doctor Who* theme into your mobile.' He said, 'The thing with this job is, you're constantly faced with these utterly bizarre scenarios.' (At this point, I was tempted to tell him about your double-decker bus! But I didn't.)

He seems pretty fearless about taking on the role. I asked him whether there's an inner turbulence. He laughed. 'Yes, it's a façade. I'm putting on an act, because it's still six months away. I'm sure if you ring me the night before the first read-through, I'll be a different man. I don't know what else I can be right now apart from very, very excited. I just so wanted to be the Doctor. I'd have been mental not to do it.' Plus, he seems keen to stay for a while. 'I'll hit 30 in 2012,' he pointed out, 'and that's an important stage of growing up. How brilliant to do that as Matt Smith, but also as Matt Smith playing the Doctor, simultaneously.'

FROM: RUSSELL T DAVIES TO: BENJAMIN COOK, THURSDAY 15 JANUARY 2009 23:55:05 GMT

RE: MATT SMITH

Ah, Matt sounds lovely. That makes everyone's jobs easier. Matt has phoned Piers, too, and said that he loved the interview – so job well done.

> Text message from: **Russell**
> Sent: 19-Jan-2009 12:05
> Julie's mum has just died, this morning. Christ. Oh, bless her.

> Text message from: **Ben**
> Sent: 19-Jan-2009 12:09
> Oh no! Isn't that incredibly sudden? How dreadful. Poor Julie. Please pass on my condolences. Will anyone be able to persuade her to take some days off work?

FROM: BENJAMIN COOK TO: RUSSELL T DAVIES, WEDNESDAY 21 JANUARY 2009 00:24:52 GMT

RE: MATT SMITH

I've just got in from the *Radio Times* Covers Party. Brilliant to see David again, looking dapper and well. ('I'm driving back to Cardiff tonight.' 'You're getting driven?' 'No, no, I'm driving myself.' 'You mean you *don't get driven*?!' 'Not any more. Matt Smith has my driver now.' Ha ha.) Freema was there, too, with her boyfriend. Full of smiles. And Piers was there. And Steven. And Susie. And Neill Gorton. And the boys from The Mill. Oh, and Kiefer Sutherland! YES, REALLY!

FROM: RUSSELL T DAVIES TO: BENJAMIN COOK, WEDNESDAY 21 JANUARY 2009 09:58:17 GMT

RE: MATT SMITH

KIEFER SUTHERLAND?! Blimey! It's a good party, isn't it? I just realised, I suppose I'll be in LA next year. Maybe I've had my last Covers Party. That's a bit sad. Mind you, once *Doctor Who* is done, I've probably had my last *Radio Times* cover full stop. David texted, saying that he was embarrassed at the number of covers he had to pick up. It's a hard life.

FROM: RUSSELL T DAVIES TO: BENJAMIN COOK, WEDNESDAY 21 JANUARY 2009 22:36:26 GMT

FW: WE'RE BACK!!! X

Ah, look what David has just sent Julie and me from set. He's back!

The 4.15 rushes so far are amazing. Christina stealing the cup is the sort of scene that would be the centrepiece of most dramas; we're just throwing it in as Scene 1! But it's really stylish and glossy. James Strong was such a good choice to direct this.

Meanwhile, Julie is coming back to work tomorrow. Of course she is. It's the Tone Meeting for 4.16, and the world will end before Julie Gardner misses a Tone Meeting. I can't wait to see her. I miss her. Her loss has put everything into perspective. She phoned up just now, as marvellous as ever, crying for her dad, but hooting at all the madness that comes with funerals, like the barmy old aunties and strange funeral directors. I remember when my mum died. It's the *size* of it, like you're trying to cram a fact that's as huge as a mountain range into your tiny head.

Hey, remember my intention – it was almost a New Year's resolution – to not kill myself smoking and slaving into the early hours in writing 4.17/4.18? To write normally, at a measured pace? According to that plan, I have to start TODAY...

PRISON DUNGEON - NIGHT 2

FX: THE MASTER, still suspended in LIGHT. Calmer, strong:

> THE MASTER
> Lucy. Oh, sweet Lucy Saxon. My ever
> faithful. Did the widow's kiss bring
> me back to life?

> LUCY
> You're killing them.

FX: GOVERNOR & GUARDS either side; still kneeling, LIGHT
pouring from their torsos - but they're weaker now, eyes
closing, heads lolling, energy being drained from them.

FX: (and REPEAT), the Master within the light -

> THE MASTER
> Let them die. Oh, let them! They're
> just the first! The whole stinking
> stupid Human disgrace can fall into
> the pit, *can't you hear it Lucy??*
> The noise? The drumming? Louder
> than ever before, the drums, the
> drums, the never-ending drums, ohhh I
> have *missed them - !*

But then...

Lucy Saxon stands. Staring up at him. Brave and clever.

> LUCY
> But no one knew you better than me.
> And I knew this would happen, one
> day, I knew you'd come back. All
> this time, your disciples were
> prepared... but so were we.

She turns to the Blonde Guard. Who's on her side! She
reaches into her pocket, hands Lucy something...

> THE MASTER
> ...what are you doing?

She's holding a SMALL PHIAL OF AMBER LIQUID. Uncorks it...

570

CHAPTER TWENTY-THREE

FOR GALLIFREY

In which Russell definitely doesn't threaten Lee Evans,
Benjamin spends the morning in a Portaloo,
and the Doctor travels to Trinity and beyond

FROM: RUSSELL T DAVIES TO: BENJAMIN COOK, SATURDAY 24 JANUARY 2009 02:40:08 GMT

EVERYONE HAD BAD DREAMS

Look! 4.17 SCRIPT!!!

I was locked away for a few days. Bit of a slump. Let's not go there. Dark day or two. But then I was having a coffee in the Bay this morning, and I thought of the Woman, the Woman that Wilf meets in the church…

```
2. EXT. SHOPPING STREET - NIGHT

CAMERA craning down a huge, outdoor CHRISTMAS TREE…

                    NARRATOR
    To the west of the north, in the season known as Winter,
    the citizens of the Human Race did gather, in celebration
    of a pagan rite, to banish the cold and the dark.

…craning down to find a SALVATION ARMY BRASS BAND. 'God Rest Ye
Merry Gentlemen'; the most mournful of carols.

Moving round to find a few ONLOOKERS (SHOPPERS in b/g). People,
just dotted about, pausing. A mother & son. Three teenagers. A
family, mum, dad & little daughter…
```

> NARRATOR (CONT'D)
> Each and every one of them had dreamt of the terrible
> things to come. But they forgot their nightmares, in the
> waking hours. They forgot their visions of fire and war.
> They forgot…

…then finding WILFRED MOTT.

> NARRATOR (CONT'D)
> Except for one.

Wilf's troubled, uneasy. Turns away.

CUT TO WIDER. Wilf wandering along. Lost in thought.

And then he hears…

Evensong. Beautiful, high, soaring chords. He looks…

A CHURCH. In the middle of town. (The Runaway Bride church.)
It's as though the music is drawing him in…

> CUT TO:

3. INT. CHURCH - NIGHT

WILFRED enters. The vaulted space filled with Evensong.

A CHOIR, at the altar, dressed in full surplices.

Candles all around. The pews are almost empty, just one or two
PEOPLE, dotted about, in prayer.

Wilf looks round. Not sure what he's doing there.

Then something catches his eye…

To the side: a STAINED-GLASS WINDOW.

He walks closer. Something in the image…

At the bottom of the window, to the left: a BLUE BOX. (FX?, image
inlaid?) A simple representation of the Tardis, stained-glass
panels of light radiating from its lamp.

The Evensong drifts into The Doctor's Theme, as Wilf walks
closer. Staring, entranced, then -

> WOMAN
> They call it, the Legend of the Blue Box.

He turns. The WOMAN behind him. She's 60, wise, kind.

```
                          WILF
Never been in here before. I'm not one for churches. Too
cold.


                         WOMAN
This was the site of a convent, back in the thirteen
hundreds. It's said a demon fell from the sky. Then a man
appeared, a man in a blue box. They called him the sainted
physician. He smote the demon. And then faded away.


                          WILF
Bit of a coincidence.


                         WOMAN
In what way?


                          WILF
                 (looks back at window)
...I've, just, heard stories like that before, that's all.


                         WOMAN
It's said there's no such thing as coincidence. Who knows?
Perhaps he's coming back.


                          WILF
Ohh, that would make my Christmas -


He turns back round -


No one there. The woman has gone; like she was never there.


Wilf chilled. He looks back at the stained-glass window.


The choir's voices soaring now.


CLOSER on the glass blue box...
```

I always knew that the opening scenes should be with Wilf, on Earth, at Christmas, with strange presentiments going on, but I couldn't tie it all together... and then I thought of the Woman. Having thought of the Woman, I then had to work out who she is. When that clicked, I was so excited, I all but ran back home. I couldn't wait to get to the keyboard. I typed out that scene in about 20 minutes. Ooh, I like that scene. (Who is she? You'll see! Ha ha. I'm not 100 per cent certain yet, but I think I can weave it in.) This has been lovely. I've really enjoyed myself. Plenty of misery to come, I'm sure. And the worry is, when this script turns out to be 500 pages long, this Wilf sequence is hugely cut-able. But we'll see.

Elsewhere, the 4.15 filming continues to be glorious. The night-time streets and the tunnel are lit like a Michael Mann movie. (The tunnel is huge!) And David is back, glory be. Everyone says that Michelle is lovely. And today I met Lee Evans. He's a hoot – completely mental, and brilliant. He'd brought along comedy false teeth to play Malcolm. We had the barmiest conversation where I talked him out of it. His version to the crew, later, was, 'Russell T Davies threatened to beat me up if I wore them!'

And Julie is okay. Back at work, of course, but genuinely okay – or as okay as you can ever be in those circumstances. Loads of us are going to the funeral – me, Phil, Ed, David – so it's a bit of a works outing, which keeps making us (and Julie) laugh.

FROM: BENJAMIN COOK TO: RUSSELL T DAVIES, SATURDAY 24 JANUARY 2009 08:04:06 GMT

RE: EVERYONE HAD BAD DREAMS

So, who's the Narrator? I want to know! (Don't tell me.) I reckon it's a Time Lord, maybe the President, but only because I know they're turning up at the top of the next episode. And who's the Woman? No idea. None at all. I'm stumped. I presume she pops up again. This is very exciting.

Interesting that you describe the Woman, simply, as '60, wise, kind' – says it all, I guess. Well, says enough. When you introduce new characters, you offer scant information about them in the stage directions. Astrid in *Voyage of the Damned* was a 'waitress in uniform', and 'young, bright, feisty'. Midshipman Frame was 'young, nervous'. Adelaide in 4.16 is 'strong, wry, 60'. And your mysterious Woman is '60, wise, kind', and no more. Why do you resist filling in further details? Is it so that you don't restrict casting directors? Or because characters should speak for themselves, through their behaviour and dialogue? Or is it just to keep the script tidy? What information *should* these succinct character sketches impart?

FROM: RUSSELL T DAVIES TO: BENJAMIN COOK, SATURDAY 24 JANUARY 2009 11:26:06 GMT

RE: EVERYONE HAD BAD DREAMS

Yes, it's partly to keep the script tidy, concise and clear. That's a big factor. Never forget that these things are designed to be read, and there is nothing more annoying than lengthy descriptions. If a paragraph says, 'Midshipman Frame is young, nervous, from a humble family background, and yet clever enough to have escaped his modest two-up-two-down hovel on Sto, and to have graduated into the Fleet; he chews his fingernails, is allergic to runner beans, and lost his virginity to Admiral Bones at the age of 17,' then it makes the script unreadable, in my opinion. (Apart from the virginity bit. I like that.) What's important is what's happening in the scenes that he's in, why Frame exists, his relationship with Captain Hardaker, and whether he will survive the crisis that you *know* is coming. Equally, what's important in the Woman's first scene is what she says to Wilf, how she says it ('wise' and 'kind' – that's important), and the mystery of who she is and what she's doing there. New scriptwriters often give you these long paragraphs of description, and while it's each to his own and all that, I really would stick to three adjectives. It's brief, concise, and accurate.

Oh, and every new writer, every single one of them, describes at least one character with the phrase 'He doesn't suffer fools gladly.' That seems to be the Number One Character Type. I'm so fed up of reading it. I mentally delete it.

>>what information should these succinct character sketches impart?<<

It's tempting to say that scripts can exist with no description or stage directions at all. Shakespeare does it! But a script is a working document that will be taken away and broken down by 57 different departments, all working very fast. They need a thumbnail. 'Wise' and 'kind' can also be applied to the Woman's clothes (Wardrobe), her hairstyle (Make-Up), any props that she may use (Design), to the actress herself (Casting) and, for the director, to the overall feel of the piece. Louise Page, and Babs Southcott, and Ed Thomas will all be scribbling notes in their books, and I bet they will all write down 'woman, wise, kind'. It simply enables work to be faster. From then on in the script, it's up to the writer to introduce some subtlety. The three adjectives are only a starting point. After that, it's up to me to find variation. Also, coming back to that teamwork thing… if you *don't* describe a character, then you're into the whole *Second Coming* red eyes/white eyes thing. The possibility of something being interpreted 57 dozen different ways. If you look *only* at the Woman's opening scene, then you could describe her as…. well, 'enigmatic', maybe 'spooky', 'prying' even. Everyone starts getting a slightly different picture, and that's not good.

As ever, that's just my way of working. I remember learning that off Paul Abbott, reading his scripts and thinking, 'Oh, I like that.' But there are lots of different ways of doing it. Some writers like to think of a nice, shiny quip to introduce someone. 'JONATHAN enters. He's a simple bloke, the sort of man who's happy if he finds a big crisp.' Actually, that's quite good! But personally I find that a bit trying and twee in a script. You can almost hear the writer too much. If you're introducing, say, seven characters, that can get quite wearing – and, frankly, you're not going to find seven lines that good!

FROM: RUSSELL T DAVIES TO: BENJAMIN COOK, SATURDAY 24 JANUARY 2009 16:08:29 GMT

RE: EVERYONE HAD BAD DREAMS

Eight pages more, and I only started at midday. I'm a-rattling through this. (I will come unstuck, fear not.) See my new plan in action! At least five pages a day, but no late nights, just steady work. I'm stopping now. No more work for Saturday. Christ, if I can keep this up, that's like a whole new life! (Although, maybe I just packed a whole day and night's worth of coffee and cigarettes into one afternoon. This is debatable.) It's all a bit steeped-in-the-past, the stuff on the Ood's home planet, with the Doctor telling them – and reminding *us* – what happened with the Master in the Series Three finale, and the Ood showing the Doctor that 'part of him survived' in the ring… but I think I'm telling the backstory well enough to be entertaining. It's nice and doom-y, I think. If you're bringing back the Master, what else can you do? And the Elder Ood, swathed in white robes, is great fun!

FROM: RUSSELL T DAVIES TO: BENJAMIN COOK, SUNDAY 25 JANUARY 2009 18:09:14 GMT

RE: EVERYONE HAD BAD DREAMS

Ha, look at me, sticking to my principles! Seven more pages. One afternoon's work. Evening off! (*Dancing On Ice*! So shoot me.) I'm typing, and I'm happy. I'm actually smiling away. Mind you, this script does show all the problems of the transmission pattern. This is strong stuff for Christmas Day. We've got the equivalent of a Black Mass on BBC One on 25 December. I've written around it where I can. Where Lucy Saxon should give blood to resurrect the Master, a small square of tissue is placed against her lips instead, gentle, like a kiss. 'You were Saxon's wife. You bore his imprint. That's all we needed, the final ingredient…' I call it 'the Widow's Kiss'. Where she was going to use a gun or a dagger to try to halt the Master's resurrection, it's a small phial of amber liquid. 'The Secret Books of Saxon spoke of the Chemicals of Life. And I was never that bright, but… there were people clever enough to calculate their opposite.' Even the Saxon disciples aren't quite chanting 'He is risen' and all that. But it's still tricky. It's Christmas! Frankly, Ben, the Master and the businessman in a public toilet ain't looking too good right now.

FROM: BENJAMIN COOK TO: RUSSELL T DAVIES, SUNDAY 25 JANUARY 2009 20:50:23 GMT

RE: EVERYONE HAD BAD DREAMS

Have you watched *EastEnders* on Christmas Day ever? Those episodes are some of the darkest, most depressing things on telly all year. Two Christmases ago, Pauline Fowler died cold, alone, and despised.[1] On Christmas Day! The Master killing someone in a toilet doesn't seem that bad, comparatively.

FROM: RUSSELL T DAVIES TO: BENJAMIN COOK, TUESDAY 27 JANUARY 2009 23:48:29 GMT

RE: EVERYONE HAD BAD DREAMS

Ah, sad day. It was Julie's mum's funeral. Although, as funerals go, that was as lovely as it could be. Strange to say, but we all had a good day out. Me, Phil and David all packed into Ed Thomas' car. (Ed was so concerned about getting there on time, he did a dry run to Julie's house last night. He's got a pregnant wife to get home to, but no, he drove for an hour up the valleys for a dry run. I've never loved that man more!) When you get to her village, you realise that it's such a tiny, tight community, there's no way her dad is going to be alone. He looked well; Julie looked wonderful. Not in denial, not in despair, but in that true and honest state of sadness.

The crematorium was packed. At least 200 people. They had to crowd outside. I realised how modest Julie is about her family. They don't just live in the valleys; they're Kings of the Valley. And all so proud of her. The Welsh sang like heroes. Hooray for the Welsh! Julie spoke at the service, a speech that was, literally, perfect – about how beautiful her mum was. Oh, it was sad. And then it was back to the house for tinned

---

1 Pauline Fowler (née Beale) – played by Wendy Richard – was a character in *EastEnders* from the show's inception in 1985 to her death in 2006.

red salmon sandwiches (so much better than real salmon), sausage rolls, Victoria sponge, and the battle of the cakes – between Julie's rock cakes and Aunty Eileen's. I preferred Aunty Eileen's. Julie is probably baking again now, determined to win. Of course, in no time at all, people were crowding in for photos and autographs with David – which he handled so magnificently. And there were so many people from the BBC there, you could see how extraordinary Julie is.

Evelyn May Gardner. As Ed said, 'What a beautiful name.'

FROM: RUSSELL T DAVIES TO: BENJAMIN COOK, WEDNESDAY 28 JANUARY 2009 16:34:50 GMT

RE: EVERYONE HAD BAD DREAMS

More script! Evening off now. And I'm still loving it. It's like the problems just solve themselves in front of my eyes. This is so strange. I am disconcerted. Of course, the Trinity Wells scene is outrageously indulgent. It might well be cut when this script is too long. But I couldn't resist…

37. EXT. PRISON - DAY[2]

CU on THE DOCTOR, running out of the TARDIS, frantic -

Into DAYLIGHT!

It hits him. He stops dead, stunned.

Wrong time of day!

He looks down…

He's standing by a burnt, battered sign, on the ground.

HMP BROADFELL.

He turns, looks round behind him…

FX: DMP WIDE SHOT, the PRISON. Destroyed. The high outer walls have fallen, the building beyond a charred, gutted ruin. No flames, no smoke; it burnt out days ago.

He missed it.

FX: REPEAT DMP, the Doctor a small figure, as he wanders into foreground, against the ruin. Knowing it's not over. Hold on this, the emptiness - long duration FX shot, because then, FX shot continued, as -

---

2   Scenes 37 and 38, which immediately follow the Master's explosive resurrection in the dungeon of HMP Broadfell (Scene 36), were deleted even before the first draft was delivered, for being, as Russell says later, 'indulgent, and also shit'. Scenes 39 to 41 – in which millionaire businessman Joshua Naismith and his daughter, 'Alice' (renamed Abigail in later drafts), watch footage of the prison burning and the Master's escape – were left in.

TRINITY WELLS, the American Newsreader, now roving reporter, steps into frame, foreground! Talking to CAMERA.

> TRINITY WELLS
> And the mystery remains. With no survivors from Broadfell Prison, we may never know Lucy Saxon's final secret, and what part she played in Harold Saxon's so-called reign of...
> (to cameraman)
> Sorry, we got a problem?

CUT TO REVERSE - a wide stretch of tarmac, once the prison car park, now abandoned, with ordinary houses way beyond. The AMERICAN CAMERAMAN lowering his camera.

> CAMERAMAN
> We got something in shot. That's weird, that box thing, it wasn't there before.

Trinity turning. The Doctor seeing her, walking over -

> TRINITY WELLS
> Hey, d'you mind? We're filming. Is that wooden thing yours?

> THE DOCTOR
> Never seen it before, but... hold on, hello! Don't I know you?

> TRINITY WELLS
> No, I get that a lot, you've just seen me on TV. Most people are surprised I've even got legs.

> THE DOCTOR
> Trinity Wells! Brilliant! So tell me, Trinity Wells... the prison. What happened?

CUT TO:

38. EXT. PRISON CAR PARK - DAY

CU STOCK FOOTAGE of a BURNING BUILDING, playing on monitor.

CUT TO WIDER: TRINITY & CAMERAMAN inside their American TV van - all playback equipment & gear, etc. A van with a sliding door on one side. THE DOCTOR outside, looking in.

> TRINITY WELLS
> They say there was something strange about the fire. It burnt for days, way beyond anything natural. Poor Lucy Saxon, that's hell of a life. Married to a madman, and then this.

                    THE DOCTOR
And no one survived? I mean, they looked, they
checked..?

                  TRINITY WELLS
That's the official story.

                    THE DOCTOR
And the unofficial?

                  TRINITY WELLS
Well. You shouldn't listen to the internet. But it's
said, the security cameras kept running. That they saw
something. Next thing you know, all the tapes have gone.
Not just wiped. Disappeared.

                    THE DOCTOR
What sort of something?

                  TRINITY WELLS
Someone running. Out of the flames.

                                                CUT TO:

39. INT. NAISMITH'S HALL - DAY

CU the STOCK FOOTAGE of the BURNING BUILDING.

Now being watched by JOSHUA NAISMITH. The playback on a terminal,
on a smart desk, with the huge, stately-home dining hall behind
him, all stark & bare elegance.

ALICE NAISMITH walking towards him. Echoing footsteps.

                      ALICE
Did you find anything?

                    NAISMITH
I think we might be in luck, darling. Take a look at
this…

On screen -

                                                CUT TO:

40. EXT. FIRE - NIGHT

SCREEN filled with FIRE. And foreground, a FIGURE, A SHADOW, just
a glimpse, a blur, rushes past -

                                                CUT TO:

41. INT. NAISMITH'S HALL - DAY

NAISMITH & ALICE studying the image.

On screen, grabbed pauses of the fleeting FIGURE.

                    NAISMITH
  That's all we've got. But I think it's enough to give us
  hope.

                    ALICE
  It really would be the most superlative Christmas
  present.

                    NAISMITH
  You just leave it to Daddy.

All smiling & kittenish, she kisses the top of his head.

                                    CUT TO:

42. EXT. DOCKLANDS/WASTELAND - DAY

Old industrial setting, disused docklands, open wasteland
beyond. The TV van pulls up - as THE DOCTOR is hopping out, with
TRINITY WELLS & CAMERAMAN all in the front -

                 TRINITY WELLS
  Funny place to stop.

                  THE DOCTOR
  Naah, it just smells right - thanks for the lift -
  whoops -

He's knocked some papers onto the floor, picks them up -

One of them is a b&w photo of Joshua Naismith.

                THE DOCTOR (CONT'D)
  Ah. Now. Hold on, who's he?

                 TRINITY WELLS
  Joshua Naismith.

                  THE DOCTOR
  Never heard of him.

                 TRINITY WELLS
  That's just the way he likes it. Billionaire, and that's
  a conservative estimate.

                    THE DOCTOR
What does he do?

                    CAMERAMAN
Everything!

                    TRINITY WELLS
Y'know how you get your Bill Gates and Steve Jobs and Henry
Van Stattens, those people running the world?[3] Like it's
said they're the front-men, while the real masterminds
sit behind them, in billionaire cabals? That's Joshua
Naismith. No one knows anything about him. I was trying to
get an interview, but no chance.

                    THE DOCTOR
…okay. Joshua Naismith.
                    (big smile)
Thanks then, Trinity! Mike!

                    TRINITY WELLS
Never even said your name.

                    THE DOCTOR
I'm the Doctor. Bye bye!

He heads off.

Head up. Searching. Keen. But behind him, the van doesn't move.
Trinity steps out.

                    TRINITY WELLS
Doctor?

He turns round. Good distance between them. Quiet, scared:

                    TRINITY WELLS (CONT'D)
Are we safe?

                    THE DOCTOR
…what d'you mean?

                    TRINITY WELLS
I keep getting these dreams. Dreams I can't remember. Past
few years, there's been enough stories about the end of
the world, but this time… Feels different.

                    THE DOCTOR
What's that got to do with me?

---

3 Although Bill Gates (co-founder of Microsoft) and Steve Jobs (co-founder of Apple) are real-life American business
magnates, Henry Van Statten is the fictional billionaire that the Ninth Doctor and Rose encounter in *Doctor Who* 1.6.

```
                         TRINITY WELLS
        I'm a good journalist. I've heard that name before. The
        Doctor.
                             (silence)
        Are we safe?


                          THE DOCTOR
        I don't know.

   Silence.


                         TRINITY WELLS
        You take care, now. Take care for all of us.

   And she turns, goes.


   The Doctor turns, with a mission. Heads for the wasteland.
```

FROM: BENJAMIN COOK TO: RUSSELL T DAVIES, WEDNESDAY 28 JANUARY 2009 19:05:04 GMT

RE: EVERYONE HAD BAD DREAMS

Um… what's American newsreader Trinity Wells doing in the UK? *Really?!*

FROM: RUSSELL T DAVIES TO: BENJAMIN COOK, THURSDAY 29 JANUARY 2009 01:22:07 GMT

RE: EVERYONE HAD BAD DREAMS

I've just been forwarded this e-mail from Jane Tranter in LA. It's from Bob Harris, the man who wrote that *Prisoner of Trebekistan* book that we mention in *The Writer's Tale* – and he's read our book! Completely by coincidence! He writes:

> *So I'm eagerly reading* The Writer's Tale, *since of course I'm a fan, and before I've barely started, there you are praising my book* Prisoner of Trebekistan, *right there in the very beginning. I had to look at it more than once, doing a cartoon-like rapid shake of the head, to be sure I was seeing that right. I'm so pleased you enjoyed the book, as in 'Hey, wow, Jane, come look at this!' followed by a small bit of dancing and repeating what you wrote aloud a couple of times. Thank you so much for the kind words. I may quote them to total strangers in cafés.*

How lovely is that? His wife is Jane Espenson, who's a writer and co-exec on *Buffy* and *Battlestar Galactica*. She's a brilliant writer! He goes on to say: 'There are so many moments in your book that feel like bits of conversations that Jane and I have almost daily. It's really cool to see that someone you admire has some of the same struggles, even a continent away.'

FROM: RUSSELL T DAVIES TO: BENJAMIN COOK, THURSDAY 29 JANUARY 2009 16:13:44 GMT

RE: EVERYONE HAD BAD DREAMS

Well, you haven't got a businessman in a toilet – it just delayed the action, sorry, it's faster to find the Master *after* that – but instead my Christmas gift to you is the Master eating a tramp and a rent boy on Christmas Eve.[4] Come on! That's not bad!

That's all I can do for today. I have to go to Upper Boat, because we've tests on the Tritovores in *Planet of the Dead* – all at night, because the crew is on night-shoot hours.[5] Meanwhile, I'm in a mild state of terror, because my back is starting to go. It starts with twinges, like bubbles rising. Then these little spasms, like warning signs. Oh God, please, no, shit, shit, shit. It is bloody awful to sit and type with a bad back. That's the last thing I need. There's nothing I can do to fight it off, except sit here, very, very still. I look like a posh secretary, all poised.

FROM: RUSSELL T DAVIES TO: BENJAMIN COOK, THURSDAY 29 JANUARY 2009 23:33:57 GMT

RE: EVERYONE HAD BAD DREAMS

Planet of the Dead is cursed. David has lost his voice! It's weird, he feels fine, no cold, it's just… gone. You can hear it fading away at the end of last night's rushes. So, we've changed tonight's scenes, cut tomorrow in half so that we can get back onto day shoots and give him a proper weekend off. But for an actor, that's terrifying.

FROM: BENJAMIN COOK TO: RUSSELL T DAVIES, SUNDAY 1 FEBRUARY 2009 18:32:15 GMT

RE: EVERYONE HAD BAD DREAMS

Are you okay? How's your back? (And what about David's voice?!)

FROM: RUSSELL T DAVIES TO: BENJAMIN COOK, SUNDAY 1 FEBRUARY 2009 18:59:29 GMT

RE: EVERYONE HAD BAD DREAMS

I've spent the last two days lying on the floor to fix my back. It's hard to watch TV, lying on your back. But I think it's worked! Sort of. A bit. More later! I'm mid rewrite on 4.16…

P.S. David's voice is holding up. Fingers crossed.

FROM: RUSSELL T DAVIES TO: BENJAMIN COOK, MONDAY 2 FEBRUARY 2009 03:52:14 GMT

RE: EVERYONE HAD BAD DREAMS

Here's the new 4.16. That was more work than I thought. I had to lose 100+ FX days and seven pages… Actually, the trickiest bit was Adelaide's gun. I was going to show it firing some sort of laser in the corridor scenes, so that we know what's happened later when she shoots herself with it. But I haven't. It made it worse. If you see any sort of laser-whatever coming out of the gun, then you later imagine that going through Adelaide's head at the end of the episode. It was horrible. I think it works by making the gun a blue-metal, then the flash is blue, tying it in. And it's obvious, anyway. But we'll have to work hard on the bang noise, so that it's more of a zap.

---

4 On some urban wasteland, the Master – in a dirty hoodie, pale-faced, wild-eyed, hair dyed punk-white – murders two homeless people, Tommo (late 40s, wry) and Ginger (18, quiet, northern), turning them to skeletons. 'Dinnertiiiiime!!!!!'
5 In *Doctor Who* 4.15, the Doctor and Christina encounter the Tritovores, humanoid fly-like creatures, on the desert planet of San Helios.

FROM: RUSSELL T DAVIES TO: BENJAMIN COOK, TUESDAY 3 FEBRUARY 2009 01:14:59 GMT

RE: EVERYONE HAD BAD DREAMS

I've only been pottering on 4.17 tonight. I needed to reduce the page count. I got rid of a lot of that Trinity Wells stuff. It was so indulgent, and also shit. And I should have introduced the Immortality Gate earlier, so I inserted a scene with Naismith and Alice in the 'Gate Room'. It comes immediately after his 'You just leave it to Daddy' line in Scene 41. Now, after Naismith kisses the top of Alice's head, I have them both walking towards a set of double doors, and then…

```
42. INT. THE GATE ROOM - DAY

JOSHUA & ALICE NAISMITH enter.

A huge, long, elegant room - all French windows, red velvet
curtains, busts on plinths, oil paintings; a stately home with
a gleaming SCI-FI LABORATORY built inside it. COMPUTER BANKS
& TERMINALS; to one side, TWO GLASS-WALLED BOOTHS. TECHNICIANS
tending to the controls. Minimal Christmas decorations, just
one, classy tree. At the far end…

THE IMMORTALITY GATE.

A huge, dark-metal, rectangular frame, bristling with technology,
as wide and as high as possible. Three sides to the frame, left,
right and top, with the left and right sides disappearing into
the floor, i.e. no bottom frame.

                    NAISMITH
     Ladies and gentlemen. It seems help is at hand. And it
     falls upon me to be somewhat Dickensian by announcing,
     with no regrets whatsoever, that Christmas is cancelled.
     Prepare the Gate!

Technicians - not complaining - press buttons, hum of power -

FX: FLICKERS OF BLUE ELECTRICITY across the GATE. Tile up -

FX: DMP WIDER SHOT OF THE ROOM & ROOF, showing the flickering
Gate set beneath a WIDE, ELEGANT, CIRCULAR, DOMED WINDOW set in
the ceiling. Sunlight streaming in.

Alice snuggles up to Naismith; admiring their empire.
```

FROM: BENJAMIN COOK TO: RUSSELL T DAVIES, TUESDAY 3 FEBRUARY 2009 01:38:11 GMT

RE: EVERYONE HAD BAD DREAMS

I'm glad that you cut poor Trinity. When Wilf's 'Silver Cloak' gang shows up (in a Sunshine Coach – ha ha!), it starts to feel like everyone on Earth knows who the

Doctor is, when he's trying to be a lonesome stranger.[6] But I knew you'd fix it.

A question: when to cut, and when not to cut…? Editing down, down, down almost always improves a script, but when is a cut a cut too far?

FROM: RUSSELL T DAVIES TO: BENJAMIN COOK, TUESDAY 3 FEBRUARY 2009 02:18:20 GMT

RE: EVERYONE HAD BAD DREAMS

Yes, cutting is good. Cut, cut, cut. Of course, that doesn't mean that everything can go. With *Doctor Who*, usually I find myself fighting like hell to cut anything, except a good joke. Jokes are often first to be chucked overboard, but they're not just accidental gags; they're vital to the whole tone of the show. They're not flippant. Or rather, they *are* flippant, but that flippancy is intrinsic to the Doctor. On *Battlestar Galactica*, it's probably the opposite – if a joke slips in there, I suspect it's the first thing to go – but that's because both shows have different aims. Other than being sci-fi, they're barely connected at all. This is something that so few sci-fi fans understand. Saying that *Battlestar Galactica* is better than *Doctor Who* is as stupid as saying that Maths is better than English. But then I think saying that *Coronation Street* is better than *EastEnders* is stupid, because they're such very different shows. Maybe I think about this stuff too much.

So, cutting isn't just about trimming the spare lines (because you could argue that jokes are going spare); it's about trimming away the stuff that isn't vital to the essence of the whole thing, not just the plot. Most cuts are simple, because they involve getting rid of ping-pong dialogue. All that back-and-forth between the Doctor and Trinity Wells can be reduced to – what? – a couple of extra lines in Naismith's opening exchange with Alice:

```
                    NAISMITH
    I think we might be in luck, darling. It's the footage from
    Broadfell Prison. The night it burnt down. Take a look at
    this…
```

That's enough, isn't it? A couple of pages reduced to 'It's the footage from Broadfell Prison. The night it burnt down.' Perfect. It's never quite as straightforward as I've made it appear, but it's one of the most important things you can do to a script – pare it right down to the bone, but keeping the jokes.

I think what I'm saying is, cutting doesn't simply mean drawing a line through speeches. That's the easy bit. It means being ruthless and concise in your approach to every line, every scene, every character. You have to keep your mind as tight as a vice. Because a commission is lucky. If you get asked to write an hour's TV, you're the

---

6   The 'Silver Cloak' gang is Wilf's posse of pensioner mates – including Oliver Barnes (65), Minnie Hooper (70), Winston Katusi (70), and half-a-dozen others. They help Wilf track down the TARDIS, leading them to the Doctor. 'It's important!' Wilf tells them. 'We've got to find it! Phone around, phone everyone – Sally, phone the Bridge Club, Winston, try the Old Boys, Bobby, get on to the skiffle band – between us, we've got this city covered!'

luckiest bastard in the world, and you shouldn't waste a single eighth of a page with ping-pong, or flim-flam, or ornate curlicues, or lengthy descriptions of a man's jumper. You must make every word count.

FROM: RUSSELL T DAVIES TO: BENJAMIN COOK, WEDNESDAY 4 FEBRUARY 2009 02:37:59 GMT

RE: EVERYONE HAD BAD DREAMS

More! I feel like I've waited all year to write that dialogue between the Doctor and Wilf on the wasteland – the old man tracking down the Time Lord to the lost and lonely edge of a city. It's about 1,000 pages long, but I can't bear to cut a word of it. (Yes, despite what I said last night about editing your own work!) Oh, and here I am back on night hours again. I just couldn't write that scene in daytime. I sat here doing nothing for hours.

FROM: BENJAMIN COOK TO: RUSSELL T DAVIES, WEDNESDAY 4 FEBRUARY 2009 03:06:41 GMT

RE: EVERYONE HAD BAD DREAMS

The 'Silver Cloak' gang continues to be brilliant! Especially Minnie. (Wilf: 'Be on the lookout for a police box. Exactly like the old ones.' Minnie: 'I got locked inside one of them, August Bank Holiday 1962.' Winston: 'Were you misbehaving, Minnie?' Minnie: 'I certainly was! Wa-hey!') But surely this exchange is inspired by our book tour, or your horrible day at the Cardiff Bay *Doctor Who* Exhibition back in October…

>   WILF
>   It is an honour to meet you again, sir.
>
> The Doctor can't help smiling, salutes back. Then:
>
>   MINNIE
>   Ooh, but you never said he was a looker, he's gorgeous,
>   take a photo!
>
> She gives her mobile to Oliver –
>
>   OLIVER
>   Not bad, is he? Me next!
>
> – and Minnie scuttles to the Doctor's side, all the old folk,
> except Wilf, gathering around him. He's trapped!
>
>   MINNIE
>   I'm Minnie. Minnie the Menace. It's been a long time since
>   I had a photo with a handsome man!
>
>   WILF
>   Now get off him, leave him alone –

MINNIE
Hush, you old misery. Come on, Doctor! Big smile! Thaaat's it!

OLIVER
Did it flash?

MINNIE
No, do it again. Smile!

OLIVER
I think the battery's gone.

MINNIE
No, there's a blue light, try again.

WINSTON
Try mine, use this one -

MINNIE
No, it's working, just press the button on top.

THE DOCTOR
I'm really kind of busy, y'know..?

MINNIE
Won't take a tick! Just keep smiling! Eyes and teeth!

THE DOCTOR
Is that your hand, Minnie?

MINNIE
Good boy!

FROM: RUSSELL T DAVIES TO: BENJAMIN COOK, WEDNESDAY 4 FEBRUARY 2009 03:11:01 GMT

RE: EVERYONE HAD BAD DREAMS

I have no idea what you mean. I imagined the whole thing. Ha ha ha. Just think how often David gets that in real life.

FROM: RUSSELL T DAVIES TO: BENJAMIN COOK, SATURDAY 7 FEBRUARY 2009 01:55:49 GMT

RE: EVERYONE HAD BAD DREAMS

Well, that was a pissy night. Something's going wrong with my screenwriter software. I put loads of changes into 4.16, went to close it, and mysterious screens came up, 'SAVING 0%', with a bar that was obviously meant to go from 0 to 100%. Except it stayed on 0. And it froze the screen. I had to turn off the computer and lose it. Turned it back on, made all the changes *again*, went to save… strange little box saying 'APPLICATION ERROR' popped up, closed down the software, all changes lost. *(cont p589)*

JOSHUA NAISMITH

Russell's first draft of *The End of Time* Part One features this extended version of Naismith and the Master's first scene together, written on 10 February 2009...

```
66. INT. NAISMITH'S HALL - DAY

JOSHUA NAISMITH strides in, all energy, ALICE following.

                    NAISMITH
     My family made its fortune out of wax. Came to England in
     the year 1890, not a penny to their names, didn't even
     need passports back then. Started work in service, good,
     honest work. But my grandfather… he noticed the wax.

Reveal, THE MASTER.

Tied to an upright trolley, Hannibal Lecter-style. Bound by
leather straps. Strap across his mouth. ARMED GUARDS & MR FINCH.¹
In the middle of the empty, echoing room.

                    NAISMITH (CONT'D)
     The kitchen maids used to rub wax into their hands. Stop
     the knuckles from splitting. Nothing more than a simple
     convenience, but my grandfather saw a business! He sold
     that wax. Began the fortune. And that's remained a family
     trait, the eye for opportunity. I imagine you're the same;
     that you'd take the first opportunity to kill me.

The Master nods, grunts 'Uh-huh.'

                    NAISMITH (CONT'D)
     If you would, Mr Finch.

Mr Finch releases the mouth-strap.

                    THE MASTER
     I'm starving.

                    ALICE
     Ohh, but look at him!

She's holding a rectangle of polaroid glass up to her eyes, the
lenses on a gold stick, like pince-nez.

FX: HER POV: the SKELETON & BULGING EYES Master.
```

1 'Mr Finch' (described as '50, thin, haughty, dry') is Naismith's valet/butler. In later drafts, the name is changed to Mr Danes, and he's '28, cool, handsome, cruel' instead.

                         ALICE (CONT'D)
        That's almost rather beautiful.

        She passes them to Naismith, he looks through them.

        FX: HIS POV: the SKELETON Master. Grinning.

                         THE MASTER
        I need feeding, don't you think?

                         NAISMITH
        I think we can help. If you help me, Mr Saxon.

                         THE MASTER
        My name is the Master.

                         NAISMITH
        I refuse to call anyone that. But you've my daughter to
        thank. She heard rumours of Harold Saxon. His disciples.
        His return. Sort of thing she finds rather thrilling.

                         ALICE
        And I was right. He's back!

                         THE MASTER
        What am I, a Christmas present?

                         ALICE
        That's exactly what I said! Oh, this is going to be
        wonderful! Mr Finch, is the Gate ready?

                         MR FINCH
        Very much so, ma'am.

Bloody bastard. (Oh, the exciting life of a writer.) I'm going to leave it for tonight, and hope that it'll just fix itself overnight. Like they do.

I was changing 4.16 because your grand plan has been wrecked! BBC One has said no to three episodes at Christmas. It's the scheduling of 4.16 on the Saturday before Christmas that they don't like. They say that it's confused, and doesn't work. Hand on heart, they have a point. It's hard to get across that episode's presence. Plus, they really want a *Doctor Who* hit before Christmas, some time in the autumn, though they can't fix a date yet – and they've promised to protect it from *The X Factor*, somehow. So, now I have to un-Christmas Mars, which is easy enough… though not when you lose your changes twice.

Interestingly, they said that the Christmas Day/New Year's Day transmission of 4.17 and 4.18 is '80 per cent fixed', though they *are* interested in showing both on Christmas Day. That's your original plan! That's fascinating, and I wouldn't mind at all.

My only worry is that when dates start shifting, they become inherently shiftable, and at the last minute you end up with something rubbish like Christmas Day and, say, 28 December, whenever that is. You're never quite sure where you stand with schedulers. They keep saying things like, 'We're lacking big movies this Christmas, so we need *Doctor Who* to be our big hitter.' Nice, fine, complimentary... but that doesn't square with showing both episodes on Christmas Day, because that's not Big Movie Day. You see? Shifting sands. That's vaguely disquieting.

But they did finally – *finally* – agree to the five-night *Torchwood*. This was, supposedly, written in stone from the moment that it was commissioned, but no, just as I suspected, they've since been talking about shifting it all over the place. Julie went in, and fought like a demon. Thank God.

FROM: RUSSELL T DAVIES TO: BENJAMIN COOK, MONDAY 9 FEBRUARY 2009 01:27:04 GMT

RE: EVERYONE HAD BAD DREAMS
There we go. More 4.17. It feels like ages since I wrote more. I've reached the big turning point – the bit where Naismith's private security troops abseil in and grab the Master, hauling him up into the air and disappearing into the night, leaving the Doctor on the wasteland, unconscious.

Hey, when are you off to Dubai? With everyone else on Tuesday morning? I want constant updates.

FROM: BENJAMIN COOK TO: RUSSELL T DAVIES, MONDAY 9 FEBRUARY 2009 01:38:21 GMT

RE: EVERYONE HAD BAD DREAMS
Yes, Tuesday morning. You're going to be writing while I'm in Dubai, aren't you? You're going to be sending me script each day, and I'm not going to be able to read it until I get back to the UK! NOOOOOOOO!!! I'll have some e-mail access out there, on my iPhone, but I can't open script attachments. Bollocks.

FROM: RUSSELL T DAVIES TO: BENJAMIN COOK, TUESDAY 10 FEBRUARY 2009 01:11:02 GMT

RE: EVERYONE HAD BAD DREAMS
Here's more. Not much more, though. It's at a weird stage, now that the action has moved to Naismith's mansion; it's practically the start of a new adventure. It takes a lot of time, getting the building blocks into place. When there's a new plot, or a new character, or a new tone, it takes time to sink in, to get a grip on it, to make myself believe it. I've been here all day – I haven't even been out for milk or papers – just pottering about, making myself believe what's happening next. Finding confidence in it. I think I'm there. It just takes time.

I reached Page 48, and shivered at how much action there is to come, so I went right back to the beginning, and went through every single bloody line, trimming it down...

until I'd cut it down to 45 pages. Good work! I keep hoping I'll finish it this week. Prep starts – on both episodes! – on 23 February, and I'm really trying to get there, because this is going to need a hell of a lot of prep.

Meanwhile, the *Planet of the Dead* rushes coming from Upper Boat are tremendous. They did the bus flying yesterday – which was only a camera swinging about on a stationary bus, obviously, but it really looks like they're flying. And you're off to Dubai in the morning! The *Confidential* team is out there already. Apparently, it's colder than they thought. They're all wishing they'd taken jumpers. One story that you should follow up out there is Mike Jones, the editor. He's going so that he can assemble each day's rushes (on his laptop!), because once they've got a rough assembly, they know if they need to pick up shots or reshoot anything, instead of waiting until they get back to Cardiff, by which time it's too late. The funny thing is, Mike does it overnight. He'll be locked away in his hotel room, working like a mad thing, pulling it all together. It could be a good story, you newshound. Mike has been with us since Series One. He did more to get that very first block made than any man will ever know.

Have fun, Ben. Safe journey

> **Text message from: Ben**
> Sent: 10-Feb-2008 19:45
> Arrived safely in Dubai a few minutes ago.

> **Text message from: Russell**
> Sent: 10-Feb-2008 19:47
> Behave now. No drugs or infidelity.

FROM: RUSSELL T DAVIES TO: BENJAMIN COOK, TUESDAY 10 FEBRUARY 2009 22:51:02 GMT

DUBAI

Okay, so as I understand it… David's minibus got stopped by scary police, and they all had to get off and stand on a verge, in the dark, while the driver was fined. While Julian's bus is lost.[7] In the desert. Right now.

It's going well. Which bus are you on?!

FROM: BENJAMIN COOK TO: RUSSELL T DAVIES, TUESDAY 10 FEBRUARY 2009 23:36:24 GMT

RE: DUBAI

Don't panic. There were three minibuses. One of them was lost in the desert (it took a wrong turning and headed for Oman), and one was pulled over by armed police, but I was on the third minibus. Score! We were the first to arrive at the hotel. Obviously, we were worried sick about the other two minibuses. Almost too worried to tuck into

---

7 Julian Howarth, *Doctor Who*'s sound recordist.

the buffet that the Holiday Arabian Resort has laid on for us. Thankfully, Julian's bus turned up a few minutes ago. He's here, eating chips and sandwiches by the pool with the rest of us. At 3.30am! Oh yes! (I'm e-mailing from my iPhone! By the pool! In the dark!) David's bus wasn't far behind ours, in the end. It was pulled over because the tail-light was broken, or something, but the driver talked his way out of it.

The hotel is… bizarre. It's an hour or so from the airport, just over the border from Dubai, in the Masfout region of Ajmân, and there's a 'nightclub' actually *in the hotel*, open till three in the morning… with, um, exotic dancers. Tracie is worried. David less so. He's laughing. 'We're in a whorehouse, in the middle of the desert,' he just said. 'What could possibly go wrong?'

FROM: RUSSELL T DAVIES TO: BENJAMIN COOK, WEDNESDAY 11 FEBRUARY 2009 00:02:39 GMT

RE: DUBAI

The Best Little Whorehouse in Dubai. That is hilarious. And why the hell didn't the bus have its lights on? With David Tennant on board?! Dear God, the insurance.

Christ, I'd love chips now, you bastards.

FROM: RUSSELL T DAVIES TO: BENJAMIN COOK, WEDNESDAY 11 FEBRUARY 2009 01:13:34 GMT

RE: DUBAI

I'm attaching more script to this e-mail, although I don't know if you can open it. You should be asleep, anyway. Hasn't it gone 5am in Dubai? Unless you're with the exotic dancers. Maybe you *are* an exotic dancer by now. It's a living. I actually thought I could finish this script tomorrow… but then, out of the blue, a friend of mine who I haven't seen for ages is going to be in Cardiff. I should have lied and said I was in Manchester, but I'm too nice. So… bah! So close, and yet so far.

FROM: BENJAMIN COOK TO: RUSSELL T DAVIES, WEDNESDAY 11 FEBRUARY 2009 19:47:15 GMT

RE: DUBAI

We don't have internet access in the hotel (well, there's Wi-Fi, but it's rubbish), so I'm e-mailing you from my phone again. I might be able to get better Wi-Fi in Reception, apparently… if I stand in the corner, on one leg… so I'll try to download the latest 4.17 script to my laptop tomorrow. Exciting!

We went on a recce into the Margham Desert today. We had to travel the final stretch on an army truck. The only way on or off was by stepladder, or swinging down on a rope. I swung down. Babs from Make-Up didn't. David and Michelle weren't even allowed on board, for 'health and safety' reasons! (That annoyed them.) The double-decker looks awesome. Seven tons of slightly damaged bus. Everyone is impressed. Ed and his design team have done the most amazing job on this episode. It's going to look beautiful in HD. He's the best designer in the business. What would *Doctor Who* do without him?

Early start tomorrow. Our coach leaves the hotel (or 'the House of Disrepute' – at least the ladies cover up in daylight hours) at 5.30am. Sob! It's almost midnight now. Breakfast on set tomorrow, in the desert. Mmm, sand.

FROM: RUSSELL T DAVIES TO: BENJAMIN COOK, WEDNESDAY 11 FEBRUARY 2009 20:03:07 GMT

RE: DUBAI

This is making me hoot! Julie and I sit here all day, wondering what you're all up to. It really is different to Rome. You're sooo far away.

Up at 5.30am? I won't keep you. Get to bed! No news from here. All is quiet.

FROM: RUSSELL T DAVIES TO: BENJAMIN COOK, WEDNESDAY 11 FEBRUARY 2009 22:51:21 GMT

RE: DUBAI

You're asleep! I hope. But I feel like writing an e-mail anyway. I'm so close to the end of this 4.17 script... but actually quite relaxed. I'm sure I can finish it by Friday, so I don't need to rush tonight. I'm tempted to stay up all night and have a marathon session... hmm, but not tempted enough.

I was thinking about what you were saying about Ed Thomas. It's true, you know, he really is the Other Producer. I remember appointing him came completely out of the blue, for all of us. We surprised ourselves! He was a stranger, and I think we'd all presumed that we'd appoint someone that Julie, Phil or I had worked with before, simply in order to have someone trusted on our side, on such a huge project. But then Ed appeared, out of nowhere. (He'd been working abroad for years, so he wasn't on the industry radar – though it turned out that Julie had been to school with him, which was a complete coincidence.) But it wasn't so much Ed's experience that counted; we booked him because we so immediately *liked* him. Bit mad, but there we go. But actually *no one* in the country had the experience that this show demanded, so we thought, what the hell, go for the nice man. (More than just 'nice'. I mean, we *profoundly* liked him.) Plus, he was Welsh. With the staffing, that's really helped.

I always remember, when I went in to meet him, one of the very first things that Ed spoke about was Health and Safety. People take the piss out of Health and Safety, like it's a joke, ignoring the fact that the words 'health' and 'safety' are pretty important, if not more important than anything else. That was burnt into me when I was quite young and starting out in TV. I was part of the BBC Children's Department that produced *UP2U*, the show on which Anthea Turner sat on a pyrotechnic and was blown up, live on air! I'm not kidding, whole lives were ruined in the repercussions of that, whole careers, whole families. It was horrific. So, good old Ed, I thought.

I'm sure if he were writing a book – I'd read it! – he would have such good tales to report from Series One, from the front line. After the first block, the budget was almost out of control. A proper emergency. I remember, for a week or so, having to look seriously at three or four episodes to see if I could gut them to become *Midnight*-style cheapos. Of course, Julie, Phil, Ed, Tracie and everyone pulled together, and somehow made it work – to this day, I don't really know how – because they're magicians. That's really when everyone gelled, and became a team, rather than just colleagues. Born out of battle! And when the show started to work, Ed started to fly... and then *Torchwood* gave him more money, to expand the team, to create an empire. He's simply the best designer I've ever worked with. Such a fine man, too. At the same time, it really is this format at work. It's the magic of *Doctor Who*. The designer is given Shakespearean London, and Pompeii, and spaceships, and 10 Downing Street. It *makes* you fly. The show demands it.

Or maybe I'm talking bollocks, and his next episode will be comprised entirely of sets made out of paper plates. Damn you, Thomas!

Right, a bit more work, then bed. Oh, and I keep musing – I'm in a musing mood! – on how comparatively relaxed I am writing 4.17. If you compare the angst of writing *Voyage of the Damned* (there's a book all about it, did you know?), then this is nowhere near as bad. But why?! Does this mean it's shit? But then the obvious thing occurred to me, only the other day: normally, I've been writing this stuff with the stress of a whole season on my back. I'd write the Christmas episode with 13 more bastards looming, and I'd write these finales in a welter of Edits, and Dubs, and problems, and transmission looming – which simply isn't there now. In other words, this is what life should be like. This is what writing should be like. I've just been working myself to death for the past four years. That's obvious, isn't it? I bet you worked that out. I've only just seen it.

Have a nice breakfast. In the sand. You could have a sand-wich. See how bloody funny I am?! I rule! Yes.

Text message from: Ben
Sent: 12-Feb-2008 07:22
It's so sandy, this isn't even funny. Sand everywhere! I know, I know, it's a desert, but this is a bloody sandstorm! They've had to go buy us all headscarves from the nearest shop. (Yeah, there's a shop. In the desert. This is mad.)

Text message from: Russell
Sent: 12-Feb-2008 09:19
Julie is worried. I've woken up to e-mails from her saying, 'They're an hour behind! We can't use the camera crane!' Oh Lordy.

Text message from: Ben
Sent: 12-Feb-2008 09:39
The sandstorm has hit! An actual sandstorm! The latest shots are unusable. The schedule is in tatters. CODE RED! ABORT! ABORT!

> **Text message from: Russell**
> Sent: 12-Feb-2008 09:45
> I've got you texting with 'SANDSTORM!' and Julie phoning with 'SANDSTORM!' I'm hooting. Save yourself, Ben.

> **Text message from: Ben**
> Sent: 12-Feb-2008 10:10
> I'm sheltering in a Portaloo. I'm no fool.

> **Text message from: Ben**
> Sent: 12-Feb-2008 12:21
> Apparently, this is the worst sandstorm to hit the region since last September. A few minutes ago, James Strong was close to abandoning the day's shooting altogether. The cameras are crunching every time they pull focus, because they're full of sand! It's pretty hellish. But they're soldiering on.

> **Text message from: Russell**
> Sent: 12-Feb-2008 12:26
> That'll teach them for pulling focus. There's no time for art! I'm sitting here cutting scenes from tomorrow's schedule. I love an emergency. I once filmed on Lindisfarne with a helicopter in a storm. I've done it all, me. Are you still buried in that Portaloo?! Is it buried in the sand?!

FROM: RUSSELL T DAVIES TO: BENJAMIN COOK, FRIDAY 13 FEBRUARY 2009 03:13:38 GMT

RE: DUBAI

I'm so close to the end of 4.17… but too tired to finish. Argh. Still, I've got all day at home tomorrow, with a Dub in the evening, so I hope I'll finish then. The Doctor has arrived at Naismith's mansion, and it's all about to kick off…

Of course, that's nothing compared to the problems out in Dubai. Lord E God. They said that David's hair had turned blond with sand. And the sand stuck to Tracie's make-up! Julie and I were laughing so much at that, she almost crashed the car. Tracie said it was stuck to her lipstick! Oh, not funny. Not funny at all.

I hope you survive today. Last I heard, it was windy, but maybe not as windy as yesterday. You won't know until you're on set. Get inside that Portaloo!

> **Text message from: Ben**
>
> Sent: 13-Feb-2008 03:51
>
> Back on set. James is reshooting a lot of yesterday's material. The weather is holding. First take of the day just completed. Only another 11 hours to go! In other news, I got my headscarf caught in my zip. The Costume Department couldn't free me. Julian had to step in and use brute force.

> **Text message from: Ben**
>
> Sent: 13-Feb-2008 04:19
>
> I spoke too soon. Filming has been disrupted by a gang of quadbikers. Try pink-paging that! Ha ha. It's Friday 13th. What could possibly go wrong?

FROM: RUSSELL T DAVIES TO: BENJAMIN COOK, FRIDAY 13 FEBRUARY 2009 08:39:02 GMT

RE: DUBAI

That is the best line EVER:

>>I got my headscarf caught in my zip. The Costume Dept couldn't free me! Julian had to step in and use brute force.<<

I forwarded that to Julie. You can probably hear her hoot.

I'm glad to hear that it's better today – so far! I only had three hours sleep. The 4.17 script was drumming through my head. I'm attaching the latest instalment, but don't worry about reading it. You probably can't even download it. I'm sending it out of habit.

The Bay has woken up now. I'm off for a coffee. It's sunny. No sand. Ha.

FROM: RUSSELL T DAVIES TO: BENJAMIN COOK, FRIDAY 13 FEBRUARY 2009 12:58:45 GMT

RE: DUBAI

I'm about a page from the end. It's very exciting. Wilf (of Donna): 'Doctor! She's starting to remember!'[8] But I have to pause. It's a hell of a mess. I'll have to edit it all down. Maybe after I deliver it, though. To hell with it.

Anyway, Mike keeps trying to send us desert footage, but the internet connection is failing, so it's still a mystery to us. We are blind. Hope you're surviving.

> **Text message from: Russell**
>
> Sent: 13-Feb-2008 14:37
>
> We've got rushes! We've got an edit! BEAUTIFUL! But Jesus, that sand. You must all be exfoliated to death.

8 In Naismith's mansion, Wilf is on his mobile to Donna, who's at home in Chiswick with her mum and fiancé, as the Master takes over the human race, turning everyone into his image. 'But they've changed,' Donna tells Wilf. 'Grandad, that's like... like the sort of thing that happened... before...' Intercut with fast, fierce images – Ood, Davros, Adipose, Sontarans, the Doctor. 'My head. Ohh, my head...'

Text message from: **Ben**

Sent: 13-Feb-2008 15:13

Most of that was re-shot today. Wait till you see today's rushes! STUNNING! A really productive day.

Text message from: **Russell**

Sent: 13-Feb-2008 15:27

I feel a little peace returning. And I'm five lines away from the end of 4.17!

Text message from: **Russell**

Sent: 13-Feb-2008 15:52

I am literally – LITERALLY – typing 'This was the day the Time Lords returned! For Gallifrey!'[9]

Text message from: **Ben**

Sent: 13-Feb-2008 17:12

Send me script! I have internet now! I'm in Reception, standing on one leg.

FROM: RUSSELL T DAVIES TO: BENJAMIN COOK, FRIDAY 13 FEBRUARY 2009 17:17:34 GMT

RE: DUBAI

Here you go. I'll spend the rest of the evening on it, but you can have this instalment while you have internet.

FROM: BENJAMIN COOK TO: RUSSELL T DAVIES, FRIDAY 13 FEBRUARY 2009 20:58:42 GMT

RE: DUBAI

TIME LORDS!!! WILF!!! DONNA REMEMBERING!!! So, so exciting… and now your final script is nigh. How do you feel? You're about to write your last ever *Doctor Who* episode, Russell! (Don't you need a break first?)

FROM: RUSSELL T DAVIES TO: BENJAMIN COOK, SATURDAY 14 FEBRUARY 2009 12:10:31 GMT

RE: DUBAI

That 4.17 script really took it out of me. Now, of course, I've sunk into the panic of thinking that I don't know what happens next. And I get so paranoid. Julie texted last

---

9 'Even as he celebrated, the creature known as the Master had no concept of his greater role in events,' explains the Narrator, as every human on Earth turns into the Master (except Wilf, who is in one of Naismith's booths and so protected by 'radiation shielding', and Donna, who is protected by the metacrisis energy that she inherited from the Doctor in *Doctor Who* 4.13). 'For this day was far more than humanity's end.' Cut to a black void, and to the Narrator in flowing robes. 'This was the day the Time Lords returned.' He lifts his staff, a warrior's cry: 'For Gallifrey!' Suspended in the void are ranks of Time Lords, above and beyond the Narrator, like the circle level of a theatre. Hundreds of Time Lords, all standing, calling out: 'For Gallifrey! For victory! For the End of Time itself!'

night and said, 'Love the script,' so I spent all night thinking, is that all? Is that it?! What's wrong with it? Why? (I think there is something wrong with it, though. But I can't quite see what it is.)

Tracie just phoned from Dubai. From a dune. She says that they've caught up. They've got time for an extra shot, even! Blimey, what a success. That crew must have worked so hard. This morning, I saw the crane shot of them stepping off the bus. It looks wonderful.

I'm in Manchester now, until Tuesday. A few days off. Nice. Safe journey home, Ben!

1. OMITTED

2. FX SHOT. GALLIFREY – DAY

FX: LONG FX SHOT, craning up to reveal the mountains
of Gallifrey, as Ep.3.12 sc.40. But now transformed;
the mountains are burning, a landscape of flame. The
valley's a pit of fire, cradling the hulks of broken
spaceships. Keep craning up to see, beyond; the
Citadel of the Time Lords. The glass dome now cracked
and open.

                                              CUT TO:

3. INT. CITADEL – DAY

FX: DMP WIDE SHOT, an ancient hallway, once beautiful,
high vaults of stone & metal. But the roof is now
broken, open to the dark orange sky, the edges
burning. Bottom of frame, a walkway, along which walk
THE NARRATOR, with staff, and 2 TIME LORDS, the latter
pair in ceremonial collars.

FX: NEW ANGLE, LONG SHOT, the WALKWAY curves round,
Narrator & Time Lords now following the curve, heading
towards TWO HUGE, CARVED DOORS, already open. A Black
Void beyond.

                                              CUT TO:

4. INT. BLACK VOID

FX: OTHER SIDE OF THE HUGE DOORS, NARRATOR & 2 TIME
LORDS striding through. The Time Lords stay by the
doors, on guard; lose them, and the doors, as the
Narrator walks on.

FX: WIDE SHOT of the Black Void - like Superman's
Krypton, the courtroom/Phantom Zone scenes - deep
black, starkly lit from above. Centre of the Void: a
long table, with 5 TIME LORDS in robes (no collars)
seated.

The Narrator - now designated THE LORD PRESIDENT -
reaches the table. He puts down his staff, loosens
his robes - underneath, a battered, black flack-
jacket; this man is a warrior. One hand is sheathed
in a BLUE-METAL GAUNTLET.

Amongst those seated; THE CHANCELLOR, male, 45, thin,
worried; THE PARTISAN, female, 50, calm, shrewd.

                      LORD PRESIDENT
            What news of the Doctor?

CHAPTER TWENTY-FOUR

THE ROAD
TO HELL

In which the Doctor's mother is inspired by Chris Rea,
Rassilon loses a diamond in the dark,
and the Master eats, shoots, and leaves

FROM: RUSSELL T DAVIES TO: BENJAMIN COOK, WEDNESDAY 18 FEBRUARY 2009 01:50:55 GMT

CARDIFF

I'm back! In Cardiff! Christ, that journey took five bloody hours. The M6 was closed. The M5 was blocked. Parts of the M4, specifically the parts leading into Cardiff, were closed. I thought I was going to have to walk.

Anyway, I'm now staring into the abyss of my last ever *Doctor Who* script. And I'm scared. What happens?! Shit, shit. shit. Still, 4.16 read-through tomorrow, with Lindsay Duncan as Adelaide. Fantastic piece of casting! She's one of the finest actors working in the UK.

FROM: BENJAMIN COOK TO: RUSSELL T DAVIES, WEDNESDAY 18 FEBRUARY 2009 13:17:34 GMT

RE: CARDIFF

It's 18 February. We've been at this Great Correspondence lark for TWO BLOODY YEARS! Can you believe it? To the day! Whole races have evolved under the sea in that time. Back then, Tony Blair was Prime Minister, Matt Smith was in short trousers, Russell Brand was allowed on the BBC, and Penny Carter was set to be the Tenth Doctor's companion. No one had even heard of iPhones, Adipose or Cyber-Strawberry flavoured Frubes. Where *has* the time gone?

How was the 4.16 read-through?

FROM: RUSSELL T DAVIES TO: BENJAMIN COOK, WEDNESDAY 18 FEBRUARY 2009 23:51:39 GMT

RE: CARDIFF

The read-through was simply magnificent. David is raising his game up, and up, and up. And it was kind of stratospheric to begin with. Lindsay Duncan was marvellous, and she was matched every inch of the way by the Great Man. David is so wild and unpredictable, like a Doctor that you've never seen before. You can just see him revving up to go out in style. It got the best round of applause I've ever heard a script get, but that was for David, really.

FROM: RUSSELL T DAVIES TO: BENJAMIN COOK, THURSDAY 19 FEBRUARY 2009 23:43:44 GMT

DALEKS

Tonight, I spent a long time wondering – I've been wondering for a fortnight now – whether to bring back the Daleks in 4.18. And I decided...

YES!!!

I bloody love Daleks. The danger of 4.18 is that villainous Time Lords amount to... well, a bunch of old bastards in cloaks. If you're eight years old, you don't want to be told that these Time Lords have turned bad; you want to *see* it. So, what could be better than a Time Lord-Dalek alliance? The final twist of the Time War, which meant that the Doctor had to destroy them all.

So. Good. They're in. I did run it past Julie, just to see her reaction. If she'd said, 'Oh, not again,' I don't think I'd have done it. But she said, 'Oh, you've got to!' Besides, if we're talking about a Time War (which we are), in which the Daleks fought the Time Lords (which we've been banging on about for four series now), you'd be so disappointed if the Daleks didn't actually turn up.

I really had better start writing it, hadn't I? Imagine if David's final episode is a disappointment. It's terrifying, Ben! But I *have* to bloody start. Soon. Not tonight. Soon.

FROM: BENJAMIN COOK TO: RUSSELL T DAVIES, FRIDAY 20 FEBRUARY 2009 01:43:03 GMT

RE: DALEKS

Isn't there a danger that you're overusing the Daleks? They've appeared in three out of your four series finales. Do you really need them again? Then again, I suppose everyone loves Daleks...

FROM: RUSSELL T DAVIES TO: BENJAMIN COOK, FRIDAY 20 FEBRUARY 2009 12:47:10 GMT

RE: DALEKS

Bollocks. Shit. Damn. Ohhh shit.

Steven is using the Daleks in Series Five.

OH, BOLLOCKS!!!

THE END OF ~~TIME~~ DALEKS

This e-mail exchange between Steven Moffat and Russell discusses the possible use of the Daleks in the Tenth Doctor's final episode...

FROM: RUSSELL T DAVIES TO: STEVEN MOFFAT, FRIDAY 20 FEBRUARY 2009 12:14:32 GMT

4.18

Look at me, facing MY LAST SCRIPT! Oh, the laughter. Yet, why does it still feel like an enormous mountain to climb? Every time?

Now, listen. I need the Daleks, I think. Does that f*** your plans? Can I have them in 4.18? Thing is, I've lumbered myself with all that stuff I told you about – Gallifrey! Time Lords! Evil Time Lords! But the problem with the Time Lords, as we well know, is that they're a bunch of men in cloaks. So, a Time Lord-Dalek alliance would spice things up a bit.

But that might interfere with your plans, and you're the boss. What do you think?

FROM: STEVEN MOFFAT TO: RUSSELL T DAVIES, FRIDAY 20 FEBRUARY 2009 12:29:24 GMT

RE: 4.18

Hello, right, yes!

Actually, we *do* have Daleks. Sorry, I really thought you knew that. Erm, I dunno, does it matter? Would kids really complain? Um, um …

I suppose, hand on my heart, I'd *rather* it was the Daleks' first appearance in a while, just to give us a boost after they've all seen what the New Guy looks like. But this is me thinking like an adult. Would my boys really mind?

We don't have Davros, if that helps.

Still thinking, hang on…

FROM: BENJAMIN COOK TO: RUSSELL T DAVIES, FRIDAY 20 FEBRUARY 2009 14:58:12 GMT

RE: DALEKS

I really don't see this as a setback. Honestly, I think the finale will work better without Daleks. You've done Daleks. Lots of times. Lots of Daleks. They're fun, and ruthless, and scary, and brilliant, but they've popped up at the end of every one of your series, except the third – and that featured the Master! Your final script shouldn't feel like a Greatest Hits package. It shouldn't feel like a Best Of. It should feel fresh and imaginative. Without the Daleks, you're allowing the script to breathe. That, I think, is why it feels different this time. The writing, I mean. That's good. The Daleks would suffocate, and upstage, and you simply don't need them… do you?

FROM: RUSSELL T DAVIES TO: BENJAMIN COOK, TUESDAY 24 FEBRUARY 2009 11:21:20 GMT

RE: DALEKS

It's 11.20am. For the record, I just opened a new file, called it '4.18', and started writing. MY LAST SCRIPT!

But no Daleks. I backed down. That was the only and instant option. Steven didn't even kick up a fuss, which was really kind. He was trying to make it work. But I don't think using the Daleks would have been fair on him. New Doctor, old Daleks, that's brilliant. You can't have seen the metal bastards just a few months earlier. It would completely devalue the impact of that launch. I'm just pissed off because I wasted time thinking about them, and weaving them in. It was a lot better than it sounded in my quick e-mails to you. I'd really given it some work, to make it different. They weren't just Daleks beetling about, squawking and killing. It was a Dalek Parliament, with a Dalek Minister – wise, whispery, and clever – entering into a political alliance with the Time Lords. Daleks as politicians. It was brilliant. It showed how low the Time Lords had fallen, to enter a treaty with them.

Anyway. Dead now.

FROM: RUSSELL T DAVIES TO: BENJAMIN COOK, WEDNESDAY 25 FEBRUARY 2009 00:54:07 GMT

4.18

Here we go, the first nine pages of 4.18. Not bad for one day. But I bloody hate this stage. You can never tell what to dwell on, how much setting-up is needed, what needs saying in what order. I thought the Doctor would have escaped from Naismith's mansion by Page 10. That was my rough plan. But I'm on Page 9, and it's still ages away. The China stuff is cut-able, I suppose, but it's a great image. Very China. And very Master...

    5. INT. NAISMITH'S HALL - DAY[1]

    CLOSE-UPS on STRAPS, being tightened.

    BUCKLES, clicked into place.

    ROPES, being tied tight.

    REVEAL THE DOCTOR. Now bound on to the upright Hannibal Lecter-
    trolley. Wide-eyed, helpless, with the leather strap across his
    mouth. THE MASTER leaning in.

                          THE MASTER
          Now, if you'll excuse me. I've got a planet to run.

---

1 Scenes 5 to 12 – which immediately follow 4.18's opening scenes of the Time Lords on Gallifrey discussing the whereabouts of the Doctor and the Master – depict the Master's conquest of the human race, but were heavily trimmed by the shooting-script stage. The sequence set in China was cut almost completely.

He walks away…

But the MR DANES-MASTER steps into his place.

> DANES-MASTER
> I've got all the time in the world!

CUT TO:

6. INT. THE GATE ROOM - DAY

THE MASTER strides in -

> THE MASTER
> Right then, what have we got?!

FX: ALL IN THE ROOM turn to face him - THREE TECHNICIAN-MASTERS, NAISMITH-MASTER, ABIGAIL-MASTER. With THREE VISORED GUARDS on duty, same height & build as the Master. NB, when not an FX shot, everyone on singles.

The Master now picks up slight traits of his originals, i.e., his Naismith is a bit grandiose, his Mr Danes is a bit subservient, his Abigail is… not feminine, but flirty.

> NAISMITH-MASTER
> Everything's quiet. As it would be, on a world without dissent!

> ABIGAIL-MASTER
> Six billion, seven hundred and twenty-seven million, nine hundred and forty-nine thousand, three hundred and thirty-eight versions of us, all awaiting orders!

> THE MASTER
> Yeah, much as I like looking at myself, I think you can get out of that dress.

> ABIGAIL-MASTER
> Is that an invitation?

> THE MASTER
> Now that would be different. And brilliant. But later!

> ABIGAIL-MASTER
> I'm a psychological minefield.

FX: ABIGAIL-MASTER walks out, passing TECHNICIAN-MASTERS.

> THE MASTER
> (looks up at CCTV)
> So! Is he watching?

SCENE CONTINUES, INTERCUT WITH SC.7-12 -

                                                    CUT TO:

7. INT. NAISMITH'S HALL - DAY

MR DANES-MASTER with THE DOCTOR, a GUARD now putting a widescreen
TV in place, with CCTV & audio of the Gate Room.

                    DANES-MASTER
    There'd be no point if he wasn't. Take a look at this,
    Doctor. The whole world pulling together!

                        WILF
    Let him go! You monster!

REVEAL WILF, tied to a chair; a great distance away from the
Doctor. They're being kept apart.

                    DANES-MASTER
                    (to the screen)
    His dad's still kicking up a fuss.

                        WILF
    I'd be proud if I was!

                    DANES-MASTER
    Hush now. Listen to your Master.

CUT TO the Doctor throughout sc.7-12. Trapped, staring,
speechless. As the world goes to hell.

CUT TO the Gate Room, the Master turning to a wall-screen -

                    THE MASTER
    Right then! Who have we got out there? Report!

                                                    CUT TO:

8. INT. WHITE HOUSE PRESS ROOM - DAY

THE PRESIDENT-MASTER to CAMERA, American accent:

                    PRESIDENT-MASTER
    This is Washington! As President of the United States,
    it's my honour and privilege to transfer the -

                    THE MASTER
    No, don't do the accent, no.

                    PRESIDENT-MASTER
    No. Sorry. So, I can transfer all United Nations protocols

to you, immediately, putting you in charge of all the Earth's defences.

> THE MASTER
> Excellent. And New York?

> CUT TO:

9. INT. UNIT HQ, NEW YORK - DAY

GENERAL-MASTER - i.e., formerly a UNIT General - to CAMERA:

> GENERAL-MASTER
> Yes sir, UNIT HQ reporting - and this place has been gathering alien technology way beyond the United Nations, we're locked and loaded!

FX: CUT TO REVERSE, FOUR DIFFERENT OPERATIVE-MASTERS sitting at workstations. After the WIDE SHOT, then cutting between them:

> OPERATIVE-MASTER #1
> We've got Compound Lasers, salvaged from the Sontaran fleet -

> OPERATIVE-MASTER #2
> - biological weapons from Antilles Major and Minor -

> OPERATIVE-MASTER #3
> - and Bitterswipe Plasma guns, rescued from a Draconian Dart -

The Master turns to the CCTV, addressing the Doctor:

> THE MASTER
> No wonder you love this place. A world full of weapons! Are you so proud of these Humans now, Doctor?
> (the Doctor gagged)
> Nothing to say?

> DANES-MASTER
> Ohh, that's his weapon. Words that can bring down governments and cause the stars to shine. But not any more.

The Doctor just staring. Furious.

CUT TO sc.7, Gate Room, NAISMITH-MASTER manning a desk:

> NAISMITH-MASTER
> Excuse me, I've got a priority call. Beijing, China.

On screen -

> CUT TO:

10. INT. CHINESE MILITARY COMMAND - NIGHT

The CHINA-MASTER to CAMERA; this one's manic and wired.

                    CHINA-MASTER
     Reporting in, sir! This is the Central Military Commission
     of the People's Liberation Army, sir!

                    THE MASTER
     And what's the priority?

                    CHINA-MASTER
     Just… the world's largest standing army, sir! Over two
     million soldiers, and all of them us!

                    THE MASTER
     I know, what's your point?

                    CHINA-MASTER
     Just wanted you to see it, sir! It's magnificent - look,
     look, look - I've gathered them on parade, sir!

CAMERA going handheld, as China-Master goes to the window. He's
on the second floor, indicates down, outside -

                                                  CUT TO:

11. EXT. PARADE GROUND - NIGHT

FX: huge stretch of tarmac, filled with the MASTER-ARMY. IDENTICAL
MASTER-SOLDIERS, all in Chinese army uniform.

The CHINA-MASTER looking down from his window:

                    CHINA-MASTER
     Preseeeent arms!

FX: THE MASTER-ARMY presents arms, all in unison.

                    CHINA-MASTER (CONT'D)
     And salute your Master!

FX: THE MASTER-ARMY salutes, in unison.

                                                  CUT TO:

12. INT. CHINESE MILITARY COMMAND - NIGHT

CAMERA swings round to CHINA-MASTER, grinning like a kid.

                    CHINA-MASTER
     Isn't that just fantastic?!

```
                        THE MASTER
Forgive  me  for  saying  it,  but…  you  seem  to  be  rather
excitable.

                       CHINA-MASTER
Oh  yes!  I  think  this  one  was  self-medicating,  sir!  Bit
too much!

                        THE MASTER
I  haven't  got  room  for  excitable.  Best  if  you  just  shoot
yourself.
```

The Doctor watching, horrified, *mmmmmmmmm*, no!

```
                       CHINA-MASTER
Yes sir, now sir?

                        THE MASTER
If you could.

                       CHINA-MASTER
Consider it done, sir!
```

On the Doctor, *mmm*, *mmm*, *mmm* - as offstage -

Bang!

His despair.

Wilf lowers his head, groans. Ashamed.

Having a file that says '4.18' is an enormous comfort. It will be better, waking up tomorrow morning, knowing that at least some of it exists. That's why idiots say that rewriting is harder than writing. Nothing is worse than all those blank pages, staring at you. They really do stare. They have a gimlet eye. I love that phrase, gimlet eye.

But just as I get started, I'm thwarted – because I'm in Upper Boat tomorrow, for the 4.17 Tone Meeting. That's when I discover that 4.18 has 27 pence left in its budget. But they did a test of the 4.16 Water Monsters on set today, and both Julie and Nikki phoned me to say that it's the Best Monster Ever. They were so excited! So, that's good.

P.S. Apparently, David had dinner with Peter Davison and Matt Smith at Steven's house the other day! Wow! Blimey. Etc.

FROM: BENJAMIN COOK TO: RUSSELL T DAVIES, WEDNESDAY 25 FEBRUARY 2009 13:21:53 GMT

RE: 4.18

Thrilling to see the Time Lords back. (Dull bastards? Hardly!) Do you feel that thrill? Or is it a dark pit of despair? Again?

FROM: RUSSELL T DAVIES TO: BENJAMIN COOK, WEDNESDAY 25 FEBRUARY 2009 18:45:32 GMT

RE: 4.18

I'd thought the Time Lords would be thrilling, but they're so hard to write, sat there in the black void, arguing away. That's why I got rid of them when I brought back the show – they spout bollocks. I tried loosening up the language, making them more real, but that made it worse. They became a bunch of chumps in posh robes, sounding glib. It reduced the whole status of the Time War. So, they're back to 'My Lord' and all that bollocks.

Great Tone Meeting today. The tone words for 4.17 were... 'the best'. Make it the best. Ever! Ha! But I must have talked for five hours solid, so to hell with work tonight. I'm going to watch TV instead. Plus, I thought it was Thursday all day, when it's Wednesday, so I feel I've been given an extra day. (I really believe that.)

FROM: BENJAMIN COOK TO: RUSSELL T DAVIES , WEDNESDAY 25 FEBRUARY 2009 19:27:45 GMT

RE: 4.18

If Andy casts a proper, heavyweight thesp or two in those Time Lord roles, with the posh robes, and the beards, and the 'My lord', it will all come together. Time Lords are supposed to be like that. That's why the Doctor ran away. Don't you think?

P.S. A five-hour Tone Meeting? You're going to miss them. No other show will ever do Tone Meetings quite like this one!

FROM: RUSSELL T DAVIES TO: BENJAMIN COOK, WEDNESDAY 25 FEBRUARY 2009 19:55:00 GMT

RE: 4.18

They're filming in 4.16's Bio-Dome tonight, actually the Great Glasshouse at Wales' National Botanic Garden.[2] It's hilarious. They switch the lights on at night, and the birds wake up. It's a cacophony! Post-sync nightmare! I've just had to add explain-the-birds-dialogue – 'You've got birds!' – and e-mail it to them, top speed, while they were rehearsing the actual scene!

FROM: BENJAMIN COOK TO: RUSSELL T DAVIES, THURSDAY 26 FEBRUARY 2009 15:14:55 GMT

RE: 4.18

How are things on Gallifrey today?

FROM: RUSSELL T DAVIES TO: BENJAMIN COOK, THURSDAY 26 FEBRUARY 2009 15:14:55 GMT

RE: 4.18

Gallifrey is slow and difficult. I keep thinking I should stop, and pick it up again tonight, but they've started prep, so I must soldier on.

---

2 The Bio-Dome on Bowie Base One is, in effect, a huge greenhouse full of lush vegetation, with walkways running between the plants.

FROM: RUSSELL T DAVIES TO: BENJAMIN COOK, FRIDAY 27 FEBRUARY 2009 02:23:16 GMT

RE: 4.18

More 4.18! I was going to write a proper e-mail to go with this – my thoughts! – but I've gone over my cigarette limit, and have to stop. But I will tomorrow, I promise.

FROM: RUSSELL T DAVIES TO: BENJAMIN COOK, FRIDAY 27 FEBRUARY 2009 12:33:54 GMT

RE: 4.18

Can I say how bloody astonished I am that I'm on the last script, and haven't had a cold or a bad back? Let alone chicken pox! I'm even hesitant about typing that out to you, because it's tempting fate. You know how you work hard, have a holiday, and then instantly get a cold? I reckon I'm going to finish 4.18, and get smallpox, and leukaemia, and CJD, and never play the piano again. I actually think I've got a cold, but I'm not letting myself have it. Is that possible? The other day, I fell asleep watching TV. When I woke up, I had a cold. A proper cold – throat and nose all bunged up. When I get a cold, it goes straight to my ears, and that's what I had, like knives going right into my head. I walked around the flat going, 'No, no, no, no, no, I CAN'T!' And then I went to bed, for two hours, and woke up… and it had gone. Completely gone. But that's bollocks. You can't actually do that, can you? Maybe it was a Phantom Cold. Yes. I've invented the Phantom Cold.

Anyway, this script is puzzling me. It's as though it's coming out of nowhere. Sometimes – mysticism alert! – it feels like I'm just transcribing it. I sit down to write, and start typing, and things come out that I was never expecting. Like that Donna sequence, with the metacrisis halo.[3] I thought of that ages ago, do you remember? I got all excited about having lots more Donna, and imagined that scene… then discarded it. Completely discarded it. I had a much smaller sequence in mind for 4.18, just to park Donna and get on with the main plot. (The Doctor was going to get on the phone, and just say one word to her – 'Sleep' – like a post-hypnotic command, to knock her out and save her). And then I sat down yesterday, and… well, I just typed out the metacrisis halo stuff. I know I always sit here with a thousand possibilities jostling for space, and I sort of surf them as I type, but that just downloaded. It was just there. It was almost easy. Even if it is eating up FX! But I'll worry about that later. It felt improvised, yet correct at the same time. (I'm not describing this very well. Maybe it's impossible to describe. I'm trying to describe writing, really.)

And you know that long conversation between the Doctor and the Master, in Naismith's mansion?[4] I had something completely different in mind. There was this

---

3 As Donna begins to remember her adventures with the Doctor ('My head! It's getting hotter, and hotter, and hotter –!'), a halo of golden energy – like the metacrisis energy that burns in her eyes in 4.13 – blasts out of her head, hitting the Masters that are chasing her, knocking them out cold. Donna is left dazed ('But what did I...?'), before falling to the ground herself, unconscious but alive. 'But really,' the Doctor tells the Master, 'did you think I'd leave my best friend without a defence mechanism?'

4 The Master urges the Doctor, in vain, to reveal the whereabouts of the TARDIS (in fact, it's parked in Naismith's stables), while the Doctor tries to persuade the Master to travel the universe with him – 'partners in time'. Of course, the Master declines.

terrific sequence where the Doctor uses his wise words to tempt the Danes-Master into rebelling against the actual Master. That's why it's the Danes-Master in the room, because he's a servant. 'You're the Master, just as much as he is. Why should you serve anyone?' The Doctor is trying to persuade all the different bits of the Master's subconscious to start fighting each other. Divide and conquer, etc. And it looks like it's going to work, like the Danes-Master is tempted... until he just bursts out laughing. Never tempted at all. 'Unfortunately for you, I think I'm wonderful!' But then none of that appeared. I mean, that often happens, I change my mind while writing... but why does this feel different?

Maybe all these options have been there for so long now that I'm cherry-picking, without being so aware of the process. But it's quite disconcerting, because I don't know what I think of the script. This script feels like a stranger. I even feel quite dispassionate about it. Not uninterested, though. It's filling my head from the moment I wake up. I can't concentrate on anything else. At the same time, look at the speed. Look how much I've done in two days! Normally, that sort of speed would leave me exhausted, and I'm a bit tired, but not knackered, not at all. It's actually physically different. (Until the smallpox and leukaemia.)

Maybe it's because I know it's my last episode. Sometimes, just for a vivid five minutes or so, I let myself imagine a few days' time – maybe a week, or ten days – when I will have finished. I keep thinking of going for a coffee in the Bay. A coffee, at Coffee Mania, like I do every morning, but without this mountain of work bearing down on me. I'm looking forward to that coffee with absolute joy. It's getting closer. It's going to be real. It feels enormous. Bloody enormous.

And 'Coffee Mania' is such a good name.

FROM: BENJAMIN COOK TO: RUSSELL T DAVIES, FRIDAY 27 FEBRUARY 2009 18:10:04 GMT

RE: 4.18

Perhaps someone up there thinks you deserve to enjoy writing this script? (No, that's silly. There is no one 'up there'. Except Julie, maybe. Is she still holed up in Upper Boat's attic?) But where are the usual problems? Should we invent some? To make *The Writer's Tale 2* more interesting? Ha ha. No, stay healthy and creative, Russell. Maybe it suits you. In LA, you'll be like this all the time.

FROM: RUSSELL T DAVIES TO: BENJAMIN COOK, FRIDAY 27 FEBRUARY 2009 19:22:24 GMT

RE: 4.18

>>But where are the usual problems? Should we invent some?<<

You had to go and say it! We watched the 4.16 rushes with the Water Monsters today. T-E-R-R-I-F-Y-I-N-G! Truly, horribly terrifying. For the first time ever on this show, I thought, 'That's too much.' I was watching the rushes and flinching. (Mind you, it's bloody brilliant.) But they're zombies. They're out-and-out zombies. *(cont p616)*

INT. HESPERUS

Russell's first draft of *The End of Time* Part Two features this extended version of the scene in which the Doctor, Wilf, Addams and Rossiter hide from the Master aboard the *Hesperus*, having teleported there from Naismith's mansion. This scene, written on 28 February 2009, was almost entirely cut from the final shooting script...

<u>66. INT. HESPERUS, FLIGHT DECK - DAY</u>

THE DOCTOR, WILF, ADDAMS & ROSSITER still tense, waiting in the dark. In whispers:

> THE DOCTOR
> I think we're safe.

> WILF
> He could still be listening.

> THE DOCTOR
> He's only got radar. We don't actually need to whisper.

> WILF
> (still whispering)
> I can stop, then?

> THE DOCTOR
> (still whispering)
> Yes you can.

They relax, Rossiter & Addams hurrying to inspect controls.

> WILF
> But we're still in space! Outer space! I don't like it, makes my knees go all shivery.

> ROSSITER
> You're not going anywhere else, mate - the teleport's blown, and the engines are fried! All we've got is auxiliary lights -

He presses a switch, LOW-LEVEL LIGHTING comes up.

> ROSSITER (CONT'D)
> - but that's your lot! Everything else is kaput, we can't move!

ADDAMS

Thanks to you. You idiot!

THE DOCTOR

Nice to meet you too.

ADDAMS

So you're not Human, right?

THE DOCTOR

Nope. Well, I was, back in 1999 for a couple of days, but
that was like catching a 48-hour bug, I got over it.[1]

ADDAMS

And you're the same species as that man, the Saxon-
thing?

WILF

They're Time Lords!

ADDAMS

Never heard of them. But tell me then, Mr Time Lord, since
you're so clever, what do we do next?

THE DOCTOR

...I don't know.

ADDAMS

No, but, you've gotta have reinforcements, what is there?
Police, Time Lordy police?

ROSSITER

A back-up squad?

ADDAMS

Special ops?

ROSSITER

An army?

THE DOCTOR

Nope.

ROSSITER

Come on though, you've gotta have something, I dunno,
weapons? Any sort of gun, or laser, some sort of anti-
Saxon device?

1 In the 1996 *Doctor Who* TV Movie, set in San Francisco on New Year's Eve 1999, it is stated that the Doctor is half-human,
on his mother's side. Thereafter, this is never mentioned in the series again.

                         THE DOCTOR
No.

                            WILF
He's got a screwdriver.

                          ROSSITER
Oh brilliant! He can loosen screws! And then he can tighten
them!

                          ADDAMS
Okay, so who's your boss? There's gotta be a higher
authority, who's in charge? Who can I talk to?

                         THE DOCTOR
Just me.

                          ADDAMS
You mean there's nothing? No one? Just you?! A major
criminal on the loose, an entire population transplanted,
a knackered spaceship, and all we've got is a man in a suit
with a screwdriver? Who's got no idea what to do??!

                         THE DOCTOR
That's about it.

                          ADDAMS
Then what are you even doing here? What's the point? What
the hell is the point of you?!

And she walks way, slams a piece of broken-computer-metal to the
floor, genuinely furious.

Silence.

Then just Wilf and the Doctor, quiet. Wilf so trusting:

                            WILF
But you've got something, haven't you? Some sort of
plan.
                    (the Doctor just looks at him)
Clever little idea? Little trick up your sleeve? Good old
bit of Doctor flim-flam, sort of thing?
                        (silence)
Oh blimey.

We've got to do emergency tests on camera tomorrow, to see if we can lessen it (take the contact lenses out, I reckon – dead eyes are the scariest thing), so that's wasted this afternoon, and I'll have to go on set tomorrow. My writing time is disappearing.

I've been thrown right out of the script today, just as I was getting a good head of steam. It's funny, you saying, 'Perhaps someone up there thinks you deserve to enjoy writing this script?' Because even I have thought that, ridiculous though it is. And I'm as atheist as… well, as Richard Dawkins. (Is *anyone* as atheist as Richard Dawkins?)

FROM: RUSSELL T DAVIES TO: BENJAMIN COOK, SATURDAY 28 FEBRUARY 2009 01:41:55 GMT

RE: 4.18

That'll teach me. As soon as I told you that I wasn't feeling tired, and was rattling through this script… I felt tired, and stopped rattling. Bollocks. So, I'm only sending you a little bit more tonight, and it's standard running-about stuff. It's a pain getting everything into the right place, setting it up for the climax… so it's all a bit dry. But I like Addams and Rossiter.[5] They're a godsend in such a dark episode. Again, I didn't plan that. They just started being funny. But I suppose that stems from the moment I made them Bannakaffalatta-like. You can hardly be serious if you look like a cactus.

That thing you said last Friday about the 'Greatest Hits' package is lingering, because, Daleks or no Daleks, this feels a little bit like 'Russell's Greatest Hits' (or 'Greatest Mistakes'). Battered old spaceship. Funny aliens. A teleport escape. The Master. A Lazarus/Torchwood technology/experiment room… hmm, maybe not. Maybe that's simply the bread and butter of *Doctor Who*. Maybe every story looks the same when you reduce it to a list. I don't know.

They're filming Adelaide's death on location tonight. It's a bastard, because there are 30 or so fans watching the filming, and the plot details in that scene are crucial. Everyone has been primed not to shout 'Bang!' when Adelaide's gun goes off, just 'Now!' or something so that it's not too clear. I hope that works. But I hate wasting time on fan defences. Screw 'em.

FROM: RUSSELL T DAVIES TO: BENJAMIN COOK, SUNDAY 1 MARCH 2009 01:51:28 GMT

RE: 4.18

The problem with Time Lords is not only do they spout nonsense, but they spout it at each other. That's why I needed the Dalek ambassadors and the Dalek Minister, so that the Time Lord President would have someone to talk to.[6] As things stand, he's stuck talking to the Chancellor, when *they both know what's going on*! But what they're doing is so complicated, so bloody complicated, so over-complicated, that they've got to talk

5 In *Doctor Who* 4.17, two of Naismith's technicians, Addams ('35, smart, cool' – aged 30 in subsequent drafts) and Rossiter turn out to be human camouflages for Vinvocci, alien salvagers with green, spiky faces. In 4.18, they help the Doctor and Wilf escape Naismith's mansion by teleporting to their spaceship, the Hesperus, in orbit a hundred thousand miles above the Earth.
6 In *Doctor Who* 4.18, the Narrator of 4.17 is revealed to be the Time Lord President.

us through each layer of the plot. Even now, I don't know if I'm explaining enough in the script. I'm simplifying as I go along. The diamond falling to Earth was originally a massive and complicated sequence, which was rather beautiful, even sort of romantic and mythic, but the page count is getting terrifying, and the Doctor still hasn't realised who the enemy really is.[7]

Rubbish day all round, really. I watched the rushes from yesterday – it's Adelaide in the snow, on Earth, shooting herself, and the Ood appearing. A vital scene, pivotal, radical… and it's rushed, because the shoot was so complicated, what with snow machines and robots, etc. You end up with the Doctor seeing the Ood by turning to his right. I mean, the Ood sends its projection all the way across space and time… and misses slightly, ending up to the Doctor's right! I think we need to do pick-ups on the Doctor's reaction. The whole thing is a bit mistimed. But it's hell to reshoot, because it's snow, and night, and the schedule is jam-packed. We will, though. At least some of it. Julie will make it happen!

And then I went out to set, to tone down the Water People – just took the contact lenses out, much better – but some people were really cynical about me calming down the monsters, like I was bowing to pressure, fearing bad press, and letting the show down. It's true that the BBC is so scared these days, and that everyone is censoring everything and being timid – but that's not why I was bloody well there! *I* think those monsters are wrong. In my heart. With all of my heart. I think children would be petrified – not scared, but sick with fear and dread. That's so wrong. It's my job, my moral responsibility, to step in. Frankly, I trust my own judgement. Sometimes in this job, you have to stand there with a thousand people telling you that you're wrong, and still believe that you're right. But then you get treated like a bloody coward.

Anyway, I'm falling way behind on 4.18. The page count is seriously adrift. I think about ten pages of those first 25 will have to go. TEN!!! All that speed, energy, and excitement – for bloody nothing! And God knows when it's going to be complete. Or even any good.

Ah well. Etc! Tra la la. It's all funny in the end.

FROM: BENJAMIN COOK TO: RUSSELL T DAVIES, SUNDAY 1 MARCH 2009 21:00:53 GMT

RE: 4.18

I hope you're okay. Is there any point in reminding you that writing is almost *always* like this? Especially these big episodes. That's not much help, is it? I feel a bit useless. I love what you're writing at the moment, but don't know whether saying so makes

---

7 The Time Lords and Gallifrey are trapped (or 'Timelocked', that is sealed as though in a bubble) beyond time and space, on the edge of the Time War, in its final day. To escape, before they die, they send a signal to the Master, a simple signal of four beats, transmitted back through time and implanted in his mind as a child. 'We need something to make the contact physical,' says the Lord President, plucking a diamond from the end of his staff, and throwing it towards an image of the Earth. The diamond burns, and vanishes in mid air… and reappears as a meteor falling to Earth. The Master senses its signal, and retrieves the diamond – in fact a Gallifreyan 'Whitepoint Star'. If he sends back the same signal, the link becomes a pathway for the Time Lords to follow, thereby resurrecting themselves and Gallifrey.

much difference. Yes, okay, it's over-length, but only a few days ago you were telling me that 'idiots say that rewriting is harder than writing'...

FROM: RUSSELL T DAVIES TO: BENJAMIN COOK, SUNDAY 1 MARCH 2009 22:17:23 GMT
RE: 4.18
Fear not, I'm okay. You're so right, of course. It *is* like this every time. But it always feels new. I suppose that's because the scripts are new, each time, so it's a brand new set of problems – but the same old misery. I think that long, dark night burnt it out of me, for now. I woke up full of ideas and resolve. Long way to go, but... there is light! I wrote one of the best scenes ever today, between the Doctor and Wilf, on the *Hesperus*, as they look out over Earth.

> WILF
> Always dreamt of seeing a view like this. I'm an astronaut!
> It's dawn over England, look.
>   (pause)
> My wife's buried down there. I might never visit her
> again, now.
>   (pause)
> D'you think he changed them? In their graves?

The Doctor appalled, stops working. Looks at the view.

> THE DOCTOR
> I'm sorry.

> WILF
> Not your fault.

> THE DOCTOR
> Isn't it?

Pause. Then, of the view, indicating the Mediterranean:

> WILF
> 1948, I was over there. End of the Mandate in Palestine.
> Private Mott! Skinny little idiot, I was. Stood on this
> rooftop, middle of a skirmish, like a blizzard, all these
> bullets in the air. World gone mad.
>   (smiles)
> Ah, you don't want to listen to an old man's tales.

> THE DOCTOR
> I'm older than you.

> WILF
> Get away.

```
                        THE DOCTOR
          I'm nine hundred and six.


                           WILF
          Really, though?


                        THE DOCTOR
          Yep.


                           WILF
          Nine hundred years. We must look like insects to you.


                        THE DOCTOR
          I think you look like giants.
```

Those lines about what Wilf was up to in 1948 are exactly what Bernard was doing during his National Service in the Parachute Regiment! I phoned him up, and he told me all that stuff. Imagine him, young Bernard, that extraordinary life ahead of him. I'm sure he said that it was actually *in* a blizzard. Well, he definitely did, because I said how remarkable that was. Then I did some research that said it would never snow in Palestine at that time of year... but I bet it did, that year! I sort of didn't want to challenge him on any details, so the image became a blizzard of bullets, which is lovely – and terrifying. I'm rather pleased with that.

FROM: RUSSELL T DAVIES TO: BENJAMIN COOK, MONDAY 2 MARCH 2009 01:39:19 GMT

RE: 4.18

I went back this morning and cut a lot out of the opening to 4.18. The American accents gag, the China-Master shooting himself... some nice stuff in there, but just delays, really. More importantly, I'd gone down an odd little tangent, at the top of the episode, where I had the Danes-Master getting all the crucial scenes with the Doctor. Funny, but he doesn't feel like the *real* Master, so I've swapped that around. It feels right, now. I wonder why I did that.

Ah, I know. I've just remembered, and come back from the bottom of this e-mail to explain. It was because I had that subplot about the Doctor tempting the subservient Danes-Master, trying to get him to rebel. Once that had gone, I'd no need for the Danes-Master, really. (And I think I liked my original description of Danes as 'cool, handsome, cruel', and fancied him, bizarrely. That's so embarrassingly true.)

Also, I put Donna's stuff in an alleyway, not outside her house. Remember when I first described that scene to you, ages ago, and I set it in an alley? She was cornered in an alley, remember? When I came to write it, I thought the street outside her house would be scarier. But I was wrong. It feels odd, leaving her unconscious in an open street. She's not parked enough. More importantly, she feels like she's moved now, since 4.17. That's vital. Otherwise, she spends the first ten pages of 4.18 offstage, having moved all of ten yards! Trust your instincts. If you imagine a scene in an alley, then that's where it should be. Probably.

I've got to stop now, because the whole story is about to go mental, and I haven't got the energy for that tonight. But I'm happier! It's still five or six pages too long, but I can monitor that. The line about why the Doctor was human back in 1999 is making me hoot, but that will be the first casualty. It's so indulgent – and yet true, in my opinion.

FROM: RUSSELL T DAVIES TO: BENJAMIN COOK, MONDAY 2 MARCH 2009 16:14:38 GMT

RE: 4.18

I'm quite good at trimming as I go along, but the costs of this episode are going through the roof – and it's all so in-built into the story, I can't shift much. Very worried. Very, very, very. Two plans of action. 1) I cut the whole multi-Master thing, so only his *mind* is inside every human being. They are him, but don't look like him. Not much of a cliffhanger to 4.17, but there you go. (It still has the Time Lords returning, I suppose). Or 2) I offer to pay for some of these FX myself. No, really. I've heard of writers doing that before, when budgets don't allow enough extras or whatever. (Although, I'm not sure it's allowed at the BBC; only with independents.) I could put some of my fee back into the show. It would make me happy – which is money well spent, in my book. Hmm. We shall see. For now, I'll just carry on, I suppose.

I'm so close to the end. That blissful Coffee Mania morning is getting closer, and closer, and closer. Must not get run over!

FROM: BENJAMIN COOK TO: RUSSELL T DAVIES, MONDAY 2 MARCH 2009 16:21:04 GMT

RE: 4.18

>>Must not get run over!<<

Which would be good advice on most days, actually.

FROM: RUSSELL T DAVIES TO: BENJAMIN COOK, TUESDAY 3 MARCH 2009 18:08:31 GMT

RE: 4.18

I just did 15 pages in one afternoon. Not bad. Unless the pages themselves are bad. Which would then be very bad. I've still got about 15 pages to go, on a script that should probably be 60-or-so pages long. Ah well.

FROM: BENJAMIN COOK TO: RUSSELL T DAVIES, TUESDAY 3 MARCH 2009 18:41:28 GMT

RE: 4.18

Fantastic stuff! The Doctor with a revolver![8] Shocking and brilliant. And you've f****d

---

8 Aboard the *Hesperus*, Wilf offers the Doctor his old Second World War service revolver. 'The Master is going to kill you,' says Wilf. 'Then kill him first. Don't you deserve it?' 'Ohh yeah,' replies the Doctor. 'I deserve it, absolutely! I so deserve to live. Everything I've done, the lives I've saved, the people, the planets, every single star in the sky. So where is it, then? Just once. Where's the reward?' At first, he refuses to take the gun; however, on learning of the Time Lords' plan to return, the Doctor changes his mind... culminating in a stand-off in the Gate Room between him, the Master and the Lord President.

over the Doctor, bruised and bloodied him.[9] I'm so pleased you've done that. We *never* see the Doctor like that. And now we do.

But poor Master! The Time Lords lodged the sound of drums in his mind as a kid, which he's endured for centuries and centuries, all so that he'd resurrect them one day, which he does (good Master!)… then when he asks them to take him with them, to ascend 'into glory', blah, blah, blah, which is fair enough, frankly, the Lord President turns around… and says no! What a bastard! 'You are diseased. Albeit a disease of our own creation.' What an utter, utter bastard! Cut the Master some slack, yeah? He spent Christmas on the streets. EATING TRAMPS!!! No wonder he comes over all righteous in the end, and shoots the Lord President in the face.

FROM: RUSSELL T DAVIES TO: BENJAMIN COOK, TUESDAY 3 MARCH 2009 18:44:40 GMT
RE: 4.18
Maybe I should just end it there, just before the regeneration. Tell Matt Smith I've changed my mind?! He he.

FROM: BENJAMIN COOK TO: RUSSELL T DAVIES, TUESDAY 3 MARCH 2009 18:52:19 GMT
RE: 4.18
Oh, and who is the Woman? The Woman who appears to Wilf in the church at the top of 4.17, then again on TV during the Queen's Speech ('Only you can see,' she tells Wilf. 'Only you stand at the heart of coincidence'), and again onboard the *Hesperus* ('I was lost. So very long ago')… who is she? Are you prepared to say? When she appears on TV in the Nobles' kitchen, and only Wilf can see her, she says, 'Tell the Doctor nothing of this. His life could still be saved. But only if you tell him nothing.' So, is she the Doctor's guardian angel? Is that it? Or his mother? She's a Time Lady, isn't she? 'Lost' so long ago? And she turns up in the Gate Room during the stand-off between the Doctor, the Master, and the President…

```
                    LORD PRESIDENT
     The final act of your life, is murder. But which one of
     us?

On the Doctor.

Looking at the President.

But aware, so aware, of the Master behind him.

Which one?

Which one??
```

9 The Doctor jumps from the *Hesperus* as it flies over Naismith's mansion, falling through the glass roof of the Gate Room and hitting the ground hard. He lands – cut and bruised, head swimming, suit torn – directly between the Master and the Lord President.

```
The Doctor, the agony.

The silence.

And then…

The Doctor's eyes just flick a fraction to the left.

As behind the President…

The FEMALE WEEPING TIME LORD lowers her hands.¹⁰

She looks up.

It's the WOMAN.

On the Doctor.

Recognising her. After all this time.
```

Also, will the actress, when she's been cast, whoever she is, be told the Woman's true identity? Does she need to know?

FROM: RUSSELL T DAVIES TO: BENJAMIN COOK, TUESDAY 3 MARCH 2009 19:15:54 GMT

RE: 4.18

The Woman! I like leaving it open, because then you can imagine what you want. I think the fans will say it's Romana.¹¹ Or even the Rani.¹² Some might say that it's Susan's mother, I suppose.¹³ But of course it's meant to be the Doctor's mother. That's certainly what I'll tell the production team. Euros knows it already. David, too. It sounds a bit dumb, a bit sentimental, a bit rubbish when you confirm it. But shame on me, getting embarrassed about beautiful and heartfelt things…

It could only be his mother, really. If I can't imagine a world in which our mothers are there, at the end of our lives, in our time of need, to help us, then what's the point? It'll never really happen, so I want to imagine it. I hadn't exactly planned it, though. In fact, I can remember, quite clearly, Wilf was going to enter the church in Scene 3, and fall into conversation with a couple of strangers – a housewife and a young lad – all drawn there because of their bad dreams; then they realise, to their horror, that they've all dreamt of the same thing. Spooky moment. End of scene. But as I went to write that, I sort of faltered. It didn't have enough size. The more I thought about the Tenth Doctor's departure, about David's departure, the more I needed to give it scale – not

---

10 Since the Time Lords voted to resurrect Gallifrey, two dissenters, one male, one female, have stood unmoving, with heads bowed, their hands covering their faces, a ritual gesture of shame.
11 Time Lady Romana (played by Mary Tamm, and then Lalla Ward) travelled with the Fourth Doctor from 1978 to 1981.
12   The Rani (played by Kate O'Mara) is a renegade Time Lady, an evil scientific genius, who encountered the Sixth and Seventh Doctors, once apiece, during the 1980s.
13 Susan (played by Carole Ann Ford) is the Doctor's granddaughter, and was his first on-screen companion, from 1963 to 1964.

just scale in terms of thousands of monsters, but in personal terms. The intimate stuff had to become huge. So I sat down and wrote the Woman, on the spot. Invented her there and then. Half my head doubting it, thinking, this is a bit extreme. (Is she his mother? Can she be? Really?!) The other half thinking, just keep writing and the story will make sense of it. And it has.

Equally, and at the other end of the story, I'd always known, as an instinct, that I'd need one Gallifreyan on the Doctor's side. I could never work out how to do it, but I knew that I needed someone there, at the end, to flick their eyes to one side, to tell the Doctor where to aim the revolver. I can't remember a time when that idea wasn't there. He couldn't know where to aim on his own. The Lord President intends to rip apart the Time Vortex, for the Time Lords to become creatures of consciousness alone, while creation itself will cease to be. But the Doctor has a gun. The Doctor. The Master. The Lord President. The choice. If he shoots the Master, the link with Gallifrey is broken – the pathway born from the Whitepoint Star. No more Time Lord resurrection. But the Lord President is part of that link, too. The Doctor could shoot him instead. What should he do? What. Should. He. Do?

```
The Woman stares at the Doctor. But then, her eyes flicker just
a fraction to the right. Meaning, behind the Doctor.

Meaning the Master.

And the Doctor pivots round, one last time, switches the gun to
his other hand, now aiming it right at the Master.

The Master terrified.

About to die.

The Doctor's finger on the trigger.

Tighter…

And then…

So calm:

                        THE DOCTOR
        Get out of the way.

Beat, on the Master. Realising. And he falls to the side -

Revealing the DIAMOND-COMPUTER right behind him.¹⁴

And the Doctor FIRES!
```

14 The Master has placed the Whitepoint Star diamond into the centre of an adapted computer bank – in a red space, a receptacle, surrounded by a bed of wires – to transmit the Time Lords' signal back to Gallifrey and open the pathway to Earth.

PRAC FX: THE DIAMOND-RED-SPACE EXPLODES!!

CAMERA SHAKE, going crazy! PRAC WIND BLASTS through the room - !
The Lord President, Chancellor & Time Lords in pain, battling
the wind, robes blowing - only the Male Weeping Time Lord and
the Woman standing tall -

                                                     CUT TO:

149. INT. BLACK VOID

CU THE VISIONARY, screaming into CAMERA:[15]

                        VISIONARY
    - Gallifrey falling! Gallifrey faaaalls - !

                                                     CUT TO:

150. EXT. FX SHOT. EARTH & GALLIFREY

FX: THE EARTH dwarfed, but GALLIFREY begins to FADE…

                                                     CUT TO:

151. INT. THE GATE ROOM & WHITE VOID - NIGHT

CAMERA SHAKE - WIND BLASTING, ferocious -

PRAC WHITE LIGHT beginning to flare, behind the TRIANGLE -

                        THE DOCTOR
    The link is broken! Go back into the Time War, Rassilon!
    Back into Hell!

CU LORD PRESIDENT, flinching against the wind, but still strong.
With all his strength, he lifts up his GAUNTLET:

The Doctor stands there.

Terrified. But not moving.

                        LORD PRESIDENT
    You'll die with me, Doctor.

                        THE DOCTOR
    I know.

                        LORD PRESIDENT
    Then die forever.

----

15 The Visionary ('female, 50, insane') – seen in the black void throughout *Doctor Who* 4.18 – is swathed in witch-like robes,
her face covered with henna tattoos, and she scribbles constantly on old parchments with a quill-like pen, muttering.

FX: THE GAUNTLET shines with BLUE LIGHT, softly.

CU the Doctor

Ready to die.

CU Lord President

A cruel smile.

And then, on CU Doctor -

The Master steps in front of him.

>   THE MASTER
>   Get out of the way.

FX: The Master savage, SHOOTS ARCS OF ELECTRICITY FROM HIS HANDS, SKELETONING as he does so - !

FX: The Lord President, wracked with ELECTRICITY, screaming -

CU on the Master, furious, righteous:

>   THE MASTER (CONT'D)
>   You did this to me! All of my life! *You made me!*

FX: The Master walking forward, SKELETON FACE & REAL FACE flickering, firing ARC after ARC after ARC after ARC, his final One! Two! Three! Four! -

- the Master walking into the PRAC WHITE LIGHT and losing resolution as he, the Lord President, the Time Lords DEFOCUS against the white -

The Doctor horrified, shielding his eyes -

Last to DEFOCUS is the Woman.

She smiles at him, so sadly.

Then all of them DEFOCUS into the whiteness, just shapes -

FULL-SCREEN WHITE FLARE -

>   MIX TO:

152. INT. THE GATE ROOM - NIGHT

THE DOCTOR. The White Void gone. The Gate back in place.

And he falls to his knees.

```
        Exhausted.

        Long, long silence. Then:

                            THE DOCTOR
            I'm alive.
```

Poor Doctor. Poor Woman. He needed someone to save him, in that moment, to put him back on the right path, to restore him. He's saved so many people; he needs saving this time. From himself. So the Woman became the Mother. Like, events are so extreme, the universe so violated, that she's been summoned. I hadn't thought of that when I started writing, but it fell into place. It took me 100+ pages to reach that moment, and believe it myself, but I got there.

Actually, it goes right back to the Master in *The Sound of Drums*, saying that he was 'resurrected'. That's always preyed on my mind. I think an awful lot about the Time War, actually, more than I'd ever quite realised – that it was so dark, so obscene, that the dead were walking, called back into life to fight the terrible fight. That's why I was free to bring back Rassilon. (The Lord President *is* Rassilon!) And that's why it felt natural to bring back the Doctor's mother. I don't imagine she's been alive all this time, but that, in the Time War, everyone was brought back to life. Horribly so. They've been there for a long time, in my head, all those dead people, walking.

There's a bit of Chris Rea in there, too. No, don't laugh. I think one of the scariest things ever is the prologue to 'The Road To Hell'. Before it gets all jaunty, there's an incredible, terrifying opening verse (often left out, when it's played) where he meets his dead mother on a highway, by the side of the road. I think she says something like, 'My fear for you has turned me in my grave.' Brrr! Really gets to me, that. It crept into my subconscious. It came out in the writing, all on its own.

FROM: BENJAMIN COOK TO: RUSSELL T DAVIES, TUESDAY 3 MARCH 2009 19:20:47 GMT

RE: 4.18

The Doctor's mother was inspired by Chris Rea! '*Well, she walked up to my quarterlight / And she bent down real slow / A fearful pressure paralysed me / In my shadow.*' As a way of framing something a bit scary, that can't be beaten.

FROM: RUSSELL T DAVIES TO: BENJAMIN COOK, TUESDAY 3 MARCH 2009 19:27:15 GMT

RE: 4.18

'*A fearful pressure paralysed me / In my shadow.*' Isn't that brilliant? Once heard, never forgotten. In my shadow. *In.* Blimey. I wish the song had continued like that, but the rest of it is all guitar-folky-road-movie-rock.

I'm really not sure if I'll continue tonight. I'm tired! But the thought of waking up tomorrow with no script to write is very lovely. It's so wet and windy tonight that I can't even go out for food. It's pissing down. Should I just carry on? I don't want to rush the ending. Also, bear in mind, WE WILL NEVER AFFORD THIS! NEVER! Seriously. I told Julie that I wanted to put money into the FX, but she says that's forbidden by the BBC. Bollocks. (Unless she's just saying that to stop me from spending my own money.) I think the Doctor will have to abandon the *Hesperus*, and just get the teleport working. Damn. Even when this script is done, it's far from over. That's a shame. Oh, I have to think of problems.

By the way, I cut the 1999 line. No loss! Silly reference – and kind of confusing, since most of the audience will remember the Doctor being human in *Human Nature*, rather than the 1996 TV Movie.

Hmm, I don't know what to do. TV for a bit, I think.

FROM: BENJAMIN COOK TO: RUSSELL T DAVIES, TUESDAY 3 MARCH 2009 19:33:38 GMT
RE: 4.18
Never mind TV. TV is rubbish! I think you should keep going. Yeah.

>>I told Julie that I wanted to put money into the FX, but she says that's forbidden by the BBC.<<

Is it? Really?! Now, why? Surely there's a loophole? Can't you do it without telling anyone? (No, obviously not. Definitely not. That would be bad.) Can't you donate it to BBC Worldwide, who then give it back to you? What if you were to buy £50,000 worth of merchandise? Yeah! Who'd stop you? (£50,000's worth of Frubes! Imagine! Now, that sounds like a party.) But tell Worldwide that you're only buying the goods on the condition that they give you £50,000 towards the budget. Or something. In all seriousness, if you want to donate your own money towards the budget, I can't imagine a single licence-fee-payer *objecting*? Then again, there's one bastard in every crowd…

FROM: RUSSELL T DAVIES TO: BENJAMIN COOK, TUESDAY 3 MARCH 2009 19:56:09 GMT
DIE, DOCTOR, DIE!
Miracle! It turns out that *Planet of the Dead* might actually be £30,000 under budget. Hooray for the heaven-sent Tracie Simpson! That can't all go to FX for 4.17/4.18; it would have to be spread out among departments, because everyone's budget is tight on this one, but… well, it's a start.

FROM: BENJAMIN COOK TO: RUSSELL T DAVIES, WEDNESDAY 4 MARCH 2009 00:48:10 GMT
RE: DIE, DOCTOR, DIE!
Hello! How's it going? Finished yet?

FROM: RUSSELL T DAVIES TO: BENJAMIN COOK, WEDNESDAY 4 MARCH 2009 00:50:29 GMT
DIE, DOCTOR, DIE!
You're there! Ha ha! I'm crying my eyes out here.

FROM: BENJAMIN COOK TO: RUSSELL T DAVIES , WEDNESDAY 4 MARCH 2009 01:09:13 GMT

RE: DIE, DOCTOR, DIE!

Me too. I haven't slept in like 40 hours. Long story. Stay up! I am! I'm not going to bed until you send me more 4.18 script. Probably. I'm interviewing Michelle Ryan tomorrow, but so what? This is very exciting. (Should I resurrect the old catchphrase from *The Writer's Tale 1*? 'STAY! WHERE! YOU! ARE!')

FROM: RUSSELL T DAVIES TO: BENJAMIN COOK, WEDNESDAY 4 MARCH 2009 01:17:56 GMT

RE: DIE, DOCTOR, DIE!

Okay, here's the next bit. At last, the ridiculously overcomplicated glass booths make sense...

152. INT. THE GATE ROOM - DAY

THE DOCTOR. Standing there. The White Void gone.

And he falls to his knees.

Exhausted.

Then:

                    THE DOCTOR
      I'm alive.

He looks round. His hands. His face. Legs!

               THE DOCTOR (CONT'D)
      I survived! I didn't... I'm still alive! Ohhhhhhh.

And he leans against a desk, so tired.

So happy.

So very happy.

Hold on him.

For a long time.

And then...

So quietly.

Behind him.

Tap-tap-tap-tap.

Four times.

The Doctor looks up.

Tap-tap-tap-tap.

Pause. Then again.

Tap-tap-tap-tap.

And all the joy drains out of the Doctor. All the hope. His entire future, gone. As he realises. Slowly, he turns around. Knowing already what he'll see.

WILF.[16]

Still in the glass booth. It was him; one more time, he taps lightly on the glass, *one-two-three-four*.

Lights flashing on the control panel behind Wilf. And now, slowly, bring up the sound of an ALARM, a red alert; it's been there from the top of the scene, but only now filtering into the Doctor's consciousness.

Wilf tries a little smile.

> WILF
> They've gone, then. Good-oh. If you could let me out…?

> THE DOCTOR
> Yeah.

> WILF
> This thing seems to be making a bit of a noise.

The Doctor strolls over. Quiet. Bitter.

> THE DOCTOR
> The Master. He left the Nuclear Bolt running. And it's gone into overload.

> WILF
> And that's bad, is it?

> THE DOCTOR
> No. Cos all the excess radiation gets vented inside there. That's Vinvocci glass. Contains it. All 50,000 rads that are about to flood into that thing.

---

16 In Scene 148, as Gallifrey was resurrected, the staff of Naismith's mansion – technicians, guards, household staff (now reverted to their original, non-Master selves, the Lord President having broken the Master's control over them) – ran for their lives, except for one technician, 'an ordinary bloke', who was trapped in the locked booth, hammering on the glass. Wilf rescued him – 'I've got you!' – by climbing into the open booth and locking the door, thereby releasing the door to the technician's booth, so he could escape. Throughout Scenes 148 to 150, Wilfred has been stuck in his booth, staring out of the glass…

                                    WILF
Better let me out, then.

                           THE DOCTOR
Except it's gone critical. Touch one control. It floods.
                           (of the sonic)
Even this. Would set it off.

Silence.

Wilf so upset.

                                    WILF
I'm sorry.

                           THE DOCTOR
Sure.

                                    WILF
Just leave me.

                           THE DOCTOR
                           (furious)
Okay! Right then! I will! Cos you had to go in there,
didn't you?! You had to go and get stuck, oh yes! Cos
that's who you are, Wilfred. You were always this. Waiting
for me. All this time.

                                    WILF
But really. Leave me. I'm an old man, Doctor. I've had my
time.

                           THE DOCTOR
Well *exactly!* Look at you. Not remotely important. But me!
I could do so much more. So! Much! More! But this is what
I get. My reward! And it's not… *fair!!!*

- proper fury, turning away to lash out, kicking something -

Then silence.

Everything still.

Then quiet, calm:

                      THE DOCTOR (CONT'D)
Lived too long.

He walks back towards the *OPEN* BOOTH.

                                    WILF
…don't, please Doctor, no don't, please don't, sir,
please…

The Doctor's hand on the door.

                              THE DOCTOR
    Wilfred. It's my honour.

                                    WILF
    But you're better than me.

                              THE DOCTOR
    Don't you ever say that.
                            (pause, deep breath)
    You'll have to be quick. Ready?

                                    WILF
    I refuse.

                              THE DOCTOR
    Three, two, one -

The Doctor enters - closes the door behind him - so fast -

- slams the RED BUTTON -

- *OPEN* and *LOCKED* switch sides, the Doctor *LOCKED* -

- Wilf running out of *OPEN* -

And FIERCE RED PRAC LIGHT, fills the *LOCKED* BOOTH. Burning. The
Doctor in agony. Wracked with pain.

Wilf horrified. Right up against the glass.

The Doctor looks at him. Tries to smile.

More pain, worse, he sinks to his knees, yelling out -

Bows his head. Curled up like a kid, in the red light.

Wilf stepping back, now, so scared.

And then the red light…

Just fades away.

The Doctor looks up.

Still himself.

But his face is hollow now, haunted.

                                    WILF
    Hello.

> THE DOCTOR
>
> Hi.

> WILF
>
> Still with us?

The Doctor standing. He seems fine, just a bit dazed, dislocated. Taps a control.

> THE DOCTOR
>
> System's dead. I absorbed it all. Whole thing's… kaput.

OPEN/LOCKED signs dead. He tries the door. It opens.

> THE DOCTOR (CONT'D)
>
> Now it opens, yeah.

He walks out.

> WILF
>
> There we are then. Safe and sound. Mind you! You're in a hell of a state. Got some battle scars there.

The Doctor's still bloodied & bruised. But now, he lifts his hands, covers his face, rubs his hands over his face, shivering a little, *brrrr*.

Takes his hands away.

Blood and bruises gone.

> WILF (CONT'D)
>
> But they've gone. Your face! How did you do that?

> THE DOCTOR
>
> It's started.

Wilf just gives a little 'Oh.' Understanding enough.

He goes to the Doctor.

He hugs him.

The Doctor accepting it, but not really hugging him back.

WIDE SHOT, the two men alone.

I can either face ten pages of the companions' farewells now, or go to bed. I'll make a cup of tea and see…

FROM: RUSSELL T DAVIES TO: BENJAMIN COOK, WEDNESDAY 4 MARCH 2009 01:24:26 GMT

RE: DIE, DOCTOR, DIE!

I have tea. I'm still typing. My cigarette count is now absurd.

FROM: RUSSELL T DAVIES TO: BENJAMIN COOK, WEDNESDAY 4 MARCH 2009 02:24:10 GMT

RE: DIE, DOCTOR, DIE!

I had to send you this bit. Scene 155 is hilarious…

<u>151. INT. NOBLES' KITCHEN - DAY</u>[17]

DONNA, unconscious on the settee. SHAUN at her side, worried.[18]
SYLVIA approaching, helpless, with a cuppa.

                   SHAUN
That's no good, she's freezing. She was just lying there,
it's like hypothermia. Try them again!

                   SYLVIA
It's engaged, everyone's dialling 999, after all that
stuff.

                   SHAUN
But we've got to do something! We've got to wake her up.
Donna? Can you hear me..?

But then Sylvia looks up. Hearing, in the distance…

The engines of the Tardis.

That magical sound.

Filling the air, stronger than ever before. Bringing life and
strength and hope.

…and Donna's eyes flicker open.

Sylvia smiling. Shaun overjoyed.

                SHAUN (CONT'D)
Donna, it's me, I'm here, you're safe, you're home.

                   DONNA
…but… what happened? I was… Did I miss something?
Again?!

17 The deletion of two short scenes (15 and 18) of a Phone-Trace-Master, in a darkened Phone-Tracing Room, attempting to track Donna's phone call to Wilf, has shifted all subsequent scene numbers, so the Doctor rescuing Wilf from the glass booth is now Scene 150, followed by this, Scene 151, in the Nobles' kitchen.
18 Shaun Temple ('tall, 30s, a kind, handsome man') is Donna's fiancé. 'He's sweet enough,' says Wilf. 'Bit of a dreamer. But he's on minimum wage, she's earning tuppence, all they can afford is a tiny little flat.'

And Sylvia hurries out, so happy -

CUT TO:

152. EXT. NOBLES' STREET - DAY

SYLVIA stepping out. For once, delighted to see -

THE TARDIS. A good distance away, down the street. THE DOCTOR & WILF standing outside it, the Doctor now in a clean, undamaged brown suit. Sylvia waves, all smiles.

CUT TO the Doctor & Wilf, the Doctor more his old self.

THE DOCTOR

Oh, she's smiling. As if today wasn't strange enough. Anyway! Don't go thinking this is goodbye! I'll see you in six days' time.

WILF

Why, what happens then?

THE DOCTOR

Wilf! Think about it!

WILF

But where are you going?

THE DOCTOR

To get my reward.

And he steps into the Tardis. On the door - *slam* - !

CUT TO:

153. EXT. ABANDONED FACTORY - DAY

PRAC SQUIBS EXPLODING on the ground! *Bang! Bang! Bang!* Someone runs through them - feet, running, running, running -

MARTHA. Gunfire, explosions at her feet - she keeps going -

It's all cement and weeds, the open area of an abandoned factory; tall, decaying buildings all around. Martha running to a hiding-hole, a small corner of ruined walls -

- she ducks down, joining -

MICKEY SMITH! With a gun & backpack.

MICKEY

I told you to stay behind!

                         MARTHA
    Looks like you need help. Besides, you're the one who
    persuaded me to go freelance.

                         MICKEY
    Yeah, but we're getting fired at! By a Sontaran! A dumpling
    with a gun! This is no place for a married woman!

                         MARTHA
    Well then. You shouldn't have married me.

And Martha Smith-Jones moves round, next to Mickey.

CUT TO POV from high up inside the factory. SONTARAN POV, the
hairlines of a gun. Targeting:

Martha & Mickey together, down below. They're not looking this
way, talking, in hiding, reckoning that the Sontaran is in a
completely different direction.

REVERSE on the Sontaran, with his gun. COMMANDER JASK.

He readies his weapon.

Rifle POV. Target zooming in on Martha.

Her forehead.

Jask licking his lips. About to fire…

Bonk!

Jask blinks. Then falls down out of frame, unconscious.

Behind him, THE DOCTOR. With a mallet.

CUT BACK TO Mickey and Martha, consulting a blueprint.

                         MICKEY
    Cos I think, if we go in here, get to the factory floor,
    down that corridor, he won't know we're there -

                         MARTHA
    Mickey.

She's looking up, he follows her eyeline.

Far above, far away, framed full-length in an open space, the
Doctor is looking down at them.

Hold the moment. They look at him, he looks at them.

Then the Doctor walks back into the factory, gone.

They stay staring up. The noise of the Tardis fills the air. And somehow, they just know he was saying goodbye.

                              MICKEY
    Hey.

Pulling Martha to him. Together. Both so sad.

                                                  CUT TO:

154. EXT. BANNERMAN ROAD - DAY

LUKE SMITH, sauntering along, on his mobile, cheery -

                              LUKE
    - but that was the maddest Christmas ever, Clyde! Mum
    still doesn't know what happened. But she got Mr Smith
    to put out this story, saying that Wi-Fi went mad, all
    across the world, giving everyone hallucinations! I mean,
    how else are you going to explain it? Everyone with a
    different face!

He's laughing away, crossing the road - not looking -

Luke foreground, A CAR SPEEDING TOWARDS HIM -

- a hand reaches out -

- pulls Luke back, out of the road - !

The car zooms past. And Luke, shaken, finds himself staring at
THE DOCTOR. Who's glaring at him, in a don't-cross-the-road-
using-your-mobile kind of way.

                              LUKE (CONT'D)
    But it's you! You're..!

But the Doctor just walks away. Fast.

Luke goes belting towards 13 Bannerman Road -

                              LUKE (CONT'D)
    Mum! Mum - !

SARAH JANE comes running round the corner, almost colliding -

                              SARAH JANE
    What is it?!

                                    LUKE
    It's him!

And she looks down the street.

The TARDIS a long way off. The Doctor a distant figure. But he
stops at the door.

Looks at her. Gives a single wave. Then steps inside.

On Sarah Jane & Luke; sound of the Tardis fills the air.

And Sarah Jane is crying.

Because she knows.

                                              CUT TO:

155. EXT. ALIEN BAR - NIGHT

CAPTAIN JACK HARKNESS sits all alone, at the bar. Deep in
thought. He's lost so much, and found nothing.

Around him, incredible life, in a dark, downtown drinking hole
in the Horsehead Nebula. Aliens galore! TWO SLITHEEN. Some HATH.
MR & MRS PAKOO.[19] A masked SYCORAX. A GRASKE. JUDOON. And MONK &
NUN-TYPE extras. FX: A VESPIFORM flies past, an ADIPOSE waddles
across the counter.

Then the barman slides a piece of paper over to Jack.

                                    BARMAN
    From the man over there.

Jack's puzzled. Looks up.

Far across the bar, THE DOCTOR. Just standing there.

Jack smiles, a little, but stays where he is. Knows something's
different. Holds up the paper, what's this?

The Doctor just nods, open it.

Jack does so.

A handwritten note, saying:

His name is Alonso.

Jack looks up again.

....
19 Mr and Mrs Pakoo were giant bird-like background aliens in *Doctor Who* 1.2.

The Doctor nods, to his left.

The man sitting next to Jack, also on his own, turns around.
It's MIDSHIPMAN FRAME.

Jack smiles at the Doctor. Gives him a salute. Farewell.

The Doctor gives that little salute back. Then turns away, into
the shadows, gone.

As the sound of the Tardis echoes away in the distance, Jack
turns to Midshipman Frame.

> CAPTAIN JACK
> So, Alonso. Going my way?

> MIDSHIPMAN FRAME
> How d'you know my name?

> CAPTAIN JACK
> I'm kinda psychic.

> MIDSHIPMAN FRAME
> Really? D'you know what I'm thinking right now?

> CAPTAIN JACK
> Oh yeah.

FROM: BENJAMIN COOK TO: RUSSELL T DAVIES, WEDNESDAY 4 MARCH 2009 03:31:10 GMT

RE: DIE, DOCTOR, DIE!

I'm here! I'm awake! Did you miss me? (What do you mean 'no'?) All right, I admit it, I just grabbed two-and-half-hours' kip. Well, I don't want to look too grisly and sleep-deprived for Michelle Ryan. But I awake to none other than MIDSHIPMAN FRAME! For it is he! Ha ha ha ha ha ha ha... and 'ha' ad infinitum. 'D'you know what I'm thinking right now?' 'Oh yeah!' Brilliant. Definitely worth waking up for.

P.S. I'm on the Red Bull already.

FROM: RUSSELL T DAVIES TO: BENJAMIN COOK, WEDNESDAY 4 MARCH 2009 03:39:48 GMT

RE: DIE, DOCTOR, DIE!

Welcome back! I thought of the Midshipman Frame bit on the spot. Literally, as I typed it. The Doctor was going to acknowledge Jack, and then Jack turns around and snogs a Slitheen – which would still be very funny. But poor Jack is so alone at the end of *Torchwood* Series Three, and deserves something happy. Plus, the episode needs a laugh. Nothing better than making the Doctor a gay pimp to get a laugh, in my book. It was a proper moment of creativity, of real invention, the words 'Midshipman Frame' typed themselves out in front of me.

Or maybe I just think about Russell Tovey all the time.

FROM: RUSSELL T DAVIES TO: BENJAMIN COOK, WEDNESDAY 4 MARCH 2009 03:52:55 GMT

RE: DIE, DOCTOR, DIE!

One more page to go!

156. INT. BOOKSHOP - DAY

A Waterstone's-type shop. A queue of PEOPLE, for a book signing. Advertising for the book on display, a blown-up cover: *A Journal of Impossible Things*, by Verity Newman.

The queue leading to VERITY, sitting at a table, a stack of books next to her. She is the image of Joan Redfern (eps 3.8 & 3.9). She's chatting to a customer, as she signs.

                    VERITY
    …it's not just a story, every word of it is true. I found
    my great grandmother's diary in the loft. And she was a
    nurse, in 1913, and she fell in love with this man, called
    John Smith. Except he was a visitor. From another world.
    She fell in love with a man from the stars. And she wrote
    it all down.

Customer moves off, next one moves in foreground - she automatically takes the book, doesn't look up.

                    VERITY (CONT'D)
    And who's it for?

                    MAN
    The Doctor.

                    VERITY
    To… the Doctor…
                    (adds her name)
    Funny, that was the name he used.

And as she hands the book back, she looks up.

THE DOCTOR standing here.

And she's breathless.

She knows. She just knows.

The Doctor so grave. So kind.

Hold the stare, the silence. She can't help it, she starts to cry, just a little. And then:

                              THE DOCTOR
    Was she happy? In the end?

                                VERITY
    Yes. Yes she was.

Hold the silence.

                          VERITY (CONT'D)
    Were you?

He gives a small smile. Takes the book. Walks away.

                                                CUT TO:

157 EXT. CHURCH - DAY

Confetti! Church bells! People smiling, laughing, throwing
confetti as the Bride and Groom, DONNA and SHAUN TEMPLE-NOBLE
come out of a perfect picture-book church.

She's never been so happy. The biggest smile!

JUMP CUT to Donna & Shaun, lining up for photos -

                                DONNA
    - come on, you lot, get in, this photo's just with friends,
    I want all of you in, that's it. And you! Friends, and
    Nerys.[20]
                          (everyone laughs)
    Only joking! Look at her!

                                NERYS
    You made me wear peach.

                                DONNA
    Because you are a peach. Furry skin, stone inside, going
    off.

CUT TO WILF & SYLVIA, standing a distance back, in all their
finery, smiling. MINNIE is there too, all saucy.

                                MINNIE
    What d'you think then, Wilfred? Never too late!

                                WILF
    Oh, give up, woman!

---

20 Donna's friend Nerys (played by Krystal Archer) appeared in *Doctor Who* 3.X.

                              MINNIE
    I'm gonna catch the bouquet!

Minnie runs off, gleeful. But Sylvia is looking across…

                              SYLVIA
    Dad.

Wilf looks.

Far away, outside the church: THE DOCTOR, and the TARDIS.

JUMP CUT TO Wilf & Sylvia, hurrying up to the Doctor.

                              WILF
    There now, same old face. Didn't I say you'd be fine? Oh!
    And they arrested Mr Naismith! It was on the news. Crimes
    undisclosed! No mention of any Gate, I bet those cactuses
    took it away. I liked those two.
                              (beat)
    But you never told me. That woman. The Time Lord. Who was
    she?

The Doctor just looks. At Wilf. At Sylvia. At Donna, in the
distance. Friends, mothers, brides.

He's not saying.

                              THE DOCTOR
    Just wanted to give you this.

He hands Wilf an envelope.

                              THE DOCTOR (CONT'D)
    Wedding present. Thing is, I never carry money. So I just
    popped back in time, borrowed a quid off a really lovely
    man. Geoffrey Noble, his name was. Have it, he said. Have
    that on me.

On Wilf and Sylvia. Overwhelmed.

JUMP CUT TO Wilf, a little shaken, back inside the churchyard
with Donna & guests, handing her the envelope -

                              DONNA
    Oh, don't tell me, it's a bill! Just what I need, right
    now!
                              (opens it, to find:)
    A lottery ticket! What a cheap present! Who was that?!
    Still, you never know, I might get lucky!

And she tucks it down her cleavage, runs off, to Shaun -

                              DONNA (CONT'D)
   Oy! Shaun! We're on a schedule, oxtail soup at 2.30
   sharp!

But stay on Wilf, with Sylvia. Both knowing what this means.

Both overjoyed. And starting to cry.

They look across.

The Doctor, and the Tardis.

He turns and goes.

Wilfred, crying, with confetti in the air, salutes him.

                                                    CUT TO:

158. EXT. TYLERS' ESTATE - NIGHT

Snow. Falling through the air. Against black.

Coming down to find the ground-floor courtyard, covered in snow.
A bell is tolling in the distance. Midnight.

No one around except a girl and her mother, walking along
together. ROSE TYLER, and JACKIE. Niggling!

                              ROSE
   I'm late now, I missed it, it's midnight. Mickey's gonna
   be calling me everything. That's your fault!

                              JACKIE
   It's not, it's Jimbo, he said he'd give us a lift, then he
   said his axle broke, I can't help it!

                              ROSE
   Get rid of him, Mum, he's useless.

                              JACKIE
   Listen to you! With a mechanic! Be fair though, my time of
   life, I'm not gonna do much better.

They stop, a little kinder:

                              ROSE
   Oh, don't be like that. You never know. Could be someone
   out there.

                              JACKIE
   Maybe. One day. Happy new year.

> ROSE

Happy new year!

And they hug.

Then head off, different ways. Calling back:

> ROSE (CONT'D)
And don't stay out all night!

> JACKIE

Try and stop me!

And Rose walks on, alone.

A good distance away, watching, from the shadows. THE DOCTOR. Silent. In the snow. His face in darkness.

She doesn't even see him, just walking on by…

But then he winces. Pain. Can't help gasping, *ow!*

She stops. Looks across. A bit wary, keeps her distance.

> ROSE

You all right, mate?

> THE DOCTOR

Yeah.

> ROSE

Too much to drink?

> THE DOCTOR

Something like that.

> ROSE

Maybe it's time you went home.

> THE DOCTOR

Yeah.

Pause.

> ROSE

Anyway. Happy new year.

> THE DOCTOR

And you.

She's about to turn and go, but -

                            THE DOCTOR (CONT'D)
    What year is this?

                                    ROSE
    Blimey, how much did you have? It's 2005.

                                THE DOCTOR
    2005. Tell you what. I bet you're going to have a really
    great year.

And she smiles, just liking him.

                                    ROSE
    Yeah.
                            (pause)
    See ya.

And Rose Tyler walks away.

The Doctor is left alone.

He turns, starts to walk.

In the distance: the TARDIS.

As he walks, he loses the pretence. He's in so much pain.
Dragging his feet. Every step.

He winces, sharp pain, *ow!*

Tries to keep going.

Walking through the show.

Then it really hits him. Agony. He falls to his knees. Desperate.
And so alone.

He heaves for breath. Can't find the strength.

He could die, right here.

But then…

A song.

A familiar song. Drifting in through the night.

The Song of the Ood.

The Doctor looks up.

Standing far away, in the snow. OOD SIGMA.

The song rising, soaring.

The Doctor gaining strength from it.

                         OOD SIGMA
    We will sing to you, Doctor. We will sing you to your
    sleep.

And the Doctor…

Stands.

The song all around him, now.

                    OOD SIGMA (CONT'D)
    This song is ending. But the story. The story never
    ends.

And the Doctor keeps walking.

To the Tardis.

FROM: BENJAMIN COOK TO: RUSSELL T DAVIES, WEDNESDAY 4 MARCH 2009 04:00:11 GMT

RE: DIE, DOCTOR, DIE!

So, *that's* how you're writing in Rose and Jackie! But it's the line about Geoffrey Noble that really got me. You've done Howard Attfield proud.

FROM: RUSSELL T DAVIES TO: BENJAMIN COOK, WEDNESDAY 4 MARCH 2009 05:52:15 GMT

RE: DIE, DOCTOR, DIE!

Here you go. Finished. Well, I'll get some sleep, and go through it all again before sending it to the office, so this is the raw version…

159. INT. TARDIS - NIGHT

THE DOCTOR steps inside, exhausted.

He stops by the doors, rests against them, lifts his hand.

FX: the faint GOLDEN GLOW.

Then he walks up the ramp. Still surrounded by Ood-song, the
unearthly choir swelling all around him.

He reaches the console. Clicks a few switches.

Watches the Time Rotor rise and fall.

                                                    CUT TO:

160. FX SHOT. TARDIS & EARTH

FX: THE TARDIS gently circling above the EARTH.

CUT TO:

161. INT. TARDIS - NIGHT

The song continues. THE DOCTOR at the console.

More pain. Fights it off. But it's time.

He stands back. Closer to the ramp.

Ready, but never ready for this.

Then, quietly:

> THE DOCTOR
>
> I don't want to go.

And then, slowly...

FX: CU THE DOCTOR, as gently, a shroud of calm GOLDEN GLOW rises up around his head, his features still visible.

FX: MID-SHOT DOCTOR, lifting his GLOWING HANDS, in amazement, his face still visible within its glow.

And then, a sudden acceleration, *wham - !*

FX: THE DOCTOR VOLCANOES!!! LONG SHOT, GOLDEN ENERGY blasting out of his head, his arms - beautiful, ferocious -

FX: GOLDEN ENERGY from one arm - ripping into the console - MASSIVE PRAC EXPLOSIONS, the whole thing going up - !

FX: GOLDEN ENERGY from the other arm, rips down the ramp - BLASTING THE DOORS, a MASSIVE SHEET OF FLAME flaring up!

PRAC FX: the door-windows shatter out!

FX: CRANING UP, WIDE SHOT, ENERGY still BLASTING OUT OF THE DOCTOR - PRAC FLAMES erupting all around, up through the floor! He's standing in the middle of an inferno!

The Cloister Bell tolling![21]

FX: CU the Doctor's head, GOLDEN ENERGY streaming out, his features finally disappearing... A new face forming...

21 The TARDIS Cloister Bell tolls, in the manner of a heavy church bell, to warn the crew of impending disaster.

```
FX: He snaps upright, ENERGY BURNING AWAY, fast, gone!
And there he is. Blinking. Dazed.

The New Man.

                                              CUT TO:


162. EXT. FX SHOT. TARDIS & EARTH

FX: THE TARDIS sparking & smoking, wrecked, spiralling down
towards EARTH, fast, faster, Cloister Bell tolling -

                                              CUT TO:


163. INT. TARDIS - NIGHT

CAMERA SHAKE! Tardis shuddering! Alarms! FLAMES all around!
SMOKE! PRAC DEBRIS falling from the roof!

The Doctor stands in the howling chaos.

Reborn.

                                   END OF EPISODE 4.18
```

And now I move to America. HOLY SHIT!!!

FROM: BENJAMIN COOK TO: RUSSELL T DAVIES, WEDNESDAY 4 MARCH 2009 06:00:17 GMT
RE: DIE, DOCTOR, DIE!
Oh my God. That's it. That's really it. Nice one, Russell! I mean that.

Never has a question been more pertinent than this, but… um, how do you feel? (Are you off to Coffee Mania? Is it even open yet?!)

FROM: RUSSELL T DAVIES TO: BENJAMIN COOK, WEDNESDAY 4 MARCH 2009 06:05:29 GMT
RE: DIE, DOCTOR, DIE!
Actually, I feel strangely anticlimactic. I thought there'd be whiskey and hookers, at least in my head. Zeppelins and elephants, as Hazel said in a deleted scene of *Queer as Folk 2*. I think it's the budget that's worrying me. I think this is going to be a nightmare. It feels like handing in a bunch of problems. Ah well. Hey, I'm done!

FROM: BENJAMIN COOK TO: RUSSELL T DAVIES, WEDNESDAY 4 MARCH 2009 06:08:17 GMT
RE: DIE, DOCTOR, DIE!
Is Steven writing Matt's first lines, to be inserted into the final scene? Or won't the Eleventh Doctor speak until Series Five, Episode 1?

THE FINAL SCRIPT

Originally published in *Doctor Who Magazine* 407, Russell describes the writing of his final *Doctor Who* scenes...

The birds go mad at night, in Cardiff Bay. Something sets them off, around two o'clock, and yet always at a slightly different time. A huge flock of seagulls rises up, all squawking and cawing. The noise is massive; I often go out and look. Lights come on in the Big Hotel. Silhouettes step out onto balconies, to gaze up at the sky. You can't see anything, against the dark. The invisible flock. Perhaps it's a trick of the sound; they might be far out at sea, or circling the city. It's slightly sinister; somewhere, Daphne du Maurier is smiling. But the almighty squall echoes round and round the Bay, then just as suddenly, stops.

They soared and cawed tonight, but that was hours ago. I'm sitting here, at my desk, the empty Bay still glittering with lights below me, and I'm about to write the last words of my last episode. Truth be told, I wasn't going to work tonight. I got ahead of myself this afternoon – for once! – and I've got no meetings tomorrow, leaving me plenty of time to finish. Except... a script never quite leaves your head. It ticks away, no matter what you're doing. I watched TV for a bit, but it just felt like heads, yapping. My mind was somewhere else, with the Gate, and Naismith, with the words 'partisan', 'carnival', 'Beijing' and the phrase 'Something is coming.' Still. Time to spare. Tomorrow.

But then! A sign! Out of the blue, a text, from lovely Mark Gatiss. Quite by chance, he's just been watching *Rose*, and texts to say how much he enjoyed it, all these years later, bless him. Hmm, my first episode, my last episode. The beginning, and the end. And then, I swear, right in that second, I flick channels, randomly finding BBC Three. And there's Mark! Wolfing down canapés, in *The Lazarus Experiment*! Okay. There are no signs and portents, except the ones we make, and that'll do me. This is a *Doctor Who* night. Back to work.

Elsewhere in Cardiff, production hasn't stopped. Things keep pinging, on e-mail. At 22.46, there's Ed's photos of the 4.16 studio sets. Wow. Blimey. Best yet! No, really, seriously, amazing, the sort of set we've never done before. Then, at 23.44, there's Nikki, signing off from the night-shoot. 'Possibly the maddest day of my career. No, the maddest day of my life!' She's not wrong. Wait till you see it! Far across the world, Julie has just arrived in LA, house-hunting, so it's daytime for her. She's working, of course, watching rushes on her laptop, e-mailing her verdict. 'That corridor looks amazing! Graeme is on fire!' (Not literally, that would be terrible.) And then silence. No e-mails, no phone calls, no texts. Twitter's probably busy, but I have enough trouble with social networking in real life. Ben Cook of this very magazine is usually around, on e-mail, at this time of night. Oh, yes, there he is, at 00.48, saying hello. I wonder to him if I should keep going? 01.09, he says, 'Stay up! I am!' But then, no more. Maybe he's fallen sleep, maybe he's out gallivanting. So. Just me.

This is always the best time to work. And for contemplation, too. [...] These are funny old times. We spend a lot of time looking forward – *Planet of the Dead* is almost finished, and yes, I'm an HD convert, it's looking gorgeous, with James Strong's most beautiful work yet. And beyond that, three more Specials, making ferocious demands on the team. But you can't help starting to look back, at the same time. Four series, five years – no, more. I started work on this in 2003. That's seven years now, blimey! We time-travel so much in our heads that I think we're getting out of sync. The other week, Julie went to her school reunion... but turned up a week too early! Then, the other day, I was about to go to the cast and crew screening of *Torchwood: Children of Earth*, Episode 1... but no, that's *next* week, seven days out again! That TARDIS has been messing with us.

Enough introspection. Work! Come on! I rattle away on the keyboard, and the words fly out. That's not a surprise. I've had these last pages ready in my head for months and months. Years, to be honest. It takes as long to write as it does to type. Well, nice sentence, but it's not quite true. Lots of new thoughts pile in, as it all becomes that bit more real. A new thrill. A new gag! And lots of unexpected problems crop up. Ah, love a good problem. So, I keep rattling away, until...

The last words.

Trouble is, last words don't really exist. In ten minutes' time, I'll change my mind about Scene 25, and go back to write something different. Then I'll get up tomorrow, and change all sorts of stuff, before sending it to the office. And then the proper rewrites start. Rewrites to make it better, clearer, shorter. Cheaper! Rewrites during filming, as budgets or locations shift and change. Even after the whole thing's been shot, there's the ADR script, for dubbing (the very last thing you type tends to be a guard shouting 'Look out!' or something). Even then, you keep writing; you think of lines that people should have said, for the rest of your life. Still, what the hell, let's allow a bit of ceremony. The last words.

Maybe I should sit here for hours, deliberating over them. But I know exactly what they are. I type them out. Times like this, typewriters would be better. Typewriters are romantic. A little metal letter should fly. It should hit the paper, *whack!* Tiny particles of ink should puff and settle. But no, there's just a plastic keyboard. I press the key. The final letter is 'n'. Then a full stop.

And that's it. Save. Done. Good.

Reproduced with kind permission

FROM: RUSSELL T DAVIES TO: BENJAMIN COOK, WEDNESDAY 4 MARCH 2009 06:12:49 GMT

RE: DIE, DOCTOR, DIE!

Yes, it's over to Steven, if he wants the Eleventh Doctor to have a first line. Last time he mentioned it, he didn't think he'd need one, but I'll let him read it and make up his mind.

FROM: RUSSELL T DAVIES TO: BENJAMIN COOK, WEDNESDAY 4 MARCH 2009 10:43:58 GMT

RE: DIE, DOCTOR, DIE!

A few hours later, and I'm still feeling quite disconnected. No great high, no great low. I'm surprised, because I thought I'd be cartwheeling. Shame, though, I wanted that Coffee Mania moment. I haven't actually been to Coffee Mania yet. Maybe it'll all happen there. Oh, I wish there was a party tonight.

I'm going to go over 4.18 one last time, dot the 'i's, cross the 't's, and deliver.

> **Text message from: Russell**
> Sent: 4-Mar-2009 11:30
> I'm in the Bay! Finally, my Coffee Mania moment. And it's beautiful. Not bad. Not bad at all.

> **Text message from: Ben**
> Sent: 4-Mar-2009 11:33
> Some men want gold, some want power, others want sex... you just want Coffee Mania! Good luck to you.

> **Text message from: Russell**
> Sent: 4-Mar-2009 11:36
> I still want sex, with the man behind the counter. This will not happen, strangely. But I have the gold and the power already, so two out of three ain't bad.

> **Text message from: Ben**
> Sent: 4-Mar-2009 11:37
> Right. Still, nice coffee?

> **Text message from: Russell**
> Sent: 4-Mar-2009 11:40
> The best!

DR WHO IV EP 17+18 SHOOTING SCHEDULE - DATED 26/3/09

DAY 1 - MONDAY 30TH MARCH: 9.30am - 8.30pm

LOCATION: TREDEGAR HOUSE, NEWPORT

17/79	INT	NAISMITH'S STABLES The Doctor and Wilf step out	Day 4 5/8 pg	1, 3	
17/77 Vfx	INT	NAISMITH'S STABLES Tardis materialises	Day 4 1/8 pg		
17/79a	EXT	NAISMITH'S MANSION The Doctor and Wilf sneak into cellar	Day 4 3/8 pg	1, 3	
18/144 Vfx	EXT	NAISMITH'S MANSION Everyone runs from house looking up to see Gallifrey	Dusk5 2/8 pg	8, 9, 10	
17/9	INT	NAISMITH'S - STUDY Naismith's have photo taken.	Day 2 3/8 pg	8, 9, 10	
17/38	INT	NAISMITH'S - STUDY Naismiths watch footage of burning building	Day 3 2/8 pg	8, 9, 10	
17/40	INT	NAISMITH'S - STUDY Naismiths optomistic over sight of figure	Day 3 3/8 pg	8, 9, 10	
18/73 Vfx	EXT	NAISMITH'S MANSION The Master runs out to see meteor streak fall to Earth	Night4 3/8 pg	2	

End Day # 1 Monday, March 30, 2009 -- Total Pages: 2 6/8

DAY 2 - TUESDAY 31ST MARCH: 8.30am - 7.30pm

17/66 Vfx	INT	NAISMITH'S - STUDY The Master bound up. Abigail see's skeleton through polaroid glasses.	Day 4 5/8 pg	2, 8, 9, 10	
18/5	INT	NAISMITH'S - STUDY The Doctor now strapped to trolley	Day 4 3/8 pg	1, 2, 3	
18/8pt	INT	NAISMITH'S - STUDY The Master recieves reports	Day 4 1/8 pg	2	
18/12	INT	NAISMITH'S - STUDY Wilf's mobile rings. Its Donna	Day 4 1 2/8 pg	1, 2, 3	
18/13pt	INT	NAISMITH'S - STUDY The Master orders to trace the call	Day 4 2/8 pg	1, 2, 3	

CHAPTER TWENTY-FIVE

THE FINAL CHAPTER

In which middle-aged men end up crying in Boots,
blue breast-enhancers are the new pink,
and Russell pirouettes for the Eleventh Doctor

FROM: RUSSELL T DAVIES TO: BENJAMIN COOK, THURSDAY 5 MARCH 2009 14:17:29 GMT

RE: DIE, DOCTOR, DIE!

I have nothing to do now.

Do you want any shelves putting up? A garden to mow?

FROM: BENJAMIN COOK TO: RUSSELL T DAVIES, THURSDAY 5 MARCH 2009 14:32:08 GMT

RE: DIE, DOCTOR, DIE!

I've a roof gutter that needs cleaning.

FROM: RUSSELL T DAVIES TO: BENJAMIN COOK, THURSDAY 5 MARCH 2009 14:36:14 GMT

RE: DIE, DOCTOR, DIE!

That'll do.

FROM: RUSSELL T DAVIES TO: BENJAMIN COOK, THURSDAY 5 MARCH 2009 14:53:25 GMT

RE: DIE, DOCTOR, DIE!

I just got a text off John Simm. He's read 4.17. 'Ha ha haaaaagh!!!' I think that means
he likes it. David left a message on my answerphone last night, after reading 4.18. He
sounded both happy and sad. That's good, then. Mission accomplished.

FROM: BENJAMIN COOK TO: RUSSELL T DAVIES, THURSDAY 5 MARCH 2009 15:03:27 GMT

RE: DIE, DOCTOR, DIE!

What did David say?

FROM: RUSSELL T DAVIES TO: BENJAMIN COOK, THURSDAY 5 MARCH 2009 15:08:21 GMT

RE: DIE, DOCTOR, DIE!

Lovely things. 'Brilliant.' He really was emotional. He was on set. He said, 'Thank God I haven't got any dialogue tonight.' And, 'What great times we've had.' There's going to be a lot of that over the next few months. And quite right, too.

FROM: RUSSELL T DAVIES TO: BENJAMIN COOK, THURSDAY 5 MARCH 2009 23:36:39 GMT

RE: DIE, DOCTOR, DIE!

I've just received an e-mail from Steven: 'Here's a go at the Matt scene. Tiny bit more than a line. Sorry.' The Eleventh Doctor's first words! History!

Meanwhile, with Julie in LA this week, she's phoning me every five minutes! Ha ha! She's finding me a flat! Sorry, an apartment. Dear God! LA! Eek!

FROM: BENJAMIN COOK TO: RUSSELL T DAVIES, THURSDAY 5 MARCH 2009 23:48:06 GMT

RE: DIE, DOCTOR, DIE!

It's all ending, isn't it? Aren't you even a little bit sad?

FROM: RUSSELL T DAVIES TO: BENJAMIN COOK, FRIDAY 6 MARCH 2009 12:04:40 GMT

RE: DIE, DOCTOR, DIE!

Am. I. Sad?

That's the question! Everyone is asking me. Julie is hilarious. Her version of 'Are you sad?' is 'Are you sad? You are, aren't you? Why won't you tell me? Is everything all right? Do you want to talk about it? I'm sad, are you? Are you okay? Seriously, really, what's wrong?' She makes me hoot.

Anyway, am I sad? I'm really, really not. And I've been thinking about it. Genuinely, I've been testing myself, because we don't always know what we feel, and that's why middle-aged men end up crying in Boots, and sometimes hanging themselves from the banister. But no. I don't. I feel happy. (No one but no one has asked me, 'Are you happy?' I'm not sure what that says about us!) That column for *Doctor Who Magazine*, in which I describe writing my final scenes, is all sentimental, because that's easy to write. It's like a Hallmark card. 'The birds go mad at night, in Cardiff Bay.' My arse that's how I felt! I felt tired, and excited that I could actually deliver the script. I think the episode is sad. I'll be crying in that final Dub, for the Doctor, for all of them. It's tempting to say that I put all the sadness into the work, but that's just cod-psychology. No, it's sad because that's the right story to tell.

So, I feel… good. I think that 4.18 script is excellent. Not in all areas, never in all areas, but it's a perfect send-off for the Doctor, and for David. I think the stand-off with the gun is great. I think the Time Lords are much better than I thought they would be, because I really tried my best with them – although they wouldn't work as a regular fixture of the show, so I feel vindicated about a decision I took six years ago. Which is important, to me!

I love all sorts of little things that no one else will ever notice, like the Time Lord Chancellor saying, 'A simple task of four beats.' I love the word 'task' there, because it doesn't actually make sense, but I sat there for ages trying different phrases, like 'a simple rhythm', 'a simple beat', 'a simple code'…? But none of those words worked. And then I thought of 'task'. Pure nonsense, yet it sounds right. I get real pleasure from moments like that. And the whole coda with the companions is wonderful. It didn't feel wonderful when I wrote it, strangely, because I'd thought of it all so long ago – except Midshipman Frame – in such detail, so concretely, that it really was a matter of typing it out as fast as I could. It felt like transcribing something from the past.

More importantly, stuff like Wilf and the Doctor sitting, watching the Earth, talking about Palestine, and rewards, and guns, and life, is why I became a writer in the first place; stuff like that proves I should be a writer, that I'm doing the right thing with my life. Also, it proves how much of this job means finding and writing for great actors. I don't talk about that much – it's kind of implicit in the whole job – but I'm not working alone. The whole point is to find actors like David and Bernard, actors who can do anything, actors who, literally, inspire me. They make writing challenging, and brave, and wonderful. Put those two in a room, and I think I can write anything. Anything. Which feels brilliant.

Oh, and Addams, too. I know she hardly matters, but she's important to me. I love Addams. There is something so vivid and right about her. I absolutely love that woman, Sinead Keenan, who plays Russell Tovey's girlfriend, Nina, in *Being Human*.[1] I think she's a stunning talent, and I found myself writing Addams as her. It's not often I do that, write for a specific actor, but she's an inspiration. She's so good. And lo and behold, she's free, so we've cast her. She's a cactus! Again, that whole process feels vindicated. That's the word. I feel vindicated. I feel like I got it right. That's more arrogant than I usually sound – all wracked with self-doubt, etc. But I don't think it's arrogant; it's just true. It goes hand in hand with all the doubt, and always has.

So, I'm not sure what I should feel sad about. Leaving? But I wouldn't leave if I didn't want to. Finishing? But I finished well! Leaving the people? That's tricky, because I love this team, but I haven't really had time to socialise with people. I don't go drinking with them. Never have. I never really want to. I'm a bit odd that way, maybe… am I? I'm happy being a bit of a recluse.

I do wonder how people see me. Steven wrote to me asking if I was sad (briskly, like

---

1 In BBC Three drama *Being Human*, Russell Tovey plays a werewolf called George, and Sinead Kennan plays his girlfriend, Nina.

you did, like a man!), but followed it up with, 'I know you won't feel a thing, you big Welsh glacier.' Ha ha. But it took me aback for a second. Is that how people think of me? I think I was really taken aback because I rather liked it. Interesting. Or is that awful?!

Brrrr, I don't know. If I find myself crying in Boots, I'll let you know. Maybe the bottom line is, I just care about myself. But doesn't everyone? Is that strange?

Love, The Glacier

FROM: BENJAMIN COOK TO: RUSSELL T DAVIES, FRIDAY 6 MARCH 2009 16:07:46 GMT

RE: DIE, DOCTOR, DIE!
You'll have to get used to everyone asking whether you're sad to be leaving. Maybe I'll print you a T-shirt that reads 'I'm not sad to be leaving. Now stop worrying, and enjoy your life.' Or one that says 'Please stop asking me if I'm all right…' on the front and 'Now piss off!' on the back. But I don't think it's odd that you're not sad. I think you'd be sad if you stayed on for another year. Or sad if you'd been pushed instead of jumped. Or if the show weren't continuing. Or if it weren't in safe hands. But I can see why you're happy, and I'm glad.

Then again, if you do burst into tears in Boots, at least they sell tissues.

FROM: RUSSELL T DAVIES TO: BENJAMIN COOK, TUESDAY 10 MARCH 2009 01:48:20 GMT

RE: DIE, DOCTOR, DIE!
Christ almighty, I've only just got in! Now! We had the 4.18 Tone Meeting from 3pm to 7pm, and then we had to go into the Edit to lock *Planet of the Dead*, literally having to stay until it was done. Normally, you sit there and give notes, like, 'Give me a closer reaction on the Doctor there, and can that line be on a two-shot?', etc, then swan off, and come back to see the results the next day. But, because transmission is so tight, we had to give notes tonight, and sit there until they were done, including tricky FX sequences. Oh, my eyes! I have brain-ache. Poor Mike Jones – imagine having to edit in front of people. That would be like me having four people sitting behind me while I type! Or like someone monitoring everything that I'm writing, all the time, every day of the… Oh.

FROM: RUSSELL T DAVIES TO: BENJAMIN COOK, TUESDAY 10 MARCH 2009 18:02:27 GMT

RE: DIE, DOCTOR, DIE!
Jessica Hynes is off to Broadway, before we even start filming 4.17/4.18.[2] Bollocks!

FROM: BENJAMIN COOK TO: RUSSELL T DAVIES, TUESDAY 10 MARCH 2009 19:19:16 GMT

RE: DIE, DOCTOR, DIE!
Isn't that the one end-of-episode cameo for which you don't *have* to cast the original

2 In the event, a day's filming was brought forward to 21 March in order to record Hynes' scene before she left the UK.

actor? It's supposed to be Joan Redfern's great granddaughter, Verity, isn't it? Alternatively, couldn't the Doctor visit Elton Pope from *Love & Monsters*? Or better still – a nice contrast with the other cameos – Jackson Lake? Yeah! Bring back David Morrissey, now living the life of a proper Victorian adventurer.

FROM: RUSSELL T DAVIES TO: BENJAMIN COOK, TUESDAY 10 MARCH 2009 20:10:46 GMT

RE: DIE, DOCTOR, DIE!

Yeah, I did think that she doesn't need to be the same actor, technically – and yet it sort of loses something. The conceit sort of makes it work somehow. Hmm, I don't know. All the other characters – even Jackson Lake – don't really have any unfinished business. The whole thing works because of Verity's final 'Were you?' to the Doctor.

Then again, the thought of the Doctor walking in on Elton and Ursula's sex life could be rather marvellous.[3] Poor Ursula. Or lucky Ursula.

FROM: RUSSELL T DAVIES TO: BENJAMIN COOK, SATURDAY 14 MARCH 2009 15:10:25 GMT

RE: DIE, DOCTOR, DIE!

I have to lose 204 FX days from 4.17/4.18. Here we go again! Plus, 4.18 is still about ten minutes too long. But I give up. For now.

I was offered another of Steven's Series Five scripts to read today… and I refused. That's enough now. I don't want to know any more. I want it to be a surprise.

I'm popping to Swansea tomorrow, to tell my family I'm off to LA. Should be fun.

FROM: BENJAMIN COOK TO: RUSSELL T DAVIES, SUNDAY 15 MARCH 2009 18:42:10 GMT

RE: DIE, DOCTOR, DIE!

Are you back from Swansea yet? What did your family make of your plans?

FROM: RUSSELL T DAVIES TO: BENJAMIN COOK, SUNDAY 15 MARCH 2009 18:48:56 GMT

RE: DIE, DOCTOR, DIE!

My sisters were happy and excited. That was nice. They're good girls, really. Even my dad wasn't too bad. 'You'll never work in this country again,' he said. 'You'll be forgotten.' Thanks! Actually, it would have been my mum's 80th today, so everyone was in a sort of nice, nostalgic mood. Unusually quiet, for my lot!

FROM: BENJAMIN COOK TO: RUSSELL T DAVIES, SUNDAY 15 MARCH 2009 18:53:56 GMT

RE: DIE, DOCTOR, DIE!

Ahh, that must be a relief. Except for the 'You'll never work in this country again' bit, but that's not true. Wales would welcome you back with open arms, any day. Oh, unless he meant England. Yeah, you're finished in England.

---

3 At the end of *Doctor Who* 2.10, Elton reveals that he and his girlfriend Ursula (played by Shirley Henderson), who was killed but reconstructed by the Doctor as a living section of pavement, enjoy 'a bit of a love life'.

FROM: RUSSELL T DAVIES TO: BENJAMIN COOK, MONDAY 16 MARCH 2009 23:02:11 GMT

RE: DIE, DOCTOR, DIE!

Tomorrow's weird. I'm in London for lunch with John Simm, Euros Lyn and Julie, but then, in the evening, I have to give a speech at BAFTA about Children's TV. I only agreed because CBBC has been so brilliant about our *Sarah Jane Adventures* budget. They've moved heaven and Earth to fund us… but then asked me to do this. That's a *big* subject, and I've given it *no* thought. Paul Abbott once had to give a talk at some TV conference in Manchester. He walked on stage, looked at them all… and walked straight off! I wish I could do that. Stupid speech.

FROM: RUSSELL T DAVIES TO: BENJAMIN COOK, TUESDAY 17 MARCH 2009 23:47:15 GMT

RE: DIE, DOCTOR, DIE!

That was a long day. I'm such an outrageous busker. I went to that microphone, and opened my gob. An hour later, they were clapping away like I'd invented television single-handedly. One day, I'll be caught out. One day, I'll crash and burn. One day, I'll do a Paul Abbott! But so far, the luck is holding. I enjoyed it, actually. I just hid on the roof for all the drinks, and mingling, and chat beforehand. I hate a crowd. Oh, I hate it. But when I'm *in charge* of a crowd, then I love it. This says terrible things about me, I know!

FROM: RUSSELL T DAVIES TO: BENJAMIN COOK, FRIDAY 20 MARCH 2009 03:59:51 GMT

THE LAST TONE

There we are, gone, done, finito. Final rewrites! (Well, there will be poxy pink pages to come, to allow for changes of location and stuff, but in essence… that's it!) And today was the last Tone Meeting, too. God, it was long and complicated (there is an e-mail about the exact chronology and continuity of the Time Lord scenes in the black void, which I'm not sending you for fear it would bleed your eyes out), but it was a hoot. I took a) my OBE and b) the Face of Boe action figure. I pinned on the OBE, and every time something got difficult, or we ran out of days or money, I'd hold the OBE with one hand, while pointing my other hand at the offending person, and claim Power of the Crown over them! Ah, you had to be there. It made me laugh. Best thing was, whenever I nipped out for a cigarette, I'd stand there with my badge still pinned on, so anyone passing by who wasn't in the meeting must have thought I was a right ponce. I looked like a Chelsea Pensioner.

And then it was done. Nice round of applause, as normal, but no big speeches. Just the way I like it. Outside Upper Boat, there were awkward half-goodbyes off a couple of people as we all drifted away, but I just said, 'Shaddup, I'll see you at the wrap party,' so any nonsense was cut short.

Mind you, I am tired. This is creeping up on me every single day. Once that engine has gone, blimey, I'm starting to run down. It's been getting like this for the past six days or so. I'm really, truly feeling 45. My knee aches for no good reason at all. It's killing me. I think I'm actually walking slower. Still, only natural after all this work. It's a deserved tiredness.

FROM: BENJAMIN COOK TO: RUSSELL T DAVIES, FRIDAY 20 MARCH 2009 04:01:18 GMT

RE: THE LAST TONE

You're still up? Me too. How much have you had to cut from 4.18? Have you managed to shave off ten minutes?

FROM: RUSSELL T DAVIES TO: BENJAMIN COOK, FRIDAY 20 MARCH 2009 04:07:02 GMT

RE: THE LAST TONE

Ha ha, hello! It's like the old days.

Nah, we're all just saying 'sod it'. I lost about three pages – yes, it's down from 75 pages to 72. Mind you, I think *Planet of the Dead* was 73 pages, and it's come in at about 58 minutes. It's an imprecise science. To be honest, we're sort of banking on the fact that the very last episode can be However Long We Want, because it's David's regeneration, on BBC One, so to hell with it! Slightly risky, maybe, because Julie always argues that stuff with BBC One, and now she'll have to argue it from LA, which is a weaker position to be in, but I think we should be okay. Too late now. Almost.

FROM: BENJAMIN COOK TO: RUSSELL T DAVIES, FRIDAY 20 MARCH 2009 04:13:15 GMT

RE: THE LAST TONE

Are you going to include the final few pages for the read-through on Wednesday? You can't, can you? David's final line will leak out. Any so-and-so can come to a read-through. Even I'll be there!

FROM: RUSSELL T DAVIES TO: BENJAMIN COOK, FRIDAY 20 MARCH 2009 04:23:55 GMT

RE: THE LAST TONE

For the read-through, Julie is cutting off the script after Scene 152, as the Doctor goes to get his reward. Boo! Although, we wouldn't have got any of those companions to the read-through, to save money, so fair enough.

> **Text message from: Ben**
> Sent: 25-Mar-2009 01:46
> Well, I've made it to Cardiff for the read-through, but they'd messed up my booking at the hotel, run out of rooms... so they've put me in a suite! A WHOLE SUITE TO MYSELF!!! I've two bathrooms and an actual throne.

> **Text message from: Russell**
> Sent: 25-Mar-2008 01:54
> A suite?! Outrageous! I think they've booked Bernard Cribbins in the other suite. He should arrive by 2am. He he.

> **Text message from: Ben**
> Sent: 25-Mar-2009 02:03
> I can hear him in the suite next door. He's playing the Ting Tings at full blast.

FROM: RUSSELL T DAVIES TO: BENJAMIN COOK, WEDNESDAY 25 MARCH 2009 16:24:42 GMT

THE LAST READ-THROUGH

That was a privilege. Literally, a privilege. It's the only word. To sit in the same room as David Tennant, as he read those final scenes with Bernard in Naismith's mansion. I had the best front-row seat ever. All of them, Bernard, John, everyone – brilliant. But especially David. What an honour. I'll never forget that.

FROM: BENJAMIN COOK TO: RUSSELL T DAVIES, WEDNESDAY 25 MARCH 2009 16:30:11 GMT

RE: THE LAST READ-THROUGH

Indeed, job well done. And for David, job magnificently done. Good times! I'm glad I was there. Really special day. So sad, too. Afterwards, Julie said, 'I cried so much, I think I've given myself a headache.' And I loved how she stressed the importance of secrecy to everyone: 'Do not tell anyone anything. Over the next 48 days of the shoot, you have no friends, you have no family…!'

FROM: RUSSELL T DAVIES TO: BENJAMIN COOK, WEDNESDAY 1 APRIL 2009 15:05:31 GMT

APRIL FOOL'S

Ed Thomas played a brilliant April Fool this morning. He sent a text saying that Michael Jackson wants to visit the TARDIS set at 4.30pm today! Oh, there were people rushing around checking security and all sorts. I missed it all, because I was asleep – recovering from a cold. The cold that you get when you stop work. Yes, that cold. Why do I always get the cold? I'm so bunged up. I haven't been to bed for two days, just sleeping in the chair, because when I lie down I can't breathe!

FROM: BENJAMIN COOK TO: RUSSELL T DAVIES, THURSDAY 2 APRIL 2009 20:08:09 GMT

RE: APRIL FOOL'S

Feeling any better? Should I post some hot soup to Cardiff in a jiffy bag?

FROM: RUSSELL T DAVIES TO: BENJAMIN COOK, THURSDAY 2 APRIL 2009 21:43:29 GMT

RE: APRIL FOOL'S

Yes. Yes, soup in a jiffy bag would be lovely. Please send.

  I'm okay. It's only a stupid cold, but I'm such a stupid smoker, the stupid cold gets stupidly worse. I hate it, when it's all my own fault. I like having someone to blame.

FROM: RUSSELL T DAVIES TO: BENJAMIN COOK, SATURDAY 4 APRIL 2009 14:03:48 GMT

RE: APRIL FOOL'S

Thank you, Noel, that's a wrap. Thank you, Freema, that's a wrap. Mickey Smith and Martha Jones have left the building. Scene completed by midday! All done and dusted. Farewell, farewell.

  I meant to go on set today, to say hello and goodbye, but it's not wise to be near actors with this cold, so I texted them instead. Noel texted back: 'I'm doing it for you, dude.' I love being called dude. So, there we go, another little bit of TV history. Well, until *The Twelve Doctors* in 2013, when everyone is called back. Funny to think that Noel was there right at the beginning. Series One, Episode 1. I remember meeting him in a car park on the South Bank on that first London shoot, back in 2004. First thing he said was, 'I'm coming back next year, yeah?' Good old Noel. And I remember Freema hiding in the St David's Hotel before her audition with David – locked away with Andy Pryor, on Valentine's Night 2006! Oh, I sound like I'm getting nostalgic. I'm not. I just felt like e-mailing, really.

FROM: BENJAMIN COOK TO: RUSSELL T DAVIES, SATURDAY 4 APRIL 2009 17:11:07 GMT

RE: APRIL FOOL'S

>>I sound like I'm getting nostalgic. I'm not.<<

  Yes, you are. And I think you're allowed to. You must get nostalgic sometimes. You're the man who brought back *Doctor Who*!

FROM: RUSSELL T DAVIES TO: BENJAMIN COOK, SUNDAY 5 APRIL 2009 14:10:19 GMT

RE: APRIL FOOL'S

Here are the latest ructions. Turns out, someone in America is about to launch a new mobile network called Neon. Yeah, just like the one on the advert on the side of the bus in *Planet of the Dead*. BBC Editorial Policy terror! It's free advertising! This is absurd, of course. It's beyond absurd. We cleared the name way back in November, when no one had claimed it; the new Neon has come along since. What are we supposed to do, clear a name that would never be used? Like 'Xffrgyxtyl'? Of course, the BBC is now scared and terrified. It must be beyond reproach. So we either a) ignore it, please, b) blur the name on the bus in every shot, or c) since The Mill has a 3D bus on their computers, they could make a 3D patch to superimpose in every bus shot, but that costs money. Julie is running with option a), of course, arguing that since Neon is in all the publicity shots that have already been released – barely visible, actually, but no one is going to check that – changing the name could create more publicity for Neon than if we left it alone.

But the time and effort that this nonsense eats up…! Bloody hell. At the same time, Editorial Policy said that the shot of the bus driver's skeleton slamming to the ground was too scary. Bollocks. But Julie was brilliant – Jana Bennett, the BBC's Director of Vision, was on a tour of BBC Wales on Friday, so Julie took her into the Dub, played her the sequence, and said, 'What d'you think of that?' 'Ooh, marvellous,' said Jana. Julie goes back to Ed Pol: reveals the Supreme Boss of the BBC has just cleared it. Ha! She is unstoppable.

FROM: RUSSELL T DAVIES TO: BENJAMIN COOK, TUESDAY 7 APRIL 2009 23:17:57 GMT

RE: APRIL FOOL'S

Euros has just been on the phone to Timothy Dalton, about playing the Lord President! TIMOTHY DALTON!!! AS RASSILON!!! Early days, of course – it's still not a definite booking – but it's as close as it can be. (I wanted the bloke from *The Five Doctors*, but apparently he was banned from acting ever again.)[4] Plus, we've cast June Whitfield as Minnie! This block is bonkers.

FROM: BENJAMIN COOK TO: RUSSELL T DAVIES, WEDNESDAY 8 APRIL 2009 05:04:55 GMT

RE: APRIL FOOL'S

Would this be the first time that Timothy Dalton and June Whitfield have appeared in the same production?! I love *Doctor Who*.

FROM: RUSSELL T DAVIES TO: BENJAMIN COOK, THURSDAY 9 APRIL 2009 00:45:17 GMT

RE: APRIL FOOL'S

Good news! Tracie Simpson and Pete Bennett have got the jobs as the Series Five producers. Isn't that's brilliant? They really are the best in the land.

Oh, and Claire Bloom is playing the Doctor's mum! (Yes, that's what she's been told, too.) To think, she was married to Rod Steiger. And now she's in *Doctor Who*. She told Tracie that she had no idea how big *Doctor Who* was until she started telling friends that she was in it and they were falling over!

FROM: RUSSELL T DAVIES TO: BENJAMIN COOK, SUNDAY 12 APRIL 2009 10:21:23 GMT

RE: APRIL FOOL'S

Planet of the Dead got 8.4 million viewers last night! That'll do me. (*Primeval* sank to 2.7 million. Ouch. They actually don't deserve that.)

---

4 In 1983 *Doctor Who* Special *The Five Doctors*, Rassilon was played by the late actor Richard Matthews.

FROM: RUSSELL T DAVIES TO: BENJAMIN COOK, THURSDAY 16 APRIL 2009 18:43:03 GMT

RE: APRIL FOOL'S

Do you know what I've got to do now? Write a *Tonight's the Night* sketch. It's Johnny B's new Saturday-night variety show. They're running a *Doctor Who* Alien Talent Search competition. The winner – basically, whoever has cobbled together the best alien costume – gets to appear in a specially written scene, in the TARDIS, with the Doctor and Captain Jack. Yes, my final work for the Tenth Doctor on TV will be writing a scene for David, John Barrowman, and a man called Tim, who has dressed himself as the alien Sao-Til using blue breast-enhancers and a wine cooler on his hand.[5] This is how it ends.

FROM: BENJAMIN COOK TO: RUSSELL T DAVIES, THURSDAY 16 APRIL 2009 23:46:32 GMT

RE: APRIL FOOL'S

Best. Monster. Ever!

Blue breast-enhancers? Really?! Oh, Russell. Prepare for brain death. Can't you refuse to do it?

FROM: RUSSELL T DAVIES TO: BENJAMIN COOK, THURSDAY 16 APRIL 2009 23:51:48 GMT

RE: APRIL FOOL'S

Too late. They've advertised it as a 'script by Russell T Davies', and they're shooting it on Monday. I have written two lines. I can't bear this. This script is killing me.

FROM: RUSSELL T DAVIES TO: BENJAMIN COOK, FRIDAY 17 APRIL 2009 00:44:50 GMT

RE: APRIL FOOL'S

Here we go. My final *Doctor Who* script. A masterpiece. MASTERPIECE! I am bleeding from the fingers. (I'm getting paid for this. It's going straight to charity. I'm not touching it.) They really, really want David as the Doctor… but I just couldn't. I literally could not type it. Let them moan if they want. I ain't doing it.

```
1. INT. TARDIS

   Tracking round, close on the central console, the hum and
   whirr of power, to find...

   SAO-TIL! A blue-faced, hat-wearing, probe-handed alien,
   operating the controls. Muttering quietly:

                     SAO-TIL
        Soon, power over Time and Space will be mine...

                     CAPTAIN JACK
        Hold it right there, mister!
```

5 *Tonight's the Night* competition winner Tim Ingham.

Sao-Til looks up -

And there's CAPTAIN JACK! At the top of the ramp, aiming his gun, *ka-chik!*

> CAPTAIN JACK (CONT'D)
> Who the hell are you, and what are you doing in the Tardis?

> SAO-TIL
> But the Tardis is mine!

> CAPTAIN JACK
> It belongs to the Doctor.

> SAO-TIL
> I am the Doctor! Look closer, Captain Jack. Old friend. Don't you recognise me?

> CAPTAIN JACK
> (lowers gun)
> D'you mean... you regenerated?

> SAO-TIL
> This is my new form.

> CAPTAIN JACK
> It's kind of blue. Is that the fashion these days?

> SAO-TIL
> Blue is the new pink.

Captain Jack relaxed, crosses over to him.

> CAPTAIN JACK
> Works for me, it's kind of... hot. If you don't mind my saying so. Nice coat. Like the hat.

> SAO-TIL
> Thank you.

> CAPTAIN JACK
> And what's with the hand?

> SAO-TIL
> My new weapon. A neural probe, capable of paralysing my prey.

> CAPTAIN JACK
> Really? Well that's fascinating.
> (close, now)
> Cos if I know the Doctor...

Jack grabs Sao-Til's hand, forces it down on the console, both face-to-face, angry:

                  CAPTAIN JACK (CONT'D)
  One thing he never does, is carry weapons! So you tell
  me, right now, who are you?!

Sao-Til breaks free, gets a few feet away, raises his weapon at Jack, and Jack raises his gun, both in a stand-off.

                  SAO-TIL
  My name is Sao-Til! From the planet Aminopia! And with
  the Tardis at my command, I will wreak havoc across the
  cosmos!

                  CAPTAIN JACK
  Oh yeah? Doing what?

                  SAO-TIL
  My species deals in arms trading.

                  CAPTAIN JACK
  More weapons!

                  SAO-TIL
  No, literally, we trade arms, legs, feet, shoulders,
  hips, and the occasional spine.

                  CAPTAIN JACK
  Body-snatchers!

                  SAO-TIL
  Legend has it that Captain Jack has donated quite a few
  organs in his time.

                  CAPTAIN JACK
  Ohh yeah, there was this party, one night, on Alpha
  Centauri, with these three -
               (serious again)
  Never mind that! No way are you getting hold of this
  Tardis, I'm gonna stop you, Sao-Til!

Both aiming, now - fast, intense -

                  SAO-TIL
  I will paralyse you and take your brain!

                  CAPTAIN JACK
  Get out of here, or I'll shoot!

                  SAO-TIL
  I'll shoot first!

                              CAPTAIN JACK
    I'm warning you!

                                SAO-TIL
    I'm warning you!!

                              CAPTAIN JACK
    You'll die, Sao-Til!

                                SAO-TIL
    You will die, Captain Jack!! Die now, and *die
    forever!!!!*

The creak of the door -

Both turn round -

And there's DAVID TENNANT. In normal clothes. Popping his head
round the door.

                             DAVID TENNANT
    Hello, John. What are you doing in here? Everyone's gone
    home.

WIDE SHOT, showing the edge of the set, black space beyond,
cables, etc. Captain Jack embarrassed.

                              CAPTAIN JACK
    ...I was just, um... Showing my friend around. This is
    Tim.

                                SAO-TIL
    My name is Sao-Til!

                              CAPTAIN JACK
    It's Tim.

                             DAVID TENNANT
    Hello Tim.

                                SAO-TIL
    From the planet Aminopia!

                              CAPTAIN JACK
    Stoke on Trent.

                             DAVID TENNANT
    ...right, anyway, I'm heading off, d'you want a lift?

                              CAPTAIN JACK
    No, we'll just... tidy up.

> DAVID TENNANT

Okay. See ya. Oh, and John? One more thing.

> CAPTAIN JACK

Yeah?

> DAVID TENNANT

My Tardis. *Mine.*

> CAPTAIN JACK

Yeah.

> DAVID TENNANT

Say sorry.

> CAPTAIN JACK

Sorry.

> DAVID TENNANT

Good.

And he goes.

> SAO-TIL

He's so cool.

> CAPTAIN JACK

I love him.
> (back into action)

So! Right! Where were we? I'm gonna stop you, evil Sao-Til, bang bang bang!

> SAO-TIL

I deflect your bullets and zap you, bzzzzzzzzz!

> CAPTAIN JACK

I am immortal, engaging super-bullets, bam bam bam!

> SAO-TIL

Zap you right back, ka-zaaaa!

And they're running around the console, like kids, all zap bang argh, etc!

Pulling out to a wide shot, both of them loving it.

> THE END

FROM: BENJAMIN COOK TO: RUSSELL T DAVIES, FRIDAY 17 APRIL 2009 00:50:38 GMT

RE: APRIL FOOL'S

Well, it made me chuckle. It shouldn't piss off too many fanboys either. And now you're free to head off to LA! Good old Sao-Til.

FROM: RUSSELL T DAVIES TO: BENJAMIN COOK, FRIDAY 17 APRIL 2009 00:57:34 GMT

RE: APRIL FOOL'S

Christ, LA! Every day, I think of changing my mind. What the hell am I doing? Maybe it's my mid-life crisis. I wake up every day determined to call it off. I do! I'm in a strange state of depression about it. It feels gloomy, and mad, and such a bloody hassle. It feels wrong. Did I tell you, I've got a flat already. Venice Beach! Not actually *on* the beach, but five minutes away. I can't believe it.

FROM: RUSSELL T DAVIES TO: BENJAMIN COOK, FRIDAY 17 APRIL 2009 14:03:30 GMT

RE: APRIL FOOL'S

I've been viewing 4.17 rushes. Return to the planet of the Ood! At the Tone Meeting, I asked for it to be bigger and better than last year's Ood episode – which was good, but so sunny that it looked like a backdrop of a white sheet. It almost felt like a studio at times. Well, blow me, they've gone and done it. Cliff-faces of ice! Euros is making it look so huge, so accurate, so beautiful. I'm truly, truly, *truly* excited. There hasn't been a dull or ordinary day's rushes.

Tracie has moved onto prep on Series Five – which I think they're calling Series One, or Series 11.1, for marketing reasons – so the on-set producer for 4.17/4.18 is now... Julie! She's taken over! It's a reign of terror. She's dusted off her wet-weather gear and is sitting by the monitor. It's just hilarious – and wonderful, because there is no one better.

But today's 4.16 Edit was terrible.

FROM: BENJAMIN COOK TO: RUSSELL T DAVIES, SATURDAY 18 APRIL 2009 00:50:38 GMT

RE: APRIL FOOL'S

Terrible how? Episodes always feel a bit shaky at the first Edit, because you're watching it to look for the faults. It's a fault-finding mission. I imagine that's why the hardcore fans suffer such agonies on a first viewing on TV, because they're concentrating, unnaturally so, on every creak, every whistle, every one-liner. Impossible viewing. Those sorts of fans, sadly, never move on from that first viewing. I wonder if a lot of them ever see it properly.

FROM: RUSSELL T DAVIES TO: BENJAMIN COOK, SATURDAY 18 APRIL 2009 15:35:07 GMT

RE: APRIL FOOL'S

You're right, it's always unsettling at the first Edit of an episode, because it's my job to find problems. Today's was fascinating. Graeme Harper and the editor, Will Oswald, had worked so hard, they'd slaved away and refined every scene, to produce a tight action thriller about Water Monsters on Mars… but that's not what the story is about. That's all set dressing. The real story is the Doctor's moral dilemma, whether to break the Laws of Time or not. It all comes down to tiny details and choices. Like, the Doctor says, 'I've got to go' – but they played this with him off-camera, choosing that line to go to a CU of Adelaide instead, so all its impact was lost. The Doctor deciding to leave Bowie Base One is huge, but it was being treated as a really ordinary thing. And because the episode is too long (about 65 minutes), they'd cut the bit where he shakes hands with all the crew and says goodbye. Again, that's massive.

When he meets the crew, he sees flashbacks of newspaper headlines showing the date of their deaths, but they'd done this with Adelaide Brooke and Ed Gold only, instead of everyone, so you didn't get the enormous impact of the story saying: Everyone Is Going To Die.[6] As a result, when you got to the end, when the Doctor is fighting time itself, you had no idea why everything was so important, why this was so different to a usual story. This ended disastrously, because Adelaide kills herself, and you just didn't know why, or what effect that was having on the Doctor. The worst bit was when the Doctor goes to leave the base, and everyone is dying. This had been edited as the story of Adelaide and her crew fighting the good fight, desperate to survive, intercut with the Doctor walking away… but that's completely wrong. It's the story of the Doctor turning his back on dying people, so Adelaide and the crew should become just voices in his head; he's hearing their screams over the comms, as he keeps walking, until he decides to break the fundamental rule of the Time Lords, and go back. It's hard to describe on paper (and just as hard to sit in the Edit and describe in pictures), because both those things are using the same images, the same events, the same order. But the emphasis tells a completely different tale. The scenes have a different reason for existing.

When I describe it like this, it comes down to a few little choices (though there were more examples), but the sum total of those glitches is a story that doesn't work. A lot of people wonder what execs do, but days like that are when Julie and I really prove our worth – because we can come in, with a bit of distance, an overall perspective, and be ruthless. And that's where all our hard work pays off, watching the rushes every day, because when we say, 'We need a CU of the Doctor on that line,' we know that it exists. We have a different version of those scenes in our heads, which we know can be edited together. I actually loved the process of repairing it, of knowing that it could make sense in the end. And I'm describing it really simply here, like 'We are right, and they were wrong,' but it's much more interesting than that, to sit with Nikki, Graeme, and Will, discussing what this story is, and how to make it work. It's not easy. It can be awkward – it's not nice, to sit facing lovely, clever, hardworking people, and tell them that they've

---

6 In *Doctor Who* 4.16, Ed Gold (played by Peter O Brien) is the Deputy Captain of Bowie Base One.

gone adrift – but it's natural. It happens. Everyone gets too close to this stuff, but a good, honest team can get the whole train back on the tracks again.

It's been re-edited twice now, and we're almost there. Almost. Another session on Monday. And I've brought a copy home for this weekend. I've already watched it twice, so I've a good insight into the final little tweaks needed to make it sing. Slowly, but surely. Even before we've finished, I think it's wonderful. David is so sensational when he walks back and tries to save Bowie Base One. He's savage and brilliant. I'm so lucky to be working with him. It's his birthday today! He celebrated it in the Ice Cave of the Ood, filming until 5am – shot at Wookey Hole, where *Revenge of the Cybermen* was filmed. That's where Lis Sladen almost died falling off a boat or something.[7]

FROM: RUSSELL T DAVIES TO: BENJAMIN COOK, SUNDAY 26 APRIL 2009 08:01:10 GMT

RE: APRIL FOOL'S

I'm off on holiday. Well, off to London this afternoon for the BAFTAs, and then from there to Spain. So, I'll be off e-mail for a week, but still on my mobile.

But before I go… listen, there are moves afoot to really close off the shooting of the regeneration on 12 May, just because people will besiege poor Matt. But Julie is fighting the good fight, and sending e-mails saying that you must be there to represent *DWM*, so we should prevail. Although, when it comes to the Matt Smith stuff, you're in Piers' hands. I was planning to be there myself, as a dyed-in-the-wool fanboy, but I'm beginning to realise that I might have to duck out, just to give poor Matt room to breathe. (He'd only fall in love with me anyway. It happens.) *Hasta la vista*, etc.

P.S. Did you know, we're getting a *Doctor Who* Christmas BBC One ident?! Like Wallace and Gromit did last year. David sitting on the TARDIS as it's pulled by reindeer!

FROM: BENJAMIN COOK TO: RUSSELL T DAVIES, SUNDAY 26 APRIL 2009 08:17:11 GMT

RE: APRIL FOOL'S

In one ident, all the reindeer should have the Master's face! Ha ha.

Have a relaxing trip.

> **Text message from: Ben**
> Sent: 29-Apr-2009 14:58
> I'm in Cardiff's Tiger Tiger with two Hath, two Slitheen, a Sycorax, a Judoon, and the Graske, amongst others. Neill Gorton: 'We need to give David a good send-off, don't we? A proper alien bar!' John Barrowman is here, too, flirting with Russell Tovey. And Euros Lyn. Oh, and the fire alarm has just gone off! How's Spain?

7 During filming of 1975 *Doctor Who* serial *Revenge of the Cybermen* in Wookey Hole, a boat carrying Elisabeth Sladen went wild, forcing her to jump into the water.

> Text message from: **Russell**
> Sent: 29-Apr-2009 15:01
> I'm in THE WRONG COUNTRY!!! Bollocks. It is sunny and lovely here, but there is nothing to compare to Russell Tovey and a Judoon.

> Text message from: **Ben**
> Sent: 29-Apr-2009 15:05
> Pete Bennett suggested that the Judoon should be arm wrestling: 'It's my fantasy. I might do it anyway later.'

> Text message from: **Ben**
> Sent: 29-Apr-2009 18:48
> That's a wrap on Johnny B! He and David are hugging. David: 'Well done, mate. That has GOT to be our last scene together.'

FROM: RUSSELL T DAVIES TO: BENJAMIN COOK, MONDAY 11 MAY 2009 11:16:21 GMT

REGENERATION EVE

I'm back in Manchester. I came up on Saturday morning. It's all part of my plan to spend more time with Andrew before disappearing to another country. Guilt trip! But I'm heading back to Cardiff late this afternoon. I'm going to have dinner with my old mate Tony Wood tonight. He produced those old Granada soaps that I worked on, and *The Grand*, but I'm around tomorrow, so I'll head on set, I think. Regeneration Day! I'm still a bit wary – it might get embarrassing, with 5,000 people on set to see the new boy – but we'll see.

> Text message from: **Ben**
> Sent: 11-May-2009 17:02
> Here in the Gate Room, Bernard is knocking on the booth door. :-(

> Text message from: **Russell**
> Sent: 11-May-2009 17:10
> Make him knock three times. That'll throw 'em.

FROM: BENJAMIN COOK TO: RUSSELL T DAVIES, MONDAY 11 MAY 2009 23:41:14 GMT

RE: REGENERATION EVE

How was dinner with Tony Wood?

I'm sat up in my hotel room, wondering how Matt Smith must be feeling tonight.

FROM: RUSSELL T DAVIES TO: BENJAMIN COOK, TUESDAY 12 MAY 2009 00:01:11 GMT

RE: REGENERATION EVE

I'm sat up in my flat, wondering how David Tennant must be feeling tonight.

I'm kind of worried that lots of people are excited by how NEW, NEW, NEW it is tomorrow, without considering David's feelings enough. They're all assuming he's fine. But I don't know. I think it will be a very strange day for him.

Have you seen the call sheet? It just calls Matt 'The New Man'. The third Doctor I've seen arrive! If you'd told me that a few years ago...

>>How was dinner with Tony Wood?<<

Dinner was lovely, thanks. I haven't seen Tony properly for years, maybe ten or so. I used to get so drunk with him. We'd arrive in a bar, and order a bottle of wine each. The same wine. Just, each. Now that we're old, greying and widening, we both had orange juice all night. He's the one who first introduced me to Julie, all those years ago. He'd been saying for ages, 'You must work with this woman. You'll love her.' And here we are today. Best of all, he was full of good wishes and excitement for LA. I'm so paranoid, I tend to assume that most people must think it's a stupid idea, so it was lovely to hear someone saying it was wonderful. That did me good.

FROM: BENJAMIN COOK TO: RUSSELL T DAVIES, TUESDAY 12 MAY 2009 00:16:18 GMT

RE: REGENERATION EVE

I've got a call sheet. It's insane, isn't it? Just when you think it can't get any madder, what with both 'David Tennant' and 'The New Man', it lists 'Timothy Dalton' as coming in for a costume fitting for Time Lord President! This call sheet is definitely a keeper.

I've been thinking about David, too. Really, I have. Have you seen today's rushes? He is, literally, amazing. I was on set for the last few hours this afternoon, and Julie played me back some of what I'd missed earlier in the day – the bit where the Doctor gets angry at Wilf, stuck in the booth – and it's magnificent, and heartbreaking, and really just mind-blowingly good. He's going out on a high. Later on, he and Bernard were having a laugh on the TARDIS set. I hadn't realised, but it was Bernard's first time on the TARDIS. Bernard (on the working Time Rotor): 'It sounds just like an Australian magpie.' David: 'Oh, is that what it sounds like?' Bernard: 'Yeah. A sort of yodel. Lovely.' Then Julian Howarth waded in: 'We've had three years of that, Bernard. Three years of us asking the Art Department whether they can fix it, and three years of them saying, yes, they can. Well, they can't.' Bernard: 'Well, I like it.'

And even in his final few days as the Doctor, David is still breaking bits of the console. Euros: 'You okay there, David?' David: 'Um... I might have just broken it.' The more things change...

LORD DAVIES AND LADY GARDNER

I'm on the iPhone, on set! (Where's Matt Smith?!) Everyone's standing around scratching their heads over how to blow up the TARDIS control room. Hey, and you've just come over and asked me what's happening. I said, 'Nothing. Very slowly.' But you know that. (Most pointless e-mail ever!) Oh, and then you asked me to e-mail you those photos that I took on my phone over lunch, of you and Julie trying on Time Lord collars. Here they are.

FROM: RUSSELL T DAVIES TO: BENJAMIN COOK, TUESDAY 12 MAY 2009 18:13

RE: LORD DAVIES AND LADY GARDNER

Ha ha ha, those photos! I've got the part, oh yes. I'm actually convinced.

I can't believe I met Matt Smith today. At last! You're right, he's lovely. Even more handsome in real life, I think – but then so am I. It was all suitably bonkers. I'd been wondering where and when that meeting would ever happen, and it turned out to be in the middle of a typical *Doctor Who*-style calamity. An Upper Boat blunder! Having decided that the studio should be emptied for the rehearsal of Matt's first scene (really nice idea – just him and Euros on set, without the pressure of 57 people staring at the new boy), we all cleared out, left the TARDIS empty, ready for the Eleventh Doctor. We all stood outside with coffee and cigarettes. It was like when I first started in TV back in the '80s, when studios actually used to stop for official tea breaks. Can you imagine that nowadays?! But as I stood there, it occurred to me... this is going wrong. Like everything that's ever been over-planned, it's going to go very, very wrong. The entire crew has cleared out, onto the tarmac, but Matt Smith has been in the Costume and Make-Up vans. In order to get to the TARDIS, he has to walk through all of us! This tarmac is his route to the studio! Oh my God! This hasn't made things better; it's made them much worse. We're all lined up like his baptism of fire.

In that second, I thought, I have to get out of here, because I can't just bump into him on some tarmac. For starters, what would I do? Go up and introduce myself? On the tarmac? I didn't want to interrupt him, not with his head full of his very first dialogue. It's such an important moment. Hardly time for me! If I stop him to chat, will everyone else? The scene will never get shot. But if I don't say hello, won't everyone think I'm rude? I swear, I was turning to go, literally, turning, to hurry away, to get out of there, and – slow-motion – as I'm turning, in that very second... I see Matt Smith. No! To be honest, I see David's suit. The Tenth Doctor's brown suit, being worn by someone else. That's weird – oh! It's him! It's Matt Smith! It's Doctor Who! To make it worse, as I see him, he sees me. I'm half-turned away, as though leaving, like I'm not bothered. Simultaneously, yes, he might well be looking at me, but I'm thinking, that doesn't mean he knows who I am. He only knows Steven and Piers, not me. Maybe he's just thinking, who's that pirouetting man? What do I do? Keep turning? Turn back? Faint?!

But then he's heading for me, and yes, bless him, he knows who I am – and we're both madly, enthusiastically, ridiculously polite. I'd sent him a card when he got cast, and he was thanking me for that, and I was saying, 'Oh, no, no, no, don't be so daft,' but all the while I'm still stuck with one leg half-turned-away, as though I'm practising my second position for ballet class. I'm a study in desperate nonchalance. And I'm thinking, the poor man, 57 people on the tarmac have noticed us and are staring, and he's about to do his first scene, so the last thing he wants to do is listen to me babbling. And I'm still staring at the suit. All I'm really thinking is, you're wearing David's suit! In the end, the fact that I was delaying him and interrupting his train of thought was so horrific, I practically pushed him away. 'Don't talk to me! Go to the studio!' And off he went, to become the Doctor, in a Cardiff shed.

Sometimes, you see people meeting David, and they go to pieces in front of him, all nerves, and bluster, and rambling – and I just did the same to the next Doctor! Still, he'd better get used to it.

FROM: BENJAMIN COOK TO: RUSSELL T DAVIES, TUESDAY 12 MAY 2009 18:26
RE: LORD DAVIES AND LADY GARDNER
Yes, I spotted you pirouetting on the tarmac! You should turn professional.

It was a strange day, wasn't it? David filming the Tenth Doctor's final moments, his heartbreaking last words, and then throwing back his head to regenerate. With that in the can – did you hear him? – he said, 'Bring in the next one! When does he start? Where is he?' And on came Matt Smith, fresh out of the Make-Up van. I'm sure he was pirouetting. (Where could he have got that from?) Lots of shaking of hands. I think that's what I'll remember most about today. Everyone shaking hands. David and Euros. You and Steven. Matt and everybody. Steven said, 'I can't deal with this much momentousness.' Even James Bo- I mean, Timothy Dalton said, 'This really is a handing-over-of-the-baton day.' (How funny was Double-O-Dalton, flirting with Julie outside the Make-Up truck? 'Can I just say, you're looking gorgeous?' 'Stop it! I'm blushing!' At this rate, she'll be the next Bond girl!)

And Matt's first words as he stepped up onto the TARDIS set – 'Hello, everybody. Lovely to meet you all. I'm Matt.' Nice. Sweet. Charming.

As David was heading to the car, to be driven home, having changed out of his costume, he bumped into Julie, Andy and me outside. Julie: 'Who are you again?' Andy: 'Didn't you used to be…?' Good job David laughed. 'Some other bloke's in there,' he protested, pointing towards the studio, all mock indignation. 'What the f***'s going on?'

FROM: RUSSELL T DAVIES TO: BENJAMIN COOK, FRIDAY 15 MAY 2009 19:09:39 GMT
RE: LORD DAVIES AND LADY GARDNER
We went out last night – me, David, Julie, Phil – for a meal, a private little farewell. In Claridge's restaurant! I've never had such a posh meal. It was like those ones you see on TV, with taster menus and things. But I'd have been happy in Burger King, with that company. It was a beautiful evening – lots of funny stories and happy memories, and the feeling of a job well done.

> **Text message from: Ben**
> Sent: 15-May-2009 19:18
> You still in London? Are you coming on set tonight, to see Billie and Camille on the Brandon Estate for one last time?

> **Text message from: Russell**
> Sent: 15-May-2009 19:21
> Sorry, but no, I'm not there. I came home. I'm back in Cardiff. I couldn't face a night wearing a stab vest in artificial snow. But have fun! Send my love to La Piper and La Coduri.

FROM: BENJAMIN COOK TO: RUSSELL T DAVIES, SATURDAY 16 MAY 2009 14:44:31 GMT

THE BRANDON ESTATE

Billie, Camille, fake snow, paparazzi, David on excellent form, a mad woman who insisted on walking her dog right through the set while shouting, 'Bollocks to the lot of yer!' – what is it with the Brandon Estate?!

FROM: RUSSELL T DAVIES TO: BENJAMIN COOK, SATURDAY 16 MAY 2009 14:50:48 GMT

RE: THE BRANDON ESTATE

'Bollocks to the lot of yer!' Well, she's not wrong, is she? I like her.

Ah, that sounds brilliant. Camille was sending me hilarious, overwrought texts all night. 'I'm so emotional, I can't breathe.' All good. End in sight.

FROM: BENJAMIN COOK TO: RUSSELL T DAVIES, WEDNESDAY 20 MAY 2009 21:26:00 GMT

MISSIVE FROM A CARDIFF HOTEL ROOM

Russell, I don't even know if this e-mail will reach you. I'm on the wireless internet back in my hotel room (no suite this time!), but the signal keeps dropping out, so heaven knows if you'll ever get to read this…

Anyway. So. Wow. That was David's final day filming *Doctor Who*. Wasn't it sad? His last scene, at Upper Boat, dangling on wires against green screen. 'I'm like an un-cool Spider-Man!' And then it was over. 'Am I free? Can I walk away?' he asked Euros, and then he disappeared, without fuss or fanfare. I was thinking, *really?!* Is that it? Then I heard Pete Bennett say, 'Let's make him think we're just calling him back for a green-screen reference.' As if he'd believe that! But back in walks David. Pete: 'Ladies and gentlemen, you'll be very sorry to hear that's a golden wrap on David Tennant, the Tenth Doctor.' He's showered with confetti, the biggest round of applause, champagne, lots of people crying… even David was fighting back the tears, wasn't he? His little speech was bang on. 'I'm very proud of everything we've done, and thank you all very, very much.' And then, 'I've changed my mind! I'm going to do Series Five after all! Is it too late?' Sniff.

So long, David. You've been beyond brilliant.

FROM: RUSSELL T DAVIES TO: BENJAMIN COOK, MONDAY 25 MAY 2009 16:30:43 GMT

BACK IN MANCHESTER

Moving country is a nightmare. I'm staring at this house, wondering what to pack, what to take, what to mothball. Ah, I'll just burn it down, that's easier.

FROM: BENJAMIN COOK TO: RUSSELL T DAVIES, MONDAY 25 MAY 2009 16:32:29 GMT

RE: BACK IN MANCHESTER

Don't take the Dalek in your hallway. That's my advice. After that, you're on your own.

FROM: RUSSELL T DAVIES TO: BENJAMIN COOK, MONDAY 25 MAY 2009 16:41:03 GMT

RE: BACK IN MANCHESTER

As well as that Dalek, I've now got a Davros head – a present from Neill Gorton. I mean, I love it, and thank you, but… what the hell will Customs say?!

FROM: BENJAMIN COOK TO: RUSSELL T DAVIES, MONDAY 25 MAY 2009 16:43:53 GMT

RE: BACK IN MANCHESTER

Davros' head? Take it to America, and leave it on the pillow of the first person out there who pisses you off.

FROM: RUSSELL T DAVIES TO: BENJAMIN COOK, MONDAY 25 MAY 2009 17:52:11 GMT

RE: BACK IN MANCHESTER

Andrew left the Davros head on the pillow last night. All tucked up with a duvet and everything. It was actually creepy.

FROM: RUSSELL T DAVIES TO: BENJAMIN COOK, THURSDAY 28 MAY 2009 20:04:12 GMT

RE: BACK IN MANCHESTER

I've delayed my flight by a week – I'm now going on 22 June – or my furniture won't have arrived! I'd be sleeping on the floor. I'm too old to sleep on the floor, though it would be a funny way to arrive in a new country.

I forgot to tell you, the Eleventh Doctor's companion is revealed tomorrow! Keep your eye on the usual news outlets around midday.

In other news, I just channel-hopped and caught *The Sound of Drums*. Am I on drugs when I write these things?

FROM: BENJAMIN COOK TO: RUSSELL T DAVIES, THURSDAY 28 MAY 2009 21:41:16 GMT

RE: BACK IN MANCHESTER

On drugs? *The Sound of Drums*? Whatever could you mean?

P.S. The new companion? I think I've exhausted the Jimmy Krankie jokes, so I'll shut up.

FROM: BENJAMIN COOK TO: RUSSELL T DAVIES, FRIDAY 29 MAY 2009 12:09:46 GMT

RE: BACK IN MANCHESTER

From the BBC Press Release announcing Karen Gillan's casting as Matt Smith's companion: 'With filming due to begin this summer, Gillan beat off dozens of hopefuls to land one of television's most coveted roles.' Now, who was responsible for that? Did she? Really?! 'Beat off dozen of hopefuls'? Ha ha ha, me so smutty. But whoever wrote it should be promoted.

FROM: RUSSELL T DAVIES TO: BENJAMIN COOK, WEDNESDAY 3 JUNE 2009 13:36:52 GMT

RE: BACK IN MANCHESTER

I've been hither and yon these past few days – the Manchester/London/Cardiff triangle. Cardiff for some *Sarah Jane* Edits and a final *Torchwood* Dub (it's kind of embarrassing walking back into the Cardiff offices after that big exit), then London for The Mill, and now back to Manchester.

But I meant to answer that question about *The Sound of Drums*, because sometimes, I swear, I can sit and watch things like a viewer, like it's all happening as new right in front of me. I can watch my stuff and get this disconcerting draught of… well, of how it must look to other people, sometimes. Of how unplanned it all seems. Like I'm making it up as I go along. I'm refusing, on screen, to do all those normal things that would make an episode more coherent, with a beginning-middle-and-end wholeness. It really struck me when the Doctor discovers the Archangel Network. That comes completely out of the blue. I mean, completely! It could have been foreshadowed – Saxon could have been talking to the Cabinet about his satellites, for example. More significantly, with the entire world hypnotised, it's interesting how little the Doctor even asks, 'How is the Master doing this?' Technically, that's a major plot strand, but I'm more interested in running on, to find new things. You're left with a Hugely Important Network that is only discovered… in the exact moment that it's revealed to be Hugely Important! No warning, no ground-laying, nothing. Then, to make it even odder, it's dispensed with in the same scene. And I'm being casual with a plot element that, next episode, saves the entire world. That's bordering on reckless!

It's the same with the discovery of the TARDIS on board the *Valiant*.[8] The Doctor opens a door… and there it is! But actually, look back, when did the Doctor last worry about where the TARDIS is? I'm not sure he's even mentioned it at all. And neither has the Master. And then we discover that the Master has turned it into a Paradox Machine… well, we had no sign of that, did we?[9] Where were the traditional scenes of the Master plotting with Lucy, or with the Toclafane? 'Soon my Paradox Machine will be complete,' etc. I don't use any of the available opportunities to explain anything, or to make the structure clear, or to reassure people that there's a plan at work here.

The *Valiant* is another good example. That's not just the reveal of a ship; it's the reveal of a different world order in *Doctor Who*. In one, big picture, I'm transforming

8 In *Doctor Who* 3.12/3.13, the Master captures UNIT's airborne aircraft carrier, the *Valiant*.
9 The Doctor's TARDIS has been 'cannibalised' by the Master to create a Paradox Machine, which prevents the universe from collapsing under the inherent logical contradiction of a grandfather paradox when the Toclafane kill their ancestors – modern-day humans.

UNIT from a secret society to a massive, expensive, sci-fi organisation, 'protecting the skies of planet Earth'! That's practically a whole new show. Conceptually, the *Valiant* is a huge leap for the show. Have I seeded it in? Built up to it? Given any sort of notion that this is the world in which UNIT now exists? No, I just throw it in as brand new. And then I don't dwell on it. I move on. Actually, the next thing you discover is that the Master helped to design the *Valiant*, which is massive – that's what allows the TARDIS/Paradox Machine to be in place, and the whole plot revolves around that – but it's thrown away. It almost sounds like a gag, to make his wife laugh.

What I'm saying is, I can see how annoying that looks. I can see how maddening it must be, for some people. Especially if you're imposing really classical script structures, and templates, and expectations on that episode, even unconsciously. I must look like a vandal, a kid, or an amateur. No wonder some people hate what I write. Of course, I'm going to win this argument. (Did you guess?) Because the simple fact is: all those things were planned. All of them were my choice. They're not lazy, clumsy, or desperate. They're chosen. I can see more traditional ways of telling those stories, but I'm not interested. I think the stuff that you gain from writing in this way – the shock, the whirlwind, the freedom, the exhilaration – is worth the world. I've got this sort of tumbling, freewheeling style that somersaults along, with everything happening *now* – not later, not before, but now, now, now. I've made a *Doctor Who* that exists in the present tense. And I think that's exactly like the experience of watching *Doctor Who*. It's happening now, right in front of your eyes! If you don't like it, if you don't join in with it, then… blimey, these episodes must be nonsensical. But those classical structures can be seen in *Primeval*, in *Demons*, in *Merlin*, in all of them – and yet we stand with millions more viewers. And I think that's partly why. So, ha!

FROM: BENJAMIN COOK TO: RUSSELL T DAVIES, WEDNESDAY 3 JUNE 2009 22:30:15 GMT

RE: BACK IN MANCHESTER

Does watching back your old episodes (okay, the Series Three finale is hardly 'old', but you know what I mean) affect how you write your next script, even in small ways? You often talk of learning from your successes, but do you learn from your mistakes? If ever you get a chance to catch a repeat or watch the DVD of Series One, Episode 1, *Rose*, and send me a critique of that, I'd be absolutely fascinated to know what you make of it. Because – and I watched it back the other day – that episode is just about the perfect first episode. I don't mean it's beyond fault (it isn't), or that it's your best episode ever (it isn't – although it's up there, maybe), but it's *exactly* what was needed back then, every beat of it, the most finely tuned opening episode that a reboot of the show could have wished for. Not a scene is wasted. Not a line. The tone is spot on and so self-assured. I'm not just saying that to be nice. It's what I think. And that's why I'd love you to watch it back, and tell me what *you* think.

FROM: RUSSELL T DAVIES TO: BENJAMIN COOK, FRIDAY 5 JUNE 2009 01:31:12 GMT

RE: BACK IN MANCHESTER

I'm off to Swansea for four days – to say goodbye to the family! – so e-mail will be intermittent. Normal service will be resumed next week. But, yes, I'll try to sit down and watch *Rose*. Good idea!

FROM: RUSSELL T DAVIES TO: BENJAMIN COOK, THURSDAY 11 JUNE 2009 16:27:11 GMT

HELLO

I booked my plane ticket to LA yesterday. It's very strange booking something for 22 June that says 'Return: 23 October' (That's when we come back for the *Waters of Mars* Dub.) That just looks so huge, on paper. OCTOBER!!!

For now, I'm back in Cardiff. I'm off to the first viewing of 4.17 – with Julie attending via iChat from LA, which should be hilarious.

FROM: RUSSELL T DAVIES TO: BENJAMIN COOK, WEDNESDAY 17 JUNE 2009 13:35:32 GMT

GOODBYE, MANCHESTER

It's like I've got forces of nature trying to stop me leaving this house in Manchester. First of all, half the electricity went. My kitchen is dead. I've got a kettle in the living room, like a student. I'm sitting in a death trap, for all I know. I keep waiting for something to ignite. Then my PC blew up. Literally, everything wiped. *Everything!* All those years of work! Thank God I've just got a new Mac laptop – talk about good timing. It's now the centre of my world. (But for Christ's sake, where's the delete key? Ben, where is it? No, not the backspace one. The normal, proper delete key. IT'S DRIVING ME MAD!!!) The stress levels with this move! You could run the national grid off my forehead.

But did you see, someone has taken a still from the wrap party DVD, and sent it to a website? And now it's in *The Sun* – a photo of David, John Simm, and Timothy Dalton, with Timothy in his full Seal-of-Rassilon garb, just in case you were in any doubt about who he's playing! Which bastard leaked that? Good old fandom. They always find new ways to let you down.

FROM: BENJAMIN COOK TO: RUSSELL T DAVIES, THURSDAY 18 JUNE 2009 14:15:37 GMT

RE: GOODBYE, MANCHESTER

All right, there's no delete button. But there are no viruses that eat up your hard drive, so swings and roundabouts.

I saw the thing in *The Sun*. Who would do that? What is the point of leaking stuff like that? I really thought you'd be able to keep the Time Lord thing a secret.

FROM: RUSSELL T DAVIES TO: BENJAMIN COOK, FRIDAY 19 JUNE 2009 00:35:56 GMT

RE: GOODBYE, MANCHESTER

The sad thing about that leak is, it wasn't for the money, because it was sent to a website first, no cash involved. But that sort of makes it worse. That means that someone didn't do it for money; they did it simply to spoil. They had a secret, and they wanted to spoil it, and did so. What is your life lacking, to think like that?

I'm back in Cardiff Bay, for the last time. (Well, until I come back for the Dub in October.) I watched 4.17 again today. It's very, very wonderful, I think. Do you remember when I was worried about bringing back the Master, and thought I didn't have a story? Ha! It's reeking of story. The Doctor and the Master are story generators. I can't imagine ending the series any other way now. It feels massive, and it feels intimate, both at the same time. And when Timothy Dalton appears, halfway through the episode... oh my God!!! So, good times. And then I went out to Pizza Express in the Bay, which has employed the Most Handsome Waiter Ever. Now! After four years, now they employ him! Bastards.

Hey ho. Onwards. Just time to pack up this flat, lock things away, grab what I need, and then I'm off. Ah, I've had good times in this flat. I wrote great stuff sitting in this chair. I've loved it here. This fantastic view. The water and the sky. I think I'll miss Coffee Mania more than anything. I wondered whether to pop in and say goodbye to the Coffee Mania staff this morning... and then decided they might think I'm weird, so I didn't. Now I wish I had. And so it goes.

But I've got 'WATCH *ROSE*' branded on my head. I haven't forgotten. I really will get that done, on Sunday, before I leave for LA. If it's the last thing I do! Which it might well be.

FROM: BENJAMIN COOK TO: RUSSELL T DAVIES, FRIDAY 19 JUNE 2009 01:02:03 GMT

RE: GOODBYE, MANCHESTER

Thanks, Russell. In the meantime, try not to go mad with all the packing.

FROM: RUSSELL T DAVIES TO: BENJAMIN COOK, SUNDAY 21 JUNE 2009 23:12:27 GMT

ROSE

This is probably the last e-mail that I'll ever send you from Cardiff Bay, so you'll be pleased to hear that I've just watched *Rose*. The last piece of telly I watch in this flat before leaving for LA is *Doctor Who*, Series One, Episode 1. Where it all began. How appropriate.

And I loved it.

Did you want more?! Sometimes I think every fan in the world wants me to say, 'Actually, we got that very wrong. I'm so sorry.' They will wait a long time. A long, long time. Of course, these episodes will age, though that's a lovely process, and there are always things that I'd have done differently, because there are always ways to do something differently. But that, frankly, was a joy – sitting down to watch a first-class episode of high-octane, big-success, primetime drama from the year 2005. Beautiful. If anything, I'm amazed that we worried, that we were scared that the show would die a death. Look at it! How could you not watch *Doctor Who* when it's that good?!

I hope you're not expecting modesty here. This is too important.

Okay, little niggles did leap out, though they annoyed me at the time. The climax could do with a tighten, of course, but we were under-running. Rose's bedroom is horribly pink, but we fixed that in later episodes. I wish we'd cut Mickey's improvised dance in Trafalgar Square at the beginning, and I'm bemused to think how reticent I must have been back then, in the Edit, not to have demanded its excision. Plus, we're in Trafalgar Square, and you can't see Nelson's Column! (Well, except in one establishing shot, without Mickey and Rose.) How mad is that? I was there on location that day, too. Nowadays, I'd just march up to the camera and turn it round. Oh, I've become a monster. And the tiniest, daftest niggle of all – the Henrik's security guard hands Rose the lottery money in a see-through plastic bag. I don't believe you'd ever do that. I'm sure the script said 'envelope'. It's simply not the sort of bag that you'd collect lottery money in. After that, we learnt to discuss every tiny prop in the Tone Meetings. And then, look, Chris whirrs the sonic against a lock – and there's a visible ripple! We never did that in future episodes, because it would have eaten up our FX budget. That's not a niggle, though. That's rather sweet. I like it.

The strangest thing about watching it now is remembering the stuff I'd get hung up on at the time, because writing this sort of thing was still new to me. For example, I remember worrying for months – *months!* – about Jackie's coffee table. Yes, Jackie's coffee table. Because Jackie's coffee table is smashed into smithereens when the Doctor and Rose are tussling with an Auton arm in her living room, and yet – here's the killer – it's never mentioned again! Now, be honest, that's never worried you, has it? But that was months of worry for me. It really bothered me. I kept coming back to it – because in 99 per cent of dramas, that would have repercussions. Well, not hugely, okay, but it would at least get mentioned. If a woman like Jackie stepped out of her bedroom to find her coffee table in pieces, she would never stop banging on about it. I worried and worried. I went through all sorts of options (when Jackie is late-night-shopping later on, should she say that she's after a new coffee table? No, really?!), before I learnt to simply let go. That's when I realised that in fantasy/action-adventure stuff, certain things fly past and are best forgotten, because the action, the characters, the audience and the writer don't want it to stop, or to obsess over details. Move on! Leave the wreckage behind you! And I never stopped doing that.

Most of all, it hit me, watching *Rose*, that this show is exactly what I wanted it to be – and it is, in its first 45 minutes, exactly what it is now. It has never fundamentally changed. There has been no mission creep since 2005, no timidity, no reversals. There has been development and exploration, but no wandering. I'm proud of that. It's hard to keep a show as it is without letting external pressures, or simply the passing of time, bend it out of shape. I've always admired the very first episode of *Coronation Street*, because it sets out what the show is with absolute precision. You can see the exact same show at work 49 years later. *Rose* is the same. It's a powerful template, still at work today. Just look, for example, at how open and visible the plots are in this fictional world, right from the start. When the Doctor blows up Henrik's, the explosion is reported on TV – and being commented on by Jackie, while her daughter was actually a witness. That's immediately, significantly, a new form of *Doctor Who*, because it's saying: this is public now. No more secret invasions of the Home Counties. The whole world is in danger, and everyone is going to know it. That persisted, to become a spine of the entire series. Four years before the human race flies right across the universe in *The Stolen Earth*, there it is, in miniature. The agenda, laid out for all to see. You'd think that was first signalled by the destruction of Big Ben in *Aliens of London*, but actually the essence of it is right here, right now, about six minutes into *Rose*.

The sexuality is there, too. Straight away, the simple, natural inclusion of sexuality. Rose kisses Mickey. Jackie flirts with the Doctor. The whole thing ends with Rose choosing a new man. Plus, the word 'gay' appears for the first time in *Doctor Who*. Oh, and look at Mickey saying to Rose, 'Don't read my e-mails!' (Some people think that Rose treated Mickey badly, like she was the selfish one, but will you look at that line?! What on Earth do you think that line means? Seriously? That boy deserved to lose his girlfriend, right from the start!) The whole thing exists in a world where sex exists, which isn't always the case with science fiction. Sex and selfishness. There is a real, vivid, selfish streak running through these characters, and that's very me. I love writing that into characters. Too many TV characters are just 'nice'. Make them selfish – naturally selfish, as we all are – and they sing. That leapt out at me, watching *Rose* again. Long before his mysterious e-mails, Mickey abandons Rose for the football down the pub. The next morning, Jackie delivers that killer line, 'There's no point in getting up.' That strand continues all the way through to Donna, who has to return to her small-town Pringles and *Heat*-magazine life, or the Sylvia who always said that Donna was no good at school – or Martha Jones, the only one who's ever truly selfless… and suffers for it! All of that is built into the very first script. A stifling world, demanding a Doctor to rescue you.

And the comedy is there. It took me four years to build up the confidence to do a complete comedy episode, with *The Unicorn and the Wasp*, but it's rattling out in *Rose*, and that's quite brave, I think. As I've said before, tragedy is straightforward, but it takes far more nerve to be funny. I laughed out loud at Jackie's 'Arianna' line. Neat bit of writing, that. It dodges the expected template, because that's an old joke, which would normally go like this…

```
                    JACKIE
    Arianna got two thousand quid off the council, just cos
    the old man behind the desk said she looked Greek.


                    ROSE
    But she is Greek.
```

<pre>
                        JACKIE
    I know, but that's not the point.
</pre>

Except, Rose's line has been cut, leaving Jackie to leap straight to the punchline unaided – 'I know she is Greek, but that's not the point' – so the joke is earlier than you'd expect. Which is good! And it makes Jackie madder, too, because she's practically talking to herself – a great character synopsis for her at the same time. Mmm, not bad. Nice.

Immediately, the Doctor is the Doctor, too. Right from the start. There's the Time War, straight away. ('I couldn't save any of them!' he yells, and it takes until 4.18 to find out why.) He's got that whole mythic side to him already. Dumbos think that I'm turning the Doctor into God, when clearly I'm saying that God doesn't exist, that we mythologise real people, events or aspirations into deities, and pay the price for it. All of that is circling around the Doctor from the off, with his 'the turn of the Earth' speech.

<pre>
                    THE DOCTOR
    D'you know like we were saying? About the Earth
    revolving?
                        (pause)
    It's like when you're a kid, the first time they tell you
    that the world's turning. And you just can't quite believe
    it, cos everything looks like it's standing still.
                    (right at her)
    I can feel it.

He holds her hand. The two of them, joined together; a gradual
tilt to the image, the feeling of suppressed power.

                    THE DOCTOR (CONT'D)
    The turn of the Earth. The ground beneath our feet is
    spinning at a thousand miles an hour, and the entire
    planet is hurtling round the sun at sixty-seven thousand
    miles an hour, and I can feel it. We're falling through
    space, you and me, clinging to the skin of this tiny
    little world, and if we let go –

He lets go. Back to normal. Rose shaken, steps back.

                    THE DOCTOR (CONT'D)
    That's who I am. Now forget me, Rose Tyler. Go home.
</pre>

I think the saltiness of the episode leapt out. There's a real vim and vigour about it. An edge. It's hard, at times. It's a tough world. Why does that surprise me? Maybe, with the passing of time, I've come to regard *Rose* as a safe opener – a thought that evolves into 'soft opener', like maybe I took some easy options. Did I hell! Look at it! Mickey gets his head pulled off![10] I'd actually forgotten that. His. Head. Pulled. Off. Wow! Clive gets shot in the face in front of his wife and child. Blimey. And the Doctor is as hard as nails – we're nothing but apes, and Mickey's death isn't given a second thought. And Rose's ditching of Mickey at the end – with a smile! – becomes the ultimate commitment to the Doctor's life.

Look how much of this show is defined by Mickey Smith. I'd never noticed that before. Rose is meant to be the everyman, the companion, the touchstone by which we measure everything – but the whole episode uses Mickey as an equal and opposite insight. I don't remember doing that deliberately. But it works.

And do you know what is staggering? What really amazed me, watching *Rose* again? Chris and Billie. Oh. My. God. And they wonder why certain other shows don't work! Christ, we were lucky. Well, lucky and clever. Those two are simply amazing together. They bristle on screen. They're sparking. Sizzling. I could watch those two forever. I just found that dazzling, Ben. That's the definition of star power right there, in those two actors.

So! I'm surprised by all of that, to be honest. I'm amazed to see that so much of what I wanted from *Doctor Who* was so present and so clear, from the opening titles onwards. I thought I'd watch something more timid, more unformed, more embryonic. I didn't remember it being that confident, that certain, right from the start. We've got so used to doing interviews in which we talk about the horrors of production, being thrown in at the deep end, the amount that we had to learn, and the steepness of that learning curve, etc, that we've forgotten: this was good. This was great! Actually, it's BRILLIANT! And the episode asserts itself again and again, even today, because those 45 minutes established an audience that grew, *for five years*. That's important, and rare. This show has drawn more and more people to it as time has gone on, and it hasn't increased its audience by changing; it's done so by staying the same, by being consistent, by never flinching. We've had some nerve. That sort of success doesn't happen often. In fact, it happens just about never.

But it happened to *Doctor Who*.

Ha!

Right. That's it. I'm off tomorrow. Bye, then. Look after TV for me. Don't let anyone break it while I'm gone.

---

10 In *Doctor Who* 1.1, the Doctor pulls the head off an Auton replica of Mickey.

THREE DAYS LATER...

Text message from: Ben
Sent: 24-Jun-2009 10:59
Since you left two days ago, *Primeval* has been axed, Irish TV broadcaster Setanta has fallen into administration, ITV are having to re-shoot the first wave of *X Factor* auditions (yes, really! I know!), and there's naff all on TV tonight.[1] You know when you told me to look after TV for you...? There will be NO TV LEFT by the time you come back to visit in October! Just a test card on every channel, or Arlene Phillips counting beans. I'm so, SO sorry.

Text message from: Russell
Sent: 24-Jun-2009 17:37
Can't I leave you alone for five minutes?

---

1 In September 2009, three months after ITV axed the series, it was announced that *Primeval* had been recommissioned for two series under a new co-production deal between ITV and digital channel Watch.

ELEVEN DAYS LATER...

HELLO AGAIN

How's LA? Have you taken up rollerblading yet? Entered rehab? No? Married Jodie Foster? (Or is it Darryl Strawberry?) Come on, Russell, you must have gone native!

RE: HELLO AGAIN

Hello! Yes! Howdy! I'm in LA!

It's strange here. Yesterday was the 4th of July ('Happy Fourth!'), so it was all parties and fireworks on the beach, which was nice. The beach is hilarious. You walk five minutes from my house, turn the corner, and there it is. Endless horizons. Palm trees. All those Venice Beach dropouts, and muscle men, and tattoos, and henna, and drugs, and holidaymakers, and *Baywatch*, and drunks, and burgers, and black kids with ginger hair, and rollerblades and everything, on my doorstep! The sun is relentless. And there are so many handsome men, you stop fancying them. Literally, you have to or you'd be twitching all day like a nervous puppy. Very odd.

But my apartment is lovely. 'Apartment' barely covers it. It must be four times the size of my Cardiff flat. And it's so cool – in terms of temperature, I mean – which is perfect for me. I dreaded coming here and boiling over, but this has got a sea breeze draughting right through the building, and glass, and patios, and sometimes, just sometimes, it's even *cold*. Bliss. I like it. It still feels odd, though. It just feels like I'm on holiday.

Everything is different. The shops are different. The milk is different. The TV schedules are different. The pace is different. The light is different. It's kind of tiring, because the simplest thing seems huge. Like, you find a shop to buy your milk – but then the questions begin. Is this the best shop? Is this what I'll do now? Buy milk here every day? Should I look further? I mean, that's tiny, but when those questions apply to everything, it's a bit wearying. (Never mind the Mac. Now, *that's* different. I still cannot believe there's no delete key!) But that, I suppose, is the kind of thing I'm doing – focusing on tiny problems, and making them huge, so I'm not actually looking at the hugeness of what I've done. Where am I?!

Still, Julie is on good form. Indomitable! She and I have an assistant called Ryan, who is ridiculously handsome. I told her not to get a good-looker, because I'd just find that oppressive. 'No,' she said, 'he's fine. You won't fancy him. He's got a beard.' Well, pah! He's got a beard in the sense that Justin Timberlake has a beard. The bastard.

Oddest of all, the supermarkets here sell chicken sausages. There's a KFC-style advert on TV, in which the company owner proudly declares, 'There's no beef in our chicken!' I'm kind of scared by what that might mean.

The hardest thing is getting used to the hours. The time difference. That's always funny on holiday – 'Ooh, they're all in bed now!' – but not when it's work. Being eight hours behind means that when I get up, the UK has had almost a full working day – and there's still plenty of work to be done back home, with *The Sarah Jane Adventures*, and the *Doctor Who* Edits, and trails to organise and stuff, let alone the *Torchwood* launch. I find 101 e-mails waiting for me each morning, all demanding to be answered before the close of business. I end up sitting here, unshaven, unshowered, bashing out replies while still half-asleep. At the end of the day, the reverse happens – I'm firing off more e-mails, needing instant replies… which never come, because you're all in bed. (Well, not you. I bet you're still up.)

Still, I was recognised last night by none other than the maître d' of our posh restaurant. 'You're Russell T Davies! I watch *Doctor Who*! I wait for the Specials!' I admit, that was nice.

And it's *Torchwood* week in the UK! That's scary. I remember when they offered a five-nighter, I made them stick to that, on transmission… but now it's here, I'm kind of thinking, it's a bit mad. Five nights in a row? This is asking for disaster. I'm kind of glad that I'm not in the country. The results could be horrific. Will *anyone* watch? That's one thing I haven't missed in the *Doctor Who* gap year, the ratings fear!

But I'm not watching any UK telly at all. I could have got a clever machine to send programmes across the world, but then I thought, what's the point? Why go all that way to stay the same culturally? So, that's been very weird. You know how much I love British TV, so it's been like having an arm lopped off. New schedules, new channels, new people, new *feel*. I can't get used to it. But I will persevere.

Right! Better do some real work.

Love from LA. (There's no beef in our chicken.)

TWO MONTHS LATER...

FROM: BENJAMIN COOK TO: RUSSELL T DAVIES, SATURDAY 5 SEPTEMBER 2009 23:39:49 GMT

AN IDEA

Russell! In compiling a second year's worth of e-mails for *The Writer's Tale 2* (I think we should call it *The Writer's Tale: The Final Chapter*. Or is that too, er, final? Would people think we've died?!), I realised something... Way back on 1 August last year (at 2.35am – oh, why didn't we keep more sensible hours?), I asked you about lying. Look, here's the e-mail:

>>I want to know more about lying.<<

See!

>>Don't you have to lie all the time in this business? At every press launch, for a start? In every interview? Even at Tone Meetings? And auditions? And every time you're asked, 'How's the writing going?'...? Isn't writing one big fat lie? Or is that the one place where the truth can out?<<

And then I asked:

>>How much have you lied over the course of this Great Correspondence?<<

But you never answered. (You bastard.) Now, I know you're in LA, and you're probably busy (have you learnt to rollerblade yet? No? Lazy!), but it's the one unanswered question – *my* one unanswered question – and I'd love you to answer it. I am, of course, especially interested in the last part, in how much you've lied during our two-year correspondence, because, well... it's *The Writer's Tale*, Russell! Is it the truth? Yes! No! A *version* of the truth? Or is it a fiction?

Honestly?

And if you're too busy to answer, get Ryan to do it.

FROM: RUSSELL T DAVIES TO: BENJAMIN COOK, SUNDAY 6 SEPTEMBER 2009 03:19:10 GMT

RE: AN IDEA

Benjamino! It's been a while. How are you? How's Camden? I imagined you'd be away this weekend – isn't there a festival on? Reading or the Isle of Wight or one of those? Obviously not.

Lying! Of course I'm happy to answer (I'm not sure why I didn't in August '08 – I must have got distracted)… but everyone lies 27 times a day. That's no surprise. 'Nice to see you.' That's just social interaction. That's politics. But when it comes to proper lying, then no, I don't think I do. I think that's why I've done well in this business. People only lie to make things easier, softer, better – and I don't care much about that. I want to make good programmes, that's all, and I'm not sure that happens by dissembling. If you don't like some aspect of the production, you've got to tell people on the team. All right, you've got a choice about *how* you tell them – 'I hate it!' might waste more of your own time than 'Perhaps there's another way of looking at this' – but if you're not straightforward with them, then your entire show will end up bent out of shape, and it's your own fault.

Press, and PR, and interviews involve lying, but that's only natural, and beneficial, and we all know it. When the presenter on *BBC Breakfast* says, 'Tell us what happens in David's last episode,' and I say, 'I can't!' – well, that's a lie, because of course I can, but imagine if I did blurt out the whole story. That would be hilarious. (Any interviewer who imagines, as they often do, that they've met the 'real' person is just an idiot. There is nothing more artificial than being interviewed about your life by a stranger for public consumption.) In the end, the PR stuff is about selling. Even then, you have to protect yourself. Promote something that's rubbish and you look like an idiot, which won't do your career any good. If we'd ever produced an episode of *Doctor Who* that was absolute bollocks, then I'd have been discreetly unavailable for that week's *Confidential*. Honestly. And I never, ever had to do that, because every episode that we've made is good. That, in turn, makes you work hard to guarantee that every episode is good, so that you never have to face the consequences of a disaster.

Of course, 'are you lying?' maybe shows how mad it is in *Doctor Who* World. I don't think you'd ask Jimmy McGovern that, or Paul Abbott, if only for the reason that they don't write genre. It's only in this barmy, enclosed sphere that the notion of me 'lying' exists. It's one of the idiocies of fandom, one of the many, and I'm tired of having to listen to it. If I deny that the Daleks are coming back, to protect the show and the stories, to maintain the surprise, so as not to reveal the twist – then I'm a liar, apparently. And you're asking me to take that seriously?! That's one thing I won't miss, that insane vocabulary. Having to talk about 'emotion' as a quantifiable thing in drama. Having to discuss a 'gay agenda' as though it's worth wasting the ten seconds it takes to type it. These stupid words and phrases proliferate, because many of those typing on message boards – which is a tiny subsection of fandom – don't have proper critical faculties, so they leap upon catchphrases as tokens of intelligence, then they parrot a phrase over and over again, repeated and repeated as though it has validity. It acquires a gloss of validity through its repetition, and it's repeated to the extent that it leaks out of fandom, and spreads, so I can end up having discussions about this stupid bollocks on Radio 4. Time after time, I get asked about shit, and have to talk shit. Ahh, of course I'm lying – every time that I'm polite!

But never mind all that. I think the real heart of your question, and this entire project, this entire correspondence, is about writing. And truth, in writing, is the only important thing. That's what it's for. The whole time, every day, all these pages, all my life, means sitting here looking for something – some line, some insight, some microsecond – that makes me think: yes. Yes, that's true. That's real. I recognise that. I know it. That's all I'm after! It might be a truth discovered ten million times before by other people, but that doesn't matter. If you discover it for yourself, then that makes everything worthwhile. No wonder writing is such hard work! You're strip mining your own head, every day, searching for this stuff – and then those moments of revelation are like a godsend.

I remember thinking, and thinking, and thinking about Vince in *Queer as Folk*, until I arrived at that crucial conclusion about him, in Episode 8, that because his boyfriend loves him, he thinks less of the boyfriend. Vince cannot love Cameron, because Cameron is stupid to love Vince. That's a great insight. Frankly, that's brilliant! It's devastating. And it's not merely analysis. It decides Vince's character, which then decides the plot, which then becomes the entire climax of the series. The discovery of a truth like that doesn't come along often, though every other moment is spent working towards it.

It's so worth it, when it happens. Oh my word. Gold dust. It feels like vindication. If you want a *Doctor Who* example, it's there when they all sing the hymn, in the traffic jam, in *Gridlock* – because, before writing that, I could have given you a hundred intellectual theories about faith and its origins, but I'd never actually felt it until that moment of writing, when I made them all sing. Or it's there in *Aliens of London* – that moment when Jackie phones the police to report the Doctor. I love the truth of that moment, that she's so shell-shocked, she betrays her daughter. An incredible thing to do, and very real. It's there in the whole 45 minutes of *Midnight*, in the accuracy of that group mentality. It's there in that tiny moment in *Turn Left*, when Donna tells Sylvia that she's tried the army for jobs, but with no luck – because this is *after* she's seen the army take her neighbours away to a concentration camp. Donna might well rage in the street, and yet she asks the same army for employment. I really believe that. A true moment of defeat.

And right at the end, it's there in the Doctor raging at Wilf. Shouting at death. 'It's not fair!' A whole two hours of galactic-spanning, Time-Lord-killing, Doctor-changing plot, which is all there for that moment. 'It's not fair!' That's exactly what the Doctor would say. That's how he'd feel. That's how any of us would feel. I wrote the whole thing to find those three words. Because they're true. And do you know what? I don't care if people hate 4.18, if they hate the plot, the acting, the sets, the set-up, the style, the length, the whatever, because there's something so true in that moment, that nothing, *nothing*, can ever stop it from being good.

As for this Great Correspondence... yes. I think it's true. Or certainly it's one part of the truth. Sometimes, I read back stuff that I wrote to you ages ago, and think, *really?!* I barely recognise myself. But that's no different to grimacing at your own photo, or flinching when you hear your own voice. 'I don't sound like that!' The real truth is, you have five billion ever-changing versions of yourself. These e-mails are just one aspect.

Imagine if someone asked you to write down everything that you think in the next five minutes. Everything. Every single nuance of every single thought. You'd fill zillions of pages, just in the first 60 seconds. So, this stuff is just one little bit of me. *The Writer's Tale* is true, and yet it's barely scratching the surface.

In the end, this book is a form of writing, and I only write to find out about myself, and I'll only achieve that if I'm honest... so yes, I stand by these e-mails. Absolutely. While always thinking of the ones I never wrote.

WORKS REFERENCED

DOCTOR WHO
AND ITS SPIN-OFFS (in chronological order)

Doctor Who (1963–present) – an alien known as 'the Doctor', a Time Lord with the ability to regenerate into a new body and personality, at least 12 times, in order to cheat death, travels through time and space in a ship called the TARDIS, which is disguised as a London police box. The show ran on the BBC from 1963 to 1989, with seven successive actors playing the Doctor. A TV movie starring Paul McGann was made in 1996. The show was revived in 2005, produced by BBC Wales (most of the show is filmed in and around Cardiff), with Russell T Davies as showrunner:

> **Series One** (2005) – starring Christopher Eccleston, Billie Piper and John Barrowman
> *The Christmas Invasion* (2005) – Christmas Special, starring David Tennant and Piper
> **Series Two** (2006) – starring Tennant and Piper
> *The Runaway Bride* (2006) – Christmas Special, starring Tennant and Catherine Tate
> **Series Three** (2007) – starring Tennant, Freema Agyeman and Barrowman
> *Voyage of the Damned* (2007) – Christmas Special, starring Tennant and Kylie Minogue
> **Series Four** (2008) – starring Tennant, Tate, Piper, Agyeman, Barrowman and Elisabeth Sladen
> *The Next Doctor* (2008) – starring Tennant and David Morrissey
> *Planet of the Dead* (2009) – starring Tennant and Michelle Ryan
> *The Waters of Mars* (2009) – starring Tennant and Lindsay Duncan
> *The End of Time* (2009–2010) – starring Tennant, John Simm and Bernard Cribbins

Doctor Who Confidential (2005–present) – BBC Three's behind-the-scenes companion show

Torchwood (2006–present) – adult-themed *Doctor Who* spin-off show, created by Russell, concerning the Cardiff branch of a covert agency, the Torchwood Institute, led by Captain Jack Harkness (Barrowman), that investigates extraterrestrial incidents on Earth. Series One débuted on BBC Three in 2006, Series Two on BBC Two in 2008, and Series Three in 2009

The Sarah Jane Adventures (2007–present) – BBC One's *Doctor Who* spin-off show for children, created by Russell, focusing on investigative journalist Sarah Jane Smith (Elisabeth Sladen)

OTHER SHOWS
WORKED ON BY RUSSELL T DAVIES

Bob & Rose (2001) – Russell's six-part ITV romantic drama focusing on a gay man falling in love with a woman

Casanova (2005) – Russell's three-part BBC drama telling the life of eighteenth-century Italian adventurer Giacomo Casanova (David Tennant)

Coronation Street (1960–present) – ITV soap, created by Tony Warren, set in a fictional street in Lancashire. Russell was a storyliner in the mid 1990s, also writing the direct-to-video Special *Viva Las Vegas*

Dark Season (1991) – Russell's six-part BBC teen drama telling of the adventures of three adolescents and their battle to save their school from the actions of the sinister Mr Eldritch

Families (1990–1993) – ITV daytime soap, created by Kay Mellor, following two families: the Thompsons, based in Cheshire, England, and the Stevens, living in Sydney, Australia. Russell wrote various episodes

The Grand (1997–1998) – hotel-set ITV period drama written by Russell

Mine All Mine (2004) – Russell's five-part ITV drama about Max Vivaldi, who believes that the city of Swansea belongs to him – and is proved right!

Queer as Folk (1999) – Russell's Channel 4 drama series chronicling the lives of three men in Manchester's gay village around Canal Street

Queer as Folk 2 (2000) – two-part TV special concluding the *Queer as Folk* story

Revelations (1994) – short-lived Granada/Carlton soap opera devised by Russell

The Second Coming (2003) – Russell's two-part ITV drama concerning the realisation of Steve Baxter (Christopher Eccleston) that he's the Son of God

Why Don't You...? (1973–1995) – BBC children's magazine show, which Russell produced and directed between 1988 and 1992

OTHER TV SHOWS DISCUSSED

The Apprentice (2005–present) – BBC reality show in which a group of aspiring businessmen and women compete for the chance to win a £100,000-a-year job working for British business magnate Sir Alan Sugar (now Lord Sugar)

Battlestar Galactica (2004–2009) – a British-Canadian-American military science-fiction TV series, and part of the *Battlestar Galactica* franchise created by Glen A Larson, which started with a TV show in 1978, followed by a 1980 sequel (*Galactica 1980*), a re-imagined mini-series in 2003, the 2004-2009 series, and a 2100 prequel series (*Caprica*)

BBC Breakfast (2000–present) – the daily, morning TV news programme on BBC One and the BBC News channel, presented live from TV Centre in White City, West London

Blue Peter (1958–present) – BBC magazine programme for children

Buffy the Vampire Slayer (1997–2003) – US drama series, created by Joss Whedon, about a young woman, Buffy Summers, chosen by fate to battle against vampires, demons, and the forces of darkness

Casualty (1986–present) – BBC medical drama, created by Jeremy Brock and Paul Unwin, based around the fictional Holby City Hospital

Charlie Brooker's Screenwipe (2006–present) – BBC Four show, created and presented by Charlie Brooker, commentating on the TV industry and reviewing current shows

Coupling (2000–2004) – BBC sitcom, created and written by Steven Moffat, about a group of thirtysomething friends

Cranford (2007–present) – BBC comedy-drama written by Heidi Thomas, based on Elizabeth Gaskell's novel of the same name woven together with two of her other works, set in the fictional village of Cranford in the 1840s

Dancing on Ice (2006–present) – ITV show created by ice-skating duo Jayne Torvill and Christopher Dean, in which celebrities and their professional partners figure skate in front of a panel of judges

Demons (2009) – six-part ITV supernatural drama series, created by Johnny Capps and Julian Murphy, following the adventures of London teenager Luke Rutherford, the last descendant of the Van Helsing line

Desperate Housewives (2004–present) – US drama series, created by Marc Cherry, following the lives of a group of women, seen through the eyes of their dead neighbour, and the secrets that lie beneath the surface of suburbia

Early Doors (2003–2004) – BBC sitcom, created and written by Craig Cash and Phil Mealey, set in a small pub, The Grapes, in Manchester

EastEnders (1985–present) – BBC soap, created by Julia Smith and Tony Holland, set in the fictional Albert Square in the East End of London

Fawlty Towers (1975–1979) – BBC sitcom, created and written by John Cleese and Connie Booth, set in a fictional Torquay hotel

Give Us a Clue (1979–1997) – ITV's gameshow version of charades, which ran until 1992; BBC One attempted a revived version in 1997

High School Musical (2006) – US TV movie musical, written by Peter Barsocchini and made by the Disney Channel, concerning students and rival cliques at a fictional high school in New Mexico

I, Claudius (1976) – BBC adaptation of Robert Graves' *I, Claudius* and *Claudius the God* novels, scripted by Jack Pulman

Jekyll (2007) – six-part BBC drama series, written by Steven Moffat, starring James Nesbitt as a modern-day descendant of Dr Jekyll, who has begun transforming into a version of Mr Hyde

Longford (2006) – one-off Channel 4 drama, written by Peter Morgan, about Moors Murderers Ian Brady and Myra Hindley

The Making Of Me: John Barrowman (2008) – Barrowman challenges scientists to explain why he is gay, in one of the BBC's *The Making of Me* series of science documentaries

A Matter of Loaf and Death (2008) – the fourth motion-clay animated TV short to feature man-and-his-dog double act Wallace and Gromit, written by Nick Park and Bob Baker, in which the iconic characters – created by Park – have started a bakery business and are embroiled in a murder mystery

Merlin (2008–present) – BBC fantasy drama, created by Julian Jones, Jake Michie, Johnny Capps and Julian Murphy, re-imagining the Camelot legend to focus on Merlin as a young wizard and his clashes with an adolescent Arthur

Most Haunted (2002–present) – Living TV show based on investigating purported paranormal activity

The National Television Awards (1995–present) – the most prominent British TV awards for which the general public votes on the results. The ceremony is sponsored by ITV, and was held annually in October until 2008. No NTAs were held in 2009 so that, from 2010, the ceremony could take place in January.

Neighbours (1985–present) – Australian soap opera, created by Reg Watson, set in Ramsay Street, a cul-de-sac in the fictional suburb of Erinsborough

Only Fools and Horses (1981–2003) – BBC sitcom, created and written by John Sullivan, focusing on brothers Derek and Rodney Trotter's attempts to get rich

Party Animals (2007) – BBC Two drama series telling the story of researchers, lobbyists and MPS in Parliament

The People's Quiz (2007) – BBC Saturday-night quiz show (full title: *The National Lottery People's Quiz*), hosted by Jamie Theakston

Pop Idol (2001–2003) – ITV talent show contested by aspiring pop singers

Primeval (2007–present) – ITV sci-fi drama, created by Adrian Hodges and Tim Haines, about a team of scientists that investigates anomalies in time and deals with creatures that travel through

The Real Hustle (2006–present) – BBC Three series demonstrating confidence tricks, distraction scams and proposition bets, performed on members of the public by presenters Alexis Conran, Paul Wilson and Jessica-Jane Clement

Reckless: The Sequel (1998) – Paul Abbot's sequel to his own ITV drama *Reckless*, concerning the love affair between a mid-30s surgeon, Owen (Robson Green), and the late-40s, estranged wife of a prominent doctor in the hospital where he works

Richard & Judy's New Position (2008–2009) – a topical primetime chat show, broadcast on UKTV digital channel Watch, fronted by husband and wife Richard Madeley and Judy Finnigan, who hosted a similar show (*Richard & Judy*), broadcast in the early evening on Channel Four, from 2001 to 2008.

***The Royle Family* (1998–present)** – BBC sitcom, created by Caroline Aherne and Craig Cash, about the working-class Royle family, who rarely do anything other than watch television, chat, eat, smoke and drink

***Skins* (2007–present)** – E4/Channel 4 drama, created by Bryan Elsley and Jamie Brittain, about a group of sixth-formers growing up in Bristol

***The South Bank Show* (1978–present)** – ITV arts magazine show

***Star Trek: Enterprise* (2001–2005)** – US science-fiction series, created by Brannon Braga and Rick Berman and set in the *Star Trek* universe created by Gene Roddenberry, following the adventures of the first Warp 5 starship, *Enterprise*, ten years before the formation of the United Federation of Planets shown in previous *Star Trek* series

***Star Wars* (set to début in 2012)** – US science-fiction series, yet to be given an official title, focusing on characters from the galaxy of the *Star Wars* movies

***Supernatural* (2005–present)** – US supernatural drama series, created by Eric Kripke, following two brothers who hunt demons and other paranormal figures

***Teletubbies* (1997–2001)** – BBC series for pre-school children; created and written by Anne Wood CBE and Andrew Davenport

***Tonight's the Night* (2009)** – Saturday night BBC talent and variety show, presented by John Barrowman

***UP2U* (1988–1989)** – short-lived Saturday morning BBC children's TV show

***The X Factor* (2004–present)** – ITV talent show contested by aspiring pop singers

MOVIES DISCUSSED

***2010* (1984)** – science-fiction film written by Peter Hyams and based on the novel by Arthur C Clarke, set nine years after the mysterious failure of the *Discovery* mission to Jupiter as depicted in 1968 movie *2001: A Space Odyssey*

***Beauty and the Beast* (1991)** – animated Disney movie, written by Linda Woolverton, based on the fairytale of the same name about a beautiful woman kept in a castle by a horrific monster

***Being John Malkovich* (1999)** – a comedy drama written by Charlie Kaufman, in which a puppeteer takes a filing job in a Manhattan office, where he discovers a door that allows him to enter the mind and life of actor John Malkovich

***Dangerous Liaisons* (1988)** – based on a play, by Christopher Hampton, about eighteenth-century French aristocracy; in turn based on eighteenth-century novel *Les Liaisons dangereuses* by Pierre Choderlos de Laclos

***The Dark Knight* (2008)** – directed and co-written by Christopher Nolan, and based on the DC Comics character Batman (played here by Christian Bale, opposite Heath Ledger as the evil Joker), this superhero movie is a sequel to 2005's *Batman Begins*

***Finding Nemo* (2003)** – computer-animated Pixar movie, written by Andrew Stanton, Bob Peterson and David Reynolds, telling the story of a clownfish, Marlin, search for his son, Nemo

***Grease* (1978)** – film musical about students at the fictional Rydell High School in 1959. Written by Bronte Woodard, and based on Jim Jacobs and Warren Casey's 1972 musical of the same name

***The Great Mouse Detective* (1986)** – animated Disney movie based on the children's book series *Basil of Baker Street* by Eve Titus. It draws heavily on the tradition of Sherlock Holmes, with a heroic mouse who consciously emulates the detective

***Hairspray* (1988)** – comedy movie, written and directed by John Waters, revolving around plump teenager Tracy Turnblad as she simultaneously pursues stardom as a dancer and rallies against racial segregation. In 2002, *Hairspray* was adapted into a Broadway musical, and a movie remake was released in 2007

***Jeepers Creepers 2* (2003)** – horror movie, directed and written by Victor Salva. The movie is a sequel to the earlier *Jeepers Creepers*

The Little Mermaid (1989) – animated Disney movie, written by Roger Allens, Ron Clements and John Musker, based on a fairytale of the same name by Hans Christian Anderson. It concerns a young mermaid willing to give up her life in the sea as a mermaid to gain a human soul and the love of a human prince

M (1931) – German thriller directed by Fritz Lang, and written by Lang and his wife Thea von Herbou, centred on Hans Beckert (played by Peter Lorre), a serial killer who preys on children in 1930s Berlin

Mamma Mia! The Movie (2008) – a big-screen adaptation of the 1999 West End musical of the same name, written by Catherine Johnson and based on the songs of ABBA

The Matrix Reloaded (2003) – the second instalment in *The Matrix* trilogy of science-fiction adventure movies, starring Keanu Reeves, written and directed by brothers Laurence 'Larry' Wachowski and Andrew 'Andy' Wachowski.

Monsters, Inc. (2001) – computer-animated Pixar movie, set in a city inhabited by monsters and powered by the screams of children

The Poseidon Adventure (1972) – concerns the capsizing of a fictional ocean liner, and the struggles of a handful of survivors to reach the bottom of the hull before the ship sinks. It is scripted by Wendell Mayes and Stirling Silliphant, and based on a novel by Paul Gallico. The movie has been remade twice: as a television special in 2005, with the same name, and a theatrical release, *Poseidon*, in 2006

Silence of the Lambs (1991) – horror thriller starring Jodie Foster and Anthony Hopkins, based on the novel of the same name by Thomas Harris, his second to feature Dr Hannibal Lecter, a brilliant psychiatrist and cannibalistic serial killer.

The Simpsons Movie (2007) – animated movie based on TV sitcom/cartoon series *The Simpsons*, created by Matt Groening, following the lives of the residents of the fictional US town of Springfield

Sliding Doors (1998) – concerning the life of a woman who's fired from her job; the plot then splits into two parallel universes, which run in tandem. It is written and directed by Peter Howitt

Thoroughly Modern Millie (1967) – a musical comedy, starring Julie Andrews and written by Richard Morris, partly set in a New York hotel

Wall-E (2008) – computer-animated Pixar movie, written and directed by Andrew Stanton (screenplay by Jim Reardon), following the story of a robot, Wall-E, who is designed to clean up a waste-covered Earth of the far future

OTHER WORKS DISCUSSED

Asterix and the Laurel Wreath (1972) – the eighteenth volume of the *Asterix* comic book series (original French title: *Les Lauriers de Cesar*), by René Goscinny (stories) and Albert Uderzo (illustrations), following the exploits of a village of ancient Gauls as they resist Roman occupation

Chain Reaction (1991–present) – host-less chat show, first broadcast on BBC Radio 5 in 1991, then revived on BBC Radio 4 in 2005. Each week, a famous name interviews another famous name; and the interviewee goes on to be the following week's interviewer

The Cherry Orchard (1904) – Anton Chekhov's last play, concerning a once-wealthy family as they return to their estate in Russia shortly before it is auctioned off

The Chris Moyles Show (2004–present) – BBC Radio 1 breakfast show

A Christmas Carol (1843) – novella by Charles Dickens, telling the Victorian morality tale of miserly Ebenezer Scrooge, who undergoes profound redemption over the course of one night as four ghosts visit him

Death in the Clouds (1935) – mystery novel by Agatha Christie, featuring Belgian detective Hercule Poirot

Doctor Who: The Highest Science (1993) – an original *Doctor Who* novel featuring the Seventh
Doctor, written by Gareth Roberts, and published as part of Virgin Books' *The New Adventures*
range

'Eleonora' (1842) – short story by Edgar Allan Poe, considered by many biographers to be
autobiographical

Goldilocks and the Three Bears – fairy tale that first became widely known in 1837 when Robert
Southey composed it as a prose story, *The Story of the Three Bears*, collected in his book *The
Doctor*, although it was probably based on an even older story in the oral tradition

Hamlet (1599–1601) – a play written by William Shakespeare, telling how Prince Hamlet of
Denmark exacts revenge on his uncle for the murder of his father. The exact year of writing
remains in dispute

Harry Potter (1997–2007) – a series of seven fantasy novels, written by JK Rowling, about the
adventures of the eponymous adolescent wizard

The Hitchhiker's Guide to the Galaxy (1979) – the first of a series of five-science-fiction novels
(published between 1979 and 1992) written by Douglas Adams, concerning an eccentric
electronic travel guide. The novel was adapted from Adams' radio comedy of the same name,
broadcast on BBC Radio 4 in 1978. In later years, the franchise became a TV series (1981), a
computer game (1984), comic books (1993–1996) and a Hollywood-funded feature film (2005)

How I Write: The Secret Lives of Authors (2007) – an anthology of writings by various provocative
authors, includes letters, essays, photographs and memorabilia; edited by Dan Crowe and Philip
Oltermann

The Little Engine That Could (1930) – a moralistic children's story that originated in the USA,
teaching the value of optimism and hard work. A brief version was published (under the title
Thinking One Can) in 1906, in *Wellsprings for Young People*, a Sunday school publication, but
the best-known incarnation of the story, *The Little Engine That Could*, appeared in 1930 and
attributed Mabel C Bragg as the author

The Old Devils (1986) – Booker Prize-winning novel, written by Kingsley Amis, about an author
who returns to his native Wales and begins associating with a group of former friends, all of
whom have continued to live locally while he was away

Peer Gynt (1867) – a play, written in verse, by Henrik Ibsen

Prisoner of Trebekistan (2005) – a book by Bob Harris, about Alex Trebek, presenter of US quiz
show *Jeopardy*

Six Characters in Search of an Author (1921) – play written by Luigi Pirandello. During
rehearsals for a play, six characters turn up and insist on being given life

Starship Titanic (1998) – a computer game designed by Douglas Adams and made by The Digital
Village, of which Adams was a founding member. The game takes place on a spaceship called the
Titanic, which has crash-landed on Earth

Ten Little Niggers (1939) – detective novel by Agatha Christie (later editions re-titled *And Then
There Were None*), about ten people, trapped on an island, killed according to an old nursery
rhyme

INDEX